AN INTRODUCTION TO POLITICAL SCIENCE

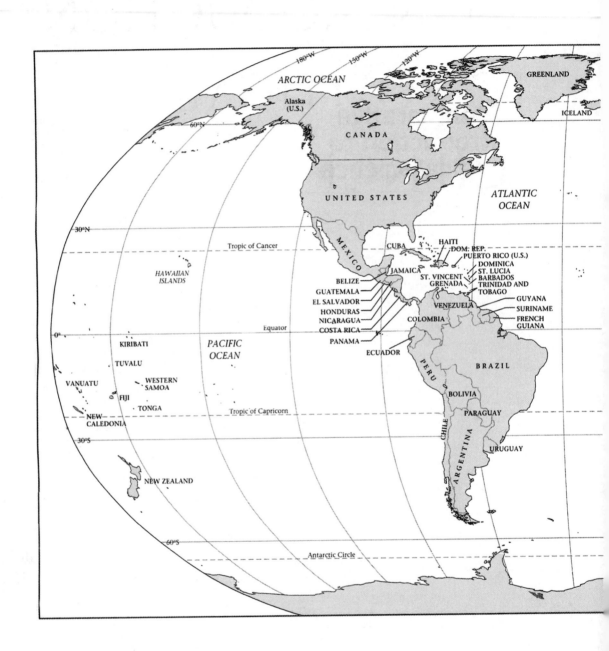

ARCTIC OCEAN

GREENLAND

Alaska
(U.S.)

ICELAND

CANADA

60°N

UNITED STATES

ATLANTIC
OCEAN

30°N

Tropic of Cancer

MEXICO

CUBA

HAITI
DOM. REP.
PUERTO RICO (U.S.)
DOMINICA
ST. LUCIA
BARBADOS
TRINIDAD AND
TOBAGO

HAWAIIAN
ISLANDS

JAMAICA

BELIZE
GUATEMALA
EL SALVADOR
HONDURAS
NICARAGUA
COSTA RICA
PANAMA

ST. VINCENT
GRENADA

VENEZUELA

GUYANA
SURINAME
FRENCH
GUIANA

COLOMBIA

Equator

ECUADOR

KIRIBATI

PACIFIC
OCEAN

BRAZIL

PERU

TUVALU

VANUATU

WESTERN
SAMOA

FIJI

BOLIVIA

TONGA

Tropic of Capricorn

PARAGUAY

NEW
CALEDONIA

30°S

CHILE

ARGENTINA

URUGUAY

NEW ZEALAND

60°S

Antarctic Circle

180°W   150°W   120°W

To Nicole Janine and Velma Marie

AN INTRODUCTION TO POLITICAL SCIENCE

Comparative and World Politics

Third Edition

ROBERT J. JACKSON
DOREEN JACKSON

Prentice Hall Allyn and Bacon Canada
Scarborough, Ontario

Canadian Cataloguing in Publication Data

Jackson, Robert J., 1936–
    An introduction to political science : comparative and world politics

3rd ed.
Second ed. published under title: Comparative government : an introduction
to political science.
Includes index.
ISBN 0-13-082199-3

1. Political science. 2. Comparative government. 3. Democracy.
4. Authoritarianism. I. Jackson, Doreen, 1939– . II. Title.
III. Title: Comparative government : an introduction to political science.

JA66.J3155 2000   320.3   C99-931228-6

Prentice-Hall, Inc., Upper Saddle River, New Jersey
Prentice-Hall International (UK) Limited, London
Prentice-Hall of Australia, Pty. Limited, Sydney
Prentice-Hall Hispanoamericana, S.A., Mexico City
Prentice-Hall of India Private Limited, New Delhi
Prentice-Hall of Japan, Inc., Tokyo
Simon & Schuster Southeast Asia Private Limited, Singapore
Editora Prentice-Hall do Brasil, Ltda., Rio de Janeiro

ISBN 0-13-082199-3

Vice President, Editorial Director: Laura Pearson
Acquisitions Editor: Dawn Lee
Developmental Editor: Laura Paterson Forbes
Marketing Manager: Christine Cozens
Production Editor: Avivah Wargon
Copy Editor: Dennis A. Mills
Production Coordinator: Peggy Brown
Art Director: Mary Opper
Cover Design: Lisa LaPointe
Cover Image: Tony Stone Images
Page Layout: Heidi Palfrey

1 2 3 4 5   04 03 02 01 00

Printed and bound in Canada

Visit the Prentice Hall Canada Web site! Send us your comments, browse our catalogues, and
more at **www.phcanada.com**. Or reach us through e-mail at **phabinfo_pubcanada@prenhall.com**.

CONTENTS

Chapter 17 Political Paries and Interest Groups: Democratic and Authoritarian   363

PREFACE TO THE THIRD EDITION

The world's states face new realities as they head into the twenty-first century. An introduction to political science must reflect these changes and make them comprehensible. With the advent of modern mass communications, students are bombarded with colourful images of the world's political events. They can ascertain quickly from international news the changing reality around them. However, to make sense of these ad hoc, seemingly disparate events, students need conceptual clarifications, interpretative tools, and a basic understanding of the wide variety of the world's political systems. They need to know how their own country fits into the world around it. They need to understand both domestic and international politics.

Today, the foremost challenge facing individual states is to establish their respective roles in the new interdependent, international environment where global economics, weapons, communications, and technology dominate. Young people who aspire to positions of political leadership need to be aware of the variety and nature of the world's political systems. Parochialism and its sister, nationalism, are not satisfactory underpinnings for successful public policy. Political leaders must deal increasingly with a multitude of different types of states and the new constraints and possibilities they present for international competition and world peace. No state, not even one's own, can be understood in isolation from others.

This book, therefore, seeks to explain politics with reference to *all* countries, not just the Western liberal democracies. The great variety of government and politics means, of course, that there is a problem of what to put into and what to leave out of a textbook. There is no practical way to avoid selectivity. However, the facts in this volume are kept to the minimum necessary for understanding government; the book does not seek to provide comprehensive material for memorization but rather offers concepts and tools with which to organize and understand the vast body of political knowledge about the world of politics that students will encounter in their studies and daily life.

With the new world situation in view, this book has two goals. The first is to introduce students in universities and colleges to the worlds of political science, politics, and government. The second is to introduce theories and methods of comparative government and international relations. With the world as a laboratory, the challenge for students is to understand the basic concepts, themes, and ideas about politics and government and apply them to the world's diverse political systems.

In striving to reach these two goals, every effort has been made to be objective and dispassionate about the systems of politics that come within the readers' purview. But one cannot and should not attempt to escape from considering values such as justice and liberty, which are inherent in the discipline of political science.

The approach of this text is eclectic. It is not dominated by any single theory of the polity that might force the analysis into a systemic straightjacket. The material is presented topically rather than on a country-by-country basis.

The first five chapters provide the background necessary to begin a comparative study of politics and government. First, they introduce the world of politics and political science. Then, the key concepts that are fundamental to rational discourse about world politics are discussed. The history and progress of political science are reviewed and placed within the context of other areas of university study.

In order to understand and interpret the various kinds of research they will encounter in political science, students must be aware of the ideas and methods of comparison. With this in mind, Chapter 4 discusses comparative theories and provides a framework with which to commence a study of the world's wide variety of politics and government. Chapter 5 introduces a typology for comparing countries according to two dimensions: their placement on a spectrum ranging from democratic to authoritarian, and the degree to which they are economically and politically developed. The chapter then develops the democratic-authoritarian dimension of comparison on which much of this book is based, providing three classifications for democratic states and five for authoritarian states.

Chapters 6 to 19 approach the topics of politics in light of this framework. The areas of culture, ideology, constitutions, government institutions, public administration, elections, parties, and interest groups are considered in two chapters for each topic. The first chapter of each pair deals with the essential concepts and theory, and the second chapter applies that knowledge to the various types of contemporary states.

The final two chapters break from this pattern. Chapter 20 deals with the exciting and difficult issues of domestic and international political change: political development and political violence, including terrorism and revolution. Because the world's states are becoming increasingly interrelated and interdependent, the final chapter, Chapter 21, deals with politics *among*, rather than *within*, states. It considers some of the dramatic changes that the late 1990s have brought to international politics and looks forward to the issues and problems of the twenty-first century.

Since the scope of this book is very wide, many topics must be touched upon. In such a limited space not all facets and complexities of each country or international organization can be covered, but the foundations are provided on which students can build in further area-study courses and specialized courses in world politics. Students are invited to explore the exciting world of politics and encouraged to pursue areas of interest and expand their knowledge. Those who take up the challenge will be rewarded by a deeper understanding of the complex political issues of everyday life. Class lectures will be vital in fleshing out issues and providing different perspectives on certain topics. Extensive, select bibliographies of the most current and useful literature in each field are provided at the end of each chapter in the Further Reading feature.

As the reader proceeds through the book and begins to compare and evaluate forms of government, he or she should constantly ask two questions. First, what constitutes good government, and how it can be achieved? This question has fascinated philosophers, historians, and political scientists for centuries. The answer continues to elude us, since there is no single form of government that is best everywhere and in every circumstance, and the variety of options is great. Second, what are the relations between domestic and international affairs and how is the process of globalization affecting world politics?

If you have Internet access, we have listed several Weblinks at the end of each chapter. They are only a sample of the interesting and useful sites which you can find over the Internet and were chosen only to give you an idea of the type of information that can be found. Explore them to discover how governments, businesses, universities, and other organizations are using this new medium to distribute information. Please keep in mind, however, that addresses do change over time. If you have comments, suggestions or questions about this book or simply want to carry on a dialogue about political science, contact the authors at **jackson@uor.edu**.

SUPPLEMENTS

- *Instructor's Manual.* This comprehensive guide includes chapter outlines, learning objectives, and lecture suggestions.
- *Test Item File.* This test file contains a variety of questions including multiple-choice, short-answer, and problem questions.

ACKNOWLEDGMENTS

Many friends and colleagues gave advice and encouragement on the preparation of this new book. In particular, intelligent and comprehensive comments were provided by the reviewers of the second and third editions—Robert Bedeski, University of Victoria; Keith Brownsey, Mount Royal College; Vincent Della Sala, Carleton University; George A. MacLean, University of Manitoba; Chaldeans Mensah, Grant MacEwan Community College, and W.A. Matheson, Brock University. Lynnae Pattison and Lesley Sebastian of the University of Redlands gave valuable assistance in preparing this manuscript. Of course much credit also must be given for the stimulating questions of thousands of undergraduate and graduate students who have studied comparative politics with us over three decades at Canadian, British, and American universities.

Lastly, we want to recognize the very excellent professional assistance offered by our friends and colleagues at Prentice Hall. Patrick Ferrier and Mike Bickerstaff initially convinced us to write the book. Dawn Lee, Laura Paterson Forbes, Avivah Wargon, and Dennis Mills deserve particular mention and genuine thanks for their outstanding contributions. While acknowledging our debt to all of these individuals, we accept full responsibility for any errors, omissions, and interpretations in the book.

Robert J. Jackson
Doreen Jackson
University of Redlands, California,
and Carleton University, Ottawa

ABBREVIATIONS

PERIODICALS

APSR	*American Political Science Review*
CJPS	*Canadian Journal of Political Science*
IPSR	*International Political Science Review*

POLITICAL PARTIES

BDP	Botswana Democratic Party
CCF	Co-operative Commonwealth Federation
CCP	Chinese Communist Party
FIS	Islamic Salvation Front
FLN	National Liberation Front
FRG	Federal Republic of Germany (the former West Germany)
GDR	German Democratic Republic (the former East Germany)
IRP	Islamic Republican Party
LCY	League of Communists
PRI	Institutional Party of the Revolution
RCD	Democratic Constitutional Party
UNIP	United National Independence Party

ORGANIZATIONS

APEC	Asia-Pacific Economic Co-operation Conference
ASEAN	Association of Southeast Asia Nations
CFE	Conventional Force Europe
CIS	Commonwealth of Independent States
EU	European Union
G-7	Group of Seven
GATT	General Agreement on Tariffs and Trade
IPU	Inter-Parliamentary Union
MMD	Movement for Multi-Party Democracy
NAFTA	North American Free Trade Agreement
NATO	North Atlantic Treaty Organization
OAS	Organization of American States
OAU	Organization of African Unity
OPEC	Organization of the Petroleum Exporting Countries
OSCE	Organization for Security and Cooperation in Europe

MINURSO — United Nations Mission for the Referendum in Western Sahara
UNAMIR — United Nations Assistance Mission for Rwanda
UNAVEM II — United Nations Angola Verification Mission II
UNDOF — United Nations Disengagement Observer Force
UNFICYP — United Nations Peace–keeping Force in Cyprus
UNIFIL — United Nations Interim Force in Lebanon
UNIKOM — United Nations Iraq–Kuwait Observation Mission
UNMIH — United Nations Mission in Haiti
UNMOGIP — United Nations Military Observr Group in India and Pakistan
UNMOT — United Nations Mission of Observers in Tajikistan
UNOMIG — United Nations Observer Mission in Georgia
UNOMIL — United Nations Observer Mission in Liberia
UNOSOM II — United Nations Operation in Somalia II
UNPROFOR — United Nations Protection Force
UNTSO — United Nations Truce Supervision Organiztion
UNUMOZ — United Nations Operation in Mozambique
UNUSAL — United Nations Observer Mission in El Salvador

MISCELLANEOUS

AV	Alternative Vote
GDP	Gross Domestic Product
GNP	Gross National Product
ICJ	International Court of Justice
IMF	International Monetary Fund
INF	Intermediate-Range Forces
LDC	Less Developed Country
MAD	Mutual Assured Destruction
MIRV	Multiple Independently-Targeted Re-entry Vehicle
MNC	Multi-National Corporation
NIC	Newly Industrialized Country
PAC	Political Action Committee
PR	Proportional Representation
SALT	Strategic Arms Limitation Talks
SDI	Strategic Defence Initiative
SEA	Single European Act
SII	Structural Impediment Initiative
START	Strategic Arms Reduction Treaty

CHAPTER 1

The World of Politics: Countries and Concepts

At the dawning of the new millennium, the study of world politics is fascinating and more important than ever. Individual states are no longer totally self-sufficient: economic, social, and political interdependence have become the most salient features of modern life. The flow of goods, services, technology, capital, and ideas around the world has changed how we live. Globalization affects levels of investment, economic prosperity, and even unemployment levels, usurping from governments, to some extent, the ability to control their own economies.

It is challenging to examine a political world that is very fluid and contains few constants. Most countries or states in existence today are relatively new, and together they provide an enormous variety of political systems, disparate economic realities, and human potentials. In 1999 the world's countries housed among them, in very uneven proportions, a burgeoning population of over five and a half billion people—a figure that is projected to reach more than eight billion by the year 2025 (see Figure 1.1). The population disparities among states are perhaps best understood through a few concrete examples. Vatican City has only 900 people while China has over 1.2 billion. Between these two extremes, the United States has a population of approximately 260 million. There are only 7 inhabitants per square mile in Canada compared to 68 in the United States, 856 in Japan, and 2073 in Bangladesh, the most densely populated state in the world. Every second, the world population grows by more than two human beings.

Technological advances in communications and transportation have, in real terms, reduced the size of the world, revolutionizing the patterns of interaction between countries and individuals. Technological developments have eliminated or reduced the significance of some social and political problems, but have also created new ones. Keeping abreast of such developments and their implications is imperative in the struggle to maintain social order and provide social justice. As societies modernize and become more complex, their only hope for long-term stability is to learn to manage the disorderliness of politics.

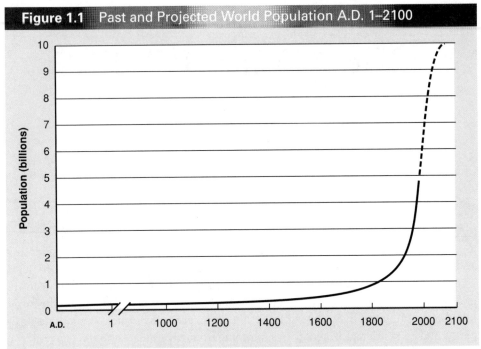

Figure 1.1   Past and Projected World Population A.D. 1–2100

Source: UN Publication: World Resources 1986 (N.Y.: Basic Books, 1986) p. 10.

The revolutions in science and technology have dramatically changed the world economy. Scientific knowledge has more than doubled in each of the four decades following World War II, and the pace of technological change has accelerated at a comparable rate. The speed of change in the twentieth century is best illustrated by a few examples. In 1900 the world was dominated by colonial empires; today those empires no longer exist, and of the powerful monoliths that replaced them as world powers—the former Soviet Union and the United States—one has disintegrated, leaving an economically impoverished Russia. In 1900 the only way to circle the globe—either for travel or for communication—was by ship. Today, sea travel has been eclipsed by vast aviation networks. Communications systems have entered the space age, making use of fibre optics, microwaves, and satellites for instant global communication. It is hard to imagine daily life without cars, radios, televisions, household appliances, computers, fax machines, the Internet, and other modern conveniences that were only science-fiction dreams at the beginning of this century.

Business corporations are increasingly transnational. In terms of global activities, ownership, and control, they are becoming "stateless," without particular links to any specific country. Because of this, a state's competitive advantage is no longer identified with its own particular group of companies as much as it was in 1900. Many multinational corporations exceed the economic strength of some states. General Motors, for example, had a revenue of $178 billion in 1997, more than Denmark, Norway, Hong Kong, and many other states. See Close Up 1.1.

CLOSE UP 1.1 The Challenge of Global Corporations

Question: What is the difference between Zambia and Goldman Sachs?

Answer: One is an African country that makes $2.2 billion a year and shares it among 25 million people. The other is an investment bank that makes $2.6 billion ... and shares it among 161 people.[1]

Many observers are concerned about what they see as the increasing impotence of liberal democracy in the face of rich and growing global corporations. Whenever possible, corporations conduct their internal international transactions in such a way as to make profits in high-tax countries but declare them in states where taxes are low. Even so, corporations regularly call for reduced taxes and "less government." Cynical observers maintain that soon states will be left only with whatever resources the global corporations and their elites are willing to contribute.

Is the concern justified that the globalization of capitalism is, in effect, killing democracy?

Technology has also brought new and enormous challenges to world peace. In 1900 rifles and cannons were the most dangerous weapons of war. Today there are atomic and neutron bombs, computerized fighter jets, tanks, heat-seeking missiles, chemical and biological warheads, nuclear submarines, and automated weapons of every description. Plans for even more sophisticated and futuristic weapons are always on the drawing board. In the first few years of the second millennium, 15 states are forecast to have the type of reconnaissance satellites that the United States used in the 1991 war against Iraq.

These kinds of economic and technological developments have shifted, to some extent, the focus of politics from the national, regional and international levels. There is an emergence of a **global economy** in terms of not just trade but all the elements of wealth creation—finance, investment, production, distribution, and marketing—which are increasingly being organized regionally and globally. The frontiers of knowledge and development—in weapons systems, communications, economics, and so on—are now on the global scale. This does not mean that country-level studies are no longer important; they are. But as countries have become increasingly interlinked and interdependent, it has also become more obviously beneficial to view such studies in a much larger comparative and international context.[1]

This book, therefore, is about world politics rather than the politics or political system of a single country. Our text invites the reader to look beyond his or her state borders to consider the similarities and differences among the great variety of political systems in the countries and regions of the world. We introduce comparative methods and examine what comparison can reveal about the world's states and how they are governed. Familiar countries such as Canada, Great Britain, and the United States are of course considered, but they are viewed in the perspective of the larger panorama. Examples are drawn from all populated continents—Africa, Asia, Australia, Europe,

North and South America. Students are encouraged to use their own political system as a reference point, comparing and contrasting it with others to judge its relative strengths and weaknesses. In this process, readers should constantly ask themselves: what constitutes good government? and how can it be achieved? No single form of government is best in every place and in every circumstance. The best form of government is relative to time, place, and other considerations.

We begin our study of politics with a brief overview of the issues in the world today, and then, to ensure a proper foundation, we define political science and then clarify several concepts that are keys to understanding how political scientists make sense of the disparate and ever-changing world that is the focus of their study. Thinking and caring about the dynamics of a changing world are central to our approach.

THE WORLD TODAY

Students of politics have a daunting task at the dawn of the twenty-first century. The world is in a new and crucial phase of its history. Shock waves from the end of the Cold War still reverberate. The sudden disintegration of the Soviet Union and the collapse of communism in the former Soviet territory and Eastern Europe destroyed the infamous "Iron Curtain" and the rigid alignment of the world's states into two confrontational camps. The initial euphoria following those dramatic events is gone, and the reality that inevitably replaced it has created uncertainties, problems, and opportunities around the world. In the former Eastern Bloc countries, people are enjoying new freedoms but also confronting harsh conditions and brutally crushed expectations. The West is adjusting to having the United States as the lone military superpower and "policeman" of the world. States everywhere are jockeying for increased economic power and influence on the world stage. As of 1999 they are also coping with economic uncertainty as crashing markets and collapsing banks cause weak economies to crumble and create havoc in global patterns of trade.

New regional, economic, or military powers now aspire to shape world events. Political actors are joining new alliances to meet the economic, security, and social challenges of a new era. The North Atlantic Treaty Organization (NATO) is restructuring and redefining its goals after losing its original purpose. In Europe, a united Germany is the foremost player in a more powerful European Union. In North America, Canada, the United States, and Mexico are working to expand free trade throughout the Americas. In Central and South America, every country except Suriname and Cuba is embracing democracy. In Africa, as well, dictators and military regimes are giving way to experiments with democracy. Nearly three-quarters of sub-Saharan African countries now offer some political choice. In North Africa, the Middle East, and Central Asia, Islamic fundamentalists are gaining social and political strength. In the southern states of the former Soviet Union, these fundamentalists are competing with Orthodox Christians as the source of moral teaching and national identity to replace the badly discredited dogma of Marxism.

The demise of the Cold War also saw a rise of ethnic and nationalist conflicts inside large countries like the former USSR, and within relatively smaller, multi-ethnic countries like Nigeria, Ethiopia, and the former Yugoslavia. Ideologies like communism that had been used to suppress ethnic and nationalist assertiveness for most of this century are now in rapid decline in many parts of the world, and demands for political rights, independence, and autonomy are rising. Kosovo has replaced Bosnia as a scene of butchery and ethnic cleansing resulting from the collapse of the former Yugoslavia and the decline of communist ideology.

The annual number of wars has been relatively constant for a decade. Regional wars rage unabated—there are approximately 82 armed conflicts in the world today, the most recent being NATO's war with Yugoslavia over Kosovo. Old fires burn brightly in Algeria, Sudan, Sri Lanka, and corners of the Caucasus. Embers smoulder dangerously in Bosnia, the Middle East, Angola, Columbia, and Cambodia. The world's foremost international body, the United Nations, is rarely more than a bystander to the carnage and terror. Sophisticated weaponry allowed conflicts such as the civil wars in Bosnia and Chechnya to be protracted and escalate. India and Pakistan openly conduct nuclear rivalry. Terrorists make sporadic attacks against the United States, and Washington responds by bombing alleged terrorist camps inside the borders of other countries.

Even when conflicts seem far away, their repercussions are evident around the world. Refugees from areas such as Afghanistan, Haiti, Hong Kong, Rwanda, and Kosovo desperately search for homes in more peaceful and secure areas. And industrialized countries are easily sucked into the vortex of armed conflict half a world away.

On the economic front, Japan and the newly industrializing countries (NICs) of the Pacific Rim flourished as centres of economic strength in the mid-1990s, helping change the traditional patterns of trade and the distribution of wealth in the world. Then, in 1998 their banks and economies suddenly collapsed, seriously disrupting the economies of countries around the globe. States can no longer govern their own economies independently. They are all affected by the same global forces.

What will the new century bring in terms of politics? Which states will endure? Which states will fragment into smaller units? Where will peace reign and where will war break out? Will states prosper or will new global forces arise to cripple economies around the world? These are just some of the crucial questions that confront political scientists at the dawn of the new millennium. They are the kinds of questions that you will be invited to consider as you read through this text. This chapter will provide some of the background needed to understand these questions better.

What is Political Science?

Everyone is affected by politics. News reports bombard us daily with details of political developments and conflicts in our immediate environment and in the world. For the casual observer, the amount of information is confusing and can be overwhelming. It is difficult to interpret political events and develop informed judgments about them; conflicts are so numerous that they often appear as major headlines one day and vanish the next, under a barrage of new crises, scandals, and revolutions.

Political scientists try to impose order on this inchoate material—to bring understanding out of the chaos, and to improve ways of thinking about political problems. Thus, topics such as governments, elections, political parties, revolutions, and wars, which are subject to much casual observation and heated discussion, are also the focus of orderly research. Political science is primarily concerned with studying dispute and its collective resolution. In definitional form, **political science** is the study of how organized disputes are articulated and then resolved by public decisions made by governments.

Political scientists describe and analyze the institutions and behaviour involved in the governance of states. But there is also an ethical, normative aspect to political science, which involves the search for the proper relationship between institutional structures and desired ends such as equality, justice, and liberty. Political scientists do not aim merely to accumulate facts and data, but to explain why events happen as they do. If they cannot be used as tools to further understanding, mere facts are not enlightening. In summary, scholars approach the study of politics with three fundamental goals: to *describe* political events and processes, seeking patterns in them that will help *explain* political behaviour and possibly *prescribe* policy.

When he introduced political science as a brand new subject in Canada in 1888, William Ashley defined the new field as "systematic knowledge concerning the state or political society ... concerning its constitution, its functions, the organs by which these functions are discharged, its relation to the individual and to other societies."[2] Political science has developed and expanded its focus and become an increasingly important subject since Ashley's day. Over the decades, citizens have increased their demands on government, and governments in turn have grown. The study of governments and how they respond to the demands placed on them has also expanded and become more sophisticated and rigorous.

POLITICS, GOVERNMENT, AND SOCIETY

The subject of this book is the dynamic, controversial, and pervasive world of politics, domestic and international. Political issues can generate the strongest of emotions, attachments, and actions. Many people absorb current information about politics, hold opinions about it, argue about it, and participate in it. Some even die for it. Everyone has a general understanding of what politics is. But when asked to be more precise, they are diffident. Some say it means "government," others "the art of compromise" or "manipulation" or "the struggle for advantage." A particularly cynical definition was given by Henry Adams: "Politics, as a practice, whatever its professions, has always been the systematic organization of hatreds."[3]

Politics has even been defined as nonviolent war. But one must not be too cynical about politics. It is the vehicle of good as well as evil: politics requires cooperation which enables individuals "to defend themselves from attack, or to attack others; to produce goods, or to steal them; to educate the youth, or to indoctrinate them with myths, or Platonic 'noble lies' that facilitate the exercise of arbitrary power by some persons over others."[4]

The variety of definitions of politics is extensive. But if we are to study and understand this pervasive phenomenon we must be precise about what it means, and take care to define and use this term and others in a generally acceptable and consistent way. Dictionary definitions may not be precise enough. Over the years a great many definitions of the word "politics" have been put forward, and among experts it would be difficult to secure unanimous agreement for any of them. The extent to which this is true indicates just how complex the word "politics" is.

A classic question which is often asked about politics illustrates the basic core of its meaning: "Was there politics when Robinson Crusoe was alone on an island?" The answer, of course, lies in the fact that politics requires human interaction and therefore politics emerged only when Crusoe and Friday were on the island together. But politics is present in all social relations no matter how small the group or society.

We should note here the distinction between "group" and "society." In normal usage, a **group** refers to "a number of persons belonging or classed together."[5] The term **interest group** has a more specific meaning in political science. It refers to a certain kind of group: an "organized association which engages in activity relative to governmental decisions."[6] **Society** has a wider meaning. It refers to a large group of people who are associated with a particular geographical area, think of themselves as possessing a common set of historical traditions, share a reasonably common culture, and engage in mutual interaction. Societal members share rules of conduct and behaviour so that there are predictable, regular patterns that integrate individuals into the social unit. The term "society" is often applied to the people of a country—as in the "Canadian society." It can also be applied to subgroups within a country, such as "French-Canadians," or even larger groups that transcend state borders, such as "North American society." An individual may be part of many different societies at the same time; the geographical boundaries of those societies may or may not be the same as those established by governments, continents, provinces, or other such units.

Although the question "What is politics?" has long been a major and perplexing topic in the discipline, other fields of study have not had the same problem. Economists, for example, have answered the question "What is economics?" by identifying it in relation to its opposite. Economics, they say, is founded on the concept of utility or usefulness (as opposed to damaging), and the behavioural unit of economics is self-serving individuals. Following this example, Carl Schmitt depicts politics on the basis of paired opposites. He says that politics is founded on the "friend–enemy" opposition, and all of politics can be perceived as conflict, or enmity.[7] Other political scientists, Giovanni Sartori, for one, declare to the contrary that this reduction of politics to "the laws of the jungle" ignores that politics can exhibit—in changing and different proportions—both "ideally motivated actors and merely self-serving ones."[8]

Most scholars of political science accept that politics has two basic characteristics:

1. It involves making common decisions for a group or groups of people; and
2. Some individuals in the group exercise power (ranging from influence to coercion) over other members in order to make those decisions.[9]

These two characteristics are implicit in two widely accepted definitions of politics. The first definition, put forward by David Easton, sees politics as "the authoritative allocation of values."[10] By values, Easton did not mean moral ideals, but rather the benefits and opportunities which people value or desire. According to this definition, the reason politics is omnipresent in societies is that resources are limited, and valued possessions such as wealth, comforts, and status are invariably scarce and unevenly distributed. Disagreements and conflict arise among individuals and groups as they attempt to satisfy their desires in attaining them. These conflicts must be resolved so that values, or resources, are distributed authoritatively—or, in other words, so that the distribution is either accepted or backed up by coercion. Politics, then, is about the resolution of dispute and conflict. For that reason, politics never ends. Each resolution of a dispute results in new relationships between resources and expectations, and these, in turn, lead to more disputes and therefore more politics.

A second widely accepted definition of politics was put forward by Harold Lasswell, who pointed out that politics always concerns "who gets what, when and how" in society.[11] Lasswell, too, saw politics as the distribution of the good things of life which people value and desire. Both of these definitions recognize the need for groups to allocate resources and exercise power or authority in doing so. Lasswell's definition, however, draws our attention more specifically to the recipients of the distribution.

In this volume we use a definition of politics that combines the insights of both Easton and Lasswell: **Politics** embraces all activity which impinges upon the making of binding decisions about who gets what, when, and how. (See Close Up 1.2.) It is an activity through which contending interests are conciliated and differences are expressed and considered. Through politics the collective welfare is supposed to be advanced and the survival of the community protected.[12]

Politics, then, exists within any group in society whenever a decision is to be taken which impinges on members of that group. This very wide view of politics can apply to all kinds of groups. A family decision to buy a house, for example, is a political decision for the family because it will impinge on all of its members. It is not, of course, a political decision for the country. Political decisions that entail wider implications for the country are the focus of studies that concern political scientists. If, of course, the house in question were to be purchased from taxpayers' money as the Prime Minister's second country retreat, it could become a wider political question, and in that case would come within the political scientist's purview.

The conflict in society which flows from making political decisions for a country requires mechanisms to enforce those decisions. We refer to these mechanisms as government. **Government** is thus the organization of people for the resolution of dispute and conflict. In the sense we know it today, government began to develop 100 centuries ago with the early civilizations in Asia Minor and northern Mesopotamia. Primitive governments were sometimes based on one individual such as a king or village chief. Today, except in remote hinterlands, government is much more extensive and often collegial.

CLOSE UP 1.2 Who Gets What?

The enormity of the wealth of some people is overwhelming. In 1997, the three richest individuals in the world had assets that exceeded the combined GDP of the 48 least-developed countries. The 15 richest individuals had assets that exceeded the total GDP of sub-Saharan Africa. The richest 32 people had wealth that exceeded the total GDP of South Asia. The richest 84 had assets that exceeded the GDP of China.

In summary, the richest 225 individuals in the world had a combined wealth of over one trillion dollars—equal to the total annual income of almost half of the world's poorest people, or almost 2.5 billion individuals.[13]

Is this distribution of wealth reasonable? Desirable? Reformable?

Modern governments not only provide order but also regulate many aspects of private and public affairs. They are very complex and important institutions in society. A society with no government would be in a state of **anarchy**; it would have no body of institutions to make and enforce public order. Of course, anarchists believe that humans can live together peacefully without government. Very few political scientists agree.

Politics and governing, therefore, both refer to organized dispute over power. However, to the degree that it is possible to distinguish between the two terms, for political scientists *politics* is concerned with influencing public officials, while *governing* consists of the actions of public officials in making and implementing decisions.

KEY CONCEPTS IN POLITICAL SCIENCE

It will be obvious by now that in order to understand politics and discuss it intelligently, we should try to understand what we mean by "power." Readers should not be too impatient to clarify and define words that are used in a very specific way in political science and which often differ from common usage. However, it is important to cope with what is meant by words in order to avoid misunderstandings and provide the basis for intelligent agreement or disagreement about the substance of what is being communicated. This is not as easy as it might seem, because words are richly textured and can have many meanings. Power is just one of many concepts that are fundamental to the study of politics. These concepts and their theoretical underpinnings form the basis of entire chapters in this book and are carefully introduced and defined before we examine them in the context of world politics. Some concepts are quite specialized and best left to be discussed in a specific context. Others apply more widely, and those we highlight briefly in this section as well as in later chapters. First, we will examine the concepts of "power," "authority," and "legitimacy," which are all intimately related. These concepts are particularly important because they apply to politics in all states, whether democratic or authoritarian, rich or poor.

Power

One cannot hold power, touch it, or even see it, yet almost everybody wants it. It is present wherever there is politics, in all social relations, no matter how small the group or society. Individuals can have it, as can institutions and states. The nature of political power in every political system is an exceedingly complex network of relationships. As students of political science, readers will be aware of recurring debates about who actually has political power and whether power is shifting in some fashion. Is the Canadian Prime Minister more powerful in the political process today than in former years? Who has more power, the Canadian Prime Minister or the American President? Analysis of what constitutes power and who holds it is complicated by the fact that power is an abstract commodity which changes in response to the dynamic political and social environment. As issues, problems, and personalities change, so do sources of power. As well, it is difficult to distinguish power from social influence. Political power can be seen as a complex mathematical equation in which there are a few constant values, but many indeterminate ones.

We noted that politics involves making common decisions for a group or groups of people, and that the exercise of power in making those decisions can range from influence to coercion.

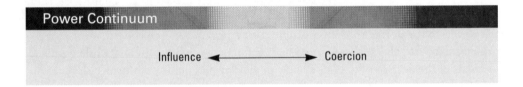

Power Continuum

Influence ←——————→ Coercion

The word "power" comes from the Latin verb *potere* meaning "to be able."[14] In its broadest sense, power is being able, physically, intellectually, or a combination of both, to achieve what one wants. The bully in the street exercises control over others by using, or threatening to use, physical coercion. Another individual might exercise power by the influence of sheer intellectual superiority and the ability to solve problems that others perceive to be important. Yet another person might employ emotional appeals to achieve desired ends.

Power may be implicit or manifest. In implicit power, B wants A to do something, and A does it simply because he or she realizes that B wants it done, and for whatever reasons wants to accommodate those wishes. When power is manifest, on the other hand, it is directly observable: B acts in an evident way to make A do what B wants. We can define **power** then, as the ability to cause others to do what one desires, using means ranging from influence to coercion. Political scientists normally restrict their focus to power situations within the field of politics.[15]

Power permeates politics. Politics, as we have defined it, is concerned with the authoritative allocation of scarce resources in society, about who gets what, when, and how. Those who control penalties and rewards are best equipped to allocate resources in competitive circumstances. Individuals (and groups) who exercise political power in society generally exhibit characteristics such as wealth, access to force (military or police), means of communication, social status, education, and often personal magnetism, or charisma. Dictators such as Iraq's Saddam Hussein concentrate these characteristics in their own person, rather than in a group of people, thus amassing great personal power. In democratic societies power is more dispersed. In the United States, for example, it is common for Congress to thwart the President's wishes by blocking legislation that he wants passed. There remains a widespread concern that perhaps Lord Acton was right when he declared, "Power tends to corrupt, and absolute power corrupts absolutely."

As important as power is in politics, many perplexing questions concerning it are still debated. Is it something that can be possessed, like gold, or handed over, as in the metaphor "the reins of power"? Or is power rather the result of a social relationship between actors? Is it absolute or relative? One thing is certain: the power to influence other individuals to act in a certain way often relies more upon bargaining than on the application of physical force.

Influence

Power and influence, then, are interwoven. Power is influence, and influence can be a form of power.[16] **Influence** is the ability to persuade or convince others to accept certain objectives or behave in a certain way. We all use both rational arguments and emotional appeals to influence others. Bribery or offering rewards, are other forms of influence, but they are often considered to be ethically questionable. For this reason patronage appointments in Ottawa and elsewhere regularly cause public reactions ranging from raised eyebrows to indignant outcries.

Influence is a component of all political interaction. Political parties and candidates seek to influence citizens to vote for them; citizens and lobby groups try to influence how members of parliament stand on certain issues; governments spend millions of dollars every year on advertising in order to influence public opinion. Influence, then, is based on persuasion and is free of threats or physical restraints of any kind. Choices are voluntary and based on personal motives.[17]

Coercion

Coercion is the opposite extreme of influence. It involves control by force; compliance is achieved through punishments or threats. Governments control the major, legitimate, coercive agents in society, including police forces, prisons, courts, and the armed forces. These agents are used when government influence alone fails to achieve its desired ends. They are powerful tools, but governments can rarely exercise a high degree of coercion for very long periods of time without encountering opposition. In democratic systems, governments would soon be overthrown by elections; in authoritarian states, opposition could culminate in a coup or revolution. In order to minimize such social problems, governments must behave within certain bounds to earn the widespread respect which comes with authority and legitimacy.

Authority and Legitimacy

Authority is government power to make binding decisions and issue obligatory commands.[18] Such power must be perceived by citizens as rightful or acceptable and therefore to be obeyed. Individuals or groups in positions of authority have power based on the general agreement that they have the "right" to issue decisions or commands that others must obey. Since citizens respect the source of decisions, they believe they should accept the decisions whether or not they agree with them. Everything else being equal, the greater the authority of the person or group, the less the need to use coercion to enforce the decision in question. The 1988 general election in Canada, for example, was fought on the central issue of the government's free trade deal with the United States. The Conservatives won the election and therefore had the authority to go ahead with the agreement.

Governments must have authority to maintain domestic stability and operate effectively. Authority enables them to make decisions for their citizens without resorting to coercion. Citizens obey laws because they agree that their government has the authority to make decisions for the larger good of society. They know that if they break the law they eventually will be coerced, but the threat of coercion alone might not be sufficient to modify their behaviour if they believe the government lacks authority.

Authority is obviously a valuable, much-sought-after commodity, but it is intangible. At an individual level, some people in society have personal qualities which enable them to initiate and lead. Other individuals and groups exercise their authority from a position or office that carries with it the right to make certain decisions. Governments rely on the latter basis of authority, generally referred to as **public authority**. In democracies, public authority is not normally based on outright coercion. When a state uses a high degree of coercion to obtain obedience, and does not allow free and competitive elections to determine the degree of support for the government, that state is considered to have authoritarian tendencies.

The concept of legitimacy is very closely related to that of authority. **Legitimacy** denotes a general belief that the state's powers to make and enforce rules are justified and proper. Legitimacy is a moral or ethical concept which involves perceptions of what is right. When governmental authority is based on legitimacy, citizens feel they have a duty or obligation to obey, or abide by, what the government legislates.[19]

In democratic systems, both authority and legitimacy are required in order to exercise power—to issue commands that will be obeyed willingly. The 1988 Canadian general election gave the Conservative government the *authority* to go ahead and sign the free trade deal even though only 43% of the electorate voted for them. This authority was based on the fact that through their participation in the election, the people had agreed that the political system was *legitimate* and that any elected government would have the right to sign or to terminate the Free Trade Agreement with the United States.

Legitimacy, although sought after, is not always achieved. For example, a government's authority to govern may be incomplete because of the nondemocratic way in which it came to power. It would be possible, as well, for an elected government to be deprived of the authority to govern by a military takeover. In Haiti in 1991 the military ousted the elected government of Jean-Bertrand Aristide. Countries around the world condemned the new military government and refused to recognize its authority because it lacked the legitimacy of an electoral confirmation of its power. In 1994 the United Nations, led by the United States, put Aristide back in power again and insisted on new elections in Haiti.

Long historical development and relative economic prosperity normally allow democracies to achieve legitimacy. Authoritarian or military regimes may initially have legitimacy but they are rarely able to maintain it for very long; citizens do not often accord these governments the moral right to govern. We think of Stalin in the former Soviet Union or President Marcos in the Philippines as examples.

The existence of a legitimate government inhibits military intervention. If the majority of the population believes that the government has a moral right to govern, and is strongly attached to civilian institutions, a strong moral barrier prevents military intervention. Military action in such a case would probably trigger popular resistance that would lead to divisions within the military. If, on the other hand, the majority of the population does not believe that the government has a moral right to govern, and they question its authority and bear no allegiance to it, no equivalent barriers exist, and military intervention might be met with gratitude and joy or, alternately, with apathy. In some countries, successive military takeovers are often based on such circumstances.

According to German sociologist Max Weber, authority (and therefore legitimacy) may be said to stem from three main sources. **Traditional authority** is derived from custom and history. It is most frequently gained through inheritance as in the case of royal dynasties or modern monarchies. **Charismatic authority** is based on popular admiration of the personal "heroic" qualities of the individual in whom it is vested. Lastly, **rational-legal** or **bureaucratic authority** is vested in the offices held by individuals and the mechanisms which placed them there.[20] This latter is the most common form of authority in Western societies. The Canadian Prime Minister derives authority primarily from the fact that he or she is leader of a government placed in power by popular election. As soon as a Prime Minister loses an election and ceases to hold that official position, the authority vested in him or her will pass to the new incumbent of the office. In Canada, as in many other modern societies, authority is vested in political institutions and offices of the state rather than in individuals.

The concept of legitimacy may also be applied to individual acts of governments. A legitimate government may do some things that are perceived to be illegitimate. Legitimacy in this sense should not be confused with legality. Legitimacy denotes the degree of subjective authority vested in the government by public opinion, but the latter relates to the constitutional or legal propriety of undertaking certain activities. Some events therefore may be quite legal, but still not be considered legitimate. The decision of the United States to have conscription in order to obtain troops for fighting in Vietnam in the 1960s was legal, but many Americans did not think it legitimate; they did not believe that the government ought to have exercised such powers. Conversely, certain events can be viewed as legitimate even though they are not legal. Some Canadians, for example, supported the 1970s action of the police in burning a barn to prevent a "subversive" meeting of a separatist group, even though the action was not legal.

A government must have the consent of its citizens, based on legitimacy, in order to resolve societal conflicts, to defend the territory against external enemies, and to maintain essential services for its citizens. Without legitimacy, it has to use coercion to maintain its authority, and in the end such a move is likely to prove self-defeating. As Close Up 1.3 shows, the concepts of legitimacy, authority, and power are vital in understanding relations among China, Hong Kong, and Taiwan, for example.

With all its complexity, politics provides a fascinating array of power relationships; a living specimen for political scientists to dissect, analyze, and attempt to understand and improve. We live in a world where resources are scarce and unevenly distributed, and where disputes and conflicts constantly arise and need to be resolved. This neverending chain of dispute, conflict, and resolution ensures that politics is an ongoing process. It takes place at the individual, societal, state, and international levels as part of a struggle for ends such as equality, liberty, justice, and economic well-being.

CLOSE UP 1.3 Legitimacy, Authority, and Power: China's Relations with Hong Kong and Taiwan

On July 1, 1997, authority over six million people in Hong Kong suddenly changed hands. Britain, which had ruled Hong Kong and the New Territories as a democratically controlled colony for nearly a century, handed the territory over to the authoritarian, communist government of the People's Republic of China (PRC).

According to the negotiated agreement, the present capitalist economic system would be retained for half a century. But China immediately disbanded the elected Hong Kong legislature and substituted a Provisional Legislature composed of pro-Bejing politicians. With little discussion and certainly no fanfare, citizens of Hong Kong lost their political identity. Did the new government have the same legitimacy as the disbanded one? (In May 1998 elections, voters returned many of the pro-democracy politicians who had been ousted by China.)

Will this be the end of Chinese expansion? Or, will it attempt to extend its authority to Taiwan? In 1949 when the communists came to power in China, the losers led by Chiang Kai–shek fled to the island of Taiwan. While a majority of Taiwanese came from China in the eighteenth and nineteenth centuries, the new arrivals claimed Taipei as the provisional capital of the new Republic of China (RC). In 1971 the PRC replaced the RC in the United Nations. While the RC had long ago given up its claim to represent mainland China, the PRC continues to claim that Taiwan and its 21 million people belong to it. Since most states of the world recognize the claims of continental China over Hong Kong, will its claims over Taiwan also prevail? Will it use its power and military force to thwart the "renegade" province's claim to sovereignty? Is there a peaceful solution?

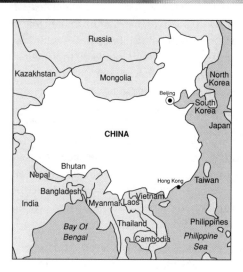

Map 1.1 China, Hong Kong, and Taiwan

Citizenship, Ethnicity, Nations, and States

Individuals belong to many organizations or institutions. At the most basic level, you may be part of a family. You may be a student in a school, or a parent of students at a school. You may belong to a church, trade union, sports and recreation club, and many other organizations.

Within a particular country an individual may also be a **citizen**—a formal member of a state and therefore eligible to enjoy specified rights and privileges. States normally consider all persons born on their territory, and their children, to be citizens. Besides these involuntary citizens, others may acquire citizenship though some specified formal action such as residing in the country for a certain length of time and carrying out some formal duties such as swearing an oath of allegiance. In Canada, for example, an immigrant may apply for citizenship after a total of three years residence in the country. Many non-citizens also live on Canadian territory. They may be settled residents or other foreigners in Canada on an extended or short-term basis. As we shall see in Chapter 3, rules concerning citizenship vary greatly among the states of the world. Some individuals even have dual citizenship. See Close Up 1.4.

Many people also consider themselves part of an ethnic group and perhaps even a nation. **Ethnicity** is primarily a subjective characteristic of groups of people who share customs, language, dialect and/or cultural heritage, and sometimes physical or distinct racial characteristics. When combined with religious, territorial, or political differences, ethnicity can be a potent political force. In Canada, for example, the country's earliest constitutional founders came from two ethnic groups, French and English, but they settled on lands that were already occupied by Native peoples.

CLOSE UP 1.4   Dual Citizenship, Multiple Allegiances

Dual citizenship is a growing global phenomenon. In the United States in 1998, a man who held passports in both the United States and Colombia tried to hold political positions in both countries and commute between them. As it happened, he lost his Senate race in the United States, but his case highlighted the growing trend of holding two or more citizenships. Years ago, voting in a foreign election was a good way to lose one's U.S. citizenship. This is no longer the case. The United States' federal government does not endorse dual citizenship, but it tolerates it—as do a growing number of other states such as Canada. A second or third passport is not just a link to a homeland, it grants privileges such as a stake in a second economy, with the ability to move in and out at will without visas.

Do you consider it to be a problem in this day and age that dual citizens pledge allegiance to more than one flag?

Nations, like ethnic groups, are *cultural* entities and are essentially subjective, containing a sense of "we-ness" or belonging. A **nation** is a politically conscious and mobilized collectivity, often with a sense of territory, which may aspire to greater autonomy or even statehood. Nations are not the same as ethnic groups, nor do they necessarily exist contiguously with the territory of a country. In Canada, some Quebec leaders claim to represent a "nation," and so do many leaders of the Native peoples. English-speaking Canadians, on the other hand, usually proclaim their loyalty to a political entity such as a city, province, or the country as a whole.

When we use the word **state**, we are referring to the political unit of an entire territory. A state comprises a territory, population, and a government. In common language, a state is synonymous with a country. However the term state can refer to more than this. A state is also an abstraction which depicts many institutions and rules. It is not possible to point at any one institution or even a number of them and say "that is the state." Actions may be carried out in the name of the state, as when laws are enforced or when countries impose compulsory taxes or go to war. For this reason some scholars assume that the state is more than an abstraction. But even when the government of a state acts in a national emergency or a war, not all state institutions are united behind them. Some of them may even actively promote policies which contradict the so-called state or government. This has often been the case, for example, with the provincial government of Quebec, when Parti Québécois ministers promoted separation from Canada.

Max Weber, the German sociologist, defined the state as a set of institutions that "successfully upholds a claim to the monopoly of the legitimate use of physical force in the enforcement of its order … within a given territorial area."[21] This definition highlights the fact that the state is able to use coercive force to issue rules that are binding on all those within its territory. Or, as a more contemporary theorist put it: the state is a "set of purposely contrived arrangements" that unify the rules, roles and resources found in governmental institutions.[22]

The state is, thus, defined in terms of its relation to power—both external and internal. A state is normally considered **sovereign** when final authority rests in the national government so that internally it is able to tax and coerce its citizens, and externally it can conduct its own relations with the international community free from outside interference by other states or governments.

The concepts of state and nation and the development of the modern state are covered thoroughly in Chapters 3, 4, and 5.

Self-Determination and Nationalism

The principle of **self-determination** is a shared belief that all peoples ought to have the right to establish their collective identity in the form of a sovereign state. Historically, this idea came from the belief that "nations" which existed as colonies should be allowed to declare independence, set up their own states, and join international organizations. Countries are normally allowed to become a member of the UN when the member-states recognize them as sovereign—that is, when they can maintain order within their territories, are free to run their own affairs, and can carry out the normal functions of government such as collecting taxes and issuing passports. Today, however, almost all of the world's population already belong to a state. Therefore, aspirants must win UN approval to break up an existing state in order to form a separate state based on the principle of self-determination. According to international law, any "nation" that is already part of a state must show that it is seeking to escape colonial status or is subject to a discriminatory regime before the United Nations will accept its status as a state and as a member of the organization.

A related concept is nationalism. **Nationalism** is the collective action of a nation in pursuit of autonomy or independence. Some members of the French nation in Quebec are nationalists; others believe that this nation can attain its goals of self-expression and identity inside the Canadian state. Those "others" may be called federalists or something else, but they are not nationalists except inasmuch as they want "more" for Quebec. Nationalists may form movements in order to demand separation or independence from the state. They may make demands which cannot be accommodated within the country, and use nationalist sentiment to support the development of a new state. The concept of nationalism is developed more fully in Chapters 3, 4, and 5 as a basis for a discussion of the development of the modern state.

Democracy and Authoritarianism

States differ greatly in their organizational forms and ideals. Democratic systems are normally distinguished from authoritarian regimes by the amount and quality of participation allowed to citizens in the determination of public policy. A **democratic political system**, therefore, is a system of government which conciliates competing interests through competitive elections. An **authoritarian political system** is a system of government which imposes one dominant interest, that of a political elite, on all others. Another term, **totalitarianism**, is used to describe an extreme form of authoritarianism.

It is said to exist when government leaders can and do impose their objectives or goals upon their people to an unlimited degree. In theory, they control all aspects of society and subordinate individuals and groups to their absolute leadership.

These concepts are all discussed in detail in Chapter 5, and they have a direct bearing on the material in every subsequent chapter. Be aware at the outset, however, of some basic difficulties with the concept of democracy. Democracy is a very simple idea which is difficult, if not impossible, to replicate exactly in the real world. In the simplest model of democracy, elections are seen as providing popular sovereignty. As the idea goes, the people elect a sample of their fellow citizens to serve for a time as the rulers. After this period, the rulers must account to the citizens for whether they have ruled properly. In the accounting process, known as an election, the people reward or punish the rulers by re-electing or rejecting them. Good government is thought to be assured because the elected rulers wish to satisfy the people in order to get re-elected. Politicians therefore serve the country in the national interests rather than in their own selfish ones.

This simple model is significant because if people *believe* in it, and act accordingly, the country can operate successfully. When citizens accept that a government has the right to make decisions for them, the political system acquires legitimacy and viability is assured. Nevertheless, this model of democracy is quite rudimentary and possibly misleading.

In the contemporary world, all states and even many autocratic organizations refer to themselves as democratic. By that they mean that they rule for the common good, regardless of the degree to which the people have a say in governing. Even inside political systems, democracy has become a very ambiguous and elastic word. For some writers it means good government or the purposes of government. This is a *substantive* view of democracy. For others, democracy is *procedural* in that it refers to the mechanics or procedures by which a country discusses and organizes political differences.

The pure or simple model of democracy assumes popular participation in law and public policy-making. But such direct, citizen influence is very rare in the modern world. The model of democracy is an ideal that is rarely actualized. Most systems today are **representative democracies**, democracies in which elected officials make decisions with the force of law because they have achieved legitimacy by some form of election. Thus democracy in Canada and elsewhere is not rule by the people themselves. It is representative democracy.

Representative democracy does not work without complex structures and a mass public with fairly sophisticated beliefs about government and politics. Governors, too, must understand the need to reconcile their authority with public influence. They must adapt to operating within a society that holds conflicting beliefs about the role of government. Let us take one example: conservatives consider individual rights to be immunities— guarantees against government action or interference in the lives of individuals and groups. A free market economy, thus, characterizes the type of economic relations desired by conservatives. Modern liberals, on the other hand, think of rights as the entitlements individuals ought to receive from the state. Modern liberals do not object to government management of the economy. They applaud it. From this simple conflict in beliefs we can see that democracy must be about a set of *procedures* that enable rules to be set despite differences in judgments about the desirable outcomes of government action.[23]

A further point in the analysis of democracy concerns its substantive qualities. At question is whether or not democracy tends to be the cause of, or is caused by, the values of liberty and equality. The principle of liberty appears to be required in democratic systems because it underlies notions about freedom of thought, assembly, and association, as well as freedom of the press. The majority principle and the idea of competing parties, rule of law, and free elections also seem to be fundamentally interlocked with democratic ideas. Furthermore, equality is embedded in the democratic notion that all individuals should be treated alike under the law and in rules about "one person one vote" in elections.

In this book we assume the existence and importance of certain values in our discussion of democratic institutions. But democracy itself is conceived as a *means* or procedure for developing public influence over politicians. Goals about economic, social, and foreign policy are seen as the output of the democratic process. While democracies may be associated with specific values, that does not mean that they should be equated with, or equal to, the "good life."

We discuss contemporary forms of government ranging from democratic to authoritarian in detail in Chapter 5. The chapters thereafter consider important topics such as political culture, ideology, constitutions, central government institutions, public administration, political parties, elections, and international politics across the entire spectrum of these forms of government. In this way students will become aware of the broad range of differences and possibilities for managing political change, depending on where a state lies on the democratic–authoritarian continuum.

Political Culture and Ideology

Politics reflects the culture of a certain time and place. What individuals know and how they feel about their political system affects the number and kinds of demands they make upon their state government and how they respond to laws and political leadership. **Political culture** refers to the broad pattern of values and attitudes that individuals and societies hold toward political objects. Chapters 6 and 7 survey the unique political cultures of different states and regions of the world and their implications of this for politics.

State politics are also affected by belief systems, which are much more systematic than political culture. These patterns of thought are known as ideologies. **Ideology** refers to a set of ideas and beliefs that clarify what is valued and what is not, what must be maintained and what must be changed, and what shapes the attitudes of those who share it. Ideologies can be very powerful: they have justified wars, repression, and even extermination of peoples. But they have also provided the underpinnings for prosperous societies and fair and orderly government. Chapters 8 and 9 consider the main ideologies that have provided blueprints for much of the world, both in the past and today.

Law, the Rule of Law, and Constitutionalism

Governments enforce their authority by making laws. That is, law is the instrument that states and their governments use to regulate behaviour. **Law** consists of a special body of rules emanating from government and backed up by the threat of state coercion. Of course, not everything governments do is made into law. Governments also act by announcing policies, spending funds, setting up structures and processes for consultation and decision-making, and steering the country in particular policy directions.

Laws come in many forms, but all concern the relationships of individuals and groups with government. In fact, most of a citizen's contact with political authorities consists of dealing with laws about taxes, business regulations, and administrative guidelines. Courts, police, and prisons all play a role in adjudicating and applying laws.

In democratic countries, law is circumscribed. Courts are separated from politics in order that judges can interpret the law in an impartial (non-politicized) manner. Recognized legal authorities such as the police enforce the law by apprehending offenders and holding them accountable before the courts for obeying the laws of the land. A prison system is constituted to set individuals apart from society when they do not conform to the laws of the land. The prison system serves several conflicting goals of state authorities such as punishing wrongdoers, safeguarding society, and correcting the behaviour of inmates so they will be able to maintain themselves legally when they emerge from captivity.

In Canada, as in other democracies, we also say that we are *ruled by law*. While laws are made by humans, these laws are to be administered impartially, and no individual (regardless of political status) is to be above the law. As we shall see in Chapter 3, the **rule of law** means that no citizen is to be deprived of due process or to be punished at the whim of an official. The courts are to ensure that these rules of law are upheld. This principle is often known by the term **constitutionalism**. In Chapters 3, 4, and 5, we discuss law in its various forms as a basic component of modern states. The specific relation of law with constitutions is covered in detail in Chapters 10 and 11.

Institutions

In the modern state, law is expressed through institutions. Political institutions reflect both the structure and the values of society. Formal institutions of government are the most visible elements of the political process. **Political institutions** define the rules, procedures, and norms that constrain and facilitate opportunities and shape expectations. They are social structures that are organized to achieve goals for society, including constitutions, legislatures, bureaucracies, and executives, and they explain much about how politics is conducted. They shape the interests, resources, and conduct of political leaders who in turn shape the institutions.

Institutions are stable configurations that normally change very slowly over long periods of time. They therefore can be studied as the organized collective behaviour of individuals. As Karl R. Popper put it, "Institutions are like fortresses. They must be well designed and properly manned."[24] In other words, the way institutions are structured affects political actors, bureaucrats, and citizens and the manner in which behaviour and institutions are intertwined. Institutions such as executives, legislatures, bureaucracies, and courts are discussed in Chapters 12, 13, 14, and 15.

Political Parties, Interest Groups, and Elections

Political behaviour in the form of political parties, interest groups, and elections provide tangible demonstrations of how culture and institutions structure individual and collective action in the political process. They provide the groups and processes through which people can participate in their political system. **Parties** are political groups that present candidates at elections and are capable of placing, through elections, candidates for public office. **Interest groups** do not present candidates for elections, but are organized associations which engage in activity relative to governmental decisions. The nature and activities of parties and interest groups are very different in democratic or authoritarian states. **Competitive elections**—those involving more than one party with a chance of forming a government—are vital to democratic government. The rules are vital because different types of electoral rules can provide very different results from the same election. Elections in authoritarian states are rarely competitive, but rather endorsements of the regime in power. Parties and interest groups are covered in Chapters 16 and 17, while the various functions and types of elections in use around the world are discussed in Chapters 18 and 19.

Political Change

States are not rigid legal/formal structures that never evolve. Throughout history, nations and peoples have contested, reformed, and even destroyed empires, absolute monarchies, and authoritarian regimes. Politics is in constant flux. Chapter 20 deals with this fascinating topic of **political change**. How do states adapt, evolve, fracture, and disappear? How are new countries created? What promotes political stability and instability in states? Here we consider domestic and international topics of political development, and various forms of political violence, terrorism, and revolution.

International Relations

States—whether democratic or authoritarian—coexist in the global arena. **International relations** is the study of the relations between and among these states. It is concerned with international law, diplomacy, and the grand issues of war and peace. It is also concerned with vital issues such as human rights, the environment, and health, which concern everyone regardless of what state they belong to. Increasingly, **globalization**—the increasing interdependence of states—impinges on the domestic affairs of states and affects their governments and politics. International politics is, therefore, also the study of how the global system affects the domestic policies of states, and vice versa. It is concerned with social, economic, environmental, military, and other issues of humanity. This book is concerned with comparing politics across a wide spectrum of the world's states and with international relations and globalization. Chapter 21 deals specifically with these exciting issues and theories of international affairs.

In the following 20 chapters we examine and compare the great variety of ways in which politics is conducted within, between, and among states. We consider the ideas and motivations behind political behaviour, and survey the kinds of institutions that have been invented to resolve political disputes. We also study what happens when political institutions fail, and coups, terrorism, violence and war are used to impose a solution through naked force. In the next chapter, however, we survey the discipline of political science and consider how early, great thinkers established the foundations on which modern political science has been built. As a branch of knowledge it has many accomplishments to its credit, although there are many limitations to overcome and problems to solve.

DISCUSSION QUESTIONS

1. What do you consider to be some of the major issues facing governments around the world? Are they similar in every country? In your country?
2. Is there a distinction between politics and government?
3. Is there a distinction between power and authority in all social relations? In the family as well as in politics?
4. To what extent would it be possible for Robinson Crusoe to engage in politics on his desert island?
5. What are the main areas a political scientist might study in the field of institutions? Political behaviour? Political change?

KEY TERMS

anarchy, p. 9
authoritarian political
   system, p. 17
authority, p. 12
bureaucratic authority,
   p. 13
charismatic authority,
   p. 13
citizen, p. 15
competitive elections,
   p. 21
constitutionalism, p. 20
democratic political
   system, p. 17
ethnicity, p. 15
global economy, p. 3

globalization, p. 21
government, p. 8
group. p. 7
ideology, p. 19
influence, p. 11
interest group, p. 7
interest groups, p. 21
international relations,
   p. 21
law, p. 20
legitimacy, p. 12
nation, p. 16
nationalism, p. 17
parties (political), p. 21
political change, p. 21
political culture, p. 19

political institutions, p. 20
political science, p. 6
politics, p. 8
power, p. 10
public authority, p. 12
rational-legal authority,
   p. 13
representative democracy,
   p. 18
rule of law, p. 20
self-determination, p. 17
society, p. 7
sovereign state, p. 17
state, p. 16
totalitarianism, p. 17
traditional authority, p. 13

ENDNOTES

1. For a critique of the globalization thesis see A. Kleinknecht and Jan ter Wengel "The Myth of Economic Globalization" *Cambridge Journal of Economics*, vol. 22 (1998), pp. 637–647.

2. W.J. Ashley, "What is Political Science?" An Inaugural Lecture (Toronto, 1888), p. 7.

3. Ernest Samuels, ed., *The Education of Henry Adams* (Boston: Houghton Mifflin, 1974), p. 7. Henry Adams was influenced by Blaise Pascal. In his *Pensées*, Pascal also says that zeal for the common good is nothing but a pretence.

4. See H. Scott Gordon, "How many kinds of things are there in the world?" Distinguished Research Lecture (Indiana University, Indiana, 1990), p. 21.

5. H.W. Fowler and F.G. Fowler, *The Concise Oxford Dictionary of Current English*, 4th ed. (Oxford: Clarendon Press, 1958), p. 534.

6. Robert H. Salisbury, "Interest Groups," in Fred I. Greenstein and Nelson Polsby, eds., *Handbook of Political Science*, vol. 4 (Reading, Mass.: Addison-Wesley, 1975), p. 175.

7. Carl Schmitt, *The Concept of the Political*, trans. of 3rd ed. (New Brunswick, N.J.: Rutgers, 1976).

8. Giovanni Sartori, "The Essence of the Political in Carl Schmitt," *Journal of Theoretical Politics*, vol. 1, no. 1 (Jan. 1989), pp. 63–75, esp. p. 74.

9. W. Phillips Shively, *Power and Choice* (New York: Random House, 1987), p. 7.

10. David Easton, *A Framework for Political Analysis* (Englewood Cliffs, N.J.: Prentice-Hall, 1965), pp. 50–56.

11. Harold Lasswell, *Politics: Who Gets What, When and How?* (New York: McGraw-Hill, 1936).

12. Bernard Crick, *In Defence of Politics*, 2nd ed. (Harmondsworth, Eng.: Penguin, 1972).

13. Human Development Report, 1998 (Oxford University Press, 1998) p. 30.

14. Fowler and Fowler, *The Concise Oxford Dictionary*, p. 936.

15. Of the many volumes dealing with the concept of power, two of the most influential are Harold Lasswell and Abraham Kaplan, *Power and Society* (New Haven: Yale University Press, 1950); and Robert A Dahl, *Modern Political Analysis* (Englewood Cliffs, N.J.: Prentice-Hall, 1950).

16. R.J. Mokken and F.N. Stokmann, "Power and Influence as Political Phenomena," in Brian Barry, ed., *Power and Political Theory* (New York: John Wiley, 1976), pp. 37–38.

17. See Robert A. Dahl, *A Preface to Democratic Theory* (Chicago: University of Chicago Press, 1970).

18. For further reading on the concept of authority, see Robert M. MacIver, *The Modern State* (New York: Oxford, 1964); Robert A. Dahl, *Polyarchy: Participation and Opposition* (New Haven: Yale University Press, 1971).

19. For further reading on the concept of legitimacy, see H.H. Gerth and C.W. Mills, eds., *From Max Weber: Essays in Sociology* (New York: Oxford, 1946).

20. Max Weber, *The Theory of Social and Economic Organization*, edited and translated by A.M. Henderson and Talcott Parsons (New York: Oxford University Press, 1947), ch. 3.

21. Max Weber, *The Theory of Social and Economic Organizations*, edited and translated by A. M. Henderson and Talcott Parsons (New York: Oxford, 1947), p. 154.

22. G. Poggi, *The State: Its Nature, Development and Prospects* (Cambridge: Polity Press, 1990), p. 19.

23. See Jean Bethke Elshtain, *Democracy on Trial* (New York: Basic Books, 1994) and Robert D. Putnam, *Making Democracy Work: Civic Traditions in Modern Italy* (Princeton, N.J.: Princeton University Press, 1993).

24. Karl R. Popper, *The Poverty of Historicism* (London: Routledge, 1961), p. 157. For neo-institutional approaches in general, see Jeffrey Pfeffer, *Organizations and Organization Theory* (Marshfield, Mass.: Pitman, 1982).

FURTHER READING

Cerny, Philip G., *The Changing Architecture of Politics: Structure, Agency and the Future of the State* (London: Sage, 1990).

Dahl, Robert, *Modern Political Analysis*, 3rd ed. (Englewood Cliffs, N.J.: Prentice-Hall, 1976).

Derbyshire, J.D. and I. Derbyshire, *World Political Systems: An Introduction to Comparative Government* (Edinburgh: Chambers, 1991).

Deutsch, Karl, *Politics and Government: How People Decide Their Fate* (Boston: Houghton Mifflin, 1980).

Gibbons, Michael, *Interpreting Politics* (Oxford: Basil Blackwell, 1988).

Kennedy, P., *The Rise and Fall of the Great Powers* (New York: Random House, 1987).

———, *Preparing for the Twenty–first Century* (New York: Harper Collins, 1993).

Lane, Ruth, *The 'Politics' Model* (Armonk, N.Y.: M.E. Sharpe, 1997).

Lindblom, C.E., *Inquiry and Change* (New Haven, Conn.: Yale University Press, 1990).

Macridis, Roy C., and Bernard E. Brown, eds., *Comparative Politics*, 7th ed. (Pacific Grove: Brooks/Cole, 1990).

Macridis, R.C., and S.L. Burg, *Introduction to Comparative Politics: Regimes and Changes*, 2nd ed. (New York: Harper Collins, 1991).

Mann, M., *The Sources of Social Power: A History of Power from the Beginning to 1760 A.D.*, Vol. 1 (Cambridge, Mass.: Cambridge University Press, 1986).

Mayer, Lawrence, *Redefining Comparative Politics* (Newbury Park, Calif.: Sage, 1989).

Morriss, Peter, *Power* (New York: St. Martin's Press, 1987).

Needler, M.C., *The Concepts of Comparative Politics* (New York: Praeger, 1991).

Nye, Joseph S. Jr. *Why People Don't Trust Government* (Cambridge Mass: Harvard University Press, 1997).

Rothgeb, John, *Defining Power: Influence and Force in the Contemporary International System* (New York: St. Martin's Press, 1993).

Rustow, D.A. and K.P. Erickson, (eds.) *Comparative Political Dynamics: Global Research Perspectives* (New York: Harper Collins, 1991).

Seidman, Harold, and Robert Gilmour, *Politics, Position and Power* (New York: Oxford University Press, 1988).

 **Weblinks**

www.unicef.org/pon96/contents.htm
The UNICEF Progress of Nations Web Page identifies the stages of social and economic development in nations of the world.

sunsite.unc.edu/expo/soviet.exhibit/entrance.html#tour
This site contains descriptions of many of the events during and documents relating to the Cold War period.

www.unicc.org/unhcr/
This site describes the circumstances and patterns in migration of many of the worlds refugees.

CHAPTER 2

Political Science Yesterday and Today

POLITICAL SCIENCE IN PERSPECTIVE

Political science is a relatively new subject in universities, but its subject material has been the object of scholarly attention for many centuries. Today, knowledge is generally categorized within the domain of the exact sciences, the social sciences, or the humanities. These artificial divisions are convenient but cannot always be maintained in a neat fashion: the groupings are often overlapping and interdependent. The humanities include literature, language, sculpture, music, dance, and painting as well as philosophy and theology. Studies in this branch of knowledge tend to rely on human judgment more than on scientific methodology. The so-called exact sciences, on the other hand, including mathematics, physics, chemistry, earth science, and biology, require a more systematic approach to the acquisition and classification of knowledge. Studies in this area must meet the standard of scientific replicability, so that, if repeated, they should always reach the same conclusions or results.

Political science belongs to the social sciences. This branch of knowledge is generally divided into eight disciplines: geography, history, psychology, sociology, anthropology, economics, communications, and political science. What these subjects have in common is the study of human behaviour. Social scientists study the "social" aspects of individuals, as do the students of the humanities, but many practitioners attempt to use scientific methodology, and pattern their research on the so-called exact sciences. While all political scientists rely on logical reasoning, the latter among them aspire to rigorous methodology and objectivity, building evidence through experiments or observations. So far, the search by political scientists for universal and enduring laws like Newton's laws of physics has been frustrated because "human behaviour is too sensitive to the fluctuations of culture and the circumstances of history to yield permanently enduring findings."[1] There is today, therefore, no agreed upon "essential scientific core" for the discipline as a whole—neither in content nor in method.

According to a leading political scientist, division over methodology in the discipline exists for two basic reasons:

1. Some political scientists are convinced that true knowledge can be found only in the "rigorous search for invariances, for the regularities we expect to find in nature";
2. Others believe that "knowledge is the search for meaning, for understanding and interpretation, that is, for what is human in the blending of mind and spirit."[2]

Greek and Roman Political Thought

Political science has evolved through a series of "surges and sags" over the centuries. As a field of study it can be traced to early classical Greece scholars such as Herodotus, Aristotle, and Plato. In fact, the word "politics" derives from the Greek word *polis*, which means city-state. Of course these early contributors did not think or write in terms of modern political science, but rather of history and, more particularly, philosophy. However, they were concerned with the enduring questions about politics and government. They wrote both *empirical* (what is) and *normative* (what ought to be) works about politics. They addressed questions such as "What form of government is best?" and "What is the good life?" They developed many of the ideas and classifications of political systems that we still use today.[3]

Herodotus, a Greek historian in the fifth century B.C., classified governments according to three types—monarchy, aristocracy, or democracy—depending on how many people wielded ultimate decision-making power; that is, rule by one, a few, or many. About a century later, Aristotle (384–322 B.C.) revised this classification, adding a new criterion—whether the rulers ruled in their own interest or in the general interest.

This perceptive classification of rule by the one, the few, or the many on a spectrum running from tyrannical rule through to democracy has become part of Western thought. It helped to introduce a degree of order into the study of the immense variety of political ideas and systems and promoted the value of unbiased observation as an approach to studying political science. On the other hand, in his *Ethics*, Aristotle observed that when human behaviour is involved, one cannot reach the same level of certainty as in the natural sciences.

Aristotle's *Politics* (eight books) had further profound effects on Western political thought. One of his most influential concepts was of the state as a social organism, in the biological sense of a living, changing unit. He believed that political systems evolve as natural social organisms from the desire to seek moral perfection. A healthy constitution, he maintained, was one to which all elements of society give assent and allegiance. And, the most stable Greek political system, he said, was one in which the middle class holds the balance of power—where they have numerical superiority and more power than the very rich and the very poor. They must, for example, hold more total wealth than the rich and physically outnumber the poor. Many of the ideas generated by Aristotle form the basis of comparative politics, an important branch of political science, which we examine closely in Chapter 4.

Plato (428–348 B.C.), another early Greek philosopher, who in fact taught Aristotle, was fascinated by the political question of what constitutes the ideal state or utopia. In his *Republic*, Plato was concerned particularly with the concept of justice, which he perceived resulted from adhering to relatively strict principles. He conceived of a "just" society as one in which every individual performs tasks for which he or she is best suited by inborn qualities and training. In return, that person receives his or her "just" due. In essence, Plato believed that justice would constitute ideal harmony for individuals and also the state.

Drawing on his knowledge of how Greek city states functioned, Plato categorized political systems according to which level of society had most influence on the governance of a given state. The ideal state, he said, would be ruled by philosopher kings who were imbued with wisdom. Of course, Plato was not naive. He posited that an "ideal" state would persist only if the people believed in their leaders. He advocated the need for a "noble lie" or myth to keep people content with their status in life. Rulers would be those with *gold* in their composition, while soldiers would have *silver*, and ordinary craftsmen and farmers would possess only *iron* or *brass*.

Timocracies, in contrast, were ruled by property-owning, ambitious men in search of honour. And oligarchies were ruled by people who sought only wealth. If the rich became degenerate, the poor, Plato said, would take over and the state would soon reflect the tendency of base individuals who yield to the pleasures of the moment. Implicitly, Plato, too, viewed the state and society as an *organic whole* in which the component parts were specialized and, like the organs of the body, had roles which contribute to the well-being of the whole.

For centuries, Aristotle and Plato's concept of the organic nature of the state dominated how people thought about the state. The concept reflected, or was reflected by, the political institutions of the day. It was accepted for centuries after the fall of the Greek city states, when the Roman Empire dominated the Western world and individuals such as Cicero (106–43 B.C.) contributed advances in law and public administration to the study of government. The concept continued even after the Roman Empire began to crumble, and through the so-called Dark Ages (A.D. 476–1000), when Christianity provided the main social and political coherence in Europe.

Western European Political Thought

When the first European states began to emerge, they coexisted with the church. Kings used the influence of the church to strengthen their own positions with their subjects. Ultimately, they adopted the concept of **divine rule**, portraying themselves as vicars of Christ with absolute, divine authority. Church and state were fused.

With the invention of the printing press, political information became widely disseminated throughout Europe. From the late fifteenth century on, politics became a popular intellectual concern. The sixteenth century brought the years of the Reformation, when Martin Luther (1483–1546) challenged the authority of the Roman Catholic Church and the supremacy of the pope. These and other attacks on the Church led to the rise of Lutheranism, Calvinism, and other Protestant denominations. Jean Bodin (1530–1596) also made his reputation during this period. Bodin is credited with inventing the term "political science," which he defined as the study of sovereignty, the functions of government, and the institutions that make law. Bodin, affected by the religious wars in Europe, wrote in his *République* that sovereignty was "indivisible," and advised that the monarchy and centralism were essential to a strong state.

By the late seventeenth century, access to written material had reached new heights, and intellectual debate about the exercise of state power flourished. This period of history, sometimes called the Age of Reason, produced several great political thinkers. Thomas Hobbes (1588–1679) was an English philosopher and an ardent Royalist. He was an acquaintance of such thinkers as Galileo, Descartes, and Ben Jonson. Hobbes had a very pessimistic view of human nature and advocated absolute government based on a social contract which would bind all citizens under a sovereign who would protect them from their own selfishness.

In *Leviathan*, Hobbes wrote that individuals did not strive for moral perfection as Aristotle had posited, but for self-preservation. For Hobbes, life in the state of nature would be "solitary, poor, nasty, brutish and short." A state would, therefore, be necessary in order to maintain order and stability. Government, he conjectured, should be developed to control personal appetites for liberty and power.

In direct contrast to Hobbes's prescription, another English philosopher, John Locke (1632–1704), advocated that governments should be limited and accountable so that people generally could be free to think and act as they wished. He conceived of humans as "free, equal and independent." Locke's optimistic views of human nature were widely popular and influential, most notably in framing the American Declaration of Independence. In France, Jean-Jacques Rousseau (1712–1778) indirectly supported Locke in his book *Social Contract* when he developed the idea that in the state of nature "Man is born free and everywhere he is in chains." In other words, he believed that man was born innocent but was corrupted by society. We shall have more to say about Locke and Rousseau in Chapter 6.

Yet another significant contribution during this period was made by the French scholar Baron de Montesquieu (1689–1755) who, after incorrectly examining the British political system, advised a "separation of powers" as a check on absolute authority. Montesquieu's views, expressed in *L'Esprit des Lois*, did not have a large following in his native France, but later greatly influenced the framers of the Constitution of the United States.

The Enlightenment also saw the development of the application of scientific principles to politics. Modern political science is indebted to the British utilitarians of the nineteenth century, including Jeremy Bentham (1748–1832), James Mill (1773–1836), and John Stuart Mill (1805–1873), who advanced the scientific principle of utility—the greatest good for the greatest number. The utilitarians wanted a scientific approach to politics so that it could be exercised for the good of the whole rather than for any particular group or elite in society.

The ultimate challenge to the organic view of the state came with the industrial revolution in Britain in the nineteenth century. The idea of the organic state and society as continuous and changeless was definitively broken at that time. People no longer believed that the relations among the three social classes—the aristocracy, the bourgeoisie, and the proletariat—were ordained by God. The repercussions of the industrial revolution were extensive. New machines were invented and new movements began. Aristocracies fell, as did forms of government. A mechanistic view of the state and society took hold. No longer understood as a fixed, organic whole, the machinery of state could be regulated, changed, and adapted, and the best way to do that was through constitutions, and finding methods of improving constitutions.

Friedrich Engels (1820–1895) and Karl Marx (1818–1883) used science in quite a different way. They developed a "scientific" philosophy of history and economics. In Marx's terms, this science could explain the historical development of mankind from feudalism, to capitalism, to socialism and eventually to a perfect condition where the state would wither away entirely. This philosophy, the basis of Marx's *Communist Manifesto*, had a profound effect on the political world and helped set the stage for the application of scientific principles of economics to politics. We will return to these and later ideas of Marxism in Chapter 8.

Some early writers, however, focused on quite different aspects of politics. Niccolo Machiavelli (1469–1527), one of the best-known political thinkers of the Renaissance (from the mid-fourteenth century to the end of the sixteenth century), emphasized pragmatism and political power. During the Renaissance, as medieval feudal societies gave way to the modern world with its growing national consciousness, political centralization, and commercial economies, a great many small, unstable, new states existed. Machiavelli searched for the rules of political stability, concentrating particularly on developing practical rules to guide politicians in obtaining and holding power. He found that power tends to be more important than ethics and morality. From his publication *The Prince*, Machiavelli's name became synonymous with these rules for princes, the best known of which today may be "It is better to be loved, but if not loved then feared." Machiavelli did not produce these rules in order to compare or analyze states but rather to instruct politicians on how to obtain or maintain power or control over the behaviour of others.

Most early Greek, Roman, and European philosophers, however, were social ethicists or social critics, rather than "scientists." A brief list of these philosophers would have to include St. Augustine (354–430), Thomas Aquinas (1225–1274), and Marsiglio of Padua (1275–1343), who combined their political advice with their theological teachings. To these few might be added the names of later philosophers of eighteenth century Europe, including Immanuel Kant (1724–1804) and Friedrich Hegel (1770–1831), and, in the United States, Thomas Jefferson (1743–1826). These philosophers of the Enlightenment were all concerned with freedom, and their ideas permeated thought during the American Revolution (1776) and the French Revolution (1789).

Early contributions to the study of politics and government came, then, largely from philosophers, but also from the fields of history and law. For many years, the subject was commonly taught in history departments. Political scientists were, in fact, often considered to be "historians of the present," and early studies of political institutions and international relations emphasized historical methodology. Since it was particularly concerned with government organization and lawmaking, the field of law, too, was important in the evolution of modern political science.

CONTEMPORARY APPROACHES AND METHODS

Political science did not appear as a separate discipline until the late eighteenth and nineteenth centuries, when departmental chairs were established in universities. The first department of political science was created in the United States at Columbia University in 1880. Even after it was officially recognized as a distinct field, however, political science continued to be taught for many years in history departments and in economics departments as "political economy." Political science thus developed as a truly interdisciplinary study. This trend continued into the twentieth century as developments in sociology, anthropology, psychology, biology, physics, and economics influenced the thinking of political scientists. Even literature can be related to the study of politics, as suggested in Close Up 2.1.

Many first-generation American political scientists, such as Harold Lasswell and Charles E. Merriam, favoured the application of scientific methods to the study of politics. At the same time, a European tradition was sustained in America by European-educated immigrants such as Carl Friedrich and many others who had been trained in the European tradition of philosophical inquiry with its traditional historical methods.[4] These two approaches to the study of politics combined to form the basis of modern political science as it exists today.

In the 1930s, and even more so in the 1940s and 1950s, the discipline of political science was reoriented as political scientists increasingly studied observable human political behaviour in the light of theories borrowed from other social sciences. Because the social sciences had developed from biological models, the concept of the political system as a political organism became popular once again, particularly in the study of subjects such as systems analysis, as we shall see below.

More recently, after World War II, political scientists relied increasingly on the fields of mathematics and statistics to help analyze political data, making political science even more interdisciplinary. But the study of philosophy was not forgotten. There is, as Lucien Pye notes, a sense that as a discipline modern political science wants to have its cake and eat it too—to be simultaneously humanistic and scientific.[5]

Theoretical Approaches to the Study of Politics

In order to escape from randomly collecting facts or relying on only one theory when none has met the complete test for scientific validity, political scientists have developed several approaches. An **approach** to a discipline is the particular orientation that one adopts when addressing the subject. It is a predisposition to adopt a particular conceptual framework

CLOSE UP 2.1   Politics and the Novel

Novelists can be particularly adept at capturing the political culture of a country. In the United States, Henry Adams began the tradition of the Washington novel with *Democracy: An American Novel*. Some classic political novels that entertain and also engage the mind about political and cultural issues would include the following — the reader undoubtedly has favourites to add to this short list:

Feodor Dostoevsky, *The Idiot*

Allen Drury, *Advise and Consent*

Umberto Eco, *The Name of the Rose*

Aldous Huxley, *Brave New World*

Arthur Koestler, *Darkness at Noon*

Hugh MacLennan, *Two Solitudes*

Gabriel Garcia Marquez, *One Hundred Years of Solitude*

V.S. Naipaul, *Guerillas*

George Orwell, *Animal Farm*

George Orwell, *Nineteen Eighty-Four*

Alan Paton, *Cry the Beloved Country*

Jean-Paul Sartre, *Dirty Hands*

B.F. Skinner, *Walden Two*

Aleksandr Solzhenitsyn, *The Gulag Archipelago*

Robert Penn Warren, *All the King's Men*

and to explore certain hypotheses in order to generate theory.[6] An approach may be implicit or explicit, but it must be identifiable because it determines the questions, perspectives, and procedures or methods that a researcher will use in his or her study. An approach provides a guide in selecting facts and in organizing them in a meaningful way.

Scholars have tended to bring approaches and methods of study from other fields to their research in political science. It is multidisciplinary. As well, different generations of scholars have developed approaches based on their unique interests, values, and methodologies. Approaches to the study of politics have therefore changed over time, with notions about which ones were best, shifting according to what was needed, or sometimes fashionable, to study specific topics or problems. However, they mostly focus now on vital questions such as who exercises power and influence in political decision-making and how politicians seek and maintain power.

Underlying all approaches to the study of politics, however, is the principle that political scientists should be analytical and comparative and should avoid basing generalizations on casual observation. Whether the research is based on experiments, statistics, or configurative case studies, it ought to be ordered by the desire to be explicit about the rules employed to describe and analyze politics.

Many modern approaches to the study of political science are based on a belief that studies of politics must employ a **general theory** of the polity; that is, they must identify all the critical structures and processes of society, explain their interrelationships with politics, and predict a wide array of governmental outcomes. Such a theory, it is argued, would allow scholars to obtain scientific-law-like generalizations about politics.

Two analogies summarize the core of this debate on the status of general theory in political science. One is that politics is like the shifting formlessness of clouds; the other is that it is based on precise, mechanical causation like a watch. Gabriel Almond and Stephen Genco conclude that "the current quandary in political science can, to a large extent, be explained by the fact that, by themselves, clock-model assumptions are inappropriate for dealing with the substance of political phenomena."[7] This conclusion comes from the belief that all theories about politics must necessarily include transient and fleeting phenomena. Almond and Genco maintain that politics is not totally predictable because, since human behaviour is involved, there can be no direct cause-and-effect relationship among all the variables. They contend that political reality "has distinctive properties which make it unamendable to the forms of explanation used in the natural sciences."[8] Therefore, the science of politics should not be seen as a set of methods with a predetermined theory, but rather, as Almond and Genco noted, as a "commitment to explore and attempt to understand a given segment of empirical reality."[9]

The Traditional-Historical Approach

We have seen that the **traditional-historical approach** was predominant in the early years of modern political science, when studies of politics concentrated on an essentially legal-formal description of governments. In Canada, this approach dominated until the 1960s. It is perhaps best illustrated by the work of R. MacGregor Dawson whose *Government of Canada* was first published in 1947.[10] Most political scientists make some use of history, but traditionalists concentrate almost exclusively in this area, emphasizing chronology and the historical development of government structures and institutions. The key idea is the study of the evolution of political institutions and processes.

By the late 1950s, the traditional approach was under severe attack. The basic criticism alleged that its practitioners were essentially *parochial* (biased toward Western thought and ideas), *formal-legal* (interested mainly in constitutions and the operations of institutions such as executives, legislatures, courts, and bureaucracies), *noncomparative* (based essentially on the configurative study of single countries), and *unscientific* (concepts, models, and theories were rudimentary, or even nonexistent). Furthermore, the approach was said to exclude informal politics and therefore ignores a large and important source of relevant information. While many of these charges were exaggerated, they did point to the simple fact that the formal-legal approach is particularly limited in comparative studies because the role of formal governmental institutions varies greatly from country to country. In some societies, legislatures may be much less important than other institutions or processes. For example, in some countries the military assumes the functions of both the government and the legislature. In others, the legislature may consist of nothing more than the extended family of the monarch.

The Behaviouralist and Post-Behaviouralist Approaches

The **behaviouralist approach** came to the forefront of the discipline in the 1960s.[11] It aimed to correct perceived shortcomings in the traditional approach to the study of politics. Concentrating on the *informal* aspects of politics, behaviouralists seek to understand how individuals behave within political institutions, and how informal behaviour contributes to policy-making. Behaviouralists are concerned mostly with **empirical theory** (which deals with the observable world) rather than **normative theory** (which involves value judgments) used by political philosophers or traditional political theorists.

The scientific approach of behaviouralists brought a new, technical vocabulary to the study of politics, a vocabulary which must be learned in order to understand much of contemporary political science. Behaviouralists made explicit many of the rules or **methodology** (the manner of gathering, measuring, and explaining political information) of the discipline that had been implicit in more traditional approaches. As in the physical sciences, these researchers begin with curiosity about some "variable" or "variables"; that is, some changeable phenomena which they are trying to understand. A **variable** is a feature of a social situation or institution that may appear in different degrees or forms in other situations and institutions. Disciplines within the social sciences stress different variables for examination. Psychologists concentrate primarily on individual behaviour; economists on scarcity. For political scientists the subject of enquiry is generally governmental power and authority—how it is obtained and used. Students might be particularly interested in variables such as how difficult university courses are in particular subjects or how rigorously essays are graded.

Political science today is a science, then, in that it aims to provide plausible explanations for phenomena. Political scientists develop "hypotheses" which offer explanations of political phenomena and then test them against empirical evidence. A **hypothesis** is a statement or generalization presented in tentative and conjectural terms. It is used to speculate about causes or effects by linking one or several variables to others. One might, for example hypothesize that levels of political stability increase or decrease depending on the possible threat of external attack on a state, and then conduct a study to see if this explanation is valid over time and in various settings. University students might hypothesize that younger professors give relatively more difficult courses, or that teaching assistants give higher grades than professors. If these concepts can be *operationalized* and measured properly, relationships (or *correlations*) may be found which confirm or refute the hypothesis.

Often political scientists combine several hypotheses into a theory. The concept of theory derives from the Greek word *theoria* meaning contemplation. **Theories** are human inventions, bold conjectures, about operations in the real world. They are intellectual "nets" used to catch or explain the real world. In scientific-behavioural terms they are defined as a "series of interconnected hypotheses which describes what we think we know about interrelationships among a series of variables."[12] A theory involves three elements: generalizations, new observations, and testability.[13] Albert Einstein put it like this: theories involve positing problems, applying a tentative theory, eliminating error, and proceeding on to a new problem.

Behaviouralists strive to use scientific methods to explain or predict political phenomena by discovering "uniformities in political behaviour."[14] They make hypotheses about politics which they verify or disprove with empirical data. The tools of their craft include statistics and computers. The most successful studies of this type have been in the area of voting behaviour, party organization, and studies of beliefs and attitudes.

In summary, the scientific enterprise encompasses:

1. identifying a significant *issue* or *problem*;
2. devising a plausible *hypothesis* to explore the phenomena;
3. finding *reliable evidence* with which to test the hypothesis;
4. exploring the *findings*; and
5. exploring how the results may be combined with other scientific explanations to form a *theory*.

The main criticism of the behaviouralist approach is that it ignores values. And by concentrating on methods and statistics, it is sometimes said to end up with very precise answers to trivial questions. Furthermore, since political science studies human beings rather than inanimate objects, it is rarely able to achieve replicable rules of political behaviour that are equivalent to those in the exact sciences. In general, political science cannot predict future events based on past behaviour; and given the immense number of variables that have to be considered, it is doubtful that this will ever be achieved to the degree possible in the exact sciences. As David Easton noted, natural sciences have the advantage of dealing with inanimate matter. "Atoms ... do not have feelings or intentions that, by their very nature are unpredictable or inaccessible to observation or prediction."[15] However, even in the exact sciences there is an extraordinary and unavoidable unpredictability. In fact, modern physicists refer to "chaos theory" as a way of studying how incredibly minute uncertainties in the initial state of a system can lead to total uncertainty in even the best conceivable predictions of the futures of those systems.

Many political scientists now rely on a combination of methods of inquiry derived from both the traditional and behavioural schools. Single theories are rarely able to capture the complexities of politics. By their very nature, different topics of inquiry require different approaches, and both schools have made important contributions to the study of politics. Efforts are often made to combine aspects of both approaches and reconcile them, retaining a concern for values, and using whatever techniques seem best suited for answering particular questions. Even advocates of other approaches to the study of politics rarely recommend discarding scientific methods. Rather, they apply such methods to new questions or to reconstruct old theories. This modified approach is sometimes labelled **post-behaviouralism**.

The Systems Approach

Yet another approach to the study of politics is the **systems approach**. The key idea in this approach concerns interrelations between society and politics and the interaction of all actors and institutions. The systems approach is based on a general theory that provides political scientists with a limited, but useful, framework for analysis. It was particularly popular in the 1960s and 1970s, and remains an implicit approach in many other ways of explaining politics. The essence of systems theory is that the politics of a country can be depicted by the interaction between the societal environment and an abstract political system which processes or converts demands and supports into outputs, producing an overall stability or homeostasis. David Easton outlined the first comprehensive systems theory for political science.[16] The study of systems entails the search for cyclical processes that govern political structures.

According to Easton, it is useful to view politics as a system of processes and relationships between the conversion processes and the environment in which they function. Political life is seen as human behaviour that operates within and responds to the environment, and thereby enables one to study political structures and functions in relation to social, economic, and cultural conditions in the environment.

The basic argument of systems analysis is that governments are the centre of political systems in which three stages of action are involved (see Figure 2.1). First, the environment affects the political system by making multiple demands on it, as well as by providing fundamental support. These might include demands for better housing or health care or lower taxes. The supports would include intangibles such as "love of country" or patriotism. In Easton's concept, these are the "inputs." In the second stage, political parties or other institutions aggregate (or try to aggregate) the inputs into wider programs. Finally, the political system (including politicians, bureaucrats, executives, legislatures, courts, and so on) makes authoritative responses. These authoritative responses are in the form of decisions, laws, or other actions as "outputs" that return to the environment as "feedback." The parts of the system interact then like, say, the boundaries of a body's circulatory system. The system is more than the sum of its parts; it is like a living organism.

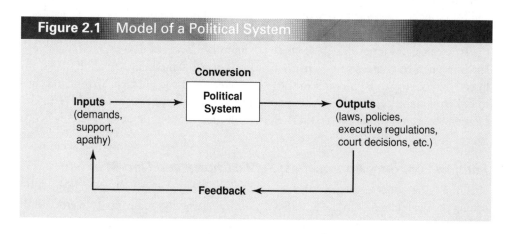

Figure 2.1   Model of a Political System

Systems analysis is frequently criticized. It is argued that the model on which it is based does not assist in discerning which parts of a political system are essential or influential. Some argue that more is learned about the various aspects of politics by studying specific components of a political system. Others say it is impossible to predict how, or even whether, a change in one part of the system will affect another part. Furthermore, political systems are not as closely interrelated as the model would make it appear. Nor are they as static as the model implies.[17] Easton's framework focused on the persistence of the system to the extent that the desire or compulsion to survive is considered a feature of all political systems. Some authors have interpreted this as a conservative bias built into the approach.[18]

The Structural-Functional Approach

Another related approach, structural-functionalism—often associated with the name of Gabriel Almond—was developed to make systems theory more open to the possibility of fundamental or developmental change.[19] In essence, **structural-functionalism** specifies the activities of a viable political system and explains how these functions must be performed to maintain the stability of the political system. If the polity cannot perform these functions, it ceases to exist. Almond and others used this approach to study the change in level of political development, from traditional to modern systems.[20]

The normally specified functions of political systems include input activities such as interest articulation, aggregation, socialization and communication, and the output functions of rule-making, rule application and rule adjudication. According to structural-functionalists, the role of the scholar is to research what "structures" various states use to perform these "functions." In some societies rule-making, rule application, and rule adjudication, for example, are all performed by the same structure. In Inuit bands, the headman performs all these output functions. In more complex systems, like Canada as a whole, these functions are performed respectively by the legislative, executive, and judicial structures.

One weakness of the structural-functional approach is that it does not accommodate well to the state as a dynamic entity. It assigns the state the mechanical role of performing functions, but the individuals who carry them out may have their own interests and priorities. Thus, some critics argue that the structural-functional approach places far too much trust in technology and "rational" procedures, and that the relation between the structures and functions is obscure.[21] Almond's "levels of development" concept left him open to charges of bias in that he considered democracy, especially Western liberal democracy, to be integral to the responsiveness of the political system and thus to political stability. He seems to be contending that all systems must evolve in the same manner and direction as did the Anglo-American democracies if they wish to "develop" to higher political stages.

Political Economy Approaches: Public Choice and Neo-Marxism

Finally, it is important to mention the political economy approach which gained popularity among political scientists in the late 1980s. **Political economy** studies are concerned with the relationship between government and economics. Politics and economics are never entirely separate phenomena: the way people earn a living as professionals, business people, labourers, or unemployed always influences politics. Economics involves conflict over scarce resources, while politics generally involves decisions about who will pay and who will benefit from the production and distribution of items ranging from highways to health care to armaments. Governments can affect the amount of resources in the hands of the poorest and richest segments of society. There is also a close interaction between the economy and government in many important issues such as tax policy, welfare policy, and so on. Governments carry out policies to protect, promote, and regulate the economy, but are themselves driven by that same economy.

The political economy approach has gained particular importance in the study of **public policy**, that is, studies of what governments do. Different ideologies and political beliefs conflict over what the role of government and politics should be. Underlying the dispute is the question: "What is the role of government concerning regulation, support, or intervention in economic and social affairs?" Those who accept values such as private enterprise, freedom, and individualism may answer the question one way; those who believe that social and political relations are largely determined or constrained by the economic basis of society may answer it quite differently.

Two opposing views, therefore, are reflected in studies of political economy: a relatively new *public choice* school, which is sometimes referred to as "liberal political economy" because it tends to follow the logic of classical economic reasoning; and *neo-Marxism*, which is based on Karl Marx's thoughts about the relationship between economic, social, and political structures. In public choice, the key idea concerns man as a rational actor, while the main idea in Marxism concerns the concept of class.

Public choice analysis is the economic study of non-market decision-making or, more broadly, the application of economics to political science. According to public choice theory, each individual is essentially a self-interested, rational actor. Individual wants are constrained by scarcity and by competition with others who want the same thing. When people engage in collective non-market decision-making in the political arena (making "public" choices), they behave exactly as many economists believe economists do when making market-oriented choices in the economic sphere. They act in a rational and calculating way to maximize their own interests. Individuals cause rules and institutions to change in order to maximize their rational self-interest. Voters support electorally the party that offers the programs most likely to maximize their individual well-being, and interest groups lobby governments for policies that will maximize their needs or desires. It is not surprising, therefore, that politicians and bureaucrats formulate policies largely to satisfy their own narrow interests.

In the public choice model, individuals do not have equal opportunities to realize their respective interests. Ordinary citizens have little impact except through elections. If they do not participate as part of an effective special interest group, they are really just consumers of public policies. According to the public choice model, therefore, powerful interest groups, bureaucrats, and politicians—especially leaders of the governing party—are the central actors in the policy-making process, even though the primary unit of political action is the individual, not the group. Individuals may join forces in pursuit of their interests, but they do so only when collective action promises greater rewards than acting alone. It is often more rational for the individual to act alone and not participate in collective action.

Public choice is still a relatively underdeveloped art as an approach to politics and public policy analysis. Its assumptions about "rationality" have been savagely attacked by many students of politics. While its application has produced some interesting insights into the policy-making process, its focus remains rather restrictive. It is at best only a partial aid for understanding how and why public policies are developed.

Neo-Marxist analysis is an alternative political economy approach to public policy. Neo-Marxism is a generic label for contemporary theories and propositions that seek to develop a systematic conceptualization of politics and the role of the state in capitalist society. This analysis is based upon assumptions originally formulated by Karl Marx concerning the relationships among economic, social, and political structures.

The details of Marxist philosophy are discussed in Chapter 8, but essentially, it argues that the primary function of the state in capitalist society is to serve the interests of capitalism. The state creates and maintains conditions favourable to profitable capital accumulation by concentrating wealth in a few hands. But, in the long run, Marx argued, capitalism cannot resist the attack of workers who will eventually become the masters of the means of production and exchange in a collectivist society. One must accept many of the Marxist premises to agree with the conclusions derived from neo-Marxist analysis.

Despite attempts to get inside the policy process and to develop a neo-Marxist approach to public policy analysis, neo-Marxism remains unclear about exactly how the state makes specific policy choices or decisions at particular moments in time.

The essential problem with systems analysis, structural-functionalism, and the political economy arguments is that they are at such a high level of abstraction that they are remote from much empirical research. That is, they are aimed at general theories, not "observation and experiment." They describe the polity in such broad terms that they neither generate testable propositions nor aid greatly in understanding concrete political problems. Besides this, the theories have also failed so far in their fundamental task of identifying all the theoretical structures and processes of the political system and explaining the relations among them—that is, they cannot be accepted as having contributed a comprehensive and predictive theory of the polity, and thus they remain only approaches to the discipline. A student must be aware of these various approaches however, in order to understand their advantages and disadvantages in the study of politics.

State-Centred Approaches and Neo-Institutionalism

A state-centred approach blossomed in the study of comparative politics and, to a lesser degree, in the examination of Canadian public policy in the late 1980s and 1990s.[22]

The key concept in this approach is institutions. Advocates of the state-centred approach object to the behaviouralist, Marxist, and public choice idea that social forces determine what state authorities do. Instead, they view the state as able to act independently of the demands of society. The state is visualized as "autonomous," independent of the public's interests, as expressed in the behaviouralist and public choice models, and certainly not derivative of class interests, as found in neo-Marxist thought.

According to the state-centred explanation of public policy, politicians and bureaucrats can act in any way they determine is best for the country—irrespective of demands from society. In other words, government policy is state-centred and not society-centred. This approach is based on the assumption that individuals with the greatest knowledge determine to a great extent the policy outputs of a society. Its practitioners tend to study public administration and other state structures such as executives, legislatures, and courts. Bureaucracy is the only permanent repository of the knowledge required to carry out modern government, and the bureaucracy uses this information to manipulate societal forces.

This approach has been attacked as being based on untenable assumptions. First, the knowledge required to govern the country is not "scientific." Those who determine the direction of public policy must convince others to accept a guiding philosophy for the direction of governmental action. After the politicians determine the priorities—which is more a question of philosophy or personal choice than scientific knowledge—the public servants are left with the administration of this choice, which is much less significant than the choice of policy orientation. Second, many members of the senior bureaucracy are as transient as some leading politicians. Third, despite the state-centred assumption that political parties do not present policy alternatives, that is not always true.

The extent to which the state-centred approach provides a new and unique paradigm for analysis is, therefore, hotly contested. Many state-centred theorists are neo-institutionalists. That is, they base their analysis on the assumption that institutions and rules control the process of choice. Rules, traditions, and structures bind policy-makers because they work within them. There are two schools of neo-institutionalists. The rational choice school argues that individuals cause institutions and rules to change in order to maximize their self-interests. Individuals cannot pursue all the interests they desire, however, because institutions and rules constrain behaviour and/or interests for the broader good of society. They encourage individuals to cooperate when trying to achieve their own interests.

The structural sociological school of neo-institutionalism bases their ideas concerning political change on the idea that institutions and rules reflect the dominant values, traditions, and ideologies of a political system and thus provide rules and institutions with longevity, resilience, and permanence. Institutions and rules evolve slowly over time to meet developments in society and thus are closely bound to changes outside formal state institutions.

Any list of approaches to political science is subject to change over time. New ideas continually impinge on the subject and restructure what scholars believe to be important.

FIELDS OF MODERN POLITICAL SCIENCE

Today there are many fields or branches within the study of political science. The most important are political theory and political philosophy; federal, provincial, and local governments; public administration and public policy; methodology; comparative government and politics; and international relations.

Political theory and **political philosophy** are terms that are often used interchangeably. Scholars in this field are concerned with questions about value judgments and the history and development of the ideas of great political thinkers. Political philosophy is sometimes called value or normative theory (as distinguished from empirical/scientific theory) because it is concerned primarily with values, norms, and morality. It attempts to examine the connections among facts, values, and judgments. Theory is an important part of all political science fields because it is used in the explanation and prediction of political phenomena. Political philosophers may also be concerned with *epistemology*—the origin, nature, and limits of knowledge.

Governments themselves make up an entire branch of political science. Scholars examine the structure and functions of federal, provincial or state, and local governments, usually within the context of a single country. As well as studying the institutions such as the presidency, they also analyze the political behaviour of the wide range of participants in the political process.

Public administration and **public policy** both concern the study of the administrative aspects of government. Public policy analyzes and evaluates policies in areas such as defence, health, education, and resource development. Public administration studies are concerned more with how these policies are formulated and implemented within the large bureaucratic infrastructure of government.

Methodology in political science is particularly concerned with empirical or scientific theory. Methodologists develop approaches and techniques to be used in all aspects of the discipline. They are especially interested in making the study of politics as rigorous as the exact sciences. Methodologists tend to work in the realm of statistical analysis, polling techniques, and computer science, or to study **epistemology** (how we know what we know) and the philosophy of science (the assumptions and general principles of science).

Comparative government and politics is a very wide field with many subdivisions. To a large extent it is the study of the macro-politics of states. While studies of single countries such as Canada may be very important in the teaching of political science, researchers are also concerned with comparing the politics and government of different states. In this field there are many area specialists who focus on regions such as the Middle East, the former Soviet Union, Asia, developing countries, and so on, as well as specialists who place their studies in the perspective of all the world's diverse political structures and practices. The argument for comparison is extremely important—only by comparing can one understand and evaluate the merits or problems of a particular political system. And furthermore, comparison is an integral part of all scientific enquiry.

International relations focuses on the foreign policies of countries, international organizations, and international law in order to learn more about the interactions among states. Scholars in this field are particularly concerned with such issues as conflict management among countries. The importance of economics is stressed in the international political economy school within this subdiscipline.

The focus of political science, then, has broadened considerably since it was formally recognized as a discipline at the beginning of the twentieth century. Much research today is designed to be relevant to current domestic and international problems. This trend is particularly evidenced in the relatively young field of public policy, which concentrates on explaining domestic and international government action.

As with the general division of knowledge into the three groups of science, social science, and the humanities, it is obvious that these fields within political science are artificial categories. There is considerable overlap of interests among them. Topics such as behaviour, parties, or violence and revolutions, for example, are studied by specialists in many of these different fields, each contributing expertise from a different perspective, as well as positing unique hypotheses and using different approaches.

POLITICAL SCIENCE IN THE TWENTY-FIRST CENTURY

It is evident from this brief survey of the development of political science that there have been a great many changes over the years in the favoured approaches and methods about how best to understand the political world. A survey of today's academic journals reveals studies based on rigorous application of scientific methodology alongside basic descriptive studies that document change in institutions or processes. This combination has led some commentators to call this the post-behavioural period of political science. They contend that political science can and should encompass a scientific approach to the discipline as well as a concern for the principles of ethics, wisdom, and judgment.

Many political scientists today could be classified as "soft" scientists. They would agree that the approach a political scientist takes to issues structures the questions that will be asked and what methods will be used in the study. Soft political scientists recognize that basic descriptive work has to be done to document changes in societies and political institutions, and that intuitive accounts are needed to supplement empirical studies in order to provide the "big picture" of society as a whole. At the same time, however, the soft approach "is based on a core adherence to the central precepts of science."[23] Modern political science seeks to discover generalizations or regularities of behaviour that govern the political process. It is a difficult exercise because human behaviour is involved and there is a multiplicity of factors in each situation. Political scientists have to work with the variation which occurs naturally in the real world. They cannot create and control experimental conditions.

Haphazard, casual observations are not part of political science; analysis must follow scientific conventions. For example, political science studies must amass evidence to support claims, clearly stating methods, results, and conclusions, and following scientific principles so that the study can come as close as possible to the goal of replication. As members of a scientific community, political scientists adopt a *critical* perspective about the causes and effects of political phenomena, constantly doubting and treating claims sceptically. As philosopher of science Karl Popper argued, the advance of science is "—towards an infinite yet attainable aim: that of discovering new, deeper, and more general problems, and of subjecting our ever tentative answers to ever renewed and even more rigorous tests."[24] The **paradigm**, or world-view which legitimates the academic consensus about what constitutes exemplary research, is constantly shifting—almost like the subject of politics itself.[25]

It is important for students to be aware of the different approaches and methods used by political scientists and of the advantages and problems related to each. Today, there is a great diversity of fields and approaches in the discipline of political science: a kind of benevolent pluralism flourishes. There remains, however, a fundamental gulf in the discipline between the "scientific" and "humanistic" tendencies; the former may be said to concentrate on explaining scientific variances, the latter on humanistic interpretations. In this text we try to take a neutral position concerning the value of the major approaches, drawing on the contributions of each where possible. In the next chapter, we develop more precisely the ideas and concepts about the state and law which provide the formal rules within which politics is conducted.

DISCUSSION QUESTIONS

1. To what extent can the study of politics be a science? Should it be studied in the faculty of humanities or the social sciences? Both?
2. Who, in your opinion, were the main thinkers who influenced the development of political thought from early Greek and Roman civilizations of the fifth century B.C. to 1880 when the first department of political science was set up in the United States? Explain your choice.
3. Explain the advantages and disadvantages of at least six different ways political scientists approach the study of politics.
4. Does "post-behaviouralism" call for adjustments in methodology or changes in states of mind? Or both?
5. Which "field" of political science do you consider to be the most interesting? practical?

KEY TERMS

approach, p. 30
behaviouralist approach, p. 33
comparative government and politics, p. 40
divine rule, p. 27
empirical theory, p. 33
epistemology, p. 40
general theory, p. 32
governments, p. 40
hypothesis, p. 33

international relations, p. 40
methodology, p. 40
neo-Marxism, p. 38
normative theory, p. 33
paradigm, p. 42
political economy, p. 36
political philosophy, p. 40
political theory, p. 40
post-behaviouralism, p. 34

public administration, p. 40
public choice, p. 37
public policy, p. 37
structural-functionalism, p. 36
systems approach, p. 35
theories, p. 33
traditional-historical approach, p. 32
variable, p. 33

ENDNOTES

1. Lucien W. Pye, "Political Science and the Crisis of Authoritarianism," *APSR*, vol. 84, no. 1 (March 1990), p. 4.

2. *Ibid.*

3. For further information see William Anderson, *Man's Quest for Political Knowledge: The Study and Teaching of Politics in Ancient Times* (Minneapolis: University of Minnesota Press, 1964).

4. The development of American political science is described in Albert Somit and Joseph Tanenhaus, *The Development of American Political Science: From Burgess to Behavioralism* (New York: Irvington, 1982).

5. Pye, "Political Science and the Crisis of Authoritarianism," p. 16.

6. See James A. Bill and Robert L. Hardgrave, Jr., *Comparative Politics: The Quest for Theory* (Lanham, Md.: University Press of America, 1982), ch. 1.

7. See Gabriel A. Almond and Stephen J. Genco, "Clouds, Clocks and the Study of Politics," *World Politics*, vol. 29, no. 4 (July 1977), p. 505.

8. *Ibid.*

9. *Ibid.*

10. R. MacGregor Dawson, *Government of Canada* (Toronto: University of Toronto Press, 1947).

11. See David Easton, "The New Revolution in Political Science," *APSR*, vol. 3, no. 4 (Dec. 1969), p. 1060.

12. Jeremy Wilson, *Analyzing Politics* (Scarborough, Ont.: Prentice-Hall Canada, 1988), p. 2.

13. See Joseph LaPalombara, *Politics Within Nations* (Englewood Cliffs, N.J.: Prentice-Hall, 1974).

14. See David Easton, "The Current Meaning of Behavioralism," in James C. Charlesworth, ed., *Contemporary Political Analysis* (New York: Free Press, 1967), p. 16.

15. David Easton, "Political Science in the United States: Past and Present," *IPSR*, vol. 6, no. 1 (January 1985), p. 142.

16. See David Easton, *The Political System* (New York: Alfred A. Knopf, 1953); and *A Framework for Political Analysis* (Englewood Cliffs, N.J.: Prentice-Hall, 1965).

17. For comments on systems theory, see Karl W. Deutsch, *The Nerves of Government: Models of Political Communication and Control* (New York: Free Press, 1966); and Harold Lasswell, "The Policy Sciences of Development," *World Politics*, vol. 17 (1965).

18. See Herbert Spiro, "An Evaluation of Systems Theory," in James C. Charlesworth, ed., *Contemporary Political Analysis* (New York: Free Press, 1967), pp. 164–74.

19. See Gabriel Almond and G. Bingham Powell, *Comparative Politics: A Developmental Approach*, 2nd ed. (Boston: Little, Brown, 1978).

20. Gabriel Almond, "Political Development: Analytical and Normative Perspectives," *Comparative Political Studies*, vol. l, no. 4 (1969), pp. 447–69.

21. Colin Campbell, S.J., "Current Models of the Political System: An Intellective-Purposive View," *Comparative Political Studies*, vol. 4, no. 1 (1971), p. 29.

22. See James G. March and Johan P. Olsen, "The New Institutuionalism: Organizational Factors in Political Life," *APSR*, vol. 78, no. 3 (Sept. 1984), pp. 734–49. For a critique, see Gabriel A. Almond, *A Discipline Divided: Schools and Sects in Political Science* (Newbury Park: Sabe, 1990).

23. Wilson, *Analyzing Politics*, p. 12.

24. Karl R. Popper, *The Logic of Scientific Discovery* (London: Hutchinson, 1968), p. 281.

25. Bill and Hardgrave, *Comparative Politics*, ch. l; and Andrew C. Janos, *Politics and Paradigms* (Stanford, Calif.: Stanford University Press, 1986).

FURTHER READING

Almond, Gabriel A., *A Discipline Divided: Schools and Sects in Political Science* (Newbury Park, Calif.: Sage, 1990).

Curzon, Mary G., ed., *Careers and the Study of Political Science: A Guide for Undergraduates*, 4th ed. (Washington, D.C.: APSA, 1983).

Finifter, Ada W., ed., *Political Science: The State of the Discipline* (Washington, D.C.: APSA, 1983).

Garson, G. David, *Handbook of Political Science Methods*, 2nd ed. (Boston: Holbrook Press, 1976).

Goel, M. Lal, *Political Science Research: A Methods Handbook* (Ames: Iowa State University Press, 1988).

Hacker, Andrew, *The Study of Politics: The Western Tradition and American Origins*, 2nd ed. (New York: McGraw-Hill, 1973).

Hall, Peter A., ed., *The Political Power of Economic Ideas: Keynesianism Across Nations* (Princeton: Princeton University Press, 1989).

Nagel, Thomas, *The Last Word* (Oxford: Oxford University Press, 1998). "Science in Culture," Special Edition, *Daedalus*, vol. 127, no. 1, 1998.

Shanley, Mary Lyndon, and Carole Pateman, eds., *Feminist Interpretations and Political Theory* (University Park: Pennsylvania State University Press, 1991).

Somit, Albert, and Joseph Tanenhaus, *The Development of American Political Science: From Burgess to Behavioralism* (New York: Irvington, 1982).

Tomm, Winnie, ed., *The Effects of Feminist Approaches on Research Methodologies* (Waterloo, Ont.: Wilfrid Laurier University Press, 1989).

Weisberg, Herbert, *Political Science: The Science of Politics* (New York: Agathon Press, 1986).

 Weblinks

The following three sites provide information about the individual associations as well as links to useful political science Web Sites.

www.sfu..ca/igs/CPSA.html
The Canadian Political Science Association Web Site

www2.dgsys.com/~apsa
The American Political Science Association Web Site

www.ucd.ie/~psa/
The International Political Science Association Web Site

CHAPTER 3

The Modern State

Politics, with its important components of power, influence, and legitimacy always takes place in a geographical setting. Today that is normally within, between, or among countries. States come in all shapes and sizes, with varying degrees of wealth and different cultures, lifestyles, and rules for their citizens. Without knowing any history, it would be difficult to find any logic behind why most state borders are where they are today. Nor would it be evident why individuals identify with their states to varying degrees—ranging from fanatic fervour to listless indifference to extreme dissatisfaction. Some individuals want into countries, some want out; some citizens are content to live within their state's territory, and some seek border changes that would subsume portions, or more, of neighbouring states. Some citizens would even like to divide their own countries into two or more new states.

All stable states conduct politics according to authoritative rules or laws. Laws define the structure and operation of a state, and determine the extent to which its government will impinge on the lives of its citizens. In this chapter we examine the features of states and the relationship between states and nations. Then we consider the meaning of the word "law" and the ways which laws embody and structure the politics of states.

STATE AND NATION

We have seen that a **state** is a political unit with a given territory. A state is usually defined as a form of political organization consisting of governmental institutions which are capable of maintaining order and implementing rules or laws (through coercion if necessary) over a given population and within a given territory.[1] The three key components of a state are a defined territory, a permanent population, and a form of government. States also possess symbols such as flags and anthems that delineate them from others.

Most states in the world belong to the United Nations. A state is normally admitted to that institution when it has satisfied the member states that it is "sovereign" both internally and externally. A **sovereign state** wields power in that it is capable of maintaining order within its territorial boundaries, it is able to tax its citizens, and it is also recognized by the international community as having the right to run its own affairs free from external interference by other states or governments when it is approved by its people—that is, seen as legitimate.[2] Modern states tend to have stable boundaries, and their populations are bound together by political ties. Under current international law, people are given their identity by the state in which they are citizens.

States normally consider all persons born on their territory, and their children, to be **citizens**. Citizenship is an involuntary membership initially that places individuals under the rule of the state. It is, as T.H. Marshall argued, conferred on those individuals who are considered full members of the community.[3] Most states also have rules by which noncitizens may acquire citizenship. In some states, citizenship is accorded to foreigners by reason of their "ethnicity"; in others it is accorded by the performance of certain "civic" acts.[4] Many states also contain a number of settled residents or foreigners whose political rights are somewhat less than those of citizens. The generosity with which citizenship is extended varies according to time, place, and economics, as discussed in Close Up 3.1.

States share few other characteristics. They range from military superpowers like the United States to countries such as Costa Rica, which do not even believe in having an army. There are populous states like China with well over a billion people and microstates like Nauru and Tuvalu, which have fewer than 10 000 inhabitants. Vatican City's population is less than 1000. There are geographically large states such as Canada and Australia and small ones such as Andorra, Monaco, San Marino, and Liechenstein. Despite these differences, however, recognition as a state remains a "powerful definition of what it means to be free and in control of one's destiny."[5]

A **nation**, as opposed to a state, is a cultural entity. It is a politically conscious and mobilized collectivity of people (often with a clear sense of territory) which possesses, or may aspire to, self-government or independent statehood. A nation is not necessarily the same as the citizenry of a state, nor is it restricted to those who possess a common language, ancestry, or cultural heritage although these components are usually involved. It is "essentially subjective, a sense of social belonging and ultimate loyalty."[6]

Another concept widely used in political science is **nation-state**. This word is now considered highly problematic in the discipline. It implies that each state consists of one nation. Yet there are very few states like that. Japan, for example, has essentially one state and one nation because 99% of the Japanese population are Japanese ethnics, speak Japanese, and belong to the Japanese culture. The remaining 1% of the population are transplanted Koreans, foreigners, and a leftover feudal class known as *bitumen*. But most of the states of the world are composed of different peoples, cultures, and languages. There are only 192 states but over 10 000 cultural groupings.

Most states, therefore, contain one or more nations. Canada, for example, contains francophone and aboriginal nations. And a nation may be dispersed in more than one state, as was the case with the German nation which, until recently, was divided between East and West Germany. Some nations, like the Palestinians and the Kurds, may not even have a state at all. Most nations and states are an ethnic mismatch: millions of Hungarians reside outside of Hungary, Chinese outside of China, Russians outside Russia, and so on. Settler states like Canada and the United States are particularly heterogeneous. Close Up 3.1 discusses the possibility of Palestinian statehood.

CLOSE UP 3.1   Is Palestine on the Way to Becoming a State?

Israel comprises much of the historic region of Palestine, known in ancient times as Canaan. Today both Arabs and Jews lay claim to the land. Many Palestinians inhabit the Israeli-occupied West Bank and Gaza Strip, land on which Palestinians have long dreamed of creating an independent Palestinian state with Jerusalem as its capital.

In 1993, an historic accord between Israel and the Palestinians gave the Palestinians limited autonomy over the Gaza Strip and the town of Jericho. Then in January 1996, Palestinians made what many called a major step toward achieving their own state. Approximately three-quarters of the voters in the Palestinian-ruled areas of the West Bank and Gaza Strip voted to elect a president and a transitional self-governing council, thus providing the Palestinians with their first freely elected leadership. PLO chief Yasser Arafat won the presidency with a landslide victory. But will he ever become the head of a recognized state?

Nationalism

Members of a nation share a sense of loyalty and psychological attachment. Normally this adherence is based on a common language, history, culture, and a desire for political independence. This identification with a nation is known as nationalism. **Nationalism** in its modern sense is defined as the collective action of a politically conscious group or nation in pursuit of increased territorial autonomy or sovereignty.

Nationalism has appeared in many forms in different states over the centuries. It has been used to justify economic expansionism, protectionism, and imperialism. As an ideology it has been employed to espouse the supremacy of particular nations or peoples; it has justified quests for emancipation from colonial rule; and it has been an operative force in newly independent multiracial or tribal societies in the Third World.[7] It has been savagely attacked. Albert Einstein called nationalism "an infantile sickness—the measles of the human race."[8]

Nationalism is sometimes the highest form of allegiance, above church, class, tribe, or other social group. It is evident that tensions will occur when national loyalties do not coincide with legal boundaries. Well-known nationalist movements include the Québécois in Canada; Irish, Scots, and Welsh in the UK; Basques and Catalans in Spain; Bretons and Corsicans in France; Sikhs in India; Flemings and Walloons in Belgium; Chechnyans in Russia; Croatians, Serbs, and Muslims in Bosnia. In these cases the ethnic minorities regularly make demands that cannot all be accommodated within the larger state. They act collectively to develop political parties and cultural organizations whose aim is to pursue fundamental changes that are not combatable with the sovereignty of the state to which they belong.[9]

The issue of statehood and nations immediately brings to the foreground discussions of the right of people to self-determination. International law is instructive but not conclusive on this question. In 1960 the UN General Assembly adopted a declaration on colonial countries. It judged that "the subjection of peoples to alien subjugation, domination, and exploitation constitutes a denial of fundamental human rights." And in two covenants passed by the UN in 1976 declared, "All peoples have the right of self-determination." However, two principles clash in these declarations. International law seems to recognize both self-determination and the inviolability of state borders. The United Nations has interfered in domestic affairs only on very rare occasions such as when it imposed embargoes on Iraq and the states of the former Yugoslavia. In the final analysis, the only thing that actually settles questions of this nature is the political action of states in recognizing a new country or in defending an old country's territory. It should also be born in mind that the right of self-determination extends only to those circumstances in which people are experiencing foreign or alien domination and exploitation, or are subject to discriminatory regimes. With the end of colonialism, the issue is not about old colonies or new territories that wish to become independent, but about groups within extant states attempting to secede.

The Arab nation illustrates a second principle about the difficulty of reconciling national loyalties with legal or state boundaries. Until about 1980, the political consciousness of modern African and Middle Eastern Arabs was dominated by the myth of pan-Arabism. The pan-Arab dream was that their common language, shared history, and culture would provide the basis for a single Arab state from the Atlantic to the Gulf. But by 1978, slowly and with a great deal of anguish and violence, a "normal" state system was established.[10] Inside each Arab state, pan-Arab rhetoric competed with a fierce state-defined nationalism. Then, in 1990, the tenuous pan-Arab dream was shattered by the Iraqi invasion of Kuwait. Although Saddam Hussein clothed his aggression against Kuwait with pan-Arab rhetoric—he said he would unite the Arabs, secure justice for the Palestinians, and bring about a more equitable sharing of Arab oil wealth—the policies of Arab states in response to this invasion were dictated by state, not pan-Arab interests.[11]

Nationalism is not the same as **regionalism**, the awareness of togetherness among a people of a relatively large area within a state. Regionalism encourages the inhabitants of a territory to demand a change in the political, economic, and cultural relations between their region and the central powers within their larger state. Such demands are often made on the basis of regional economic equalization, and they do not directly challenge territorial sovereignty. Persistent neglect to resolve regionalist tensions may, however, result in serious loss of state legitimacy in these parts of the country, or even stimulate the development of a group with a distinct national identity that seeks separation from the state. Regionalism is an important dimension of political life in many countries like Canada, Nigeria, and India which are geographically, economically, and/or ethnically diverse. Recent events in Britain highlight the significant role of regionalism in that country. See Close Up 3.2.

Although many organized ethnic demands may be accommodated within the confines of an existing state, some may not be. Such ethnic activity can be considered as a continuum moving from those movements that achieve accommodation at one ex-

> ### CLOSE-UP 3.2 Regionalism and Nationalism in the United Kingdom
>
> The United Kingdom of Great Britain and Northern Ireland was put together by England over a period of centuries. Wales was added between 1536 and 1542, Scotland in 1707, and Northern Ireland in 1921. No level of government exists between local or municipal governments in these regions and the Parliament at Westminster. Scotland, Wales, and Northern Ireland are all governed from London.
>
> When Prime Minister Tony Blair's Labour government came to power in 1997, it promised to use referendums and elections to create a separate parliament with tax-raising powers for Scotland by the year 2000. The move, it said, was a means of recognizing Scotland's distinctive identity while keeping it in the United Kingdom. The Welsh are to have a somewhat less powerful assembly, as will Northern Ireland when the political crisis between Protestants and Catholics there has been resolved.
>
> The move to devolve power to the regions is not viewed as positive by everyone. For example, some say this enhancement of regional powers will fan the flames of nationalism in Scotland and lead to constitutional turmoil—even possibly leading to the breakup of the United Kingdom.
>
> Did the Labour government do the right thing in this case?

treme to those which seek increased autonomy through to total separation at the other extreme. Nationalism in the modern sense does not usually apply to demands that can be accommodated within a state; it is restricted to demands for political (and usually economic and cultural) autonomy through to separation.

Continuum of Ethnic Activity

Political Integration ⟷ Separation

Since nationalist groups within a state create divisions which may cause disintegration, governments actively foster a strong "national identity" at the state level. There are several ingredients or components of a strong **national identity**:

1. Emotional attachment to the geographical features of the territory;
2. A common past with heroes and myths which inspire and promote pride;
3. Special kinship through a common language (bilingual or multilingual nations such as Belgium, Canada, and Switzerland are rare; most have one major, official language);
4. A unique culture with shared values and a common literature that generate pride in traditions and custom and create a sense of familiarity and belonging.

New states in particular need to develop a broad national identity which will bind their citizens together. They accomplish this in a variety of ways. Sometimes, as in authoritarian states like China or Cuba, children are vigorously politically socialized in schools and youth organizations, and the media is tightly controlled to present the governmental point of view.

Nation-building in authoritarian states is often dismayingly brutal. Take for example the state of Indonesia after 1965 when General Suharto took over as President. During his first few months in power, Suharto carried out a horrific anti-communist purge. In the ensuing years, he attempted to build a stable state by employing the following measures typical of an authoritarian state: arbitrary arrests, a shackled press, and military-dominated politics. Three decades later the 180 million Indonesians on 13 000 islands have been fairly successfully knit into one country. While they used to speak in dozens of different vernaculars, they now communicate to a large extent in a single, simple national language, Bahasa Indonesia. Ninety percent of the population is Muslim, and they basically tolerate the minorities, including the commercially dominant ethnic Chinese (although brutal suppression of Timorese in East Timor continues). Suharto's tough methods of nation-building created a state that, until he was forced to resign in 1998 for alleged corruption and authoritarianism, many thought capable of producing another economic miracle in Asia.[12]

In democratic states, national identity is fostered by governments in more subtle ways, such as with flags, national day celebrations, setting national content rules for television, grants for artistic endeavours, and so on. Canada, for example, has a national flag, special Canada Day celebrations and a state body to regulate the degree of Canadian "content" in broadcasting and television. The goal is to build strong feelings of national identity that will subsume and temper the aspirations of smaller groups within the country.

National identity is fostered by governments in order to promote cohesion and stability. However there is a point at which such attachments can become virulent, divisive, and threatening. This development, often called **hypernationalism**, occurs when nationalist sentiment fosters the belief that other nations or states are both inferior and threatening. At this point hypernationalism threatens domestic peace. Hitler's Germany promoted a classic example of nationalism which crossed the threshold to hypernationalism. The government preached the purity of the German race with attacks on Jews, gypsies, homosexuals, communists, and other "enemies of the state." It asserted the right to annex other states. German propaganda nourished contemptuous beliefs about the nations of surrounding states and promoted hatred toward those groups in order to garner support for the national security policy and eventually a wave of aggression against other states. Hypernationalism tends to thrive under three conditions:

1. The country in question is composed of people mainly of one ethnic group;
2. Anarchic, aggressive continental, or world conditions exist;
3. The country relies on mass armies which are constantly in need of recruitment.

DEVELOPMENT OF THE MODERN STATE

Because the concepts of state, nation, and nationalism are so familiar today, there is a tendency to believe that they have always been present. But that is not true. The state as we know it is relatively new in the history of world politics. The modern idea of state did not exist until the sixteenth century. Then there was a gradual increase in the number of states until World War II. Decolonization and the dissolution of empires then led to a rapid increase. And the last surge of new states came with the emergence of post-communist regimes in eastern Europe after the collapse of the USSR in 1991, providing the approximately 192 states that exist today. Figure 3.1 illustrates the rate of the formation of countries throughout modern history.

The European Model

It is instructive to consider how and why the modern European state became the accepted worldwide form of territorially defined government. At various times in history, tribes, bands, city-states, empires, and religious or other authorities, which may or may not

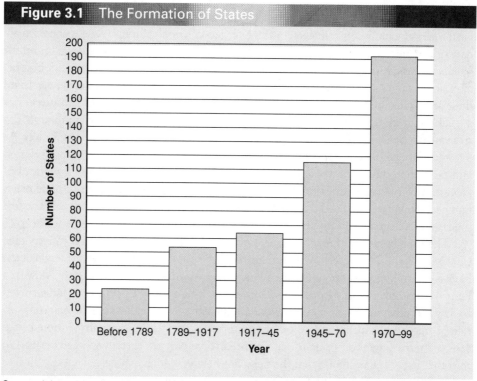

Figure 3.1 The Formation of States

Source: Adapted from data found in *World Handbook of Political and Social Indicators*, 2nd ed. (New Haven: Yale University Press, 1972) pp. 26ff., *Political Handbook of the World: 1990* (Binghampton, N.Y.: CSA Publications, 1990), and *The New York Times*, 1991 to 1999.

have been based on territories, performed many of the functions of the modern state. How did the state become predominant—even in Asia, where more than two centuries ago powerful, prestigious empires were the norm?

The answer is that the state as we know it today originated in Europe, and European colonists carried the model with them when they settled in the Americas, Australasia, and Africa. In these far-off lands, states were formed either for self-defence, or in emulation of European states, or both.[13]

The modern state made its first appearance in Western Europe in the sixteenth and seventeenth centuries. Until that time, individuals on that continent owed their loyalty to feudal lords or religious authorities to whom they were economically and/or spiritually bound. Feudal and religious loyalties were both trans-territorial, that is, without territorial boundaries. Gradually, as communications and technology advanced and modern economies were established, allegiances to feudal lords and the Church were displaced by a new sentiment that developed and encompassed these traditional loyalties. The new sentiment was nationalism. Nationalism required that the nation be awarded the greatest loyalty; the self, and even religion, had to be subordinated to it. This substitution of the secular for the sacred created a situation the Roman Catholic Church called "whoring after strange Gods." It marked a dramatic new era in church-state relations.[14]

There were two distinct steps in the European transition to territorially defined states. First, rulers gradually consolidated control over feudal vassals through such means as marriage or conquest, and established larger territorial units, as occurred in French- and Spanish-speaking areas in the late thirteenth and fourteenth centuries. In some parts of Europe, most notably in German- and Italian-speaking areas, similar attempts were unsuccessful, and these areas remained fragmented into multiple territorial units for several centuries.

The second step in the transition to statehood was a product of the Reformation, the sixteenth-century movement against the authority of the Roman Catholic Church. As a result of this movement, people began to define themselves in terms of both religion and language. They identified with Roman Catholicism or a particular brand of Protestantism. And when the Bible was translated from Latin into German and other European languages, it paved the way for new, linguistic identities to develop. For the first time, people began to define themselves as English-, French-, or German-speaking.

The final break between church and state came with the 1648 Peace of Westphalia, which ended the Thirty Years War in Europe. This treaty brought to an end the role of the Holy Roman Empire as the linchpin of European solidarity and gave rise to the view that Europe consisted of legally equal states, each controlling a specific population and territory.

By this time, rulers and statesmen found it increasingly difficult to follow their old practice of trading European and colonial territories at will for strategic or economic reasons. Citizens now took pride in, and wanted to be part of, certain specific states. On the other hand, leaders found that the new, larger states, which manifested nationalist sentiment, were a boon because they facilitated the process of mobilizing populations to support wars. It became much easier to institute conscription and build a citizen's army, as France later did in 1791, enabling Napoleon to "liberate" and conquer much of Europe.

The new states provided a strategic and economic unit. The boundaries of the state formed a valuable "hard shell" that "rendered it to some extent secure from foreign penetration, and thus made it an ultimate unit of protection for those within its boundaries."[15] At the same time, as agrarian societies were transformed into industrial ones, the state became the major locus of economic activity and the guarantor of economic autonomy.

As the notion grew that the boundaries of the state and nation should coincide, states like England and France tried to incorporate inside their borders other territories in which people spoke their language. In Italian- and German-speaking areas, movements rose to unite small units into single national territories. In multi-ethnic, multilanguage empires such as Austria, the Russian Empire, and the Ottoman Empire, the movement was to smaller, rather than larger units. The many small nations that had been subsumed under common dynasties created nationalist revolutions and tried to form separate states. As Close Up 3.3 shows, boundaries in Europe continue to shift and be redefined. Map 3.1 shows the European boundaries in 1999.

The form of the European state was original in three major respects: legalism, mutability, and a multi-state system.[16] Samuel Finer points out that although some of these characteristics could be found in other parts of the world at this time, nowhere else did they all appear at the same time as they did in Europe.

Legalism

The essential difference between the newly emergent European states and those in other parts of the world was in the central notion that the relationship of the government to the individual must be based on law, that the individual possessed certain inherent rights, and consequently could be deprived of these only by due process.[17] The concept of **legalism** incorporated several important conditions: law developed a paramount sanctity so that the power relationships between public authorities and individuals were based in law. Individual citizens were no longer merely subjects, but citizens with certain inherent rights to life, liberty, and property; penalties for crimes were restricted to the perpetrators of the crimes; private property was respected by governments; and means existed to sue government officials for alleged wrongdoings. Thus, in several very important respects, government powers were restricted by legal means.

Mutability

The second respect in which the new European form of state was original was in its **mutability**, or its predisposition to change. A state achieves durability when its social structure, political structure, and belief system all reinforce each other. When reinforcement does not occur, the state becomes mutable or susceptible to innovation. This was the case in Europe in the fifteenth and sixteenth centuries. The traditional Christian belief system, which underpinned the medieval political and social structures, was attacked first by Protestant religious nonconformists and then by the Greco-Roman revival of the Renaissance, which represented an entirely new way of thinking and living.[18] The breakdown of traditional belief systems and the consequent political and social instability

Close Up 3.3   Boundary Changes in Europe 1974–99

From the Former USSR:

Armenia: Declared sovereignty August 1990. Voted for independence September 1991.

Azerbaijan : Declared independence August 1991.

Belarus: Voted for independence August 1991.

Georgia: Declared independence April 1990.

Moldova: Voted for independence August 1991.

Russian Republic of the USSR: The largest part of the former USSR became Russia.

Ukraine: Voted for independence December 1991.

Baltics:

Estonia: Voted August 1991 to reassert independence.

Latvia: Declared effective independence August 1991, just after the botched coup attempt in the Soviet Union.

Lithuania: The first republic to reassert independence, in March 1990.

Changes Due to Conflict in Yugoslavia:

Bosnia and Herzegovina: Achieved independence in 1992. A civil war ensued.

Croatia: Declared independence from Yugoslavia in June 1991.

Slovenia: Declared independence from Yugoslavia in June 1991.

Macedonia: Declared independence from Yugoslavia in April 1992.

Yugoslavia: Now made up of Serbia, Montenegro, and the provinces of Vojvodina and Kosovo. Currently at war.

Other Changes:

Czechoslovakia: Divided into the Czech Republic and Slovak Republic in 1993.

Present-day Germany: Formed in 1991 by the merger of two former countries: West Germany, or the Federal Republic of Germany (FRG), and East Germany, or the German Democratic Republic (GDR).

gave rise to new ways of thinking about the state, and a wide range of new institutions and social structures become possible. The year 1648 was a transition point in the growth of the European idea of the state. In that year the Peace of Westphalia terminated the Thirty Years War of religion in Europe. The Holy Roman Empire had disintegrated, and in its place were established autonomous, legally equal states that no longer were subject to higher secular or religious authority.

Map 3.1   Europe in 1999

Independent states:

Albania	Liechtenstein
Andorra	Lithuania
Armenia	Luxemburg
Austria	"Macedonia"
Azerbaijan	Malta
Belarus	Moldova
Belgium	Monaco
Bosnia-Herzegovina	Netherlands
Bulgaria	Norway
Croatia	Poland
Cyprus	Portugal
Czech Republic	Romania
Denmark	Russia
Estonia	San Marino
Finland	Slovak Republic
France	Slovenia
Georgia	Spain
Germany	Sweden
Greece	Switzerland
Hungary	Turkey
Iceland	Ukraine
Ireland	United Kingdom
Italy	Vatican City
Latvia	Yugoslavia

Detached provinces:

Arquipelago dos Acores
Isal Canarias
Kaliningrad
Madeira
Naxçivan
Svalbard

Dependencies:

Føroyar
Gibraltar
Guernsey
Isle of Man
Jersey

In other parts of the world such mutability was not possible because stable belief systems underpinned the social and political institutions of the states, creating durability and a seamless and continuous culture.[19] By the fifteenth century, Islam, for example, had achieved a stable relationship among social organization, political structures, and the belief system in its society. The lack of mutability made it difficult for Islamic states to rapidly adjust to the Industrial Age. China, under the equally closed system of Confucianism, also achieved this condition by the fifteenth century. As a result, their belief systems, unequal and authoritarian social structures, and absolute monarchies buttressed one another to produce almost total sociopolitical immobility, even stagnation.[20]

> "The great Islamic empires reached peaks of civilization, science and the arts long before Europe. But the Industrial Revolution transformed European military power, while liberal democracy unlocked the power of its populations."
>
> "The World of Islam"
> *Understanding Global Issues*
>
> What would it take for the Islamic world to regain its former glory?

Multi-State System

The third respect in which the new European-style state was original is that it was a **multi-state system**. In the European feudal system, allegiance was to a feudal lord, not a given territory. And the Roman Catholic Church, which spread its thought across Europe, did not act in terms of territorial borders. When new states developed in the fifteenth and sixteenth centuries, they did so as multiple, competing, territorially defined sovereign political units.

In other parts of the world, multiple territorially based states did not occur until much later. This development was hampered in the Islamic world by common religious beliefs; in China by a firm dynastic domination of one vast territory; and in the Indian subcontinent by the competing belief systems of Hinduism and Islam.

Some European states, such as Britain, Spain, and France, established large colonial empires over the years, which gradually gained economic and political independence. By the end of World War II, little remained of these empires, and a proliferation of new states, following the models of statehood established in Europe, created today's political map of the world. The efforts of Germany and Japan to establish empires by military force failed in 1945 and resulted in drastic changes to their own statehood. In both cases the Allies attempted to ensure that their enemies were demilitarized and democratized, so that they would not become aggressive again.

The example of Japan illustrates what the victorious Allies envisaged to be a model state, and shows how they tried to create new states for their wartime enemies based on this ideal. Japan was occupied from 1945 to 1952, shorn of its conquests and even some of its territories over which other states had no valid claims. The army and navy were demobilized, and their ships and weapons destroyed; military leaders were tried for atrocities and executed. American leaders took measures to democratize Japanese society and re-establish a viable economy. General MacArthur and his staff drafted a new constitution for Japan based on the British parliamentary form of government. It included Article 9 in which Japan renounced forever "war as a sovereign right" and even the maintenance of "land, sea and air forces." Today Japan is restricted by its own law to possessing a military force and alliances only for self-defence, although, as of 1992, troops are allowed to participate in UN peacekeeping duties abroad.[21]

Thus, following the war, Japan submitted to drastic changes in the two key components of statehood—its defined territory and its form of government. For a time, while it was occupied by the allies, it was deprived of its sovereignty, and was not recognized by the international community as having the right to run its own affairs free from interference. It was forced to conform to the European model of what a state ought to be like.

LAW

We have clarified what states are, but what do they do? The answer is they all make rules for their societies which are enforced or backed up by the threat of coercion. They control their populations and regulate conflict over resources by making laws that are enforced by a criminal justice establishment of courts, police, and prisons.

Law is a body of rules emanating from government institutions and enforceable by the courts.[22] In stable liberal democracies, law provides rules which resolve disputes for the collective good of society and thereby improves people's chances of living together peacefully. In such countries the law applies to all individuals and groups in society equally, so that the outcomes of various actions are predictable. It is used to punish those who violate the rules and also to compensate those who have been harmed by rule breakers. Where it is functioning well, law may be a deterrent to others who might be tempted to break society's rules. In democracies, laws are interpreted and applied by judges who impartially mete out justice accordingly.[23] Recognized legal authorities such as the police and sometimes the military enforce their decisions. The first recorded code of laws, the Hammurabi Code, is described in Close Up 3.4.

CLOSE UP 3.4 The First Recorded Code of Laws

Hammurabi, King of Babylon, who reigned 2067–2025 B.C. was one of the great rulers of antiquity. He governed much of Mesopotamia, and created a code of laws for which he is famous. The Code of Hammurabi is found today in the Louvre Museum in Paris. A black basalt stele, about eight feet high, is inscribed with 282 laws in the Akkad language. The stele shows the King receiving the laws from the god of justice.

There are two main types of law; customary and legislative. **Customary law** develops over time through trial and error; it is never really "made" at any specific point in time but develops through habit and custom. It emerges from social conflict, and it may or may not be written down, but it exists and is enforced. **Legislative** or **statutory law** is created according to a specific plan to resolve actual or potential social conflict and can replace customary law.[24] It is created by a high organ of government such as a Congress or a Parliament.

Students of **jurisprudence** (legal philosophy) are divided about the essential nature of law and what makes it different from other customs, habits, and basic rules affecting human behaviour. Is it different because of its content or because of the procedures involved in making and enforcing it? Some theorists argue that laws are (or should be) based on **natural law**—"a body of principles for human behaviour ordained by God or Nature.[25] Thus we see, for example, Mosaic law embraced by orthodox Jews; Islamic law based on the Koran, held by followers of Islam; and the teachings of Christ as interpreted by Christians having an influence even in secular countries. These natural-law theorists believe that eternal principles of right and wrong should guide the behaviour of moral people in the event that man-made laws conflict with them. They try to distinguish law from the "wrong" principles for human behaviour.[26]

Other theorists argue that since people cannot absolutely identify right and moral principles, the law should be defined by the procedures or rules that governments make and enforce. This human-made law is known as **positive law**. American Supreme Court Justice Oliver Wendell Holmes, Jr. wrote that he considered law to be "the prophecies of what the courts will do in fact."[27] As an advocate of positive law, he tried to distinguish law from the rules set out by established customs and religious traditions.

In the English language the word "law" covers both natural law and positive law. However, the French language accords them different words—*droit* meaning eternal principles of correct conduct and *loi* meaning the rules enforced by a government. This separate nomenclature is also true in other languages including Latin, German, and Spanish.

Since many government agencies make laws, there are several types of positive law, including legislation, treaties, constitutions, administrative law, roman and civil law, and also court decisions. Early British theorists such as Thomas Hobbes believed that the sovereign was, and should be, the sole creator of laws. From this view developed the doctrine of **legal positivism**, which declares that all law is the command of the sovereign (or the state acting in the name of the sovereign) who may create any law so long as the proper procedures are followed. Legal positivists view the state as the legitimate power ruling over the people, imposing rules. They believe that as long as law is specifically enacted by a proper authority, then it is legitimate and ought to be obeyed. They do not see it in the reverse sense as being the expression of social development based on the people's or the judge's conception of justice.

In Europe a controversial case gained international publicity in January 1992. In a decision reminiscent of the post–World War II Nuremberg trials for crimes against humanity, two young former East German border guards were tried for shooting to death the last of more than 200 people killed who attempted to flee from communist East Berlin to democratic West

Berlin. The judge ruled that it did not matter that the guards had only done their jobs and acted according to the former East German law. "Not everything that is legal is right," he said. "At the end of the twentieth century no one has the right to turn off his conscience when it comes to killing people on the orders of the authorities." The guards who had fired the fatal shot were sentenced to three and a half years in prison.[28] The judge went beyond the use of positive law. He justified his decision on a higher moral, or natural law.

Law in Western Societies

In Western societies there is a belief that both rulers and the ruled should be subject to the same laws. In these societies the authority of the state is to be exercised rationally and without malice, with all citizens being protected from the abuse of power. This notion is embodied in the concept of the **rule of law**, meaning that the citizen, no matter what his or her transgression, cannot be denied due process of law. No individual or institution is to be above the law or exempted from it, and all are equal before it. The courts are to play a vital role as guardians of the rule of law.[29]

Several principles flow from this belief in the rule of law. Since all citizens are to be protected from the abuse of power, the government must maintain law and order, restraining individuals and also the government itself from transgressing on citizens' rights. The "rule of law" also means that individuals cannot be punished at will, but only when they have broken a law. People can do what they want as long as there is no law preventing it. And laws cannot be made or changed willy nilly, but only according to accepted procedures. If those rules are not followed, the laws are not binding.

There is a significant element of discretion in the enforcement of legal rules, of course. This is evident when judges must interpret the intent of a law as, for example, when they are allowed to assign sentences within a certain latitude. The government also has a certain latitude in which to conduct its affairs, as evidenced in the area of defence where it can command the military; in the field of domestic security where it can use emergency powers; or even in carrying out its day-to-day functions such as when it expropriates land necessary for building highways. In all of these cases, however, the government and its employees are also bound by the law of the country. Police and security forces work for the state, but this gives them no dispensation to act outside of the law.

The rule of law thus assures that the state uses coercion sparingly and equally. It restricts the freedom of action of the few who might harm or take advantage of their fellow citizens, but in doing so maximizes the freedom of the many whose rights and way of life are protected. As in any human engagement, the rule of law is an ideal, and thus vulnerable to human failings. Some criminals do escape punishment and sometimes the innocent are punished; sometimes political leaders take advantage of their power to commit unethical or illegal acts. But these actions do not destroy the validity of the ideal.

Common Law and Civil Law

Two separate legal systems developed and continue to dominate in Western countries; one is based on English Common Law, the other on Roman Civil Law.

We have briefly referred to **common law** as customary law. This unique legal practice was established during the reign of Henry II in twelfth-century England. The king dispatched royal judges to travel about the country and settle local disputes based on their interpretation of the customs of the realm. This innovation was deemed fairer and more predictable than the older local courts that had been established prior to the Norman Conquest of 1066. These new judges created a "common" body of law for the kingdom by following the principle of *stare decisis*, or "standing by former decisions." That is, they applied established rules from previous decisions or precedents rather than formulating new ones with each new case. This adherence to precedents allowed the law to grow in an orderly, predictable, and flexible manner, and a large body of law grew up without being issued as commands by the government. As social change occurred, judicial interpretations, based on the common law, helped to adjust law to the new realities. As British culture spread to other parts of the world, common law was transported and became an important feature of law governing contracts, personal property, and family matters in the United States, Canada, Australia, New Zealand, and India.

Over the years, as societies grew and advanced technologically, interpretations of common law became burdensome because of the great complexity of accumulated precedents, which sometimes conflicted. Eventually, other types of law, such as legislative and administrative law, incorporated a great deal of general common law. But common law remains the basis of many decisions not covered by statutes or constitutions. It is often called **case law**, and is developed by court interpretations and decisions over time. This unenacted common law may be superseded by constitutional and statutory law when necessary.

Roman civil law was a body of rules based upon the "codified" laws of ancient Rome that were rediscovered and served as models in Europe in the early Middle Ages. The Romans **codified**, or ordered and systematized, their common law in order to reveal its principles more clearly. Justinian's Code was produced in the sixth century A.D. and served as a model in 1804 when Napoleon I ordered French customary law codified in the manner of early Rome. The result came to be known as the *Code civil* or *Code Napoleon*, which serves as the basis of law in France, and in other European countries such as Belgium, Spain, and Italy. It has also been adopted and adapted in a great many other countries in the world. In Quebec, and in Louisiana in the United States, civil law is used instead of common law in the courts. Civil law follows specific rules and procedures and is more "rationalistic and deductive" in tone than is common law.

Civil law must be distinguished from "criminal law." **Civil law** is concerned with private law—wrongs committed against individuals rather than the whole community. **Criminal law** is concerned with crimes which are considered to damage the whole community, generally by threatening basic security or safety.

Legislative Law

Two types of legislative law are common to modern states: constitutional law and statutory law.

Constitutional law is based on the constitution of a state. A constitution is a body of fundamental rules, written and unwritten, according to which its government operates. Constitutional law is fundamental, in that any other type of law which contravenes it is superseded and annulled.

Statutory law consists of legislation or rules enacted by the legislature. Today, statutory law exists in the fields of both public law (which creates agencies of the state and controls relations between individuals and the state) and private law (which applies to relations between individuals). Statutory law supersedes common law. It can be created or changed relatively quickly, and can be used to anticipate problem areas before they arise, unlike common law which can be applied only after a problem has arisen. Judges develop common law and interpret statutory law. As in common law, statutes are interpreted in the light of particular disputes as they are brought before the courts, and follow the rules of precedent, or *stare decisis*.

Administrative Law

Like legislated law, administrative law constitutes an important feature of most modern political systems. Many executive and administrative agencies are authorized by their legislatures to provide sub-rules and regulations within certain limited areas and under the authority of other laws. This is referred to as subordinate or delegated legislation.

Laws are constantly made, revised, and interpreted to reflect the current mood of society. As social change occurs, judicial interpretations help to adjust laws to the new realities. When common law becomes seriously outmoded, it has to be replaced by new legislation. If law lags too far behind social change it may become widely disobeyed and require higher levels of coercion to enforce it.

Culture, Ideology, and Religion in the Development of Law

Historical events, culture, ideology, and religion give character to the customs and usage of all countries, and have an impact on the law in constitutions, statutes, and regulations. The idea that the relationship between the government and the individual must be based on law (i.e., individuals possess inherent rights and can be deprived of them only by due process) was central to the development of the law in Western societies. This important concept made the development of law in the Western world quite different from that in areas where absolutist rulers were not impeded by legal restraints or other social influences such as strong aristocracies. In early Chinese and Japanese societies, for example, the individual was simply a subject, and law was used only to enforce the power and policy of the ruler.[30]

Over time, Western legal concepts have had considerable influence in other parts of the world, and states have adopted certain procedures and codes and blended them with their own customs. This is true in most states in Asia, Africa, and Latin America. Often the influence came from colonizing or conquering powers; in Africa, legal systems reflect civil law codes of Germany, France, and the Netherlands as well as British common law; in Latin America they reflect civil codes from France, Germany, Switzerland, Spain, and Portugal, and also English common law. Japanese law has been based on the codified law system of continental Europe since the 1890s; but since 1945 it has been greatly liberalized, and many constitutional safeguards have been introduced from American law.

Religion provided many of the values which underlay the development of law in the Western world. European monarchs were circumscribed by divine law as interpreted by the Church, as well as by "natural law," which conferred the right to private property, life, and liberty, and by the laws of the state itself. Adherence to principles based on religion is found even in the modern constitutions of some secular societies. In Canada, for example, the *Charter of Rights and Freedoms* begins with the idea that "Canada is founded upon principles that recognize the supremacy of God and the rule of law," which harks back to Judeo-Christian influences. Other secular societies, concerned to avoid the divisiveness of competing religions, have been more adamant in separating church and state. In the United States, the framers of the Constitution sought to separate government from religious practice. The First Amendment stipulates that Congress is prohibited 1) from establishing a national religion and 2) from interfering with religious practice. Freedom to *believe* is absolute, but freedom to *practise* that belief may, in certain circumstances, be circumscribed by government.

The relation between religion and the development of law can be seen throughout the world. A unique legal system based on the religious precepts of Muslim countries, for example, is prevalent today in many states in the Middle East, Asia, and Africa. It is based on Islamic law, which originated, along with Islam itself, in the seventh century, and is founded on the revelations of Mohammed, as written in the Koran. Since it developed at a time when there were very few social and governmental institutions, Islamic law assumed the role of regulating all areas of human conduct, not just religious behaviour.[31] In Islamic states, no distinction was made between the person of the ruler and the state, and the law was conceived as simply a means to maintain official power and policy. This is the origin of the Sunni Muslim doctrine of passive obedience, that:

> ... any Muslim ruler, whoever he was and however he came to power, who was able to protect the territories of Islam and impose civil peace was entitled to obedience. Obedience to such a ruler, whether bad or mad, was a religious duty.[32]

By the nineteenth century, many Muslim states decided to modernize their legal systems to cope with new demands on them. European legal codes, for example, were adopted in Egypt and Turkey to supplement Islamic law. In the twentieth century, Turkey abolished Islamic law altogether. Egypt abolished it as well in 1956, but then in 1980 amended the constitution to reinstate Islamic revelations as the foundation of Egyptian law. Today, approximately two dozen Muslim states use a blend of Islamic law and European civil law codes to soften the stern teachings of the prophet and meet the needs of their culturally varied populations. One of these is Indonesia, which contains almost a fifth of the world's Muslims, but where Islam is not the state religion. There the official ideology of *pancasila* prescribes a belief in one god, but not necessarily Allah. In Afghanistan, the new Taliban rulers have taken an extreme view of how law should be based on religious dogmas. See Close Up 3.5.

CLOSE-UP 3.5 Islamic Law and the Taliban

Today in Afghanistan, law is determined entirely by the Taliban leadership's strict interpretation of the teachings of Islam—an interpretation not accepted elsewhere in the Muslim world.

By 1998, after nine years of civil war, the Taliban religious army had extended its control over more than 95% of Afghanistan. They brought relative peace to the civil-war-torn country, but also tyranny and fear imposed by an Islamic movement so extreme that those who violate its ways are beaten, maimed, or killed in public ceremonies echoing with verses from the Koran.

Taliban rules are so sweeping that they touch every aspect of life. Women must wear tent-like burkas that cover their bodies entirely and provide only a screen-covered opening for their eyes. They are forbidden to work, read, or walk the streets alone. Girls may not attend schools. Men must trim their mustaches just above their lips, trim their bangs neatly along their foreheads, and wear beards at least as long as a clenched fist, under the chin. If any deviation is found in this respect, the men are imprisoned and given compulsory lessons in religious law. Harsh punishments are meted out for sins such as gambling, alcohol, drugs, watching television, and even listening to music. Homosexuals are buried alive under walls of brick, adulterers are stoned to death, and thieves have their hands amputated.

What should the United Nations or the leaders of individual states attempt to do about this situation? Should NATO act here as it has in Bosnia and Kosovo?

In secular authoritarian states, ideology may be used to determine the content and administration of the law. Legal systems in communist countries differ fundamentally from those in democracies because the Communist party determines what is in the best interests of the country.[33] In these countries the accepted doctrine of socialist legal consciousness requires that lawyers and judges adhere to party policy and ideology when deciding cases. Criminal behaviour, for example, covers a very wide range of activities. At one end of the scale, crimes such as theft are handled relatively similarly to the West, while at the other end of the scale, the difference is considerable. Severe punishments are meted out for crimes against the state such as inefficiency and poor-quality production. The harshest penalties are reserved for political crimes, which traditionally have been interpreted as political protest.

Readers should now have an understanding about where political science is today, what it is trying to accomplish, and how. The study of politics is based on the concepts of power, authority, influence, state, nation, and law that we have covered in the first three chapters. With this foundation we are now ready to impose some order on the seemingly infinite range of politics that is conducted in states. In the next two chapters we will outline the benefits of analysis and discuss how to make interesting and proper comparisons of the world's states.

DISCUSSION QUESTIONS

1. Is Canada a state, a nation, or both? Justify your answer.
2. To what extent are states "independent" today? Even from their larger neighbours?
3. "Nationalism is the political manifestation of ethnicity; ethnicity is an enduring social formation through which interest is pursued." Debate.
4. Distinguish between natural and positive law. Consider how the concepts apply to the Nuremberg trials in which post–World War II Nazis were tried for crimes against humanity.
5. How does the development of law differ in democratic and authoritarian states?

KEY TERMS

case law, p. 60
citizens, p. 46
civil law, p. 60
codified laws, p. 60
common law, p. 60
constitution, p. 61
constitutional law, p. 61
criminal law, p. 60
customary law, p. 58
delegated legislation, p. 61
hypernationalism, p. 50

jurisprudence, p. 58
law, p. 57
legalism, p. 53
legal positivism, p. 58
legislative or statutory law, p. 58
multi-state system, p. 56
mutability, p. 53
nation, p. 46
nationalism, p. 47
national identity, p. 49

nation-state, p. 46
natural law, p. 58
positive law, p. 58
private law, p. 61
public law, p. 61
regionalism, p. 48
Roman civil law, p. 60
rule of law, p. 59
sovereign state, p. 45
state, p. 45
statutory law, p. 61

ENDNOTES

1. See, for example, David Beetham and Max Weber, *The Theory of Modern Politics*, 2nd ed. (Cambridge: Polity Press, 1987).
2. K.J. Holsti, *International Politics: A Framework for Analysis*, 4th ed. (Scarborough, Ont.: Prentice-Hall Canada, 1967), p. 65.
3. T.H. Marshall, *Class, Citizenship and Social Development* (Garden City, N.J.: Doubleday, 1965).
4. See William Rogers Brubaker, ed., *Immigration and the Politics of Citizenship in Europe and North America* (Lanham, Md.: University Press of America, 1989).
5. Robert H. Jackson and Alan James, eds., *States in a Changing World* (Oxford: Clarendon Press, 1993), p.11.
6. George De Vjos and Lola Ramanucci-Ross, *Ethnic Identity: Cultural Continuities and Change* (Palo Alto, Calif.: Mayfield Publishing, 1975), p. 3.
7. On the types of nationalism, see Anthony D. Smith, *Nationalism in the Twentieth Century* (Oxford: Martin Robertson, 1979). On the "new" nationalism see Michael Ignatieff, *Blood and Belonging: Journeys into the New Nationalism* (Toronto: Viking, 1993).
8. Attributed to Albert Einstein in Martin Levin, "Nationalism, disease or plague?" *The Globe and Mail*, June 15, 1995.

9. See Ignatieff, *Blood and Belonging*; and E. Gellner, *Nations and Nationalism* (Oxford: Basil Blackwell, 1983).

10. Fouad Ajami, "The End of Pan-Arabism," *Foreign Affairs*, vol. 57, no. 2 (Winter 1978–79), p. 355; and also, by the same author "The Summer of Arab Discontent" in *Foreign Affairs*, vol. 69, no. 5 (Winter 1990–91), pp. 1–20.

11. See Shaul Bakhas, "How Saddam is Dividing the Arab World," *The New York Review of Books*, vol. xxxvii, no. 17, (November 8, 1990), pp. 49–51.

12. See for example "Suharto and the reins of power," *The Economist*, 17–23 Nov. 1990, pp. 37–41. In 1998, Suharto was forced to resign during an uprising against his 32-year rule and his method of stifling opposition and amassing a personal fortune. His successor, B.J. Habibie has ordered an investigation into how Suharto and his children accumulated holdings estimated at $40 billion (U.S.), but he, too, has to contend with internal violence and upheaval due to the collapse of the economy.

13. S.E. Finer, "Problems of the Liberal-Democratic State: An Historical Overview," *Government and Opposition*, vol. 25, no. 3 (Summer 1990), p. 358.

14. *Ibid.*, p. 350. Church-state relations in this period are explored in John A. Hall and G. John Ikenberry, *The State* (Minneapolis: University of Minnesota Press, 1989), pp. 34–41.

15. John H. Herz, *The Nation-State and the Crisis of World Politics* (New York: David McKay, 1976), p. 101.

16. Finer, "Problems of the Liberal-Democratic State," pp. 335–43.

17. *Ibid.*, p. 340.

18. See R.W. Southern, *Western Society and the Church in the Middle Ages* (London: Penguin, 1970).

19. See Hall and Ikenberry, *The State*, ch. 3; and Finer, "Problems of the Liberal-Democratic State," p. 341.

20. Finer, "Problems of the Liberal-Democratic State," p. 341. Also see James R. Townsend and Brantly Womack, *Politics in China*, 3rd ed. (Toronto: Little, Brown, 1986), ch. 2.

21. Edwin O. Reischauer, *The Japanese Today* (Cambridge, Mass.: Harvard University Press, 1977), ch. 10.

22. Austin Ranney, *Governing*, 4th ed. (Englewood Cliffs, N.J.: Prentice-Hall, 1987), p. 293.

23. This is of course the ideal. One notorious exception was the judiciary in Nazi Germany in which many judges ingratiated themselves ideologically and professionally with Hitler's dictatorial Third Reich. To a very large extent they gave up their autonomy, welcomed the removal of Jewish and liberal colleagues and embraced the "new Germany." See Ingo Muller, *Hitler's Justice* (Cambridge, Mass.: Harvard University Press, 1991).

24. Michael Zander, *The Law-Making Process* (London: Weidenfeld & Nicolson, 1989).

25. Ranney, *Governing*, p. 291.

26. Jeffrie Murphy and Jules Coleman, *Philosophy of Law* (Boulder, Colo.: Westview Press, 1989).

27. Oliver Wendell Holmes, Jr., *Collected Legal Papers* (New York: Harcourt Brace Jovanovich, 1921), p. 173.

28. *The New York Times*, January 26, 1992, p. E6.

29. See Jerold Waltman and Kenneth Holland, *The Political Role of Law Courts in Modern Democracies* (New York: St. Martin's Press, 1987).

30. J. Hall and M. Jansen, *Studies in the Institutional History of Early Modern Japan*, (Princeton, N.J.: Princeton University Press, 1968), pp. 214–215.

31. See John Esposito, ed., *Islam and Development: Religion and Sociopolitical Change* (New York: Syracuse University Press, 1980); and J. Schacht, *An Introduction to Islamic Law* (Oxford: Oxford University Press, 1982).

32. E. Kedourie, "Crisis and Revolution in Modern Islam," *The Times Literary Supplement*, May 19–25, 1989, p. 549.

33. See, for example, Frederick C. Barghoorn and Thomas F. Remington, *Politics in the USSR*, 3rd ed. (Toronto: Little, Brown, 1986), ch. 9.

FURTHER READING

State and Nation

Alter, Peter, *Nationalism* (London: Edward Arnold, 1989).

Anderson, Benedict, *Imagined Communities*, 2nd ed (London, Verso, 1991).

Bialer, Seweryn, *Politics, Society, and Nationality inside Gorbachev's Russia* (Boulder, Col.: Westview Press, 1989).

Eisenstadt, S.M., and S. Rokkan, eds., *Building States and Nations*, Vols. I and II (Beverly Hills, Cal., and London: Sage Publications, 1973).

Fieldhouse, D.K., *The Colonial Empires: A Comparative Study from the Eighteenth Century*, 2nd ed. (London: Macmillan, 1982).

Gellner, Ernest, *Nations and Nationalism* (London: Basil Blackwell, 1983).

Ghayasuddin, G., ed., *The Impact of Nationalism on the Muslim World* (London: Open Press, 1986).

Grass, Gunter, *Two States—One Nation?* trans. Krishna Winston and A.S. Wensinger (San Diego: Helen and Kurt Wolff, 1990).

Greenfield, Liah, *Nationalism: Five Roads to Modernity* (Cambridge, Mass.: Harvard University Press, 1992).

Hall, J.A., ed., *States in History* (Oxford: Basil Blackwell, 1986).

Horowitz, Donald, *Ethnic Groups in Conflict* (Berkeley: University of California Press, 1985).

Ignatieff, Michael, *Blood and Belonging: Journeys into the New Nationalism* (Toronto: Viking, 1993).

Kaplan, William, ed., *Belonging: The Meaning and Future of Canadian Citizenship* (Montreal: McGill-Queens' University Press, 1993).

Mayall, James, *Nationalism in International Society* (Cambridge: Cambridge University Press, 1990).

Pfaff, Wilson, *The Wrath of Nations: Civilizations and the Furies of Nationalism* (New York: Simon & Schuster, 1998).

Poggi, C., *The Development of the Modern State* (London: Hutchinson, 1978).

Smith, Anthony D., *Theories of Nationalism*, 2nd ed. (London: Duckworth, 1983).

———, *National Identity* (Las Vegas: University of Nevada Press, 1991).

Sovereignty

Morgan, Edmund S., *Inventing the People: The Rise of Popular Sovereignty in England and America* (New York: W.W. Norton, 1988).

Walker, R.B.J., and Saul H. Mendlovitz, eds., *Contending Sovereignties: Redefining Political Community* (Boulder, Colo.: Lynne Rienner Publishers, 1990).

Law

Carter, Lief, *Law and the Judicial Process* (Glenview, Ill.: Scott, Foresman & Co., 1988).

Gall, Gerald, *The Canadian Legal System* (Toronto: Carswell, 1990).

Murphy, Jeffrie, and Jules Coleman, *Philosophy of Law* (Boulder, Col.: Westview Press, 1989).

Russell, Peter, *The Judiciary in Canada: The Third Branch of Government* (Toronto: McGraw-Hill Ryerson, 1987).

Tiruchelvam, Neelan, and Oki Ombaaka, *The Role of the Judiciary in Plural Societies* (New York: St. Martin's Press, 1987).

Waltman, Jerold, and Kenneth Holland, *The Political Role of Law Courts in Modern Democracies* (New York: St. Martin's Press, 1987).

 **Weblinks**

haynese.winthrop.edu/index.htm
This site contains information about the Arab League.

canada.justice.gc.ca/index_en.html
The Canadian Department of Justice and Canadian Law site outlines the department's structure and contains copies of many important Canadian Laws.

www.law.cornell.edu/supct/supct.table.html
This site contains rulings by the United States' Supreme Court on important aspects of American law.

CHAPTER 4

Modern States and Forms of Government

It was a major historical landmark when the state emerged as the dominant form of political organization in the sixteenth and seventeenth centuries. Other types and combinations of political organizations such as local governments, empires, and international structures had existed before and continued to exist after the rise of the state, but none have rivaled it in importance or ubiquity. Most state borders were determined by historical accidents or were settled by wars or colonization.

Today, the arbitrarily drawn borders of the world's states define countries which differ dramatically in ways that affect the prosperity and quality of life of their citizens. We touched on some of these differences in Chapter 1 when we spoke of the great disparity in area, wealth, and population size among the states of the world. Here, we will pursue some of these differences further before considering why it is important to use a comprehensive approach in the study of states and forms of government.

Several environmental factors provide possibilities and also set limitations on what governments can do to provide security and prosperity for their citizens. These factors, with features unique to individual states and regions, help to shape and set priorities among political issues. They include the territory, climate, natural resources, and population which a state possesses. Level of economic development is also an important part of the environment in terms of its influence on political issues and government policy.

This book is concerned primarily with world politics, with the similarities and differences in forms of government among the states of the world. Such a study is necessarily comparative. The second part of this chapter explains why and how political scientists study states and governments comparatively.

INDEPENDENCE, INTERDEPENDENCE, AND GLOBALIZATION

A majority of today's states were established after 1945 when the process of decolonization was at its zenith. In 1945 there were only 65 states; today there are 192.[1] In recent years the total number of states has still been increasing, but only slowly. With less than 1% of the world's population and territory remaining with no self-government, new states will undoubtedly have to reach independent statehood either peacefully through secession or violently by revolution or war.[2]

There is a primary difference between the newly emerging states of the 1950s and 1960s and those of recent years. The former, as we have noted, were, in effect, granted recognition of their right to self-determination as the total population of a colonial territory. International law recognized their right to self-determination, to allow them to escape external determination by their "mother country." Today, "such limitations as laid out in international law are not acceptable to many sub-state groups as they push for self-determination up to and including secession."[3] They want the right to break away from existing states. An example would be the Basque separatist movement that demands independence from both France and Spain. Such sub-state groups want to emulate other former nations, forced into states by war, which successfully claimed the right to regain their independence. Lithuania, Latvia, and Estonia, which were forced into the Soviet Union for many years, are three examples of nations which recently have become states for the second time.

Two other major changes are occurring in the pattern of states in the contemporary world. First, although they emphasize territoriality and sovereignty, modern states are increasingly vulnerable to outside influences due to the political, economic, and technological changes that have come with globalization. These focuses include international trade, finance, and communications, as well as the effects of modern science and technology and other elements of modernization. Second, sovereignty still prevails in many domestic areas, but international forces are gradually affecting how governments act in all fields. These international variables continue to impinge on the priorities of governments. Authoritarian governments, particularly the economically weaker ones, are especially vulnerable and are being undermined in many parts of the world.[4]

In other words, states are becoming increasingly interdependent.[5] Three basic tendencies are promoting these changes. First, the world has shrunk because of increased free trade in goods, services, and capital and the international use of modern forms of communication, especially the Internet. Second, there has been a growth of regional groupings such as the European Union (EU), the Organization for Security and Cooperation in Europe (OSCE), and the North American Free Trade Agreement (NAFTA). We are witnessing the gradual evolution of the state to supranational units of government. The reason is largely economic. World trade today accounts for nearly one-fifth of the Gross World Product, which is the total value of goods and services produced in the world. Economies are more interlinked than they were at the beginning of the 1990s, and these economic links have increased prosperity. The third reason for interdependence and globalization is that many noneconomic problems are now best resolved internationally. Problems such as terrorism, environmental pollution, drugs, and so on require concerted international action.

At the same time as large regional groupings are forming, a second trend is to smaller groupings, sometimes called a "downward drift." Many countries currently on the map owe their shape to the collapse of larger empires—the Hapsburg, Ottoman, French, and British empires, for example. Today some large states are breaking up again largely because of the rise of nationalism. Examples include the 1991 breakup of the Soviet Union as a federal state of 15 republics into Russian and other smaller units, and the 1993 collapse of Yugoslavia into many states and warring factions. In these and other cases the large states were forged out of conquest, not consent, and a national identity at the state level did not develop sufficiently to subsume sub-national identities.

THE PHYSICAL, DEMOGRAPHIC, AND ECONOMIC ENVIRONMENT

Territory is the physical unit that unites the people of one state and separates them from others. It provides a tangible homeland and a foundation of economic resources. For these reasons territory is highly valued and is often the cause of disputes and war. Canada, at nearly 10 million square miles, has the largest territory in the Western Hemisphere, and is second only to Russia as the largest country in the world. Compared to small states such as Vatican City or Monaco at less than one square mile, Canada is indeed enormous. But size is deceiving; territory alone is no insurance that a country will be prosperous, well governed at home, or influential abroad.

Hospitable climate, population, and natural resources are other crucial factors; but, like territory, they too are grossly maldistributed among the world's states.[6] Human settlements do not thrive where temperatures are consistently below freezing in winter, because the cold imposes extra burdens on the economy. There are 30 countries in which subzero temperatures are regularly recorded; the most intense cold is in regions such as Siberia, Alaska, the Northwest Territories of Canada, and Greenland. At the other extreme, 43 countries have experienced temperatures over 43.3 degrees Celsius, and are considered to be among the most inhospitable to human life. The hottest recorded temperature in the world was recorded at 54.4 degrees Celsius in Mali. Only 29% of the globe is land and most of the habitable part cannot be used to produce food. Almost half the land is ice-capped, desert, or wasteland, and a third is forest, marsh, or mountain. When urban areas are subtracted, only about 10% remains that can be used for agriculture, and even this is unevenly distributed among states of the world.

Water is vital for human settlement, agriculture, and all forms of economic activity. It, too, is maldistributed among states. Most states border on seas or oceans, but a few are landlocked with no easy access to the international marketplace. Some receive almost no rain. Some places in the Sahara desert receive tiny amounts of rain only once in several years, yet others like Cherrapunji in India receive an average of 1.2 inches every day of the year. The three regions that receive the most rainfall are Southeast Asia, southern West Africa, and the West Indies and Central America.

People are a state's key resource, but here, too, disparities are enormous. China is by far the world's most populous state, with approximately 1.5 billion people. China and India alone contain almost 40% of the world's population. Some states and regions are densely populated while others have almost no inhabitants.[7] Population size alone cannot be used to predict prosperity. Bangladesh and the Netherlands are among the most densely populated states in the world; yet Bangladesh is one of the world's 20 poorest countries while the Netherlands belongs to the richest 20. At the other extreme, the United States has a very low population density and relatively high income level, while several African countries have similarly low densities but suffer from poverty and famine.

Population becomes a better indicator of prosperity when one examines larger, regional units. The most industrialized regions of North America, Europe, and Asia contain only about 15% of the world's population; the rest of Asia, Africa, and Latin America contain about 77%. The areas of the former Soviet Union and Eastern Europe, which are in transition from communist to market economies, contain about 8% of the world's population. This current pattern of population will become even more distorted between industrialized and nonindustrialized regions if today's birth rates remain constant. The rate of **population replacement**—that is, a sufficient increase for the number of inhabitants to remain stable—has been set at 2.1 births per female. In all of the industrialized capitalist countries,[8] (and also in the region that constituted the former Soviet Union and Eastern Europe), fertility rates have fallen well below replacement level, averaging 1.5 births per female in 1995. This means that unless these countries accept immigrants, their populations will shrink over time.

In the poorest, nonindustrialized countries, on the other hand, the regions of Africa and Asia, where population levels are already the highest in the world, the annual growth rate of population is well above the replacement level at 2.4 births per female. About 36% of the people living in developing countries are under 15 years of age. Their fertility as adults will make an enormous difference to population growth rates and consequently to global resources.

According to World Bank projections, the inhabitants of the developing countries today could more than double to over 8 billion by the year 2025. The *Human Development Report, 1998*, indicates it could double even sooner, in 2023[9] (see Figure 4.1 for the World Bank's projected regional population figures up to the year 2100). Population growth that is too high can severely hamper economic development. High population countries like China and India often seek ways to cut their rapid rate of growth. China, which contains approximately one out of every five people on earth, has an official policy of one child per family, which only recently has been somewhat modified (see Close Up 4.1). In India, when Indira Gandhi was Prime Minister (a country that contains about one out of every seven humans), individuals were jailed and their ration cards confiscated if they had more than the statutorily permitted quota of children.

The 1994 World Bank population projections illustrate in a graphic manner how population growth will be greater in some continents than others (see Figure 4.1). Africa, for example, is projected to grow dramatically over the next century because of its current extremely high birth rates. China, on the other hand, has undergone a drop in its total fertility rate, which means that its projections are lower than might be intuited from the fact that it is has the largest population of any country in the world.

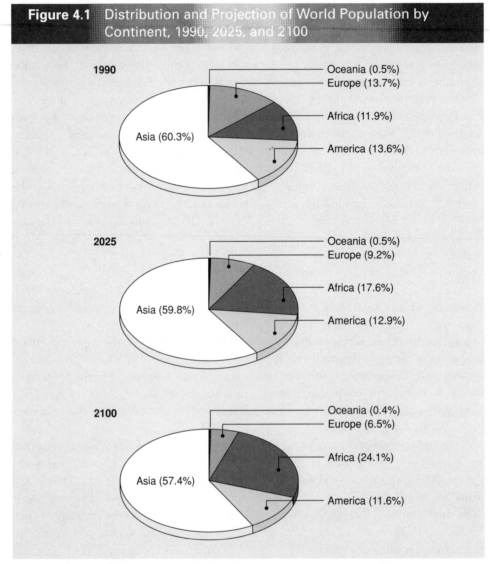

Figure 4.1 Distribution and Projection of World Population by Continent, 1990, 2025, and 2100

1990

Oceania (0.5%)
Europe (13.7%)
Africa (11.9%)
America (13.6%)
Asia (60.3%)

2025

Oceania (0.5%)
Europe (9.2%)
Africa (17.6%)
America (12.9%)
Asia (59.8%)

2100

Oceania (0.4%)
Europe (6.5%)
Africa (24.1%)
America (11.6%)
Asia (57.4%)

Source: World Bank, *World Population Projections, 1994–95* (Washington, D.C.: The International Bank, 1994), p. 6.

Another problem of world demography is aging. The world is facing a looming old-age crisis. A 1994 report by the World Bank claims that the number of people over 60 years of age will triple from 500 million during the years 1990 to 2030. The challenge confronts all continents but will be most pronounced in the developed democracies, including the United States and Canada (see Table 4.1).

The dilemma posed by rapidly increasing population and the world's inability to cope is graphically illustrated on a large computer display at the International

CLOSE UP 4.1 China's Population Policy

To help curb its burgeoning population (1.2 billion in 1998), China has had an offi-cial policy of one child per family. Exceptions have been allowed for ethnic mi-norities such a Tibetans, and couples whose first child is handicapped. Peasants whose firstborn were female were also allowed to have a second baby in order to try to get a son (a policy that has caused the death of many baby girls and changed the national male-female birth rate of 114 to 100, compared with a statistical norm of 106 to 100). Parents who had a second child in defiance of the law risked the wrath of the state with such punishments as stiff fines and loss of state jobs and housing. Many have been subjected to forced abortions and sterilizations.

In 1998, however, following considerable internal and external pressures about human rights violations, Bejing modified the national population-control regula-tions. Forced abortions and sterilizations are now prohibited. As well, in some test regions wealthy women may now have a second child without fear of punishment if they pay a steep "family planning" fee—in Shanghai the fee is three times the com-bined annual salary of both parents.[10]

Given that the Chinese population is rising even as birth rates decline, do you think China is acting humanely and responsibly in its population policy?

Development Research Centre in Ottawa. It displays a "Doomsday equation"; two or three times a second the numerator in the equation increases, indicating an increase in the pop-ulation. At the same time, the denominator, which represents the number of hectares of arable land on the planet, is relentlessly decreasing.

The list of disparities between states goes on. Natural resources are extremely un-evenly divided. Only four states possess an abundance and diversity of mineral resources:

Table 4.1 The Aging World: 1990 and Future Projections of Percentage of Population Over 60 Years of Age

	1990	2010	2030
OECD (countries)*	18.2	23.1	30.7
Latin America and Caribbean	6.9	9.3	16.0
Eastern Europe and the former USSR	15.3	18.2	22.7
Middle East and North Africa	5.7	6.5	9.8
Sub-Saharan Africa	4.6	4.5	5.9
Asia	7.4	9.5	16.3

*Organization for Economic Cooperation and Development
Source: Adapted from World Bank data published in *The Globe and Mail*, October 4, 1994.

Australia, Canada, South Africa, and the United States.[11] Just four states, the United States, Canada, Australia, and Argentina, have an agricultural base sufficient to allow them to dominate the export of staple grains in the world.[12]

Level of economic development is another important factor in the environment of a political system. **Gross Domestic Product (GDP)** per capita is one way to compare economic development across countries. GDP is an estimate of the total value of goods and services produced by the people in a country in a given year. This indicator is used by economists to measure economic activity and growth from year to year within a country, or to compare the relative wealth or poverty of different states. GDP is only a general indicator; it can be misleading to distinguish among states in only this one respect. The indicator may conceal significant inequalities that sometimes exist in the distribution of economic and social amenities and opportunities for citizens, who may not share equally in a country's prosperity. In Brazil, for example, half the total wealth of the country is in the hands of just 10% of the population.

GDP is also a deceptive measure for those instances where goods and services are not counted if they are not commercialized on the market. Unpaid labour (usually done by women) such as child care, cooking, housework, and community volunteer work is not counted in either developed or developing countries. In developing countries the hard work of daily life—gathering firewood, carrying water, subsistence farming, and so forth—does not figure into the calculation. However, even exercising caution in interpreting these figures, the range of difference in GDP between rich and poor regions is enormous, as Table 4.2 shows. In 1995, Luxembourg had the highest per capita GDP in the world at $34 004 and the Democratic Republic of the Congo had the lowest at $355.[13] The poorest people in opulent societies like the United States and Japan have larger incomes than those of the rich in many developing countries.

The seven most industrialized countries are Britain, Canada, France, Germany, Italy, Japan, and the United States. Richer states generally enjoy more rapid economic growth than poorer countries. Industrial states are relatively rich and heavily urban; poor, nonindustrial states are comparatively rural. To be rich, industrialized, and urbanized also means to be literate, educated, and healthy. Life expectancy varies, from

Table 4.2 Real Gross Domestic Product Per Capita by Region 1995 ($U.S.)	
Region	**GDP**
All developing countries	$3 068
LDCs	1 008
Industrial countries	16 337
World	5 990

Source: United Nations Development Program, *Human Development Report 1998* (Oxford: Oxford University Press), p. 130. Copyright © 1998 United Nations Development Program. Used by permission of Oxford University Press, Inc.

country to country, from 52 years to about 80. A mother in a developed country can expect her baby to live; only about 15 of 1000 babies who are born alive will die in infancy. See Figure 4.2. In developing countries, however, mothers have reason to be more fearful: 78 of every 1000 babies born will die early. Figure 4.3 shows the upward trajectory of life expectancy in industrial, developing countries, and LDCs from 1970–1995. A child born today in a developing country can expect to live 16 years longer than one born 35 years ago.

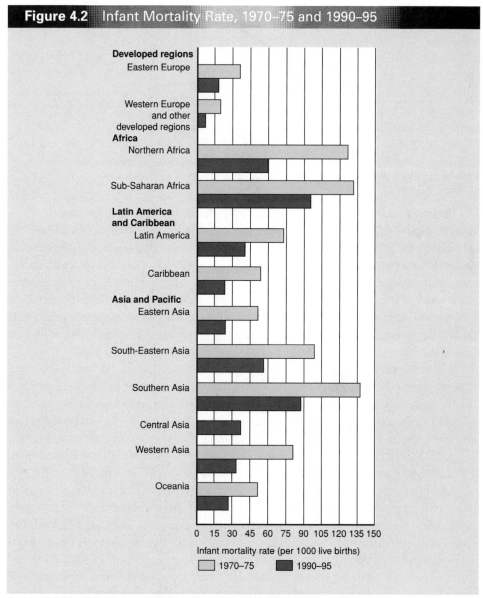

Figure 4.2 Infant Mortality Rate, 1970–75 and 1990–95

Source: *The World's Women 1995* (New York: United Nations, 1995), p. 69.

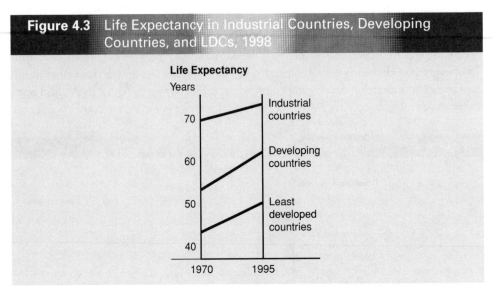

Figure 4.3 Life Expectancy in Industrial Countries, Developing Countries, and LDCs, 1998

Source: United Nations Development Program, *Human Development Report 1998* (Oxford: Oxford University Press), p. 19. Copyright © 1998 United Nations Development Program. Used by permission of Oxford University Press, Inc.

Illiteracy rates are nearly eight times higher in developing than developed countries. As Figure 4.4 shows, these rates are significantly worse for females than males in all parts of the world. In the developing countries, where the number of illiterates is about 45% for females—and up to nearly 70% in some areas—the repercussions for society are particularly serious. Education in the Northern Hemisphere is, in general terms, vastly superior to that in the Southern Hemisphere. Lack of education is detrimental, for example, to practising basic hygiene and health care, and severely curtails job opportunities for women, who still support the majority of the world's children. Adult literacy rose about 20% from 1970 to 1995 in both developing countries and LDCs.[14]

There are various ways to measure standard of living. Table 4.3 uses the United Nations Human Development Index (HDI) to depict the quality of life of the 10 best and the 10 worst states in the world in which to live in 1995. This measure aggregates the factors of life expectancy, literacy rates, educational attainment, and real purchasing power into one index. Canada places first on the HDI. A gender-related development index, which includes human development achievements of women, still places Canada first. The 16 worst places for women to live are by this measure, all in Africa.[15]

Our brief overview illustrates the enormous discrepancies existing among states in terms of their physical, demographic, and economic environment. However, despite these differences, as we have already noted, all states also have a core of features in common. In particular, all are managed by political systems that rest on fairly similar foundations of political organization, so that many newly emerging states have authority structures similar to those already in existence. Exactly what the state apparatus will look like in any particular case depends on the historical evolution that has taken place

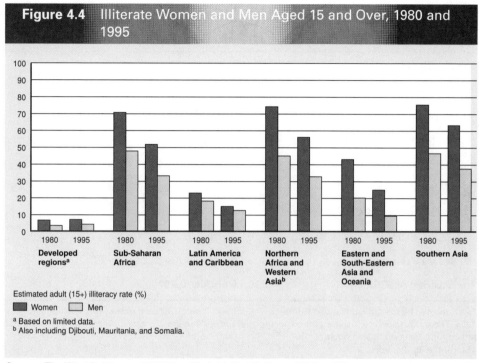

Figure 4.4   Illiterate Women and Men Aged 15 and Over, 1980 and 1995

Estimated adult (15+) illiteracy rate (%)
■ Women   □ Men

a Based on limited data.
b Also including Djibouti, Mauritania, and Somalia.

Source: *The World's Women 1995* (New York: United Nations, 1995), p. 90.

in the relations between society and politics. These similarities and differences among states provide the basis for comparison. Before beginning our study of the world's states, we next consider why comparing states is important, and examine the major approaches and techniques political scientists have adopted in that endeavour.

COMPARING STATES AND FORMS OF GOVERNMENT

Why Compare?

The field of political science is premised on the idea that comparing one state to another will yield a better understanding of politics than can be achieved by outlining the facts about only one country. By comparing states for their similarities and differences, we discover the advantages and disadvantages of specific institutions and make judgments about their impact on public policy. Widespread public knowledge about one's own government and those of foreign countries is an important aspect of the democratic ethos.

In order to avoid a narrow, ethnocentric view of the world based solely on one's own culture, nationality, religion, and so on, it is important to look beyond state borders for comparisons. Comparison provides standards by which to measure and evaluate. When the Canadian Prime Minister declares that "The economy is in good shape," for

Table 4.3 The Best and Worst Places to Live in 1998

The 10 Best	The 10 Worst†
1. Canada (0.960)	1. Sierra Leone (0.185)
2. France (0.946)	2. Niger (0.207)
3. Norway (0.943)	3. Burkina Faso (0.219)
4. United States (0.943)	4. Mali (0.236)
5. Iceland (0.942)	5. Burundi (0.241)
6. Finland (0.942)	6. Ethiopia (0.252)
7. Netherlands (0.941)	7. Eritrea (0.275)
8. Japan (0.940)	8. Guinea (0.277)
9. New Zealand (0.939)	9. Mozambique (0.281)
10. Sweden (0.936)	10. Gambia (0.291)

*As indicated by the United Nations Human Development Index, 1998, a measure of conditions in 1995. The Index takes into account life expectancy at birth; adult literacy rates; mean years; educational attainment; real purchasing power.
†Starting with the worst.
Source: United Nations Development Program, *Human Development Report 1998* (Oxford: Oxford University Press, 1998), p. 128–130. Copyright © 1998 United Nations Development Program. Used by permission of Oxford University Press, Inc.

example, what does he mean? Does he mean that compared to the 1930s (during the depression) Canada has a higher standard of living today? Or, does he mean that compared to Switzerland (which has a higher per capita income than Canada) Canadians are doing well? When politicians and commentators make such statements we should always ask the question "Compared to what?" One should not accept the self-ascription of politicians or of states. For example, just because a country declares itself democratic or prosperous does not make it so.

It is because states share certain characteristics and differ on others that they can, and should, be compared. And, because no state can be described as unique, a key question in comparative politics is whether political systems tend to fall into, or can be placed into, distinguishable categories or classes. To do this we must look beyond our state borders. In any given country there is only one national government, a circumstance which makes every country appear unique in its "class." To be meaningful, however, the number of cases and classes must be increased—"This is why the search for comparison is central to the study of government and why comparative government is necessarily the cornerstone of a rigorous and scientific study of government."[16] Simple classifications based on distinctions such as democracy versus communism, monarchy versus tyranny, and traditional versus modern economies are familiar and useful. Such classifications help political scientists to examine, account for, and even suggest improvements for the structure and behaviour of governments.

Among academics there is little disagreement about the need for comparison in political science. The purposes can be summarized under four general headings: description, explanation, evaluation, and reform.

Description

Through comparison, descriptive knowledge can be expanded to provide detailed information about relatively unknown aspects of individual and systemic behaviour. When we study another culture we often see things that native dwellers may take for granted. Comparing also helps us learn more about ourselves. It is often difficult to achieve accurate comparisons even at the descriptive level, but problems can be minimized when information about individual countries is readily available, known to be accurate, and collected following the same rules—as is the case in most developed countries. Some theoretically interesting questions cannot be tackled in many parts of the globe because of insufficient statistical data. Better description can and does affect how public affairs are conducted. Governments are human inventions—faulty understanding creates faulty policies.

Explanation

Attempts to identify and explain fundamental patterns of political behaviour across different states and cultures may help us to arrive at useful theoretical generalizations. Explanatory statements clarify general relationships among variables. It is often easier to identify which particular independent variables provide an explanation of a political behaviour when comparisons are made across states. Since explanations of political behaviour are more likely to come from a number of independent variables, they may prove easier to isolate or apply in some country comparisons than in others. Some countries are more amenable than others to particular kinds of studies. Ideas or hypotheses that have been tested and proven useful in one country may have utility when applied to another country with similar conditions. However the more variables that can be controlled in the comparison, the more likely the study is to provide interpretations based on strong, statistical relationships.

Scholars seek explanatory statements applicable to all societies, but there is a strong case for beginning with explanations in two, or a manageable number of, countries. Then, as new information is accumulated, arguments or theoretical assumptions can be revised and the number of countries expanded. The eventual goal is to understand more about the performance of individuals and politics in widely different types of countries.

Evaluation

In order to evaluate governments it is necessary to make qualitative judgments based on accurate description and explanation. Such evaluation is necessary to help one decide what is valid or good and, therefore, worth replicating. Evaluation, like description and explanation, may be more fruitful in making comparisons in some countries than in others. Also, there is more likely to be agreement on what values are worth and how to measure abstract values such as freedom or justice in similar systems.

Reform

Political science is more than just an intellectual exercise; it is also an ethical one. The impetus to promote political reform—in the sense of the peaceful enhancement of liberty, justice, and democracy—is intrinsic to the profession. Accurate description, valid explanations, and acceptable evaluations lay valuable groundwork for the reform of institutions and changes in public policy. If Canadians want to reform their Senate, for example, it makes good sense to study how the Senate works within a similar system such as Australia. There is also a vital link between the search to expand knowledge of comparative politics and efforts to develop broad social goals and public purposes such as the promotion of liberty, order, and justice.

As we saw in Chapter 1, political scientists seek to learn how things work in practice, to determine whether there is a gap between reality and how things ought to work. Once a gap is indicated in research findings, few political scientists will be satisfied with the status quo and are likely to become committed to reform. As Samuel P. Huntington put it:

> Political science has helped, can help, and should help by generating understanding of political processes, by illuminating the feasibility and consequences of alternative governmental arrangements, and by enhancing appreciation of the potentialities and the limits of political engineering.[17]

How to Compare

In order to compare states for their similarities and differences we need to provide criteria for the task. We can neither make sense of the multitude of facts nor make generalizations unless we find a way to group the world's states along some dimensions. One way is through the **synchronic** or **cross-national approach** in which a comparison is made between one state and another or between several states *at the same time*. Another way is through the **diachronic approach** that calls for comparisons within one or more states *over time*. (See Figure 4.5 for a graphic representation.) The study of patterns *within* individual states is often referred to as the **configurative approach**.

The difference between synchronic and diachronic approaches is fairly straightforward. In the synchronic design, the purpose is to explain an attribute of politics by comparing several states at the same time. It calls for an effort to make empirical generalizations that hold for all the states examined. In configurative designs, on the other hand, the purpose is to explain a variety of attributes *within* a particular state. With the configurative approach, one attempts to make generalizations about sets of conditions and specific attributes of the state in question. When such a study is carried on across time within *one* state, it is called the diachronic approach.

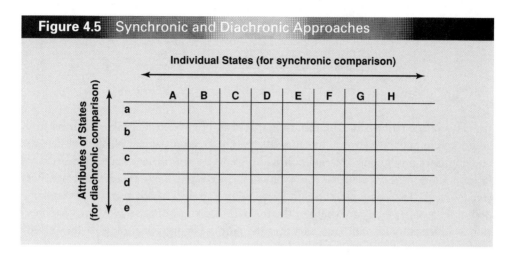

Figure 4.5 Synchronic and Diachronic Approaches

Individual States (for synchronic comparison)

Attributes of States (for diachronic comparison)

	A	B	C	D	E	F	G	H
a								
b								
c								
d								
e								

The choice of either a synchronic or diachronic approach leads to further questions about which aspects of politics and government should be emphasized in the study. These answers lie at the heart of the discipline and tend to involve ethical or normative evaluations about what constitutes the most important ideas in the study of politics.

The classic framework for cross-national analysis was provided by Aristotle as summarized in Table 4.4. We have seen in Chapter 2 that he argued for a classification of the Greek city-states by employing two criteria—who rules the city-state and in whose interest they rule. States could be ruled by one, a few, or many people. And, this rule could be in the general interest of everyone, or it could be in the self-interest of the rulers. The classification thus provided six cells for analysis.

Aristotle used this classification to examine the extant 158 Greek city-states. He found that only two types—aristocracy and polity—were reasonably stable, and concluded that stability depended on both the active participation of a large proportion of the population and on rule-making exercised in the interests of all the people. Arbitrary rule could not be stable because it was not based on law, but rather on the whims and private interests of individual leaders.

Table 4.4 The Aristotelian Classification

Number of Rulers	Rule in the General Interest	Self-Interested Rule
One	Monarchy	Tyranny
Few	Aristocracy	Oligarchy
Many	Polity	Democracy and Ochlocracy

Types of Government

Authoritarian ◄────────────► Democratic

This classification and the resultant spectrum of government types running from authoritarian rule through to democracy has become an essential part of Western thought and civilization. Of course, actual political systems do not fit neatly into such a classification. One of the worst mistakes in political science is to confuse **theoretical constructs** (models, classifications, typologies, etc.) with politics itself. These constructs or *ideal-types* do not necessarily exist anywhere in the real world. By its very nature, then, classification is arbitrary, rigid, and temporary. But the purpose of classification is to draw attention to certain aspects of the political system.

In other words, classifications and other scientific methods, such as modelling, provide political scientists with devices somewhat comparable to what physicists or chemists obtain with controlled experiments. The human world does not provide opportunities for experimentation in politics such as found in the physical sciences. The political scientist must extract comparison from the patterns of variation found in the real world. In searching for comparable states, behaviours, and policies, the researcher attempts to maximize *ceteris paribus* (if everything else were held equal) principles in order to be as scientific as possible.

Another common method of classification is based on the concept of political development. States are considered "modern" by the degree to which they establish viable political systems and economies. Classification of states in terms of political development is often based on Max Weber's three-fold method of comparison that he developed to classify leadership according to traditional, charismatic, or bureaucratic features, discussed in Chapter 2. The reader will recall that traditional authority arises from custom and history and gives leaders such as monarchs or aristocracies the right to rule through their status or heredity. Charismatic authority is derived from popular admiration of the personal "heroic" qualities of the individual in whom it is vested. And bureaucratic or rational-legal authority is vested in the offices of a political regime, not in individuals. In such a system the legal rules are established and officials adhere to the rules while exercising authority according to known procedures. Rational-legal authority is regarded as the most modern type of rule.

Scholars have also constructed classifications of two types of systems depicted by the categories "modern" and "traditional." In this preliminary sense, **modern states** are those with relatively highly organized societies, and **traditional states** are those with relatively low standards of organization in which people are ruled by custom or the personal standards of leaders. We shall discuss these two concepts further in Chapters 5 and 20, but even based on this simple distinction alone many comparisons have been made of the world's states. They include comparative studies of the political attitudes and values of mass populations—for example, the degree of public support given to the political system and its leaders; studies of the economic system—for example, the degree to which agricultural or industry forms the Gross Domestic Product; and studies of types of leadership—for example, the degree of rational-legal as opposed to traditional form of authority in traditional as opposed to modern states.

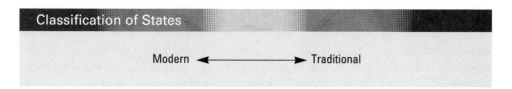

An important point to note is that these classifications are not intended to be based on ethical or normative considerations. That is, the distinction between traditional and modern is not meant to imply any superiority or inferiority about the systems studied. All states combine some elements of tradition and modernity, and they can be arrayed on an axis of tradition/modernity even if determining a precise cut-off point for categorization is difficult.

This leads to another important conclusion. A proper classification scheme, or **taxonomy**, calls for the development of classes of objects to be based on a rule of mutually exclusive and mutually exhaustive cells. That is, a country should be considered either democratic or not, either modern or not. Classifications are most useful when they are based on manifest characteristics such as the type of legislature, or when used with precisely measurable data such as is found in census reports and atlases. However, since not every state or government fits neatly into any one category in a classification, political scientists often use other devices to enable comparison.

A **typology** is a taxonomy in which classificatory distinctions are graded or ordered rather than "pigeon-holed." They are based on the scholar's abstract conceptualization of qualitative indicators. Since no country exhibits every characteristic in a classification, typologies are combined with **spectrum classification**. That is, the "ideal" types of systems are posited to be at the end of a range or dimension, and actual systems of government are arranged on the resulting spectrum to illustrate how close they come to possessing those ideal characteristics. For example, democratic and authoritarian may form the extreme ends of a spectrum, and actual systems such as Canada and China may be placed somewhere along the dimension depending on their degree of "democracy" or "authoritarianism." We shall discuss in Chapter 5 how these and other words are used to understand the world of politics.

Methods and Research Designs

The field of comparative politics has been characterized by the lack of absolute agreement about concepts, frameworks, and even subject matter. Yet despite this, there is substantial agreement about the core of the discipline, and also about the fact that there should be congruence between the purpose of an analysis and the type of research design adopted.

The wide variety of comparative research designs can be categorized under three basic types: single-country studies; and two forms of synchronic comparison—most-similar-system and most-different-system.

Single-Country Study

The first of these, the **single-country study**, which examines one country in depth, is the most popular among social scientists. The literature is replete with volumes on the governments of Britain, France, and the United States, for example. Such research encourages the in-depth study of single countries and the comparison of these units to provide parallel, descriptive, country-by-country comparisons. The advantage of single-country studies is that they provide context for determining how certain events have occurred, and a degree of realism that is vital for correcting overly high-level abstractions that would distort or oversimplify an understanding of the political process.

This type of study dominated the discipline most thoroughly in the years before 1960. During the 1960s it was attacked as lacking a valid "comparative" perspective. As Anthony King pointed out, with such single-country studies "One does not know what is peculiar to a specific country, what is general to a number of countries; one has no means of discovering which correlation among phenomena are accidental or spurious, which are genuinely causal."[18] Because of this type of criticism, some scholars today argue that such approaches should be considered comparative only if they provide "inter-unit comparisons within the country, or, for that matter, undertake intra-unit longitudinal comparisons." However, many academics believe that such a test may be too rigid. More often, research is considered comparative if it is used to formulate explicit hypotheses and considers propositions that are *comparable*.[19] As Lawrence Mayer said of single-country studies—if they "have theoretical or potential applicability to other contexts—such studies clearly contribute to the goals of cross-national analysis."[20]

Another powerful reason for conducting single-country studies and following the diachronic approach is that it is practical. Social science surveys and large-scale data collections are overwhelmingly expensive and fraught with design complexities. Moreover, in collecting data to determine the relative plausibility of ideas or hypotheses, whether from written or visual records, observation, interviews, or questionnaires, problems of language are minimized in single-country studies. Confusing such simple words as "bonnet," "boot," and "schooner," for example, would lead to difficulties in comparing even countries as similar as the United States and Britain.

Most-Similar-System Comparison

The second basic design in comparative studies is based on **most-similar-system analysis**; that is, comparing political systems which are as "similar" as possible with respect to as many features as possible.[21] Most research based on this design focuses on intersystemic similarities and differences; in other words, it is synchronic. The whole system constitutes the original level of analysis, and within-system variations are explained in terms of whole-system factors.

As an example, take the case of two or more countries such as Canada and Australia, which have developed from the same parliamentary model of democracy and possess similar federal systems.[22] The terminology and institutions are similar enough that it is possible to "control" certain variables to determine which relationships (correlations) are causal and which are accidental or spurious. Subtle differences should also be easier to identify. At a minimum, such a design provides generalizations that may be further explored in depth by expanding the number of states examined.[23]

The student must always bear in mind, however, that such a design is only "quasi-experimental," and that there may be other factors influencing the variables and outcomes. Most comparative studies "should not attempt to replace causal analysis, because they can only deal with a few cases and cannot easily isolate the variables (as causal analysis must)."[24]

Most-Different-System Comparison

The third basic approach employed in comparative political research is called **most-different-system analysis**. It calls for the comparison of states that have "dissimilar" political systems—such as democratic with authoritarian, or parliamentary with monarchical. A comparison of Canada (with a democratic parliamentary system) and China (with an authoritarian communist system) would be an example. While there are some exceptions, much of this research is focused at the individual or group level because systemic factors are not considered to play a role in the observed behaviour. In other words, in this type of synchronic approach it is assumed that whole-country factors can be disregarded or eliminated if valid general statements can be formulated without regard to the social systems from which the samples were drawn.

Cross-national comparisons of most-different systems classify states in terms of such factors as Gross Domestic Product or degrees of civil violence, and then attempt to gauge the extent to which they are associated with political stability, political participation, or other similar ideas. Technology has made such studies increasingly possible. However, basic problems remain even though computers have reduced the amount of slogging required. Reliable, aggregate data are simply not available for many countries, and concept formulation at the required high level of abstraction is fraught with difficulty.

Bearing in mind these purposes and types of designs, we are ready to explore the nature of the world of states with which we began this chapter.[25] The ensuing chapters draw on the best and most pertinent synchronic and diachronic studies. We make use of single-country studies, most-similar-system comparisons, and most-different-system comparisons. The student should by now be acquainted with the main benefits and limitations of each type of design and the overall advantages of comparative analysis.

DISCUSSION QUESTIONS

1. Give four significant benefits of doing comparative research.
2. Can only whole states be compared?
3. Can and should your country be compared with other similar states? With different kinds of countries? With no other countries?
4. What are the benefits of single-country studies?
5. Suggest some topics that would benefit from a synchronic rather than a diachronic approach, and vice versa.

KEY TERMS

configurative approach, p. 80

cross-national approach, p. 80

diachronic approach, p. 80

Gross Domestic Product (GDP), p. 74

modern states, p. 82

most-different-system analysis, p. 85

most-similar-system analysis, p. 84

population replacement, p. 71

single-country study, p. 84

spectrum classification, p. 83

synchronic approach, p. 80

taxonomy, p. 83

theoretical constructs, p. 82

traditional states, p. 82

typology, p. 83

ENDNOTES

1. See Appendix A.
2. These include, for example, the Sovereign Military Order of Malta, which is confined to small properties in Rome since the 1830s, and Western Sahara, which is mostly under Moroccan administration.
3. David B. Knight, "Territory and People or People and Territory? Thoughts on Postcolonial Self-Determination," *IPSR*, vol. 6, no. 2 (1985), p. 248.
4. Lucian W. Pye, "Political Science and the Crisis of Authoritarianism," *ASPR*, vol. 84, no. 1 (March 1990), p. 6.
5. See the issue of *IPSR*, vol. 6, no. 1 (1985), devoted to "The Future of the State," especially Karl Heinz-Roder, "Global Problems, A Challenge to Cooperation Between States of Different Social Systems," pp. 35–43.
6. George Thomas Kurian, *The Book of World Rankings*, 3rd ed. (New York: Facts on File, 1991), ch.1.
7. Information for this section comes from *Third World Guide 91/92* (Uruguay: Instituto del Tercer Mundo, 1990), pp. 12–17.
8. "Industrialized economy" refers to an economy that relies primarily on mechanized production.
9. United Nations, *Human Development Report, 1998* (Oxford: Oxford University Press, 1998), p. 177. World Bank, *World Population Projections, 1994–95* (Washington D.C.: The International Bank, 1994), pp. 5–7. The concepts "developed" and "developing" are defined and discussed in Chapters 5 and 20 of this text.
10. *The Globe and Mail*, Nov. 5, 1998.

11. The former Soviet Union was included in this list, but now its resources are fragmented among the 15 new states.

12. A fascinating collection of maps illustrating disparities not only in natural resources and economy but also in areas such as social development, arms in the world, and so on, is by Michael Kidron and Ronald Segal, *The States of the World Atlas* (London: Pan Books, various dates).

13. *Human Development Report*, 1998, p. 130.

14. *Ibid.*, p. 14.

15. *Ibid.*, p. 133.

16. Jean Blondel, *An Introduction to Comparative Government* (New York: Praeger, 1969), p. 3.

17. Samuel P. Huntington, "One Soul at a Time: Political Science and Political Reform," *APSR*, vol. 82, no. 1 (1988), p. 9.

18. Anthony King, "Executives" in Fred I. Greenstein and Nelson W. Polsby, eds., *Handbook of Political Science*, vol. 5 (Reading, Mass.: Addison-Wesley, 1975), p. 248. See also Veronica Ward and John Orbell, "Sherlock Holmes as a Social Scientist," *PS* (Fall 1988); and Jeremy Wilson, *Analyzing Politics* (Scarborough, Ont.: Prentice-Hall Canada, 1988).

19. Lee Sigelman and George H. Gadbois Jr, "Contemporary Comparative Politics; An Inventory and Assessment," *Comparative Political Studies*, vol. 16, no. 3 (1983), p. 284.

20. Lawrence Mayer, "Practicing What We Preach; Comparative Politics in the 1980s," *Comparative Political Studies*, vol. 16, no. 2 (1983), p. 175.

21. Adam Przeworski and Henry Teune, *The Logic of Comparative Social Enquiry* (New York: John Wiley, 1970), pp. 31–47.

22. An excellent example is Malcolm Alexander and Brian Galligan, *Comparative Political Studies: Canada and Australia* (Sydney: Pitman, 1992).

23. G.K. Roberts, "The Explanation of Politics: Comparison Strategy and Theory," in P.G. Lewis et al., eds., *The Practice of Comparative Politics*, 2nd ed. (London: Open University, 1978), p. 293.

24. Reinhard Bendix, *Kings or People: Power and the Mandate to Rule* (Berkeley: University of California Press, 1978), p. 15.

25. The literature on comparative theory and the state continues to grow but is much too detailed to be discussed here. See, for example, Gabriel A. Almond, "The Return to the State," *APSR*, vol. 82, no. 3 (1988), pp. 853–901; James Caporaso, "Introduction to a Special Issue on the State in Comparative and International Perspective," *Comparative Political Studies*, vol. 21, no. 1 (1988), pp. 3–12; James G. March and Johan P. Olsen, "The New Institutionalism: Organizational Factors in Political Life," *APSR*, vol. 78, no. 3 (1984), pp. 734–749.

FURTHER READING

Bertsch, Gary K., et al., *Comparing Political Systems*, 3rd ed. (New York: Macmillan, 1986).

Chandler, Andrea, "The Interaction of Post-Sovietology and Comparative Politics," *Communist and Post-Communist Studies*, vol. 27, no. 1, (1994), pp. 3–17.

Cornelius, Wayne, et al., eds., *Controlling Immigration: A Global Perspective* (Stanford, Calif.: Stanford University Press, 1995).

Dogan, Mattei, and Dominique Pelassy, *How To Compare Nations: Strategies in Comparative Politics*, 2nd ed. (Chatham, N.J.: Chatham House, 1990).

Fleron, Jr., Frederick J., and Erik P. Hoffmann, eds., *Post-Communist Studies and Political Science: Methodology and Empirical Theory in Sovietology* (Boulder, Colo.: Westview Press, 1993).

Giddens, Anthony, *The Constitution of Society: Outline of the Theory of Structuration* (London: Polity Press, 1984).

Gonzalez de la Rocha, Mercedes, *The Resources of Poverty: Women and Survival in a Mexican City* (Oxford: Basil Blackwell, 1994).

Holt, Robert T., and John E. Turner, eds., *The Methodology of Comparative Research* (New York: Free Press, 1970).

Jackson, Robert J., and Michael B. Stein, *Issues in Comparative Politics* (New York: St. Martin's Press, 1971).

Katzenstein, Peter J., Theodore J. Lowi, and Sidney Tarrow, eds., *Comparative Theory and Political Experience: Mario Einaudi and the Liberal Tradition* (Ithaca, N.Y.: Cornell University Press, 1990).

Kidron, M., and R. Segal, *The New State of the World Atlas*, rev. 1st ed. (London: Pan Books, 1987).

King, Gary, Robert O. Keohane, and Sidney Verba, *Scientific Inference in Qualitative Research* (New York: Cambridge University Press, 1993).

Lane, Jan-Erik, and Svante Ersson, *Comparative Politics* (Cambridge: Polity, 1994).

Lane, Ruth, *The Art of Comparative Politics* (Needham Heights, MA: Allyn & Bacon, 1997).

Lichbach, Mark Irving, and Alan S. Zuckerman, *Comparative Politics: Rationality, Culture and Structure* (Cambridge: Cambridge University Press, 1997).

Macridis, R.C., and B. Brown, *Comparative Politics: Notes and Readings*, 6th ed. (Chicago: Dorsey Press, 1986).

Migdal, Joel S., *Strong Societies and Weak States* (Princeton, N.J.: Princeton University Press, 1988).

Nagle, John D., *Introduction to Comparative Politics*, 5th ed. (Chicago: Nelson-Hall, 1988).

General Reference

Banks, A. et al., *Political Handbook of the World* (Binghampton, NY: New York State University, annual).

Bogdanor, Vernon, ed., *The Blackwell Encyclopedia of Political Institutions* (Oxford: Basil Blackwell, 1988).

Boulton, C.J., ed., *Erskin May's Treatise on the Law, Privileges, Proceedings and Usage of Parliament*, 21st ed., (London: Butterworths, 1989).

Europa World Year Book (Rochester, Kent: Staples Printers, annual).

Facts on File (Weekly U.S. News digest) (New York: Facts on File, annual).

Kaleidoscope: Current World Data (Santa Barbara, Calif.: ABC-Clio) (card file reporting the domestic and foreign affairs of every country and activities of major international organizations).

Keesing's Contemporary Archives (UK news digest) (London: Longman, weekly).

Keesing's Record of World Events (London: Longman, monthly).

Mackie, T.T., and Richard Rose, *International Almanac of Electoral History* (New York: Facts on File, 1988).

Political Handbook of the World (New York: McGraw-Hill, 1997).

Statesman's Yearbook (London: Macmillan, annual)

Taylor, C.L., and D.A.A. Jodice, *World Handbook of Political and Social Indicators*, vols. 1 and 2, 3rd ed. (New Haven Conn.: Yale University Press, 1983).

United Nations, *Statistical Yearbook* (New York: United Nations, annual).

World Economic Survey 1991 (New York: United Nations, 1991).

 **Weblinks**

www.unicef.org/sowc96/cover.htm
The UNICEF State of the World's Children site contains information on world population, infant mortality, and literacy rates.

lanic.utexas.edu/la/region/government
This site provides information about countries in Latin America.

Japan   www.ntt.jp/japan/
Israel   www.israel.org/
These sites provide information about Japan and Israel.

CHAPTER 5

Contemporary Forms of Government

All states have features comparable to other states. While each exhibits unique institutions, organizational features, and behaviour based on its history, society, and economy, the overall pattern of each is similar (though not identical) to others. These regularities and differences provide the basic information for understanding and generalizing about politics and government.

In the last chapter we mentioned two important dimensions for comparison in political science. One is classification by political criteria whereby the form of government in a state is located relative to others on a spectrum ranging from democratic to authoritarian. The second dimension is both economic and political. This traditional-modern spectrum classifies states by the degree to which they are economically and politically developed. This continuum is also referred to as the developed-developing spectrum. Figure 5.1 illustrates the four cells that result when these two dimensions are combined. It provides an abstract, hypothetical typology that can guide comparison in the real world.

THE WORLD OF STATES

As we survey the states of the world in the light of the first of these dimensions of comparison, we find that there is great variety in forms of governmental rule.[1] These forms are commonly differentiated by familiar terms such as liberal-democratic, totalitarian, dictatorship, and authoritarian. On the second dimension we find that states also demonstrate a considerable range of economic development from primitive to highly industrialized. It is also possible on this dimension of political development to grade and compare the relative sophistication and diversity of political institutions in each state. By combining indicators of political and economic development, political scientists used to group states into three basic types of political "worlds," commonly referred to as First, Second, and Third Worlds. Today, as we shall see, these categories have been largely abandoned in favour of purely economic measures.

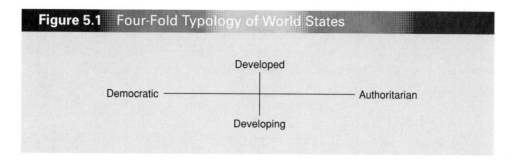

Figure 5.1 Four-Fold Typology of World States

In this book we are primarily concerned with the democratic-authoritarian dimension of comparison; however, we shall refer to the developed-developing dimension when it is appropriate and useful to do so. We turn first to a consideration of the democratic-authoritarian dimension of comparison, and then to some important aspects of the developmental dimension before we begin our overview of forms of government and politics in the world's states.[2] The concept of development is discussed in relation to political change and international politics in Chapter 20. Appendix A provides a list of all 192 contemporary states.

THE DEMOCRATIC–AUTHORITARIAN DIMENSION
Liberal Democracy

Today everyone claims to love democracy; it is almost synonymous with the word "good." Practically every government calls itself "democratic," no matter how authoritarian it may actually be. Bernard Crick wryly concluded that democracy has become the most promiscuous word in the world of public affairs.[3] It is so widely and loosely used that careful definition is required in order for it to be helpful in studying contemporary forms of government.

Democracy is a concept derived from two Greek roots—*demos*, meaning the people, and *kratos*, meaning authority. In ancient Greece, democracy meant government by the many. Aristotle, as we have seen, was not well-disposed to rule by democracy. For him it signified the "poor" or "masses" ruling in their own self-interest without regard for the concerns of others or following the rule of law.

In the pure model of Athenian democracy in the fifth century B.C., citizens ruled through popular assemblies. They assembled in small groups to make major policy decisions for the polity. Higher officials were not elected but were chosen by lot. Athenians believed that if the choice were made by a vote then the richer, or better known, candidates would win. Not much has changed!

Since those early days and debates, democracy has acquired quite a different meaning. Today, it is applied by political scientists to political systems which manage to *reconcile* competing political interests rather than *impose* one interest on another.[4] In practice the test for this is often taken to be whether opposition parties have a fair chance of winning governmental office in an open election. Very few commentators believe that direct democracy, in which citizens actually meet to make public policy, can be practical in complex societies. Instead, all state-level democracies are representative systems in which citizens choose individuals to represent them and make policy between elections. Today, democracy demands that all individuals should have equal access to public policy through participating in fair and competitive elections, but the policies themselves are made by their representatives. Of course, some small political entities such as towns and villages still maintain direct democracy through such means as town-hall meetings.

An essential characteristic of **democracy**, therefore, is the reconciliation of the need for order and stability with a degree of influence for competing political interests. Representatives are elected by a form of majority rule to make legislation which has the force of law. They are allowed to do so because success in an election accords the winners the *legitimacy* required to govern. A *majority principle* is required so that decisions can be taken by the people and their representatives even when division continues to exist.

A primary argument or defense for representative democracy is that it is the best form of government for governing a complex society with different and pluralistic interests. It is preferable to any other system because it allows citizen participation in determining the orderly succession of rulers. As Aristotle put it, an expert cook knows best how to bake a cake, but the person who eats it is a better judge of how it tastes. Elected representatives should, therefore, make the laws but they should be held accountable to the people for them in elections.

Winston Churchill declared democracy to be "the least worst" system of government. He felt that since decisions about which public policies are "best" cannot be scientifically determined, it is necessary to put our faith in the machinery of democratic and representative government. Democracy is a "means" of governing. For some commentators this argument for democracy as a "means" or "technique" of government is not sufficient. They believe that democracy is a "good" in itself because it incorporates desirable political values. Or, as they argue, it is the best system to promote capitalism. In fact, the values implicit in the democratic ideal are fervently debated. They tend to cluster around ideas that are embedded in the notion of reconciling diverse interests through the majority principle. This means the inclusion of such values as freedom of opinion and the press, contested elections, and competing political parties. Limited terms of office for those who are elected, constitutional limits on government authority, and a military that upholds the government without interfering in politics all help to make democracies function. Civil rights are protected because the rule of law ensures impartial justice.

In almost all representative democracies, the political rights of citizens are spelled out in the highest law of the land—the constitution—and limits are placed on the extent of government authority either by the constitution or by the existence of a set of conventions or norms about political behaviour. We shall return to the question of constitutions and their institutions in later chapters. It is sufficient to note here that different democratic states have established quite different political rights for their citizens and various limits to government authority, but every democracy has at least some limitations on pure majority rule.

More fundamental yet may be the debate over the values of liberty and equality and their roles in democracy. In fact, the term "liberal" democracy is often used instead of "pure" democracy to depict systems that are democratic but do not allow the majority complete freedom to do as it chooses. In a **liberal democracy** even the majority is bound to accept certain limits to its behaviour and to govern within the rule of law. We have seen that this principle is known by the term **constitutionalism** (discussed further in Chapters 10 and 11).

The concept of equality, too, is circumscribed in democracies. While equality of political rights—voting, participation, equal treatment before the law, and so on—are considered part of representative democracy, there is no requirement for the economic equality of all citizens in a democracy. It is for this reason that liberal democracy can co-exist with a socialist economy, as in Sweden, or a capitalist economy, as in the United States. This contention means that we adopt the *minimalist* or *procedural* conception of democracy rather than the *maximalist* or *substantive* definition of democracy, which embraces considerations of economic equality and social justice.[5]

A final justification for democracy may be found in its impact on foreign policy. In this respect, the foreign policies of democracies differ significantly from those of authoritarian countries. As the political process is relatively open and representative of various interests, democratic leaders find it very difficult to convince large numbers of participants to go to war, as this would mean spending more taxpayers' money and possibly causing their children to be killed. Only on the rarest occasions have democratic countries gone to war with other democratic countries. However, they do make war on nondemocracies; they sometimes even start them. The United States "invaded" Haiti in 1994 in order to reinstate Jean-Bertrand Aristide as President and replace the military council. For that matter, the United States has often acted in the Western Hemisphere to prevent authoritarian regimes from damaging perceived U.S. interests or setting up a communist system.[6]

Contrary to its appeal as a concept for propaganda reasons, democracy as a system of government is not accepted everywhere in the world. In some areas, the term "peoples' democracy" is used to denote a state with democratic trappings but authoritarian realities. As defined above, democracies—with free competition of political parties—have persisted only in Western Europe, North America, Australia, New Zealand, and a few places in Asia. Until the mid-1980s, democracy remained the exception rather than the rule in many parts of the globe. Since then, however, the number of democracies has more than doubled. But even so, democracy is a fragile system of government, and disenchantment, even violence, can set in quickly when an economy fails to deliver expected material improvements.

The so-called third wave of democratization (recall that the first wave of democracies came in the nineteenth century, and the second wave with the end of colonization after World War II) has been extensive in terms of the number of both states and people involved. It has swept across Latin America, Eastern Europe, and many parts of Africa and Asia. It has affected the transformation of authoritarian regimes based on cultures and religions as diverse as communism, Confucianism, and Islam.

Many scholars have attempted to explain these recent and varied transformations to democracy. Two sets of facilitating factors have been found. At the domestic level, steady decline in the *legitimacy* of authoritarian rule and a strengthening of *civil society* (the development and strengthening of interest organizations and associations) have accompanied the shifts to democracy. Increasing education and income have also exposed many people to the advantages of democracy. At the international level, international organizations and democratic countries have weakened the bases of authoritarian rule by cutting off military and economic assistance. As well, there has been a "snowball" effect caused by one transition to democracy affecting others, especially in Eastern Europe.[7]

Varieties of Liberal Democracy

Within the democratic family there are many different types. In this volume we employ the following three categories.

Established—Approximately half of the world's states are democratic (i.e., conduct open and competitive elections), and even fewer have managed to persist over a substantial period of time. In this book we consider "established" democracies to be those which have had two successive, free, competitive, and relatively violence-free elections.[8] Examples would include Canada, the United States, and most states in Western Europe.

Transitional—Some declared democracies have very short life spans. The roots of democracy in these countries do not go very deep in their histories. Some of these democracies persist for a short time and then recede back to authoritarianism. Still others oscillate from democratic to authoritarian and then back again to democratic. In this volume we also use this category to depict those countries that have very recently left communism and adopted democratic constitutions. Such examples include the Czech Republic, Slovakia, Hungary, Poland, and many states of the former Soviet Union. In 1994, South Africa also became a transitional democracy as we discuss in Close Up 5.1.

Facade—Some declared democracies are nothing but facades for authoritarian regimes of one type or another. They may be military or dynastic regimes which provide the trappings of democracy in order to control their populations, or to achieve international respectability. Sometimes both factors are behind decisions to present an image of competitive elections, even though there is no real significance to the democratic institutions. Recent examples would include Bolivia, Colombia, and Honduras. Other examples would include the militaristic Republic of South Korea or the on-again-off-again democracy of Peru.

Democracy and its Critics

Democracy is often attacked for its elitism. This is an important but simple and misplaced contention. In all states a relatively small number of people dominate the political process. As we have seen, Aristotle's sixfold classification was based on the typology

CLOSE UP 5.1 South Africa Becomes a Transitional Democracy

Isolated for many years by the international community because of its policies of apartheid, South Africa experienced its first-ever, fully democratic elections in April 1994. The election was relatively free of violence and repression. The transition from a facade to a transitional democracy was accomplished quite smoothly, given the problems to overcome.

The election placed Nelson Mandela, who had been imprisoned for 27 years during apartheid, in the President's chair and established an interim and democratic constitution. The policy of apartheid (a policy of racial segregation which violated the rights of blacks, coloureds, and Asians) was finally over and the homelands were abolished. The 43 million South Africans (70% black, 16% white, 10% coloured, and 3% Indian) now confront the challenge of improving an economy harmed by years of neglect and foreign embargoes.

The first task of the Parliament, however, was to write a permanent constitution. In December 1996 President Mandela signed into law a new constitution that guaranteed equal rights to all people, regardless of race. It was designed to take effect gradually over the next three years and become a permanent fixture with the next national elections in 1999. The document says that the party that wins more than half the seats in Parliament in a national election will choose the President.

that states are ruled by one, few, or many people. In his terms, the ruling group, or **political elite**, may therefore be fairly closed, or it may be open to many interests. Two schools of thought dominate the discussion in political science about this issue—elite and pluralist theories.

Elite theories are based on the contention that all states, even democracies, have a maldistribution of power within them. Vilfredo Pareto (1848–1923) and Gaetano Mosca (1858–1941) both argued that all societies possess a small governing elite which obtains its authority because of a set of attributes such as money or prestige. Robert Michels (1876–1936) extended this argument. After studying political parties, especially in Germany, he concluded that "who says organization, says oligarchy." In other words, even supposed democratic institutions such as political parties have an elite.[9]

Many studies of democracy have confirmed the basic thesis that some people have more power than others. The best known of these studies at the level of the United States as a whole was *The Power Elite*, by C. Wright Mills, which contended that power in the U.S. was dominated by a military-industrial complex led by top military, corporate, and political leaders.[10]

Pluralist theorists, by contrast, contend that power in democracies is not held by a single ruling class or elite. These theorists maintain that while democracies may not allow all the people to govern (or even to take part in the major decisions), power is reasonably diffused in society. In his path-breaking book *Who Governs?* and later in *Polyarchy*, Robert Dahl showed that there is never a cohesive, single ruling elite in the United States. According to Dahl, different minorities rule on different issues over time.[11] This idea that the state is an arena of political struggle in which the people may choose their rulers but may not actually govern is articulated best by J. Schumpeter. His classic definition is that democracy is a process in which elites engage in a competitive struggle for people's votes.[12]

This issue cannot be resolved in this book, but even in democracies it is clear that "the people" rarely rule and, therefore, this type of political system should not be equated with "good" government. Democratically elected governments may do wicked things. They may interfere in the affairs of other countries, as the United States did in Grenada in 1984. They may preside over an unjust society because of the way money is distributed within the country (as is clearly the case in many countries). But we do contend that the people's ability to "throw the rascals out" distinguishes democracies from authoritarian regimes. For that reason, we have deliberately adopted a procedural or *minimalist* conception of democracy.

Authoritarianism

The term **authoritarianism** is used to depict political systems that contrast with democracy by resting more upon obedience of the citizens than upon their consent. Such regimes impose one political group or interest on everyone else. They restrict pluralism and limit public participation, calling for obedience and no dissent. Authoritarianism is considered to be a very old form of government because of its association in Western culture with tyrants, despots, monarchs, sultans, and czars.[13] Of course, as we have seen earlier, all states rely on authority, but the authoritarian state sets itself apart in that it uses a high degree of coercion to obtain obedience and does not allow free, competitive elections to determine the degree of support for the government.

In authoritarian countries, power is organized by the elites through the military, bureaucracy, religious leaders, or similar authorities. All political activity is dominated or manipulated by these elites. Institutions such as the media are carefully controlled or censored. Usually, little effort is made in such regimes to mobilize the population to political action because the leaders prefer apathy. And although the economy, educational institutions, churches, unions, and other cultural institutions may ostensibly be free, they, too, are often subordinated to the authoritarian machine. Parties are frequently banned and opponents are imprisoned. The threat of state violence is never far behind any significant political activity. The German playwright Bertold Brecht, came close to depicting these attitudes of leaders in authoritarian states when he wrote:

> Would it not
> then
> Be simpler, if the government
> Dissolved the people and
> Elected another?[14]

Authoritarian governments come in several varieties. The ideologies of such regimes differ greatly; these states may be on the right or the left of the political spectrum. Ideology is defined and discussed at length in the next chapters (see especially Chapters 8 and 9), but here it is important to understand that ideology refers to belief systems that aim to cure the ills of societies. Twentieth-century ideologies are often seen as shaded on a spectrum with communism at the extreme left, through social democracy, to liberalism and conservatism, which would be relatively central, to Nazism and fascism on the extreme right. (See Figure 8.1 in Chapter 8.) The intellectual godfather of authoritarianism is sometimes said to be Thomas Hobbes, the seventeenth-century British philosopher. In his book *Leviathan* he contended that the people owe their absolute obedience to the sovereign state. The state, in turn, must provide security for individuals and property so that citizens are able to pursue their individual desires and interests.

With such an underpinning to these political systems, it should be no surprise to discover that ideology may be less important than leadership in authoritarian regimes. Some authoritarian systems require total subservience to the state and its elite leadership. The arguments for maintaining absolute obedience may include the necessity to retain law and order in order to avert civil war, or the need to build large armies to fend off foreign invaders, or simply to solve a difficult economic problem.

Authoritarian countries have included such historic right-wing states as the Franco regime in Spain (1936–75) and Salazar's Portugal (1931–68). They also include military systems and **juntas** (military councils—often pronounced "hunta" as it would be in Spanish) such as those that dominated Brazil from 1964 to 1984. Many states in Africa and Asia fall into this category today. On the left wing of the political spectrum, we find regimes such as that of Muammar Qadhafi in Libya and others that espouse varieties of socialism, such as Iraq and Syria.

We shall return to the varieties of authoritarian regimes after an examination of two specific concepts associated with authoritarian, nondemocratic regimes—dictatorship and totalitarianism.

Two Types of Authoritarianism

Dictatorship—Aristotle called political systems that consist of an individual ruling in his or her own self-interest tyrannies. Over time this word has acquired a more general meaning, and the Greek philosopher's word has generally been replaced by the term **dictatorship**. The concept of a dictator or absolute ruler comes from ancient Rome where it applied to the appointment of a chief magistrate who was given absolute power on a temporary basis to deal with a war or other emergency. When the emergency was over, the dictator was supposed to give his authority back to the Senate. Some statesmen, such as Lucius Quinctius Cincinnatus, did so, but many other individuals seized the office of dictator by force and tried to hold on to it for long periods of time.

Dictatorship is an "ideal-type," since, in the real world, no leader ever has absolute power over each and every decision in his or her society. Leaders may aspire to absolute power, but it is never obtained completely. Authority must be delegated to associates, and

Map 5.1 Democracy and Authoritarianism in Africa

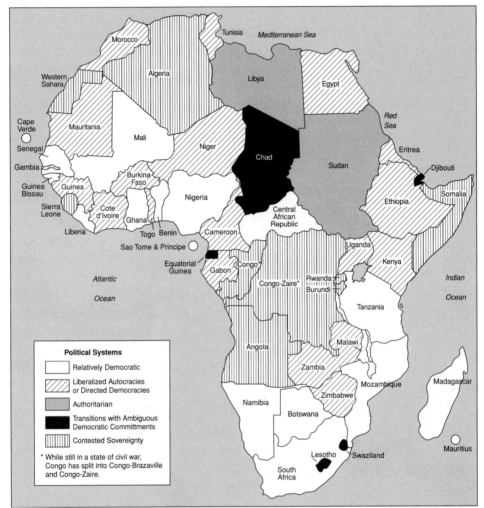

Political Systems

- ☐ Relatively Democratic
- ▨ Liberalized Autocracies or Directed Democracies
- ▩ Authoritarian
- ■ Transitions with Ambiguous Democratic Committments
- ▦ Contested Sovereignty

* While still in a state of civil war, Congo has split into Congo-Brazaville and Congo-Zaire.

Source: Originally created by the African Governance Program, The Carter Centre. Updated to 1999 by Professor Richard Joseph, Emory University.

a set of rules must be developed by which they operate. Dictators must constantly be wary that coteries of associates might turn against them.

The concept of dictatorship, however, draws our attention to that end of the spectrum where ultimate power rests in the hands of an individual or small elite. Leaders such as Hitler in Nazi Germany, Stalin in the Soviet Union, Mao Tse-tung in China, and Ayatollah Khomeini in Iran were often referred to as dictators. Other examples help to show how tyrants or dictators may rely on personal rule rather than ideology or religion. Modern dictators have included such well-known tyrants as "Papa Doc" Duvalier in Haiti, Emperor Bokassa in Central Africa, Idi Amin Dada in Uganda, Sam Doe in Liberia, Jerry Rawlings in Ghana, Hafez al-Assad in Syria, Manuel Noriega in Panama, Alfredo Stroessner in Paraguay, Anastazio Somoza in Nicaragua, and Saddam Hussein in Iraq.

The degree of personal control by such dictators varies. Some lead countries so divided by strife that the dictator's control is fairly weak. Others such as Saddam Hussein in Iraq have near "total" power. In that country, a small Revolutionary Command Council regularly meets and makes formal policy decisions in secret, but all power flows from Saddam. As President and Commander-in-Chief, his power is based on the secret police, the militia, and the regular army.

Totalitarianism—By contrast with other forms of authoritarian rule, **totalitarianism** is a twentieth-century phenomenon. The concept is used to describe those states in which leaders impose their objectives or goals upon their people to an unlimited degree. Brutal, pre-modern dictatorships tended to place limits upon dictators' aspirations to control all aspects of society. Rarely, except in wartime, did they try to extend their political demands into private spheres of people's lives, such as family or religion.

In totalitarian systems, however, efforts are made to control all aspects of society; to subordinate individuals and groups to the dominant leadership. The total concentration of authority is justified in terms of some basic necessity—such as the need for rapid industrialization, social transformation, mass mobilization, or even war. Of course, in the real world such a "total" control cannot be exercised by single leaders, though some have tried.[15] If we contrast Benito Mussolini's goal with reality, we can see this relationship more clearly. Believing that there should be no distinction between the Italian state and society, he declared: "Everything in the state, nothing outside the state, nothing against the state."[16]

The total power Mussolini established for himself in law in December 1925 was reinforced by repressive measures which Martin Blinkhorn summarized as follows:

> Political opposition and free trade unions were banned; the free press surrendered to a combination of censorship and fascist takeover; elected local governments were replaced by appointed officials; and the essentials of a police state were created by extending the government's powers of arrest and detention, increasing the scope of the death penalty, introducing a special court for political "crimes," and forming a "secret" police force, the OVRA.[17]

In Hitler's Germany, Stalin's Soviet Union, Mao's China, and Khomeini's Iran, special institutions such as those constructed in fascist Italy were set up in an attempt to establish a totalitarian regime. In all cases, the dictators' actions were supported by single parties or movements with committed ideologues. But it is especially in Nazi Germany and Stalin's Soviet Union that the closest approximation to the totalitarian model is found. From the Nazi concentration camps to the Soviet gulag (forced labour camps), extreme brutality and violence existed and may be said to have distinguished these to-talitarian systems from other tyrannies.

In Western thought, the intellectual roots of totalitarian government are often credited to Jean Jacques Rousseau (1712–78). In the *Social Contract* he argued (in contrast to Hobbes) that the population should govern itself. In his argument the people are sovereign, not the state. But when one group of leaders can claim they rule in the name of the people they obtain absolute power. This argument is said to have provided the democratic origins of totalitarianism and to have pointed to the importance of ideology in totalitarian states. Contrary to the popular image, totalitarianism is not outside modern philosophy; in fact, a commitment to modernity is at the centre of the philosophy, as it tends to emphasize release from tradition and adherence to moral relativism.

Leaders in totalitarian states use ideology—usually utopian in style—to control society. One scholar has even concluded that "Totalitarianism is utopianism come to power."[18] Ironically communism, for example, was first conceived not as a centrally planned society or economy, but as a system of local community control of production and distribution. Words we normally associate with democracy such as "the sovereignty of the people" are used in communist ideology to convey the notion of popular control. In reality, however, state or party officials control all social relations, and institutions such as churches, schools, and universities are all used to spread the ideology of the regime. If such institutions do not bring their teachings into line with the ideology, they are disbanded and replaced by others that will bend to the authority of the political elite. However, even in a totalitarian state it is more effective if the people feel part of the system. They need to be convinced to accept the state ideology as the official truth. As Hannah Arendt put it: "Wherever it [totalitarianism] rose to power, it developed entirely new political institutions and destroyed all social, legal and political traditions of the country."[19] State and society must be fused.

The hallmark of this type of system is total domination of one group over the rest of society. One set of tyrants asserts total control over the country, basing its control on a state-imposed ideology. They make use of modern communications technology and advanced social control methods to manipulate citizens. Political liberties and human rights are suspended. Political dissidence and nonconformity are outlawed. The state controls all social activities, engages in continual surveillance of its citizens, and makes extensive use of terror. As Jeffery C. Goldfarb so succinctly expressed it: "Ideology explained that some beings who gave every appearance of being human were not."[20] The leading Nazi ideologue, Heinrich Himmler, provided an illustration when he instructed his leading officers to be "'superhuman,' to be 'superhumanly inhuman.'"[21]

Many significant efforts have been made to summarize the components of totalitarianism. One of the most succinct summaries is Carl J. Friedrich and Zbigniew Brzezinski's six conditions of totalitarianism:

1. An official ideology covering all aspects of human endeavour;
2. A single mass party based on this ideology;

3. A secret police for dominating the population;

4. Control of the means of mass communication;

5. A monopoly of coercive mechanisms such as the military and police; and

6. Central control of the economy.[22]

Varieties of Authoritarianism

Bearing in mind these distinctions made above, we shall now examine some existing varieties of authoritarian governments—communist, one-party states, military, dynastic and court, and theocratic. (All states are listed in Appendix A.)

Communist—States that best exemplify the extreme totalitarian end of the authoritarian spectrum are those led by communist leaders with strict adherence to the Marxist-Leninist doctrine. In 1917, Nickolay Lenin's Bolsheviks seized control of Russia and attempted to transform it into a communist paradise. With the guidance and support of the Union of Soviet Socialist Republics (USSR), communism spread throughout the world. At its height, communist regimes came to power throughout Eastern Europe and in parts of the underdeveloped world such as China, Cuba, Vietnam, and much of Africa.

At the institutional level, this regime type is characterized by an almost complete lack of institutions that can compete with the Communist Party and its leaders. Although no pure totalitarian situation has ever existed—that is, one in which there was complete domination of all societal relationships by one party—the Stalinist period of violent control of the Soviet Union, especially during the Great Purges of 1936–38, is usually taken as a proximate example. The centrepieces of communist institutions are **democratic centralism**—in which all important decision-making is handled by the central core of political leaders—and a **centrally planned economy**—in which, in principle, an egalitarian society can be set up by political authorities using the force of the state and the abolition of the free-market economy. While other institutions such as professional associations, schools, and the media may have some freedom of action, in the final analysis all must adhere to government policy rather than put forward their own political views.

In such systems political power and violence are largely controlled by a relatively few individuals. In China, human rights have been violated countless times since the Revolution. The government has forced the compliance of dissident citizens by harassment, imprisonment, and torture. The suppression of the Tiananmen Square demonstrations in May 1989 is only one example of state repression.

In communist systems, party leaders dominate most, if not all, government positions. In principle, the members of these positions are not elected in competitive elections but are selected through a special process dominated by the party elite. As individuals they are forced to accept the principles of democratic centralism, a centrally planned economy and the dominant role of the Communist Party. (See Chapters 15, 16, and 17.)

In the last decade communist governments have been changing and disappearing. The legitimacy and competence of their leaders as economic managers have been questioned and many of these countries have become transition democracies. Even China, which retains a communist regime with strict party and military control, has had to accept a degree of capitalism, with aspects of a free market, the import of foreign capital, and even stock markets. In the early stages of the regime land was parcelled out to collective and state farms, but today a degree of privatization is allowed and encouraged.

Communist systems have simply failed to produce the economic results that their theories have suggested. But not all have adapted. As Lucian W. Pye put it, China shook the world

> ... first with the heartwarming spectacle of students demonstrating for democracy in Tiananmen Square and then with the horrors of an autocratic regime flaunting its powers by massacring its citizens and hypocritically pretending that the nonviolent demonstrators were "thugs" and "hooligans" and that the casualties were mainly the heavily armed soldiers.[23]

As everyone familiar with recent events in the former USSR and Eastern Europe knows, communist principles of organization broke down throughout the region. All Eastern European countries have allowed competitive elections since 1989, and the new states formed from the Soviet Union have set up multi-party systems. For that reason these countries are considered to be transitional or fledgling democracies. Some of these states are part free and part authoritarian. They present a challenge of categorization to all political scientists. A new typology may be needed to encompass them. Some scholars will wish to place them in the same category as other modern authoritarian regimes which have recently become democratic, such as Portugal and Spain.[24]

Rapid transformation of former communist states has also been taking place in much of Africa. In recent years, several communist states have adopted democratic constitutions and multi-party systems. Many others have promised major reforms during the next decade. There is no doubt that communist authoritarianism is on the wane on the African continent, but a final assessment of the genuineness of recent changes may take some years.

While the number of communist states is diminishing, the type retains vital significance in understanding the variety of political regimes in the world today. Authoritarian communist states remain in place in China, Cuba, the Democratic People's Republic of Korea, Laos, and Vietnam. Remnants of this type of regime are found in Southeastern Europe, states of the former USSR, and parts of Africa.

One-Party States—Many non-communist states are also run by only one party. In such authoritarian countries the party and the state are fused. The state supports one particular party, and that party alone is allowed to run for office. It is this latter fact which distinguishes such states from democracies with one strong, or even a single dominant, party.

One-party states emerged for several reasons. Many developed from anti-colonial movements which became associated with the newly independent state—such as in Tanzania with Julius Nyerere's African National Union. Others resulted from the aftermath of military takeovers in which the military usurped government control but then decided to return to the barracks and allow one party to become dominant in the system. In Sierra Leone, for example, Dr. Siaka Stevens seized power by way of a military takeover in 1968, but soon set up the All-People's Congress as the only political party allowed to exist in the country. (That one-party system collapsed in 1992 following yet another military coup).

Such political systems are distinguished from communist regimes because they are not based on a philosophy of Marxist-Leninism with its doctrines of democratic centralism and a centrally planned economy. The single party usually shares political power with other institutions in society such as the military, bureaucracy, and societal institutions such as churches, tribal leadership, and so on. These political systems are often quite fragile, and it is not surprising that many of them fluctuate between military and single-party control. Indeed, it is sometimes quite difficult to distinguish them from facade democracies. Movement may take place in the direction of democracy, but such changes may be illusionary. Today many of the former one-party states are in some form of transition to multi-party systems. The transition is generally turbulent. Sierra Leone, for example, following a military coup in 1992, held multi-party legislative and presidential elections in 1996. Ahmed Kabbah won the presidential elections. There was another military coup in 1997 and all political parties were banned. Kabbah was restored as President in 1998, and the multi-party system reinstated, but civil war resumed again within months.

Military—When a group of officers takes over a government it is called a military government. Actual takeovers differ from one country to the next, but the most dramatic is the **coup d'état** in which some officers and their troops use violence, or the threat of it, to overthrow the government. We discuss coups in Chapters 14, 15, and 20, but here let it suffice that these types of military regimes have been extremely widespread in the modern world. One author has described military control as "the most common, and thus characteristic, aspect of non-Western politics."[25] Our survey of modern states shows military governments continue to be one of the important types of political systems today, but they appear to be somewhat on a decline since the mid-1990s. Examples today include countries such as Algeria, Fiji, Iraq, Myanmar (Burma), and, until recently, Uganda and Nigeria. States which have frequent military interventions in politics are often called **praetorian states**.

Two basic forms of government—direct and indirect military rule—emerge from these interventions. In **direct rule**, the military actually assumes the role of government. Generals act as cabinet ministers, and the military runs the bureaucracy, police, and other government institutions. In **indirect rule**, the military leaders do not assume all, or perhaps not even many, dominant positions in the political hierarchy. Instead, they "remain in their barracks" but are called upon to help puppet administrators and cabinet members make the most important political decisions. This latter category is extremely difficult to appraise in the abstract. In some cases, a democratic facade is introduced to give the appearance of democratic influence on the country. A classic illustration was the Iraq referendum of October 1995 in which 99.96% voted to keep

Saddam Hussein as President for the next seven years. In others, there is actually a sharing of political responsibility: the military is the most powerful institution, but a democratic constitution exists alongside elections and free political parties. This category, therefore, is closely related to what we earlier called facade democracies.

In fact, many regimes oscillate back and forth between these two forms—at one time the military rules, only to be replaced by a civilian government, and then later a military group takes over again. These countries are sometimes referred to as **crypto-democracies**. The degree of democracy is difficult to assess in such countries.

Dynastic and Court—These regimes are close to ancient forms of tyranny and dictatorship in which a single person, such as a king, held almost complete political power. Scholars have traced the origin of kingship back over 5000 years. Often the characteristics of such regimes resemble those found in the governments of European monarchs in France, England, and Spain before the rise of popular consent and democracy in the eighteenth century. While monarchs still *reign* in some countries such as Britain and the Netherlands, they no longer actually *govern* their countries. These countries have become **constitutional monarchies** in which the monarchs are constrained by constitutions and governing is left to elected politicians.

In dynastic or court regimes, the rulers govern their peoples much the way that monarchs did until modern times. Legitimacy and authority is accorded to a king or sultan based on custom and inheritance, and often is backed up by fear generated by the possible use of repressive force. Monarchs inherit their absolute power by birth and often assert their right to rule as being eternal, inviolable, and God-ordained. In medieval Europe such arrangements were justified by a philosophy of **divine right of kings** claimed by Christian monarchs.

In such monarchical states there is little recourse to the rule of law, and the personal desires and even the whims of the ruler are supreme. Access to the ruler is sought by all members of the elite. Friends of the ruler may play major roles in the determination of public policy. The influence the fanatic Rasputin held with the Tzar and Tzarina of Russia before the 1917 Revolution is a good example (see Close Up 5.2).

Today, many dynasties are based in the Middle East, where most of the rulers have been fortunate enough to have extensive oil resources to back up their authority. It is at least partially because of such resources that these states have not known the instability often associated with nondemocratic countries. The traditional leadership in Saudi Arabia exemplifies these types of regimes. As King Fahd put it: "The democracy systems do not suit this region and our people."[26] Traditional authority of this type is also accorded to oil-rich kings in Bahrain, Kuwait, and Oman, and to the powerful Sultan of Brunei. Other kings such as Hussein—and now Abdullah—in Jordan, Hassan II in Morocco, and the descendants of George Tupou in Tonga have had to rely more on tradition and less on economic might to back up their monarchical rule.

The tenuous nature of dynasties is illustrated by events in Nepal, one of the economically least developed states in the world. Historically, Nepal had been governed

CLOSE UP 5.2 Rasputin (1871–1916)

Rasputin was a Russian monk, a sinister character with a notoriously bad reputation. However, he attracted the attention and support of the Tsarina, wife of Tsar Nicholas II. The Tsarina took comfort in his pronouncements and even medical council, particularly concerning her ill son. Through the Tsarina, Rasputin became so influential in the royal family that he could exercise significant control on the affairs of state. His presence in court made even the supporters of the monarchy uneasy. In the end, he was assassinated by a group of Russian nobles in 1916. The reign of Nicholas II ended just one year later with the abolition of the monarchy and the Russian Revolution.

by a monarch but in 1960 there was a brief experiment with democracy. This failed and was followed by a reassertion of royal autocracy. In 1990, Nepal underwent another revolution in which the people demanded, and obtained, a form of representative democracy alongside the monarchy. For a short time, following a Marxist-Leninist party victory in 1994 elections, Nepal had the distinction of being the world's first communist monarchy. In 1997, the King approved a coalition government. Today, the political system is shaky but remains in place.

Theocratic—While religion plays an extremely important role in many countries of the world today, very few states are governed essentially as religious entities. Many democratic countries have constitutions which cite the importance of God or religion. Israel, while a democracy, calls itself a state based on Judaism. But in this book the word **theocracy** is reserved for states that are actually governed by religious leaders. The Vatican state, which is governed by the Pope and leaders of the Catholic Church, is an example. Much less controversial in this categorization is the state of Iran.

In Iran, the 1979 revolution ousted the traditional monarchy and ushered in an era of absolute control by the clergy. Based on Islamic fundamentalism and led by the late Ayatollah Khomeini, a state was set up based on Shiite Muslim principles. The Islamic Republican Party, dominated by the clergy, controlled all political institutions, including the Parliament. Two decades after the revolution, Iranians have an elected President (a cleric, Muhammad Khatami) and have begun to openly challenge the orthodoxy that dominates their lives. However, religious structures still dominate in Iran, and repression can be swift. Political power remains in the hands of the Supreme Religious Guide, who is also Iran's spiritual leader. That Guide, currently Ayatollah Ali Khamenei, controls the armed forces, the security and intelligence services, radio and television, and the judiciary. The Supreme Religious Guide's advisors, consisting of clergymen, are known as the Assembly of Experts (elected for the first time in 1998) and the Council of Guardians (which is dominated by hard-liners and determines the elegibility of candidates for the Assembly).

They act as the spiritual guides for high political decision-making. A secular arm of Revolutionary Guards acts as the enforcers, using intimidation and even murder to enforce Islamic law.

In short, such a theocracy has the ingredients of an extreme authoritarian system. Religion provides the ideological glue for holding the state and its institutions together. Readers will wish to consider the role of religion in other types of states as well. (Refer back to Close Up 3.5 on the Taliban in Afghanistan.) No one could deny the role of religion in countries such as Israel.

THE DEVELOPMENTAL DIMENSION

In this book we concentrate primarily on the political dimension of states, but it is also vital for students to be aware of schema that classify states based on their level of economic modernization. The schema that was used for many years prior to 1990 was based on the concept of First, Second, and Third Worlds. However, after the collapse of the Soviet Union and the end of the Cold War that had divided states into communist or capitalist camps, that schema suddenly became inadequate. The new states that arose from the old Soviet Union abandoned communism, with its distinctive economic features, and became fledgling democracies. The distinction between First and Second Worlds blurred and became meaningless. As we shall see, only the Third World category continues to have much relevance today, and many scholars find the word itself pejorative and unhelpful.

States of the **First World** category were considered to be both politically and economically modernized. They were liberal democracies with open, competitive elections, and were based, to a large degree, on a free market. Almost all of the states in this category had maintained stable, democratic institutions over many decades. The United States was usually taken as the prototype of political systems in this category as it has been politically stable since the Civil War of 1861–65. All states in the First World category also had free market economies so that to a high degree the forces of supply and demand operated without government regulation, and the profit motive provided incentives for diligence and entrepreneurial activity. (Of course, in reality, no pure market economy exists anywhere—to some extent all countries have mixed economies with governments controlling the money supply and regulating the economy through taxation and expenditure.) In a nutshell, First World countries were relatively very rich and stable by comparison with other states.

States of the **Second World** included those that were, broadly speaking, communist and had neither a competitive party system nor a free market. On the whole, they were based on one-party dominance and had controlled or centrally planned economies. Both First and Second Worlds were based essentially on industrialized economies. But the Second World adhered to a philosophy based on socialism—or some form of Marxist-Leninist ideology—and backed it up with the command structures required for authoritarian leadership.

The sudden downfall of Soviet and Eastern European communism in 1991 depleted the number of states in the Second World category. The political distinction between the

First and Second Worlds faded, so that today many of the post-communist states differ from the First World primarily on economic levels. Today, the states that comprised the Second World are now commonly described as "economies in transition." There are only three large communist states remaining: China, North Korea, and Vietnam, and their economies are desperately poor. North Korea retains a Soviet-modelled dictatorship, but political leaders in Beijing and Hanoi have begun to pursue market reforms by introducing capitalist practices in state-run economies.

In the earlier classification, the **Third World** included all the countries that remained outside of the first two categories. The term *le tiers monde*—the Third World—was coined by French demographer Alfred Sauvey in 1952. It was almost a shorthand term for powerlessness and poverty.

The concept of the Third World was a typical product of the Cold War era. It reflected an obsession with the superpowers and a lack of interest in the less powerful, more populous states. The approximately 3.5 billion people living in the buffer zone between the great global rivals were deemed part of the Third World, yet there was considerable disparity within this category. For example, it included the oil-rich Gulf state of Saudi Arabia, industrializing countries such as South Korea, Taiwan, Singapore, and Hong Kong as well as many dozens of poor states scattered throughout Africa, Asia, and Latin America.

The political and economic heterogeneity of this "catch-all" category made generalization difficult, but on the whole these states were not industrialized (hence they were called traditional rather than modern), were found in or close to the Southern Hemisphere, and were often, but not always, characterized by an important role for the military in political affairs. In most of the Third World, government structures and institutions were generally weak, whether they were based on capitalist or socialist models. Economic problems, including sheer survival, were more significant than the structures and processes associated with democracy or communism.

Most, but not all, Third World states resulted from collapsed empires and colonialism. In the nineteenth century, Latin American states obtained their independence from Europe, and in the twentieth century much of Africa and Asia threw off the yoke of Western political domination. The organizations of the new states were often patterned on the institutions of their colonial history and hence were inappropriate for local conditions. Often the resulting states were based on illogically drawn geographical borders or ignored hostile tribal divisions, which made governing difficult.

Democratic stability often proved impossible to achieve in many Third World states. Government legitimacy, and even geographical borders, remained subject to question and debate. Loyalties were more with tribes, regions, or even families than with the states itself. Military governments frequently held power. The states in this category had little relevance internationally, and after the Cold War they lost what leverage they had as ideological allies of the superpowers. As well, the industrialized nations began to increasingly focus their attention and aid dollars on Eastern Europe so that the Third World countries became even more marginalized.

Levels of Economic Development

Today, political scientists tend to categorize the world's states more generally accord-ing to level of economic development. The term **development** is used because it implies that if a country can produce economic wealth it will transform society from a subsistence- or agricultural-based economy to one where manufactured goods and services create wealth. The logic is that with economic wealth generated by the manufacturing and service sectors, a country can develop a literate, urban, well-fed population. Using de-velopment, then, as the key concept, the world's states can be categorized into developed and less developed countries.

Developed countries are defined by the World Bank as those whose GNP per capita averaged (in 1993) more than $8626 annually. (The GNP per capita is reached by di-viding a country's total production of goods and services by its population.) This high-income category includes principally the 21 member states of the Organization of Economic Cooperation and Development (OECD)—countries characterized by "peace, wealth and democracy." It also includes some countries that have wealth but lack the po-litical, technological, or demographic characteristics of the OECD members, and so in spite of their relatively high GNP per capita are often regarded rather as developing countries. These include four oil exporting countries—Brunei, Kuwait, Qatar, and the United Arab Emirates; and three newly industrialized economies—Hong Kong, Singapore, and Taiwan; and Cyprus and Israel.

Less developed countries (LDCs) are defined by the World Bank as those with a GNP per capita less than $8626 annually (in 1993). This category produces a list of countries essentially the same as the one defined formerly as the Third World. The very **lowest of the LDCs** are sometimes referred to as **LLDCs**. These LLDCs in 1993 had a GNP per capita of $695 or less. The United Nations identified 45 LLDCs in 1995. More than two-thirds of these countries are in Africa, and most of the rest are in Asia. Haiti is the only such country in the Americas.

Thus the terminology has changed from a pejorative sounding "Third World" to LDC or LLDC, but the countries concerned and their main characteristics remain the same. The extreme poverty that characterizes the LLDCs has many implications. Their population growth, at 2.8 percent in 1995, is far in excess of the average world wide rate of 1.5 percent. At 2.8 percent, the population of the LLDCs will double in only 25 years, while it will take two and a half *centuries* for developed countries to double. Although the population of LLDCs is burgeoning, however, their economic growth rate is extremely low, averaging less than one-tenth of one percent per year in recent years. With this persistent disparity in population growth and economic growth between the LLDCs and the developed countries, the rich simply get richer and the poorest of the poor never improve their wretched condition. Life expectancy is only 51 years in the LLDCs compared with 76 years in developing countries. Infant mortality rates and illiteracy rates are among the highest in the world.[27]

The LDCs as a group lag behind the developed countries in terms of technological advances. Research and development for technology are funded by and geared to the interests of the richest states. The LDCs therefore depend for their economic well-being, to a large extent, on multinational corporations transfering technological know-how to them. Moreover, one of the main characteristics of the LDCs, besides their comparatively low economic performance, is their tendency to be "zones of turmoil" in which poverty, war, tyranny, and anarchy dominate people's lives.[28] Violent conflict is often present both within and between countries in this category. In fact, one study showed that more than 90 percent of the conflicts and 90 percent of the casualties of inter- and intrastate violence in the past half century were inflicted in developing countries.[29]

Perhaps the main question that specialists in development studies seek to answer is why some countries and areas of the world have so much wealth while others are so poor. What are the origins of this inequality and what, if anything, can be done about it?[30] It is a complicated but fascinating study, and we resume our discussion of theories and explanations of development in Chapters 20 and 21. See "boxed quotes" below for some dramatic and important observations and questions about development.

> "We live in a world of inequality and diversity. This world is divided roughly into three kinds of nations: those that spend lots of money to keep their weight down; those whose people eat to live; and those that don't know where the next meal is coming from."
>
> David Landes, *The Wealth and Poverty of Nations*
>
> "...questions about inequality in the modern world can be reformulated as follows. Why did wealth and power become distributed as they are, rather than in some other way? For instance, why weren't Native Americans, Africans, and Aboriginal Australians the ones who decimated, subjugated, or exterminated Europeans and Asians?"
>
> Jared Diamond, *Guns, Germs and Steel*

Overall, the decade of the 1990s brought massive economic and political change to the LDCs. Many parts of the underdeveloped world have democratized while others have stagnated in authoritarian rule. In Latin America, most countries, with the exception of Cuba, have had democratic elections in the past few years. Although the trappings of democracy are found almost everywhere in Latin America, the level of human rights abuses remains high in some countries such as El Salvador and Guatemala. Less democratic progress has been made in Africa and Asia, but considerable movement to democracy is visible there as well. However, much of Africa has remained under military or one-party rule. Even Nigeria has gone back to military dictatorship. The end of apartheid in South Africa has been the major shining example of success. Despite their economic problems, China, Laos, Vietnam, and North Korea retain their communist governments. Democracy and economic progress have not advanced together in the world as many optimists had hoped. Famine, hunger, and war continue to devastate peoples throughout most of Africa and Asia.

There are of course other ways to categorize states, particularly within basic types. Such distinctions as presidential versus parliamentary government, geographical distributions of power, and categories such as unitary, federal, and confederal systems can be very useful and will be discussed in appropriate chapters. By now, however, the reader will be aware that the basic types of states vary from democratic to authoritarian and from developed to developing. With these distinctions we can proceed to examine the patterns of cultures and ideologies that exist in the world and how they intersect with the types of states found on the democratic–authoritarian axis.

DISCUSSION QUESTIONS

1. Since all governments must have the authority to act, are they all authoritarian?
2. Analyze the various types of democracy.
3. Is democracy "rule by the people?" Was Hitler a democrat?
4. Distinguish between "authoritarian" and "totalitarian" governments.
5. What, if anything, is wrong with the use of the terms First, Second, and Third Worlds?

KEY TERMS

authoritarianism, p. 96
centrally planned economy,
   p. 101
constitutionalism, p. 93
constitutional monarchies,
   p. 104
coup d'état, p. 103
democracy, p. 92
democratic centralism,
   p. 101
developed countries, p. 108

development, p. 108
dictatorship, p. 97
direct rule, p. 103
divine right of kings, p. 104
elite theories, p. 95
First World, p. 106
juntas, p. 97
indirect rule, p. 103
less developed countries
   (LDCs), p. 108

liberal democracy, p. 93
lowest of the LDCs
   (LLDCs), p. 108
pluralist theorists, p. 95
political elite, p. 95
praetorian state, p. 103
Second World, p. 106
theocracy, p. 105
Third World, p. 107
totalitarianism, p. 99

ENDNOTES

1. As a distinct type, the relics of empire—colonies, dependencies, and semi-sovereign states—are disappearing. See J. Denis Derbyshire and Ian Derbyshire, *World Political Systems* (London: Hutcheson, 1991), ch. 9; and D.K. Fieldhouse, *The Colonial Empires: A Comparative Study from the Eighteenth Century*, 2nd ed. (London: Macmillan, 1982).
2. No list that assigns countries to particular categories can be definitive forever. States may move from one category to another over time, and there is no mutually exclusive and mutually exhaustive categorization that will determine the placing of all of them perfectly over time.
3. Bernard Crick, *In Defence of Politics* (London: Penguin, 1964), p. 56.
4. Bernard Crick, *Basic Forms of Government: A Sketch and a Model* (London: Macmillan, 1973).

5. See Doh Chull Shin, "On The Third Wave of Democratization: A Sythesis and Evaluation of Recent Theory and Research," *World Politics*, vol. 47 (October 1994), pp. 135–70.

6. Bruce Russett, *Grasping the Democratic Peace* (Princeton, N.J.: Princeton University Press, 1993); G. Sorensen, *Democracy and Democratization* (Boulder, Colo.: Westview Press, 1993); David Lake, "Powerful Pacificists: Democratic States and War," *APSR*, vol. 86, no.1 (1992), pp. 24–37; and Mancur Olson, "Dictatorship, Democracy and Development," *APSR*, vol. 87, no. 3 (Sept. 1993), pp. 567–76.

7. Doh Chull Shin, "On the Third Wave of Democratization," pp. 150–54. Several reversals of the democratization process have recently taken place in countries such as Nigeria, making the idea of a "snowball effect" somewhat tendentious.

8. This measure is fairly similar to Samuel Huntington's somewhat less practical "two-turnover test" for consolidated democracies. See his *The Third Wave: Democratization in the Late Twentieth Century* (Norman: University of Oklahoma Press, 1992), p. 267.

9. Geraint Parry, *Political Elites* (New York: Routledge Chapman & Hall, 1969).

10. C. Wright Mills, *The Power Elite* (New York: Oxford, 1956).

11. Robert Dahl, *Who Governs?* (New Haven, Conn.: Yale, 1961) and Robert Dahl, *Polyarchy* (New Haven, Conn.: Yale, 1971).

12. J. Schumpeter, *Capitalism, Socialism and Democracy* (New York: Harper & Row, 1943).

13. Eli Sagan, *At the Dawn of Tyranny* (New York: Alfred A. Knopf, 1985).

14. Quoted in Timothy Garton Ash, "East Germany: the Solution," *New York Review of Books*, vol. xxxvii, no. 7 (April 26, 1990), p. 14.

15. See Michael Curtis, *Totalitarianism* (New Brunswick, N.J.: Transactions, 1979).

16. Giorgio Pini, *The Official Life of Benito Mussolini* (London: Hutchinson, 1939).

17. Martin Blinkhorn, *Mussolini and Fascist Italy* (London: Methuen, 1984), p. 20. On Stalin see Robert C. Tucker, *Stalin in Power* (New York: W.W. Norton, 1990).

18. Jeane Kirkpatrick, *Dictatorships and Double Standards* (New York: Simon & Schuster, 1982), p. 101.

19. Hannah Arendt, *The Origins of Totalitarianism*, 2nd ed. (New York: World Publishing, 1958), p. 460.

20. Jeffery C. Goldfarb, *Beyond Glasnost: The Post-Totalitarian Mind* (Chicago: University of Chicago Press, 1989), p. 38.

21. Hannah Arendt, *Eichmann* (New York: Viking, 1970), p. 105.

22. Devised from Carl J. Friedrich and Zbigniew Brzezinski, *Totalitarian Dictatorship and Autocracy*, 2nd ed. (Cambridge, Mass.: Harvard University Press, 1965), pp. 9–10. For later discussions of the concept of totalitarianism, see Robert Nisbet, *The Twilight of Authority* (New York: Oxford, 1975); and Jean-François Revel, *The Totalitarian Temptation* (New York: Doubleday, 1977).

23. Lucian W. Pye, "Political Science and the Crisis of Authoritarianism," *APSR*, vol. 84, no. 1 (March 1990), p. 5.

24. Students will wish to examine the evolution in the former USSR by reading Mikhail Gorbachev, *The August Coup: The Truth and the Lessons* (New York: Harper Collins, 1991).

25. Eric Nordlinger, *Soldiers and Politics: Military Coups and Governments* (Englewood Cliffs, N.J.: Prentice-Hall, 1977), p. 6.

26. *The Commercial Appeal*, March 29, 1992, p. 2.

27. Data in this section are from *The World Bank Atlas 1995* and the Population Reference Bureau (1995 World Population Data Sheet). Data for the LDCs are often incomplete and are intended to be estimates only.

28. See Max Singer and Aaron Wildavsky, *The Real World Order: Zones of Peace/Zones of Turmoil* (Chatham, N.J.: Chatham House 1993).

29. Lester R. Brown, Nicholas Lenssen, and Hal Kane, *Vital Signs* (New York: Norton, 1995) p. 111.

30. Two fascinating books on this topic by historians are Jared Diamond, *Guns, Germs and Steel* (London: Jonathan Cape, 1997) and David Landes, *The Wealth and Poverty of Nations* (London: Little, Brown, 1998).

FURTHER READING

Bebler, A. and Seroka, J., eds., *Contemporary Political Systems: Classifications and Typologies* (Boulder: Lynne Rienner, 1990).

Brzezinski, Zbigniew, *The Grand Failure: The Birth and Death of Communism in the Twentieth Century* (New York: Charles Scribner's, 1989).

Dabashi, Hamid, *The Theology of Discontent: The Ideological Foundation of the Islamic Revolution in Iran* (New York: New York University Press, 1993).

Dahl, Robert, *Democracy and Its Critics* (New Haven, Conn.: Yale University Press, 1989).

Dahrendorf, Ralf, *Reflections on the Revolution in Europe* (New York: Random House, 1990).

Diamond, Larry, Juan Linz, and Seymour Martin Lipset, *Democracy in Developing Countries: Persistence, Failure and Renewal* (Boulder, Colo.: Lynne Rienner Publishers, 1989).

Elster, John, *Deliberative Democracy* (Cambridge: Cambridge University Press, 1998).

Gereffi, Gary, and Donald Wyman, eds., *Manufacturing Miracles: Paths of Industrialization in Latin America and East Asia* (Princeton, N.J.: Princeton University Press, 1990).

Jackson, R., and C.G. Rosberg, *Personal Rule in Black Africa: Prince, Autocrat, Prophet, Tyrant* (Berkeley, Cal.: University of California Press, 1982).

Mainwaring, Scott, Guillermo O'Donnell and Arturo Valanzuela, *Issues in Democratic Consolidation* (Notre Dame: University of Notre Dame Press, 1992).

Marks, Gary, and Larry Diamond, eds., *Reexamining Democracy* (Newbury Park, Calif.: Sage, 1992).

O'Donnell, G.A., P.C. Schmitter, and L. Whitehead, *Transitions from Authoritarian Rule: Prospects for Democracy* (Baltimore: Johns Hopkins University Press, 1987).

Landes, David S. *The Wealth and Poverty of Nations: Why Some are So Rich and Some So Poor* (New York: W.W. Norton, 1998).

Sartori, Giovanni, *The Theory of Democracy Revisited* (Chatham, N.J.: Chatham House Publishers, 1987).

Schmitter, P., and L. Whitehead, eds., *Transition from Authoritarian Rule* (Baltimore: Johns Hopkins University Press, 1986).

Watson, Patrick, and Benjamin Barber, *The Struggle for Democracy* (Toronto: Lester & Orpen Dennys, 1988).

Useful Comparative Volumes on the History and Politics of Different Regions

Baxter, Craig, Yogendra K. Malik, Charles H. Kennedy, and Robert C. Oberst, *Government and Politics in South Asia* (London: Westview Press, 1987).

Bebler, A. and Seroka, J., eds. *Contemporary Political Systems: Classifications and Typologies* (Boulder: Lynne Rienner, 1990).

Beinart, William, *Twentieth–Century South Africa* (Oxford: Oxford University Press, 1994).

Bill, James A., and Carl Leiden, *The Middle East: Politics and Power* (Boston: Allyn and Bacon, 1974).

Brass, Paul R., *The New Cambridge History of India: The Politics of India Since Independence* (Cambridge: Cambridge University Press, 1990).

Bremmer, Ian and Ray Taras, eds., *Nations and Politics in the Soviet Successor States* (Cambridge: Cambridge University Press, 1993).

Chehabi, H.E., *Iranian Politics and Religious Modernism: The Liberation Movement of Iran Under the Khah and Khomeini* (Ithaca, N.Y.: Cornell University Press, 1990).

Chilcote, R.H., and J.C. Edelstein, *Latin America: The Struggle with Dependency and Beyond* (New York: Wiley, 1974).

Diamond, L., J. Linz and S. Lipset, eds., *Democracy in Developing Countries*, 4 vols. (Boulder: Lynne Rienner, 1989).

Dunn, J., *West African States: Failure and Promise* (Cambridge: Cambridge University Press, 1978).

Fish, Steven, *Democracy from Scratch: Opposition and Regime in the New Russian Revolution* (Princeton: Princeton University Press, 1995).

Hardgrave, Robert, and Stanley Kochanek, *India: Government and Politics in a Developing Nation* (Fort Worth: Harcourt Brace Jovanovich, 1993).

Harnecker, Marta, *Cuba: Dictatorship or Democracy?* (Westport, Conn.: Lawrence Hill & Co., 1980).

Hourani, Albert, *A History of the Arab Peoples* (Cambridge, Mass.: Belknap/Harvard University Press, 1990).

Lewis, Bernard, *The Middle East: A Brief History of the Last 2000 Years* (New York, Scribner, 1998).

Murray, Martin J. *The Revolution Deferred—The Painful Birth of Post-Apartheid South Africa* (London: Verso, 1994).

 **Weblinks**

home.fog.net/frankw/dictator.html
This site contains information about some of the world's most famous dictators.

www.arablink.com/saudi-arabia/
Information about Saudi Arabia can be found at this site.

www.pitt.edu:80/~cjp/rspubl.html
This site provides information about Russia and other Eastern European countries that have recently witnessed the transformation from communist regimes to transitional or fledgling democracies.

CHAPTER 6

Political Culture: People and Politics

To understand contemporary forms of government and their politics, one must be familiar with the organization and functions of political institutions. It is also important to be aware of the physical and cultural circumstances within which politics operates. These external dimensions provide the environment of politics and help to shape attitudes and values which influence political behaviour. Elements of the physical, demographic, and economic environment of politics were discussed earlier; in this chapter we focus on the cultural environment.

A survey of the world's states reveals a rich pattern of diverse cultures which have evolved through history. These cultures have been conditioned over time by factors such as geography, religion, language, ethnicity, and types of economic activity to produce wide varieties of behaviour. In an engaging observation of behavioral differences, Ian Robertson noted that:

> Americans eat oysters but not snails. The French eat snails but not locusts.
> The Zulus eat locusts but not fish. The Jews eat fish but not pork. The Hindus
> eat pork but not beef. The Russians eat beef but not snakes. The Chinese eat
> snakes but not people. The Jalé of New Guinea find people delicious."[1]

Studying cultural differences is a fascinating venture. In a broad sense, culture includes intellectual development in many areas including art, architecture, cuisine, literature, music, and politics. It delineates distinctive attributes of groups and societies, masses and elites, nations and states. Political culture is one aspect of overall culture.

A well-known American professor of political science, Samuel P. Huntington, considers culture to be such a vital force that he hypothesizes in a controversial article that world politics is entering a new phase, in which the fundamental source of conflict will not be primarily ideological or economic but cultural:

> Nation states will remain the most powerful actors in world affairs, but the
> principal conflicts of global politics will occur between nations and groups of

different civilizations. The clash of civilizations will dominate global politics. The fault lines between civilizations will be the battle lines of the future.[2]

Over time, 21 major civilizations have been differentiated by history, language, culture, tradition, and religion. According to Huntington, only a few of them still exist: Western, Confucian, Japanese, Islamic, Hindu, Slavic-Orthodox, Latin American, and possibly African civilizations. He argues that the most important conflicts of the future will occur along the cultural fault lines separating these remaining civilizations. Whether or not this comes about, it is clear that increasingly the forces of globalization and the massive flow of ideas and information across state borders and around the world is impinging on state cultures and creating a homogenizing effect on previously differentiated state cultures.

WHAT IS POLITICAL CULTURE?

Political culture refers to the broad pattern of values and attitudes that individuals and societies hold toward political objects.[3] These objects include institutions such as the executive, legislature, bureaucracy, judiciary, political parties, pressure groups, and also the individual's view of him- or herself as a political actor, and in relation to others. Political culture is one of the most powerful influences that shape a political system. It creates **norms**—beliefs about how people should behave—and those norms influence social behaviour.

Politics, therefore, always reflects the culture of a certain time and place. Political acts are embedded in the wider culture of a society and can be understood only in that context. They "reflect and exemplify society's deepest-held values."[4] Understanding political action, therefore, requires one to understand political culture. The rationale behind politics is not always self-evident. Because it is largely conducted in terms of signals, coded language, and symbolic behaviour. Words mean different things in different cultures. The word "democracy," as we have seen, is a prime example.

CLOSE UP 6.1   **Reconciling Cultural Differences**

The European Union unites 15 European states into a community that can benefit from free trade and large-scale planning. However, reconciling cultural differences has been a difficult obstacle to securing unity. Initially, problems of standardization and quality control came over such unlikely items as condoms, the content of bangers (English sausages), the ingredients in beer, and the bacterial content of cheese. Before the Swedes voted to join the European Union in 1994, for example, they won concessions over their favourite tobacco—moist snuff. Moist snuff is prohibited in the rest of the union, but Sweden received an exemption allowing for its continued use in that country.

Cultures change extremely slowly over decades and even centuries. Since political change generally occurs *after* cultural change, it, too, changes slowly unless some major, traumatic event alters historical patterns. A country like Canada with deep, democratic roots and a tradition of peaceful changes in the political process is unlikely to suddenly adopt an authoritarian pattern of government. Similarly, an authoritarian country like China with a tradition which stresses hierarchy, order, submission to authority, and rule by a few is unlikely to change its political style quickly. Broad cultural patterns persist, and therefore political forms do too.

What individuals know and how they feel about their political system affects the number and kinds of demands they make on the state and how they respond to laws, political leadership, and decisions made within the political system. The extent to which they appreciate the political institutions of their country has other practical ramifications. When citizens accept the *legitimacy* of their state—that is, when they accept that the government has a moral right to govern—this provides a significant barrier to radical change. And if there is a strong belief in civilian authority, there is a built-in barrier to intervention by authoritarian structures or institutions such as the police and military. On the other hand, if there is little attachment to civilian institutions, allegiance to the government of the day can be expected to be low, and the possibility of intervention by police and military will be high. Political culture, therefore, demarcates the boundaries within which governments can legitimately act.

The political culture of a state, then, encompasses values and attitudes which pertain to its political system. These provide an invisible, overarching bond that unifies its citizens (see Figure 6.1). That bond includes ideologies, values, traditions, customs, beliefs, myths, and symbols—all of which influence the political life of a country—and "are part of the particular pattern of orientations to political objects in which a political system is embedded."[5]

A political culture is passed on to succeeding generations through various forms of socialization, and thereby lends cohesion and continuity to politics and institutions. Socialization studies, discussed later in this chapter, examine how attitudes and values are learned and transmitted. To a great extent they move beyond the description of beliefs and values to develop explanations for their development and acceptance.

Figure 6.1   The Overarching Bond of Political Culture

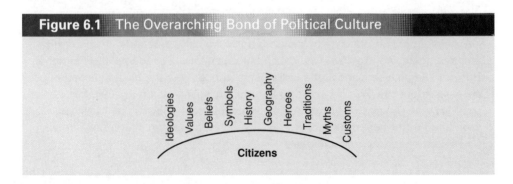

The political culture of a country is not monolithic. It is like a tapestry made up of many interwoven fibres or strands. One strand is composed of the values and attitudes common to all citizens of the state. The remainder are made up of the many subcultures or divisions that exist within a country including ethnic, linguistic, religious, and regional groups. In this chapter we examine the components of state-wide political cultures and consider the effect that subcultures have on them. As in a tapestry, the strands of subcultures can strengthen, but in some respects also weaken, the larger unit, depending on how they are incorporated. The political culture of a country is intimately related to how and when individuals act politically. We therefore consider the connection between political culture and political participation. We also examine the field of political socialization to consider how values and attitudes are learned and passed from one generation to another. First, however, we will trace the development of the concept of political culture in political science, and consider some of the methods used to study political culture.

HISTORY AND METHODS

Culture has been used as an explanatory variable for as long as humans have been studying politics. However the scientific field of "political culture" itself is relatively new, and was not established under that name until the 1950s when it was introduced in the United States. Until that time, one common form of study, linking values and attitudes to behaviour, was the "national character" study, which was typically conducted by various forms of observation within a single country. These studies generally offered such crude and impressionistic blanket descriptions as Asians are "inscrutable," Germans are "authoritarian," Americans are "rugged individualists," and Canadians are "peaceful, honest and boring."[6]

Needless to say, such stereotypical generalizations may be based on erroneous impressions. In fact, they may tell more about the observer than the observed! In the 1890s, for example, Anglo-Saxons were certain that the Japanese were "too indolent and pleasure-loving to succeed at anything requiring hard work."[7] Anglo-Saxons constantly underestimated Japan and were completely taken by surprise when it defeated China in 1895 and won victories over Russia in 1904 and 1905. Obviously it is important to distinguish between stereotypes and recurring real-life observations.

Other early studies relating values and behaviour approached the topic through the history of ideas, documenting the flow and clash of ideas across time and space. These were not known as political culture studies, but as political philosophy or political theory. Chapters 8 and 9 discuss the history of such ideas.

It was partly historical circumstance that brought political culture studies to the forefront in the 1950s. With the end of World War II, French, British, Dutch, Italian, and then Portuguese colonies moved toward independent statehood, and decisions had to be made about what kind of political forms these new countries would adopt. Generally it was decided to model the new institutions after those of the respective "mother" country. As a consequence, new countries sprang up in Asia, Africa, and South America with ambitious Western-style constitutions, political institutions, and legal systems.

Most of them foundered within a very short period and gave way to authoritarian, military, or single-party regimes. Too late, well-meaning Westerners realized that the ideas and institutions that served their own countries had evolved over generations and were inappropriate for the new states. Constitutions that appeared suitable on paper did not work in practice in many Third World states because the new states lacked societal support for the essential elements of democracy.

Nigeria provides a good example. During the 1950s the British combined about 250 different Nigerian tribes, tried to teach them English as a common language, trained their leaders in parliamentary democracy, and finally, in 1960, launched Nigeria as an independent country with a democratic constitution. Six years later there was a military coup. Instability persisted and a cycle of tribal, military, democratic, and then military governments ensued. In 1999 civilian government was returned, but with a former General as President.

With a practical impetus coming from problems such as how to advise developing states like Nigeria, a new emphasis arose. New methods of research were needed to describe and analyze political culture, so political scientists turned to research that had already been done in the field by sociologists, anthropologists, and psychologists.

By the late 1950s, many political scientists had shifted their emphasis from the study of institutions to the study of attitudes—how attitudes determine government functioning. Researchers began to examine how political culture affects support for the community, regime, and government. Unlike the impressions, stereotypes, and generalizations of national-character studies, political-culture studies endeavoured to determine objectively "what kinds of orientations are held by *which* people towards *which* political objects" and what, if any, impact this has on political stability.[8]

A primary method employed in the study of political culture is **survey research**, in which data is collected in interviews with a large "sample," or selection, of individuals. The responses are aggregated, and the researcher looks for patterns or configurations that provide the political culture of the "sample." It is inferred, using statistics, that the **sample** characterizes the overall political culture of the region or state from which it is drawn.

Gabriel Almond and Sidney Verba conducted the first such cross-national study of political culture in 1959, publishing their results in *The Civic Culture* four years later.[9] This landmark study became a reference point for further studies. Borrowing ideas and methods from other disciplines, these scholars examined public attitudes and values across five states in an attempt to measure and compare national political attitudes. The data from Britain, the United States, West Germany, Italy, and Mexico provided rich descriptions of the political cultures of the five countries.

Almond and Verba encountered many of the problems common to social science, which we discussed in Chapter 2, and exposed many strengths and weaknesses of survey research.[10] But, the development of survey technology "was the catalytic agent in the political culture conceptualization and research that took place in the 1960s" and in subsequent decades.[11] As increasingly sophisticated sampling, interviewing, scoring, and scaling techniques were developed, it became possible to determine:

... whether and in what respects and degrees nations [states] were divided into distinctive subcultures: whether social classes, functional groups, and specific elites had distinctive orientations toward politics and public policy ...

The development of statistical analysis made it increasingly possible to establish the patterns of interaction among attitudes, the relations of social-structural and demographic variables to attitude variables, and the relations of attitude variables to social and political behaviour.[12]

A major contribution of cross-national surveys is that they can reveal enduring, distinctive characteristics and allow fairly precise comparison between states. Besides possible faults in design construction, perhaps the most serious drawback of cross-national survey research is the considerable financial expense it entails. To circumvent these and other problems, studies of political culture are often conducted by area specialists within particular states or regions.

Alternative methods of studying political culture include examining the opinions of the political elite rather than the mass population. The **political elite** consists of individuals who participate extensively in organized politics and thereby exercise considerable influence in political decision-making.[13] Elites in democratic countries normally include distinct subgroups with control in the areas of politics, economics, and the bureaucracy. The exact composition of such elites is often controversial; however, they clearly constitute an extremely small percentage of the population even though they exercise very considerable influence in the country's decision-making process.

Some researchers study elites to discover what motivates them to participate politically, trying to identify the connection between values, attitudes, and participation. Researchers may study groups such as government or cabinet members, senior bureaucrats or judges, where a small sample could still be considered representative of the wider universe. Or they might concentrate on political activists who work inside the system, extremist-activists who advocate a dramatic shift in the existing system, or top political leaders such as presidents or prime ministers. Some elite studies even focus on the single political actor, a strategy which allows data gathering and analysis to be intensive and precise. However, to be useful, such studies must move beyond idiosyncratic explanations to find broad explanatory factors, and on the whole that is easier to do from studies of larger groups.

Other methods used to study political culture include **content analysis,** by which the researcher studies the "content" of speeches, newspaper articles, other writings and broadcasting as well as television clips in order to provide an empirical measure of specific attitudes or values. As well, **projective techniques,** in which subjects are required to project their imagination to complete sentences or stories are often used to discover the orientations of people, especially children.

More traditional methods and avenues of research are also available to determine the content of the individual citizen's knowledge and awareness of the political system, as well as the generalized attitudes held about politics and political objects in society. Even the literature and films a country produces can offer insights into political values and attitudes.

THE OVERARCHING POLITICAL CULTURES OF STATES

In Chapter 3 we discussed how political leaders attempt to develop and foster a broad national identity in order to bind together the citizens of their state and promote stability. This is much more difficult in some societies than others. State boundaries are artificial and may encompass a highly differentiated territory and populace. There are, however, many components of a national culture, including a widely accepted ideology, common values, symbols, history, geography, heroes, traditions, and myths.

Ideology is one part of the broader political culture. Chapters 8 and 9 focus extensively on this topic, but it is important here to differentiate between the two. **Ideology** refers to an explicit doctrinal structure that provides a particular diagnosis of the ills of society, plus an accompanying "action program" for implementing the prescribed solutions. Political culture studies are much broader; they are concerned with the views and values of citizens whether or not they embrace any explicit, formal ideology.

Typically, ideologies are the intellectual creation of an educated elite, and political leaders use their arguments to dispense simplified ideological propaganda to influence the beliefs and behaviour of the mass population. Some political systems, such as in China or Iran, are based on ideologically explicit norms of communism or religion; others are less overt, such as the attachment of British Conservatives to classic laissez-faire liberalism, or French Socialists to economic modernization. Ideologies, then, are action-oriented programs that are specific to individual actors or collective actors such as organizations or elites, rather than the collective thought of a whole community such as a society or a nation.

The traditional values and ideologies that underlie a country's political culture are found in its history. The roots of political thought in Canada, for example, have been traced by Louis Hartz who put forward a thesis that North America, like other societies founded by European settlement, is a "fragment society."[14] Hartz said that the New World societies based their political cultures on single European ideologies brought as "cultural baggage" during colonization. Immigrants to the new land did not represent all elements of the society that they left, but they set up institutions and myths which perpetuated their beliefs and values. Kenneth McRae argued further that because it has two founding nations, Canada is a classic instance of a "two-fragment" society.[15]

In pre-revolutionary United States, the liberalism of British philosopher John Locke was the prevailing ideology. Locke's ideas were based on the importance of the individual, free enterprise, and the right of the individual to pursue personal interests without government interference. Loyalists who left the United States for Canada at the time of the American Revolution took these liberal values with them—along with strong anti-American, pro-British sentiments. These ideas strongly affected the political culture of English-speaking Canadians. The cultural differences that developed between English Canada and the United States were, therefore, relatively minor. In both cases, the liberal ideology "congealed" before socialism developed in Europe; therefore socialism did not take hold in North America.[16]

A country's political values form the broad base of its political system. Though generally taken for granted and not articulated, they set the parameters of acceptable behaviour and underlie the attitudes of citizens toward specific political objects, providing guidelines to define what is right or wrong, what is or is not valuable or acceptable. As we see below, states vary in the degree to which there is unity with respect to fundamental political values.

Throughout Western Europe and North America the basic values of democracy, human rights, and political freedoms are part of the political culture and often are enshrined in state constitutions. The political values of individual states are symbolized in flags, anthems, historical heroes, and monuments that reinforce respect for, and emotional attachment to, political institutions. The symbols provide a focal point for national unity. Myths grow around them and are believed because they make people feel good— usually by confirming prejudices or reinforcing convictions of moral superiority.

Political leaders often use such symbols to unite and even manipulate their fellow citizens. A relevant example can be found in Japan where the traditional role of Emperor has had very special symbolism. The Meiji Constitution and culture of modern Japan are still based on a theory of the state known as *kokutai*. For theoretical and legal purposes, the Emperor and the state are fused—the Emperor embodies the state. Formerly, spiritual authority was also embodied in the Emperor, who was considered to be a "living god," the linear descendant of the Sun-Goddess.

When, under U.S. tutelage, the Japanese established a new constitution and democratic government in 1946 after the war, the Emperor remained the traditional symbol for the state and for the unity of the Japanese people, even though he had formally lost his status as a god. In November 1990, Emperor Hirohito's son Emperor Akihito was invested in a ceremony grounded in animistic Shinto religion. The event drew considerable criticism from liberal academics, Buddhists, and Christians in Japan, exemplified by a Japanese historian who claimed that the ceremony clearly intended to deify the Emperor.[17] The writer claimed that the ceremony violated the constitutional separation of state and religion in modern Japan. Modern Japanese culture is rejecting the old symbolism partly because it was in the name of the Emperor (and therefore by divine order) that Japan invaded other countries during the Second World War. This Japanese myth which posits a link with the gods through the Emperor engendered belief in Japanese racial superiority, a belief which, in the past, justified genocide in China, forced labour and prostitution in Korea and Taiwan, and brutal Japanese administrations in East and Southeast Asia. Few believe in this myth today.

History, geography, shared symbols, heroes, traditions, and other facets of historical memory, along with ideology, provide the basis of relatively durable beliefs and values that set the general parameters of political behaviour. Also important to political culture are the specific attitudes or orientations of citizens toward political objects such as politicians. These attitudes may be less widely accepted than basic beliefs and values, and more fleeting, but they may be more immediate determinants of political behaviour depending upon the intensity with which they are held.

At the national level then, political culture serves many purposes. As the set of values within which the state operates, it draws individuals together; provides rationale for judgment and action; constitutes the character and personality of a community; and helps determine the form of government that will exist in a country and how stable that government will be. In some states ideological diversity and free expression of ideas is a basic feature of the political culture; in others one ideology is a dominant force directing and limiting political thought, behaviour, and institutions. This is the case in communist states such as China and Cuba and also in religious theocracies like Iran. Confucianism is another fascinating example of a culture that for centuries has greatly influenced political behaviour in large parts of Asia. We shall examine these and other specific political cultures in more detail in the next chapter.

Political Subcultures

The strength of a state-wide political culture is greatly affected by elements in the environment, which may work against it. Factors such as geography, language, ethnicity, religion, and economic resources that help shape the political culture of a country can also be the basis of conflicting attitudes and values. They may help create **subcultures**, or cultures which exist within the overarching national culture of the state.

Large and complex states are rarely monolithic; rather they are almost always pluralistic. Within the framework of the wider political culture there may exist a variety of subcultures in which significant numbers of people hold distinctive values and attitudes toward political objects. When different cultural groups, which are aware of their distinctiveness and are impervious to change, coexist within a national state, the phenomena is known as **cultural** or **social pluralism**.[18] One author has described plural societies as "a medley of stateless societies: an assemblage of contiguous, closed communities in which membership is ascriptive and mandatory."[19]

Countries that lack broad agreement on how political life should be conducted, and base it instead on factors such as ethnicity, class, region, or religion are often said to have **fragmented** political cultures. Nigeria and the former Yugoslavia are extreme examples of countries with fragmented political cultures. In such states, patriotism and national identity are weak to the point that the unity of the country is threatened. States with a strong consensus about a core of political beliefs, on the other hand, are said to have **integrated** political cultures. They are characterized by a high degree of patriotism; a strong national identity; a high level of social trust; and a general acceptance of social, economic, and political arrangements. They are relatively stable politically.

There is a wide spectrum of countries with gradations of pluralism.[20] Some states consist of vertically divided communities that are conscious of their distinctive identities. Others form a "melting pot" so that although individuals may speak different languages, belong to different races, and so on, they are fairly well integrated into the mainstream of the country's population; they have accepted a common set of fundamental values and basic beliefs that provide an overarching bond for society. The United States is a good example of a "melting pot" society which is highly integrated even though it is socially complex and composed of different races and immigrants from many lands. Americans enjoy a strong sense of national identity and unity of political outlook. In countries like Nigeria and India, at the other extreme, subcultures do not overlap as they do in the United States. There, the social segments are separate and impervious and they are more likely to challenge the political viability of the country. Figure 6.2 illustrates the common bases of political culture and subcultures.

Within every state, there are class divisions which form the basis of socioeconomic subcultures, and also divisions along such cultural lines as ethnicity, language, caste, region, and religion. A great many states are divided along some or several of these lines into antagonistic sections often referred to as "political cleavages." A **political cleavage** is a set of attitudes that divides the state's citizens into major political groups.[21] Sometimes such cleavages are strictly political in that they represent groups that have attitudes which are developed, sustained, and organized by political leaders; sometimes they are not.

Class is sometimes a source of distinctive political attitudes and beliefs. In some countries the divisions between classes are not well defined, but indicators such as level of income, education, and occupation tend to produce a degree of class identity. Class is discussed further in Chapter 8 as the basis of Marxist thought. It can be a powerful basis of political cleavage, particularly when linked to group identities such as trade unions or political parties. Labour parties which seek to improve the lot of blue-collar workers exist in many countries.

Political cleavages are often based on ethnicity. When individuals and minorities share cultures distinct from those of other groups, social scientists label them "ethnic

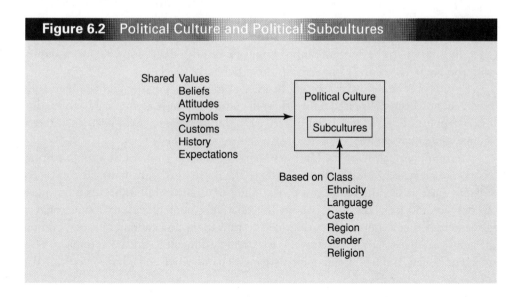

Figure 6.2 Political Culture and Political Subcultures

Shared Values
Beliefs
Attitudes
Symbols
Customs
History
Expectations

Political Culture

Subcultures

Based on Class
Ethnicity
Language
Caste
Region
Gender
Religion

groups" or "ethnic minorities." **Ethnicity** is a largely subjective characteristic that defines groups of people who share customs, language, dialect and/or cultural heritage, and sometimes distinct physical or racial characteristics. Like national identity, ethnicity is primarily a subjective phenomenon. In many societies, such as the United States, ethnic groups live together as one nation. In others, however, such as Canada, some ethnic groups define themselves as separate nations.

Ethnic characteristics are often, but not always, bonded to a specific religion. French ancestry and Roman Catholicism go hand in hand; Arabs are predominantly Muslim (although there are significant Christian populations in Syria, Iraq, Iran, and elsewhere); most but not all Jews are followers of Judaism. When ethnic/religious groups exist inside a country where the dominant religion is not their own, they tend to segregate themselves and hold values distinct from the dominant social system. If such differences become politicized, the results can be detrimental to national unity. In addition, if radical members of a religious sect break away, there is a danger that it may give rise to a religious fanaticism unacceptable to the dominant society. Religious values may be uncompromising, and when such religious issues enter into the public agenda there is a danger of activities which undermine democracy. History is replete with examples of religious wars, inquisitions, crusades, and massacres. Today, examples of violent ethnic rivalries are still in evidence, such as between Catholics and Protestants in Northern Ireland, Sikhs, Hindus, and Moslems in India, and, of course, Orthodox Christians, Catholics, and Muslims in the war-torn remains of the former Yugoslavia and especially Kosovo.

Language is another feature which distinguishes groups in culturally plural societies. Fewer than one state in five have only one shared language. In the vast majority, an array of languages are spoken. Language divisions are frequently part of political cleavages and are particularly divisive when they correspond with strong ethic identities.

Yet another common political cleavage is based on region. Different regions of a country often have unique patterns of settlement, geographic, and economic factors that are politically significant. They produce regional economies and can be particularly divisive when they correspond to linguistic or ethnic divisions, as, for example, with the French-speaking Canadians in the province of Quebec.

Subcultures endure with varying degrees of intensity. Gender and age identities have recently been politicized. Like other subcultures these groupings may exhibit distinctive political behaviour and also often support distinctive political parties, interest groups, and public policy.

Certain political theorists, Marxists being the most prominent, have argued that economic cleavages, manifested in class, are the most significant political cleavages. Others, such as G. Bingham Powell, Jr., argue that cultural pluralism is a far more serious factor in social divisions because it is relatively more difficult to find reasonable agreements on cultural conflicts than it is to find them on economic issues.[22] When religious principles clash, for example, it is extremely difficult to find compromises. This problem is seen in the contemporary abortion debate, which some have even called a "cultural civil war." There is also a tendency for cultural pluralism to diminish class conflicts. That is, perceptions of class division tend to be inhibited by the strong cultural segmentation of a society.

If subcultures become too strong vis-à-vis the national political culture, the fabric of the society is weakened and the state may break apart. In a subculture community within a plural society the individual may reserve loyalty more for his or her own group than for the state as a whole. This divided loyalty is the basis of links between segmentation and instability, intensity of conflict and violence.[23] Subcultural characteristics create an identity or sense of selfhood that may threaten the state or other groups, causing fear and hostility.[24] Studies have shown that rioting or political violence is not much more common, on a per capita basis, in ethnically divided nations than in more homogeneous nations. However, when political violence does occur, it is more serious and causes more deaths.[25]

Some high divided societies such as the Netherlands, Austria, and Switzerland have survived by adopting **consociational** or **consensus democracy** despite strong cultural cleavages. In such countries the ruling elites are not divided to nearly the same degree as society as a whole and they learn to cooperate in spite of societal differences. Arend Lijphart, who introduced these terms to the discipline, says that the essential characteristic of consociational democracy is the "overarching cooperation at the elite level with the deliberate aim of concentrating disintegrative tendencies in the system."[26] The impact of consociationalism is discussed further in Chapter 12.

Leaders of newly emerging states have to be particularly wary of the possibility of instability, conflict, and violence that accompanies cultural pluralism. To promote cohesiveness, they often try to enforce a common language and exercise strong control over communications through the educational system and media. And of course, they are particularly interested in establishing and celebrating common national symbols such as flags, anthems, and national holidays. Sometimes they adopt political rhetoric such as "imperialists" and "bourgeois capitalists" or "reds" to identify a common, exterior enemy in order to promote unity. As Close Up 6.2 indicates, promoting cultural integration is not a simple matter.

Economic, social, and political development do not necessarily eliminate the negative effects of political pluralism. Often economic disparities and rivalries between groups increase: for example, greater differences may arise between urban political centres and the periphery, creating a privileged elite at the centre and an isolated, insecure population at the periphery. This may reinforce other cultural segments and deepen political cleavages. It must also be noted that while subcultures are potentially disruptive to a country, there are also forces from without that can put stress on a country's political culture. A relatively small country in terms of population, economic power, and military strength is particularly vulnerable to pressures from larger countries which are proximate to it. Canada and Mexico, for example, must each continually struggle to maintain an economic, political, and cultural identity separate from that of the United States.

CLOSE UP 6.2   Integrating Ethnic Minorities: Indonesia

Since Indonesia took control of Irian Jaya (the former West New Guinea) from the Netherlands in 1963, it has been attempting to socialize the natives. In one of its first attempts, in the 1970s, the army launched Operation Penis Gourd, airlifting jogging shorts and dresses to encourage wearing clothes. The operation failed. In fact, shortly thereafter, an American missionary observed men wearing the shorts on their heads and the women using the dresses as shoulder bags. By 1995 however, only about 5% of the residents in remote highland areas still prefer to walk around semi-naked. Today, they speak in a mixture of Bahasa Indonesia, the national language, and their own dialect. They are taught the national education curriculum, including the *pancasile* ideology, which stresses national unity. They are taught that loyalty is due not just to their god, or to their clan, but to a culturally diverse state of millions of people—Indonesia.[27]

Do you think the strategy has worked? Was it ethical?

POLITICAL PARTICIPATION AND POLITICAL CULTURE

Political culture is intimately linked to political participation. The term **political participation** applies to all political actions of individuals. In ancient Athens, direct participation in the political affairs of the city was deemed to be the essence of democracy. However even though informed participation is desirable, it is not a necessary condition of democracy. Today, with states forming ever larger units encompassing millions of people, democracy and direct public participation in decision-making are not inextricably bound together.

Nonparticipation is not necessarily an indication of alienation or dissatisfaction, nor is it necessarily a bad thing. It could indicate hostility or indifference, but it might also mean satisfaction and consent with the way elected, responsible politicians are carrying out their tasks. What is important is that democracies provide opportunities for participation, so that when individuals or groups feel strongly about an issue—such as nuclear energy, pollution, abortion laws, and the like—they are free to generate political activity, mobilize people, and actively promote their interests.

A government can take many measures to encourage participation by its citizens. It can structure electoral systems in order to make voting easier, or even make it compulsory as in Australia and other countries. Or, it can make voting relatively more difficult through registration laws as in the United States. A government can put in place laws encouraging individuals to join political groups. It can help ensure that citizens have the educational skills required to participate. And it can develop efficacious citizens who believe they can and should engage in political activities effectively. The Almond and Verba *Civic Culture* study showed that participant political values tend to be fairly widespread in industrial democracies.

POLITICAL SOCIALIZATION

Political culture is the product of the history of a society; collective orientations are re-inforced and passed from generation to generation through families, educational systems, the work place, the media, and various other institutions, including the political system itself. The process by which political culture is transmitted and maintained, transformed, or created, at both the individual and community levels, is called **political socialization**. It is a lifelong process. It comprises casual, informal learning from peers and family, who are the primary agents of political socialization. It also includes both informal and overt political indoctrination by secondary sources such as educational organizations, the media and other institutions including governments. The content and manner of political so-cialization is subject to debate because what may be considered proper civic training by one population or individual may be viewed by another as indoctrination and brainwashing.

Talcott Parsons and David Easton were among the pioneers of political socialization theory.[28] They reasoned that the process of political socialization, which builds citizen support for the state through positive norms and beliefs, is a major ingredient of polit-ical stability. To varying degrees, governments deliberately attempt to inculcate values that will enhance popular support for the country's political institutions. In Western democracies this tends to be relatively subtle. However, as we shall see in the next chap-ter, authoritarian regimes regularly control and use schools, mass media, and other means at their disposal, including sports and art, to socialize their citizens.

Institutions which shape individual and collective attitudes and values are known as **agents of political socialization**. Some of the most important agents include the family, educational and religious institutions, and the mass media. There are, of course, others in-cluding peer groups, friends, work places, and even governments (see Figure 6.3).

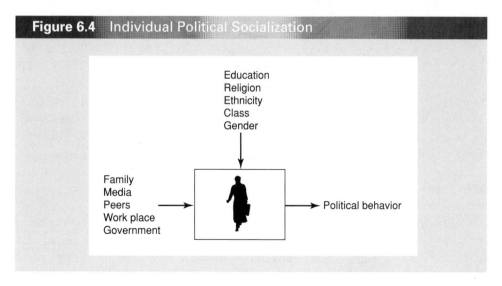

Figure 6.4 Individual Political Socialization

Societies vary a great deal in the extent to which they actively socialize their citizens politically. At one extreme, where central institutions are not strong or do not choose to exercise control, socialization is left to spontaneous action by families and other primary and secondary agents. At the other extreme, political socialization is exercised with absolute control by an authoritarian state, and all agents of socialization are harmonized. But no socialization, even the most assiduous, is perfect; it suffers many discontinuities. People are not entirely passive, and social groups are not always malleable. In addition, the values of the different subcultures to which an individual belongs may conflict with those of the dominant culture.

All governments, democratic and authoritarian, old and new, try in varying ways to create and maintain national symbols and myths to unify their people and provide a strong national identity that will promote emotional allegiance to the state. Symbols can be a divisive force if they are not carefully designed to encompass major groups. In Britain, for example, the present Union Jack dates from the union with Ireland in 1801. The flag joins traditional symbols of England, Scotland, and Ireland—the red cross of England, the Scottish white diagonal cross on a blue field, and the red diagonal cross of Ireland. The flag is layered so that the colours of the cross of St. Andrew (for Scotland) and the Cross of St. Patrick (for Ireland) are each uppermost in two quarters. Imperialism carried and planted the Union Jack around the world, but the flag was never officially adopted by the British Parliament. Today it is said that only the English wave the flag with enthusiasm. Ireland is no longer part of the Union, Wales is left out, and the Scottish Nationalists prefer their own version. The Flag Institute is trying to get a standard version adopted by Parliament by 2001, the flag's 200th birthday. It may not be easy. On the other hand, flag selection has been relatively easy for the new Russia, but as we see in Close Up 6.3, choosing a suitable new anthem has proved a daunting task.

The Family

The family is an important socializing agent in the early years of an individual's life. Family influence is not absolute, however. Parents have to possess firm convictions in order to transmit them in the first place (and many do not), and they must also communicate them to their children (which, again, many do not). Political preferences which are learned early tend to persist. However, they may be held more or less strongly by individuals depending on the constancies or discontinuities in their political socialization. If, for example, a long time elapses between primary socialization and the assumption of a political role, then attitudes may be weakly held. As well, exposure to a great number of agents or political situations which transmit contradictory messages may cause change and discontinuities in attitudes.

Differences of opinion exist concerning when political learning takes place. Some psychologists, for example, emphasize the importance of the family with regard to what is learned at a young age. Assumptions and orientations learned during this period can "become inarticulate major premises which then exercise a background effect on thought and overt behaviour precisely because they are not made sufficiently conscious to become

CLOSE UP 6.3 **Developing Symbols in Russia**

The new, democratically oriented Russia that emerged after 1991 needed new national symbols to replace those of communism. Choosing a new flag was easy—it became a red, white, and blue tricolor which had once been the official banner of the Russian Imperial Navy. However the stirring national anthem was harder to replace. Political correctness required deference to all of Russia's different nationalities and religions. Lamented the chairman of the national composers union, "We can't have lyrics about Christ or about Slavs and we don't want this false patriotism or the stupid rhetoric that was in the Soviet hymn."

When the first competition for new words and tune failed in 1995, the committee suggested a new sweepstake to come up with something suitable. "A country needs a good anthem to boost patriotism and just to make people feel better about themselves and their lives."[29]

open to challenge."[30] That is, children learn attitudes in nonpolitical contexts that are later carried over to political life. Other psychologists believe that socialization experiences that are closer in time to the relevant political context have the greatest impact. They therefore assign relatively more importance to the socialization that takes place in adolescence or adulthood, stressing the importance of issues, personalities, and events. A compromise is possible—as Dennis Kavanagh concludes: "The durability of the early impressions depends to some extent upon their usefulness in the new circumstances— particularly the political and social conditions—to which a person is exposed."[31]

The influence of the family is disputed by Marxists, who interpret the world in terms of class struggle. They regard the family as relatively insignificant as a socializing agent compared to adult experiences. They believe that socialization is largely a systematic and pervasive effort by middle-class elites to produce social consensus by using social agencies such as the media.

Educational and Religious Institutions

A country's education system represents an important path to political power. In developed societies political leaders tend to be the product of a few elite universities, and individuals who attain such an education are primarily from the middle class. Screening biases typically leave the working classes politically underrepresented even in countries where schools are free and open to all.

However, schools are an important source of attitude formation for the masses as well as the elite. In democratic societies the educational curriculum may socialize students through implicit teaching of values in history and other subjects, and more explicitly in civics courses designed to produce informed, participatory citizens. In authoritarian countries the curriculum is likely to emphasize indoctrination or more overt teaching of "correct" political answers based on a specific political ideology.

Informally, schools provide regular social contact with peer groups and teachers who exercise pressures on individuals to conform, accept authority figures, and behave in a certain way. They reinforce views and attitudes already absorbed, including those having to do with the political sphere. Sometimes they provide conflicting orientations that cause individuals to defer political commitment. Classrooms themselves can be organized in a rigid, authoritarian manner or in a more relaxed, democratic fashion.

Apart from this latent socialization, schools also attempt to instill specific attitudes. Course material and texts present themes and points of view with the aim of having students internalize certain knowledge and beliefs. Textbooks and lessons are selective and thus contain biases. Even at the university level, ideas and course material are far from value-free. When the Berlin Wall fell and Germany was reunited in 1989, universities in the former Eastern sector were in a state of turmoil. Professors who taught Marxist-Leninist courses in East German institutes became redundant, and much of the rest of the educational system was systematically expunged of communist influences. In many university departments, professors had been trained only in Marxist-Leninism or the now-irrelevant legal structures and economic principles of a communist state. Some students were caught in the middle of their university careers. The law, political science, and history they had learned was no longer relevant, and they were told to forget much of what they had learned and begin again using new, imported Western books and ideas. Even university names were changed: The Karl Marx University became, once again, the University of Leipzig.

In the new, interdependent world, parochial influences of state educational systems are weakened by international exchanges between schools and universities and the ability of students to work and pursue graduate degrees abroad. The European School in Brussels is an example of an attempt to reach beyond the socialization of a single state. Here, students from the 15 states of the European Union come to be educated not as products of a motherland or fatherland but as Europeans. This is also true on the various campuses of the United Nations University.

As with educational institutions, religious institutions exercise a significant informal influence on the political culture of states and also wider regions of the world. Some religious institutions, such as fundamentalist Islam, are very rigid and authoritarian in their structure, organization, and teaching. Others, such as the Unitarian Church, are very flexible and democratic. Some churches or religious groups actively promote political attitudes or ideologies, while such teachings are quite peripheral to others. In theocratic states such as Iran and the Vatican City, politics and religion are inseparable. We will consider religion and political culture in detail in the next chapter.

The Mass Media

The growth of communications technology in recent decades has dramatically increased the impact of the mass media on the political culture of states. By **media** we mean communication media—agents of communication such as radio, television, newspapers, and magazines. Television and newspapers in particular shape public opinion and its expression. Communications guru Marshall McLuhan noted decades ago that "the medium is the message" by which he meant that we must look beyond the content of the media to understand the effects of the medium itself on our lives and our thinking. Mass media are crucial sources of political information in most modern societies, suggesting the topics citizens think about, and often also what to think about the topics. Media have enormous access to the public. By the time American children finish high school, for example, they have watched on average almost twice as many hours of television as they have spent in classrooms.[32] Television reaches adults as well as children, and offers a useful means of socialization that is crucial to political modernization in developing countries.

Media are not neutral. Like textbooks and school lessons, they are selective in subject and content. They are used to inform and persuade. They are extensive but not comprehensive. There is little depth of coverage, and stories appear and disappear as if by magic. They may be biased. Journalists in Western democracies today are commonly criticized for their tendency to see world events through "liberal" eyes, to report on events as a game that is largely about winning and losing. Reporting, it is said, is based on cynicism rather than a more neutral scepticism, so that public figures and political events are only discussed in negative terms. This magnifies the bad and ignores or underplays the good, casting doubt and even distorting events to suggest scandal even when there is none. Journalists have learned that they get more personal rewards for outrageous opinions, so they tend to oversimplify and sensationalize.

All political news is delivered to the public through media intermediaries—journalists and media owners—and they have their own biases and agendas. Sometimes major media outlets are owned by only a few members of the wealthy, dominant class; sometimes they are controlled by the government. It can be expected that biases of the owners will be reflected in the presentations.[33] And the more chain–owned newspapers there are instead of independents, for example, the more newspapers will appear to be stamped from a giant corporate cookie cutter, taking the same point of view.

In democratic countries the media are relatively free and independent. However one study has estimated that governments in more than 85% of the states of the world substantially censor their media.[34] In authoritarian countries, such as China, state-owned networks generally mean outright government control of the news, making it almost a commercial for the party leadership. In these countries journalists have far less legal protection when they engage in free speech. In Cuba, for example, unofficial print and broadcast outlets are banned. Independent journalists trying to send stories to foreign media are treated as political dissidents and often put in jail. Close Up 6.4 provides examples of journalistic restrictions in Saudi Arabia and Iran.

The political bias of the news media is overt in authoritarian regimes, and easily spotted. By political bias we mean deliberate manipulation of the content and presentation of news so as to favour certain political interests over others. In Western liberal democracies this process is more subtle. Sometimes it is through omission—as when

CLOSE UP 6.4   Print Media in Authoritarian Political Systems

In absolute monarchies, restrictions on the print media may be very severe. In Saudi Arabia, for example, all foreign magazines for sale are previously read by the country's religious censors, known as the *mutawa*. This is an independent religious body sanctioned by the government. The *mutawa* even combs magazines such as *People* and *Better Homes and Gardens* to paint out exposed arms and legs with black markers. Sometimes its members draw black robes over pictures of women. All baggage entering the country is searched at entry and any books and magazines suspected of containing explicit or subversive material (such as *Time* or *Newsweek*) are seized. In Iran, in 1994, the parliament banned satellite dishes and placed an austere revolutionary at the head of Iranian television with instructions to turn the medium into an "open university" for Islamic thought.[35]

American broadcasters only briefly mentioned the civilian deaths in Iraq during the Gulf War, but at the same time stressed the small numbers of American casualties. Sometimes it is contained in an implicit, unquestioning acceptance of the system in place—for example, basic capitalism or socialist principles.

As intermediaries between governments and the population of a country, the media play a significant role in legitimizing government, making it more effective, and preventing abuse of power. The journalists take seriously their role of exposing wrongdoing, pursuing leads with sometimes fanatical fervour. On the other hand, political leaders and parties learn how to use and manipulate the media to maximum advantage. Media exposure is vital, and experts are hired to assure that the message conveyed is the right one. Examples abound. Former British Prime Minister Margaret Thatcher enjoyed a significant boost in popularity following extensive media coverage of her handling of the Falklands invasion by Argentina in 1982. In 1983, massive media coverage is credited with boosting the popularity of U.S. President Ronald Reagan following his order to invade Grenada.

Political leaders have learned standard "tricks" to obtain media coverage. Announcements are carefully timed for optimum exposure and generally delivered in a carefully prepared setting with a phalanx of cameras and journalists with notebooks in hand. Some specialists teach leaders how to improve their image on television. Other specialists produce just the right "sound clips" for television and radio news. Such as former British Prime Minister Margaret Thatcher's famous soundbite "The lady's not for turning."[36] Political "spin doctors," too, routinely try to ensure that their "interpretation" of events is disseminated to foster the "appropriate" attitudes and opinions in the public.

Mass media may play a less significant socializing role in developing countries, particularly in rural areas where there is less television exposure. However even there leaders recognize the potential impact of the media and use it extensively. Authoritarian countries that use the media to legitimize government actions make great efforts to ensure it is accessible to all. In Cuba, for example, the government supplies televisions to most recipients of public housing, thus enabling Fidel Castro a vehicle to "enter" as many homes as possible. Media control is considered to be so important by military leaders that in planning a *coup*, one of the first things revolutionary leaders do is take over the means of communication so that all messages to the public can be censored and tightly controlled.

Media socialization does not stop at artificial borders. Globalization forces in recent years have dramatically increased the scope and reach of the media. Economically powerful countries exercise an enormous socializing impact on others. Through CNN, newspapers such as *The New York Times* and the *International Herald Tribune*, and the Hollywood film industry, the United States disseminates American culture abroad. This role is taken seriously by the U.S. media. When the American marines landed in the beaches of Somalia in late 1992, camera crews were there waiting for them. In Canada, where most of the population is thinly spread within 100 miles of the long Canada/U.S. border, the country is deluged with U.S. radio and television signals. Almost all foreign reporting is bought from U.S. media so that by the time it reaches the public it has been filtered through American eyes and given American viewpoints. There are symbols of American cultural penetration in even more remote locations. Isolated places in the Pacific like the Cook Islands often have no television reception, but they do have large stocks of U.S. videos for their VCRs. Of particular interest at the turn of the century is the electronic media, which appears to be practically limitless in its capacity to carry information around the world.

The academic literature about political culture, then, has been concerned primarily with the role of values in maintaining stability in democratic regimes. It is clear that norms and beliefs are central to an explanation of stability and change, but so far a complete explanation is elusive. It remains difficult to provide unambiguous, empirical evidence that a specific agent of socialization or feature of the environment is the direct cause of political behaviour and government performance. Political culture, as an explanatory variable, sets limits to the range of outcomes. It does not determine specific outcomes. Moreover, there is no absolute proof that a particular culture must prevail over time. Past political culture is not destiny—people can change. Today, throughout Eastern Europe, the Commonwealth of Independent States (the former USSR), Latin America, Asia, and in Africa, for example, fragile new democratic political cultures are emerging in which citizens have entirely new expectations and beliefs concerning their government and their own role in society. Their political views are not totally "conditioned" by their country's history.

DISCUSSION QUESTIONS

1. Is literature part of a country's political culture? Movies? Comic books?
2. Does your country have an overarching political culture which helps to hold it together despite problems of economics or leadership?
3. Which of the following have had a greater influence on your political ideas: your family? School? Church? Professors?
4. Identify the main subcultures that impact on politics in your country.
5. Is a world or global culture developing? Why or why not?

KEY TERMS

agents of political socialization, p. 127
consociational or consensus democracy, p. 125
content analysis, p. 119
cultural or social pluralism, p. 122
ethnicity, p. 124
fragmented political cultures, p. 122

ideology, p. 120
integrated political cultures, p. 122
media, p. 130
norms, p. 115
political cleavage, p. 123
political culture, p. 115
political elite, p. 119

political participation, p. 126
political socialization, p. 127
projective techniques, p. 119
sample, p. 118
subcultures, p. 122
survey research, p. 118

ENDNOTES

1. Ian Robertson, *Sociology* (New York: Worth Publishers, 1981) p. 63.
2. Samuel P. Huntington "The Clash of Civilizations?" *Foreign Affairs* (Summer 1993), pp. 22–49. Several responses to this controversial article appeared in the September–October 1993 issue of *Foreign Affairs*, and Huntington responded to the critics in the article, "If Not Civilizations, What?" in the November–December 1993 issue, pp. 186–194. Others criticize Huntington's effort to group Islamic states. Fred Halliday, for one, maintains that Huntington has simply reinforced the stereotype that there is one binding Islamic answer to all political questions. See his *Islam and the Myth of Confrontation* (New York: St. Martin's Press, 1996).
3. Political culture has been defined a great many ways. Our definition is influenced by Sidney Verba, "Comparative Political Culture," in Lucian W. Pye and Sidney Verba, eds., *Political Culture and Political Development* (Princeton, N.J.: Princeton University Press, 1965), p. 513; and Gabriel A. Almond and G. Bingham Powell, *Comparative Politics: A Developmental Approach* (Boston: Little, Brown, 1966), p. 50.
4. Oliver H. Woshinsky, *Culture and Politics: An Introduction to Mass and Elite Behaviour* (Englewood Cliffs, N.J.: Prentice Hall, 1995), p. 41.
5. Dennis Kavanagh, *Political Science and Political Behaviour* (London: Allen and Unwin, 1983), p. 50. For further discussion of the concept of political culture, see Stephen Chilton, "Defining Political Culture," *Western Political Quarterly*, vol. 41, no. 3 (September 1988).

6. Examples are found in essays in *National Character in the Perspective of the Social Sciences*, Annals of the American Academy of Political and Social Science, March 1967.

7. James Fallows, "Is Japan the Enemy?" *The New York Review of Books*, vol. xxxviii, no. 10 (May 30, 1991), p. 34, in a review of Endymion Wilkinson, *Japan Versus the West: Image and Reality* (London: Penguin, 1991), p. A3.

8. Kavanagh, *Political Science and Political Behaviour*, p. 50.

9. Gabriel Almond and Sidney Verba, *The Civic Culture* (Princeton, N.J.: Princeton University Press, 1963).

10. See the essays by Almond, Lijphart, and Verba in Gabriel A. Almond and Sidney Verba, eds., *The Civic Culture Revisited* (Boston: Little, Brown, 1980). Note particularly Gabriel A. Almond, "The Intellectual History of the Civic Culture Concept," p. 1.

11. Almond, "The Intellectual History of the Civic Culture Concept," p. 15.

12. *Ibid.*

13. See Sidney Verba and Norman Nie, "Political Participation," in Fred I. Greenstein and Nelson W. Polsby, eds., *Handbook of Political Science*, vol. 4 (Reading, Mass.: Addison-Wesley, 1975), pp. 24–25.

14. Louis Hartz, ed., *The Founding of New Societies* (New York: Harcourt Brace, 1964).

15. Kenneth D. McRae, "The Structure of Canadian History" (Chapter 7), in Louis Hartz, ed., *The Founding of New Societies* .

16. See Robert J. Jackson and Doreen Jackson, *Politics in Canada*, 4th ed. (Scarborough, Ont.: Prentice-Hall Canada, 1998), pp. 74–76.

17. *The Globe and Mail*, Nov. 23, 1990, p. 2.

18. Mattei Dogan and Dominique Pelassy, *How to Compare Nations* (Chatham, N.J.: Chatham House Publishers, 1984), pp.59, 60.

19. R. Jackson, *Plural Societies and New States: A Conceptual Analysis* (Berkeley, Calif.: University of California Press, 1974), p. 8.

20. Dogan and Pelassy, *How to Compare Nations*, p. 60.

21. G. Bingham Powell, Jr., *Contemporary Democracies: Participation, Stability, and Violence* (Cambridge, Mass.: Harvard University Press, 1982).

22. Powell, *Contemporary Democracies*, ch. 1.

23. See D.G. Morrison and H.M. Stevenson, "Cultural Pluralism, Modernization and Conflict," *CJPS*, vol. 5, no. 1 (1972), pp. 82–103.

24. See Robert A. Dahl, *Polyarchy: Participation and Opposition* (New Haven, Conn.: Yale University Press, 1971).

25. Powell, *Contemporary Democracies*, p. 47.

26. A. Lijphart, "Typologies of Democratic Systems," *Comparative Political Studies*, vol. 1 (1968) p. 21. Lijphart's important works on the topic are: *Democracy in Plural Societies: A Comparative Exploration* (New Haven, Conn.: Yale University Press, 1977); and *Democracies: Patterns of Majoritarian and Consensus Government in Twenty-One Countries* (New Haven, Conn.: Yale University Press, 1984).

27. See *The Economist*, July 29 – August 4, 1995, p. 28.

28. See T. Parsons, "Family Structure and the Socialization of the Child," in T. Parsons and R. Bales, *Family, Socialization and Interaction Process* (Glenco, Ill.; Free Press, 1955), pp. 35–131; and D.E. Easton, "The Function of Formal Education in a Political System," *School Review*, vol. 65 (1957), p. 309; and by the same author, "The New Revolution in Political Science,"

APSR, vol. 63, no. 4, (December 1960), pp. 1051–61; and D. Easton and J. Dennis, *Children and the Political System* (New York: McGraw-Hill, 1969).

29. Quotations from Vladislav Kazenin, Chairman, National Composers Union, quoted in *The Globe and Mail*, July 22, 1995.

30. F. Greenstein, U. Herman, R. Stradling and E. Zureik, "The Child's Conception of the Queen and Prime Minister," *BJPS*, vol. 4, no. 3 (1974), p. 285.

31. Kavanagh, *Political Science and Political Behaviour*, p. 46.

32. Austin Ranney, *Channels of Power: The Impact of Television on American Politics* (New York: Basic Books, 1983), p. 60.

33. See for example studies of the Glasgow University Media Group, *Bad News* (London: Routledge & Kegan Paul, 1976); *More Bad News* (London: Routledge & Kegan Paul, 1980); and *Really Bad News* (London: Routledge & Kegan Paul, 1984).

34. See Raymond Gastil, ed., *Freedom in the World, 1987–88* (New York: Freedom House, 1988).

35. See *The New York Times*, August 14, 1994, p. E4.

36. See Nicolas Jones, *Soundbites and Spin Doctors* (London: Cassell, 1996).

FURTHER READING

Political Culture

Almond, Gabriel, and Sidney Verba, *The Civic Culture* (Boston: Little, Brown, 1965).

———, eds., *The Civic Culture Revisited* (Boston: Little, Brown, 1980).

Chinn, Jeff, *Russians as the New Minority: Ethnicity and Nationalism in the Soviet Successor States* (Boulder, Colo.: Westview Press, 1996).

Diamond, Larry, *Political Culture and Democracy in Developing Countries* (Boulder, Colo.: Lynne Rienner Publishers, 1994).

Holland, Henry M., Jr., ed., *Politics Through Literature* (Englewood Cliffs, N.J.: Prentice-Hall, 1968).

Kavanagh, Dennis, *Political Culture* (London: Macmillan, 1972).

Kaplan, Robert, *The Ends of the Earth: A Journey at the Dawn of the Twenty-First Century* (New York: Random House, 1998).

Powell, G. Bingham, Jr., *Contemporary Democracies: Participation, Stability and Violence* (Cambridge, Mass.: Harvard University Press, 1982).

Putnam, Robert D., *Making Democracy Work: Civic Traditions in Modern Italy* (Princeton N.J.: Princeton University Press, 1993).

Pye, Lucian W., and Sidney Verba, *Political Culture and Political Development* (Princeton, N.J.: Princeton University Press, 1965).

Warwick, Paul V., *Culture, Structure or Choice: Essays in the Interpretation of the British Experience* (New York: Agathon Press, 1990).

Woshinsky, Oliver H., *Culture and Politics: An Introduction to Mass and Elite Behaviour* (Englewood Cliffs, N.J.: Prentice Hall, 1995).

Political Socialization

Dawson, Richard E., Kenneth Prewett, and Karen S. Dawson, *Political Socialization*, 2nd ed (Boston: Little, Brown, 1977).

Eaman, Ross A., *The Media Society: Basic Issues and Controversies* (Toronto: Butterworths, 1987).

Fallows, James, *Breaking the News: How the Media Undermine American Democracy* (Toronto: Random House, 1996).

Graber, Doris A., *Mass Media and American Politics*, 4th ed. (Washington, D.C.: Congressional Quarterly Press, 1993).

 **Weblinks**

www.umich.edu/~nes/resourcs/nesguide/gd-index.htm
This site provides information about the nature of political participation around the world.

www.freenet.msp.mn.us/govt/e-democracy/
This site is an example of an electronic democracy and chronicles new methods of political participation.

CHAPTER 7

Political Culture: Democratic and Authoritarian

Every state has a unique political culture and embraces a variety of political subcultures. It is a daunting, if not impossible, task to compare the political cultures of all the world's states and to relate those findings to particular forms of political behaviour. Culture knows no borders. It is not confined inside the artificial boundaries of states. Cultural patterns can be found within countries and also across large regions and even continents where populations have shifted and share such factors as language, ethnicity, history, religion, and language. There are broad similarities in the overall patterns of political culture inside specific regions such as Western Europe, North America, South America, and parts of Asia and the Middle East because of such factors as shared history, cultural and religious experiences, and economic development.

Belief and value systems in the countries of Western Europe and North America are relatively similar. There is widespread emphasis on individualism in the form of ideas about equality and the importance of rights and freedoms. Many Asian countries, by contrast, manifest essentially collectivist cultures based on their heritage of Confucian thought. Individuals in such societies may view themselves as part of a social order that is hierarchical, and view those in authority as the natural leaders of an extended family. Opposition to authority is considered to be essentially inappropriate behaviour, whereas in Western Europe and North America challenges and conflict are seen as a natural part of the fabric of a democratic society.

Some broad similarities are also found across developing countries. Many of these countries experience social turmoil when their national political cultures are brought into confrontation with the political cultures of more modern states. As states adopt international standards in order to achieve competitive economic performance with other states, they often jeopardize the parochial values that are the basis of local loyalties and politics. Modern technology, economics, and principles of efficiency, for example, are parts of a world culture that may weaken the sense of self-identity and dignity that comes from "a fundamental belief in the collective uniqueness of the national entity and its spirit of community."[1] Such clashing values pose a serious problem for many developing nations and also for poorer areas within developed states where modern technologies and values are imposed on traditional societies.

To provide an overview of political culture in the range of democratic and authoritarian countries, this chapter is divided into five main parts. The first part examines political culture at the state level in developed liberal democracies, reviewing some significant findings of political culture studies. Part two considers the impact of religious and cultural belief systems on national politics. The discussion of Christianity is followed by sections on Islam and Confucianism. The third part explores aspects of two important subcultures that exist within many states: ethno-linguistic groups, and a gender-based group—women. The fourth part of the chapter explores comparative political socialization; the fifth considers political participation as a behavioral manifestation of political culture.

POLITICAL CULTURE IN DEMOCRACIES

The practical and interpretive difficulties of making comparisons across cultures are considerable. Such inherent problems have restricted most cross-national survey research comparing political cultures to a few developed, democratic countries with relatively similar political systems. For the same reasons, studies of political culture have often been confined to single counties. In Canada, for example, studies have concluded that Canadians, like those of most developed democracies, share many fundamental values. **Values** are shared beliefs that provide standards of judgment about what is right, important, and desirable in society. They are deeply held convictions. Though generally taken for granted and not articulated, widely accepted values about what is good and worthwhile set the boundaries of acceptable behaviour and underlie citizens' attitudes toward specific political goals. They provide guidelines for defining what is right or wrong, what is, or is not, valuable or acceptable. Some of the overarching values that bring Canadians together include traditions of personal freedom and civil liberties, respect for the law, and a belief in the peaceful coexistence of heterogeneous communities. Many of these political values are even enshrined in the Constitution.

National Identity

A sense of **national identity**—of attachment or loyalty to the state and its institutions—provides the spiritual glue that helps keep countries united. The degree to which it is manifested varies significantly among states. When citizens have a weak national identity, states tend to be less stable and effective politically than when such attachment is strong. For this reason, leaders of new and developing countries try to promote a sense of national identity among their people, encouraging them to think in terms of belonging to the larger state unit rather than smaller units such as provinces or regions. As we shall see below, there are a number of ways political leaders can promote a strong national identity through development and promotion of unifying symbols such as flags, anthems, military decorations, military parades, and so on.

As we noted in the last chapter, the extent to which citizens appreciate the political institutions of their country has practical ramifications. When citizens accept the legitimacy of their state, there exists a stable political environment and a significant barrier to violent change. In recent years the world has witnessed the violent disintegration of several states that were unable to maintain a strong national identity in the face of ethnic or religious division. In Lebanon, for example, the larger state was torn apart by groups determined to identify themselves primarily as "Muslim," "Christian," or "Palestinian." In Nigeria, Ibo tribesmen sought to break away and form their own country of Biafra; they failed but much blood was shed. And in the former Yugoslavia, ethnic and religious divisions created a bloody civil war that United Nations peacekeepers were helpless to prevent. The conflict continues in Kosovo.

Trust

A sense of **trust**, or a general belief in the honesty and veracity of people outside the immediate family, including neighbours, acquaintances, and also individuals involved in politics, is required as an underpinning to successful, stable political systems. The degree of trust in society varies widely among states. Social trust is the basis of confidence in political institutions. A government needs a degree of voluntary compliance to its laws and directives. Where such compliance is high, the government need only exercise minimal force to carry out its activities and does not, as a matter of policy, need to resort to having individuals imprisoned or tortured because of subversive activities. The public's expression of trust in political institutions varies, depending on the popularity of the politicians in power, or major events such as war or external threats to the state, but throughout such events trust remains an important indicator of political stability.[2]

Political Efficacy

Political efficacy, the extent to which individual citizens feel they can affect political decisions, varies a great deal among and within states, ranging from apathy to activism. For example, Almond and Verba's study, *The Civic Culture*, found higher levels of political efficacy in Great Britain and the United States than in the former West Germany, Italy, and Mexico. It also found that differences among different educational groups *within* those states (except Great Britain) were even greater than the overall differences *between* states.[3] Within states generally, more highly educated individuals feel considerably more efficacious than those with only primary education; and consequently, as a group, they participate more in politics than the less educated who are more passive.[4] Political efficacy, therefore, is intimately related to political participation. The aim of most political participation is to influence the selection or actions of political rulers.[5] Differences in kind and rate of participation among democratic and authoritarian countries are discussed in the last section of this chapter.

The Civic Culture

A strong national identity, trust in one's compatriots, and a degree of political efficacy, then, are basic ingredients of a stable society. Almond and Verba used these concepts to identify the type of political culture that would be most conducive to sustaining a liberal democracy. This ideal culture, they concluded, would be a **civic culture**—a blend of three pure types of culture that they identified as participant, parochial, and subject cultures (see Figure 7.1). **Participant political cultures** are highly efficacious—citizens believe that political decisions affect their lives and that they can contribute to their political system. In **parochial political cultures**, on the other hand, people are distanced from their national government to such an extent that they feel it has nothing to do with them. The state does not penetrate deeply into such societies. Citizens in **subject political cultures** do not feel efficacious either. They view themselves simply as subjects whose lives are directed by a political process above them.

Almond and Verba concluded that a participant political culture was vital to a stable democracy, but they also posited that it was best if there was also a degree of parochial and subject culture. Citizens would therefore participate but at the same time would leave much of political decision-making to their elites. They would willingly give legitimacy to the decisions of the elite even if they did not agree with them. Such a balance between governmental power and governmental responsiveness, they said, was necessary to maintain a stable democracy.[6]

Critics of the civic culture concept point out that there is no proof that a civic culture *causes* a stable democracy. It might, in fact, be the other way round: a stable government may create a civic culture. They point out that given the diversity of subcultures of class and ethnicity in most countries, one cannot identify a national culture that would be any more accurate than the stereotype that national character studies offer. For their part, Marxists consider political culture to be the outcome of the efforts of the dominant classes to legitimize their social and economic power over the masses. Marxists consider that national identity is fostered simply to create a sense of unity across the social classes. In spite of such criticisms, however, Almond and Verba's *Civic Culture* study remains highly respected and essentially unrefuted.

The third wave of new democracies in the period after Portugal's authoritarian regime was forced out of office by the military in 1974 provided a test for the importance of civic culture in promoting stable democracy. Despite some evidence that they lacked a civic culture, a large number of countries became democratic in Latin America, Eastern

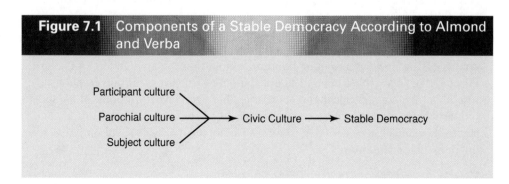

Figure 7.1 Components of a Stable Democracy According to Almond and Verba

Participant culture

Parochial culture   ⟶   Civic Culture   ⟶   Stable Democracy

Subject culture

Europe, and to a smaller extent in Africa and Asia. However, many have proven to be extremely fragile, which indicates that an establishment or consolidation of democracy requires the masses to believe in democracy for its own sake and not only for its offers of better economic and social performance.[7] In other words, a set of attitudes about governing similar to that found in the civic culture pattern is required for the long-term stability of democratic institutions. As indicated in Close Up 7.1 many culture studies today are focusing on the concept of civil society which accomodates this idea.

INTERNATIONAL POLITICAL CULTURES

Religion is one of the most important forces that shape political culture, but it is not necessarily limited by state boundaries. Religion has played an important role in the evolution of civilizations and the founding of many states. As well, it has provided moral principles that underlie basic cultural values such as trust, compassion, justice, and honesty. Religions throughout history have provided a social order necessary for human survival; they encouraged people to integrate and live together cooperatively—to repress individual instinctual drives in favour of the good of the community. They provided a force

---

CLOSE UP 7.1   Civil Society

The study of political culture has, in recent years, been enhanced by the concept "civil society." **Civil society** refers to the social and economic arrangements that counterbalance the powers of the state by providing an alternative source of power and prestige to that offered by the state itself. They include a complex web of "intermediate institutions"—private groups that exist between the state and the family. They include associations such as charities, book clubs, volunteer agencies, human rights chapters, and so on, that help create public-spirited citizens. They exist outside of the state and exercise restraint on it. According to proponents of the civil society argument, democracy grows from the grass roots of society upward through these intermediate structures of community life.

In the West, liberal, pluralist, scientifically-oriented modern states have created civil societies based on several centuries of religious upheaval and economic and technological change. On the other hand, the Soviet Union crushed or stifled civil society in many countries in Eastern Europe and inside its own borders. Since the habits and attitudes that a liberal democracy depends on were destroyed in these countries, the new leaders must build or rebuild them. Many leaders in Eastern Europe, thus, want to go beyond establishing new governments and create a culture able to sustain political and economic liberalism. Western political leaders, too, are expressing the need to revitalize civil society in their own countries and across the globe. It is evident that countries cannot build a civil society simply by rebuilding their economies.[8]

for social integration, a "universal" family for believers. They help preserve family values and provide continuity of these values between generations. As well, early systems of law originated with religions, establishing the notion that individuals are equal before a god and divine laws. Secular laws later amended this assertion so that all persons "are considered equal before the laws of man."

Cultural "Families"

In some parts of the world, political culture is based primarily on a cultural force (such as Confucianism) that can underlie a variety of religions. Samuel P. Huntington has identified nine cultural families which encompass a great many of the world's countries: Nordic, Latin, Arab, Slavic, Indian, Sinic, Japanese, Malay, and African.[9] To this list we add Jewish culture (see Table 7.1). Huntington relates these cultural families to the principal religions that provide many of the important ideals, aspirations, and goals of the countries or regions. Some states, of course, do not fit any of these categories exactly. However, Huntington estimates that at least 85% of the world's population is in national societies that fit reasonably well into one of his categories.[10] Since cultural differences among and within countries are important for the political analysis of states, Huntington says political scientists should ask whether each of these cultural group-

Table 7.1 Cultures, Religions, and Regions		
Culture	**Principal Religion**	**Region/Countries**
Arab	Islam	North Africa, Middle East
Indian	Hinduism	India
Japanese	Confucianism/Buddhism/Shinto	Japan
Jewish	Judaism	Israel
Latin	Catholicism	Southern Europe, Latin America
Malay	Islam/Buddhism/Catholicism	Malaysia, Indonesia
Nordic	Protestantism	Northwest Europe, British settler countries, America
Slavic	Orthodox	Eastern Europe, Russia
Sinic	Confucianism	China, Taiwan, Korea, Singapore, Vietnam
African	Christianity/Paganism	Africa south of the Sahara

Source: Adapted from Samuel P. Huntington "The Goals of Development" in Myron Weiner and Samuel P. Huntington, *Understanding Political Development* (Boston: Little, Brown, 1987), p. 24

ings has its own pattern of political and economic development and goal achievement. He suggests that cultural identity may be the single most important factor in predicting the extent to which any one country "was likely to achieve growth, equity, democracy, stability and autonomy."[11]

Huntington goes on to point out that the ideal image of developed Western society is to be wealthy, equitable, democratic, stable, and autonomous, but that for countries with different cultures the image of a good society may be quite different—for example a good society may be considered one that is simple, austere, hierarchical, authoritarian, disciplined, and martial. Western goals therefore may not provide a meaningful model for a modern Islamic, Confucian, Pagan, or Hindu society. He suggests that the time may have come to "stop trying to change these societies and to change the model, to develop models of a modern Islamic, Confucian or Hindu society that would be more relevant to countries where those cultures prevail."

We consider next the impact of three of these belief systems—Christianity, Islam, and Confucianism—on national political cultures.

Christianity

About one in four people in the world belong to religious organizations.[12] Christianity is the largest religion today; nearly 33% of those with religious affiliations belong to a Christian church. The Christian Church was founded by followers of Jesus Christ, known also as Jesus of Nazareth. Jesus, born between 6 and 4 B.C., and crucified about A.D. 28, was considered by them to be the Messiah predicted by the Old Testament prophets.

Over time, the Christian Church has divided into many different branches. In Europe, the basic division of Christians has been between Protestants and Roman Catholics. Protestantism had an immense impact on the countries of the north; the Roman Catholic Church exercised most influence in the south. Both Protestant and Catholic churches sent missionaries throughout the world. In 1900 about two-thirds of the world's 500 million Christians lived in the United States and Europe. However, the centre of Christianity has changed. By the year 2000, two-thirds of the world's two billion Christians will live in South America, Africa, and Asia. Missionaries now come mainly from the LDCs.

In communist states, the Communist party and ideology fills many of the same functions as religion. It even offers elements of salvation as in Christianity. As we shall see in the next chapter, instead of a god, the "dialectic of history" provides an inescapable historical plan and promises the perfection of the historical process. Utopia, in communist terms, is the inevitable withering away of the state, with complete equality for all individuals. Between 1989 and 1993, belief in the communist ideology disintegrated in many European communist states, along with the regimes that had supported them. Christians and Muslims scrambled to fill the vacuum. After decades of persecution, Orthodox Christianity and other kinds of missionary activity have reemerged from Russia to Romania and Albania to provide moral teaching and strengthen national identity (see Close Up 7.2).

CLOSE UP 7.2   Religion in Albania

The case of Albania illustrates the impact that the fall of communism has had on religious life in the countries of Eastern Europe. In 1967 the tiny communist state of Albania proclaimed itself the first official atheist state despite the fact that 70% of the population had historically followed the principles of Sunni Muslim and that there were Greek Orthodox and Roman Catholic minorities. Just over two decades later, after the collapse of communism, missionaries poured into the country. Ninety orthodox churches reopened, several hundred Catholic churches were built along with over 500 mosques. By 1995 there were 12 orthodox priests in the country, as well as about 450 missionaries from 70 evangelical churches (mostly American), 200 Roman Catholic nuns, 80 Catholic priests, and several hundred mullahs from the Gulf states. In 1992 the Albanian government became the first European country to join the Islamic Conference of Nations.

Islam

The second largest religion in the world, in terms of both the number of adherents and the number of countries where it is professed by the majority of the population, is Islam. There are about 850 million Muslims in the world. Most followers of Islam are in the Arab states of the Middle East, however there are substantial numbers in 21 other countries including Indonesia, countries of North Africa, and Central Asia including Pakistan, Afghanistan, and three of the newly independent states of the former Soviet Union.

In most countries today, church and state are separate institutions, with religious leaders exercising varying degrees of influence on the behaviour of citizens, political leaders, and policy issues. However, in some parts of the world, religion is the driving force of political institutions as well as the backbone of cultures. The church and the state are one, and religious law governs both government institutions and the political rights of individuals. This is the case in Iran where the spiritual leader is also the head of state, and Shiite clerics fill all political offices. Islam does not coexist easily with democracy. The mullahs hold that any system which places the will of the people above the will of Allah destroys the soul and the nation. Powerful religious parties manipulate largely illiterate populations in much of Africa, the Middle East, and Central Asia.

Islam is the religion of Mohammed (A.D. 570–632), who claimed to be the true prophet of God among the Arab people, the last of the prophets and successor to Jesus. The adherents of Islam, called Muslims, follow the revelations and teachings of Mohammed as contained in the Koran. After the death of Mohammed, Arabs from the Arabian peninsula carried the faith of Islam through the Middle East, across North Africa and into Spain. Islam reached into the Balkans and Eastern Europe, establishing great civilizations and making significant cultural, artistic, and scientific achievements. The three principal languages of the Islamic tradition were Arabic, Persian, and Turkish.

Today, there are 21 Arab states including Palestine. They include about 200 million people, or 5% of the world's population. Another 6 million Arabs live outside the Arab states. About 10% of all muslims are members of the ideologically oriented Shiah sect. Shiites are concentrated mainly in Iran and Iraq. The vast majority of Muslims are Sunnites, or Sunnis. They include most Muslims among the Turks, Arabians, Afghans, North Africans, and East Indians.

The Turkish, Iranian, and Arab nationalisms which developed during the late nineteenth and twentieth centuries never wholly superseded the bonds of Islam. During that time secular nationalisms developed in the Arab world, but nationalists often drew on Islam as a source of cultural strength to oppose encroachments of the West.[13] Even

Map 7.1   Middle East

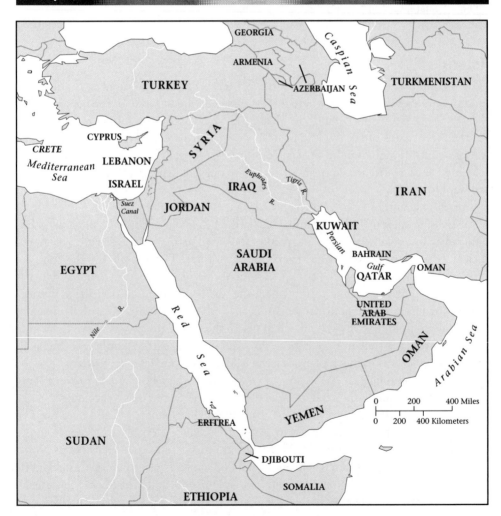

today, pan-Arab nationalism and Islamic faith are often called on in times of crisis to mobilize the population across national borders. President Saddam Hussein of Iraq called in vain for a *jihad*, or holy war, against the UN forces when they declared war on Iraq in 1991 after his troops had invaded Kuwait.

In 1999, Islam is exercising a profound effect inside the Middle East, and also in Africa and Central Asia. Iran, Sudan, and Afghanistan have adopted Islamic administrations, and Algeria, Egypt, and Turkey could follow. Islamic movements are active in the Palestinian territories, Lebanon, Jordan, the Gulf, and across northern and Central Africa.

Throughout the 1980s, after the Shah of Iran was ousted in 1979 and replaced by a vehemently anti-Western Islamic regime, Iran was a showcase of Islamic fundamentalist rule. However, by 1994, popular dissent with the rule by the mullahs was raising calls for the Islamic clerics to step down so free elections could be held. As we noted in Chapter 5, Iran now has an elected President, and the Assembly of Experts—clerics who advise the Supreme Religious guide—was elected for the first time in 1998. Pressures for change continue, but religious structures still dominate in Iran.

In some predominantly Muslim countries today (e.g., Algeria and Egypt) outlawed political parties formed by fundamentalist groups are engaging in violence against secular authorities. In others, the fundamentalists are playing by the rules of the game and being coopted by a secular political system.[14] In Turkey's 1991 municipal elections for example, the secular republic faced its first electoral losses to Islamic fundamentalists since it was established by Ataturk in 1924. In the December 1995 national elections, the Islamic Welfare Party won the biggest share of the vote and 158 of the 550 seats in Parliament. Turkey faced a period of political turbulence as some of the country's main secular parties agreed to share government with the pro-Islamic Welfare party, (see Close Up 7.3).

There are now 25 countries where the population is expected to be more than 90% Muslim by the year 2000.[15] With the collapse of the Soviet Union in 1991, Iran moved to fill the political and religious vacuum left by the Communist party and its ideology in several of the southern republics including Kazakhstan, Tajikistan, and Azerbaijan. The slow march of Islamic fundamentalism is also eroding the traditional political patterns of authoritarianism, socialism, and military rule in the region of the Sahara. In the inland states of Mali, Chad, and the Sudan, despotic authoritarianism is being replaced by fundamentalism, as if the dry ergs (lakes of sand) in the Sahara region were being slowly replaced by water.[16] In the littoral states of Mauritania, Morocco, Algeria, and Tunisia, traditional political forms are also being challenged by the persuasive, egalitarian ideology of this religious movement.

In Algeria, Islamists fought alongside secular liberation fighters to achieve that country's independence in 1962. Until 1988 they were content to let the National Liberation Front (FLN) rule the country as an Islamic state with a Marxist-oriented government. Government actions in 1988, however, led to a rise in Islamic fundamentalism and the Islamic Salvation Front (FIS). The FIS swept the initial round of Algeria's first multi-party election in 1991 but a military takeover deprived them of victory. This

> ### CLOSE UP 7.3   Background to Religion and Secularism in Turkey
>
> Turkey is 99% Muslim, yet it is a secular state. After World War I, Turkey was defeated and partitioned. However, Mustafa Kemal rallied the Turkish military, drove out the occupying forces, and took political control. The next year he founded the Republic of Turkey in 1923 from the ruins of the 600-year-old Ottoman Empire. Kemal abolished Islamic-based laws and separated church and state in Turkey. In doing so he paved the way for peaceful coexistence of the Muslim factions and liberated women to participate openly and freely in society. Mustafa Kemal was given the name Ataturk (father of the Turks) by the national assembly.
>
> Today, Turkey's 15 million Alawis, who are Shiah Muslims, are particularly fearful of a resurgence of Islamic fundamentalism and renewed persecution from the country's 40 million Sunni population. The military sees itself as the guardian of the secular state, and has a strong say in the National Security Council, the senior policy-making body. It engineered the overthrow of Turkey's first Islamic-oriented government in 1997 and banned the pro-Islamic Welfare Party. Welfare's successor, the Virtue Party, was a leading contender in the general election in 1999. The military tried to delay the election date but it went ahead and the Virtue Party did poorly.
>
> In such a circumstance, should the Turkish military intervene to maintain a secular government, or should it support a democratically elected, pro-Islamic party's right to govern?

gave rise to radical Islamic movements, the Armed Islamic Group and the Islamic Salvation Army, which joined forces to battle Algeria's military government. Violence and massacres continue. Military-supported candidates won the presidential election in 1995 and the parliamentary elections in 1997.[17]

The change caused by Islamic fundamentalism in many countries is so pervasive and all-encompassing that social traditions and political forms are being swept aside in its wake. In Afghanistan, for example, the Taliban consolidated their control of the state by 1996. Their take-over followed ten years of brutal Soviet occupation and then seven years of civil war. The Taliban's edicts are all-encompassing, and violators are treated summarily and brutally. When government is based on "God's word" it cannot be challenged.

Even moderate fundamentalists espouse practices that many in the West find difficult to accept, especially curbs on freedom of expression and the segregation of women. At best, Islamic movements aspire to a just society without exploitation where obedience to God's teachings as recorded in the Koran is the rule. It represents compassion, hope, order. Veiled women are free from sexual attack. At worst, however, it means religious intolerance. Throughout North Africa, women have been killed for not wearing prescribed head covering. In Turkey, Egypt, and Algeria nonconforming districts have been bombed. Individuals who dare to criticize fundamentalist teachings or actions, like British author Salman Rushdi, are sentenced to death (see Close Up 7.4).

CLOSE UP 7.4   Actions of an Islamic Fundamentalist Government

In 1989 the late Ayatollah Ruhollah Khomeini broadcast a "fatwa" (religious decree) on Teheran radio concerning author Salman Rushdie:

> I inform the proud Muslim people of the world that the author of *The Satanic Verses* book, which is against Islam, the Prophet, and the Koran, and all involved in its publication are sentenced to death.

The author, a citizen of Britain, was forced to live in hiding until 1998 when the leaders of Iran, anxious to receive Western approval, dissociated the government from the fatwa and a $2.5 million bounty placed on Mr. Rushdie's head by a radical religious foundation in Iran. However, under Iranian law the government has no authority to revoke a fatwa, and defiant hardliners claimed that all Muslims are still duty-bound to execute the sentence on Rushdie. Even though it wants to improve relations with the West, the Iranian government can do little in the face of the fundamentalist backlash.

Confucianism

For centuries, Confucianism has been a cultural force in Asia where it has had a particularly powerful impact on politics. Confucianism is a Chinese political and moral philosophy based on the teachings of the scholar Confucius (551–479 B.C.) who advised rulers that they could obtain stable government by instilling correct moral behaviour in both rulers and the ruled. Confucianism is not a religion—in fact it is agnostic in outlook. It is, however, compatible with formal religions and political philosophies, and this important fact assisted its spread throughout Asia. It still permeates politics and society and has been called "the ideology par excellence of state cohesion."[18]

Confucianism was the official creed of China in the second century B.C.—a guide for statecraft and moral instruction. It became the official state belief system for the Han dynasty in 136 B.C. and dominated Chinese political and ethical thought until the early twentieth century.[19] As an abstract guide to a way of life, it stresses management of society through a carefully defined system of social and familial relationships. It teaches that each person has a role to understand and perform obediently. Sons are subservient to fathers, wives to husbands, and subjects to rulers. As the highest authority, rulers must set a moral example by a pure spirit and manners above reproach. If the ruler has good thoughts and is utterly sincere, good government will follow. When things go wrong, it is an indication that rulers have not been sincere. The emphasis on right thinking remains important in China today, even though Confucianism has been replaced by Marxist thought as the state orthodoxy. Today, the government emphasizes the need for revolutionary, pure thoughts.

Confucianism as a cultural tradition is extremely varied. Each Asian country developed its own distinctive version, and these diverged further as the countries modernized, modifying the doctrinal teachings of Confucianism without eliminating its essence.[20] In this way the evolution of Confucianism contributed to distinct political cultures.[21] Strands of Confucian culture are visible throughout Asia and are said to be conducive to economic achievement. Some cultural characteristics and socialization patterns of Confucianism have significant political consequences. They include the following six important aspects.

- *Respect for authority*—Hierarchy is important. All social relations are structured by the status of subordinate and superior (child to parent, subject to ruler, etc.) and due respect and obedience are necessary. There is a translation of loyalty and obedience from family to state.
- *Loyalty and obedience*—These are primary virtues from the family grouping outward.[22]
- *Closely knit family*—Good treatment of old people is maintained through extended families, where they are honoured and respected.
- *Less emphasis on the individual*—There is a "family self" which "promotes the feeling that what shames the child shames the family."[23]
- *Dissent is a sign of weakness*—Consensus is highly respected, protests are rare.
- *Absolutism is honoured*—There is a long history of absolutist dynasties in Asia.

The effects of Confucian thought on some Asian economies are apparent: economic activities are relatively less conflictive than in the West; only a low proportion of the work force is unionized; there is low unemployment; there is low inflation; and GNP growth is comparatively high. Some political scientists speculate that this positive economic performance can at least partially be attributed to cultural characteristics including "ambition for self and family; high value on education and learning by copying exemplars; frugality; the family as an economic unit; and entrepreneurship."[24] See Map 7.2, Southeast Asia.

The tiny city-state of Singapore illustrates the relation between Confucianism, culture, and politics. When Lee Kuan Yew was elected Prime Minister in 1959, Singapore's future was uncertain. Its two-year federation with Malaysia had collapsed and many doubted Singapore's ability to exist as an independent nation. Today, however, 2.7 million Singaporeans enjoy one of the highest living standards in Asia. Yet the Western goal of democracy played little role in this remarkable transition. Lee's 31-year leadership was based on strict, authoritarian methods. He did not believe that democracy had a place in his country, or anywhere in the developing world, because, he said, checks and balances interfere with governing in a developing country, "where executive action must be swift to forestall disorder."[25] In the three decades in which he transformed Singapore, the tightly controlled structure which he crafted rested heavily on his own incorruptibility and "the innate entrepreneurship and pragmatism of the ethnic-Chinese majority and its Confucian father-knows-best ethic."[26] In late 1990, Lee Kuan Yew installed his protégé, Goh Chok Tong, as Prime Minister, but Lee remains a force in Singapore's political life. Authoritarian capitalism still directs the thriving Singapore economy.

As Samuel Huntington argues, "Islamic, Sinic, African, Latin, and other societies have developed in very different ways. It is hard to see much convergence among them

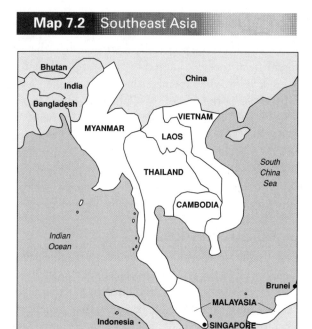

Map 7.2 Southeast Asia

in their patterns of development between the 1950s and the 1980s or between any one of them and the commonly accepted Western pattern (which is largely a Nordic pattern)."[27] He points out that in 1962 Ghana and South Korea were virtually identical in terms of economy. Thirty years later, the South Korean economy was booming while Ghana's was stagnant. The divergence was not predictable in terms of economic or political variables, but cultural differences provided very different environments and probably were an important factor in accounting for the differences in development.

Japan is another example where religion and Confucianism exercise an important influence on politics. A democratic form of government was introduced there after its defeat and occupation at the end of World War II. However evidence of Confucian influence is still to be found in political and social relations. Characteristics such as obedience, achievement, and respect for authority are important in Japanese society, and are reinforced by intense competition in national examinations for students at all levels of education and by loyalty to corporations in the work place. The Japanese culture includes both Buddhist and Shinto religions, which inspire habits of cleanliness and extraordinary discipline, and are often credited with playing a significant role in the Japanese economic "miracle." It is common, for example, for priests and engineers to gather in a ceremony outside a temple to burn pictures of worn-out computer chips to thank the chips and other electronic devices for their uncomplaining service.[28] The Japanese culture is basically consensual—an attitude considered vital in the conduct of political parties and cabinet formation.[29]

SUBCULTURES AND POLITICAL CULTURE

Subcultures within a society become politically relevant when the attitudes and values they hold are different from those promoted by the state and shared by the majority. Serious consequences develop when members become strong enough to challenge the overall political culture. Since the end of the Cold War, international hostilities have relaxed and there has been a corresponding rise of ethnic rivalry and escalating demands within states. Ethnic intolerance is surfacing on a scale unseen since the period before World War I. The Soviet Union and Yugoslavia disintegrated in the wake of challenges by ethnic minorities. In addition, extremist political parties, which advocate policies such as deporting citizens of different colour and ethnic heritage, are gaining strength in many European countries and also to some degree in North America.

Ethno–Linguistic Subcultures

We noted in the last chapter that ethnicity is primarily a subjective phenomenon, although it usually is reinforced by the presence of objective traits such as different languages dialects, customs, and/or cultural heritage, and often distinct racial or physical characteristics. Ethnicity is reinforced by historical experiences that are unique to each particular ethnic group or subculture and which create a complex of shared values. Ethnic diversity, when combined with region, religion, and language differences, can be a powerful force that may tear a state apart.

In only about half of the world's states do more than 75% of the population speak the same language. Few states consist, as does Japan, of basically a single ethnic group with a single language. The political manifestations of ethno-linguistic subcultures typically appear in a range of behaviour from bloc voting and separate political parties to separatist movements. Many states, such as Canada, contain aspiring nations within them (see Close Up 7.5). The politicization of demands to redraw state borders along ethnic lines frequently results in highly emotional and even violent conflict.

Closely related to ethnicity are issues of race. **Race** is "an arbitrary social category, consisting of persons who share such inherited physical characteristics as skin colour and facial features, which characteristics are charged with social meaning in some societies."[30] **Racial discrimination** is the imposition of handicaps, barriers, or different treatment on individuals solely because of their race. Behavioral and psychological differences are attributed to the genetic nature of a racial grouping. History is replete with examples—there has been discrimination of gentiles against Jews, whites against blacks, Japanese against Koreans, and so on—on the unwarranted basis that a particular "race" is inherently inferior or that one's own is superior.[31] Racial conflicts tend to become political, with discriminators trying to enact legislation against the discriminated, and encountering group protests, anti-discrimination movements, and affirmative-action groups taking the opposite stand. Racist ideologies such as Nazism have served as rationalizations for even the extermination of minority groups.

CLOSE UP 7.5   Ethnic Nationalism in Canada

Canada's confederation arrangement in 1867 was essentially a bargain between the French and English in British North America to create one strong political unit that would protect the rights and assist the advancement of two culturally diverse peoples. It was on this basis that linguistic duality was embedded in the Constitution. This duality has consistently evoked social and political tensions between French- and English-speaking Canadians. At the same time, however, the establishment of two official languages has provided one of Canada's most distinctive traits and, for many, enriches the experience of being Canadian.

In the province of Quebec, however, the fear that French language and culture is threatened in Canada, or may soon be, is used by Quebec nationalists to create insecurity and rally support. Historical defeats and injustices are magnified and mythologized to build an invisible wall around the French-speaking community and encourage separatism. In 1995, a referendum calling for the eventual independence of Quebec was narrowly defeated (50.6 to 49.4%). Shortly thereafter, Lucien Bouchard, the new premier of Quebec vowed to continue the struggle to separate Quebec from Canada. In November 1998 he led the Parti Québécois to another victory.

A classic example of a very complex multi-ethnic society in which issues of race and ethnicity are highly politicized is India. It has a caste system—a hereditary system, delineated in terms of certain occupations, rules of marriage, and rules of interaction with other castes—which dates back to the origins of Hinduism more than 2000 years ago.[32] Hindus make up about 83% of India's 850 million people; 11% are Muslim, 3% are Christian, and 2% are Sikh. There are also Jain, Buddhist, and other minorities.[33] These ethnic and religious differences are reinforced by different languages. The constitution of India recognizes 14 major languages, and hundreds of other languages and dialects are spoken in the rural areas.[34]

The Hindu population is divided further into four main castes which contain hundreds of sub-castes based on descending levels of ritual purity. Within the broad caste groups are *jati* – the thousands of occupation-based groups. The jati observe strict rules about social contact and intermarriage.[35]

Brahmins (12%) are the highest caste, traditionally the caste of Hindu priests, now found in most professions; *Kshatriyas* (13%) are soldiers, governors, and landowners; *Vaishyas* are tradespeople and farmers; and *Shudras* are the service castes or artisans including land tillers, barbers, craftspeople, and menial labourers (25% combined). Over time, an underclass also emerged. The *Harijan* (Untouchables), who are outcasts, and tribes who belong to none of the castes, make up the remaining 50% of Hindus. Caste discrimination begins early in life and extends to all parts of life; untouchables are often barred from wells and temples and live in the semi-slavery of debt-bonded labour.

Attempts to eliminate even some of the worst injustices of the Indian caste system regularly meet with resistance and create significant political ramifications. In 1990, for example, Indian students staged violent protests over the Prime Minister's proposal to raise the number of government jobs reserved for so-called "backward castes" from 22% to 49%. The students wanted to keep favoured access to the 18 million jobs provided by the government.[36]

The existence of different subcultures can have serious and violent consequences for the politics of a country. One Indian subculture, the Sikh population, which is differentiated from the Hindu majority by ethnic, linguistic, and religious differences, has been in and out of the international news spotlight in recent years as it has struggled to create a separate state of its own. Historically, the Sikh separatist movement makes an interesting comparison with the creation of Pakistan—a state with a Muslim majority—which was founded in the wake of Indian independence from Britain in 1947.

The Indian Sikh population is heavily concentrated in the north of the country, in an area known as the *Punjab*, and is relatively prosperous economically. The struggle for independence in this region has led to violence several times by Sikh extremists and more violence in anti-separatist backlashes. In 1984, for example, Sikh extremists occupied the Golden Temple in Amritsar. The recapture of the temple by the Indian army led to many deaths. Also that same year Prime Minister Indira Gandhi was assassinated by her Sikh bodyguards, and the anti-Sikh riots that followed caused over 1000 deaths. The struggle also reached the level of international terrorism with the bombing of one Air India plane and the attempted bombing of a second, both taking off from Canadian airports on June 22, 1985.

Even in states with relatively homogeneous societies, there are ethnic divisions. Japan has one of the most homogeneous societies in the world, yet there, too, racism is embedded in parts of society. A group called the *burakumin* (hamlet people), who are racially identical to most other Japanese were, until the middle of the last century, held to be legally inferior to other citizens.[37] They number about 3 million people in a total Japanese population of more than 123 million. The *burakumin* had untouchable status, which originated centuries ago from "unclean" jobs such as handling leather or burying the dead. Japan has an elaborate system of permanent official records of ancestry so that it is almost impossible for a *burakumin* to conceal his or her origins, to work for major companies, or to marry outside of the caste.

Authoritarian states normally try to destroy or forcibly subjugate regional and ethnic subcultures within their borders to the dominant culture. There are many examples. The former Soviet Union excelled at forcing distinctive subcultures underground. After disintegration of the Union in 1991, however, it quickly became apparent that subculture identities had not been destroyed, and in many cases had become defiant towards Russia. Today, China imposes strong controls over Tibetan culture, making sure that Tibetan children learn the standard communist Chinese version of history—that Tibet was "peacefully liberated" by China in 1951. However, Tibetans carefully guard elements of local culture including language and the Buddhist religion.

Women and Political Culture

Of the world's five and a half billion people, slightly fewer than half are female.[38] The 1980s witnessed an unprecedented politicization of women in many of the world's states. In many countries today, young women can aspire to be elected political leaders, to assume leadership positions in law, medicine, education, business, or the sciences. They can enter occupations from architecture to firefighting that were closed to their mothers only a few years earlier.

Around the world and throughout history, however, women have often been treated as inferiors to men. Discrimination has been enforced by social customs and laws. As the bearers of children, endowed with less obvious physical strength than men, women have been assigned, and have generally accepted, primary responsibility for children and the family. Until relatively recently, even in developed countries, women have been barred from such societal participation as owning property, holding public office, and voting.

Until the last decade there was little hard evidence to back up claims of women's relative deprivation, because statistics that were collected tended to ignore the contributions of women to the family and the economy. Since 1991, however, statistical portraits and analyses of the situation of women have been released by the United Nations, providing comparative information on the condition of women around the world. The profile of women in terms of education and training is instructive and revealing.

Around the world, both households and governments spend fewer resources to educate and train girls than boys, reducing the potential social, economic, and political contribution of women to society, and leaving women at a disadvantage in making major life decisions. Womens' ability is therefore not translated into recognized economic contributions to society.

The UN study shows that in much of the world women have progressed toward equal educational enrollment rates with men. Primary education has been accepted as a fundamental goal by all countries, and enrollment of girls in primary and secondary schools is now comparable to that of boys in most countries except those in southern Asia and sub-Saharan Africa.[39] (See Figure 7.2.) The 1998 *Human Development Report* confirms that gender gaps in education have continued to narrow as education levels—especially for females in developing countries—have been steadily rising.[40]

At the university and college level, female enrollment is also increasing around the world. In the developed regions, western Asia, some countries of southern Africa, and in Latin America and the Caribbean, gender enrollment is now nearly equal. However in other regions, such as sub-Saharan Africa, southern Asia, the Pacific region, and some countries such as China and Indonesia, female percentages are lower. Although equality is being achieved in enrollments, it will take considerably longer to reach parity in male and female literacy rates. To be classed as literate in the UN study, a person must be able to read and write, with understanding, a short, simple statement about everyday life. Illiteracy rates are falling for young women, but they are still much higher than for men. Literacy is a better measure of education than enrollment in developing regions since it usually indicates a minimal level of successfully completed schooling.

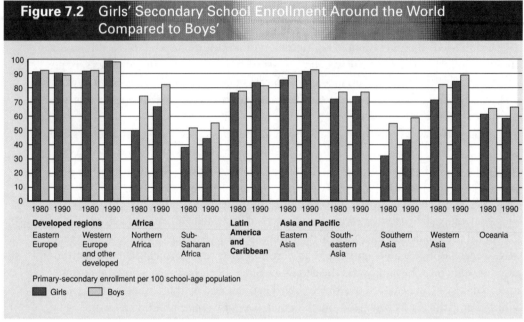

Figure 7.2   Girls' Secondary School Enrollment Around the World Compared to Boys'

Source: *The World's Women 1995* (New York: United Nations, 1995), p. 92.

Most Western states acknowledged women's right to vote around the time of World War I. Women in the communist states of the former Soviet Union and China were awarded new roles in the work place about that same time, but still only about 10 to 20% of the members of the prestigious Communist Party of the Soviet Union were women. As in the Western democracies, most were employed in the lower echelons of society. After the collapse of the Soviet Union and the traumatic shift to a capitalist economy, women were the first to lose their jobs, and many of the gains they had made were lost. In 1995, more than two-thirds of Russia's unemployed were women. The average woman earned only 40% as much as the average man, compared to 75% in 1991.[41] In China, soon after proclaiming the People's Republic in 1949, Chairman Mao Tse-tung wrote that women should "hold up half the sky" in the new country. It was only rhetoric. Forty-five years later, in 1995, women in Bejing even had trouble holding a news conference announcing the United Nations' World Conference on Women. Eight of nine head table participants at the event were men. The lone woman did not speak and left before the conference was over.

In some countries, particularly theocracies like Iran and Afghanistan today which purport to encompass a complete religious way of life and system of government, women are subject to governmental laws that restrict their freedom profoundly (see Close Up 7.6). In her recent book Geraldine Brooks examines the complex world of women in Islamic countries. She points out that many customs attributed to Islam come from *pre*–Islamic customs, politics, and resistance to modernization.[42] The most notorious of these customs,

CLOSE UP 7.6   A Woman's Life in Saudi Arabia

Saudi Airlines flight 312 from Cairo to Riyadh in the authoritarian monarchy of Saudi Arabia regularly carries at least one young woman decked out in bridal regalia. These young women marry immediately upon arrival. Most of them are poor, and have met their future husbands only once, when their family exchanged them for cash. Once in Saudi Arabia they may be one of four wives. Like other women they will be required to wear a long black robe, the *abaya*, and cover their faces completely. Based on the religious establishment's interpretation of the Koran, women in Saudi Arabia are required to avoid all contact with men other than their fathers, brothers, husband, or sons. This means they cannot work where men work, which means they can hardly work at all. They cannot drive a car. In 1991 when 40 Saudi women protested their lack of right to drive they were all arrested; those with jobs were dismissed and in many cases the women and their husbands were confined to the kingdom for more than two years. The women's names were read from the pulpit of every mosque in the country and all were denounced as "whores."

When asked about the incident, a prince of the royal family is quoted as saying "let's be honest, deep down all men have a macho-sexual complex. They want to control women. It's a question of where to draw the line."[43]

the mutilation of female genitalia, seems to have originated in the Stone Age in central Africa. Today, it is practised by specific groups across the Muslim world and, on occasion, even in North America.

Women are traditionally responsible for the health and well-being of their families, and because of this they participate extensively in community affairs. Although they have been systematically cut off from men's traditional routes to political leadership (see Figure 7.3 for statistics on elected representatives), women in both developed and developing regions have made significant headway in recent years in terms of entering political life through nongovernmental organizations, womens' movements, and associations. Women are increasingly active in the politics of their local communities in such areas as discrimination, poverty, health and environmental issues, violence against women, and peace movements. As of January 1997, the Scandinavian countries and the Netherlands led the world in national parliaments—roughly 30 to 40%. (Canada had 18%.) However, the human development achievements of women fall below those of men in every country.[44]

Routes to power in government decision-making are traditionally through political candidacy and the civil service. Around the world, women are usually more successful in local than national elections. Statistics on women in bureaucratic careers are not generally available, but one pattern is clear: significant numbers of women work at the lower echelons, and their representation dwindles rapidly as pay and status increase.[45] Everywhere there is a need to end occupational segregation and wage discrimination

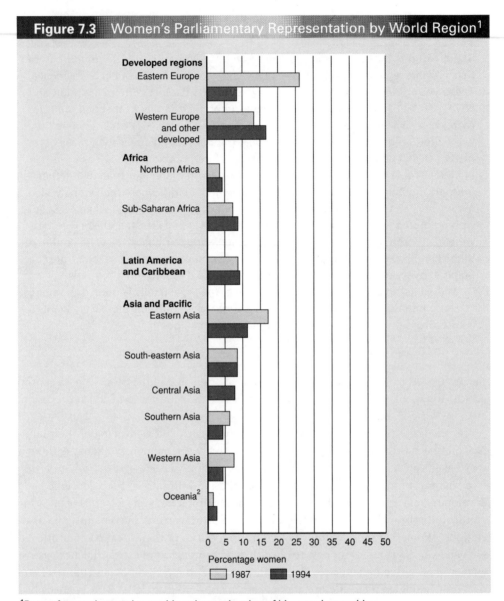

Figure 7.3 Women's Parliamentary Representation by World Region[1]

Developed regions
Eastern Europe

Western Europe
and other
developed

Africa
Northern Africa

Sub-Saharan Africa

Latin America
and Caribbean

Asia and Pacific
Eastern Asia

South-eastern Asia

Central Asia

Southern Asia

Western Asia

Oceania[2]

0   5   10 15 20 25 30 35 40 45 50

Percentage women

☐ 1987   ■ 1994

[1]Data refer to unicameral assembly or lower chamber of bicameral assembly.
[2]Oceania includes Fiji, French Polynesia, Guam, Kiribati, New Caledonia, Pacific Islands, Papua New Guinea, Samoa, Solomon Islands, Tonga, and Vanuatu.
Source: *The World's Women 1995* (New York: United Nations, 1995), p. 154.

and to recognize women's unpaid work as economically productive. The International Women's Movement is playing a major role in developing awareness of these kinds of problems and stimulating political action at national and international levels. Little girls in China may no longer have their feet crushed by foot binding, but female infanticide is not uncommon and prenatal scans enable abortions of female fetuses. Widows in India are still occasionally burnt alive on the funeral pyres of their husbands. Unequal status and discrimination in the LDCs can mean neglect and death. In the West women are more likely to have inferior earnings compared to men and unequal representation in political and decision-making bodies.

The status of women has improved dramatically in the twentieth century, at least in the developed nations, but there is still a long way to go before gender equality will be reached socially and politically. The UN's 1998 *Human Development Report* says that on every continent women work longer hours, earn less money, and are more likely to live in poverty than men. It estimates that 70% of the world's poor are women. In fact, it says that the human development achievements of women fall below those for men in every country.[46]

POLITICAL SOCIALIZATION

Political Socialization in Democratic and Authoritarian States

Political socialization in democracies is indirect and implicit. It is carried out by agents such as families, schools, peer groups, work groups, and the media. Families help to shape the political orientations of children through direct means, such as observational, imitative learning, and also through indirect means such as being part of a particular sociopolitical milieu. The government's role in socialization, too, is usually indirect. Appeals to loyalty and patriotism often fall on deaf ears. In all democracies, however, there is a reliance on the school system to provide basic civic instruction and to integrate immigrants into society. The political systems stress pride in civic affairs, history, and culture. There is a strong emphasis on patriotism and the "goodness" of the country's way of life.

Political culture in authoritarian states is more openly manipulated by political elites than it is in democratic states. For example, in the early stages of their regimes, the communist states of China, the Soviet Union, and Eastern Europe each tried to impose a cultural revolution to buttress industrial and technological revolutions. Primarily through education and persuasion, the political elite tried to create model citizens of a classless, socialist, atheist society.

In authoritarian states, political socialization is more overt and less subtle than in democracies. At the totalitarian extreme it is state controlled. Many authoritarian states try to reduce the influence of the family on their youth, often actively promoting defiance between parents and children. Hitler's youth groups, for example, were encouraged to report to their group leaders about any "disloyal" activities of their parents. Years later, after the collapse of the communist regime in East Germany, authorities discovered proof that the state had forcibly removed the children from families when it had deemed the parents "unfit." Loyal communist families adopted the children.

Authoritarian states attempt to dominate institutions such as schools, political parties, and the military. They forbid churches and educational institutions to voice thoughts that compete with the official line, and they simplify political discourse into slogans which are learned at school and reinforced in youth groups, at work, and in the media.

One of the most extreme examples of this was in Cambodia from 1975 to 1979 when the Khmer Rouge government fractured not just families, but the entire country by forcing individuals back to what they called an "ideologically superior," "primitive" culture. Educated Cambodians were maltreated or murdered; families were broken up and dispersed in an effort to erase historical memory. Ironically, the leaders of the Khmer Rouge had developed their own ideas about ideology in France.[47]

Socialization in communist states is intense and direct, although rarely as extreme as by the Khmer Rouge in Cambodia. Communist countries screen, recruit, and socialize the future ruling elite while they are still young. Older members of the elite endow themselves with prestige, power, and legitimacy and use their position to inculcate respect, obedience, and submission. They set up youth organizations, and extend their influence even beyond these specialized groups into families and schools, mobilizing and teaching young people, and providing a way to select the "best" for leadership positions.

Before its collapse in 1991, the Soviet Union maintained three major organizations to socialize the young in the spirit of communism—the *Octobrists* (boys and girls seven to nine), the *Pioneers* (nine to 14), and finally, the *Komsomol*, or Young Communist League (14 to 28). The Komsomol had extensive control of socializing agents including radio and television programs, special newspapers for Soviet youth, supervision of school curriculum and activities, and leadership of the Pioneers and Octobrists. Membership in the Komsomol served as an apprenticeship and was necessary to become part of even subordinate elite positions.[48]

In the Soviet Union at that same time, the media also served as an important agent of socialization for the Communist Party. A central agency in charge of propaganda assisted party leaders to assess, censor, or present both domestic and foreign news, maintaining total control of communications. All media were controlled by the party, from the daily press to weekly or monthly publications and scientific or literary journals. This monopoly allowed events to be portrayed and interpreted in a uniform fashion, with no conflicting opinions presented.

The study and understanding of history, too, was manipulated in the former USSR. According to historian Edward L. Keenan, now that the Soviet Union has collapsed, much of the content of the standard Soviet culture will be swept away quickly, but the "contrived national histories that were provided to all nationalities by Soviet propagandists will linger on." He elaborated:

> In their modernizing zeal, Soviet administrators invented for many nations still emerging from a traditional culture full-blown national cultures of a nineteenth century type, modeled quite consciously on that of Russia; each nation was assigned, often quite arbitrarily, its heroes, national poets and the like. These were not only artificial; in suppressing authentic national memory, they were mendacious.[49]

The crumbling of the Soviet Union has lent credence to the argument that even extensive control of communications can never be complete, and eventually may create an indifferent and resentful populace. Such efforts at socialization may cause a state to lose, rather than gain, the support it seeks.

Similar patterns of formal socialization still exist in China. When the communists came to power in China following the revolution of 1949, traditional Chinese culture was nearly destroyed by the party's attack on religion, art, and the intelligentsia. The highly centralized Chinese Communist Party (CCP) still maintains its authoritarian command of politics and intellectual life. In 1991, on the seventieth anniversary of the Chinese Communist Party, and as the Soviet Communist Party was falling into disrepute, the aging CCP leadership took the opportunity to enforce enthusiasm for the party. Across China it showed a new movie on the life of Mao; it sent officials back to party school to study Marxism; and it ordered workers to copy in their own hands the latest version of the party's official catechism. In recent years the government has attempted to do the same with the ideas of Deng Ziaoping; today a Mao-Deng philosophy dominates the socialization process.

POLITICAL PARTICIPATION: DEMOCRATIC AND AUTHORITARIAN

A wide range of behaviour can be classified as political participation—from total inactivity, to engaging in conventional activities such as voting or signing petitions or working for a political party, to less conventional behaviour such as civil disobedience, violence, or even revolutionary activities. Some political systems provide more opportunities and encouragement to participate politically than others.

Democratic systems in general have what has been called a participant political culture in which individuals have an explicit political role, with widespread opportunities to participate. In spite of this, however, most people in democracies do not engage in regular, high levels of political action. Voting is the most frequent political act, followed by other conventional contacts with publicly elected or appointed officials, in order to achieve political objectives. At the other end of the spectrum, some citizens in democracies (about one fourth to one half) have engaged in, or are willing to engage in, lawful demonstrations of protest against government policy. But very few of them are prepared to participate in violent protest against persons or property in order to achieve their political objectives.[50]

There is substantial variation among Western democracies in regard to degree of participation in conventional or unconventional political activity. Education is the strongest predictor of political participation. University-educated citizens vote and participate in politics more than those who have not graduated from secondary school—a correlation that applies to both conventional and unconventional participation.[51] Gender, too, is often related to conventional political participation, with men more likely to participate than women: the correlation is weaker, but still valid in the case of unconventional participation.

As in democratic states, authoritarian governments try to develop a broad consensus in society, promoting a specific value system and instilling pride, enthusiasm, and support for the regime. In totalitarian states, leaders develop an official ideology which they promote vigorously to legitimize the system. These regimes differ fundamentally from democratic regimes in that participation is not voluntary but induced, sometimes by physical coercion, in order to build support for the ideological goals of the ruling elite. The role of the individual is to be passive and obey the decisions of the state.

Other authoritarian systems that are closer to democracies on the spectrum do not strive as much for consensus. They are not as concerned to develop or follow the rationale of an official ideology, and have not assigned any particular role for the individual in the system. They tend to rely on the charisma of a leader. They are primarily concerned with obedience, which they consider to be the essence of stable government, and they seek to maintain the status quo. In such states apathy or acquiescence are therefore more attractive characteristics of citizenry than is participation.

There has been little systematic comparative study of socialization in less democratic or authoritarian countries: for obvious reasons survey research is not appropriate. In these situations, however, there is considerable evidence that reliance on nongovernmental channels and unconventional forms of political behaviour is greater and more varied than in democracies. State repression often deters conventional political participation. When established channels of participation are weakened or eliminated, the citizens must find other outlets for their dissatisfaction. Political violence, strikes, insurrections, and revolutionary activities therefore are more apt to occur in countries that are oppressive economically and politically. (See Chapter 20 on political violence, terrorism, and revolution.)

The overarching political culture and the layers of subcultures within a state provide the environment for politics. They influence collective behaviour and governmental policies indirectly through the complex channels of governmental structures, systems of group interaction, and formal decision-making processes. We turn to an examination of these institutions and processes after a closer look at ideologies, a particularly important part of political culture.

DISCUSSION QUESTIONS

1. Name several political symbols in a democratic country and an authoritarian country.
2. Distinguish between the terms "civic culture" and "civil society."
3. Do women have a distinctive political culture?
4. Is socialization by the state possible? Justifiable?
5. What are the most effective agents of political socialization in your country?

KEY TERMS

civic culture, p. 141
civil society, p. 142
national identity, p. 139
parochial political
   cultures, p. 141

participant political
   cultures, p. 141
political efficacy, p. 140
race, p. 152
racial discrimination, p. 152

subject political cultures,
   p. 141
trust, p. 140
values, p. 139

ENDNOTES

1. Lucien W. Pye, "Political Science and the Crisis of Authoritarianism," *APSR*, vol. 84, no. 1 (March 1990), p. 11.
2. Gabriel A. Almond and Sidney Verba, *The Civic Culture: Political Attitudes and Democracy in Five Nations* (Princeton, N.J.: Princeton University Press, 1963), Table 4, p. 267.
3. Almond and Verba, *The Civic Culture.*
4. *Ibid.*
5. See Joan Nelson, "Political Participation," Myron Weiner and Samuel Huntington, eds., *Understanding Political Development* (Boston: Little, Brown, 1987), pp. 144–45.
6. Almond and Verba, *The Civic Culture.*
7. For an extensive review of the vast literature on this subject see Doh Chull Shin "On the Third Wave of Democratisation: A Synthesis and Evaluation of Recent Theory and Research," *World Politics* vol. 47 (October 1994) pp. 135–70.
8. See Ernest Gellner, *Conditions of Liberty: Civil Society and its Rivals* (New York: Allen Lane, 1994; and Francis Fukuyama, *Trust: The Social Virtues and the Creation of Prosperity* (New York: Free Press, 1995). Also see Robert D. Putnam, *Making Democracy Work: Civic Traditions in Modern Italy* (Princeton, N.J.: Princeton University Press, 1993).
9. Samuel P. Huntington, "The Goals of Development," in Myron Weiner and Samuel P. Huntington, *Understanding Political Development* (Toronto: Little, Brown, 1987), p. 23.
10. *Ibid.*
11. *Ibid.*, p. 24.
12. George Thomas Kurian, *The Book of World Rankings*, 3rd ed. (New York: Facts on File, 1991), p. 44.
13. Paul Cammack et al., *Third World Politics* (Baltimore, Md: Johns Hopkins University Press, 1988), p. 42.
14. Western democracies are continually facing choices in the Middle East over whether to support autocratic Arab governments or popular Islamic movements. So far, in Algeria, Egypt, and Saudi Arabia they have chosen secular governments—and hoped the Islamic movement would die out.
15. Kurian, *The Book of World Rankings*, p. 46.
16. See Bernard Lewis, "The Roots of Muslim Rage," *Atlantic Monthly* (September 1990), pp. 47–60.
17. In 1995 Liamine Zeroual, the military's candidate, won Algeria's first contested presidential election. He resigned in 1998 amid rumours of military in-fighting. Parliamentary elections in June 1997 gave the country a three-party coalition government again led by the

army-backed party, and local elections in November 1997 were widely denounced as fraud-ulent. Violence continues with civilians almost exclusively its targets.

18. Roderick MacFarquhar, "The Post-Confucian Challenge," *Economist* (February 9, 1980) pp. 67–72. An excellent study of the cultural biases of power and authority in Asian society, using the approaches of both area specialists and comparative politics is Lucien W. Pye, *Power and Politics: The Cultural Dimensions of Authority* (Cambridge, Mass.: Harvard University Press, 1985).

19. James B. Hsiung, "*East Asia,*" in James B. Hsiung, ed., *Human Rights in East Asia* (New York: Paragon House, 1985), p. 7.

20. Lucien W. Pye, *Asian Power and Politics* (Cambridge, Mass.: Harvard University Press, 1985), p. 55.

21. *Ibid.*, p. 254.

22. Fox Butterfield, *Alive in the Bitter Sea* (New York: Times Books, 1982), pp. 203–4.

23. Alan Roland, quoted in Enz Schmitt, "Growing up Asian in America," *New York Times*, March 7, 1989, p. C8.

24. Thomas Gold, *State and Society in the Taiwanese Miracle* (Armonk, N.Y.: M.E. Sharpe, 1986), p. 55.

25. Quoted by Lewis M. Simons in "Brave New Singapore," *The Atlantic*, vol. 268, no. 1, (July 1991), p. 26.

26. *Ibid.*

27. Huntington, "The Goals of Development," p. 24.

28. *The New York Times*, December 11, 1990.

29. See Edwin O. Reischauer, *The Japanese Today: Change and Continuity* (Cambridge, Mass.: Harvard University Press, 1988), Part 3.

30. James J. Teevan, *Introduction to Sociology* (Scarborough, Ont.: Prentice–Hall Canada, 1986) p. 196.

31. This notion has been invalidated by many scientific studies. See Brewton Berry and Henry L. Tischler, *Race and Ethnic Relations* (Boston: Houghton Mifflin, 1978).

32. See, for example, Craig Baxter, Yogendra K. Malik, Charles H. Kennedy, and Robert C. Oberst, *Government and Politics in South Asia* (London: Westview Press, 1987), pp. 20–57; Rajni Kothari, *Caste in Indian Politics* (New Delhi: Orient Longman, 1970).

33. *Ibid.*, p. 45. India stopped collecting statistics on caste in the 1931 census, so all figures about caste are extrapolations from that time.

34. Baxter et al., *Government and Politics in South Asia*, p. 45.

35. See, for example, Lloyd Rudolph and Susanne Rudolph, *The Modernity of Tradition* (Chicago: University of Chicago Press, 1967). See also Hamish McDonald "India, Pride and Prejudice," *Far Eastern Economic Review* (November 3, 1994), pp. 24–28.

36. *The Globe and Mail*, October 13, 1990, p. D3.

37. Reischauer, *The Japanese Today*, p. 35.

38. *The World's Women 1970–1990: Trends and Statistics* (New York: United Nations, 1991), p. 11.

39. In developing countries enrollment figures can be deceiving. For example, although roughly 60% of rural Indian boys and girls enter primary school, five years later only 16% of the girls are still enrolled, while almost 50% of the boys still remain.

40. *Human Development Report, 1998* (New York: Oxford University Press, 1998), p. 31.

41. See, for example, Helena Goscilo and Beth Holmgren, eds., *Russia—Women—Culture* (Bloomington, Ind.: Indiana University Press, 1996).

42. Geraldine Brooks, *Nine Parts of Desire: The Hidden World of Islamic Women* (New York: Anchor Books, 1995).

43. Quoted by Patrick Martin, Middle East Bureau, Riyadh, *The Globe and Mail*, January 11, 1995.

44. The lack of equal opportunities for women to participate in economic and political life is reflected in the Gender Empowerment Measure (GEM) in the *Human Development Report, 1998*. The GEM shows that some developing countries do better than industrial countries in respect of equal opportunities. For example, Trinidad and Tobago and Barbados score higher than the U.K. and Ireland.

45. *The World's Women*, p. 34.

46. United Nations, *Human Development Report, 1998*, pp. 31, 32, 54.

47. For a first-hand account of Cambodia during this time, see James Felton, ed., *Cambodian Witness: The Autobiography of Someth May*, (New York: Random House, 1986).

48. See, for example Frederick C. Barghoorn and Thomas F. Remington, *Politics USSR*, 3rd ed. (Boston: Little, Brown, 1986), ch. VI.

49. Edward L. Keenan, "Rethinking the U.S.S.R., Now That It's Over," *The New York Times*, September 8, 1991, p. E3.

50. Joan Nelson, "Political Participation," in Myron Weiner and Samuel Huntington, eds., *Understanding Political Development* (Boston: Little, Brown, 1987), p. 117.

51. Alan Marsh and Max Kaase, "Background of Political Action," in Samuel H. Barnes, Max Kaase, et al., *Political Action: Mass Participation in Five Western Democracies* (London: Sage, 1979), pp. 97–135.

FURTHER READING

Democratic: Political Culture and Socialization

Almond, Gabriel A., and Sidney Verba, *The Civic Culture, Political Attitudes and Democracy in Five Nations* (Princeton, N.J.: Princeton University Press, 1963).

———, eds., *The Civic Culture Revisited* (Boston: Little, Brown, 1980).

Bell, David V.J. *The Roots of Disunity: A Study of Canadian Political Culture* (Toronto: Oxford University Press, 1992).

Bissoondath, Neil, *Selling Illusions: The Cult of Multiculturalism in Canada* (Toronto: Penguin, 1995).

Cohen, Jean L., and Andrew Arato, *Civil Society and Political Theory* (Cambridge, Mass.: MIT Press, 1992).

Huntington, Samual P., *The Clash of Civilizations and the Remaking of World Order* (New York: Simon & Schuster, 1996).

Inglehart, R., *Culture Shift in Advanced Industrial Society* (Princeton, N.J.: Princeton University Press, 1990).

Kohli, Atul, *Democracy and Discontent* (Cambridge, Mass.: Cambridge University Press, 1990).

Kumagi, Fumie, and Donna J. Keyser, *Unmasking Japan Today: The Impact of Traditional Values on Modern Japanese Society* (Westport, CT: Praeger, 1996).

Lipset, Seymour Martin, *Continental Divide* (London: Routledge, 1990).

———, *American Exceptionalism*, (New YorK: W.W. Norton, 1996).

Maré, Gerhard, *Brothers Born of Warrior Blood—Politics of Ethnicity in South Africa* (Johannesburg: Ravan, 1992).

Moen, Matthew, and Lowell S. Gustafson, eds., *The Religious Challenge to the State* (Philadelphia: Temple University Press, 1992).

Solzhenitsyn, Aleksandr, *The Russian Question at the End of the Twentieth Century* (New York: Farrar, Straus and Giroux, 1995).

Authoritarian: Political Culture and Socialization

Al-Khalil, Samir, *Republic of Fear: The Inside Story of Saddam's Iraq* (New York: Pantheon, 1990).

Esposito, John L., and John O. Voll, *Islam and Democracy* (New York: Oxford University Press, 1996).

Lewis, Bernard, *The Political Language of Islam* (Chicago: University of Chicago Press, 1988).

Mottahedeh, Roy, *The Mantle of the Prophet: Religion and Politics in Iran* (New York: Pantheon, 1985).

Petro, Nicolai N., *The Rebirth of Russian Democracy: An Interpretation of Political Culture* (Cambridge, MA: Harvard University Press, 1995).

Polk, William R., *The Arab World Today* (Cambridge, Mass.: Harvard University Press, 1990).

Remnick, David, *Resurrection: The Struggle for a New Russia* (New York: Random House, 1997).

Roy, Olivier, *The Failure of Political Islam* (Cambridge, Mass.: Harvard University Press, 1994).

Women

Brooks, Geraldine, *Nine Parts of Desire: The Hidden World of Islamic Women* (New York: Anchor Books, 1995).

Gelb, Joyce, *Feminism and Politics, A Comparative Perspective* (Berkeley, Cal.: University of California Press, 1989).

Inter-Parliamentary Symposium on the Participation of Women in the Political and Parliamentary and Decision-Making Process: Reports and Conclusions (Geneva: Inter-Parliamentary Union, 1990).

Political Participation

Milbraith, Lester W., and M.L. Goel, *Political Participation: How and Why Do People Get Involved in Politics?* 2nd ed. (Chicago: Rand McNally, 1977).

Verba, Sidney, Norman H. Nie, and Jae-on Kim, *Participation and Political Equality: A Seven-Nation Comparison* (Cambridge, Mass.: Cambridge University Press, 1978).

 **Weblinks**

www.umich.edu/~nes/cses.html
Information about electoral systems throughout the world can be found at this site.

www.undp.org/fwcw/daw1.htm
This site contains information from the United Nations Fourth Conference on Women, identifying the social, economic and political status of women throughout the world.

www.yahoo.com/Society_and_Culture/Religion
This site contains links to hundreds of other sites about many different world religions.

CHAPTER 8

Contemporary Ideologies and Philosophies

In the last two chapters we discussed the variety of political cultures and subcultures that provide the environment for politics and political systems around the world. We now focus on ideologies, that specific part of political culture which relates culture to action in the political sphere.

In this chapter we examine the philosophical roots and basic tenets of the ideologies of liberalism, conservatism, socialism, communism, democratic socialism, Nazism, and fascism. These ideologies, which originated in Europe, exercised a powerful influence around the world during the twentieth century, providing the rationale and impetus for political action. The economic and political strengths of the Western world, and of the former Soviet Union as leader of the communist world, ensured that ideologies were exported to developing countries through colonialism and economic penetration. Before beginning our exploration of the ideas which motivate a good deal of the political activity in the world today, let us define more precisely what we mean by ideology.

IDEOLOGIES: BLUEPRINTS FOR ACTION

In casual conversation and political debate the term "ideology" is often used in a pejorative sense—as a derogatory comment to disparage or dismiss an argument with which the speaker disagrees. The implication is that the argument in question is based on beliefs that are not well thought through, or perhaps, is merely a convoluted rationalization of self-interest or a justification for maintaining the status quo. This popular usage of the word "ideology" bears little resemblance to the way it is used in political science. Most political scientists would agree that **ideology** refers to a set of ideas and beliefs that clarifies what is valued and what is not, what must be maintained and what must be changed, and what shapes the attitudes of those who share it.[1] In other words, political ideologies are belief systems which aim to cure the ills of societies. As such they are abstractions—broad, amorphous bodies of thought which provide the motivating force for individuals and groups in society to act politically. They are action programs.

Pure ideologies tend to be limited to an educated elite and the attentive public; they are relatively rarely held by mass publics. On the other hand, almost everyone has beliefs and values of some sort, and often they contain elements of an ideology. Individuals can espouse an ideology, but ideas can also be integrated within larger groups such as a class or society.[2] Ideologies can be distinguished by four implicit or explicit elements:

1. A negative perception of where society is headed;
2. A reasoned view of what is wrong and why;
3. A prescription to reform or overthrow the present system; and
4. An attempt to form a movement which will follow the prescription to its natural conclusion.

Generally, ideologies are based on the teachings of significant thinkers or philosophers who are engaged in a search for truth through logical argument derived from first principles. As the original ideas are molded to accommodate specific circumstances and turned into slogans to provide the basic framework for political action, the ideas may be simplified, popularized, and distorted. This is most evident when ideologies are used to mobilize political movements and parties. To attract followers they transmit messages by propaganda techniques such as repetition and oversimplification. And they provide simple answers to social, economic, and political problems, offering identifiable enemies as scapegoats. Jews, infidels, capitalists, and communists have been some groups traditionally singled out as responsible for societal problems.

Ideologies all promise perfection, although they can never provide it. They are not necessarily neat, tidy, and consistent in their details. As held by individuals they are generally full of inconsistencies because of personal experience and self-interest. But even though they end up as a hodgepodge of political beliefs at the individual level, ideologies are useful because they provide assumptions and values as common denominators or frameworks from which to derive political debate and persuasion. They are useful in helping individuals respond to diverse events in a consistent way, so that one position logically leads to another. Often, a special vocabulary is shared by adherents of an ideology and it simplifies communication among them. Words or phrases such as "communist conspiracy," "Reds," "freedom of the individual," or "the universal class," are all shorthand, coded ways of expressing ideas shared by a given group. Ideologies also help justify or give legitimacy to political regimes, their institutions, and the groups which support them. Conservatism, for example, may be used to justify elite groups, liberalism to justify the middle classes, and communism to justify the "vanguard" of the workers leading toward a classless society.

Understanding the main ideologies is useful because a society's prevailing ideology affects how the government works. Political leaders must select, define, and rank order which issues they will address. Their choices to a large extent are guided by ideology which provides them with a coherent set of rules and a mental organization for ordering political circumstances—a framework to interpret and understand reality. Ideology also helps individuals to decide for themselves what they think about political decisions and issues.

The Left-Right Ideological Spectrum

Ideological positions are often placed on a left-right spectrum. The concept of left-right stems from politics in France after the Revolution (1789) when the different political factions sat in different locations in a semicircular legislative chamber. The most radical elements, who wanted considerable social change and maximum equality, sat on the far left side of the chamber, while the most conservative elements, who wanted no change and maximum inequality, sat on the right. The moderate, middle-of-the-road groups occupied the centre seats. Over time these groupings became known as the left, centre, and right. Gradually the same labels were applied to groups and ideas outside of Parliament, and over time they were adopted in other countries as a shorthand way to identify and explain various groups or ideas in relation to each other.

The most important twentieth-century ideologies are thus often seen as shaded on a spectrum with communism at the extreme left, through social democracy, liberalism and conservatism, which would be relatively central, to Nazism and fascism on the extreme right (see Figure 8.1).

It is difficult to apply the left-right ideological spectrum accurately in the real world because ideologies are never manifested in a pure form; rather they vary considerably over both time and place. One conservative or liberal regime may be considerably further "left" or "right" than another. Ideologies do not always proceed neatly on a continuum when one examines specific issues such as freedom of speech or racial equality. An ideology might be relatively extreme in respect to one issue but not another. The left–right notion does, however, prove useful as a very general method of categorizing political ideas.

Dominant Ideologies of the Twentieth Century

Liberalism, conservatism, and socialism, including communism, all originated in Europe. They have changed considerably over time, often with new branches breaking away from the original, classical body of thought as they adapted to new social and economic conditions. Liberalism and conservatism developed in the nineteenth century as philosophers and thinkers struggled to create logical and consistent patterns of thought about

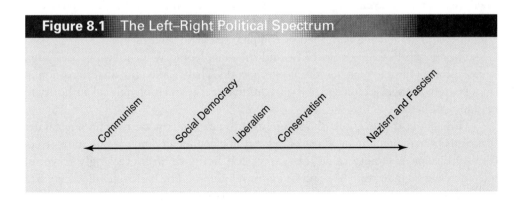

Figure 8.1 The Left–Right Political Spectrum

Communism   Social Democracy   Liberalism   Conservatism   Nazism and Fascism how to restructure the medieval social and political order that new technological developments had rendered obsolete. **Liberalism** became the ideology of the rising commercial class whose members chafed under the confines of the old social order, while **conservatism** justified the positions of the aristocracy and the church.

Both ideologies spawned political parties, namely, the Liberals and the Conservatives. The Liberals became dominant in the Western world in the latter part of the nineteenth century, and for that reason some see the nineteenth century as the century of liberalism. **Socialism** developed slightly later, but again in response to fundamental changes in society; the technological advances of the industrial revolution had brought the growth of a large urban working class, whose wretched condition socialists sought to ameliorate. By the beginning of the twentieth century, the ideological and party battlefield was a three-way contest as the socialist ideology produced Socialist, Labour, and Communist parties.

Today, at the beginning of the twenty-first century, Conservative parties and their ideology are still with us. Liberal parties, though greatly weakened in Europe, are still strong in the "new world" states of Canada, the United States, and Australia. Socialist parties have been transformed into milder Social Democratic parties, having accepted the civil libertarian positions of the liberal ideology. That is, they, too, seek to have persons, property, and opinion protected by the constitution against arbitrary government actions. Extremist and moderately extremist variations of these three great ideologies have not done well. **Nazism** and **fascism**, which were extremes of the conservative ideology, have been rejected; **communism** and other extreme Marxist variations of socialism were rejected in the West, and more recently in Eastern Europe and the former Soviet Union itself; and more moderate libertarian parties, which derived from the Liberal Party, have never commanded a large following.

It is necessary to recall something of the social, economic, and political conditions which prevailed before and during the time these ideologies were born. In medieval society the king, nobility, and church completely dominated social and political affairs. Feudal societies were largely rural, and peasant farmers were literally tied to the land by a system of heavy taxes and other obligations to the local nobility and church. Land ownership, like other feudal privileges and social classes, was static and entrenched. Upward (or downward) social mobility was uncommon; individuals generally were born, lived, and died in the same strata of society. Communications were difficult, industry was strictly controlled by guilds, and trade was limited and hampered by complex taxes and tributes.

The French Revolution in 1789, and the Napoleonic Wars a few decades later, were historical turning points in the Western world. They marked the final transition in Europe from the social bondage of the traditional feudal and monarchical authority to a new, legal basis.

Throughout the seventeenth and eighteenth centuries, modern technological developments facilitated the rapid rise of industry and commerce, and the old, static structure of European society came into direct conflict with an increasingly powerful commercial and industrial class and its business interests. The basic rules of society had to change in order to accommodate modern developments; the question was how.

Behind this revolutionary activity, philosophers, and statesmen in particular, were concerned with finding the best answer to the fundamental question of politics: "What is the proper role of the state?" As the British philosopher Edmund Burke later phrased it—what ought the state to "take upon itself to direct by public wisdom, and what ought it to leave, with as little interference as possible, to individual discretion?" [3]

The question subsumes many others: to what degree should governments regulate the economy or morals? How much, for example, should they exercise control over issues such as censorship, abortion, and capital punishment? How much should they tax their citizens and redistribute income? How much should individual freedoms be restricted by governments in making laws for the state?

There is, of course, no simple "right" answer to these questions. Over the centuries the debate that has taken place in the Western world has tended to fall into the three main ideological positions: liberalism, conservatism, and socialism. All describe what governments do and prescribe what they *ought* to do. All have adapted their answers to changing social, economic, and political circumstances over time, but their basic forms are still with us today and offer quite different answers to these fundamental questions.

In this chapter we will examine the early development and main tenets of these great ideologies and their extremist challengers—communism, Nazism, and fascism—which represented a reaction against democracy and liberal institutions. The latter two were discredited and destroyed as living ideologies after the allied victory in Europe in 1945, but given the proper conditions they could resurface again. The German and Italian political situations following World War I remain powerful illustrations of how leaders can use ideology to manipulate and motivate populations to do their bidding. We will consider how the leaders of Nazism and fascism proposed to solve the ills that they perceived in society by outlining and logically justifying a particular role for the state.

Keep in mind that ideologies are not static; they are adaptable to changing social and economic circumstances in different countries and over time. In this chapter we focus on the patterns of ideas and early development of these ideologies. In Chapter 9 we will examine the state of ideology around the world today and discuss the latest types of ideology.

WESTERN IDEOLOGIES

Liberalism

Liberalism was the intellectual haven of the new commercial class that wanted freedom to change the old social order. It provided guidance in moral, political, and economic spheres. The historical root of "liberal" is the Latin *liber* meaning "free (man)." The concept of freedom is at the heart of the liberal ideology. Originally, to be free was not to be a slave. It still means that one has legal, guaranteed control over what one does. One is neither prevented from doing what one wants nor forced to do what one does not want.

Yet even in the freest democracies individual freedoms are subject to many limitations. No one is allowed to act exactly as he or she pleases in all circumstances, without restrictions. One must still stop at red lights when driving and refrain from physically attacking rude neighbours or taking things that belong to others.

Leading exponents of liberalism in the seventeenth and eighteenth centuries provided answers to this dilemma. They believed profoundly in rights as ends in themselves and called for freedom (absence of coercion, or negative freedom) in all areas of life, social, political, and economic.[4]

John Locke, an English political philosopher, was the most influential of these early liberals, who are generally referred to as **classical liberals**. His ideas spread rapidly throughout the Western world; they animated the industrial revolution in Britain, became the rationale for the *Declaration of Independence* in the United States, and were affirmed by the *Declaration of the Rights of Man and of the Citizen* by the French National Assembly in 1789. In 1948 Locke's ideas were enshrined, once again, in the *Universal Declaration of Human Rights* adopted by the United Nations.

Locke's ideas were spelled out in his *Two Treatises on Civil Government* (1690). He argued that all human beings have the right to life, liberty, and property and that they create government to protect and preserve these basic rights. If the government fails in this task, Locke said, the people have the right to overthrow it.[5] He wrote: "Freedom is ... to have a standing rule to live by, common to everyone of that society and made by the legislative power erected in it."[6] Civil liberties, or freedoms such as freedom of expression, freedom of speech, freedom to publish and disseminate one's ideas, have been enshrined in the constitutions of most liberal democratic countries.

Classical liberals called for equality before the law and equality of right in respect to person and property. In reflection of the social and historical circumstances of the day, classical liberals did not call for equality of political participation or economic equality. Their ideas concerned only males who owned property—a tiny fraction of society at that time. However, their premises gradually led to universal suffrage. They believed that individuals must be free, and have the opportunity to develop their capacities to the fullest extent, and that the degree to which they are able to do so determines the essential goodness of the society in which they live.

Locke believed, then, that legislatures elected by the people (at that time still a very limited, male franchise), should make decisions for society. He based his idea of representative government on the notion that political authority derives from the people. The elected majority can make decisions, but it must respect the natural rights of all citizens.

Another early liberal, John Stuart Mill, asserted in his famous essay *On Liberty* (1859) that the only justification for restricting the freedom of any individual is to prevent harm to others. The state should therefore not restrain individual actions that are not coercive of others. However, if the role of government were uniquely to protect and preserve the basic rights of men, it would have to be restrained by law so that it could not interfere with human freedom. The extreme of total freedom without such protection would mean anarchy, which would therefore increase the danger that the strong would usurp the rights of the weak.

Classical liberals, therefore, faced a dilemma; governments were needed to preserve human rights from private organizations that might usurp them, but governments also represented a principal threat to those rights. They noted that in the past, governments which relied on social privilege or divine right often used their powers arbitrarily to take away citizens' rights. Therefore, liberals wanted to organize government to maintain law and order, but not to infringe on human rights. The way to accomplish that task was to make governments operate under the strict limits of a constitution.

Liberalism also had important economic implications for the state. The principle "the government is best that governs least" was espoused not only by John Locke and other British philosophers but also by a group of French economists known as the physiocrats. As well, it provided the basis of a full theory of the market by Scottish economist Adam Smith. Published in 1776, Smith's *The Wealth of Nations* became a major influence on the development of Western states.[7] The principle he expounded was known as "laissez-faire," or "let alone," which essentially means there should be minimum intervention by government in economic affairs.

Adam Smith's basic argument for laissez-faire complemented Locke's political ideas. Society, Smith said, is governed by natural laws, just like the physical universe. There are laws of social order which human reason can understand. One of them is the law that prices in a free market are determined by supply and demand. If a government interferes with this law by such means as attempting to regulate markets, restrict competition, or assist the inefficient or unsuccessful, the natural balance of the economic system will be upset. Ideally, Smith said, the government should leave the economy entirely to adjust itself through the free market.[8]

This was an economic reflection of the classical liberal idea that unrestricted individual initiatives will serve the common good, and that state direction is not necessary even in the economic sphere. Thus, the protection of the market is the key element of classical liberalism.

Adam Smith maintained that governments had only three duties, summarized as follows:

1. To defend against foreign attack;
2. To establish an administration of justice; and
3. To undertake providing goods or projects that are not profitable in a free society, but which will provide collective benefits (such as a beautiful, clean city) and to ensure that all individuals pay a fair share toward them.

These three deviations from the general rule of noninterference were considered justifiable only on humanitarian and nationalistic grounds, not from the standpoint of economic efficiency.

Smith's ideas about free trade and open competition were adopted and extended by John Stuart Mill in the economics textbook *Principles of Political Economy* which helped to consolidate the virtues of the market system in Europe and North America. In more recent times, two other economists, Milton Friedman and Friedrich Hayek, developed arguments for economic freedom even further, and for their efforts won Nobel prizes in 1974 and 1976 respectively. Their writing, premised on the notion that people must be free of coercion in order to attain other goals of human society, maintains that governments simply cannot be as efficient as individuals in directing complex societies and therefore the market should be free of government regulation to the largest extent possible.[9]

Classical liberalism, then, holds that spontaneous individual choice is more effective than deliberately imposed government direction in coping with the demands of complex societies. In an economic context this means that the marketplace should not come under the control of any individual or group, but should be allowed to adjust itself naturally to bring supply and demand into equilibrium. Only minimal interference is needed by governments in enforcing basic rules of conduct for the general welfare, such as respect for individuals and contracts. To protect the market, the state should promote competition, prevent monopolies, and promote consumer information. By enforcing these rules, governments make spontaneous order possible. Coercion may be necessary for those who violate such rules, but apart from that, individuals should be free to pursue their own interests. They may not understand what is in their own best interest, but classical liberals believe that individuals will at least know better than the state will, and that they can learn from, and build on, their failures.

Beyond providing a few basic public projects such as roads, classical liberals did not want governments to interfere with or provide benefits for society. Even collective goods were a problem in that governments had to finance them by taxing the people, and that took revenue which could have been invested in the private market. It follows that a government would have no mandate to transfer wealth by subsidizing the weak or poor. Classical liberals acknowledged that poor people exist, but they said that advantages generated by the rich would filter down to the poor. They objected to redistribution because it was not only economically inefficient but was also incompatible with equality of rights in that it treated people differently before the law. In the same vein, they advocated the abolition of special privileges and discrimination that prevented people from being treated equally by the law.

Classical liberalism was deemed harsh to the poor and unfortunate in society because it opposed redistribution of wealth; but at the same time it defended the principle of equality before the law for all individuals. Economic inequality was unavoidable, classical liberals said, but eventually the free market system would create wealth and raise living standards for everyone.

In summary, there are three important aspects to classical liberal thought—political, moral, and economic. Politically, it is concerned with basic political rights such as the right of representative government. Morally, it affirms basic values including freedom and dignity. Economically, it is dedicated to the right to private property and free-enterprise capitalism.

Conservatism

As the classical liberals of the eighteenth and nineteenth centuries developed their ideology of change and new direction for social reform, those who defended the status quo resisted social change and developed an opposing ideology: conservatism. The term comes from the latin *conservare* which means to save or preserve, a concept which appropriately depicts the basic core of beliefs around this ideology. Conservatives seek to conserve such elements as power, property, status, or way of life.[10]

Edmund Burke (1727–1797) was the earliest major figure to attempt to refine and clarify the ideology that became known as conservatism. Like Locke, Burke was a British philosopher and professional politician. His thought was profoundly affected by the turmoil and excesses of the French Revolution, and in his book *Reflections on the Revolution in France* (1790) he argued against the dramatic break with the customs and traditions of the past in that country.[11]

Burke, and other early conservatives, insisted that society must have a stable order and structure so that individuals could know their place in it and live and work within those confines for the good of the whole. He believed that being a responsible member of the social whole allowed an individual to achieve greater happiness than could be gained individually.

Whereas classical liberals judged society by the extent to which individuals were free to develop their capacities, conservatives believed that it was not individuals but rather the social group that was most important. Society, they said, is more than the sum of all the individuals in it. For them, the highest good of society is to maintain an ordered community. As a group, people can create greater happiness than the individuals in it can achieve on their own. They accused the liberals of being too individualistic and selfish.

Because their goal was to achieve a stable order, early conservatives were skeptical of the value of change. They considered that the basic limitations of human nature make it unlikely that sudden change would be for the best in the longrun. It is not that they rejected all change; they agreed that innovations are necessary and could be valuable. But they argued that one must be cautious of the untried and unproven, and respect the habits and customs that have served well in the past. Burke wanted change to be gradual.

Whereas liberals were suspicious of state power and wanted to limit it, conservatives believed that, appropriately arranged, state power was necessary in order to achieve social order. Burke opposed extending the right to vote beyond the narrow, elite base that was already established. He defended the social hierarchy with its hereditary aristocracy and established church. As bastions of power in traditional society, these groups rightfully had power, he said, but they did not have the right to abuse it. Rather, Burke viewed such power as providing a responsibility to help the weak and less fortunate in society. He rejected the concept of the redistributive state, but conservative governments in Britain in the late eighteenth century did establish a guaranteed minimum income for citizens. Bismarck's conservative government in Germany also established an elaborate social security system. In this way, conservatives were, in spite of their support

for social distinctions, able to argue that their approach was better for the less fortunate of society than that of the liberals who believed that everyone, including the poor,
should be free to look after themselves.

Burke and the early conservatives held basically the same economic views as Adam
Smith and the classical liberals. Burke believed in the inherent ability of the free market
system to produce an equilibrium between supply and demand. This blend of social
conservatism—respect for the past combined with economic liberalism—represents the
core of conservatism as it developed over the years in Europe and also North America.[12]

Like liberalism, conservatism adapted and changed with the times and issues of the
day. It was strong in Europe in the nineteenth and early twentieth centuries, although it
developed differently on continental Europe than it did in Britain. On the continent, conservatism generally applied to those who harkened back to the ideal of medieval Europe
before the French Revolution. In Britain, too, it originated as a reaction against the
sudden, state-directed change of the French Revolution, but in that country the revolution
of 1688 had already established what early reformers in France still wanted: parliamentary supremacy and religious toleration. A relatively structured class system with an aristocracy still existed, but it was now closely tied to the new business class. Much later, after
World War II, by which time the former social order had broken down, the nobility and
church which had formed the nexus of the conservative social order were largely discredited. Continental European conservatism also adapted to the new circumstances.
We discuss modern, postwar conservatism and liberalism in the next chapter.

Socialism

Within the first few decades of the nineteenth century, another group of political
thinkers began to challenge the idea that governments should not be involved in directing
the economy of the country. Socialism was born; this powerful new ideology presented
fresh answers to the economic problems caused by industrial development in capitalist
systems—economic systems in which the means of economic production were privately
owned. Socialism championed public ownership, a planned economy, and state intervention in market forces.

We have seen that the rising group of shopkeepers and small businessmen in Western
Europe was attracted to the basic tenets of liberalism as these entrepreneurs struggled to
advance their positions in society. Workers, who were beginning to congregate in the
towns and cities, also found many of the precepts of liberalism appealing. They particularly liked the idea that people were politically equal and should have equal opportunity to develop their talents. However, by the latter part of the century this attachment
to liberalism was waning as the lot of urban workers worsened. Liberalism increasingly
came to be seen by this group as the tool of the new capitalist business class against the
workers. Workers wanted help from the state, but liberalism held that they should be
helped as little as possible; they had to struggle for even the most basic government
protection against such abuses as child labour, unsafe factories, and long working hours.
The working class was thus fertile ground for the advancement of a new ideology.

Threads of socialist ideals are identifiable in the works of early Greek philosophers, in some themes of the New Testament, and in the organization of early Christian communities. In the early nineteenth century, two versions existed: the "utopian" version found in Britain, and especially France, and the "scientific" version of Karl Marx in Germany. To improve the lot of the working class in society, the utopian socialists wanted industrial technology to advance by government planning. In Britain, Robert Owen (1771–1858) and others organized model factories to demonstrate the conditions under which labour could be more efficient and productive. In France, Louis Blanque (1805–1888) and others wanted the government to set up workshops to employ the jobless.

The scientific socialists, led by the very influential German intellectual, Karl Marx (1818–1883), dominated socialist thought by the end of the century. Within this group, however, a doctrinal split emerged over the appropriate means for achieving agreed-on ends. Those who wanted to work within the framework of parliamentary democracy became known as democratic socialists. Those who clung to the Marxist revolutionary prescription came under the label of "communist." Both groups sought public control of the means of production and the abolition of the exploitation of labour under capitalism. But communism went beyond this to promise equalization of material conditions for everyone.[13]

Karl Marx and the Origins of Communism

Marx's socialism was based on purported scientific claims that social and historical development are determined by basic economic laws which lead to an inevitable revolutionary transition to socialism. Marx's thought was easily simplified and adapted into a political program that promised power to the working class. As defined by Marx, a **class** is a group of people who share the same relationship to the means of production. He attributed the misery of the working class to oppression and exploitation by the rich capitalist class. He maintained that, in capitalist systems, workers are psychologically **alienated**—cut off from their creative potential, from the products of their labour, and from their fellow citizens, as a result of the material conditions of their working life. To end this exploitation, he said, the working class would and should take control of the government and government should, in turn, take control of all industry. In this way the workers would control the industries themselves and share their benefits equally.

Marx based this prescription on a dialectical theory of historical materialism that offered great hope for the working class.[14] According to this theory, conflict generates change and accounts for historical development. There are two types of conflict: man against nature, and man against man in the class struggle. Because of these conflicts, Marx said, societies pass through a series of predictable stages, eventually culminating in a communist utopia. History progresses according to a pattern; the domination of one group eventually leads to revolution against that group, followed by domination by the successful new group, which in turn leads to another revolution, until a perfect state is reached. As proof, Marx noted that the earliest societies lived a primitive, communal existence until some individuals acquired control of the means to produce things people needed. They created an underclass of slaves to perform the labour they required.

Marx noted that in Europe a feudal society based on a nobility-serf relationship had dominated Europe in the Middle Ages. This system, he said, created, and then eventually was overthrown by, the capitalist class in the industrial revolution. The capitalists in turn created a working class to supply cheap labour for their factories. Eventually, he said, as the workers were exploited more and more to provide the ruling class with ever greater profits, they, too, would stage a revolution. The workers would seize the means of production, end the alienation of their class, and finally establish majority rule. This point would be the apex of historical development. In the final stage, according to Marx, the proletariat would do away with private property—which is the basis of class. Without classes there would no longer be any need for the state since it is the instrument of the dominant class. At that point the state would "wither away" (see Figure 8.2).[15] It is understandable that the working class and left-leaning intellectuals found Marxist ideas appealing.

The four basic elements in Marxist ideology can be summarized as follows:

1. Capitalism is unjust and doomed;
2. Capitalism has internal contradictions which create economic depressions;
3. Capitalism should be abolished and replaced with collective ownership of the means of production; and
4. The Communist Party, the instrument of the working class, will provide the means to carry out the overthrow of capitalism, which will lead to the new society and the withering away of the state.

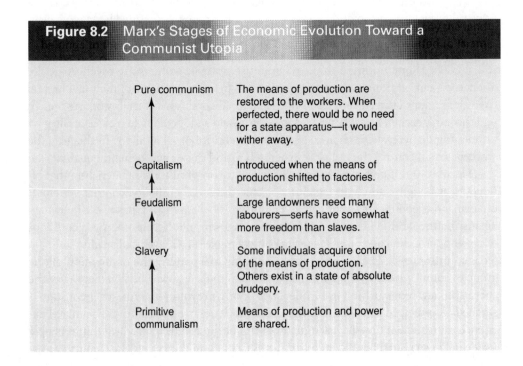

Figure 8.2 Marx's Stages of Economic Evolution Toward a Communist Utopia

Pure communism — The means of production are restored to the workers. When perfected, there would be no need for a state apparatus—it would wither away.

Capitalism — Introduced when the means of production shifted to factories.

Feudalism — Large landowners need many labourers—serfs have somewhat more freedom than slaves.

Slavery — Some individuals acquire control of the means of production. Others exist in a state of absolute drudgery.

Primitive communalism — Means of production and power are shared.

Marx saw communism as a higher, more radical stage of socialism. Only under communism would there be equalization of material abundance that would provide true freedom for all human beings. His goal was to establish a revolutionary, international working-class movement. When Marx met Friedrich Engels in 1844, they began a close intellectual collaboration, which lasted until Marx's death in 1883. In 1847, their ideas were published in *The Communist Manifesto*, a small document that held that the evils of capitalist society cannot be abolished by reform, but only by destroying the entire capitalist economy and establishing a new, classless society. The tract was to have enormous influence in the development of communist ideology. Twenty years later, Marx published *Das Kapital*, his major work. Friedrich Engels took over Marx's mission when he died. At that point, they had still not agreed on whether the working class should take over the state peacefully by elections or violently through revolution. Marx thought that revolution would generally require mass insurrection in order to succeed, but he also thought that where democratic traditions were well-established, revolution could take the form of electoral victories.

In 1917 Nikolay Lenin (1870–1924) and the Bolsheviks took control of the Russian Empire and turned it into a socialist state—the Union of Soviet Socialist Republics.[16] This was a turning point in socialist development. Lenin was greatly influenced by Marxist thought, and the revolution gave him the opportunity to implement it. Socialists who supported progress through revolution established Communist parties, and the Communist party in the USSR became the inspiration and leader of revolutionary communist groups throughout Europe. Lenin revised Marx's theory in that he said Marx's conception of socialism as a mass democratic struggle was not sufficient to achieve the desired ends; there also had to be outside revolutionary leadership from an efficient, tightly controlled professional elite in the Communist Party.[17]

In the short run, Lenin said, an emerging socialist society would need a strong state to defend itself against capitalist counterrevolution. Eventually, however, classes would disappear, the means of production would be held by all, and there would be no further need for the state. Lenin claimed that advanced capitalist economies had managed to postpone social and economic chaos only because they had expanded into new markets in developing economies in other parts of the world. Imperialism and colonialism, he claimed, were a consequence of monopoly capitalism; they were methods to delay the severe social disintegration and economic collapse that would otherwise take place in capitalist nations. He outlined these ideas in *Imperialism: The Highest Stage of Capitalism*, which he published in 1916.

In 1917 Leon Trotsky (1879–1940) provided the brilliant organization of the Red Army with which Lenin secured the Bolshevik victory in the Russian civil. Trotsky's ideological approach differed from that of Lenin (and also Stalin who followed) in that Trotsky believed Russia should be the base for world revolution.[18] He therefore was not satisfied to concentrate on consolidating the Russian state and wanted to immediately export the revolution beyond the borders of the Soviet Union, uniting the working class in all countries to establish a world communist commonwealth. Only then, he said, would the Russian Revolution succeed. When Lenin died in 1924, Stalin successfully attacked Trotsky, deprived him of position and influence, exiled him to Turkistan, and eventually banished him from the USSR.

Joseph Stalin (1879–1953) became ruler of the Soviet Union shortly after Lenin's death. By 1927 he was in uncontested command of the party and the government. Rather than actively working to spread international revolution, Stalin concentrated on building Russia as a model and base from which communism would eventually spread. Stalin deviated from Marxist orthodoxy by gradually abandoning the notion of a stateless society and promoting an active role for the state in furthering the class struggle. He said the Soviet state would remain "unless the capitalist encirclement is liquidated, and unless the danger of foreign military attack has been eliminated."[19]

Stalin established a near-totalitarian state. He tried to modernize and reach socialist economic and political goals through state coercion and terror. He purged the government and the army in the 1930s and had complete control of Russia at the outbreak of World War II. By the time he died in 1953, the Soviet economy seemed to have passed through the stages of early industrialization; it had made massive investment in capital goods to produce products such as steel, iron, cement, and coal that were necessary for development. However, as Stalin's most scathing critic, Yugoslav communist Milovan Djilas, wrote, for all the terror imposed by his authoritarian regime none of the expectations had been fulfilled; there had been no economic improvement, and the dream of a classless society was no closer. The Communist Party and the huge state bureaucracy, he said, had become a new class which "can do nothing more than to strengthen its brute force and pillage the people. It ceases to create. Its spiritual heritage is overtaken by darkness."[20] Close Up 8.1 illustrates another writer's response to Stalinist Russia.

CLOSE UP 8.1   Orwell's *Animal Farm*

Stalin's Russia was the focus of *Animal Farm*, a brilliant, trenchant satire by British author George Orwell. The book appeared in 1945, just after World War II. In many quarters Stalin was still regarded as "Uncle Joe," and communism in Russia was something of a "sacred cow," particularly among left-wing intellectuals. In this atmosphere *Animal Farm* was shocking. The Bolsheviks were portrayed as pigs, supported by an entire cast of barnyard characters. Stalin was a bullying boar called Napoleon—the idealistic Trotsky was a softhearted pig called Snowball. The Russian masses were sheep and donkeys. Many early readers found the characterization unduly offensive and missed the message that egalitarianism is good, but power corrupts. Only in the years to come did they see the tragedy of the human condition acted out by these beasts.

Orwell found it nearly impossible to publish the book in Britain in the 1940s. And, of course, it was banned in the USSR. Today, however, there are countless editions of the book sold throughout the world.

Democratic Socialism

Democratic socialism, the second strain of socialist thought traced to Karl Marx, is sometimes referred to as socialism "by ballots rather than bullets." This evolutionary approach to socialism espoused by social democrats was originally labelled "revisionism" because it professed to revise some basic principles of Marxism.[21] Socialism as propounded by Marx rejected the political goals of liberalism, including popular sovereignty and majoritarianism, in favour of centralized, public control of the means of production to prevent the exploitation of the workers by capitalists. Social democrats and their communist colleagues had essentially the same goals, but the social democrats wanted to reach them by peaceful political means and established democratic procedures.

By the end of the nineteenth century, socialist parties in France, Germany, England, Belgium, the Netherlands, and the Scandinavian countries began to accept the goals of democracy.[22] One of the most influential socialist groups at this time was the Fabian Society, established in Britain in 1884. According to George Bernard Shaw, one of their most important leaders, the Society had two tasks: "first, to provide a parliamentary program for a Prime Minister converted to Socialism," and second, to make it "easy and matter-of-course for the ordinary respectable Englishman to be a Socialist ..."[23] They wanted to socialize the means of production, and institute state controls and broad welfare measures to facilitate maximum social equality. In 1901 the Fabians and the leaders of the major British trade unions formed the Labour Party. As a measure of their success, they increased their share of the vote steadily from 1900 to 1945, when Clement Atlee formed the government.

Democratic socialism rejected the elitist and dictatorial methods adopted by Lenin, in the belief that the interests of the proletariat lay in the perfection of democracy. They, too, wanted to redistribute resources in favour of the disadvantaged classes. However they did not believe it was necessary to have a major redistribution of power as well in order to achieve this end; their goals could be achieved in an openly democratic way. Democracy, they said, would enable classes that were weak to use their superior numbers to win power and make the necessary redistributive decisions.

Social democrats also differed from communists in that they did not accept that progress depended on the deterioration of social conditions.[24] They rejected Marx's theory both as a description of history and as a political strategy for the future. According to Marx, as the condition of the proletariat worsened the workers would galvanize and revolt. However social democrats believed that the progress of socialism depended on eliminating abuses, not letting them build. As conditions gradually improved, they said, the workers would become more aware, win power, and achieve their goals peacefully.

Social democrats, like the revolutionary socialists, held that public ownership of the means of production and exchange was necessary to create social justice. They wanted to nationalize at least the significant sectors of the economy—such as banking and utilities.[25] As we shall see in the next chapter, modern social democrats are much less identified with the need for public ownership.

By the early 1900s, the Social Democratic Party was the largest political party in Germany, and social democratic precepts were rapidly gaining strength in many other Western European countries, particularly through the Labour Party in Britain. In Canada, the Co-operative Commonwealth Federation (CCF), the forerunner of the modern New Democratic Party (NDP), held its founding convention in 1933. We will examine the modern development of social democracy in the next chapter.

Nazism and Fascism

Fascism burst dramatically upon the European scene in the early twentieth century. It provided the ideological underpinning for highly organized and structured right-wing movements, particularly in Germany and Italy, after World War I. German Nazism and Italian fascism were the two major fascist regimes of the twentieth century. Both relied on the ideological tenets of fascist political systems: opposition to liberal democracy and communism; unity of the state into a single, organic whole; leader and state as the embodiment of national will; and protection for private ownership of property.

Nazism was the brainchild of Adolf Hitler (1889–1945). After World War I, the embittered Hitler founded a nationalist party—the National Socialist Party—which later became known as the Nazis. Following an abortive attempt to overthrow the Weimar Republic and seize power in Germany in 1923, he was imprisoned. In jail he wrote *Mein Kampf* (My Struggle), a manifesto or complete political program, in which he outlined the principles of Nazism. The destruction and ensuing economic depression following World War I had created fertile conditions for right-wing extremism in Germany. By January 1933, only a decade after his arrest, Hitler had completed his dramatic ascent to become Chancellor of Germany, assuming absolute power until his suicide in the ruins of Berlin in April 1945.

Socialist pledges were abandoned when the Nazis came to power—in fact many of the party's socialist leaders were massacred in 1934.[26] The official ideology of Nazism was pervasive in that it extended into all branches of life—cultural, political, and scientific—prescribing what was true, right and permissible. In the field of art, for example, all non-Aryan influences were expunged.[27]

In politics, the ideology justified expansionist policies that led to the annexation of the Rhineland, Austria, and Czechoslovakia, and finally to the invasion of Poland in 1939 and the beginning of the World War II. Economic policy consisted of little more than improvisations to meet the objectives of war.

Italian fascism incorporated many of the same features as Hitler's Nazism, but was less coherent and pervasive as an ideology. It was what writer Umberto Eco called "fuzzy totalitarianism, a collage of different philosophical and political ideas, a beehive of contradictions."[28] The Partito Nazionale Fascista did not enter office in 1922 with a clear-cut ideology, and its principles were developed in an ad hoc manner by its leader, Benito Mussolini (1883–1945). When the Allies invaded Italy near the end of World War II, Mussolini was deposed and imprisoned but then rescued by the Germans, who installed him as head of a puppet state in northern Italy. He was subsequently forced to flee, but was recognized by partisans who captured and killed him in 1945.

The resounding victory for the Allied forces in 1945 discredited the leadership and the ideological underpinnings of Germany and Italy so thoroughly that neither Nazism nor Italian-style fascism have ever been revived except by tiny pockets of radical fringe groups.

The intellectual roots of Nazism and Italian fascism were borrowed from philosophers, political scientists, sociologists, and other intellectuals and were often grossly distorted to justify totalitarian methods. These included the ideas commonly associated with fascism: racial superiority, Social Darwinism and elitism (which were the backbone of Nazism), irrationalism, nationalism, anti-communism, subordination of business and economic enterprise to the state, glorification of violence, and a strong military.[29] The core of fascism is its appeal to national rebirth through the instrument of a charismatic leader.[30] Italian intellectuals were relatively enthusiastic about fascist thought and generally defended its economic and social philosophy; it was considerably more respectable intellectually than Nazism was in Germany.

The Nazis and Italian fascists both carried themes of nationalism to extremes; the glorification of state and nation was carried to the point of obsession. The nation, not the individual, was considered supreme. Both Hitler and Mussolini used themes of cultural and racial glorification, resurrecting past glories as the rationale for territorial aggrandizement through war. For Italian fascists, the state was the embodiment of the national will, and as such was of paramount importance—much more than it was for Hitler. For Hitler the state did not represent an end, but a means. He said that the state is "the premise for the formation of a higher human culture, but not its cause, which lies exclusively in the existence of a race capable of culture."[31] For Mussolini, the state and nation were one, and he would not tolerate liberal individualism. Mussolini said: "For Fascism the State is absolute, individuals and groups relative. Individuals and groups are admissible in so far as they come within the State."[32] The individual was to be subordinated to the ends of the state, for which purpose he or she should be coordinated and directed (see Close Up 8.2).

Racism was a key component of Hitler's nationalist ideology. We defined **race** in Chapter 7 as "an arbitrary social category, consisting of persons who share such inherited physical characteristics as skin colour and facial features, which characteristics are charged with social meaning in some societies."[33] Nazis based nationalism on theories of racial superiority, while Italian fascists appealed to the past greatness of ancient Rome.[34] Hitler justified racism by distorting Darwin's theory of evolution and the notion of the survival of the fittest. He applied it to human society and claimed that those who survive or suc-

---

CLOSE UP 8.2   Instilling Fascist Ideas

Author Umberto Eco recalls winning a literary prize when he was a 10-year-old child. The contest was for young Italian fascists and the topic was "Should we die for the glory of Mussolini and the immortal destiny of Italy?" Eco was, he says, a smart boy. His answer was "yes."[35]

ceed are superior to those who perish. He used this theory of **Social Darwinism** to legit-imize the supremacy of white-skinned people on the basis of biological superiority, and to substantiate his claim that the German "Aryan race" was the "master race." Once in power, Hitler introduced anti-Semitic policies that advanced gradually from legal dis-crimination against Jews to internment of Jews (as well as gypsies, homosexuals, and any other individuals who it was said might dilute the purity of the Aryan race), and finally, to the Holocaust, which claimed 6 million lives, carried out during World War II.

Elitism was another component of Nazi and Italian fascist thought. Hitler rejected liberal assumptions of equality and participation in favour of conservative elitist arguments that hold that some people are more qualified to lead than others because of their nat-ural skills. In this respect he also followed Lenin's teaching that elites should organize and lead the workers. Like Nazism, Italian fascism provided a totalitarian, dictatorial role for the leader of the state. And like Hitler, Mussolini created a personality cult around himself; as the leader he claimed the unique capacity to discern the national will. One of the 10 rules of Italian fascism was "Mussolini is always right."[36] Mussolini chose lead-ers in society to be his collaborators. Italian fascism also denied that elected parliaments could represent the essential will of the people. It maintained that only a strong exec-utive or dictator could bypass the interest groups which form barriers between people and state and determine the true national will.

Nazi **irrationalism** had its intellectual roots in the writings of the German philoso-pher Arthur Schopenhauer, who advocated the idea that rational and scientific dis-course is inadequate to provide an understanding of the world, and that intuitive communication alone can provide true understanding.[37] In this light, intuition can be seen as more important than reason, measurements, and observations; knowledge is subjective, and therefore subject to manipulation. The Nazi and Italian fascist regimes used this logic to justify creating myths, slogans, and symbols based on stereotypes and prejudices in order to appeal to peoples' emotions and unite and move the masses. Nazi myths included racial purity, national superiority, heroic leadership, and the resurrection of a glorious German past.

In using science to support myths that were part of their ideological claims, Nazism discounted certain ideas in modern physics because Jews, including Albert Einstein, had developed them. Biologists suppressed environmental factors in their research and developed theories of racial eugenics to support the racist Nazi ideology. Hereditary and genetic differences were determined to be the root of different cultures, and since the German culture was perceived as the purest and highest form, it was argued that it had to be nourished, expanded, and protected from adverse influences.

Nazis and Italian fascists glorified violence as a tool to reach utopian goals. They taught that a perfect end-state or society could be reached. Hitler and the Nazi party, for example, believed they had a mission to lead the German people to a condition where the purity of the superior Aryan race would be freed from the contaminating influences of lower cultures. This mission justified violence and the role of the totalitarian dicta-tor in German society.

There were considerable differences in the role that ideology played under the totalitarian governments of Hitler and Mussolini and the powerful central position it enjoyed under Soviet leaders.

Hitler did not come to power because of a revolution, nor did he have a well-defined ideology other than notions of racial supremacy as outlined in *Mein Kampf*. Rather, he took over a government that was already in place. His economic policies were not ideologically driven, and only after the war began were Hitler's anti-Semitic, racist ideas consolidated and acted upon. The Nazi party was not the single focus of authority in Germany; there were other competing centres of power, particularly the SS, the state police. The propaganda ministry under Joseph Goebels was also beyond control of the party.[38] Loyalty was to Hitler personally, not to an ideology. Once he was in power, Hitler had little use for the party, unlike Lenin in the Soviet Union and Mao in China, who used the party as an organizational weapon to reshape and control society.[39] The government bureaucracy was not restricted to members of the Nazi party; professional criteria were considered ahead of party membership; purges of the civil service, except for Jews, did not take place.

Extreme right-wing ideologies like Nazism and Italian fascism have deep roots, and could surface again depending on conditions. The themes of nationalism, anti-liberalism, and anti-individualism continue to be attractive to elitist and authoritarian movements. The word "fascist" tends to be used very loosely in popular parlance to label regimes that are simply authoritarian tyrannies lacking the economic philosophy and racist–nationalistic ideology to be truly fascist. However, neo-fascist parties advocating hostility to immigrants and ethnic minorities have arisen again, particularly in postwar Europe. It might take only a serious economic crisis or a dramatic international event to set the stage for a charismatic leader to establish another such regime. Bringing down Nazism and Italian fascism required the mobilization of the world, an uneasy alliance of the democratic West with the Communist Soviet Union, and the deaths of more than 30 million people.

THE EXCESSES OF IDEOLOGY

We have seen that ideologies provide consistency, logic, and coherence for individual and group action. They promote political participation. However, they can also create great problems.

In politics, as elsewhere in everyday life, it is natural for people to defend their own belief system even when evidence contradicts it.[40] They block out contradictory evidence because it would mean changing their established way of looking at life. People sometimes even strengthen their resolve and belief in the ideology in the face of contradiction. In this way, ideologues are often blind to information that is against their beliefs, and this can cause intolerance and rigidity leading to dispute, hostility, and conflict.

Ideology can be manipulated into propaganda. After coming to power, a movement may require a coherent ideology to justify its policies, and may adopt one in an ad hoc fashion. Once a set of leaders or a movement has established an ideology, it often reinterprets the early history of the group in the light of that ideology. An often cited case is Italian fascism. When the fascist movement was established by Mussolini in 1919 it had little discernable ideology; a pattern of ideas only took shape gradually after the takeover in 1922.

Ideology plays an important role in revolutions. In the past century Marxism provided the ideological underpinning of many revolutions around the world. Today, the ideology of Islamic fundamentalism projects a similar revolutionary fervour. It was a major mobilizer of the 1979 revolution to overthrow the Shah of Iran.[41] It continues to haunt Algeria, Egypt, Turkey, and other countries of the Middle East and central and northern Africa, and it is the justification for despotic government in Afghanistan.

Ideologies are based on utopian goals—conflicting ideologies present different ideas about how to perfect society. No political party, movement, or regime in the real world perfectly embodies any ideology. Ideologies are part of the general political culture of states, and are adapted by leaders to the existing historical, social, cultural, and economic circumstances. The major ideologies we discussed in this chapter concerned the role of the state in the production and distribution of wealth, so that politics and economics are inextricably intertwined. The pure capitalist ideologies of liberalism and conservatism argue that the profit motive encourages acquisition of wealth, and this, through the "trickle down" effect, leads to collective economic growth and stability. Socialist ideologies argue that the means of production cannot be left in private hands because the rich get richer and the poor get poorer. There is, however, some middle ground between these ideological positions, which has been sought out by political parties as they adapt their platforms to fit with the political culture of their electorates in order to win political power.

DISCUSSION QUESTIONS

1. Do only radical governments such as those found in Nazi Germany or Fascist Italy have an ideology?
2. Does the Canadian government have an ideology? The Quebec government? The Alberta government?
3. Do you have an ideology? Do your classmates?
4. How do ideologies promote collective action?
5. Do all political parties have an ideology?
6. Is "consumerism" an ideology?

KEY TERMS

alienated, p. 177
classical liberals, p. 172
communism, p. 170
conservatism, p. 170
elitism, p. 184

fascism, p. 170
ideology, p. 167
irrationalism, p. 184
Italian fascism, p. 182
liberalism, p. 170

nazism, p. 170
race, p. 183
racism, p. 183
socialism, p. 170
Social Darwinism, p. 184

ENDNOTES

1. Roy C. Macridis, *Contemporary Political Ideologies: Movements and Regimes*, 4th ed. (Boston: Scott, Foresman/Little, Brown Series, 1989), p. 8.

2. Karl Mannheim, *Ideology and Utopia* (New York: Harcourt, 1961).

3. *The Writings of Edmund Burke*, vol. 5 (Boston: Little, Brown, 1901), p. 166.

4. Isiah Berlin, *Four Essays on Liberty* (New York: Oxford University Press, 1969).

5. John Locke, *Two Treatises on Civil Government*, Peter Laslett, ed. (New York: New American Library, 1965).

6. *Ibid.*, *Second Treatise*, ch. 4.

7. Adam Smith, *The Wealth of Nations: Representative Selections* (New York: Bobbs-Merril, 1961).

8. For a more detailed discussion of the economic theory of early liberalism, see George H. Sabine, *A History of Political Theory* (New York: Henry Holt, 1959), pp. 688–90.

9. Milton Friedman, *Capitalism and Freedom* (Chicago: University of Chicago Press, 1963); Friedrich A. Hayek, *The Road to Serfdom* (Chicago: University of Chicago Press, 1944) and *The Constitution of Liberty* (London: Routledge & Kegan Paul, 1960).

10. See Robert A. Nisbet, *Conservatism* (Minneapolis, Minn.: University of Minnesota Press, 1986), or Russell Kirk, *The Portable Conservative Reader* (New York: Penguin Books, 1982).

11. Edmund Burke, *Reflections on the Revolution in France* (New York: Bobbs-Merril, 1955). See also, for example, Donald Kagan et al, *The Western Heritage* (New York: Macmillan, 1983), pp. 663–65.

12. See Rod Preece, "The Political Economy of Edmund Burke," *Modern Age*, vol. 24, no. 3 (1980), pp. 266–73.

13. See, for example, Albert Fried and Ronald Sanders, eds., *Socialist Thought: A Documentary History* (Garden City, N.Y.: Anchor Doubleday, 1964).

14. Marx developed his theory of history and change from the ideas of the German philosopher G.W.F. Hegel (1770–1831). G.W.F. Hegel, *The Philosophy of History* (New York: The Colonial Press, 1900).

15. See Robert C. Tucker, ed., *The Marx-Engels Reader*, 2nd ed. (New York: W.W. Norton, 1978).

16. Nikolay Lenin was the pseudonym of Vladimir Ilyich Ulyanov.

17. See A.J. Polan, *Lenin and the End of Politics* (London: Methuen, 1984).

18. Trotsky's real name was Lev Davidovich Bronstein. He was first arrested in 1898 for revolutionary activities and sent to Siberia, but escaped under the alias of Leon Trotsky and kept his new name.

19. Joseph Stalin, "Report to the 18th Party Congress of the CPSU" (March 1939), in Bruce Franklin, ed., *The Essential Stalin*, (Garden City, N.Y.: Anchor, 1972), p. 387.

20. Milovan Djilas, *The New Class: An Analysis of the Communist System* (New York: Praeger, 1957), p. 69.

21. See Eduard Bernstein, *Evolutionary Socialism* (New York: Schocken Books, 1961), originally published in English in 1900.

22. Macridis, *Contemporary Political Ideologies*, p. 58.

23. George Bernard Shaw, ed., *The Fabian Essays in Socialism* (London: Allen & Unwin, 1948), p. xxxiii, first published 1889.

24. See, for example M. Markovic, *Democratic Socialism: Theory and Practice* (New York: St. Martin's Press, 1982).

25. See, for example, Peter Gay, *The Dilemma of Democratic Socialism* (New York: Columbia University Press, 1952).
26. Macridis, *Contemporary Political Ideologies*, p. 211.
27. Joseph Goebbels, "Freedom and Organization," in G.L. Mosse, ed., *Nazi Culture* (New York: Grosset & Dunlap, 1968), p. 154.
28. Umberto Eco, "Eternal Fascism," *The New York Review of Books*, vol. XLII, no. 11 (June 22, 1995) p. 12.
29. Roger Griffin provides more than 200 extracts on fascism written by its precursors, its practitioners, its critics, and its supporters from Richard Wagner, a notorious anti-Semite, to Vladimir Zhirinovsky, the Russian populist. See Roger Griffin, *Fascism* (London: Oxford University Press, 1995).
30. Roger Eatwell, *Fascism: A History* (London: Chatto, 1995).
31. Adolf Hitler, *Mein Kampf* (Boston: Houghton Mifflin, 1943), p. 391.
32. Benito Mussolini, "Political and Social Doctrine," in *Fascism: Doctrine and Institutions* (New York: Howard Fertig, 1968), p. 27.
33. James J. Teevan, *Introduction to Sociology* (Scarborough: Prentice Hall, 1986), p. 196.
34. Mario Palmieri, "The Philosophy of Fascism" in C. Cohen, ed., *Communism, Fascism and Democracy*, (New York: Random House, 1966), p. 384.
35. Eco, "Eternal Fascism," p. 12.
36. From "The Doctrine of Fascism" in Carl Cohen, ed., *Communism, Fascism and Democracy* (New York: Random House 1962), p. 349–364.
37. Arthur Schopenhauer, *The World as Will and Idea*, trans. E.P. Payne (New York: Dover, 1968).
38. Amos Perlmutter, *Modern Authoritarianism* (New Haven, Conn.: Yale University Press, 1981), p. 29.
39. *Ibid.*
40. Psychologists call the ability to maintain belief in the face of continual definite evidence to the contrary *cognitive dissonance*. Leon Festinger, *A Theory of Cognitive Dissonance* (Stanford, Calif.: Stanford University Press, 1957).
41. Paul Cammack et al., *Third World Politics* (Baltimore: Johns Hopkins University Press, 1988), p. 175.

FURTHER READING

Adams, Ian, *Political Ideology Today* (New York: Manchester University Press, 1993).
Apter, David E., ed., *Ideology and Discontent* (New York: Free Press, 1964).
Baradat, Leon, *Political Ideologies: Their Origins and Impact*, 5th ed., (Englewood Cliffs, N.J.: Prentice-Hall, 1994).
Barry, Norman, *On Classical Liberalism and Libertarianism* (New York: St. Martin's Press, 1987).
Berlin, Isaiah, *Four Essays on Liberty* (New York: Oxford University Press, 1969).
Collins, Peter, *Ideology after the Fall of Communism* (New York: Boyars and Bowerdean, 1993).
Earwell, Roger, and Anthony Wright, eds., *Contemporary Political Ideologies* (New York: St. Martin's Press, 1993).
Ebenstein, William, and Edwin Fogelman, *Today's Isms: Communism, Fascism, Capitalism, Socialism*, 10th ed. (Englewood Cliffs, N.J.: Prentice-Hall, 1994).

Griffin, Roger, ed., *The Nature of Fascism* (London: Pinter, 1991)

Hampsher-Monk, Iain, *The Political Philosophy of Edmund Burke* (Toronto: Copp Clark Pitman, 1987).

Heywood, Andrew, *Political Ideologies* (New York: St. Martin's Press, 1992).

Horowitz, Asher, and Gad Horowitz, *Everywhere They Are in Chains: Political Theory from Rousseau to Marx* (Scarborough, Ont.: Nelson Canada, 1988).

Robin, Martin, *Shades of Right: Nativist and Fascist Politics in Canada 1920–1940*, (Toronto: University of Toronto Press, 1991).

Rosenbaum, Ron, *Explaining Hitler: The Search for the Origins of His Evil* (New York: Random House, 1998).

Skidmore, Max, *Ideologies: Politics in Action* (Chicago: Harcourt Brace Jovanovich, 1989).

 **Weblinks**

www.keele.ac.uk/depts/po/thought.htm

This Web Page provides links to sites describing different types of political thought.

www.knuten.liu.se/~bjoch509/noframes/philosophers/philosophers.html

This is another useful site which provides links to examples of the work of great political thinkers.

CHAPTER 9

Contemporary Ideologies and Philosophies: Democratic and Authoritarian

The three great Western ideologies of the twentieth century spread quickly and easily across state borders around the world, sometimes withering among local cultures, sometimes mutating, adapting, and flourishing in new conditions to the extent that they occasionally even overpowered local patterns of thought.

Looking across the democratic-authoritarian spectrum of states, we find that ideologies are employed in distinctive ways by different kinds of governments. The ideas often differ, and so do the ways they are manifested in and by political institutions. This chapter surveys the modern influence and development of the three great ideologies, and some of their derivatives, within the broad range of democratic and authoritarian regimes in the world today. Our survey includes political systems in Canada, the United States, Great Britain, the former USSR, China, and countries of the Middle East.

In World War II, and later during the Cold War, ideologies confronted each other with dramatic and sometimes horrifying consequences. Now the appeal of those ideologies is waning, and in their place are rising narrower philosophies, such as environmentalism, deconstructionism, and feminism, which are directed at resolving more specific societal issues. Islamic fundamentalism and nationalism are arguably the most dynamic ideologies today. These topics, and arguments about the excesses and the decline of ideology, are considered in the second half of this chapter.

IDEOLOGY IN DEMOCRATIC REGIMES

Politics and political institutions in the world's democracies have been shaped primarily by the liberal ideology. Western constitutional order has a "liberal" core, as does the working of the market economy. The underlying logic of liberalism is that individuals should be free to pursue their own interests, and this pursuit renders political conflict inevitable.[1] Freedom is a fundamental commitment of democratic societies, and it is the task of political institutions to resolve resulting conflicts peacefully.

Contemporary Liberalism

In the last chapter we examined the historical roots and ideas of classical liberalism. Today, many liberals have moved away from some of the classical tenets of the ideology to a new position, often called **reform liberalism** because it "reformed" the classical approach to the concept of freedom. The initial motivation for this change was the need to relieve the extensive poverty of the new working class in the cities of Britain.

There are three essential differences between classical liberalism and reform liberalism. First, the idea of classical liberals that government should be left to the propertied class gave way to democratic principles of mass participation. Second, the concept of freedom was intensified and changed to mean not only freedom from coercion but also "positive power or capacity of doing or enjoying" something worthwhile.[2] In practice, this means that the state may have to curb some liberties in order to provide a higher standard of living for the least-well-off in society. British philosopher T.H. Green and American philosopher John Dewey were key figures in developing the liberal rationale to support a stronger role for the state in modern society.[3] Their new interpretation of what freedom implies provided the justification for the Liberal Party in Britain, and later in Canada, to lay the foundations of the welfare state. More recently, the rationale for assisting the poor in society has been extended by reform liberals to encompass other groups in need of assistance, including racial minorities, aboriginals, women, and the disabled. Apart from this modification to help the less fortunate in society, reform liberals continue their fundamental commitment to freedom of expression, including condemning censorship in all forms.

The third way that reform liberalism differs from its classical roots is in the field of economics. In classical liberalism the role of the government in the economy was essentially limited to rule enforcement for laissez-faire capitalism; competition, private entrepreneurship, and the profit motive were seen as the driving forces of the economy. This premise was contested in England and continental Europe by various groups including socialists, Christian reformers, monarchists, and the aristocracy, who argued that the democratic state should act to prevent extreme inequalities.

Reform liberals accepted the teaching of economist John Maynard Keynes who argued that reliance on market spontaneity could result in a permanent economic depression, and that this could be avoided by governments adopting appropriate fiscal and monetary measures.[4] Liberals who accepted this thinking reconciled economic intervention with their notion of freedom by saying that economic intervention was necessary to enable individuals to fulfill their desires. They realized that state intervention was needed to make the market work. Many governments, including those of Britain, Canada, and the United States followed this liberal reasoning after World War II.

Reform liberals also advocate that governments should protect individuals when large corporations reduce competition in key markets. They maintain that when effective competition is no longer possible, the government must play a regulatory role to protect society. Again, they see the role of the state as being to correct the injustices of the marketplace as well as other social problems.

Contemporary liberal values include the importance of individual rights and freedoms, political equality, limited government, rule of law, minimum conditions of life guaranteed by the state, and modified economic freedom. In other words, modern liberalism favours minimum government intervention in the private lives of citizens, but considerable government intervention in economic affairs.

Adherence to these values is far from uniform across the Western democracies, largely because of different political cultures. In the eighteenth and nineteenth centuries liberalism was strong in Britain where it originated, and somewhat less strong, though still important, on continental Europe. However, liberalism in Europe declined throughout the twentieth century as socialists adopted the more moderate philosophy of social democracy, and conservatives adopted some progressive tenets. In Britain, the Liberal Party, which alternated in office with the Conservatives for the early years of this century up to World War I, declined in the 1920s and 1930s as it lost ground to the social democratic Labour party. Today it is a relatively weak third force.

In North America, however, liberalism has been a dominant ideology for much of the nineteenth and twentieth centuries. In 1789, the United States based its constitution on liberal ideas, including guarantees of individual freedom and the decision to limit the power of government by not allowing powers to be too concentrated in any one branch. Free enterprise and a free market, competition and profit are still widely accepted, although there has been marked disillusionment with "welfare liberalism" in the United States in the late 1990s.

In Canada, reform liberalism was particularly popular in the period following the Great Depression in the 1930s when the trend was to social welfare policies that promised a more just and equitable society. Canada has had Liberal governments for most of the period from 1921 to 1999. However the party system in Canada is not highly ideological, and there is not always a well-defined policy difference between Liberals and Conservatives whose basic ideas are both firmly lodged in the centre of the political spectrum. In the United States, there is no sharply defined ideological conflict between the Republican and Democratic parties either, but rather a pragmatic approach to find the solution that works best for any particular issue. In the 1930s, and thereafter, the ideas of social democracy were absorbed into the Democratic Party. As we noted in the last chapter, the range of ideological expression is quite limited in the United States—even more than it is in Western Europe and Canada.

Liberalism is not usually a popular ideology in developing countries, partly because poorer countries are unable to establish economic and political stability without strong governmental control of the economy and society.

Conservatism

Conservatism, like liberalism, has undergone considerable revision since its inception. In Europe, conservatism was a strong force in the nineteenth and early twentieth centuries. Then, after World War II, when the old social order had been destroyed, European conservatism changed. In adapting to the new circumstances, it gave qualified acceptance to the notion of the welfare state, but still sought to preserve traditional moral values and a social structure that would provide leadership for society. When, for example, the British Conservative Party replaced Labour as the government in 1951, it did not dismantle the welfare system that Labour had built. Instead, it tried to slow the pace of reform until society had time to adjust to a new direction.[5] Under Margaret Thatcher's leadership in the 1980s, however, the Conservative government quickly reduced state intervention in the economy. British Conservatives retain their commitment to democratic principles and representative government, and have built a wide base of support from all levels of society—although they retain elitist principles that authority should be entrusted to natural leaders, and reject the egalitarianism of their opponents.

On the European continent, conservatism appeared under different labels. Post–World War II conservative parties moved to the centre and took over Christian or Catholic movements. In countries such as Germany and Italy, Christian Democratic parties took up the traditional conservative theme of preserving the established church. In France, the conservative Gaullist party dominated politics from 1958 to 1981.

There was a perceptible rise in conservativism throughout the Western democracies in the 1980s and early '90s; parties espousing conservative ideology governed in Great Britain, the United States, Canada, Japan, Italy, and Germany during much of this time. Under British Prime Ministers Margaret Thatcher and John Major, Presidents Ronald Reagan and George Bush, Canadian Prime Minister Brian Mulroney, and German Chancellor Helmet Kohl, conservative thought in Britain, the United States, and Canada and Germany largely converged.

Historically, European conservatism had never been a strong part of American culture because the United States was founded and populated largely by "liberals." There was no aristocracy or "old order" to defend. However, in the 1930s those who opposed the welfare-state philosophy of liberalism adopted the conservative label. Today, American conservatism stands predominantly for the preservation of traditional moral and religious values, and for the economic laissez-faire ideas of economists such as Milton Friedman and Friedrich A Hayek. American conservatives are now mostly found in the Republican party, which has melded together traditionally conservative moral values with the core ideal of completely free markets—originally defended by nineteenth-century liberals. "They are liberals who subscribe by and large to the tenets of nineteenth-century capitalism ... they believe in economic individualism, competition, and the free enterprise system."[6]

In direct contrast to their liberal counterparts, American conservatives encourage government intervention in the personal lives of citizens to defend moral and religious values, but minimum intervention in economic affairs. In the 1980s religious fundamentalism gained strength in the United States and became a political movement designed to promote conservative views. When he became Speaker of the House of Representatives in 1994, Newt Gingrich set the agenda of the following Congress with his "Contract with America," a coherent party platform with the theme of "less government," and the idea that a crumbling social fabric can be mended by government opprobrium, balanced budgets, school prayer, private charity, and a return to past values. Conservatism has become inherently pessimistic, returning to themes of cultural decline, moralism, and the need for greater state control in the field of ethics. In defending the market economy and economic individualism, modern conservatism includes promoting reduced social spending, deregulation of business (lifting government controls on market activity), privatization (sale of government-owned assets to the private sector), and downsizing of government activities. Projects of the welfare state are selectively opposed.

In general terms, conservatives today still seek to preserve the status quo, or look to aspects or conditions from the past that they would like to revive. They tend to see the state as the protector and promoter of morality, social responsibility, and traditional institutions and practices. They are therefore against pornography and abortion, and are supportive of the "traditional" family. Modern conservatives tend to oppose affirmative-action policies for women or homosexuals on the grounds that, as advocates of human rights, they support equality of treatment. They also tend to be against legalization of drugs such as marijuana because it involves pleasure-seeking for individuals rather than the good of society as a whole.

In international relations, conservatism in the United States advocated tough opposition to the spread of communism, which it viewed as a major threat to the Western capitalist world. Under former President Ronald Reagan, the American military arsenal was built up and support was given to anti-Marxist regimes and counterrevolutionary groups in Central and South America and throughout the world.

In continental Europe today, there is little distinction between liberalism and conservatism; both accept existing political, economic, and social institutions. Conservatives oppose state regulation and redistribution of resources somewhat more than do liberals, who tend to advocate moderate reforms. In Canada, conservatism is now the basis of two parties—the Progressive Conservatives and the Reform parties (see Chapters 16 and 17).

In developing countries, aspects—but not a wholesale philosophy—of conservatism are often advocated by traditional leaders. This is true, for example, where there is a religious and aristocratic hierarchy such as in Saudi Arabia, Kuwait, or Iran. Aspects of conservatism are found in all dynasties and theocracies, in most authoritarian military regimes, and in some one-party states where tradition, hierarchy, and authority are related justifications of the political system.

Democratic Socialism

Socialism developed later than liberalism and conservatism, but by the early 1900s it had a major following in Europe. Early in the twentieth century the Social Democratic Party was the largest party in Germany, and its counterparts had wide appeal throughout Western Europe where, in most countries, democratic socialism was the driving force in introducing the modern welfare state. It sapped the strength of the Liberal Party in Britain where the welfare state was introduced in 1945 on the initiative of the Labour Party. In North America, however, democratic socialism was less attractive. It did not take root in the United States. Since the 1930s, however, it has had a relatively small but persistent following in Canada, represented today by the New Democratic Party. (The NDP has never been in power federally, but, in 1999, it formed two of the ten provincial governments.)

There have been significant changes to socialist thought in recent decades. While many socialists maintain a "warm place in their hearts" for public enterprises, nationalizing industries is no longer a key component of their doctrine. In fact, they have all but abandoned the idea, and have even moved, grudgingly, to selective privatization along with slimmer government and lower taxes.[7] According to C.A.R. Crosland, a leading social democratic spokesman in Britain, it is no longer valid to identify socialism with public ownership "because the alienation of the workers is an inevitable fact whether ownership is 'capitalist' or 'collectivist,' and ... because even capitalist ownership is increasingly divorced from effective control."[8] Crosland maintains that the essence of socialism today is rather a set of what he calls "moral values." These can be summarized as recognizing the need to:

1. Ameliorate the material poverty and physical squalor produced by capitalism;
2. Contribute to the social welfare of those in need;
3. Support equality and the classless society;
4. Promote fraternity and cooperation; and
5. Fight the negative effects of capitalism such as mass unemployment.

Seen in this light, social democrats believe they can achieve progress toward these "moral goals" within the modern welfare state. They are not, however, monolithic in this belief. Some advocates argue that reducing the inequities caused by capitalism does nothing to eliminate their underlying causes. Another spokesman, G.D.H. Cole, for example, argued many years ago that softening the abuses of capitalism simply undercuts support for socialism and the goal of a classless society.[9] Today, Social Democratic and Labour parties are active and popular throughout most of Western Europe.

Modern democratic socialism strives to preserve individual freedom and to promote peaceful constitutional change, social equality, and the need to alleviate the negative effects of capitalism. Apart from that, today's Socialist parties have all but abandoned many of their old policies. They have been forced to grudgingly advocate smaller governments, lower taxes, and privatization, all of which they once bitterly opposed. In recent years social democratic parties have embraced pollution as a major issue and are actively looking for a new public philosophy. Where parties called "socialist" are doing better, it is partly because they no longer espouse the traditional tenets of socialism.

In Europe, and also to a lesser degree in Canada, political parties are more readily identified with political ideologies than they are in the United States. In the United States, there are relatively few ideologues in the more "left-wing" Democratic Party. As we have noted, the membership of both majpr parties is predominantly centrist. In Western Europe the left-right expression of opinion in political parties is considerably wider, with relatively smaller percentages of voters being found in the centre—even when the active Communist parties are not considered.[10] Chapters 16, 17, 18, and 19 discuss the relations between parties and electorates more thoroughly.

IDEOLOGY IN AUTHORITARIAN REGIMES

Ideologies in authoritarian regimes cover a wide range, with some such as fascism, Nazism, and Islamic fundamentalism on the right of the spectrum and variants of socialism and communism on the left.

In totalitarian regimes, ideology is all-encompassing and utopian. It reaches into all aspects of life, making prescriptions about what is just and providing principles to judge what is good or bad. It is formulated exclusively by, and is an important tool of, the leadership, who use it to control all aspects of society and to provide and justify the goals of the state. Such ideologies are highly mobilizing, calling for action and sacrifice. Soviet communism under Stalin was a prime example.

These generalizations are basically true of all authoritarian regimes; the difference is a matter of degree. When authoritarian regimes are not totalitarian, official ideology is less pervasive. In this circumstance political demands tend to be for acquiescence and obedience rather than submission and a "believer" mentality. In tyrannies such as the classic example of General Trujillo in the Dominican Republic (1930–1961), for example, coercion and complicity are used to obtain support and consent. Dynastic monarchies such as the current one in Saudi Arabia appeal to traditional religious values, hierarchy, and deference. Military regimes such as the one that took over Algeria in 1992 rely on coercion or manipulation, and sometimes limited representation. When a single mass party based on an authoritarian ideology takes control of a country, as in Iran, it normally exercises strong central control over communications, law enforcement, the military, and the economy.

While there is no organized, worldwide Communist party, and no single "communist ideology," communist parties share a certain body of theory. Their common theme is a strong Communist party that defines the ideology and revolutionary principles: collectivism, centralization of power, and elite rule. There are, however, many variations in communist ideology.

Following World War II, most of Eastern Europe established communist regimes and came under the Soviet Union's control. This included East Germany, Hungary, Czechoslovakia, Romania, Bulgaria, and Poland, as well as the small, conquered, border states of Latvia, Estonia, and Lithuania. The former Yugoslavia had organized its own socialist revolution during the war, without direct Soviet military involvement, and remained relatively independent.

Ideological differences between communist and capitalist democratic countries became sharply defined after World War II, creating the Cold War. In this period the Soviet Union and its Eastern European satellite countries formed a united communist bloc, and, following their ideological precepts, assisted the spread of communism throughout the world. At its height, communism was the official ideology of 16 countries. They achieved power through revolutionary force, guerilla warfare, or elections. In many other countries communist parties kept the dogma alive. Communist governments were established in China, Cuba, Vietnam, and several developing countries. The Soviet Union became the centre of world communism, and the undisputed ideological leader. Ideological differences (discussed below) soon emerged between the Soviet Union and China, and caused a break between the two. However, efforts continued to bring other communist regimes and parties under Soviet leadership and control, and to impose the Soviet model of communism in other countries. By the late 1980s it was clear that both of these efforts had failed. The collapse took the world by surprise. The Soviet Union, as such, officially ceased to exist in December, 1991.

Communist Ideology in the Soviet Union

The late 1980s brought remarkable change to the face of Soviet communism before the Soviet Union abruptly disintegrated. In 1985, Mikhail Gorbachev became the first Soviet leader in the postwar era to attempt to reform the communist ideology on which politics and economics in the Soviet Union were based. At the twenty-seventh Congress of the Communist Party of the Soviet Union (CPSU) in 1986, he officially launched a new era of *perestroika* (restructuring) and *glasnost* (openness), which were symbolic of the new thought. **Perestroika** aimed to dismantle and decentralize the enormous bureaucracy that controlled industry, agriculture, and trade. **Glasnost** aimed to liberalize the political regime by allowing open public debate in the party and in society generally.[11]

On this basis, Gorbachev initiated reforms aimed at overcoming the stagnant economy and technological backwardness and corruption of his country. He declared that the central planning process at the heart of the Soviet economy did not work—it had failed in agriculture, in technological modernization, in satisfying consumer demand, and in distribution. He advocated replacing the state-directed economy with a market economy based on the natural forces of supply and demand.[12] This "new thinking" dominated all government policies and moved Soviet society toward economic and political freedoms at home and cooperation abroad. Meanwhile, the Communist Party gave up its monopoly of political expression, and a plethora of movements and parties emerged.[13]

Reforms in the Soviet state left interdependent communist states in a crisis over their economies, ideology, and political institutions. The countries of Eastern Europe were the first to abandon communism. As the ideological reins of communism loosened, the political map of Eastern Europe changed.

> Stalinist power in the Soviet bloc was an extension of the false Soviet claim to be the ascendant world power that was riding the tide of historical inevitability. When Gorbachev abandoned that claim, he removed the keystone from the structure of Stalinist control. The walls came tumbling down—literally in Berlin, figuratively all across the Soviet empire.[14]

The speed of change was astonishing. In November 1989, the world witnessed the dramatic opening of the Berlin wall. East and West Germany were reunited; democratic elections were held in the Soviet satellite states of Poland, Hungary, and Czechoslovakia; the Albanian, Bulgarian, and Romanian dictatorships were overthrown; and Eastern Europeans generally struggled to rid themselves of the burdens of extreme state control as dictated by the communist ideology.

Within the Soviet Union itself, the republics which had been kept under tight control by the Communist Party were restive with the slow pace of economic and political reform. Ideological turmoil was rampant. By December 1991, after an aborted takeover of the Soviet Union by hard-line elements, the new reformers, headed by Boris Yeltsin, had won. Gorbachev resigned, the CPSU and communist ideology were discredited, and the Soviet Union itself was dissolved (see Map 11.1). The dismantling of the Communist Party in the Soviet Union and its later resurgence is discussed in Chapter 17.

Variations in Communist Ideology: China

The Chinese Communist Party (CCP) adopted the basic elements of Marxist-Leninism from Soviet communist thought, and on that foundation created a distinctive ideology adapted to achieve its own goals. Chinese communists regard their comprehensive ideology as consisting of two major components: Marxist-Leninism and the thought of Mao Tse-tung.[15]

Mao Tse-tung (1893–1976) was a founder of the Chinese Communist Party in 1921. He became Chairman of the People's Republic of China in 1949 and was the undisputed leader until his death in 1976. A fervent admirer of the thinking of Marx and Lenin, Mao accused the Soviets of distorting the true Marxist vision. He believed that Marxist principles had to be "sinified," or blended with themes of Chinese culture, thus adapting, or "nationalizing" socialism, and also socializing the nation.[16] Mao wrote:

> China has suffered a great deal in the past from the formalist absorption of
> things foreign. Likewise, in applying Marxism to China, Chinese
> Communists must fully and properly unite the universal truth of Marxism
> with the specific practice of the Chinese Revolution.[17]

Marxist-Leninism provided the basis of a new moral order to replace the eroding Confucian order in China. The resulting distinctive system is sometimes referred to as Confucian-Leninism, in which the rulers claim to have a monopoly on virtue, and this moral superiority gives them the right to defend the moral order of Chinese society.[18]

Marx and Lenin believed that the peasantry could be helpful at times, but that only the working class and its leaders in the Communist Party could develop the proper revolutionary consciousness to establish socialism. Mao accorded peasants a much greater role in his theory; he said the revolution would be made in close association with them, and in great part, by them. Unlike Marx, he stressed the role of peasants and populism, of national self-sufficiency. The transition to communism, he said, required not only a class revolution but a social and cultural revolution, and this meant permanent political struggle. To this end, unlike Marx, he supported guerilla wars in agrarian societies in order to spread communism abroad. He believed that as the most populated of the world's underdeveloped countries, and as the first to have undergone total social revolution, Chinese Communists had a duty to work for the "proletarianization" of the world.

By the 1950s, China was seeking to advance the cause of world communism by supporting wars of national liberation in Third World countries such as Cambodia, the Philippines, and Vietnam. The class struggle was manifested in the fight of emerging nations against "foreign imperialists." Communists organized revolutions in poor countries in the belief that discontent eventually would spread to capitalist countries. Latin America, for example, was often viewed as "the testing ground" of their view on contemporary world history.[19] At home, Mao developed the People's Liberation Army into an effective political and educational tool with which to buttress his ideas.

We have noted that whereas Marx's ideology was deterministic, Lenin and, even more so, Stalin disassociated themselves from economic determinism. Mao stressed **voluntarism**, that is, that man is not necessarily dominated by impersonal forces; human will and effort can affect the outcome of historical events. Mao said that:

> while we recognize that in the general development of history the material determines the mental and social being determines social consciousness, we also—and indeed must—recognize the reaction of mental on material things.[20]

Mao believed that the safeguard of socialism was the popular involvement and participation of the people; support of and identification with the peasantry was paramount in his thinking.

The ideological gulf between China and the former USSR remained after Mao's death, although great changes took place in China after that event. There was a relaxation of ideological rigour and an end to the worst forms of repression. Excesses were blamed not on Mao but on his advisors. The four fundamental principles of Chinese communism were, however, upheld—socialism, single–party leadership, dictatorship of the proletariat, and modified Marxism–Leninism. In October 1987, at the party's thirteenth Congress, the leadership was rejuvenated and the communist ideology seriously qualified; decentralization and dismantling of bureaucratic controls were undertaken to open the way to new capitalist incentives in the economy. And China opened its doors to foreign trade and investment. However the Communist Party remains paramount in China, and the economy remains under state control. China disassociated itself from the ideological chaos and disintegration in the former Soviet Union.

In 1991, the country's top leaders announced that China would stick with orthodox socialism, and play down the role of economic reform. As usual, they asserted that socialism would make China "strong" and its people "rich," and outlined a new five-year plan and a ten-year economic blueprint emphasizing socialist ideology.[21] At the same time, however, they continued to liberalize the economy. Enterprise zones were set up and stock markets developed.

Some similarities in how China and the Soviet Union used Marxist ideology to guide their revolutions are worth noting. Lenin and Mao both relied heavily on ideology to build their governments and create more integrated, authoritarian societies. The fact that dedicated communists had helped overthrow the previous regimes gave their communist governments considerable legitimacy. Once in power they used that legitimacy to purge and eliminate opposition by removing dissidents from government and other positions of responsibility.

In both countries the Communist Party was the vehicle to teach and enforce ideological conformity. Communist parties strictly control their membership. In China today, as in the former Soviet Union, membership in the Communist Party is by invitation only; one cannot simply choose to join.[22] The party therefore has been composed of a select core of individuals who owe allegiance to it. In China, the party still controls all positions in the government bureaucracy. Under Mao, expertise, knowledge, and technical skills were less important than ideologically "correct thought" in filling bureaucratic positions.[23] Emphasis was placed on obedience to the party and conformity to ideology according to Mao rather than efficient technical performance. Accordingly, leadership in China, as in the former USSR, disparaged and often brutalized the intellectual classes. During the Cultural Revolution, which began in 1966, Mao taught that all knowledge must be subordinate to ideology, and banished many students and intellectuals to the countryside to "learn from the people." As we shall see in Chapter 15, he tried but failed to replace bureaucracy with revolutionary ideology. Since his death, Mao's ideas have been used selectively by China's leaders rather than as a dogma.

Neither the former Soviet Union nor China retained totalitarian regimes. They both retreated early from the ideological obsession necessary for totalitarianism. Communist ideology teaches people that through their hard work and sacrifice they are helping construct the first real utopia. While that ideology is now in disrepute in the new states of the shaky Commonwealth of Independent States (CIS) which was formed from the Soviet Union, in China, the idealism has crumbled and widely been replaced by cynicism and resentment toward what is viewed as a tenacious, corrupt, privileged elite. In Beijing, the capital of China, the brutal 1989 Tiananmen Square massacre of students demonstrating for democratic reforms revealed problems that will continue to hamper that country's modernization (see Chapter 17).

Today, China enjoys the combination of relatively free market economics and authoritarian one-party rule. Many areas of life have been freed from state control. Signs of individualism in ideas as in fashion are clearly evident. The old men at the top of the party hierarchy are dying. The belief in communism is also fading, but for now, however, over one billion Chinese people still live under a form of communist ideology.

Variations in Authoritarian Regimes: Islamic Fundamentalism and Baath Party Socialism

Elements of Western thought have had strong appeal in some authoritarian Arab and Muslim states in North Africa and the Middle East. While Saudi Arabia and Iran can be viewed as manifestations of conservatism, Libya, Iraq, and Syria are examples of countries with indigenous varieties of socialism. Saudi Arabia is an absolute monarchy ruled by King Fahd Al Saud: it has only rudimentary political institutions and did not have political parties until 1987. Iran, whose population is 95% Shiah Muslim, is ruled by the Islamic Republican Party, which allows some controlled opposition and some freedom of the media.[24] Libya is a dictatorship, and Iraq is a dictatorship buttressed by the country's only effective legal party, the Arab Baath Socialist Party. Syria, too, is firmly ruled by Arab Baath Socialists. When Baathist leader Hafiz al-Assad came to power in Syria in 1970, he allied the country with the former USSR.

Baath party socialism, the second major ideology of the Middle East, provides the ideology and principles behind the political activities of Iraq and Syria. The Arab Baath Socialist Party was founded in Damascus in the 1940s. It set as its task the creation of a new Arab man: disciplined, incorrupt, and committed to Arab nationalism and mild socialism.[25] The secular principles of the ideology were always vaguely stated. The ideology took root in Iraq where the party structure is dominated by Saddam Hussein and in Syria under Hafiz al-Assad. Each asserts the right to lead the Baath Socialists. In both countries socialism is a tool used by the political party to penetrate all aspects of life, sometimes using repression and terror.

In Libya (predominantly Sunni Islam), Muammar Qadhafi also took a strong socialistic approach after the coup that brought him to power in 1969. He abolished the mixed economy that had existed in Libya. He nationalized private corporations, transforming the wholesale and retail trade in Libya into state enterprises, putting small shopkeepers out of business, and he suppressed all opposition.

Similar socialist ideals were part of the rhetoric that helped to overthrow the Shah of Iran in 1979. These were not pursued, however, largely because an ensuing eight-year war with Iraq consumed much of Iran's resources. As leader of the fundamentalist Islamic political ideology in the 1980s, Ayatollah Ruhollah Khomeini set up a revolutionary Islamic government in Iran. He held the office of *Faqquih*, which is the earthly representative of the Imam. The Shiite fundamentalist sect personified by Khomeini describes the Imam as a divinely inspired, infallible spiritual leader. The Imam is

... both sinless and absolutely infallible in his supposed pronouncements on the dogma and indeed on all matters ... belief in the Imam and submission to him is ... the third cardinal article of faith, after a belief in God and his apostle.[26]

Khomeini maintained that "there is not a single topic in human life for which Islam has not provided instruction and established norms."[27] With the help of the Islamic Republican Party (IRP), Khomeini instigated a cultural revolution and oversaw the "Islamization" of educational institutions, city planning, media and entertainment, and also such details as clothing, food habits, manners, and family relations. Terror was an accepted tool of government under the IRP, and the Revolutionary Guards were established to attack anyone who threatened Islamic unanimity. When Khomeini died in 1989, Iran became somewhat less ideological and more traditionally authoritarian. The new President, Muhammad Khatzami, tends to emphasize pragmatic policies, including attempts to heal the diplomatic rift with the West. Today, Islamic fundamentalists in Iran speak of wanting a classless society and promoting collective choice over the rights of the individual, however the fundamentalist rulers tolerate a "middle class" and allow private property that is "non-exploitative."

As we saw in Chapter 7, Islam is a territorially expansionist religion that is powerful and growing in force. There are 34 countries where Muslims are expected to form a majority of the population by the year 2000; in 25 of them it will be the religion of more than 90% of the people.[28] Following the Gulf War in 1991, a wave of Islamic fundamentalism swept North Africa. A highly organized fundamentalist minority would have come to power in Algeria in January 1992 had the election not been stopped by a military takeover. Fundamentalists are also a strong force in Morocco and Tunisia, but they have not made any significant political gains. In Turkey, as well, there has been a resurgence of Islamic fundamentalism. In the 1995 national elections the Islamic Welfare Party won 21%—the biggest share of the vote—and 158 of the 550 seats in Parliament. By 1996 it shared government power. In early 1997, concerned by what it saw as too much religious influence, the military engineered the overthrow of this government and banned the Welfare Party. In early 1999 a new coalition government was set up under Bülent Ecevit to lead the country until new elections were held. The Virtue Party, Welfare's successor, did poorly in the April 1999 election. (See Close Up 7.3 in Chapter 7.)

THE END OF IDEOLOGY?

In the mid-1950s and '60s, the idea that ideology was in decline in the West became popular.[29] As one author expressed it, "Ideology, which once was a road to action, has become a dead end."[30] This proposition maintained that ideology had been the fundamental cause of the devastating wars of the first half of the twentieth century. Ideological systems, it was said, bred political intransigence, which led to totalitarianism and war. The wars had brought disillusionment with grand ideologies, and consequently the appeal of ideological systems was waning, and they would disappear. Proponents of this idea noted that concepts such as the welfare state and representative democracy had taken the place of ideology. Differences in support for or against such concepts were of degree rather than being based on diametrically opposed positions. In the place of ideology a more *pragmatic* approach to political issues was arising, such as "how much" and "how fast" to move on social or economic problems.

The ideological transition of the Soviet Union, for example, can be viewed in the contrasting statements of two Soviet leaders, one at the beginning and the other at the end of the twentieth century. Lenin said, "national wars against the imperial powers are not only possible and probable; they are inevitable, progressive, and revolutionary."[31] Gorbachev, in his 1988 speech to the United Nations, said it is "obvious that the use or threat of force no longer can or must be an instrument of foreign policy."[32]

Marxism has lost much of its fervour almost everywhere. As the People's Republic of China tentatively moves toward a market economy, Marxism's greatest popularity is in countries such as Cuba and in some academic circles. Market capitalism, the economic goal of both liberalism and conservatism, is widely accepted as "natural," but in many parts of the world it is "associated with selfishness, exploitation, inequality, materialism [and] war."[33]

The apparent ideological triumph of the West and the lack of viable alternatives to Western liberalism prompted the following controversial observation by American State Department official Francis Fukuyama:

> The century that began full of self-confidence in the ultimate triumph of Western liberal democracy seems at its close to be returning full circle to where it started; not to an "end of ideology" or a convergence between capitalism and socialism as earlier predicted, but to an unabashed victory of economic and political liberalism.[34]

He argues that the West has won the Cold War, and, therefore, we may be witnessing not just the end of the ideologies, but in fact the end of the progression of history as such. As we have seen, Karl Marx believed that the direction of historical development was determined; the clash of opposing ideologies would end with the achievement of a communist utopia at which point the state would wither away, and, in that sense, there would be no more history. Fukuyama argues that the communist dream has been discredited, but the end of history has still been reached. The endpoint of mankind's ideological evolution was not the communist utopia, according to his argument, but the universalization of Western liberal democracy as the final form of human government.

It is not certain that the "victory" of liberal democracy and consumer society will dominate the future. As we have seen, religious fundamentalism—particularly Islam, is still a thriving ideology. In many Western democracies, conservatism has adopted high moral positions on topics such as family values and anti-abortion platforms. To a large extent countries like Canada and the United States have adopted a much more conservative set of values in recent years. And many new ideologies on the scene are already vying for followers. Although some of the traditional ideological confrontations of the twentieth century have subsided, the appeal and usefulness of ideology in societies may mean that it is only in temporary remission.

New Ideologies and Philosophies

Recent decades have given rise to new, though as yet less comprehensive, philosophies that provide the momentum for several social movements. These include capitalism, environmentalism, post-modernism, right-wing extremism, feminism, and communitarianism. Some of those ideas have affected the teaching and scholarship of political science.

Capitalism

Capitalism reigns as the economic system that has most transformed societies in the modern world. It refers to both an economic system and an ideology. Recall that Marxist thought holds that capitalism contains flaws that make its demise inevitable. German sociologist Max Weber argued against Marx's determinism. Weber believed that ideas impact independently on political change and that the rise of capitalism was in part the impact of Protestantism. The Protestant religion encouraged thrift and the saving or reinvestment of profits. These values embedded in society, he said, facilitated the growth of capitalism in the West—that is, ideas affected economics, not the reverse.[35] In a capitalist system the major means of production are owned by individuals rather than by the state. The economic philosophy which underlies capitalism, as we noted earlier in the discussion of Adam Smith, emphasizes private ownership and a laissez-faire market economy that is little regulated by governments. It also emphasizes individualism and promotes the right of individuals to seek their own economic self-interest. Believers in individualism and laissez-faire economics still find a role for government in society—to regulate taxes, for example. Capitalists do not like steeply progressive taxes that require the rich to pay more. As an ideology, capitalism is a set of ideas that provides philosophical and analytical support for a certain kind of public policy-making. It is not a fully complete ideology, but today it is a powerful force in political movements, parties, and government policy-making in many countries.

Environmentalism

Environmentalism has been a natural successor to parts of utopian Marxism. Environmentalists criticize traditional ideologies as supporting industrialism, which exploits people and the planet alike. Europe's Green parties, which have increased their following in the past decade and now share the government in Germany, have led the way, linking opposition to unrestricted technological development with anti-nuclearism and anti-imperialism. Whereas Marxists advocated social control on behalf of the working class, environmentalists advocate social control on behalf of preserving nature.[36] They reject unsustainable industrialization that feeds continuous expansion of goods and services:

> If the system works, i.e., we achieve full employment, we basically destroy
> the planet; if it doesn't, i.e., we end up with mass unemployment, we destroy
> the lives of millions of people ... From the green point of view ... we hold
> true to the most important political reality of all: that all wealth ultimately
> derives from the finite resources of our planet.[37]

Moderate environmentalists criticize pollution, waste, and environmental degradation. Fundamental environmentalists go further to reject consumerism and economic growth, because they lead to environmental decay. They advocate a world approach that aims to achieve a new lifestyle based on conserving nonrenewable resources. To this end they tend to advocate not only international integration but also decentralization and democratization so that there are smaller units of production which are closer to the people. (For more on environmental issues, see Chapter 21.)

Post–Modernism

Another movement that has picked up support from flagging left-wing ideology consists of **post-modernism**. This movement, launched in France, is now current in the intellectual and ideological debates in both European and North American universities. The movement bases its arguments on philosophical **deconstructionism**. At its essence, this philosophy attacks the central values of Western culture. Post-modernists ridicule the academic ideal of disinterested, objective research on the ground that outsiders can never understand or interpret thought from group experiences to which they do not belong.

Post-modernists proclaim and champion new oppressed groups—not the working classes but certain ethnic and gender groups, including blacks, Hispanics, women, homosexuals, and Native peoples—who are seen to be politically dispossessed. They believe, for example, that no white person could write an account of the Zulu nation—or for that matter, no non-German Jew could write German history. Post-modernists reject North American society as a white, male-dominated system of cultural oppression. And they treat all ideas as equally deserving of respect—except those coming from Western civilization. Close Up 9.1 illustrates the kind of pressures post-modernist thought can have on traditional university courses.

Post-modernists do not believe there is any compelling standard for judging facts—or, for that matter, for determining what a fact is.[38] Following the precepts of the late French intellectual Michel Foucault, they maintain that knowledge about other people always devolves into power over them. Many post-modernists reject science as "male interests"—a product of the power structure it serves (see Close Up 9.2). For them, one narrative account of the world has as much validity as any other: "The task of the historian is not to discover ultimate truth, but rather to construct a convincing explanation of selected aspects of human behaviour."[39]

Right–Wing Extremism

In the last decade, **right-wing extremism** including racism and fascism has been revived on a small scale in many countries including the United States, Germany, France, Spain, and Italy. Far-right racist groups erupted with new vigour after the fall of communism in Eastern Europe, the collapse of the Soviet Union, and the reunification of

---

CLOSE UP 9.1 Should "Western Civilization" Courses be Taught?

In 1991 in the United States, it was announced that M. Bass would make a $120 million (U.S.) donation to Yale University to fund a course of studies in Western Civilization. Post-modernists and multiculturalists found any emphasis on Western Civilization studies offensive, and four years later no such curriculum had materialized. The administration decided, therefore, to do away with the original implementation plans and find a more "acceptable" use for the money on the basis of academic freedom. Mr Bass withdrew the grant.[40] Did the university make the correct decision?

CLOSE UP 9.2   Post–Modernism at the Smithsonian

Post-modernists and some environmentalists share a profound hostility to modern science. Some see disaster in new technologies, others argue that the laws of physics were constructed to maintain white male dominance. In 1995, the renowned Smithsonian Museum of American History's permanent exhibit "Science in American Life" displayed what amounted to a litany of environmental horrors. Exhibits included weapons of mass destruction, displays of pesticide residue, air pollution, acid rain, ozone holes, radioactive waste, and food additives. These are evils for which modern science is responsible, but there was no reference in the exhibit to positive facts such as that life expectancy in the United States more than doubled in the twentieth century, much due to modern science. "What century," *The New York Times* asked, "would the Smithsonian historians prefer to have lived in?" It is an astute question.[41]

Germany. In France, the racist demagoguery of Jean-Marie Le Pen and his extreme right-wing National Front political party is a good example. Le Pen's National Front party is dedicated to the preservation of the purity of the French nation and its culture. Its attack is on the more than 4.5 million immigrants in France today.[42] In Britain the neo-Nazi British National Party has also been active throughout the 1990s. Racists share the belief that races are inherently unequal and should be kept pure. They tend to be drawn to simplistic, often violent, solutions. Typical of these far-right groups are not only racist but also sexist and anti-intellectual ideas.

Feminism

Feminism is yet another system of beliefs. It emerged first with the suffragettes, who sought and won voting rights for women. The goals have been expanded and intensified by a "second wave" of feminists in the last quarter century who argue that orthodox theories about politics tend to ignore gender and harbour unconscious assumptions about the role of women. Today there are many different schools of feminist thought. All would oppose discrimination and active oppression against women. They seek more active representation by women in all aspects of life including politics, and have forced a range of policies onto the public agenda, particularly in Western democracies. These include equal pay for work of equal value, wider employment opportunities, child-care facilities, and the like.

There are various types of feminists. *Liberal* feminists support policies aimed at opening up equal competition between the sexes, and claim that this requires government support for such amenities as day care and policies to encourage equal representation in male-dominated professions. *Radical* feminists argue that social revolution is needed to restructure society. These radical feminists argue that gender is a more important social cleavage than class or race. Women, they say, are subjugated because of their biological function—having babies and raising families. Some radical feminists go so far as to advocate test-tube babies and child rearing by social institutions to break the patriarchal social pattern.[43] Feminism exists as a social movement, but like the other new ideologies it also has influenced traditional socialist and liberal thought—and has raised a counter-reaction among conservatives.

Communitarianism

Communitarianism is yet another rudimentary modern ideology—one which seeks a middle way between capitalism and socialism—between an ever-expanding welfare state and an unbridled free market. The communitarian philosophy was included in President Bill Clinton's election campaigns and has found interest in Europe as well. Amitai Etzioni says that Western politics have become obsessed with rights and has forgotten responsibilities. Consequently, society has disintegrated into a raw competition between individual claims. He believes that society needs an ethical basis—to build a sense of responsibility, institutions such as family, school, neighbourhood, and community that stand between the individual and the state must be revived. Communitarians say that these "closer" institutions are the answer to today's social and economic problems. Big government should be replaced by small government. Families should be made more responsible and divorce made more difficult. Communitarianists advocate workfare, community service, moral education in schools, and the public humiliation of criminals.

The great, comprehensive ideologies of the twentieth century—liberalism, conservatism, and socialism—have impacted on countries around the world. All countries have borrowed heavily from at least one, and often more, of them. Often, elites have tried to retain traditional values and also combine them with new ideological systems of thought in order to provide a new blueprint for political development. Today, however, these major ideologies are in decline; the simple divisions of the past—communism versus capitalism and liberal versus conservative—are losing much of their usefulness as ways to demarcate the states of the world. Ideologues, obsessed with the pursuit of grand, unrealistic goals in the names of their ideologies, are currently in disrepute. But new ideas continue to emerge and sometimes they generate new approaches to the study of political science. In recent years, branches of some of these new ideologies have appeared in new university institutions such as Departments of Afro-American Studies, Race Studies, Environmental Studies, and Gender Studies. As the discipline of political science evolves, fragments of these ideologies are also added to the corpus of the discipline, and sometimes even affect the core approaches.

DISCUSSION QUESTIONS

1. Is socialism dead? Marxism?
2. Is "feminism" an ideology? Is it radical or conservative?
3. Is post-modernism an ideology? Or is it an amalgam of social ills and dissatisfactions without a sense of goals or directions?

4. Is "communitarianism" going to become the one ideology which will replace all the others?

5. Was old-fashioned puritanism behind the effort to impeach President Bill Clinton following his affair with Monica Lewinsky?

KEY TERMS

capitalism, p. 203

communitarianism, p. 207

environmentalism, p. 204

feminism, p. 206

Glasnost, p. 197

Perestroika, p. 197

post-modernism, p. 204

reform liberalism, p. 191

right-wing extremism, p. 205

voluntarism, p. 199

ENDNOTES

1. Mark E. Kann, *Thinking about Politics: Two Political Sciences* (New York: West, 1980), pp. 15–42.

2. T.H. Green, "Liberal Legislation and Freedom of Contract" (1881) in John R. Rodman, ed., *The Political Theory of T.H. Green* (New York: Appleton-Century-Crofts, 1964), pp. 51–52.

3. John Dewey, "The Future of Liberalism," *Journal of Philosophy* April 25, 1935, pp. 225–30.

4. John Maynard Keynes, *The General Theory of Employment, Interest and Money* (New York: Harcourt Brace, 1936).

5. See Roy C. Macridis, *Contemporary Political Ideologies*, 4th ed. (Boston: Little, Brown, 1989), pp. 92–94.

6. *Ibid.*, p. 97.

7. See "The Left's New Start, a Future for Socialism," *The Economist*, June 11, 1994, pp. 11–12.

8. C.A.R. Crosland, *The Future of Socialism* (New York: Schocken, 1963), p. 67.

9. G.D.H. Cole, "Socialism and the Welfare State," in I. Howe, ed., *Essential Works of Socialism* (New York: Bantam, 1971), p. 777.

10. Giacomo Sani and Giovanni Sartori, "Polarization, Fragmentation and Competition in Western Democracies,: in Hans Daalder and Peter Mair, eds., *Western European Party Systems* (Beverly Hills, Calif.: Sage 1983), pp. 307–41.

11. Mikhail Gorbachev, *Perestroika* (New York: Harper & Row, 1987).

12. See Marshall I. Goldman, *Gorbachev's Challenge: Economic Reform in the Age of High Technology* (New York: W.W. Norton, 1987).

13. Macridis, *Contemporary Political Ideologies*, p. 155.

14. Robert G. Kaiser, "The End of the Soviet Empire: Failure on a Historic Scale," *The Washington Post National Weekly Edition*, January 1–7, 1990, pp. 23–24.

15. Franz Schurmann, *Ideological Organization in Communist China* (Berkeley, Calif.: University of California Press, 1968), p. 27.

16. E.H. Carr, *Nationalism and After* (London: Macmillan, 1945), p. 19.

17. Mao Tse-tung, "On New Democracy," in *Selected Works*, vol. 3 (New York: International Publishers, 1954), p. 154.

18. Lucian W. Pye, "China: Erratic State, Frustrated Society," *Foreign Affairs*, vol. 69, no. 4 (Fall 1990), pp. 60–63.

19. Schurmann, *Ideology and Organization in Communist China*, p. 42.

20. Mao Tse-tung, quoted in Frederick Wakeman, Jr., *History and Will* (Berkeley, Calif.: University of California Press, 1973), p. 299.

21. "China's leadership sticks with socialist orthodoxy," *Financial Times*, Jan. 2, 1991, p. 4.

22. Darrell P. Hammer, *The USSR* (Boulder, Col.: Westview Press, 1986), p. 82.

23. See Schurmann, *Ideology and Organization in Communist China*.

24. Only about 10% of all Muslims are Shiite, the most ideologically oriented sect, and they are located mainly in Iran and Iraq; the 80% who are Sunnis are concentrated in the Middle East, Africa, Pakistan, and Southeast Asia. *World Facts and Maps* (New York: Rand McNally, 1995) p. 129.

25. Paul Cammack et al., *Third World Politics* (Baltimore, Johns Hopkins University Press, 1988), pp. 34–44.

26. Thomas W. Lippman, *Understanding Islam* (New York: Mentor, 1982), p. 144.

27. Quoted in Cheryl Benerd and Zalmay Khalilzad, *The Government of God* (New York: Columbia University Press, 1984), p. 115.

28. George Thomas Kurian, *The New Book of World Rankings*, 3rd ed. (New York: Facts on File, 1991), p. 46.

29. Chaim I. Waxman, *The End of Ideology Debate* (New York: Simon & Schuster, 1969).

30. Daniel Bell, *The End of Ideology*, (New York: Collier, 1961), p. 393.

31. V.I. Lenin, "The Economic Base of the Withering Away of the State," in V.I. Lenin ed. *State and Revolution*, (Moscow: Foreign Languages Publishing House, 1968), p. 233. (Originally published in 1932)

32. Quoted in Harmon Zeigler, *The Political Community* (New York: Longman, 1990), p. 377.

33. Michael W. Doyle, "Liberalism and World Politics," *APSR*, vol. 80, no. 4 (December 1986), pp. 1151–1170.

34. Francis Fukuyama, "The End of History?" *The National Interest*, no. 16 (Summer 1989), pp. 3–18.

35. Max Weber, *The Protestant Ethic and the Spirit of Capitalism* (London: Allen & Unwin, 1930).

36. Ronald Inglehart and Hans D. Klingemann, "Ideological Conceptualization and Value Priorities," in Samuel H. Barnes and Max Kaase, eds., *Political Action* (London: Sage, 1979).

37. J. Porrett, *Seeing Green: The Politics of Ecology Explained* (Oxford: Basil Blackwell, 1984).

38. See Clifford Geertz, *After the Fact* (Cambridge, Mass.: Harvard University Press, 1995).

39. John Lankford, historian at Kansas State University quoted in *The New York Times*, July 9, 1995, p. 15.

40. See *The Wall Street Journal*, March 14, 1995.

41. See *The New York Times*, July 9, 1995.

42. Macridis, *Contemporary Political Ideologies*, p. 231.

43. Germaine Greer, *The Female Eunuch* (London: Paladin 1971); Kate Millett, *Sexual Politics* (Garden City, N.Y.: Doubleday 1970).

FURTHER READING

Albright, David E., ed., *Communism in Africa* (Bloomington: Indiana University Press, 1990).

Burton, Charles, *Politics and Social Change in China Since 1978* (New York: Greenwood, 1990).

Coole, Diana, *Women in Political Theory: From Ancient Misogyny to Contemporary Feminism* (Boulder, Colo.: Lynne Rienner Publishers, 1988).

Dobson, A. Green, *Political Thought* (London: Unwin Hyman, 1990).

Gellnor, Ernest, *Conditions of Liberty: Civil Society and Its Rivals* (New York: Allen Lane 1994).

———, *Post Modernism, Reason and Religion* (London: Routledge, 1992).

Gingrich, Newt, *To Renew America* (New York: Harper Collins, 1995).

Girvin, Brian, *The Right in the Twentieth Century* (London; Pintner, 1994).

Harris, Geoff, *The Dark Side of Europe: The Extreme Right Today* (Savage, Md.: Barnes and Noble, 1990).

Kristof, Nicholas D., and Sheryl WuDunn, *China Wakes: The Struggle for the Soul of a Rising Power* (New York: Times Books/Random House, 1994).

Lijphart, Arend, *Democracy in Plural Societies: A Comparative Exploration* (New Haven, Conn.: Yale University Press, 1977).

Lind, Michael, *The Next American Nation: The New Nationalism and the Fourth American Republic* (New York: Free Press, 1995).

Milner, Henry, *Sweden: Social Democracy in Practice* (Oxford: Oxford University Press, 1989).

Moaddel Mansoor, *Class, Politics and Ideology in the Iranian Revolution* (New York: Columbia University Press, 1993).

Nevitte, Neil, and Roger Gibbins, *New Elites in Old States: Ideologies in the Anglo-American Democracies* (Toronto: Oxford University Press, 1990).

Pierson, Paul, *Dismantling the Welfare State: Reagan, Thatcher and the Politics of Retrenchment* (Cambridge, Mass.: Cambridge University Press, 1994).

Toffler, Alvin and Heidi Toffler, *Creating a New Civilization: The Politics of the Third Wave* (Atlanta: Turner Publishing, 1995).

Ulam, Adam B. *The Communists: The Story of Power and Lost Illusions* (New York: Charles Scribners, 1992).

 **Weblinks**

english-www.hss.cmu.edu/feminism/
Links to numerous sites dealing with feminist thought and activities can be found at this site.

ernie.lang.nagoya-u.ac.jp/~miura/Postmodern_Sites
This site provides links to postemodern sites around the world.

www.greenpeace.org/
The is the Greenpeace International Web Page.

CHAPTER 10

Constitutional Frameworks

Establishing a stable and orderly state which is able to adjust to change in the social and economic environment is a necessity for all modern social systems. To this end, all states create rules or principles with which to guide the deliberations between the rulers and the ruled. These principles describe how power is to be distributed among citizens, delineate the organizations of the state, and grant leaders the legitimacy required to act authoritatively.

Such rules take a variety of forms depending on the level of political development in a state. In primitive societies they develop only through custom and usage. In complex, modern political systems these higher principles are almost invariably embodied, and often codified, in a constitution. A **constitution** provides the highest set of principles or laws in a country, creating the structures used for the resolution of conflict and imposing obligations on citizens and rulers.[1]

The idea of a constitution has been traced to ancient Greece and imperial Rome. Most modern constitutions, however, can be said to have their intellectual origins in the eighteenth and nineteenth centuries when autocracies were overthrown and replaced by representative institutions. Today, leaders in both democratic and most authoritarian political systems share the idea that to be considered legitimate they should have a constitution.

In modern times a constitution is said to include both normative guidelines and practical rules for governing. That is, it depicts at least the key institutions of governmental organization and lists the rules that restrain political leaders from engaging in arbitrary action. Most constitutions also stipulate how the constitution itself can be amended.

The existence of a constitution does not mean that its rules or obligations will last forever or that it will actually be effective in determining the relations between the rulers and the ruled. Some constitutions merely list philosophical platitudes that have little, if any, bearing on how the political system actually works. Politicians in authoritarian countries may not even believe they should be subject to a constitution.

Political scientists employ the word **constitutionalism** to depict the belief that everyone, including the government, should be subject to the rules of the constitution.[2] Constitutionalism sees the government as the servant of society, not its master. The government may exercise authority and even use coercion but it does so according to the rules set out in the constitution and abides by judicial interpretations of its actions.

WRITTEN AND UNWRITTEN CONSTITUTIONS: LAWS AND CONVENTIONS

Today, most constitutions are of the *written* type.[3] That is, most countries have a specific, written document that can be pointed to as their constitution. For that reason, in many countries the word is capitalized when it refers to the specific document or body of laws. A few countries such as Britain, Israel, and New Zealand, however, have not codified their constitutional laws into a single document.

The American constitutional document is the world's oldest continuing constitution. This "sacred" document, drawn up in 1787, continues to be authoritative in outlining the key institutions of the country. In fact, it is the only constitutional document resulting from the revolutions of the eighteenth century that is still in effect today.[4]

The German Constitution is unique. When West Germany was founded in 1949 the founding document was called *Grundgesetz* (basic law) rather than *Verfassung* (constitution) because the law was only to be provisional—that is, valid only until West and East Germany were reintegrated. One of the ironies of history is that in 1989, when the democratic and communist parts of Germany were reunited, the word *Grundgesetz* remained.

In traditional, autocratic systems, written constitutions were rare, and even today in many authoritarian regimes no written document depicts the authority of the government. No document restrains a dictator such as Saddam Hussein in Iraq or Hafiz al-Assad in Syria. In some systems a constitution is suspended by a tyrannical government, as was the case in Germany under Hitler. In other cases the human rights articulated in the constitution are ignored, as was the case in the USSR under Stalin or even more recently in Russia in 1993 when President Yeltsin ordered a military attack on the Duma (the Parliament) and then temporarily suspended the governing body.

Britain provides an interesting example of a democratic country which evolved from an absolute monarchical system to a democracy without a revolution and without preparing a "single" document called a constitution to depict the way it conducts its affairs or the relations between the government and its citizens. It is for this reason that Britain is often said to possess an *unwritten* constitution. There are, however, documents and statutes that explain Britain's constitutional laws. The most important parts of these British documents date from conflicts between citizens and the state. For example, the royal powers were restricted by the Magna Carta. This charter, forced on King John in 1215 and later adopted by Parliament, declared that even the King had to act within the laws of England. Among other documents that make up the British Constitution is the Bill of Rights of 1689, which prevented the King from levying taxes without the consent of Parliament.[5]

Canada has both a written and an unwritten constitution. A 1982 constitutional amendment codified all past constitutional laws into one document, provided for a Charter of Rights and Freedoms, and set up amending formulae for future revisions.

Because of Canada's British heritage, however, many of the most important parts of the small "c" constitution are not written down but require reference to historical precedent for direction. These include conventions such as how the Governor General names the Prime Minister and all of the rules about the relations of the executive to Parliament.[6]

In most countries a distinction is made between constitutional laws and conventions. A **convention** is a custom or practice that, while not necessarily a legal necessity, is nevertheless based on good reasons and time-honoured practices. As constitutions develop over time, the norms or customs of a society become incorporated into the rules for governing, but not all of them are written down in constitutional documents. In fact, for practical reasons not all the rules for conducting the affairs of a state can possibly be written down in any constitution, regardless of how detailed the document is. When conventions that are not laws conflict, the courts cannot make a final, legal determination concerning them (even though in some countries the courts may declare what conventions exist at any given time). Conventions are enforceable only in the sense that the government would lose the support of the people if they were not obeyed.

In general, the more precise a written constitution is about the machinery of government and the relations between citizens and the state, the less conventions are needed. In Britain and other countries that have adopted parliamentary systems (often called the **Westminster model**), constitutional conventions are extremely important. In Britain and Canada, for example, even the monarch's duty to choose the leader of the party with the most members in the House of Commons as Prime Minister is based on convention.

But unwritten constitutional conventions exist even in countries with written constitutions. In the United States, the Supreme Court is allowed to overturn acts of Congress, not because this principle is in the written constitution, but because of a convention developed from early cases in American history that this action could be appropriate. Because of this convention, it is often said that although the amending process in the United States has not permitted many actual or formal amendments, the Court, acting as the final arbiter, has changed the constitution on many occasions by its interpretation of the written word.[7] Similarly, according to the Constitution, the electoral college is authorized to select the President, but the members of the college almost without exception cast their ballots according to the way the people have voted in general elections.

Individual and Collective Rights

Constitutions are a product of their historical development as well as a reflection of contemporary values and beliefs about how governments should function. They convey **rights**—entitlements owed to individuals as duties by others. In this regard, most constitutions contain a statement extolling such values as natural rights, religious beliefs, life and liberty, and political rights such as freedom of speech and assembly. The stress on individual rights clearly differs from country to country, but most constitutions today give this concept a high degree of significance.

Individual rights are defined as individual claims against the state. The French *Declaration of the Rights of Man and Citizens*, the United States' *Constitutional Bill of*

Rights, and the former Soviet *Constitution* all include the principle of the rights of individuals. These rights are based on the principle that the constitution should draw no distinction among citizens because of their cultural, social, religious, or linguistic background or socioeconomic status. All individuals should be treated equally. According to this tradition, the constitution should not provide privileges or impose obligations on groups as such. However, many constitutions also specify **collective rights**. In other words, they call for distinctions to be made among "groups" in order to ensure equality of condition or of resources and bargaining power. The Canadian Charter of Rights and Freedoms lists both individual and collective rights, while other parts of the Constitution provide collective educational rights for specific denominational groups and language rights for others. In short, collective rights and entitlements have been granted to some groups and not others.[8] The fact that such individual or collective rights, or for that matter other higher principles, are mentioned in a written constitution is no guarantee that they will be acted on in the real world.

Another value often mentioned in constitutions is the goal or goals of the state. The constitutions of the former Soviet Union and, to an extent, Portugal both declare that the state is "socialist" and committed to a major transformation of society. Other governments are devoted, as is the Canadian Constitution, to "peace, order and good government." Such instrumental goals give the illusion that they can be obtained if people are diligent, whereas ideals such as "life, liberty, and the pursuit of happiness" (found in the American Constitution) are broad transcendental goals which herald a country's dominant values and beliefs.

We have already mentioned in Chapter 2 that a constitution also implies the **rule of law** or a guarantee that the state's actions will be governed by fairness and without malice. Put another way, according to the rule of law no individual is supposed to be above the law and no one ought to be exempted from it. Obviously, the rule of law and the adherence to a constitution are among the primary distinguishing features of a democracy. In authoritarian regimes citizens come to expect that the rulers may act against their own constitutions. That is, they may act autocratically—which was one of the distinguishing principles of an authoritarian regime as defined in Chapters 4 and 5.

However, on the practical level, every state has to have a means of dealing with emergencies such as wars, civil unrest, or natural disasters. Thus, even when a constitution stipulates that individual rights are to be upheld under normal conditions, there are usually constitutional provisions for the suspension of these same rights during a crisis. Of course, in any particular case the temporary suspension may, on occasion, turn out to be nothing less than a pretext for arbitrary action on the part of leaders.

A constitution, thus, is only a code about how government ought to operate. The formal institutions may or may not function according to the normative prescription of this code. In fact, a constitution may be devised and then discarded. Its institutions may be used, suspended, or even demolished. In short, we have to understand how constitutions and institutions operate in the real world in order to formulate any reasonable judgments about them.

Constitutional Amendment

All constitutions ought to include built-in mechanisms to accommodate future changes in society. The economic and social conditions of all states change over time, and it is important that the manner of conducting the affairs of the country remain in touch with contemporary realities. Thus, a constitution should be reasonably easy to change. But if the constitution is too easy to change, or if it is amended too often, or too drastically, its citizens will not be able to develop stable expectations about the relations between the rulers and the ruled. A compromise between these two goals is required. A primary question, then, is "What manner of amendment is reasonable?"

In political science a constitution that is easy to change is referred to as **flexible**, and one that is difficult to amend is called **rigid**. Rules for amendment must be structured in such a way that the people will not believe that their traditional way of doing things has been changed too greatly if there is an amendment. Put simply, the citizens must perceive any amendment and the new rules to be as legitimate as the old rules were.

The most flexible constitutions are unwritten; one body, such as the Parliament, is empowered by the people through tradition and custom to change the constitution by the mere passage of a resolution or bill. Britain and New Zealand have flexible constitutional amending formulae. The London and Wellington legislatures may amend the constitution simply by passing an ordinary law.

Rigid constitutions embody restrictions to formal constitutional change and special rules about how such changes are to be brought about. The United States, for example, possesses two rigid constitutional amendment procedures. In the usual form an amendment must be passed by a two-thirds majority of both houses of Congress and then ratified by three-quarters of the states. This rigid formula has resulted in only 27 formal amendments in well over 200 years. The second formal method of amending the United States' Constitution has never been used: it requires a national convention, convened by Congress upon petition of two-thirds of the states, and a ratification process similar to the first method of amendment.

Constitutional amendment has been a controversial problem in Canada for many years. After Confederation in 1867, Canada could not amend the important parts of its Constitution without asking the British Parliament to pass an act. This procedure was used a total of 17 times. However, in 1982 the Canadian Constitution was amended to provide domestic procedures for amendment. The formulae are very rigid as some of the most important details of the system of government can be amended only by the approval of both houses of Parliament and *all* 10 provincial legislatures. In 1990, a single elected legislator in the province of Manitoba delayed a constitutional amendment long enough that the three-year timetable on the proposed changes ran out. This action terminated the resolution and showed how profoundly difficult it is to achieve unanimity for constitutional amendments.

It is clear that countries such as Canada and the United States, which have rigid amendment formulas, will not pass very many constitutional amendments over the years. This rigidity, however, is intended to prevent governments from changing the constitution too readily. The special majorities and procedures prevent arbitrary actions by minimum majorities. Other countries have even more rigid rules. Some countries have constitutional rules that prevent amendments from becoming law until either a referendum is passed or an election is called to ratify the amendment. Even more rigid are the rules found in Australia and Switzerland, where a constitutional amendment is not adopted unless the proposal is approved by both a majority of voters *and* a majority of the states or cantons. In Belgium, the Netherlands, and Sweden a constitutional amendment must be approved by two legislatures: the one that initiates the legislation and the one that is in office after a *compulsory* election.

Constitutions may be changed by court decision as well as by formal amendment. Many countries adjust to changing social realities and new philosophies of governing in this manner. In their judgments on individual cases, judges interpret the vague or elastic clauses in a constitution and over time their piece-meal decisions add up to new constitutional dictums. In the United States the Supreme Court has dramatically changed the Constitution over the years by its decisions on specific cases. A celebrated case in modern times was in 1954 when the Court reversed earlier decisions and declared that separate schools for blacks and whites were not acceptable under the laws of the Constitution.[9]

Court decisions which affect the Constitution are highly charged political events in the United States. There are often complaints, for example, that the Supreme Court has "legislated" rather than simply interpreted the document "as it is." Judges who make their decisions according to the language or "letter" of a constitution rather than its "spirit" are called "strict constructionists." Since the courts may, in fact, be initiating major public policies when they make judgments on major cases, it is not surprising that ideological charges from liberals, conservatives, or others are raised on practically every issue of this type. The point is made by naming a few emotionally charged issues on which the Supreme Court has "legislated"—school segregation, school busing, school prayers, and capital punishment.

KEY GOVERNMENT INSTITUTIONS

All constitutions depict which institutions will be responsible for carrying out the tasks or functions of government. Institutions define the rules, procedures, and norms that constrain and facilitate opportunities and shape expectations. Depending on the nature of the constitution, these descriptions may range from highly precise to extremely vague. The descriptions usually cover three broad topics—the structure of central government, the territorial division of powers, and the court system. The constitution normally outlines how these organizational features ought to function and conveys legitimacy to the leaders at the top of these structures.

The role of executives, legislatures, the judiciary, and even the bureaucracy are often specified in a constitution. Some systems call for a **separation of powers** between executive, legislative, and judicial functions, while others do not. In general, the role of the executive is to steer the country and to apply the rules made by the legislative body.

The role of the legislature is to make laws for the country, while the courts are to adjudicate the laws by resolving disputes between citizens and between citizens and the state. However, these simple descriptions may prove highly inaccurate when any particular country is analyzed.

An example of how the structures may be outlined in the constitution is provided by the type of legislature a country possesses. One elementary way of depicting the constitutional structure of governments is by the number of chambers the legislature of a country possesses. **Unicameral legislatures** have one chamber while **bicameral legislatures** have two. Most countries today have only one chamber, but a sizable number—all federal countries—have two levels of legislative authority.

In most countries where there is more than one chamber, the lower house is elected directly by the people, while the second or upper house, as in Britain and Canada, is hereditary or appointed. In some rare cases, as in the United States, the upper house is elected in large constituencies. In the United States, two Senators are elected per state regardless of its size. Representation in the lower house, the House of Representatives, is determined by the principle of representation by population. Hence, the greater the population of the state, the greater its numbers of representatives.

In most cases, where there are two extant houses, the upper chamber has had its powers severely restricted over time. This is especially true when the upper house is unelected. Since 1949 the British House of Lords has not been able to block legislation passed by the House of Commons for more than one year. Such a restricted legislative power is called a **suspensory veto**—that is, one house may be able to hold up legislation for awhile, but not indefinitely.[10] In Canada, the appointed Senate has complete power to block any bill emanating from the House of Commons. But it almost never does so.

Some upper houses, however, do remain powerful. The elected United States' Senate is as powerful as the House of Representatives and, in many respects, even more so. Not all powerful upper houses are elected. In the Federal Republic of Germany, the members of the *Bundesrat*, or upper house, are appointed by the governments of the *Laender*, or provinces. Since the provincial and federal governments share most jurisdictions, *the Bundesrat* is quite powerful and its concurrence must be sought regularly.

After this brief sketch of one of the primary distinctions in constitutions we can examine some of the principles in more detail. The relation between these constitutional features and political realities in democratic and authoritarian governments will be discussed in Chapter 11. Leadership, executives, and legislatures are discussed in detail in Chapters 12 and 13.

Forms of Central Government

Two basic types of central government institutions exist in modern democratic constitutions. The **presidential** form is found mainly in the United States, Africa, and Latin America while the **parliamentary** system tends to dominate in Western democracies, especially in Europe and in those countries that were once part of the British Empire—such as Canada, Australia, New Zealand, and India.[11]

In presidential systems a single head of state, often elected, dominates the executive and appoints all members of government such as cabinet ministers and senior public servants. He or she is both the ceremonial *head of state* and the actual political *head of government*. The president is directly elected by the people for a fixed period of time or, as in authoritarian countries, is self-appointed for an unlimited duration.

The vast majority of authoritarian systems in Latin America, Asia, and Africa use the term "presidential." The reasons these regimes adopt the presidential form are complicated, but political scientists have given two basic explanations. First, a large number of these countries, especially in Africa, are autocratic, and the dictators do not want to share their authority with other leaders. And, secondly, even when political power is shared, some regimes wish to emphasize their unity and cohesion under a single leader. Since many of these countries are sharply divided on racial, tribal, and linguistic lines, adherence to the presidential form allows a group of leaders, often based on one tribe, to present an appearance of unity to the public.

Parliamentary systems are of two types—*cabinet-dominated* or *assembly-dominated*. In both varieties the senior politician tends to be a Prime Minister who, while he or she may dominate the cabinet ministers, is also responsible to the legislative body whether it is an assembly or Parliament. In other words, in the usual case the ministers are members of an elected legislative body and, while they owe their precise position in the executive to the Prime Minister, they also retain power from their positions as members of the assembly. This executive-legislative link is one of the vital concepts that distinguishes models of presidential government from parliamentary government.

In cabinet-dominated systems the ministers and the Prime Minister are collectively responsible to the legislature for their actions. The classic example is the Westminster model which is used in Britain, Canada, Australia, New Zealand, and India to name only a few.

When the government cannot dominate the legislature, political scientists tend to call the system *assembly-dominated* rather than *cabinet-dominated* to indicate the relative weight of the legislative body in policy formulation. In assembly-dominated systems the members of the legislature make and un-make cabinets and Prime Ministers at will. Classic examples of such systems existed in the Third (1870–1940) and Fourth (1944–1958) French Republics. Despite changes in the electoral system, this unstable type of cabinet system has tended to persist in contemporary Italy where governments continue to be changed annually.

In all parliamentary systems the legislature holds final decision-making power over lawmaking and the finances of the country. In principle, the legislature is the supreme body, but it, too, is subject to the constitution and the judicial process, so its real power may appear exaggerated on paper. We consider this and how parties interact with the executive and legislatures in Chapter 13.

While the Prime Minister is the actual head of government in parliamentary democracies, the ceremonial functions are performed by a nominal head of state. In Britain, the Queen is head of state. In Canada, Australia, and New Zealand, the Governor General, acting in the name of the monarch, performs this symbolic role. In other countries the same functions of the head of state are performed by a President as in Germany, India, and Italy, or by a monarch as in the Netherlands.

A few democracies *combine* parliamentary and presidential systems. In Europe, France and Russia are obvious contemporary examples, but Portugal and Finland also have elected Presidents with some independent powers. In France, for instance, the Constitution of the Fifth Republic (which began in 1958) provides both an elected President and a Prime Minister. The President, elected for seven years, selects the Prime Minister from the majority party or coalition in the National Assembly. The President also selects the members of the Prime Minister's cabinet. If the National Assembly passes a vote of censure, the cabinet and Prime Minister must resign. The strength of the President is illustrated by the fact that he remains in office even if there has been a vote of censure. A President who does not approve the actions of the legislature can simply dissolve Parliament and force new legislative elections.[12]

Presidential and Parliamentary Democracies

The differences between presidential and parliamentary forms of government are vital. The basic constitutional principle that distinguishes them is "separation of powers." In principle, the presidential system divides the powers of government into three distinct executive, legislative, and judicial branches to prevent the arbitrary use of power by any one body. This division is termed **separation of powers**. The seventeenth-century British philosopher John Locke constructed an elaborate explanation of the importance of separation of powers, and the French constitutionalist Montesquieu gave it such strong endorsement in *The Spirit of the Laws* (1748) that the creators of the American Constitution adopted it as one of the basic principles of the United States. The United States is the oldest, classic form of presidential government, and its philosophy of separation of powers has been adopted by many other countries including Costa Rica, Mexico, the Philippines, and Venezuela.

In the United States, James Madison and the other founders of the Constitution set out to establish a government which was strong enough to maintain law and order but sufficiently divided to keep it from becoming tyrannical. For them a tyrannical government was one where executive, legislative, and judicial powers were held by the same people—that is, as in Britain. As Madison put it:

> No political truth is certainly of greater intrinsic value, or is stamped with the authority of more enlightened patrons of liberty, than that the accumulation of all powers, legislative, executive, and judiciary, in the same hands, whether of one, a few, or many, and whether hereditary, self-appointed, or elective, may justly be pronounced the very definition of tyranny.[13]

In the United States this separation is accomplished by the separation of the personnel of the various branches of government. The Constitution specifies that no person may hold office in more than one of the three branches of government at the same time. If Senators wish to join the cabinet they must resign their seats in the upper house. If judges wish to take up ambassadorial positions they must resign from the bench.

This traditional classification of powers of government is misleading, however. In the real world each of these branches of government performs multiple roles. Executives make **subordinate** or **administrative legislation**—laws created under the auspices of statutes passed by legislatures at earlier periods. In the United States, the Congress acts like an executive when its committees carry out investigations. And courts regularly add to the laws of the country by interpreting the Constitution or other laws. The accumulation of these court decisions constitutes a large part of American "legislation" and the laws of other countries as well.

In order to buttress the theory of separation of powers, a constitution may also provide each institution with brakes on the other. In the United States this system is called **checks and balances**.[14] The Constitution declares that the President may veto bills from Congress. But Congress can refuse to pass bills proposed by the President, withhold financial measures (known as appropriations), deny some appointments, and even impeach and throw the President out of office (see Chapter 12). Through the practice of declaring some legislation unconstitutional the Supreme Court, too, has come to be part of the checks and balances system.

In parliamentary systems such as those following the Westminster model, by contrast, there is neither a principle of separation of powers nor one of checks and balances. In parliamentary systems, governments are organized by a principle of **fusion of powers**; that is, the unification of the executive and legislative branches. In principle, such a system requires an overlap between the individuals who are in the executive and in the legislature; that is, they follow the rule of compatibility. To use the Canadian nomenclature, everyone who is in the cabinet is also expected to be a member of Parliament or to be in the process of trying to get into Parliament.

In such systems the constitution often provides for Parliament to be the supreme organ of government. In Canada the executive derives its authority from the unwritten rules of the constitution, and the Prime Minister and cabinet ministers all must be supported by Parliament. In the Westminster-type Parliaments, if the executive cannot keep a majority of supporters in the lower house, then it can be deposed by a **vote of no confidence.**

The rules for controlling executive authority vary from country to country. In Germany a majority of members must be found to "support" a new Chancellor (equivalent to a Prime Minister) *before* an established government can be deposed. In other words, the onus is on the members of the *Bundestag* not only to want to get rid of a government but also to determine who will replace the outgoing leaders. This procedure, called a **constructive vote of confidence**, prevents the legislature from deposing the incumbent government without proposing which leaders will replace it.[15]

Geographical Distribution of Authority

The second most important distinguishing institutional feature of a constitution is the geographical distribution of authority. For practical reasons all countries—of any size—

distribute the power to carry out governmental functions across their territories in some manner. Political power may be arranged in such a way as to provide one strong, central state with insignificant local authorities (i.e., with a centre and peripheries) or the centre may be weakened by dividing authority into the hands of city or regional governments.[16] In some countries, the constitution gives all final decision-making authority to one level of government, and its authorities decide how to distribute responsibilities. In others, the constitution provides for more than one level of final authority over the same people in the same territory.

Among the many institutional arrangements to accomplish this task, two are most prevalent in the modern world. The first is called **unitary government**. In such a system the constitution provides for one level of government to be in control of all policy fields over the whole country. It is the only sovereign power in the country. If other levels of government exist—such as cities and regions—they are under the constitutional jurisdiction of the unitary government. The central government may delegate powers to regional or local administrative units, but it alone remains, in constitutional terms, the supreme law-making institution. Examples of unitary governments are Britain, France, and Japan.

In a **federal system** the legal powers are divided constitutionally between a central government and regional governments.[17] This means that there is more than one level of government over the same geographical territory. In the standard design, the constitution specifically divides jurisdictional powers between a central government and regional government(s), neither of which owes its authority to the other level of government. In this sense, **federalism** has been defined as a political organization in which the activities of government are divided between regional governments and a central government "in such a way that each kind of government has some kind of activities on which it makes final decisions."[18] Federal countries tend to have a large territory, many ethnic or language groups, and a historical tradition of local government. As well as the United States, examples of federal countries include Australia, Canada, Germany, India, and the former Soviet Union.[19]

It is also possible to conceive of nonterritorial federalism, although such a contention is somewhat controversial. The usual examples cited are Estonia in 1925 and Cyprus in 1960. In these cases, legal jurisdiction over cultural and linguistic affairs was accorded to groups wherever they lived, and was not based on a geographical division of the state.[20] Such a definition may lead one away from rigid, formalistic definitions of federalism, but it may also confuse the student by making the concept of federalism so loose that almost any political arrangement could be called federal.

The manner of dividing jurisdictions between federal and territorial governments differs greatly from state to state. But one key point is whether the specific *powers* are clearly circumscribed or intentionally left vague. A second important consideration is whether the **residual powers**—those not specified in the constitution—are assigned to the federal government or the provincial authorities. In the United States and Switzerland the residual powers belong to the states or cantons, whereas in Canada the residual powers are left to the federal government. Judicial interpretation of residual powers is vital.

In the United States the residual powers have not allowed an enhancement of state powers, whereas in Switzerland they have.

Federal systems are usually required when there are major divisions along ethnic, tribal, linguistic, or other such lines. Differences based on economic, geographical, historical, and religious cleavages may also play a part. As a general proposition, it can be hypothesized that when societal pluralism is low, a unitary, majoritarian model of democracy may suffice, but as pluralism increases a more consensual model of democracy seems to work better. When societal cleavages become extreme, only a federal form of union can succeed—otherwise the chances for continued unity will approach zero. Of course, the extent and depth of the cleavage has to be taken into consideration in such an analysis. However, diversity may not be a barrier to stable and effective government if the proper institutional forms of government are constructed—and this requires that the elites appreciate the dangers of fragmentation and transcend the bounds of hostility. Whether this can be achieved in any given situation depends upon how conflicts have been managed in particular historical circumstances and the current motivations of the elites toward overall unity.[21]

It is usually agreed that federalism allows unity with diversity; or, in other words, that it provides harmony in the face of territorially based loyalties. The degree of federalism is measured by the level of centralization and decentralization in the country. All federal systems require a written constitution which describes the jurisdictions of central and regional governments; in other words, it outlines the **division of powers**. The names of the regional governments differ from country to country but in English-speaking jurisdictions the most familiar are province and state.

If several unitary governments are linked together without any agreement to cede final authority to the central organization, the system is called a **confederation**. Canada and Switzerland today call themselves confederations, but in both cases the name is a misnomer. They are actually federations. If we contrast these two countries with the early history of the American confederacy the point will be clear. In the first United States' constitution of 1781, each state retained sovereignty; there was no enduring central government—it could neither raise taxes nor make laws for the states—and the role of Congress was, in practical terms, restricted to receiving delegations from the states. It was a true confederacy because it consisted of several unitary states so that power rested in the states.

At the present time the European Union is a type of confederacy. It is a supra-national association of independent states that have both separate and common interests. Although the Union has its own institutions, including the powerful European Commission of bureaucrats, an elected Parliament, and a common market, it is not yet a federal system since the most important decision-making functions still depend on the member governments and are worked out in the Council which has equal representation from all 15 members.[22] Some individual countries are also evolving toward federalism. Belgium and Spain are examples of "federalizing" states. Both have recently accorded a high degree of autonomy to their constituent units. But neither yet meets the definitional requirements for a federal state, nor has either actually defined itself as federal.[23]

There are many more unitary than federal countries, but approximately half of the world's population live in federations. Federal states constitute some of the largest and most powerful countries in the world, including the United States, Germany, Canada, Australia, Mexico, Nigeria, India, and Brazil (see Table 10.1). One scholar postulated that federalism has replaced empire as a means of governing diverse peoples over a large land mass.[24] However, it may turn out to be only a transitory stage as many federal systems seem to be experiencing the types of difficulties that lead to fragmentation.

The Constitution of the United States outlines a complex federal system. In a nutshell, Washington has only those powers given to it by the Constitution. The states have all the reserve powers not delegated to the federal government. Washington possesses power over fields such as external affairs and matters of national concern such as regulating interstate commerce. The states' reserve powers are in ordinary fields, such as controlling elections and local government. Both federal and state governments are denied some powers—in particular by the Bill of Rights. Both levels of government share jurisdiction in fields such as taxes, health, and auto safety. Within the scope of its operations, however, the courts have ruled that the federal government is supreme.

Overtime, the country evolved from a highly decentralized system of **dual federalism** in which each level basically looked after its own interests through to what has been called an integrated **marble-cake federalism** of shared responsibilities. Today it is highly *centralized*, but fiscal restraint and rivalry between Washington and the states has made the system very *competitive*.

Table 10.1 States with Federal Constitutions, 1999	
Argentina	Islamic Republic of Pakistan
Australia	Malaysia
Austria	Mexico
Bosnia & Herzegovina	Nigeria
Brazil	Russia
Canada	Saint Kitts and Nevis
Ethiopia	Switzerland
The Federated States of Micronesia	Tanzania
Germany	United Arab Emirates
India	United States of America
Islamic Federal Republic of Comores	Venezuela

Source: Arthur S. Banks, ed., *Political Handbook of the World*, 1997 (Binghamton, N.Y.: CSA Publications, 1997); and *The New York Times*.

In a federal country such as Canada the powers of government are divided between the federal government (central) and the provinces (regional). The Canadian Constitution gives the federal government control over such broad topics as commerce and defence and assigns the provinces jurisdiction over all items such as education and welfare that are local or regional in nature. A few jurisdictions are constitutionally divided between the federal and provincial governments, such as the power over agriculture and immigration.

In other words, in federal systems like Canada and the United States each level of government has jurisdiction over the same people but with regard to different, or sometimes shared, political responsibilities. A somewhat contrasting arrangement is found in Germany. There, the *Grundgesetz* (Constitution) gives only a very few powers to each level and then makes all the remainder **concurrent powers**, to be held by both levels of government. The federal government in the city of Berlin has independent power over defense and foreign policy while the *Laender* (provinces) have control over education. All other jurisdictions are shared between the two levels of government.[25]

The degree of centralization or decentralization of a state is, to some extent, determined by these types of constitutional rules over jurisdictions. But many unitary countries also devolve powers to their constituent units. When such devolution exists, the central government retains a monopoly of authority, and delegates responsibility and power to local or regional government. Britain, for example, is a unitary government, but London increasingly allows important administrative functions to be performed by authorities in Scotland and Wales and will soon have referendums to allow greater autonomy for the regions (see Close Up 10.1).[26]

While there is no written constitution in Britain, the country operates on the principle that all final authority resides with Parliament in London.[27] Certain powers have been devolved to the regions and even local governments, but the final decision-making powers remain at Westminster. An extreme example of the unitary power of the British government was provided in its handling of Northern Ireland. Stormont, as the Northern Ireland legislature was known, was set up in 1920 to deal with local issues, but it was stripped of its powers by Westminster in 1972 when the local politicians could not halt the violence between Protestants and Catholics. After that period, Northern Ireland was governed from London until the signing of the peace accord between Britain, Ireland, and the parties to the dispute in Northern Ireland in 1998.[28]

We consider the question of centralization and decentralization more closely when we examine the various unitary and federal states in comparative perspective in the next chapter. Close Up 10.2 summarizes the way in which federalism broke down in the former Yugoslavia (see also Map 10.1).

Judiciary And Constitutional Courts

While all constitutions describe the institutions of government authority, some of them also contain clauses that restrain governments from taking certain types of actions. We

CLOSE UP 10.1 **Centralization and Decentralization in a Unitary State: The Case of the United Kingdom**

The complex and controversial history of the United Kingdom illustrates how states can be consolidated into highly centralized systems and then fragment. First, the English subjugated the Welsh over many years, leading finally to the 1536 Act which incorporated Wales into England. Secondly, the tortuous wars between England and Scotland abated when James VI of Scotland also became James I of England in 1603. A century later, in 1707, Scotland and England were united as a "union" of crowns and legislatures. Thirdly, after centuries of enmity and suppression, Ireland was brought into the Union in 1801. The United Kingdom was then complete.

The union of Ireland with England came to a bloody end with the completion of the civil war in 1921. The Catholics of the southern part of the Island received what they wanted from Britain, but the agreement left Northern Ireland, which had a majority of Protestants, lodged inside the United Kingdom.

Despite the fact that the Westminster Parliament was supreme and the United Kingdom was a sovereign state, a degree of administrative decentralisation existed in Wales, Scotland, and Northern Ireland. In 1998, Tony Blair, the Labour Prime Minister, promised referendums in Wales and Scotland, to determine if these entities would like to have greater autonomy *inside* the United Kingdom. Nationalists in both areas continue to demand outright independence.

have already employed the word *constitutionalism* to depict a constitution that limits government power and protects human rights. We have also seen that the constitution may *separate* powers between the executive and legislative branches and *divide* power between central and regional governments.

In each of these cases a body must be set up to resolve disputes that arise between the state and its citizens and between the various levels of government. It is for this reason that every country with a constitution also possesses a court system. However, only in democratic countries are such courts allowed to exercise these powers in a meaningful way. In authoritarian systems judges are simply replaced, if not murdered, if they attempt to overrule their autocratic leaders.

Historically, the courts did not always have separate functions to perform. Lawmaking and law implementation were not always separate as they are now. Before the late Middle Ages, kings and their courts made and enforced laws. Later, when more specialized forms of organization took over the function of law-making, the ancient "courts" were left with the functions of interpreting and applying the law. By the eighteenth century, the theoretical and institutional distinction between executives and courts or judiciary had been made in most states of Europe.

CLOSE UP 10.2   The Violent Breakdown of Federalism in the Former Yugoslavia

The territory of the former Yugoslavia has had a violent history. Divided ethnically into Serbian, Albanian, Montenegrin, and Hungarian ethnic groups, and religiously into Orthodox, Catholic, and Muslim religious groupings, the area has been wracked by violence, war, and various political systems for over a 1000 years.

After World War II, Josip Broz Tito assumed political leadership and declared Yugoslavia a communist state. Following his death in 1980, the country was ruled as a federal state and governed by a collegial executive — headed by a presidency that rotated among the republics.

In June 1991, the federation began to fall apart. Croatia and Slovenia declared their independence, and several countries leaped to recognize them. Macedonia and Bosnia-Herzegovina followed. All that was left as Yugoslavia was Serbia, Kosovo, and Montenegro. As Croatia and Serbia stabilized to a degree, ethnic/religious/nationalist conflict inside Bosnia broke into full-scale war and overflowed into the surrounding area. The collapse of the former federal state of Yugoslavia was complete.

The tragedy of Bosnia cannot be comprehended without some knowledge of its historical past. Bosnia has been governed by outsiders for hundreds of years. The peacekeeping efforts of the United Nations and NATO represent only the latest "invasion." The Ottoman Empire, the Austro-Hungarian Empire, a Serbian monarchy, a puppet-Nazi Croatian regime, and Yugoslavian communists have all taken turns at governing the beleaguered area.

But who does the land of Bosnia belong to? Historically, the Serbs say the land belongs to them because the Muslims are actually Serbs who converted to Islam under the Ottoman Turkish rule. The Croats argue that the Muslims are actually Croats who have lost their faith. The Muslims claim that they are simply Bosnians and so are the Croats and Serbs who form the population of Bosnia.[29]

The problem does not end there. The new Yugoslavia itself is divided ethnically. Kosovo, for example, was over 90% populated by ethnic Albanians. It was not surprising, therefore, that an independence movement, led by the Kosovo Liberation Army, began fighting for a separate state against the forces of President Slobodan Milosevic. In 1999, the conflict intensified to such an extent that NATO bombed Yugoslavia (Serbia, Montenegro and Kosovo) in an attempt to dislodge Milosevic from power. He in turn "cleansed" Kosovo of most of its Albanian people.

Can states persist, even those with federal systems, when they are highly divided among hostile ethnic groups?

Today, the power of the courts to interpret the constitution in order to resolve such disputes, and on occasion even annul legislative and executive actions, is called **judicial review**. The power to engage in judicial review of the government (in other words, to review the constitutionality of laws), was proclaimed in Britain as early as the seventeenth cen-

Map 10.1   The Territory of the former Yugoslavia

tury, but the philosophy of court power received its modern significance in the United States only in 1803 with the case of *Marbury versus Madison*. Despite the fact that judicial review was not in the written constitution, American politicians of the day accepted the decision, and this famous case determined once and for all the power of the courts to engage in *judicial review*—to rule some actions of the American government unconstitutional.

Acting as the final arbiter of such issues, the courts decide whether legislation is constitutional or not, and whether one level of government has overstepped its authority and is **ultra vires**—that is, outside its constitutional jurisdiction. Since all constitutions include vague clauses, and most constitutions contain some form of recognition of citizens' rights and/or a federal form of government, the courts are always busy sorting out rival claims. As Chief Justice Hughes remarked, "We live under a constitution. But the constitution is what the judges say it is."[30]

In all countries, courts also adjudicate nonconstitutional disputes between citizens, and between citizens and the state. That is, they apply the law to particular civil or criminal cases. In this text we discuss courts when they have political and/or constitutional significance. Suffice it to say that both civil and criminal laws need to be adjudicated by a court system, and that the nature of this system depends on the structure of the political system. Unitary countries tend to have one legal structure while federal countries require a dual form of court structure to apply the different types or levels of law.

The court system plays a major role in both law-making and the adjudication of legal cases. In the accumulation of judgments in particular cases, judges make laws that are just as enforceable as statute law. In this way judges are an important part of the functioning of the whole political system, not just the legal system. As Robert A. Dahl put it about his country:

> To consider the Supreme Court of the United States strictly as a legal institution is to under-estimate its significance in the American political system.
> For it is also a political institution—an institution, that is to say, for arriving at decisions on controversial aspects of national policy.[31]

In authoritarian countries, the courts are not as independent of the political system as they are in the United States. In countries ruled by single parties, the military, the clergy, or royal families, the courts may be under the thumb of the political elite. Since these authoritarian structures are thought to represent the "will of the people" or have the coercive power to enforce their wishes, it is not surprising to find that the courts regard themselves as the virtual servants of their leaders (see Close Up 10.3).

Communist systems have unique legal systems and courts. In the former USSR, **procurators** were appointed to investigate and bring to justice those deemed to have contravened state security. They had extensive powers in interpreting and applying the law, and like most judges and advocates in communist systems, they were members of the Communist Party, legally bound to uphold the interests of the state. Today, the legal system of the former states of the USSR, like the political system itself, has undergone profound and liberal changes. In Russia, reform of the legal system is beginning to emerge: judges are starting to assert a degree of independence, and trial by jury, abolished in the USSR, has returned. Nevertheless, the rule of law is far from established, and criminal activity impinges on the everyday lives of Russians.

CLOSE UP 10.3 Political Correctness in the Iranian Theocracy

The powerful Iranian Council of Guardians combines religious and legal institutions. Its 12 members are appointed. The faqih (spiritual guide Ali Hoseini-Khamenei) names six Islamic clerics to the Council, and the supreme court names six more. All Guardians must be approved by the Majlis (the Islamic Consultative Assembly or parliament).

The Council has formal authority to ensure that no legislation violates Islamic principles. Moreover, the Council judges candidates for the Majlis and can disqualify them. In the 1996 elections the Council eliminated almost half of the candidates, calling them inadequate in their support of Islam.

The distinction between courts in democracies versus courts in authoritarian regimes can be overdone. Even in democracies the court system tends to have a bias in favour of the status quo and the regime in place. They are not the neutral "nonpolitical" instruments they are often characterized to be. As L.J. Edinger said of the Federal Republic of Germany, "The constitutional courts and particularly the Federal Court are quite explicitly judicial structures for legitimizing and preserving the present political system."[32]

A significant role of the courts is to act as the guardians of constitutional order. In some countries all courts may interpret the constitution, while in others specialized constitutional courts are set up for this specific task. Regardless of the institutional structure, however, if a country has a spirit of constitutionalism, the appropriate court may approve or strike down government laws or actions as unconstitutional and declare them null and void. In order to ensure proper hearings and fairness, court systems are set up in a hierarchical fashion so that appeals may be made until the appellant finally reaches the supreme or superior court. In Canada (since 1949), and in the United States, this body is called the Supreme Court. In democracies where Parliament is supreme, as in Britain, there can be a constitutional challenge in the courts only in very special cases. In other words, if Parliament is considered the "highest court of the land" and it has approved or disapproved of a law then there can be no further legal challenge.

The method of selecting and dismissing judges for the court system is also important. They may be appointed, co-opted by the legal system itself, or elected. In addition, the procedures for choosing or recruiting judges greatly affects the degree of independence and impartiality that these individuals possess when handling cases against the state. In authoritarian countries, it is extremely unlikely that judges are able to maintain neutrality in partisan politics. In fact many, if not most, are appointed because of their membership in the particular party, tribe, or religion which controls the state apparatus.

Beyond country level no law is enforceable. Although institutions do exist to interpret international law, these courts have no power to enforce their decisions. We shall examine this question further in Chapter 21. In the next chapter, we focus on the interaction between legal constitutional structures and political realities in democratic and authoritarian regimes and analyze some of the controversies about the role of constitutions in providing stable political systems.

DISCUSSION QUESTIONS

1. Is it better to have a written or an unwritten constitution?
2. Should legislators be elected? Cabinet Ministers? Judges? Dog catchers? Professors?
3. Why do federal systems require a written constitution?
4. Which would be more efficient for waging a war—centralized or regionalized government?
5. What is the role of judicial review in a constitutional democracy?

KEY TERMS

bicameral legislature,
   p. 217
checks and balances, p. 220
collective rights, p. 214
concurrent powers, p. 224
confederation, p. 222
constitution, p. 211
constitutionalism, p. 211
constructive vote of
   confidence, p. 220
convention, p. 213
division of powers, p. 222
dual federalism, p. 222
federal system, p. 221

federalism, p. 221
flexible constitution, p. 215
fusion of powers, p. 220
individual rights, p. 213
judicial review, p. 226
marble-cake federalism,
   p. 222
parliamentary system,
   p. 217
presidential system, p. 217
procurators, p. 228
residual powers, p. 221
rights, p. 213
rigid constitution, p. 215

rule of law, p. 214
separation of powers, p. 216
subordinate or
   administrative legislation,
   p. 220
suspensory veto, p. 217
ultra vires, p. 227
unicameral legislatures,
   p. 217
unitary government,
   p. 221
vote of no confidence,
   p. 220
Westminster model, p. 213

ENDNOTES

1. Charles M. McIlwain, *Constitutionalism: Ancient and Modern*, 2nd ed., (Ithaca, N.Y.: Cornell University Press, 1947); James R. Pennock and John W. Chapman, *Constitutionalism* (New York: New York University Press, 1979).

2. For the relation between constitutionalism and democracy see Henry B. Mayo, *Introduction to Democratic Theory* (New York: Oxford University Press, 1960); and Giovanni Sartori, *Democratic Theory* (New York: Praeger, 1965).

3. K. Wheare, *Modern Constitutions* (London: Oxford University Press, 1964); and L. Wolff-Philips, *Comparative Constitutions* (London: Macmillan, 1972).

4. See S.E. Finer, ed., *Five Constitutions* (Baltimore: Penguin, 1979); and Carl Friedrich, *Limited Government: A Comparison* (Englewood Cliffs, N.J.: Prentice-Hall, 1974).

5. Ivor Jennings, *The British Constitution*, 3rd ed. (Cambridge, Mass.: Cambridge University Press, 1950).

6. See Robert J. Jackson and Doreen Jackson, *Politics in Canada*, 4th ed. (Scarborough, Ont.: Prentice-Hall Canada, 1998), ch. 5.

7. Sheldon Goldman and Thomas P. Jahnige, eds., *The Federal Courts as a Political System* (New York: Harper & Row, 1976).

8. Khayyam Zev Paltiel, "Group Rights in the Canadian Constitution and Aboriginal Claims to Self-determination," in Robert J. Jackson, et. al., eds., *Contemporary Canadian Politics* (Scarborough, Ont.: Prentice-Hall Canada, 1987), pp. 26–43.

9. *Brown v. Board of Education*, 347 U.S. 483 (1954).

10. See R.M. Punnett, *British Government and Politics*, 5th ed. (London: Heinemann, 1987).

11. For a sophisticated analysis of all parliamentary and presidential regimes, see Alfred Stepan and Cindy Skach, "Constitutional Frameworks and Democratic Consolidation," *World Politics*, vol. 46, no. 1, (Oct. 1993), pp. 1–22.

12. Henry W. Ehrmann and Martin Schain, *Politics in France*, 5th ed. (New York: Harper Collins, 1992).

13. James Madison, "Federalist No. 47," *The Federalist Papers*.

14. For constitutional rules see Chapter 20 of Stephen E. Frantzich and Stephen L. Percy, *American Government* (Madison Wis: Brown and Benchmark, 1994). For informal rules see Richard E. Neustadt, *Presidential Power*, rev. ed. (New York: John Wiley, 1976).

15. David P. Conradt, *The German Polity* (New York: Longman, 1978), ch. 6.

16. For a description of the centre–periphery dimension see Stein Rokkan and Derek W. Urwin, *Economy, Territory, Identity* (London: Sage, 1983).

17. The classic treatment of comparative federalism is found in K.D. Wheare, *Federal Government*, 4th ed. (Oxford: Oxford University Press, 1963). For an extensive discussion of federalism in multicultural societies see Wolf Linder, *Swiss Democracy* (London: Macmillan, 1994), and for an excellent summary see Daniel J. Elazar, "International and Comparative Federalism," *PS: Political Science and Politics*, vol. 26, no.2 (June 1993), pp. 190–195.

18. William H. Riker, "Federalism," in Fred I. Greenstein and Nelson W. Polsby, eds., *Handbook of Political Science*, Vol. 5: *Government Institutions and Processes* (Reading, Mass.: Addison-Wesley, 1975), p. 101.

19. For detailed comparisons of Canada with the United States, see Roger Gibbins, *Regionalism: Territorial Politics in Canada and the U.S.* (Scarborough, Ont.: Butterworths, 1982).

20. See details in Jackson and Jackson, *Politics in Canada*, p. 242.

21. For a general discussion of the concept of "integration," see Robert J. Jackson and Michael B. Stein, *Issues in Comparative Politics* (New York: St. Martin's Press, 1972).

22. For an overview see N. Nugent, *The Government and Politics of the European Community*, 2nd ed. (Basingstroke: Macmillan, 1991).

23. For a discussion and excellent summary of "federalizing" states, see Dwight Herperger, *Distributions of Powers and Functions in Federal Systems* (Ottawa: Supply and Services, 1991), ch. 1.

24. William H. Riker, *Federalism: Origin, Operation, Significance* (Boston: Little, Brown, 1964), p. 1.

25. Conradt, *The German Polity*; and Lewis J. Edinger, *Politics in West Germany*, 2nd ed., (Boston: Little, Brown, 1977).

26. Vernon Bogdanor, *Devolution* (New York: Oxford University Press, 1979).

27. Some scholars today distinguish between "unitary" states like Japan that are forged out of one nation and "Union" states which meld together more than one nation such as the United Kingdom. See Rokkan and Urwin, *Economy, Territory, Identity*, pp. 181–87.

28. Richard Rose, *Governing Without Consensus* (Boston: Beacon Press, 1971).

29. A complete objective history of the fall of Yugoslavia has still not been written. Students would be wise to consider the views of Richard West in *Tito and the Rise and Fall of Yugoslavia* (New York: Carroll and Graf, 1995); Laura Silber and Allan Little in *The Death of Yugoslavia* (London: Penguin, 1995); and Norman Cigar in *Genocide in Bosnia: The Policy of "Ethnic Cleansing"* (College Station, Tex.: A&M University Press, 1995).

30. Cited in R. Hague, et al., *Comparative Government and Politics*, 3rd ed. (London: Macmillan, 1992), p. 282.

31. Robert A. Dahl, "Decision Making in a Democracy: The Role of The Supreme Court as a National Policy Maker," *Journal of Public Law*, vol. VI (1958), p. 279.

32. Edinger, *Politics in Germany*, pp. 322–23.

FURTHER READING

Ajzenstat, Janet, ed., *Canadian Constitutionalism: 1791–1991* (Ottawa: Canadian Study of Parliament Group, 1992).

Bogdanor, V. ed., *Constitutions in Democratic Politics* (Aldershot: Gower, 1988).

Bogdanor, V., and Finer, S.E., *Comparing Constitutions* (Oxford: Clarendon, 1995).

Conklin, William, *Images of a Constitution* (Toronto: University of Toronto Press, 1993).

Cook, Curtis, ed., *Constitutional Predicament* (Montreal: McGill-Queen's Press, 1994).

Elazar, Daniel, Jr., *Exploring Federalism* (Tuscaloosa: University of Alabama Press, 1987).

Elkin, Stephen L. And Karol Edward Soltan, eds., *A New Constitutionalism: Designing Political Institutions for a Good Society* (Chicago: University of Chicago Press, 1993).

Elster, Jon and Rune Slagstad, eds., *Constitutionalism and Democracy* (Cambridge, Mass.: Cambridge University Press, 1988).

O'Brien, D. *Storm Centre: The Supreme Court in American Politics* (New York: Norton, 1986).

Riker, William H., *Federalism: Origin, Operation, Significance* (Boston: Little, Brown, 1964).

Sartori, Giovanni, *Comparative Constitutional Engineering* (New York: New York University Press, 1995).

Scheiber, Harry, ed., *North American and Comparative Federalism* (Berkeley: University of California Press, 1992).

Seligman, Alan, *The Idea of a Civil Society* (New York: Free Press, 1992).

Tushnet, Mark, ed., *Comparative Constitutional Federalism: Europe and America* (New York: Greenwood Press, 1990).

Weaver, Kent and Bert Rockman, eds., *Do Institutions Matter? Government Capabilities in the United States and Abroad* (Washington D.C.: The Brookings Institution, 1993).

Wheare, K.C., *Federal Government*, 4th ed. (Oxford: Oxford University Press, 1963).

Wrong, Dennis H., *The Problem of Order: What Unites and Divides Society* (New York: Free Press, 1994).

Federalism and Ethnicity:

Cigar, Norman, *Genocide in Bosnia: The Policy of Ethnic Cleansing* (College Station, Tex.: A&M University Press, 1995).

Malcolm, Noel, *Kososvo: A Short Story* (New York: New York University Press, 1998).

Rhode, David, *Endgame: The Betrayal and Fall at Srebrenica* (New York: Farrar Strauss & Giroux, 1997).

Vickers, Miranda, *Between Serb and Albanian: A History of Kosovo* (New York: Columbia University Press, 1998).

 **Weblinks**

www.cc.ukans.edu/carrie/docs/docs_con.html
This site contains links to the constitutions of countries around the world.

www.soc.umn.edu/~sssmith/Parliaments.html
This site contains links to parliamentary governments around the world.

www.droit.umontreal.ca/opengov/s-courtf/sc.home.html
This site describes the Canadian Supreme Court and how the Canadian judiciary works.

CHAPTER 11

Constitutional Frameworks: Democratic and Authoritarian

The comparative study of formal, written constitutions provides an important starting point for the examination of comparative politics. These documents are theoretical blueprints of the institutional structures of modern states. Yet a study of comparative politics limited to these documents would be sterile.

Most modern constitutions are similar in their basics. To a remarkable degree every constitution in the world describes its system as containing legislative, executive, and judicial institutions, and almost all hail their country's rights and freedoms. But, aside from these constitutional basics, the actual institutional combinations and political behaviours around the world differ greatly. In some states the real world of politics does not even reflect the constitution.

A formal, written constitution may be permanently in place in one country yet easily discarded in another. A military government may temporarily replace a civilian government and suspend the constitution only to resign a short while later and put the constitution in force again. In some states constitutions are reflected in institutional arrangements, while in others there is such a distortion between the written codes and political reality that the document is not even a sketchy organizational map for the country.

In Chapter 10 we examined the terms and usage of constitutions. We paid particular attention to how important "constitutionalism" is in liberal democratic states. In this chapter we examine how constitutional dictums are put into practice in both democratic and authoritarian countries, paying particular attention to communist regimes. We also examine constitutions in action: their impact on government functions, the degree of centralization and decentralization in states, and their impact on human rights around the globe.

CONSTITUTIONS IN ACTION

Constitutions are important documents, but they remain imperfect guides to the "workings" of individual countries.[1] Important institutions such as parties, police, and the military are not mentioned in most of them. The principles of the constitution may or may not be operative, and in any particular country there may be no perceptible relationship between the written document and the actual machinery of government. Yet the study of constitutions is important even where the constitution is otiose or superfluous.

The history and culture of each state shapes and is shaped by the constitution in multiple and sometimes quite bizarre ways. A country's constitutional rules can work only if they are in line with the traditions of the society and what people want them to be. Liberal democracies require elections, but dynastic systems allow their leaders to rule by divine law, custom, inheritance, and sometimes wealth. The economic underpinnings of societies and the development of parties and interest groups also greatly affect constitutional development. Because of these and other factors, a constitution should be understood as part of the whole system of politics.

Some countries faithfully follow the basic contours of their constitutions while others do not. S.E. Finer, in his book *Five Constitutions*, divided constitutions into two categories.[2] In the "realistic" category he placed those states with constitutional documents that do, to a large extent, affect political institutions and processes. The constitutions of liberal democratic countries such as the United States, Australia, Canada, France, and Germany are in this category. These constitutions channel and constrain governmental power and protect individual and certain collective rights. Such constitutions may or may not indicate in precise detail how a state functions—how its electoral system operates, for example. However, in many of the most important processes they determine the parameters of political behaviour. The minimum number of years between elections may be cited, for example, even though the method of election may not be mentioned.

In the second, or "fictive" category, Professor Finer placed those constitutions that contain decorative passages and omit many of the real powers and processes.[3] Such distortions may occur because of specific developments in the country's history or economy. The evolution and pattern of interest groups or party systems may also be the cause of incongruities between political life and the written constitution. For example, extra-constitutional institutions may have arisen over time which are actually more significant than the institutions mentioned in the fictive constitution. The written documents of communist countries and many authoritarian countries would fit in this fictive category.

Enduring constitutions are present only in certain parts of the world. Elsewhere, constitutions are regularly overturned. With the exception of those in the Caribbean countries, for example, the constitutions of Third World states have not lasted very long. Often they were mere copies of constitutions from their colonial powers. It is not surprising, therefore, that in most areas, especially Africa, constitutions have been constantly changed by governments. As Christopher Clapham put it:

> In some respects, independence constitutions reflected a balance of power which became anachronistic with the act of independence itself ... Newly drawn up indigenous constitutions, which might be expected to reflect the realities of the domestic power structure, nonetheless rarely fared much better.[4]

But even in "non-colonial" states such as Thailand and Turkey, constitutions have been radically altered on many occasions to suit the needs and whims of their leaders.

The law-bound societies of the West must be contrasted with those countries where little adherence to "constitutionalism" exists and also to those where the most important institutions are not mentioned in the constitution. Attention should also be paid, however, to the fictive part of all constitutions. For example, the powers of the Prime Minister and Cabinet are not listed in the written part of the Canadian Constitution, and the role of political parties is not mentioned in the U.S. Constitution.

Authoritarian Constitutions

Constitutions in most authoritarian states resemble ideological manifestos more than they do organizational descriptions and limitations on governments. Communist systems, in particular, are characterized by the fact that the party is above the constitution. Unlike democratic systems where the constitution and rule of law are not subordinate to the wishes of the party, in communist systems the demarcation line between the governing party and the state organization is blurred. The degree of "party-state" fusion differs from one country to the next. In order to further comprehend constitutions in action and transition, we examine the defunct constitution of the former Soviet Union as well as its stable counterpart in China.

While to a large extent functioning democracies follow the rules of their constitutions, this is not the case in communist countries. The former Soviet Union was particularly significant not only because it was the leading example of a communist state for more than seven decades but also because many other countries copied its form of communism and constitution. Cuba, for example, has virtually the same constitution and continues to function in a fairly similar manner today.

The Former USSR

The Soviet Union had four new constitutions between 1917 and 1991. The last became law in 1977 and was then abandoned in the breakup of the union in 1991. It outlined the institutions of authority and guaranteed freedom of speech, press, assembly, and immunity from arbitrary arrest. It also provided religious freedom and guaranteed separation of church and state. These rights were given "for the purpose of strengthening and developing the socialist system." As a socialist constitution it also provided various economic rights such as the right to employment and housing. And yet it is well known that such rights were never upheld in the Soviet Union. In 1956 Nikita Khrushchev revealed that for three decades under Stalin's rule, arrests, torture and execution without trial had been common. Despite some loosening of state terror after that period, labour camps and mental hospitals continued to be used to incarcerate political dissidents. What should we make of a constitution that promised so much and provided so little?

It is important to understand that reading the Constitution of the USSR explains very little about how the country actually worked. There was a world of difference between formal political authority and actual political power. Informal, real power was exercised by the Communist Party that gained control of the country in the revolution of 1917. After that date the party *alone* controlled the state's formal decision-making institutions.

Clause 108 of the Constitution specified that laws were to be passed by a parliament (the Supreme Soviet) composed of elected members; it was to be the "highest organ of state power in the USSR." There were to be no institutional checks on its authority; yet, the reality was quite different. This formal structure was actually insignificant. The Supreme Soviet met only infrequently, and its members were elected on ballots that offered no real choice to the voters. The Communist Party controlled all nominations, and the electorate was given an opportunity only to approve or disapprove of candidates.

Thus, despite some liberal clauses in the Constitution, the Communist Party was the supreme decision-making unit in the former Soviet Union. When its power was combined with Article 3, which proclaimed "democratic centralism," it is clear that the remainder of the Constitution was mere decoration. The Soviet Communist Party is discussed in Chapter 16.

China

By comparison with the former USSR, the People's Republic of China (PRC) has remained constitutionally stable. This was not always the case. In the early years after the revolution in 1949, Mao Tse-tung's philosophy was the dominant force in the politics of the country, but there was considerable institutional fluidity. There were four different constitutions after 1954 when the first one was adopted. These fundamental changes occurred each time a new powerful group gained control of the "party-state" apparatus.[5]

After the death of Mao and the downfall of the "Gang of Four," the present, or fourth, Constitution was adopted in 1982 by the National People's Congress. Led by Deng Ziaoping and his pragmatic reformers, the new Constitution set out to make up for the "excesses" and mistakes of the Cultural Revolution. It was the product, it is said, of millions of meetings and one million suggestions for revision of the first draft.

The 1982 Constitution deleted all praise of Mao and the Cultural Revolution from the preamble, and inserted four fundamental principles of socialism. These are:

1. the people's dictatorship;
2. Marxist-Leninism and Mao's thought;
3. the socialist road; and
4. the leadership of the Communist Party.

The Constitution, which Deng depicted as "socialism with Chinese characteristics," outlines the institutions of government—a President, a Premier, a National People's Congress, and a Military Council to control the armed forces. The party's role is not as explicitly described as in earlier constitutions, but it continues to control and direct the state organization. The parallel structures of party and state institutions are still in place, so that a "party-state" is still the best way to describe the system. The party and military hierarchies are also linked together, as every military officer is a party member.

As in the former USSR, the 1982 Constitution of China contains provisions for freedom of speech, of the press, of assembly and of demonstration. However, none of these rights are observed in reality. Some former rights have been explicitly dropped. For example, the right to "write big character posters" allowed in earlier constitutions is now prohibited. Article 51 of the Constitution says these rights "may not infringe upon the interests of the state, of society and of the collective, or upon the lawful freedoms and rights of other citizens." Moreover, these individual rights may not be used to challenge any repressive measures of the state in the courts. The Constitution is merely a legitimizing document for party control of China. It reaffirms the ideological and organizational leadership of the Communist Party.[6] The party acts as the coordinating cadre for the country and the actual governing system remains clouded in intrigue and secrecy.

Centralization/Decentralization of Power

The concentration or dispersal of power among the territorial components of states is one of the major constitutional issues concerning all modern polities. How much political authority is, and should be, distributed between the central government and the regional governments? When written into a constitution, this distribution of authority is called the **division of powers.**

By definition, a unitary government is more centralized than a federal one. But, for practical reasons, every state of any size, regardless of its constitutional form, must delegate a degree of implementation authority to its regions or local authorities. This means that, although it may appear as a contradiction, it is logically possible to have a federal country that is highly centralized or a unitary government that is greatly decentralized.[7] William Riker has provided a continuum for assessing the degree of centralization and decentralization within countries (see Figure 11.1).[8] The continuum ranges from centralized federalism, in which the central government dominates or encroaches on the sub-units, to what he calls decentralized federalism, or peripheralized federalism, in which the sub-units dominate. Countries may oscillate on the continuum over time.

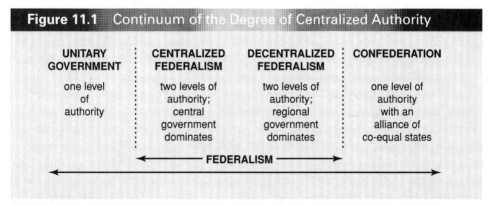

Figure 11.1 Continuum of the Degree of Centralized Authority

UNITARY GOVERNMENT	CENTRALIZED FEDERALISM	DECENTRALIZED FEDERALISM	CONFEDERATION
one level of authority	two levels of authority; central government dominates	two levels of authority; regional government dominates	one level of authority with an alliance of co-equal states

◄———— FEDERALISM ————►

Source: Adapted from concepts proposed by William H. Riker in *Federalism: Origin, Operation, Significance* (Boston: Little, Brown, 1964).

In practice, the division of powers is handled quite differently in each federal state. There is no uniform approach. The listing of powers differs from state to state by subjects, numbers, and specificity. However, the constitutions of all federal states enumerate the specific powers to be assigned to the federal and/or regional governments and leave others as residual powers. **Residual powers** are defined as the authority over jurisdictional fields that do not fall under the subjects enumerated specifically in the constitution. In the United States the states are given the residual powers whereas in Canada residual powers belong to the federal government. All federal constitutions also provide for **concurrency**—that is, a shared jurisdiction by both levels of government over some topics. And, some federal states have developed **asymmetry**—that is, a division of powers which allows some particular units (states, provinces or cantons) to have powers that other units do not have. Table 11.1 lists some of the powers of the established federal systems as an illustration of the variety and complexity in this field.

We have seen that power or legal jurisdictions can be arranged to provide for unitary or federal systems of government. But the degree of centralization within a polity is determined by many factors in conjunction with the precise phrases in the constitution.[9] Besides the legal constitutional constraints, the degree of centralization and decentralization is also modified by the way public money is shared and by the nature and formation of ethnic groups and political parties within the country.

Fiscal Relations and Dispersion of Power

Let us take a hypothetical example of how the fiscal arrangements of a state can affect the degree of dispersion of political authority within the territory. If, for example, a state had a federal system in which jurisdictions were divided, and yet the ability to tax and to spend money were *only* in the hands of the federal government, it would mean that, despite the constitutional division of powers, all significant authority would rest with the central government.

The United States is a case in point. At the Philadelphia Constitutional Convention in 1789, the 13 original states were adamant that the constitution should assign precise functions to each level of government. The federal government was assigned only those jurisdictions that were clearly national, such as foreign affairs, defence, currency, and the regulation of commerce between the states and with foreign countries. The residual powers—that is, all those left unspecified—were to remain in the hands of the state governments.

Today, this distinction between state and federal powers is blurred and bears little relation to the deal struck in 1789. By the twentieth century, a form of "cooperative" or "marble-cake" federalism was grafted onto the basic constitutional structure in the United States. Over time, Washington collected a greater and greater proportion of all government revenues and handed them back to the states in the form of grants. The use of these payments is controlled by standards set by the national government which, according to some critics, distort state interests. This fiscal relationship has made the country much more centralized than one would expect from a study of the constitutional document itself.

On the other hand, the American Constitution continues to provide a high degree of decentralization in other respects: the states play a major role in the election of

Table 11.1	Patterns in the Division of Powers in Established Federal Systems

	Australia	Austria	Canada	Germany	India	Malaysia	Pakistan	Switzerland	United States
Primary Characteristics									
Residual Power	P	P	F	P	F	P	P	P	P
List of Provincial Powers	No	Yes	Yes	Yes	Yes	Yes	No	No	No
Specific Powers									
Agriculture	PC	F*	C	C*	PC	PC		FP	P
Fisheries	FP		FP	C*	FP	FP	FP		P
Mineral Resources	P	F	FP		FP	FP			P
Civil Law	FP	FP	P	C*	C	FP		F	P
Criminal Law	P	FP	F	C*	C	F		F	P
Corporation Taxation	C	F	FP	C*	F	F	F	F	C
Personal Income Tax	C	F	FP	C*	FP	F	FP	FP	C
Citizenship	F	FP*	F	FC*	F	F	F	F	F
Defence	FP	F	F	F	F	F	F	F	FP
Immigration	C	F	C	C*	F	F	F	C	C
Treaty Implementation	F	F¹	F¹	FP	F	FP	F	F	F
Currency	F	F	F	F	F	F	F	F	F
External Trade	C		F		F	F	F	F	F
Hospitals	FP	C*	FP	C*	P	F		P	FP
Post-Secondary Education	FP	F	P	C*²	FPC	F		FC*P	FP
Primary and Secondary Education	P	FP	P	P	CP	F		C*P	P
Aboriginal Affairs	C		F		FP	F	FP		F
Culture		FP				C		C*	
Environment	FP	FP	FP	C*				C*	FP
Language			FP		FP	FP		F	
Municipal Affairs	P	P	P	P	P	FP		P	P

Key:

F	=	federal
P	=	provincial, state, canton, or *Land*
C	=	concurrent
*	=	province administers federal legislation
1	=	requires consent/implementing legislation by province
2	=	the federal government can enunciate general principals, leave the *Laender* to provide further details through their own legislation and executive action.

the President; two Senators are elected from each state; and three-quarters of the states are required for ratification of a constitutional amendment. As well, the party system is highly decentralized and buttresses a kind of regional alliance system.

The German Constitution is much more explicit in setting out the "financial" arrangements between the central government and the *Laender* (provinces) than the United States is, and is decidedly more decentralized as a result of it. Despite the fact that most jurisdictions are shared, the Constitution, or *Grundgesetz*, minutely outlines the division of finances between the federal government and the *Laender*. Berlin and the *Laender* are required to split individual and corporate income taxes in equal 40% shares; the cities get an automatic 20%. In other words, the regional governments can be certain what share of the taxes they will receive and have no need to ask the politicians from the central government for funds. Clearly this system decentralizes the country regardless of the fact that in many other respects policy is made in the federal capital.

The degree of centralization or decentralization in a country can vary greatly over time. One of the basic reasons is the changing nature of **fiscal federalism**—in other words, the financial arrangements and transfers between governments at different levels in a federal system. Take Canada, as an example. Among the Western liberal democratic states with federal constitutions, Canada is one of the least centralized. That is, the proportion of the country's financial resources which the federal government spends is lower than in comparable federal systems. And yet, the federal government collects the great bulk of the taxes for the provinces and the "residual powers" are in its hands.

The degree of centralization or decentralization in Canada has varied greatly over time. Why? Two different types of financial arrangements link the federal and provincial governments in Canada—conditional and unconditional grants. "**Conditional**" **grants** are payments from the federal government to the provinces with strings attached; that is, provinces must spend the money in designated areas. "**Unconditional**" **grants** come in the form of block or general revenue-sharing payments; they have no conditions attached to them, so the recipients may spend the funds in the way they choose. It is obvious that the more conditional the payments are, the more centralized the system is and the opposite is true for unconditional grants. It is also clear that provincial politicians prefer to receive grants without restrictions.

For about one hundred years after Confederation, Canada moved to a greater and greater use of conditional grants, but in the mid-1970s the provinces began to receive most of their funding from Ottawa in the form of unconditional payments called **bloc grants**. This tendency continues today. Provinces became more free from federal control than they had been. Thus, ironically, as the country centralized via constitutional change in 1982, it decentralized in terms of funding throughout the same period.[10]

Ethno–Regionalism, Parties, and the Dispersion of Power

Besides the division of constitutional power and the realities of fiscal federalism, the degree of centralization or decentralization in federal states is also affected by subcultures, cleavages, and political parties. Few large federal states can claim to be homogeneous.

Most countries have a greater difficulty with regionally based ethnic groups that are inadequately assimilated into the general culture or language of the country.

When such groups are territorially based, political scientists call them **ethno-regional movements**. On occasion they become **separatist movements**, which wish to divide from their parent countries and form their own states. In Canada, separatist movements in Quebec and regionally based parties in the west of the country have occasionally claimed the right to a more decentralized country or even complete independence. What concerns us more directly in this chapter is the degree to which such ethno-regional movements decentralize the country by their political organizations and electoral behaviour. In Western Europe, ethno-regional movements are common. In Britain, Scottish, Welsh, and Irish nationalists have formed their own political movements and, although Britain remains constitutionally united, the government has often had to respond with forms of administrative decentralization and devolution to Wales and Scotland. This was also the case in North Ireland until the Stormont legislature had its power clipped in 1972 because of continued turmoil and violence between Protestants and Catholics. Today, a degree of self-government has re-emerged in Belfast because of the Anglo-Irish Peace Accord.

For years in Spain, the Basques—who span geographical territory between France and Spain—have demanded a separate state. Employing violence and terrorist tactics, they have forced various concessions from the state. Another ethnic group, the Catalans, has demanded and received a degree of autonomy for its state and a powerful legislature in Barcelona. Such pressures also exist in France with the Bretons and Corsicans, and in Belgium with the Flemings and Walloons.

Approximately half of all federal states are in the Third World. Their degree of centralization differs greatly. Most of them have very high ethnic tension, and the party system or the military provides the only cohesive force in the country. Mexico, Brazil, and India are three of the most significant of these federal countries to examine.

Mexico, Brazil, and India

Mexico is characterized by a mixture of democracy and authoritarianism. Despite the division of the country into 60% Mestizo, 30% Amerindian, and 9% white, the country operates as a single political system. Constitutionally a federal country, Mexico is so tightly linked together by the control of the one powerful party—the Institutional Party of the Revolution (PRI)—that the country functions almost as a unitary system. Reversing the normal party role of organizing government, the PRI can be considered an instrument of the state for organizing society. The President's power is illustrated by his authority to control the appointment of many of the governors in the 31 states.

Brazil's federalism, too, has historical roots but little validity as a functioning system today. In the sixteenth century the Portuguese King Dom Joao gave 15 royal grants or *capitanias* to encourage feudal leaders to settle the land. The boundaries established by these grants continue today in the form of states. However, military government occurred so frequently until 1985 in Brazil that the states were often mere appendages of central government.

Federalism does not count much if the major decisions are taken by generals. Today, under President Henrique Cardoso, Brazil is in an advanced transitional stage toward stable democracy, and it remains to be seen what role will be played by federalism over the years.

In India, the federal system is superimposed on a territory with a large number of languages and cultures. There are 16 official languages, but a million or more persons speak 24 other languages, and there are numerous other languages and dialects. The language differences combine with the federal system to make the country very decentralized. But as in Mexico, the strength of one party—in this case the Congress Party—and the personality of Prime Minister Jawaharlal Nehru kept the country fairly unified after independence from Britain in 1947 until Nehru died in 1964. The country remains united, but the Congress Party lost its dominant role in 1977 when an opposition coalition won a massive victory in parliamentary elections. The Congress Party has formed governments since then, but has never regained its former dominance, and all governments now tend to be fragile. In 1998, Atal Bihari Vajpayee of the Bharatiya Janata Party (Hindu nationalist) became Prime Minister with only 178 of the 543 seats but the government only lasted a few months. As in many Third World federal countries, the central government in New Delhi is very powerful, but allows local elites to control a share of power in their regions. The Indian Constitution allows states to be brought under the direct authority of the central government if necessary, and on several occasions New Delhi has simply ruled a state by **fiat** or decree. The central government can alter a state's boundaries or even abolish them. On the whole India, like other developing states, tends to concentrate administration in the centre—exasperating local elites and spawning regional jealousies.

It must be said, however, that in these same three countries the existence of regional governments also decentralizes the country to an extent. Each state has its own bureaucracy and its own budget, and this provides paid positions as administrators, educators, and so on, for the members of the elite, and menial jobs for the poorer people in each region.[11] Business owners are also dependent on local government contracts for their livelihood, and thus owe loyalty to local elites.

The role of political parties in centralizing or decentralizing federal and even unitary systems is very complex. In this section we have seen how federalism can be enhanced or distorted by the party system. A thorough study of party systems is found in Chapters 16 and 17.

Authoritarianism and the Dispersion of Power
Communist Governments and Federalism

In authoritarian socialist countries, such as the former states of the USSR, Yugoslavia, and Czechoslovakia, federal constitutions were instituted because of the pressures of ethnic and regional diversity. However, it was not adherence to the constitutional system that enforced unity in these countries. It was the Communist Party and its control of the military which upheld or forced national unity, and all of these federal countries functioned as if they were unitary states. Final legislative and financial authority was centralized in Moscow, Belgrade, and Prague.

The Soviet Union was populated by several dozen major, and several hundred minor, nations. As one expert put it: "Their cultures are not colourful regional variations upon Russian culture; most are fundamentally different by every standard ethnographic measure."[12] And the borders of the USSR were drawn arbitrarily, with no respect for ethnic groups. In order to accommodate this vast number of ethnic groups and nationalities under one banner in the former Soviet Union, the Bolsheviks adopted a federal Constitution soon after the revolution of 1917. They even declared that all the republics that comprised the Soviet Union were sovereign, and Article 72 permitted each republic the right to secede from the Union. Republics also had the right to engage in international affairs and conclude treaties with foreign countries. Two of them—Belarus and the Ukraine—even had independent seats in the United Nations. Of course, what really happened was that they simply followed Soviet policies at the United Nations without any deviation in speeches or votes.

Despite its formal federalism, the USSR was, in fact, totally centralized until the 1980s and the beginning of the democratization program. Until then the Communist party tried to maintain absolute control throughout all 15 republics. While the republics had the right to secede they never did so. Moreover, party control was exercised through **democratic centralism**, which meant that although the republics and other local entities were encouraged to show some initiative, final authority in all significant policy fields belonged to the central authorities.

Article 14 of the Soviet Constitution listed the powers of central government and was virtually exhaustive of all policy-making. Moscow also maintained its constitutional control by Article 77, which asserted that the republics were to "implement the decisions of the highest bodies of state authority and administration of the USSR." Moreover, and possibly most important, there was no constitutional court with the power to resolve jurisdictional disputes.

Since the central principle of communism was to create a planned economy, and since only the highest political institutions had budgets, the Soviet state was a highly centralized federation. When the discipline of the Communist Party was added to this structure of democratic centralism it became clear that the Soviet Union was one of the most centralized federations anywhere.

After the death of Stalin a decentralization process began and proceeded from Nikita Khrushchev to Mikhail Gorbachev. Today, decentralization is complete as the union has splintered into several independent republics—perhaps indicating that only a totalitarian party with a dogmatic ideology could actually hold the cultural pieces of the former USSR together.

Even today about 24 million Russians live outside of Russia. When the central government in Moscow disintegrated in 1989, the territorial claims of neighbour against neighbour multiplied. Ethnic rivalries *within* the new republics became so intense that at least one study concluded that their long–term prospects of surviving as independent democratic states—except for Russia, Ukraine, and the Baltic states—range from "highly doubtful to nonexistent."[13] Map 11.1 shows the collapsed Soviet Empire.

Map 11.1   The Collapsed Soviet Empire

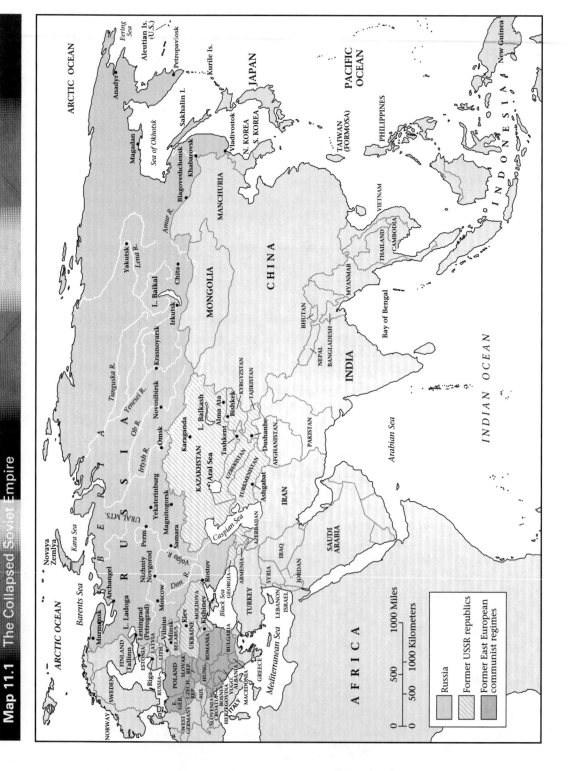

Legend:
- Russia
- Former USSR republics
- Former East European communist regimes

Elsewhere, ancient ethnic-based animosities suppressed during four decades of Soviet imperialism reemerged following the collapse of communist regimes in Eastern Europe. They destroyed two federations and continue to threaten the stability of other fledgling democracies. In Czechoslovakia, for example, Czechs and Slovaks initially competed for advantage, seeking a compromise that would satisfy both sides within the federation. However, the efforts quickly failed and independence for Czechs and Slovaks was peacefully achieved in January 1993 (see Close Up 11.1). The former Yugoslavia, on the other hand, quickly broke into a state of civil war. Slovenia, Croatia, and Serbia attained self-governing institutions and international recognition for their sovereignty. Bosnia-Herzegovina, however, continued to be the battleground for internal war between Muslims, Croats, and Serbs. After the deaths of over 200 000 people, massacres of civilians, systematic rapes and "ethnic cleansing," a peace treaty was finally signed in Dayton, Ohio, in November 1995. New state institutions were formed in Bosnia-Herzegovina, but despite elections and the support of international organizations, NATO troops are still required to patrol the borders between the three ethnic groups.

In Hungary, which along with Poland and Albania is one of Eastern Europe's most ethnically homogeneous states, an old, divisive debate over "who is a Hungarian" has been revived. Millions of ethnic Germans who were left behind in Poland, Hungary,

CLOSE UP 11.1   The Peaceful Break-up of Czechoslovakia

Czechoslovakia is the most recent example of an established federal state to undergo a peaceful secession. That does not mean, however, that it was without costs.

In January 1993, without any consultation with the people, the elected government of Czechoslovakia divided the country in two, forming the Czech Republic and Slovakia. It was a quick, peaceful, amicable divorce for both partners.

However, it was not easy for everyone, and the transition is still underway. Many, particularly the Slovaks, now see the event as a self-serving deal hatched by politicians and top civil servants who had a great deal to gain personally. The euphoria that politicians had raised by their appeals to ethnic nationalism—the wonder of having their own state for their own "people" is gone.

Slovakia is the eastern, less-industrially developed, primarily agricultural area of the former Czechoslovakia. Today it is mired in a spiral of debt with a devalued currency. There is little money or political will to privatize the farming collectives that grow increasingly uncompetitive. Prices rise, but salaries on the whole are shrinking. Much capital and many highly qualified professionals left in 1993.

Overall, the Czechs are satisfied with their new state. The Czech Republic is relatively well off compared to Slovakia, but, economic dislocation is felt. Overnight the Czech Republic lost about 30% of its population. Families were divided and forced to choose between citizenships. The Czech Republic is now in NATO; Slovakia has been denied membership.

Czechoslovakia, Romania, and the Soviet Union when the map of Europe was redrawn after World War II are increasingly asserting their sense of nationality.

Where should self-determination begin and end? In principle, each of these ethnic groups should have the right to form a separate state. However, the choice is often made to appear much less complex than it is. People are asked to choose either self-determination with freedom and democracy, or the status quo with order, stability, and dictatorship. Reality is not that simple; the problem is complicated and fraught with emotion. Unfortunately, oppressive nationalism, in which minority rights are disregarded, is a frequent byproduct of self-determination; stability and order, though less dramatic, can provide a better context for peaceful change. Those on the sidelines can do little but encourage peaceful transitions over time that will allow all parties to reflect on the rewards and risks of independence.

Military Governments and Federalism

Nigeria and Ethiopia provide pertinent examples of military governments and federalism. The stresses and failures of democratic federal systems that are taken over by the military can be illustrated first by the case of Nigeria. This country of 100 million people has oscillated between military government and a federal constitution since it became independent in 1960. The country's basic problem results from the fact that it has over 250 ethnic groups with three main tribes, the Yorubas, Hausa-Fulani, and Ibo, and two dominant religions, Islam and Christianity. In an attempt to accommodate these sharp differences, Nigeria formed a democratic and federal government after independence, but soldiers have run the country for all but nine years since then. The country quickly developed a pattern of replacing each civilian government with a military government, escalating to "coup culture" with one military government following another since 1983 (see Chapter 20).

As early as 1966 the Nigerian government was replaced by a military government after anarchy and bloodshed followed corrupt elections. In 1979 a second civilian government was set up only to collapse again in 1983 amid economic crises and allegations of electoral fraud. In 1991 the military government announced that a civilian government and elections would be allowed after 1992. In order to offset the impact of diverse tribes and regionalism the military proposed drastic steps. All past holders of elected or key appointed offices would be prohibited from future political or party activity. And the military commanded that there would be only two broadly based parties—the Social Democratic Party and the National Republican Convention—and each party was to include different tribes and religions.

The military claimed that these changes would result in a viable democratic state. However, in a 1993 coup, General Sani Abacha declared himself leader of the country and annulled the elections. He ruled as a military dictator and was condemned by the international community. The Commonwealth suspended Nigeria's membership after the 1995 execution of the poet Ken Saro-Wiwa and eight colleagues from the Ogoni people for advocating freedoms and environmental reforms. Abacha died in June 1998, ending one of the most repressive periods in Nigeria's history. General Abdulsalam Abubukar was sworn in as the country's new military ruler. He held elections in 1999 which were relatively fair and resulted in General Olusegun Obasanjo becoming President.

Finally, consider the use of federalism in the impoverished state of Ethiopia. This country of 56 million people is divided into hostile ethnic groups (including Oromo 40%, Amhara and Tigrean 31%, Sidamo 9%, Shankella 6%, and Somali 6%) and 83 language groups. It is one of the poorest states in the world with 95% of the population working as subsistence farmers. One of the oldest countries on earth, Ethiopia began to take its modern form when Haile Selassie became Emperor in 1930. His regime lasted off and on until 1974 when he was ousted by the military and the monarchy abolished. Civil war (the Ethiopian province of Eritrea eventually became an independent country in 1993), poverty, massive famine, and repressive Marxist governments followed. Finally, in 1991, Meles Zenawi, a leftist-guerilla leader, overthrew the military dictatorship, declared himself Prime Minister, and began to implement democracy and regionalization. He disbanded the one-party state and to a degree parties and a free media were permitted. By 1994 the country had a new constitution for a parliamentary government over nine partially autonomous regions. Border wars continue, but what is important here is that Zenawi implemented a *federal system with power to be divided along ethnic lines*. The classic use of federalism!

Failed Federations

Since constitutional federations combine both diversity and unity it is not surprising that they often prove to be highly unstable. In recent years some federations have fallen apart and many others seem constantly on the verge of doing so. Since most federations are large countries they tend—with the primary and important exception of China—to contain wide varieties of cultures, linguistic groups, and even nations within them.

Scholars have traced the failure of federations to four common conditions. They find that federal systems fail when they have regional divergences in their political demands; weak communications; a diminution of the original impetus to federation; and external influences.[14] The fallacy in this summary is that such strains and stresses are present in all federations over time, and the question remains: "Why do some federations succeed while others fail?"

States do not fall apart easily or peaceably. Around the world, in all kinds of states, there have been three dozen secessionist movements since World War II, but only two of them achieved their goal of independence in a relatively peaceful manner. Both examples were federal countries. Singapore separated from Malaysia in 1965, and Slovakia and the Czech Republic formed separate countries in 1993. Most of the other attempts deteriorated into various degrees of violence or civil war. One has to go back to the turn of the century to find another example of a peaceful division of a politically stabilized country with political arrangements similar to federalism. This was when Norway divided from Sweden in 1905.[15]

Historically, state breakdowns involved political violence or involved the termination of colonial regimes without contiguous territory with the parent countries, such as Algeria's breakaway from France. Yugoslavia is a pertinent example today. After World War II, a federal, communist state based on the Soviet model was set up in Yugoslavia. The League of Communists put in place a system of democratic centralism under Marshal Tito. The federation of six republics and two provinces worked fairly well as a united country until Tito died in 1981. After that the nationalist forces in Serbia, Croatia, Slovenia, Bosnia, Macedonia, and Montenegro as well as in the provinces of Vojvodina and Kosovo reasserted themselves. And when the Communist Party lost its cohesion, there was no force except the army to counteract the centrifugal forces in the regions. As we discussed in Close Up 10.1, a civil war concluded with the final destruction of Yugoslavia and the setting up of several new states.

The lesson is clear—civil war has been the usual means by which federal and other kinds of states divide. But it is also true that constitutional federalism requires more than a formal legal framework of institutions and laws; it requires an appropriate culture, with economic and party systems to buttress it. Even established federations can fall apart if the right conditions prevail.

> "Over several centuries, Moscow has got used to ruling a wide variety of peoples— some 140 different nationalities in the Soviet Union which Gorbachev inherited— and then 'gave away'. The Russian Federation itself still has numerous national groups within its borders, from Chechens to Vakuts ...
>
> "Now Russia is having to redefine its identity and learn to live within narrower borders. Will it leave its newly independent neighbours in peace?"
>
> "Russia and Its Neighbours"
> *Understanding Global Issues*, vol. 96, no. 5

HUMAN RIGHTS AND CONTROVERSIES

As we have seen, constitutional provisions for the rights of citizens exist in many countries. But in practice there is tremendous variation in the degree of adherence to these principles, even when the rights are documented in the supreme law of the state.

In communist countries the rights of the collectivity are often given precedence over the rights of individuals, and the individual rights specified in the constitutions have not been subject to court jurisdiction. While the Soviet Constitution was in effect, Stalin arbitrarily arrested literally millions of citizens.[16] Soviet dissidents were exiled to foreign countries, placed under house arrest, exiled to Siberia, stripped of their citizenship, and put in prison. China has also severely repressed citizens, as with the dissident students who participated in the Tiananmen Square demonstration in 1989.[17] And despite economic reforms in China, there is little sign of a significant change in China's appreciation of citizen's rights today.

Liberal democracies, on the other hand, make the rights of citizens justiciable in ordinary courts of law. The Canadian Charter of Rights and Freedoms asserts citizens' rights to fundamental liberties such as freedom of conscience and religion; freedom of thought, belief, opinion, and expression; freedom of peaceful assembly; and freedom of association. It also provides for basic democratic, mobility, legal, equality, and language rights. The U.S. Constitution contains within its text, and in the ten amendments attached to it, a bill of rights of citizens, which declares similar freedoms and the French Constitution mentions in its preamble adherence to the *Declaration of the Rights of Man* of 1789.

The German *Grundgesetz* (constitution) follows these precedents in setting forth strong individual rights. A bill of rights is found at the beginning of the Constitution and, unlike the early German Weimar Constitution or that of China and the former Soviet Union, no list of the duties of citizens is included. Moreover, in Germany these rights are not amendable. They stand over and above the Constitution itself, and in this respect are even more entrenched than those in the American Constitution.[18] The Canadian Charter of Rights and Freedoms goes even further. It not only asserts citizens' rights to fundamental liberties such as freedom of conscience and religion; freedom of thought, belief, opinion and expression; freedom of peaceful assembly; and freedom of association, but also provides "equality" rights in that "every individual is equal before and under the law ... without discrimination based on race, national or ethnic origin, colour, religion, sex, age, or mental or physical ability."[19]

How are these constitutional liberties defended in the real world? The answer is mixed. The "degree of freedom" is assessed annually by an American organization called Freedom House. It ranks states by such factors as the degree of freedom citizens have to speak and write what they wish; the freedom of their press, radio, and television to criticize the government; and the frequency and severity of violations against journalists. In 1998, Freedom House found that 1.2 billion people in 67 states possess a free press (36% of the 186 countries surveyed), 2.2 billion people in 54 states (29%) have a partly free news media, and 2.5 billion people in 65 countries live in a country in which the print and broadcast media are not free.[20]

The Freedom House data also show quite conclusively that those systems we classified as democratic in Chapter 5 are, on the whole, either free or partly free, while those in the authoritarian category are ranked as not free. Of course, great changes have occurred in many of the former communist countries during the last few years: some can now be classified as "free" while others remain under despotic regimes. On the other hand, some countries have not adjusted at all. As an example, Myanmar attempted to regain democracy by instituting elections in 1990. However, the military government refused to accede to democratic control and put the leader of the main opposition party, Aung San Suu Kyi (winner of the Nobel Peace prize), under house arrest. To appease opposition demands Suu Kyi has since been released by the military authorities, but she, and others, continue to be thwarted by oppressive measures.

Much of the debate over rights comes down to a conflict between collective rights and individual rights. In communist countries, for example, we have seen that the values of socialism may take precedence over individual rights. Further, in countries with pluralistic interests, collective rights may be placed ahead of individual rights. In fact, even in democratic countries today rights are viewed as encompassing entitlements such as claims for state services in health, education, and employment. In other words, rights are now being defined as encompassing the basic services governments should provide for their citizens. The 1948 United Nations *Declaration of Human Rights*, for example, includes both types of rights.

Since citizens in all countries cherish both individual freedoms and other values it is clear that the fight over human rights will continue to be at the heart of politics. Government decisions about what rights will be allowed and what policies will be used to protect them will remain one of the major distinguishing characteristics of democratic and authoritarian regimes. However, even within democratic states, major conflicts between individual and collective interests continue unabated.

DISCUSSION QUESTIONS

1. Why is a constitution necessary?
2. Is your country's constitution more similar to that of the United States or Britain? Russia?
3. Does your central government have adequate financial resources to keep the people in the regions and provinces satisfied?
4. What is the relationship between the degree of centralization and the nature of the constitution in a country? The party system and the degree of centralization?
5. Can power be decentralized in an authoritarian state? Totalitarian?

KEY TERMS

asymmetry, p. 238
bloc grants, p. 238
common market, p. 251
concurrency, p. 238
"conditional" grants, p. 238
customs union, p. 251

democratic centralism, p. 243
division of powers, p. 237
ethno-regional movements, p.241
free trade area, p. 251
fiat, p. 242

fiscal federalism, p. 240
residual powers, p. 238
separatist movements, p. 241
"unconditional" grants, p. 238

ENDNOTES

1. For documentation on the constitution of every country see the multi-volumed works of A.P. Blaustein and G.H. Flanz, eds., *Constitutions of the Countries of the World* (Dobbs Ferry, N.Y.: Oceana, annually).

2. S.E. Finer, *Five Constitutions* (London: Penguin, 1979).

3. *Ibid.*, p. 16

4. Christopher Clapham, *Third World Politics* (London: Croom Helm, 1985), pp. 45–46.

5. See James C.F. Wang, *Contemporary Chinese Politics*, 2nd ed. (Englewood Cliffs, N.J.: Prentice-Hall, 1985); James R. Townsend and Brantly Womack, *Politics in China*, 3rd ed. (Boston: Little, Brown, 1986); and Jonathan D. Spence, *The Search for Modern China* (New York: W.W. Norton, 1990).

6. Various models have been adopted to try to understand modern China. One persuasive argument is found in Weizhi Xie, "The Semihierarchical Totalitarian Nature of Chinese Politics," *Comparative Politics*, vol. 25, no.3 (April 1993), pp. 313–30.

7. For significant contemporary studies of regionalism see William D. Coleman and Henry Jacek, eds., *Regionalism, Business Interests and Public Policy* (London: Sage, 1989); Sidney Tarrow, Peter J. Katzenstein and Luigi Graziano, eds., *Territorial Politics in Industrial Nations* (New York: Praeger, 1978); Peter J. Katzenstein, *Disjointed Partners: Austria and Germany Since 1815* (Berkeley, Calif.: University of California Press, 1976); and L.A. Picard and Raphael Zariski, eds., *Subnational Politics in the 1980s* (New York: Praeger, 1987).

8. William H. Riker, "Federalism" in Fred I. Greenstein and Nelson W. Polsby, eds., *Handbook of Political Science, Vol. 5: Government Institutions and Processes* (Reading, Mass.: Addison-Wesley, 1975), p. 101.

9. There are also levels of political and economic integration lower than that found in federal states. A **free trade area** joins two or more states with no internal tariffs, but the participant states set their own tariffs for the rest of the world. A **customs union** has no internal customs and a common external tariff. A **common market** is a customs union buttressed by laws which require the free movement of goods, services, capital, and labour.

10. Robert J. Jackson and Doreen Jackson, *Canadian Government in Transition*, 2nd ed., (Scarborough, Ont: Prentice Hall, 1998), ch.4.

11. Clapham, *Third World Politics*, ch. 5.

12. Edward L. Keenan, *The New York Times*, September 8, 1991.

13. Study by the Deutsche Bank. See *The International Herald Tribune*, September 11, 1991.

14. R.L. Watts, "Survival or Disintegration," in Richard Simeon, *Must Canada Fail?* (Montreal: McGill-Queens University Press, 1977), pp. 42–60.

15. In a few instances in the post-World War II period, states joined together to form new federations and then quickly disintegrated. They include the weakly organized regimes of Syria-Egypt, Senegal-Mali, Rhodesia-Nyasaland, and the federation of the West Indies.

16. The reader may wish to read Alexander Solzhenitsyn's *The Gulag Archipelago* (New York: Harper and Row, 1974) which vividly describes these prison camps.

17. Spence, *The Search for Modern China*, p. 739 ff.

18. Finer, *Five Constitutions*, p. 25.

19. See Robert J. Jackson and Doreen Jackson, *Politics in Canada* (Scarborough, Ont.: Prentice-Hall, 1994), p. 210.

20. Freedom House, *Press Freedom* (Toronto: Ifex Clearing House, 1998).

FURTHER READING

Constitutions

Conklin, William, *Images of a Constitution* (Toronto: University of Toronto Press, 1993).

Finer, S.E., ed., *Five Constitutions* (London: Penguin, 1979).

Foley, Michael, *The Silence of Constitutions: An Essay in Constitutional Interpretation* (New York: Routledge, 1990).

Hennessy, Peter, *The Hidden Wiring: Unearthing the British Constitution* (London: Indigo, 1996).

Jackson, Robert J., and Doreen Jackson, *Canadian Government in Transition* (Scarborough, Ont.: Prentice-Hall Canada, 1996).

Jowell, J., and D. Oliver, eds., *The Changing Constitution*, 3rd ed. (Oxford: Clarendon Press, 1994).

Lieberthal, Kenneth, *Governing China* (New York: Norton, 1995).

O'Brien, David, *Constitutional Law and Politics* (New York: W.W. Norton, 1993).

Sartori, Giovanni, *Comparative Constitutional Engineering* (New York: New York University Press, 1995).

Federalism

Aitken, Robert, et al., eds., *Dismantling the Mexican State* (London: Macmillan, 1995).

Burgess, M., ed., *Federalism and Federation in Western Europe* (London: Croom Helm, 1986).

———, ed., *Canadian Federalism: Past, Present and Future* (Leicester: Leicester University Press, 1990).

Chandler, William M., and Christian W. Zollner, eds., *Challenges to Federalism: Policy-Making in Canada and the Federal Republic of Germany* (Kingston: Institute of Intergovernmental Relations, Queen's University, 1989).

Coleman, William D., and Henry J. Jacek, eds., *Regionalism, Business Interests and Public Policy* (London: Sage, 1989).

Dittmer, Lowell, *China under Reform* (Boulder, Colo.: Westview Press, 1994).

Djilas, Aleksa, *The Contested Country: Yugoslav Unity and Communist Revolution, 1919–1953* (Cambridge, Mass.: Harvard University Press, 1990).

Gray, Gwendolyn, *Federalism and Health Policy: The Development of Health Systems in Canada and Australia* (Toronto: University of Toronto Press, 1991).

Jeffrey, Robin, *What's Happening to India: Punjab, Ethnic Conflict and the Test for Federalism*, 2nd ed. (London: MacMillan, 1994).

Katzenstein, Peter J., *Disjointed Partners: Austria and Germany Since 1815* (Berkeley, Calif.: University of California Press, 1976).

Lieberthal, Kenneth, *Governing China* (New York: Norton, 1995).

Picard, Louis A., and Raphael Zariski, eds., *Subnational Politics in the 1980s: Organization, Reorganization and Economic Development* (New York: Praeger, 1987).

Rokkan, Stein, and Derek W. Urwin, *Economy, Territory, Identity: Politics of West European Peripheries* (London: Sage, 1983).

Schram, S.R., ed., *The Scope of State Power in China* (New York: St. Martin's Press, 1985).

Stevenson, Garth, ed., *Federalism in Canada: Selected Readings* (Toronto: McClelland and Stewart, 1989).

Tarrow, Sidney, Peter J. Katzenstein, and Luigi Graziano, eds., *Territorial Politics in Industrial Nations* (New York: Praeger, 1978).

Whitely, Paul, *Political Control of the Macroeconomy* (London: Sage, 1986).

Human Rights

Mandel, Michael, *The Charter of Rights and the Legalization of Politics in Canada* (Toronto: Wall and Thompson, 1989).

Saich, Tony, ed., *The Chinese People's Movement* (Armonk, N.Y.: M.E. Scharpe, 1990).

Shugart, Matthew, and John Carey, *Presidents and Assemblies: Constitutional Design and Electoral Dynamics* (Cambridge, Mass.: Cambridge University Press, 1992).

Thompson, Judith Jarvis, *The Realm of Rights* (Cambridge, Mass.: Harvard University Press, 1990).

Weiner, Myron, *The Global Migration Crisis: Challenge to States and to Human Rights* (New York: Harper Collins, 1995).

 Weblinks

www.wavefront.com/~homelands/

This site contains links to the Web Pages of secessionist movements around the world.

www.un.org/Overview/rights.html

Information about the United Nations Declaration of Human Rights can be found at this site.

www.government.de/ausland/index_e.html

This site provides information on Germany's system of government.

CHAPTER 12

Design of Central Government Institutions: Leadership, Executives, and Legislatures

Every society and every type of state, democratic or authoritarian, requires leadership. And there seems to be a natural tendency for political systems to be run by a relatively small group of individuals. This elite may be based on one person and his or her relatives or cronies, or it may be based on the principles of democracy. Leadership is inherent in all systems.

LEADERSHIP

Changing leaders in an orderly manner is one of the greatest challenges in politics. Whether it is a president, prime minister, king, emperor, emir, or fuhrer, every system is headed by an incumbent who does not want to be replaced, but who has to contend with newcomers who want to get control of the reins of government. In most countries, the legitimation of political leaders by democratic elections is not well established. It is not surprising, therefore, that many leaders rise to their positions through heredity, charismatic appeal, or military coups.

Authoritarian leaders often hang on to power too long—often until they are driven out of office and sometimes in a body bag! Democratically elected leaders, too, are subject to the frailty of believing they are infallible; they tend to prefer not to transfer authority to other leaders. However, in the established democracies, institutional rules make changes of leaders both possible and probable.[1]

In light of the definitions and classifications of constitutions and their key institutions discussed in Chapters 10 and 11, we can surmise that leadership in modern democracies tends to be of the rational-bureaucratic type.[2] Even in authoritarian states, few leaders claim to receive their inspirations from a god, while a somewhat greater number account for their authority by referring to the customs and traditions of their countries. Some manage to control their populations with their own personal charisma or magnetism. Such leaders usually base their legitimacy on some heroic deeds—real or mythical—that they have performed for the people. But by far the greatest number of state leaders derive their legitimacy from some form of constitution or through the barrel of a gun.

Before the development of the modern European state in the sixteenth century, leadership was seen as holistic. The monarchs, or their equivalents, represented the totality of regime authority; they were **absolute monarchs**, deriving their authority from the principle of the divine rights of kings. From that period onward the internal structures of European states evolved toward democracy. Assemblies, parliaments and other forms of public participation arose to protect the interests of groups in society. With this change in structure came a distinction between making the laws, executing them, and interpreting them. This distinction led to the tripartite division known today as legislatures, executives, and the judiciary.

We have already discussed the role of constitutions and the judiciary in Chapters 10 and 11; here we concentrate on the various forms of executives and legislatures. In the next chapter we examine the relations between these structures and political realities in the modern world.

EXECUTIVES

Political leadership today is usually the responsibility of an **executive**, which can be defined as the institutions and individuals who "steer" the country by formulating the most important political decisions.[3] The institutional terms used to depict the core executive differ from country to country. Even determining which people should be included by the term may prove contentious. In Canada the executive normally refers to the Governor General, Prime Minister, cabinet, and senior bureaucrats, most of whom are career civil servants. In the United States the term "administration" is used to describe the President, his or her cabinet, and the dozen or so political appointees who run each government department.

In nondemocratic systems the executive always proves to be the major, and sometimes the only, organ of government.[4] In communist systems, ultimate authority resides in a party hierarchy which parallels a less powerful official government hierarchy. (See Figure 17.2 in Chapter 17.) Sometimes, individuals hold powerful positions in both the government and the party. For example, for a short time before the Soviet Union broke up, Mikhail Gorbachev was Secretary General of the Communist Party and President of the state. In military regimes the executive may be a junta, composed of a number of senior military personnel. In theocracies, leading clergy form the nucleus of the core executive.

In all political systems the executive or top decision-makers are supported by a phalanx of individuals who provide the **public administration**. The executive consists of those individuals who are politically responsible for government actions, whereas the public administration is, to a large extent, composed of neutral public servants. In Chapters 14 and 15 we discuss the role of this latter group in policy-making, but here we concentrate on the political executive including heads of state such as kings and presidents, prime ministers, cabinets, or the central core of top political decision-makers, and their immediate staff and advisors.

Forms of Executives

The names and responsibilities of executives vary greatly around the globe, but, at a minimum, they all perform the two functions of ceremonial representation and government decision-making.

Every country has a degree of conflict within it. In durable states this conflict is mitigated by cultural and social forces that encourage national unity. Often, a symbol, such as an individual—sometimes acting as head of state—signifies the unity or cohesion of the state. This individual acts in the name of the state on ceremonial occasions by giving out honours, for instance, or by reviewing military parades. This "symbolic" and "dignified" activity also includes formal tasks such as meeting foreign dignitaries and officiating at holiday celebrations. If this figurehead role is adequately integrated into the nation's consciousness, its representative may perform an important function in symbolizing the history, customs, and unity of the country.

By contrast, the "effective" work of executives consists of making and implementing laws and regulations. In institutional terms the ceremonial work is carried out by a "head of state" or "chief of state" and the governing is done by the "head of government."

When the head of state is separated from the governing function, the individual may represent the unity of the state and be above party bickering. On the other hand, when the functions are combined the individual has more "power" to accomplish things—for good or ill. In most democratic countries it is considered an advantage to keep the symbolic and effective functions of government separated. Ceremonial tasks are carried out by individuals who are above politics, "symbolizing unity and continuity"[5] while governing is left to "bickering politicians." Sometimes, of course, as in the case of the United States, the same individual performs both tasks.

Heads of State

The precise title of the head of state may or may not be enlightening about the nature of a country's politics. While President and Prime Minister are the most commonly used titles today, there are also Kings, Queens, Emperors, Chancellors, and Emirs. A very few states possess collective or collegial executives.

Monarchs may be hereditary or elected. **Hereditary monarchs** inherit their positions from family ties while **elected monarchs** obtain their roles by some form of democratic process. Heads of state such as the British, Belgian, and Dutch monarchs derive their positions from families that were once the authoritarian leaders of their respective countries. Japan is an interesting example as for centuries it was headed by a person who was considered a living god. The current Japanese head of state, Emperor Akihito, is the 125th emperor and the first one to be enthroned without being considered a supreme being. Akihito is considered a symbol of the postwar constitution and unity of the Japanese people, but the emperor is no longer considered superhuman.

Some of these titles convey significant meaning of real power in the government while others are merely symbolic. In countries such as Britain, Canada, Australia, and New Zealand, the role of the Queen or her representative, the Governor General, is basically ceremonial (see Close Up 12.1). Or put another way, the monarch reigns rather than governs. The monarch represents the customs and traditions of government but does not actually run the country. However, even in these systems, some monarchical duties are more than merely ceremonial. When the head of state is called upon to proclaim laws, agree to subordinate legislation, summon or dissolve parliament, the role is both ceremonial and functional.

On rare occasions, such as in the case of a divided or fragmented parliament where no individual can easily be selected as Prime Minister, a major political role may be played by the monarch or his or her representative. For example, in most cases the head

---

CLOSE UP 12.1   Elizabeth II, Queen of Great Britain, Northern Ireland, and members of the Commonwealth, including Canada

Elizabeth II assumed the throne in Britain in 1952. She is the personal embodiment of the Crown — the composite symbol of the institutions of the state. The powers of the British monarch can be traced to the period of authoritarian rule in Great Britain, when the Crown possessed wide discretionary authority. These have been reduced to a very few reserve powers. Although the monarchy is of necessity personified in an individual, one must separate the two. Individuals come and go, but the Crown is permanent. It provides history, tradition, and an institutional framework that can promote political stability.

Although Parliament and the political executive govern in the name of the Crown, the powers of the monarch are severely limited. Even the monarch's ability to stay on the throne is no longer a right but subject to acceptance by British ministers and Parliament. The functions of the monarch are largely ceremonial and strictly non-partisan. The subjects of Elizabeth II include the citizens of the 50 member states of the Commonwealth.

Elizabeth's II became the monach only because her father, King George VI died without sons. Her eldest son, Prince Charles, is heir. However in 1998 Queen Elizabeth agreed to abandon the age-old hereditary custom of primogeniture which says the eldest son ascends to the throne. Once this becomes law, sons and daughters will be treated the same in the determining the line of succession.

Many well-publicized scandals involving Prince Charles and the other young royals have blemished their own reputations and even that of the monarchy. In Australia there is a strong movement to drop the royal connection and become a republic. Even in Canada and England there are grumblings of discontent about whether the monarchy should be continued after Elizabeth II.

of state in Canada, the Governor General, merely chooses as Prime Minister the individual with the majority or plurality of seats in the House of Commons. When there is a complication, such as when no party can demonstrate that it can control the House, the Governor General may use his or her royal prerogative to select someone to act as head of government. But such solutions are temporary and last only until the parties or the electorate have had another chance to determine who should be Prime Minister.

In other words, in some countries the head of state may be called upon to aid in the transfer of power from one democratic leader to another. Most heads of state, however, perform mainly ceremonial acts for their country. They represent the historical continuity of the state and are symbols of official authority. Examples include the British Queen, other monarchs in Europe such as the Queen of the Netherlands, and the Japanese Emperor.

The type of government in which the monarch is both the ceremonial and political head of government is becoming almost extinct. Only in the few dynasties in the Middle East and scattered throughout the developing world are actual ruling monarchs still to be found. In Bahrain, Kuwait, Oman, Qatar, Saudi Arabia, and the United Arab Emirates monarchs possess the same complete power that was held by authoritarian leaders in feudal Europe during the Middle Ages. Bhutan, Brunei, and Swaziland also have absolute monarchs (see Close Up 12.2). Somewhat more restricted as monarchs are the kings of Jordan and Morocco.

In some cases where monarchies have been abolished, there continues to be a need to separate the symbolic and effective functions of government. The heads of state in Austria, Germany, Iceland, India, and Italy, for example, are selected by politicians or elected by the people as heads of state. These positions of elected monarchs convey little real power in the policy-making process except in constitutional crises or other emergencies.

We shall deal with individual elected heads of state who *do* play a vital role in the policy process, but there is one more interesting type of head of state that fits none of the

CLOSE UP 12.2   The Sultan of Brunei

The Sultan of Brunei is another example of a contemporary autocrat or absolute ruler. In 1984 the Sultanate of Brunei became independent of colonial rule. This newly independent country on the northern half of the island of Borneo was one of the richest countries in the world until it was hit by slumping global oil prices in 1998. (Brunei's economy relies almost entirely on oil.) Brunei is also one of the few countries actually governed by a hereditary monarch whose family forms the top administration of the country. The Sultan, Hassanal Bolkiah, is one of the most powerful heads of state today and until 1998 was allegedly the richest man in the world. He rules by decree, assisted by a Council of Ministers appointed by himself. His government employs 80% of the work force at one of the highest average salaries in the region. There are no political parties.

usual categories. Unique among political systems today is the **collective executive**. This system is found in only one liberal democracy—Switzerland—where a collective seven-member federal council is the prime policy-making body. It is chosen every four years by the bicameral legislature, and it, in turn, selects one of its own members to act as President of the Swiss Confederacy for a one-year period. The communist regime of Yugoslavia possessed a similar "collective" arrangement for running its federal system until civil war broke out in 1991.

Ceremonial heads of state provide continuity that may not be possible in most democratic states. Table 12.1, for example, shows that Queen Elizabeth II began her rule in 1952. From the beginning of her reign to 1996 she has dealt with nine British Prime Ministers, nine Canadian Prime Ministers, and ten American Presidents. When Elizabeth II came to the throne, Stalin was in power in the Soviet Union; she watched as the Cold War gripped the world and was still the Queen when the Soviet Union disintegrated in 1991 and U.S. President Bill Clinton was impeached by the House of Representatives and nearly thrown out of office by the Senate in 1999.

Heads of Government

Most governments around the world today are headed by a President or Prime Minister, and sometimes both. These executive leaders have substantial power to steer the entire political process of their countries. Among the Western democratic systems, somewhat more countries are headed by Prime Ministers than Presidents, while in the authoritarian parts of the world, particularly in Africa, Presidents are more common.

Presidents

As absolute monarchies have declined around the world they have tended to be replaced by republics—many of which have chosen a President as head of state and government—following the model of established Presidential systems such as the United States. In the United States, the President heads the state in a ceremonial sense and is also the actual head of the government. He or she reigns and rules.[6] In this sense, the President is often thought of as the one person who unifies the country. This feature makes this particular institutional design attractive in less developed countries, divided as they often are along ethnic and linguistic lines. In one-party systems, military regimes, and theocracies, presidential systems are usually established in order to illustrate that the head of state and government obtains authority directly from the people and not from some particular group or ethnic community in society.

Many presidential regimes are highly personalized forms of government. In Mexico, for example, the President is almost like an absolute monarch for a six-year mandate. The post can be held for only one term, but during that term the President is a virtual autocrat. In many Third World countries the office of President is so closely linked to the personality of the incumbent that only a military uprising can rid the country of the individual. Such, for example, was the fate of Jean-Bédel Bokassa who ruled the

Table 12.1	Continuity Provided by the British Monarchy: Forty-seven Years in the Reign of Elizabeth II, 1952–1999			
Date	**British Monarch**	**British Prime Ministers**	**Canadian Prime Ministers**	**American Presidents**
1952	Queen Elizabeth II	Winston Churchill	Louis St-Laurent	Harry Truman
		Anthony Eden	John Diefenbaker	Dwight Eisenhower
		Harold Macmillan	Lester Pearson	John F. Kennedy
		Sir Alec Douglas-Home	Pierre Trudeau	Lyndon Johnson
		Harold Wilson	Joe Clark	Richard Nixon
		Edward Heath	John Turner	Gerald Ford
		James Callaghan	Brian Mulroney	Jimmy Carter
		Margaret Thatcher	Kim Campbell	Ronald Reagan
		John Major	Jean Chrétien	George Bush
1999		Tony Blair		Bill Clinton

Central African Republic for 13 years. For the last three years he proclaimed himself Emperor, also assuming the positions of Life-President and President of the government. His self-proclaimed empire lasted only from 1977 to 1979, before he was thrown out in a coup d'état.

Among the democracies, there are, however, several constitutionalized presidencies. The best known is the United States, but in Europe three countries—France, Finland, and Portugal—have powerful presidencies. Stable presidential rule is also found in states such as Costa Rica, Mexico, Senegal, Venezuela, Brazil, Argentina, and Sri Lanka to mention a few (see Close Up 12.3).

Russia, too, chose a presidential form of government after the collapse of authoritarianism.

Prime Ministers

As we have seen above, the head of government in many countries is called the Prime Minister, or, less often, premier or chancellor. The Prime Minister obtains his or her position by maintaining a majority of supporters in the legislature—in other words by keeping the **confidence** of the legislature.[7] In the British model, the leader of the party that wins an election becomes Prime Minister. The government is formed from members of Parliament and it must retain the confidence of the majority of members of the House

CLOSE UP 12.3 Boris Yeltsin, Russia's First Democratically Elected President

Boris Yeltsin took on an awesome task when he set out to establish a stable free market economy in Russia. Initially, he appeared to many to be the only person capable of steering Russia through its post-communist turbulence. He fought for economic reform and closer ties with Western countries. He was a reforming strongman who held fragile political coalitions together and ushered in the constitutional changes needed to bring Russia's chaos to order. And he struggled to tear down the monopoly of Russia's state-owned industry in order to make way for the market economy.

Many times he showed courage in a crisis: he stood on top of a tank to defy putschists; he presided over the Russians' humiliating retreat from empire both in the former Soviet states and Eastern Europe. However, critics soon complained that he did not have a clear sense of where he wanted to go, and could not provide steady and sustained leadership. He created a strong presidency with a vast array of legal tools to guarantee his position above the Prime Minister and Parliament. He often ruled by decree rather than negotiating compromises with Parliament. When the Duma opposed his reforms he set up rival centres of power to try to bypass Parliament. He even sent tanks to subdue parliamentary rebels. Perhaps what damaged his popularity most was that he mired Russia in a bloody civil war in Chechnya.

By 1996 the pressures had taken their toll. He had suffered at least two heart attacks, and the reform parties had lost to the communists in the legislative elections of December 1995. There was a large question mark about his ability to win the spring 1996 presidential elections, but he did so by a comfortable margin. His inability to name the Prime Minister of his choice in late 1998 and his acceptance of the Duma's nominee marked the beginning of the end for Yeltsin's powerful presidency.

of Commons. In Britain, Canada, Australia, and New Zealand, for example, this is reasonably easy because of the principle of cohesive and disciplined political parties.[8]

This form of government is called **responsible government** because the Crown acts only on the advice of the executive or cabinet which, in turn, must retain the confidence of a majority of members of the lower house. After a defeat in a general election or in the legislature on an important matter, the Prime Minister submits his or her resignation or asks the Crown to call an election and remains in office until it is called. In the case of a resignation, the head of state appoints someone to attempt to form a majority from members of the legislature. If a majority of members will not support a government, a cabinet based on a minority of members is set up. In Anglo-American systems these are called **minority governments**. Such governments are usually quite fragile and tend to last only for limited periods. A **majority government**, on the other hand, is one backed by a majority of members in the legislature and which, in principle, can last until an election is required under the constitution.

In many other countries, particularly on the European continent, parties are factionalized and/or a multi-party legislature prevails. In such cases, a coalition of factions or parties is necessary to allow someone to obtain majority support in the assembly, form a cabinet, and assume the title of head of government. In these **coalition governments,** the Prime Minister must sustain a majority in the house, or he or she can be deposed even before an election takes place.

Authoritarian Leaders

Authoritarian executives come in a variety of types: some are led by single leaders, others by collective leadership. Many authoritarian governments consist of one-person dictatorships. In Europe, for example, Franco's regime in Spain (1936–1975) and Salazar's and Caetano's regimes in Portugal (1931–1973) were one-person dictatorships. In each case the leader had absolute control of the military which had come to power after a civil war.

In Africa many of the military regimes were, and continue to be, one-person dictatorships. Idi Amin in Uganda (1971–1979) is possibly the best known example of this autocratic type of leader. Moreover, the leaders who followed after his demise also set up personal dictatorships in Uganda. Similar examples in other countries in Africa would include Bokassa in the Central African Republic, Doe in Liberia, and Qaddafi in Libya. Close Up 12.4 recounts the recent history of another dictator, Saddam Hussein.

Aside from one-person dictatorships, military executives often take the form of a **junta,** a group of officers who run the country after a coup d'état or other form of military takeover. A few of these regimes have one person at the head of government, but the structure of authority is often based on a collective leadership.

In Myanmar (formerly Burma) a military junta seized power in 1988 after a period of civil upheaval against the one-party tyranny of the Burmese Socialist Program Party. The junta immediately set up a collective leadership called the State Law and Order Restoration Council (SLORC). Even today it has not restored power to civilians despite the 1990 elections which resulted in a landslide victory for the National League for Democracy party. Currently, a collection of officers rules by fiat. The 1991 Nobel Peace prize went to Aung San Suu Kyi, leader of the democratic opposition, who remains in permanent opposition within the country.

In communist countries there tends to be a duality of state and party institutions so that leaders hold positions in each organizational hierarchy. In other words, the constitution of the state is closely integrated with the organization of the Communist Party. Such a duality gives the party either complete or almost complete "political" authority over the state organizations. China is currently the most powerful communist country in the world (see Close Up 12.5).

In communist countries the central *apparat* determine the organization and personnel of sensitive positions. In the former Soviet Union, for example, a system know as *nomenklatura* (see Chapter 15) provided party control throughout the Soviet bureaucracy. The First, or General, Secretary of the party was the most powerful member

---

CLOSE UP 12.4   Saddam Hussein, President of Iraq

Saddam Hussein is a dictatorial President of a troubled Arab state. Iraq became a republic after a 1958 military coup in which the royal family was murdered. Ten more years of terror and coups brought the Ba'athist (pan-Arab nationalist) officers to power.

Saddam is not only a dictatorial but also an aggressive leader. He attacked Iran in 1980 and entered a long, drawn-out war that left his country in economic ruin. In 1990 he tried to restore his fortunes by invading oil-rich Kuwait. This resulted in the Gulf War in which forces from the United States, Canada, the United Kingdom, and more than 20 other countries participated. After only 100 hours Saddam was forced to agree to a ceasefire. The Iraqi President was effectively demonized in the Western media, and went from relative obscurity to become a highly recognized world figure. After the war, the United Nations Security Council imposed sanctions on Iraq, hoping to hasten Saddam's departure by turning Iraqis against him. However, Saddam remained in power. The cease-fire that ended the Gulf War requires Iraq to destroy all of its weapons of mass destruction including chemical and biological weapons. Saddam's non-compliance has brought his country to the brink of another war several times.

Iraq imports most of its food and is dependent on a single export commodity: oil. With oil sanctioned, the country is desperately poor. Food is severely rationed, and infant mortality has more than tripled since the war. Many people are dying from diseases related to malnutrition and lack of medicine.

In typical dictatorial fashion, however, Saddam continues to spend money on his retinue and palaces. He retains an army of elite soldiers kept loyal by favours. Army deserters are punished like criminals, with the loss of an ear and a tattoo on the forehead. Ba'ath informants, estimated to be one in 20 Iraqi adults, form a secret police to keep dissidents in line.

In 1995 Saddam held a presidential referendum to confirm his leadership. Not surprisingly, he won over 99% of the vote.

---

of the executive, but not the titular head of state. That role was usually performed by a President. Mikhail Gorbachev combined the role of President (the most important role in the Soviet system) with that of General Secretary of the Communist Party. This allowed him to chair the *politburo* (party cabinet) and also the Central Committee of the CPSU (party legislature). Today, the presidency of Russia is formed on a more typical democratic structure.

LEGISLATURES

Today almost every state has a legislative body of some kind. Not every one of them, however, consists of elected individuals or parties; in a small handful of traditional states

CLOSE UP 12.5   Leadership in China

China, the world's most populous country, is a communist state. The country's elected National People's Congress elects a Central Committee, which in turn elects a Politburo. The latter two bodies are the most powerful political bodies. They are guided by Jiang Zemin, who took over the leadership of China after the death of Deng Ziaoping in 1997. Jiang is head of the Communist Party of China (General Secretary), President of China (heading the National People's Congress) and Chairman of the Central Military Commission.

Deng had initiated economic reform, restructuring and privatizing China's huge state-owned industrial sector. He endorsed a 1993 plan to put China's large industries on the same footing as Western corporations by making them responsible only to shareholders and not the party, and to the demands of the market. However, little progress was made in this area. When Jiang took control, no major policy changes ensued, largely because the succession issue had been clear for some time. However, conservative ideologues in the party leadership appear to be attempting to reverse the reform strategy. In 1998, for example, faced with a slowing economy, China declined to join the World Trade Organization (WTO) a 132-country organization dedicated to open markets and free competition.

Jiang Zemin has adopted the language of reform initiated by Deng, but his actions support delay and deferral. In the meantime, the egalitarianism in society established under Mao has given way to vast income disparities and conspicuous consumption. China continues to be highly criticized in the West for human-rights violations and worker exploitation.

legislators are appointed because of their family, religious, or military connections. Separate **representative assemblies**, parliaments, legislatures, diets, or dumas do exist in most contemporary political systems, however.

On the whole, modern legislative bodies have evolved from an executive authority that sought or required some degree of advice or mandate from a wider public. It is for this reason that in modern democracies these bodies consist of "representatives" who govern on behalf of the people. In democracies they are chosen in free elections and are held accountable to the public for their actions in future elections.

In some cases, legislatures are powerful decision-making bodies, while in others they are merely advisory institutions. Unlike political parties and interest groups, legislative bodies are official agencies of government. Of course, the historical development of the party system plays an important part in determining the significance of the legislature in each country. In some states, parties are so disciplined that an individual member has very little freedom of action, while in others the members are more concerned with local or constituency concerns than they are with their party interests. We shall return to the role of parties in legislatures throughout this chapter and Chapter 13. Those questions which concern parties directly will be dealt with in Chapters 16 and 17.

Legislatures have been defined many ways. The simplest definition is that they are deliberating bodies.[9] However, Nelson Polsby has argued that they can be distinguished from other institutions of government by six specific characteristics: they are official agencies of government; they are multi-membered; they are directly elected by their citizens; in the legislature their members are formally equal in status; they deliberate; and they make decisions by counting votes to determine what issues have majority support.[10]

While this definition helps to focus the student on the basic functions of legislatures, it is biased toward legislatures of the Western or liberal democratic tradition such as those found in Canada, the United Kingdom, the United States, or Western Europe. Even there, however, the British and Canadian Parliaments have upper houses as part of their legislatures that would not accord with Polsby's definition. In this book, therefore, we shall remain with the broadest concept of legislatures as deliberative bodies. We should bear in mind, however, that in Western liberal democracies these institutions are supposed to have a central role to play in making the system work. Through elections the members of these bodies are given the legitimacy to act in the name of the people in creating laws for the state.

Functions of Legislatures

Legislatures are multi-functional institutions.[11] They perform many tasks, the best known of which is **law-making**. To a greater or lesser degree each legislative institution in the world is involved in the law-making function. In the United States, the two houses of Congress make the final decisions about laws subject only to a presidential veto. In the British and Canadian systems, law-making is legally the responsibility of Parliament although in reality it is controlled by the executive. But even such generalizations are simplistic, as law-making itself is a multifaceted task. Law must be initiated, made, and implemented. As well, the role of the legislature differs from country to country, and conclusions about the role of legislatures also depend on the precise type of law-making discussed. In some countries the legislature must pronounce on all laws; in others the legislature may be prevented from acting in some spheres of law-making. In some countries legislatures are mere rubber stamps for the executive, while in others they actually draft legislation.

Even in democracies legislatures are not the only, or even the most important, law-making body. We have already seen that executive power exists in every political system and is almost always the most vital institution. Power over policy-making is thus shared between these two bodies in some manner. The legislature may guard the final decision-making authority, but the role of initiating legislation usually rests with the executive and bureaucracy. Legislators commonly have neither the time nor the expertise to develop the technical, economic, and specialized information necessary for writing legislation.

As executives have gained more and more power over the years they have increasingly tended to resort to the use of "**subordinate**" **legislation** to carry out many of their tasks. Subordinate legislation consists of the detailed rules, regulations, or ordinances used to govern society under the auspices of a regular statute or piece of legislation. Increasingly, modern state governments adopt regulations to flesh out the details of laws. In Canada, for example, the Fisheries Act gives the government authority to make annual regulations and set quotas and limits on commercial fishing to protect off-shore fisheries. Parliament would not have the time or inclination to pass statutes with such details, so the responsibility is left to the government and administration.

Such sharing of law-making authority between the legislature and the executive also takes place over other functions such as controlling budgets, surveillance of the bureaucracy, and educating the public about government.

The power to raise taxes and to spend public money was the fundamental issue that gave rise to the development of parliamentary democracy in Britain. It became one of the crucial issues in the relations between the executive and legislature in every state. However, the growth in broad and complex functions of the modern state has reduced the power of legislatures to maintain absolute control over government budgets. But democratic legislatures continue to affect the raising and spending of taxes to a large degree. Usually, as in Canada, the executive prepares the details of the budget—both revenue and expenditure sides—and presents this to the legislature for deliberation and final determination. Only in countries such as the United States is the power to increase expenditures given to the legislature. Legislatures are also given responsibility to oversee the executive in various ways. They investigate and publicize government malfeasance. They commission studies and publish reports which may have major importance or be shelved as insignificant.

In his famous book *The English Constitution*, Walter Bagehot provided a different way of explaining the roles of legislatures.[12] To the usual tasks of helping to elect a government and law-making, he added *expressive functions*, including teaching and informing the public. Other scholars have added functions such as *legitimation* to this list.[13] In this respect the formal deliberations, hearings, and surveillance activities of the legislature make the public more aware and appreciative of the powers of government. These activities are sometimes referred to as *representative functions* because they relate to the articulation of the people's needs and desires. In the long run such activities help prepare the people to determine which party should be chosen in elections.

In the final analysis, the most powerful legislatures are those that share law-making authority with the executive, as in the United States. The second most powerful are those which can control the legislative process by making and un-making governments, as in some European multi-party parliamentary systems. The primary examples of the latter systems are found in Italy and smaller European countries such as the Netherlands, Austria, and Switzerland. In some countries such as Germany, Italy, and Greece, the assembly actually chooses the head of state as well as having a say in the choice of the head of government.

The functions of legislatures in authoritarian regimes are even more differentiated. In communist systems the party controls the legislature, which performs ceremonial and ritual functions. During most of the communist period in the USSR, the Congress of the Supreme Soviet was a toothless tiger and the present National People's Congress of China, although more powerful than it was during Mao's leadership, is not much more than an appendage to the Communist Party. Legislatures in LDC authoritarian countries tend to be democratic showplaces for conflicts over poverty, religion, ethnicity, region, and language, but only rarely do they have any significant power in policy-making.

Organization of Legislatures

The structure of legislatures is one of the best-documented areas of political science. The role of elected politicians and the institutions that support their activities is very well described in most countries of the world, but the consequences of their activities are hotly contested.

To begin with, legislatures may have one or two houses; they may be **unicameral** or **bicameral**. Bicameral systems are set up to limit the power of the lower house or to provide special representation in a federal constitutional system. In almost every system, the lower house is based on direct election by the people, and the upper house is hereditary, appointed, or elected in a manner different from the lower house.

In every case, upper houses are based on a principle other than "representation by population." The principle of "rep by pop" is the rule for the lower house, but in all cases the number of representatives in the upper house is not proportional to the population of the region or state they come from. For example, no matter how large or small a state is, each American state has two members in the Senate and each Australian state receives ten members. In Canada, Senators are appointed by the federal government on a regional basis—24 each from the Maritime provinces, Quebec, Ontario, and the West. Newfoundland gets six Senators, and one is appointed from each of the Yukon and Northwest Territories. Another Senate seat will be created in 1999 for the new Territory of Nunavit. The 1993 provisional constitution of the new South Africa provided for a bicameral legislature in which the lower house is elected by proportional representation while the upper house is chosen by the nine provincial legislatures.

While about two out of every three contemporary legislatures have two chambers, the second or upper house is usually insignificant in the policy process. The prime exception to this generalization is the United States, where the House of Representatives and Senate both play a critical role in policy-making. The U.S. Senate, which is elected for six years on the basis of two Senators per state, is probably the most powerful upper house in the world.

In those countries that follow the British model of Parliament, all have retained their second houses with the exception of New Zealand. Britain has an unelected House of Lords. The upper house or House of Lords consists of about 1100 members. Over half of them are hereditary peers and the remainder are individuals appointed by the British government as life peers.[14] Since the Parliament Acts of 1911 and 1949, the Lords continue to have the power to initiate legislation as in the House of Commons, but they can delay bills passed by the lower house for only up to one year. Even this limited theoretical power has little practical import. In 1998 the Blair government promised to abolish hereditary peers in the House of Lords. But, instead of deciding what type of body would replace them, he promised a Royal Commission and a "transitional arrangement."

Canada has an appointed Senate, and Australia has an elected upper house also called a Senate. All members of the Canadian Senate are officially appointed by the government, but its counterpart in Australia consists of elected members from each of the states and territories. These two upper houses are quite powerful, at least in terms of their theoretical constitutional responsibilities, but in reality the Canadian institution is much, much weaker. In some countries the upper house is used for functional representation; the Irish Senate (Seanad) has members nominated by the Prime Minister but also elects representatives from the universities and public fields such as the arts, languages, literature, agriculture, banking, labour, and industry.

The Canadian Senate, which under normal circumstances consists of 104 members appointed by the government until the age of 75, shares with the lower house almost all powers except that it can delay constitutional bills for only six months. While it cannot introduce financial legislation (known as money bills), it has the same theoretical ability to introduce all other legislation and to amend or block Commons bills. The Senate has no constitutional authority to throw out governments, but its ability to block legislation can cause an election. In practice, however, while the unelected Senate often delays or amends House legislation, it only rarely actually vetoes it.

The major exception was the initiation of the 1988 general election. That election was forced by the Liberal-dominated Senate over the issue of the Free Trade Agreement with the United States. Since the Senate was able to block the legislation indefinitely, the Prime Minister had to call an election to resolve the impasse. Later, in 1990, the Conservatives used a special technique provided for in the Constitution, which allowed the government to appoint an additional eight Senators to the upper house, in order to prevent the Liberals from blocking a highly controversial Goods and Services Tax bill.[15] In 1991, however, a bill which would have seen abortion returned to the Criminal Code was overturned by the Senate in a tie vote. The previous legislation had been overturned by the Supreme Court on January 28, 1988, as it was deemed contrary to the Canadian *Charter of Rights and Freedoms*. By 1992 the law had still not been replaced. This example provides a particularly good illustration of how constitution, court, and Senate can affect Canadian politics.

In terms of control over legislation, the Senate in Australia is equal to the lower house, called the House of Representatives. In 1975, for example, when the Senate refused to pass a financial bill from the House and the Prime Minister would not amend the legislation, the Governor General felt he had to dissolve both houses and call for dual elections. This meant that the upper house had brought down the government even though the Prime Minister retained control of the lower chamber. In the ensuing election the voters chose the opposition which, to some extent, justified the actions of both the Senate and the Governor General.[16]

In Germany, the Constitution (*Grundgesetz*) determines that the upper house, or *Bundesrat*, possesses powers somewhere between the powerful U.S. Senate and the weaker upper houses discussed above. The members of the *Bundesrat* are appointed by the leaders of the states (the *Laender*). Its members—three or four from each *Land*—cast their votes as a bloc. It may accept or turn down any legislation emanating from the lower house, or *Bundestag*. If the *Bundesrat* defeats a bill by a simple majority, the *Bundestag* may override the decision by a simple majority. If, on the other hand, the upper house defeats a bill by a two-thirds majority, the lower house is required to obtain a similar vote to override the action.

In practical terms, the *Bundesrat* is most powerful over **concurrent legislation**—that is, when the national and state government have overlapping jurisdiction in a field—but this power is vital as most jurisdictions in Germany are concurrent. The power of the *Bundesrat* provides a major link between the *Laender* and the federal government.[17]

In summary, what is the purpose of maintaining two houses in a democratic system? Four reasons have been given. Firstly, an upper house may help the lower chamber carry out its duties, by tidying up legislation or by carrying out assigned functions such as oversight of the executive. Secondly, the upper chamber may act as a check on legislation passed by the lower house. This idea is based on the contention that the upper chamber should prevent hasty actions by a popularly elected lower house. This essentially conservative argument is usually rejected by those who advocate strong government. Thirdly, an upper house may allow territorial or other special representation. Accordingly, the second chamber ought to be chosen from a special constituency—a social category such a local elite or a functional category such as business people or trade unions or regions or territories. Fourthly, an upper house may represent the constituent parts of a state as in a federal union where the States, provinces, *cantons*, or *Laender* are given special powers.

Internal Rules for Legislatures

The internal rules for deliberation in legislatures are important in the determination of members' activities and their effectiveness. In all legislatures an individual is selected to chair the meetings and preside over the decision-making process in the chamber. Called a Secretary General, or Speaker, this person presides over the plenary sessions, has a significance in the proceedings of committees and other bodies of the house, and normally controls, or at least guides, its administration. In Britain the Speaker is appointed by the government, but in Canada, as of 1986, the Speaker is elected by a secret ballot of the members of the House of Commons.[18] In the United States, the Speaker is the presiding officer of the House of Representatives. He or she is formally elected by the House members but is actually selected by the majority party.

In liberal democracies the procedures of a legislature are set up to accomplish two basic purposes—to allow a government based on a majority to govern and to allow the voices of the minority to be heard. In order to meet these conflicting demands, democratic legislatures have procedures to allow the opposition to make its points of view known. These may include the right to **filibuster**—delay or obstruct the proceedings in order to prevent a vote. But they also have rules such as time allocation, "guillotine," or closure, which allow the government or majority party to cut off debate and force decisions.

When a prospective law is introduced in most legislatures it is called a **bill**. This terminology comes from early British history. When Parliament was convened by Edward I in 1295, it would not approve new taxes on the people unless the King would hear the members' lists of demands, or bills. Today, in order to become law, a bill or initial legislation must pass several stages. The normal process is an introductory **first reading**, a debating stage called the **second reading**, a stage for detailed **study in committees,** and a **report** back to the whole assembly where a final **third reading** calls for the final decision on the principles of the bill. After the bill has passed these stages it goes to the second chamber, if there is one. In countries such as Britain which are constitutional monarchies the bill may also have to go to the monarch to receive a ceremonial **royal assent**. At some time later, the bill will be **proclaimed** by the government as a law of the land.

The executive retains some powers of discretion however. Although the British Parliament became supreme in 1689, the executive continues to hold some **prerogative powers** as the monarch's representatives. Equivalent executive power normally exists in presidential regimes as well. The classic example is the power of the American President to veto legislation which has been approved by Congress. If the President chooses this option, Congress can pass the bill only if the legislation obtains a two-thirds majority in each of the houses.

In parliamentary regimes with a dominant cabinet system, most bills are introduced by the government. These are known as **government bills**. Provision may also exist, however, for ordinary or private members to put forward their own **private members' bills**. In Parliaments with disciplined political parties, such as Australia, Britain, Canada, and New Zealand, very few private members' bills ever become law. Figure 12.1 illustrates how a bill becomes law in Canada.

Every legislature carries out its functions by forming a number of committees to deal with different types of business. The relative importance of these committees determines to a large degree the kind of power the legislature will have in policy-making and surveillance of the executive. Committee powers are often tabulated under the three headings of making laws, scrutinizing the executive's authority to spend money, and carrying out investigations of the administration.

The legislative body as a whole could carry out these tasks but committees are often more efficient. In principle, smaller bodies should allow for greater specialization and reduce partisanship. The reality is more complex. In the United States Congress, these principles sometimes allow the committees to become power centres in Congress. This is because American parties normally lack a high degree of party cohesion, and the role of the individual representative or senator is enhanced by rules that reward seniority and committee activity in the legislature. Fewer than one in five bills introduced ever gets out of the committee stage.

In Parliaments of the British model, a high degree of party cohesion and discipline overshadows the committees and reduces their overall significance. In modern Westminster-style legislatures, the committees tend to emphasize the scrutinizing and investigation functions, rather than law-making, in order to avoid fields dominated by party politics.

These few examples indicate how necessary it is to evaluate the importance of the committee system in relation to other institutions such as parties and the executive,

Figure 12.1   How a Bill Becomes Law in Canada

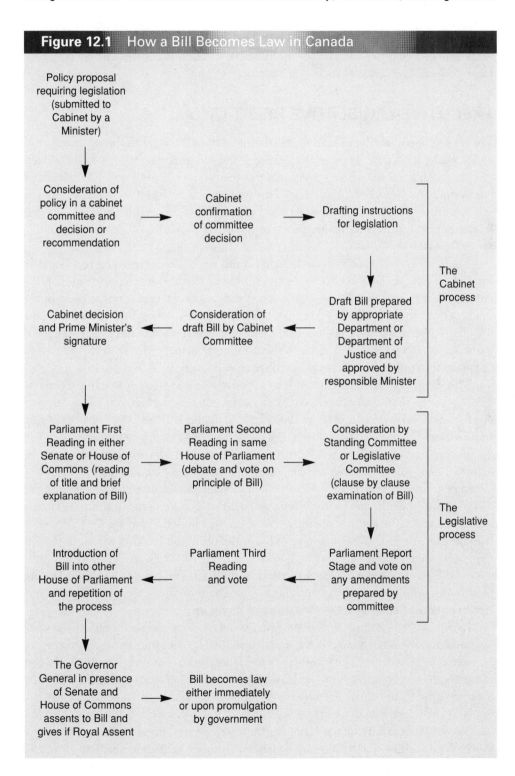

and to bear in mind the constitutional arrangements of each country in any assessment of the role of committees. While the United States' committee system is very powerful, many countries possess very weak committees.

EXECUTIVE-LEGISLATIVE RELATIONS

The relation between the executive and the legislature is crucial to the way a political system works. In fact, the so-called dominance of the executive over the legislature is often used to characterize the whole system. For this reason the United States has sometimes been termed an "Imperial Presidency." This term is used to depict an overly strong executive. In this sense, too, Germany has been called "Chancellor Democracy," and countries of the British-parliamentary type are often criticized as "Prime Ministerial" governments.

There are two main schools of thought on this topic. One is based on the idea that legislatures have *declined* over time and thus allowed executives to become more powerful in the policy process. This argument is countered by the position that there never was a period when legislatures dominated executives; legislative institutions have always been relatively weak. Depending on the country, each position has its advocates and has a degree of validity. Both schools also contain reformers who wish to strengthen the main representative bodies of their respective countries.[19]

These types of arguments are, at least superficially, easier to explore in parliamentary systems. In these governments a majority of members of the legislature must support one particular group or executive in order for it to obtain and retain political authority. In such cases the party system determines the longevity of each government.

In countries that follow the British model, the Prime Minister and executive remain in office unless they lose the *confidence* of a majority of members of the House of Commons. This is of particular concern when a single party does not have a majority of members and there has to be a minority or coalition government. In some countries, such as Germany, the lower house must choose another person to replace the Chancellor (head of government) *at the same time* as his or her dismissal. In other words, in Britain the government can be defeated without being replaced, while in Germany any government that is defeated must simultaneously be replaced. The first system is called a **vote of lack of confidence** in the government, while in the latter case a positive or **constructive vote of confidence** in someone else is required.

In presidential systems, executive-legislative relations are circumscribed by the written constitution and to a large extent are determined by the structure and influence of parties in the legislature. The interplay of influence and power between the American Congress and the President "ebbs and flows." This flow of influence can be examined by looking at the ability of the President or Congress to declare war.

The U.S. Constitution uses the word "declare" war rather than "make" war. This has caused considerable difficulty as it implies that the Congress must pass an act declaring war before it can be started. But, as American history has made eminently clear, the

President can involve the United States in a war before it is declared. As Commander-in-Chief of the U.S. Armed Forces, the American President may take the position that he or she can engage American troops in action without Congressional approval. In fact, in only five of the approximately 120 times that American forces have fought did Congress actually declare war.[20] In December 1995, President Bill Clinton committed 20 000 U.S. troops to "peacekeeping" in Bosnia *before* Congress voted on the issue.

One difficulty with this form of analysis is that it is based on the idea that the relations between the legislature and the executive are always like a teeter-totter. If the executive gains power it is seen to be a loss for the legislature, and vice-versa. It assumes that power is tangible and omits the idea that in most political situations influence is more important than legal power.

There may have been a "golden age" of Parliament in Britain in the nineteenth century, but it neither lasted very long nor existed in many other parts of the world. Legislatures have had some degree of power in most countries, but with differing intensities at various times and in different countries.[21] In the next chapter we explore this question in both democratic and authoritarian states.

DISCUSSION QUESTIONS

1. Where does political power lie in presidential systems? In parliamentary systems?
2. Do legislatures and assemblies have adequate control over their executives?
3. Can the legislature in your country be reformed? How could this be accomplished?
4. What is the role of the committee a system in the Canadian legislature? United States?
5. Have legislatures "declined" in Western parliamentary systems? In the United States' presidential system?

KEY TERMS

absolute monarchs, p. 255
bicameral, p. 267
bill, p. 269
coalition government, p. 262
collective executive, p. 259
concurrent legislation, p. 269
confidence, p. 260
constructive vote of confidence, p. 272

elected monarchs, p. 256
executive, p. 255
filibuster, p. 269
first reading, p. 270
government bills, p. 270
hereditary monarchs, p. 256
junta, p. 262
law-making, p. 265
legislatures, p. 265

majority government, p. 261
minority government, p. 261
monarchs, p. 256
prerogative powers, p. 270
private members' bills, p. 270
proclaimed, p. 270
public administration, p. 255
report, p. 270

ENDNOTES

1. James MacGregor Burns, *Leadership* (New York: Harper & Row, 1978).

2. Discussed in Chapter 1.

3. Whether individuals matter in the history of a polity is discussed in Valerie Bunce, *Do Leaders Make A Difference? Executive Succession and Public Policy Under Capitalism and Socialism* (Princeton, N.J.: Princeton University Press, 1981).

4. For a fascinating study of the power of an authoritarian leader, Franco, see Juan J. Linz, "An Authoritarian Regime: Spain," in Erik Allardt and Stein Rokkan, eds., *Mass Politics* (New York: Free Press, 1970).

5. Gabriel A. Almond and G. Bingham Powell, Jr., *Comparative Politics*, 2nd ed. (Boston: Little, Brown, 1978), p. 260.

6. James MacGregor Burns, *Presidential Government* (Boston: Houghton Mifflin, 1966).

7. Robert J. Jackson and M. Atkinson, *The Canadian Legislative System*, 2nd ed. (Toronto: Gage, 1980); and Richard Rose and Ezra N. Suleiman, eds., *Presidents and Prime Ministers* (Washington, D.C.: American Enterprise Institute, 1980).

8. For an excellent summary of the role of Prime Ministers see the special edition "Western European Prime Ministers," in *West European Politics*, vol. 14, no. 2 (April 1991).

9. See for example, Jean Blondel, *Comparative Legislatures* (Englewood Cliffs, N.J.: Prentice-Hall, 1973); Gerhard Loewenberg and Samuel C. Patterson, *Comparing Legislatures* (New York: Little, Brown, 1979); and Michael Mezey, *Comparative Legislatures* (Durham, N.C.: Duke University Press, 1979).

10. Nelson Polsby, "Legislatures," in Fred I. Greenstein and Nelson W. Polsby, eds., *Handbook of Political Science*, Vol. 5 (Reading, Mass.: Addison-Wesley, 1975), pp. 257–319.

11. The literature on the function of legislatures is voluminous. See, for example, Blondel, *Comparative Legislatures*; and Loewenberg and Patterson, *Comparing Legislatures*.

12. Walter Bagehot, *The English Constitution* (Oxford: Oxford University Press, 1936).

13. Loewenberg and Patterson, *Comparing Legislatures*.

14. The House of Lords also includes certain bishops of the Church of England.

15. See G. Bruce Doern and Brian W. Tomlin, *Faith and Fear* (Toronto: Stoddart, 1991).

16. Dean Jaensch, *An Introduction to Australian Politics*, 2nd ed., (Melbourne: Longman, 1988).

17. Mark Kesselman and Joel Krieger, *European Politics in Transition* (Lexington, Ken. : D.C. Heath, 1987), p. 275.

18. Robert J. Jackson "Executive-Legislative Relations in Canada," in Robert J. Jackson, et al., *Contemporary Canadian Politics* (Toronto: Prentice-Hall Canada, 1987), pp. 111–24.

19. See Bernard Crick, *Reform of Parliament*, rev. ed. (London: Penguin, 1966).

20. James MacGregor Burns, J. W. Peltason, and Thomas E. Cronin, *Government by the People* (Englewood Cliffs, N.J.: Prentice-Hall, 1978), pp. 286 ff.

21. Loewenberg and Patterson, *Comparative Legislatures, passim*.

FURTHER READING

Leadership and Executives

Blondel, J., *Government Ministers in the Contemporary World* (Beverly Hills, Calif.: Sage, 1985).

Crossman, R.H.S., *The Myths of Cabinet Government* (Cambridge, Mass.: Harvard University Press, 1972).

Englefield, Dermon, Janet Seaton and Isobel White, *Facts about the British Prime Ministers* (London: Mansell, 1995).

Janis, Irving, *Crucial Decisions: Leadership in Policy Making and Crisis Management* (New York: Free Press, 1988).

King, A., ed., *Both Ends of the Avenue: The Presidency, the Executive Branch and Congress in the 1980s* (Washington, D.C.: American Enterprise Institute, 1983).

Lijphart, A., *Democracies: Patterns of Majoritarian and Consensual Government in Twenty-One Countries* (New Haven, Conn.: Yale University Press, 1984).

Narkiewicz, Olga, *Soviet Leaders: From Cult of Personality to Collective Rule* (New York: St. Martin's Press, 1986).

Neustadt, Richard E., *Presidential Power: The Politics of Leadership*, rev. ed. (New York: John Wiley, 1976).

Rhodes, R.A.W. and Patrick Dunleavy, eds., *Prime Minister, Cabinet and Core Executive* (New York: St. Martin's Press, 1995).

Rosenbach, W., and Robert Taylor, *Contemporary Issues in Leadership* (Boulder, Col.: Westview Press, 1989).

Strom, Kaare, *Minority Government and Majority Rule* (Cambridge, Mass.: Cambridge University Press, 1990).

Thatcher, Margaret, *The Path to Power* (New York: Harper Collins, 1995).

Weller, P., *First Among Equals: Prime Ministers in Westminster Systems* (Sydney: Allen & Unwin, 1985).

Legislatures

Davidson, Roger H., *The Postreform Congress* (New York: St. Martin's Press, 1992).

Davidson, Roger, and Walter Oleszek, *Congress and Its Members*, 3rd ed. (Washington, D.C.: CQ Press, 1989).

Fisher, Louis, *Presidential War Power* (Lawrence: Kansas University Press, 1995).

Hahn, Jeffrey W., ed., *Democratization inb Russia: The Development of Legislative Institutions* (Armonk, NY: M.E. Sharpe, 1996).

Lees, J., and M. Shaw, eds., *Committees in Legislatures: A Comparative Analysis* (Durham, N.C.: Duke University Press, 1979).

Lowenberg, Gerhard, and Samuel C. Patterson, *Comparing Legislatures* (Boston: Little, Brown, 1979).

Mezey, Michael M., *Congress, The President and Public Policy* (Boulder, Colo.: Westview Press, 1989).

Norton, P., ed., *Legislatures* (Oxford: Oxford University Press, 1990).

Olson, David M., *The Legislative Process: A Comparative Perspective* (New York: Harper & Row, 1980).

Radice, Lisanne, Elizabeth Vallance, and Virginia Willis, *Member of Parliament: The Job of the Backbencher* (New York: St. Martin's Press, 1987).

 **Weblinks**

www.odci.gov/cia/publications/chiefs/
This site identifies Chiefs of State and Cabinet Ministers of different world nations.

thomas.loc.gov/
This is the Web Page of the United States Legislature.

www.senate.gov/
This is the Web Page of the United States Senate.

senate.aph.gov.au/index.html
This is the Web Page of the Australian Senate.

CHAPTER 13

Design of Central Government Institutions: Democratic and Authoritarian

The design of central government provides the framework for the activities of the numerous elected and unelected officials who initiate, determine, and implement policies and decisions for a state. The organization of the executive, legislative, and judicial branches of government circumscribes how these officials are to perform their duties and how they are to be made accountable to the public at large.

In democratic systems the rules, regulations, and constitutional norms about these functions are carefully described in various documents. But the history, culture, ideology, interest groups, and party system determine how the design works in practice. In authoritarian countries the actual functioning of central government is highly variegated, ranging from the personalized dictatorship of a kingship or theocracy through to the large machinery and deliberations that may characterize communism or military juntas.

In Chapter 12 we examined the concepts and basic machinery in the design of governments. In this chapter we survey how these forms are reflected in extant processes around the world, and in particular discuss some relevant issues such as the relations between executives and legislatures, the strengths and weaknesses of parliamentary versus presidential government, and the decline of legislatures. The role of executives and legislatures in authoritarian regimes and in the process of development concludes the chapter.

PARLIAMENTARIANISM IN PRACTICE

In democratic systems two basic types of executive-legislative relations exist: parliamentary and presidential. In this chapter we shall also refer to these patterns as the **fusion** and the **separation of powers** models. In the first, the executive and legislative branches are united, while in the second they are separated (see Figure 13.1).

The number of parliamentary democracies is smaller than might be expected. Fewer than one-third of all states in the Inter-Parliamentary Union (IPU) have a parliament with a Prime Minister and a cabinet who are dependent on the confidence of a majority party or a coalition of parties.[1] Almost all of these are industrialized, liberal democratic countries found in the developed, northern hemisphere. The United States, Portugal, Finland, and France are exceptions in this region as they have presidential systems.

In the British parliamentary model—essentially followed by countries such as Australia, Canada, and New Zealand—the executive and legislative functions are fused. The Prime Minister and his or her cabinet sit in the House of Commons to which they have been elected as members. Their authority rests on an ability to maintain the support of a majority of members in the House. **The Crown**, the composite of executive authority, acts only on the advice of these ministers. These two principles combine to provide what is known as **responsible government**—that is, although a monarch or governor general exists, they (the Crown) act only on the advice of those who have the confidence of Parliament.

In Britain the Queen (in Australia, Canada, and New Zealand the Governor General, acting in the name of the Queen) asks the leader of the party with the most seats in the

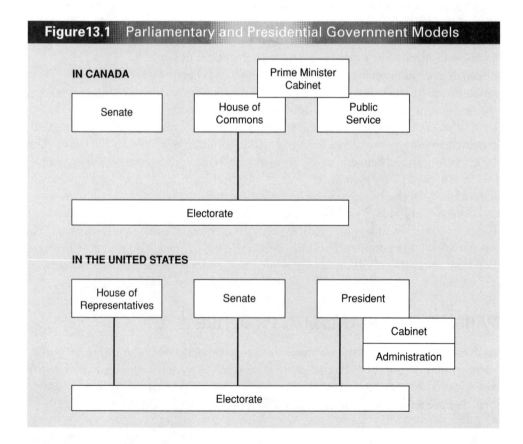

Figure 13.1   Parliamentary and Presidential Government Models

IN CANADA

Prime Minister
Cabinet

Senate

House of
Commons

Public
Service

Electorate

IN THE UNITED STATES

House of
Representatives

Senate

President

Cabinet

Administration

Electorate

House of Commons to become Prime Minister. The Prime Minister is neither elected directly by the people nor is necessarily the leader of a party that received the most votes in an election. The Prime Minister is simply the person chosen by the Crown to lead the country, based on his or her command of majority support in the lower chamber.

The Prime Minister and cabinet retain executive power as long as they have the **confidence** of the legislature—that is, as long as they can control a majority of votes. In principle, the government falls whenever it is not able to keep such a majority. In reality, what the government requires to remain in power is that there be no majority vote against it. If the government is defeated on an important matter, such as the budget, the Prime Minister may ask the monarch or the governor general to dissolve Parliament and call an election, or ask that a different individual or party take over the offices of government.

The Prime Minister names the members of the cabinet from among his or her followers in the House or, on occasion, from the upper chamber. On rare occasions the Prime Minister may nominate someone to the cabinet who is not in either house, but by convention such nominees are expected to find a seat as a member of Parliament, or a place in the upper house, as soon as possible. In Britain and Canada, not all of the ministers are in the cabinet. Many are appointed members of a "ministry" to head departments or agencies of government, but are not assigned positions in the cabinet, the central executive body.

The Prime Minister is technically *primus inter pares*—"first among equals"—or the same as the other ministers. But this is mere fiction as the Prime Minister has the ultimate power to nominate or fire any member of his cabinet. He or she is in charge of the government's overall policy thrust, and is the leader of the party that won the election that brought the ministers to power in the first place. The Prime Minister's actual powers differ from state to state. In Britain he or she may be very powerful when supported by a cohesive single party, whereas in, say Switzerland, Prime Ministers are only figureheads in a highly decentralized multi-party country.

In the countries that follow the British model, the cabinet acts as a collegial body and, after coming to a decision in private, acts in a united fashion when facing the opposition in the House and the public. This practice of maintaining cabinet solidarity, known as **collective ministerial responsibility**, allows ministers to be critically frank in private but actively support the government in Parliament.

In theory each individual minister is accountable for all activities in his or her own ministries or departments. The personal accountability of each minister is referred to as **individual ministerial responsibility**. Cabinet members set the policy priorities and agenda for their departments and the legislature. In practice, strict adherence to the principle of ministerial responsibility is rare. While ministers may resign from their posts because of criminal or other questionable activities, they usually do not accept accountability for everything that transpires in their departments. This does not mean that ministers do not have overall control of their departments. In the final analysis, it is they who must defend their department in cabinet and in Parliament.

Ministers originate the vast majority of bills introduced in Parliament. Their bills normally become the law of the land in countries such as Canada, Britain, Australia, and New Zealand. Only rarely do bills emanating from non-ministers or backbenchers get passed. On occasion, however, **private members' bills** actually do become law.

In legislatures of the British type, the largest opposition party in the lower house is called the **official opposition**. This party, like all the other parties in the lower house, is highly cohesive—that is, the party members stick together on votes in the House regardless of their own personal viewpoint on the subject matter. Only on extremely rare occasions do parties call for a **free vote** to allow members to vote as they choose.

The **party caucus** consists of the members of Parliament from each of the parties. In Britain the caucuses are called the **1922 Committee** for the Conservatives and **Parliamentary Labour Party** for the Labour party. But in other similar systems, like Canada, Australia, and New Zealand, they are simply called the *caucus*. This grouping of the members of Parliament, and in some cases the upper house, is used to provide opportunities for ordinary backbench members to voice their opinions and to question their leaders about party or government policy.

The government caucus is particularly important because theoretically it could bring down the government. This happens very rarely. But on occasion a caucus may actually vote a Prime Minister out of office. In 1991 the Australian Labor caucus simply deposed Bob Hawke and replaced him with Paul Keating. That same year in Britain the Tory 1922 Committee replaced Prime Minister Margaret Thatcher with John Major (see Close Up 13.1). In New Zealand the caucus of the Labour Party not only decides who will be the party leader but also determines which politicians will be in the government. Furthermore, a Prime Minister in the Australian Labor Party or the New Zealand Labour Party may determine which portfolio each minister gets, but it is the whole caucus that determines who will be in cabinet.[2]

In all Westminster parliamentary systems, after caucus has deliberated on a policy, solidarity is supposed to emerge and the members lose their freedom to object publicly to the party position without being labelled as rebels or dissidents. On occasion they may be deprived of promotion, membership in the caucus, or perks.

The cornerstone of the parliamentary system, therefore, is that the government, supported by a majority of members of the legislature, acts as the executive between elections. Headed by a Prime Minister, this government can be prevented from holding office only if it loses the confidence of the lower house or if it is defeated in a general election. It negotiates with its own legislature.

PRESIDENTIALISM IN PRACTICE

While fusion between the executive and legislature is the essential characteristic of parliamentary systems, precisely the opposite principle characterizes presidential systems. Of course, this statement does not apply to presidential systems that are simply facades for authoritarian governments, as for example in the Philippines during the long

CLOSE UP 13.1   Margaret Thatcher, John Major, and Tony Blair: Retaining Prime Ministerial Leadership in Great Britain

Prime Ministers in Britain have to do more than win elections to retain their positions. They must also keep enough support among the backbenchers of their party to overcome leadership challenges.

Margaret Thatcher, a formidable politician, was toppled in a leadership challenge in 1990. Her support melted away when she failed to win a leadership vote in her parliamentary caucus. In the first ballot, she received more than 50% of the vote, but she didn't beat her rival, Michael Heseltine, by the required 15%. Because of this she was seriously weakened, so she withdrew from the contest and anointed John Major. Heseltine, who was labelled a traitor to the party because he had challenged Thatcher, lost in the second round to Major.

Later, when Prime Minister John Major in turn came under fire from opponents in the Conservative Party, he opted for a preemptive strike. In 1995 he resigned as Conservative Party leader and called a leadership election — four months before the annual challenge required in the party rules. His move was intended to stop party infighting and consolidate his government before the next general election. Major won and resumed his post as Prime Minister, but the infighting continued and damaged the party's popularity. Major lost to Tony Blair in the 1997 election.

"emergency" rule of Ferdinand Marcos. In legitimate democratic systems, presidentialism means that the executive and legislature are both responsible for making laws and yet each is independent of the other.[3]

Since the United States is the prime example of successful presidential government, we will examine it more closely. The first principle is clear—there is a **separation of powers** between the executive and legislative branches of government. Members of the House of Representatives, the lower house, are elected in districts based on population, and the Senate or upper house consists of two senators elected from each state. The President, on the other hand, is elected separately in a national campaign. After all eligible Americans have had a chance to vote, the winning candidate is officially proclaimed as President by an electoral college. This procedure is explained in further detail in Chapter 19.

The United States Congress has two houses—that is, it is bicameral. Every two years, all 435 members of the House of Representatives are elected from geographical districts based on "representation by population." That is, each district has approximately the same number of people and each elects one member of Congress. The Senate is composed of one hundred members, two elected from each state for a six-year tenure. It is correct to say that the lower house is based on the principle of representation by population while the Senate adds a regional principle that allows smaller states to have equal representation with the larger ones.

Elected members of Congress are prohibited from holding executive office of any kind, including a cabinet position. If a member of the House of Representatives or Senate is appointed to the cabinet, he or she must immediately resign from any elected office. This incompatibility rule effectively separates the two branches of government.

The two branches of the United States' government are also separated by the fact that each has its own electoral rules. The set terms of four years for the President, two for the House of Representatives, and six for the Senate cannot be affected by the actions of another branch. The President cannot decide, for example, to dissolve Congress earlier than anticipated in order to discipline its members. Nor can Congress affect the tenure of a President except by using the extraordinary impeachment process. The very heart of the parliamentary system, the right of the legislature to get rid of a cabinet if it cannot survive a **vote of confidence** (that is, obtain a majority of votes in the legislature) is omitted in the American system of government.

These two different electoral routes to high office politically separate the executive from the legislature in the United States, but other legal mechanisms also mandate a separation of powers. The legislative *process* is effectively divided. Congress and the President have checks and controls on each other. Only Congress can pass legislation, but even if a bill is passed in both houses, the President possesses the power to block the legislation. The President has the choice of signing the bill, delaying it for ten days by not signing, or vetoing the measure. If the veto power is used, however, Congress can override the executive only by re-passing the bill with a two-thirds majority. There is also a "pocket veto" whereby a President allows a bill to die at the end of a session by not signing it, but not vetoing it either.

The principle of separation of powers is also upheld in the budgetary process. Presidents propose a budget to Congress, but this must be approved before money can be appropriated, as public funds cannot be expended without congressional authorization. The **power of the purse** gives Congress the final authority over government expenditure. The President may use his veto over all such legislation but even this power can be negated if a two-thirds majority can be found in each house to override the executive action. In December 1995 such power plays between the President and Congress over a balanced-budget philosophy caused the government to be shut down for several weeks. The complete set of relationships between the President and Congress is called **checks and balances**.

The President steers or governs the country. He or she appoints a cabinet from chosen supporters or other political experts, and submits much of the major legislation that Congress eventually passes. The President controls the whole administration of public servants, and the White House staff consists of a phalanx of personal advisors.

As it happens, the American party system also buttresses the separation of powers. In Congress the parties are rarely cohesive. Representatives and Senators regularly oppose their party leadership and are more responsive to their own views and their constituents' interests than those of their party. Traditionally, the Democratic and Republican parties break apart on congressional votes except those on organizational issues, and dissidents cannot be disciplined by the President even if he happens to be of the same party as they are. Some scholars have even contended that this is the most important single fact to know about the United States' form of government.

Given these principles of separation, how does such a ramshackle system actually work? The answer is that often it does not. But surprisingly, it often does. Leaders in both branches know they must compromise. "Whirlpools" of influence and power unite the two branches when it is necessary to get something done.

The House of Representatives and the Senate are each run by leaders elected by the party that controls the majority in that chamber. These leaders—the Majority leader in the Senate and the Speaker in the House—have considerable power. Through their close relations with the White House (even if the President is not of their party persuasion) and with members of their house, they influence the flow of legislation and committee assignments. Since power is diffused among so many institutions and the party system has little if any cohesion, these leaders must persuade and cajole their colleagues to get anything accomplished.

Iron Triangles, Issue Networks, and Public Policy

In presidential systems, in particular in the United States, policy concepts have been developed to explain how policy emerges from a divided Presidential-Congressional system especially when the two branches are held by different parties, as is often the case. The first of these—**Iron Triangles**—refers to the stable pattern of interactions among Congressional committees, specific interest groups, and government departments or agencies. This idea may be more important in the United States than in other countries, particularly those with parliamentary systems where party control of both the executive and legislative branches is the regular pattern.

In the U.S. an often-cited example is the three-sided relationship among the Congressional committees concerned with Veterans Affairs, the department of Veteran Affairs, and such veterans organizations as the American Legion and the Veterans of Foreign Wars. Such examples, however, exaggerate the importance of such relationships which exclude the executive itself, including secretaries, their subordinates, and the White House itself. In many fields, different relationship persist. Perhaps even in the United States such interactions should also encompass the individuals in the executive branch. This extension would make the appropriate concept not Triangles but Iron Quadrangles.

Another concept for discussing such divided government patterns is that of **Issue Networks**. Perhaps much more important for the discussion of all developed democracies, this concept has both strengths and weaknesses. The broad idea is that policy is affected by a loose and informal relationship among a large number of specific actors who affect policy in their specific fields. This concept is of great interest as it directs our attention away from pure institutional analysis and towards more amorphous and informal pressures in the policy process. For example, environmental experts in the private sector spend a lot of time with their equivalents in government departments, and the same is basically true in all policy fields.

But the term policy networks is also woolly as it does little to direct scholars to the source of policy or its implementation. That many people are involved in making policy is a given in the open and democratic societies. Moreover, the party variable is almost totally omitted in this framework, and that omission would be ridiculous in countries such as Australia, Britian, Canada, and New Zealand, and perhaps even in the United States if we were to extend party to mean the partisanship of the President and his top advisors. While the President is not the only actor in the policy process, he certainly is powerful in it.

MERITS AND DEMERITS OF PARLIAMENTARY AND PRESIDENTIAL FORMS OF GOVERNMENT

Many comparative studies have assessed the strengths and weaknesses of these two fundamental types of government. On the whole, this important exercise is unlikely ever to be definitive. Each system has its own merits and demerits.

The parliamentary system concentrates power. With a majority in the lower house, the Prime Minister and cabinet can be highly effective. They have the power and authority to govern. The parliamentary system also provides an important check on government authority. If the Prime Minister and cabinet act arbitrarily, the opposition and some government backbenchers may join together to vote down the government by denying it the confidence it requires to continue in office. Moreover, if there is no majority then the government may be based on an unstable grouping, and this means that it can be brought down at any time. In such situations a high degree of cooperation between parties is required, and a minor party, which is unlikely ever to hold power except in a coalition government, can have a profound effect on policy and legislation.

If the coalition government is constructed out of diverse and hostile interests, it may produce coalitions that constantly fall apart. The now defunct Italian system provided the classic case as its multi-party system resulted in 55 new governments between 1946 and 1996. It is also argued by some commentators that one of the causes of Hitler's ascendency to power was the weak coalition governments of the Weimar Republic (1918–1933). However, in some countries, such as Austria, the Netherlands, and Switzerland, coalition governments hold together despite having parties that are highly competitive. Such countries are called **consociational democracies** to distinguish them from countries with fragmented party systems and cabinet coalitions that constantly break down.[4] Elites in consociational countries are able to compromise enough to solidify the cabinet coalition for some time.

Since legislatures and executives are assumed to be united in parliamentary systems, it follows that governments based on such an arrangement should be more effective than those based on fragmented party systems. However, when a single party does have an absolute majority in the legislature, it may also be regarded as either advantageous or disadvantageous depending on the circumstances. If, for example, citizens do not want their government to accomplish very much, then a weak, unstable government is more beneficial than a stable, effective one. On the other hand, such a weak government would not be considered valuable if the people wished the legislature to act effectively. In other words, evaluations on this topic are replete with ideological bias.

In most political science writing, it is assumed that parliamentary systems will possess cohesive parties. When that is the case, it makes sense to argue that the lines of responsibility for government decisions will be fairly clear and consistent. According to this argument, the government is based on one party. It controls its backbenchers and they support its policy proposals. Then, as the argument goes, the voters know exactly which party to credit or blame when the next election takes place.

The reality is much different, however. In parliamentary systems a coalition of parties is often required to support the government. The leaders of each party have to make compromises on some issues in order to get others through Parliament. The public cannot know which party has adhered to its principles and which has compromised. Moreover, the model assumes the existence of well-informed voters who decide how to cast their ballots based on the parties' actions in specific circumstances and on particular issues—a dubious assumption in most instances.

The presidential system, too, has strengths and weaknesses. The framers of the American Constitution did not wish strong government. They wanted a weak government in the capital: one that could be slowed down or prevented from taking action altogether. They therefore wrote a constitution that, for example, first requires the President to negotiate all treaties, but then requires that they be ratified by a two-thirds majority of the Senate. The United States' government is considered beneficial precisely because it separates powers and discourages the concentration of authority in one institution.

The checks and balances possessed by the President over Congress, and Congress over the President, diffuse power; they limit the opportunities for independent or hasty action by any one individual, group, or branch.[5] This contrasts with the parliamentary system, where relatively few protections exist against a government that is backed by majority support in Parliament.[6] Of course, such an argument will be opposed by those individuals who wish decisive presidential action.[7] Such advocates of strong executives also appreciate the fact that the Congress cannot dismiss the President because he or she is elected for a set four-year term.

To some extent, Congress has the ability to right the balance. The Constitution allows a majority of members in the House of Representatives to **impeach** the President—that is, make a formal accusation of a crime by a majority vote. After articles of impeachment are passed by the House, the President is tried by the Senate acting as a court. If a two-thirds majority can be mustered in the upper house in support of accusation, the President is convicted and removed from office. One President, Andrew Johnson, who succeeded Abraham Lincoln, was impeached for violating the Tenure-of-Office Act but was never convicted. President Richard Nixon resigned in 1974 when it became clear that he would be impeached for his role in the Watergate affair. In 1998 the House voted for the impeachment of Bill Clinton, but the Senate could not muster the two-thirds majority required to remove the President from office.

Committees of the United States Congress also contrast with committees in Westminster-model parliamentary democracies. American committees are independent and powerful bodies that can defy Presidents, cabinet members, and bureaucrats alike. Bills, for example, are often delayed or killed by committees. Congressional committees tend to be composed of members who serve on the committees for long periods and develop specialized knowledge about the committee's activities. They have permanent staffs and funds, can subpoena witnesses, and hold open hearings on legislation and administrative action.

Comparative research on legislatures has shown that committees are strong only when they are few in number, their membership is limited, their ability to investigate subjects is unhampered by the government, they have their own paid officials, and they have their own budgets. These conditions do not prevail in parliamentary democracies of the British type. In these bodies there is an assumption that strong committees would weaken the executive too much, whereas in the United States the intention is precisely to weaken the independent power of the executive.[8]

By contrast with U.S. committees, Canadian and British "standing committees" are poor cousins. In the United Kingdom they are set up only for deliberation on specific bills and die after the discussions are concluded. The members on the committee are not subject-matter experts. The committees have no significant staff or independent funding, and although witnesses may be called, the hearings are carefully controlled by the government. In Canada, the standing committees are multifunctional. They examine legislation, proposals to spend money, and investigate government departments, and policy committees. But they are always controlled by the government of the day and only rarely take any independent action.

Lastly, the parliamentary system appears to allow for more unity of action. But the same can be said of presidential systems—except that different machinery is used. A President, unlike a Prime Minister, is elected by the population as a whole. The American President can claim to represent the totality of the American people against the fragmented interests of Senators and members of Congress. The cabinet is appointed by the President to work for him or her. It is not a group of ministers who represent various factions, regions, or interests, as in the parliamentary system.

In principle, the whole bureaucracy works for the President. Directly under the President is the Executive Office, which comprises almost two thousand employees in the White House Office (consisting of immediate staff or aides), the Office of Management and Budget, the Council of Economic Advisors, and the National Security Council. Not counting the armed forces, another three million people work indirectly for the administration in departments, bureaus, offices, and divisions.

In conclusion, each type of system has strengths and weaknesses and can be manipulated for better or worse by elected politicians. The touchstone on this is whether the system (presidential or parliamentary) fits congruently with the political culture, traditions, and customs of the country.

The French and Russian Adaptations

Both the French and Russian systems are hybrids of the parliamentary and presidential systems. In each case the President is considerably more important than in parliamentary types of government.

After the Second World War, French politicians set up a new Constitution similar to that of the Third Republic, which had lasted from 1870 to the Second World War. Like its predecessor, the Fourth French Republic was highly unstable—it manifested all the classic problems of a parliamentary system with a fragmented party system. Cabinets fell apart about every half year, and when the country was confronted by an independence movement in Algeria in 1958, the Constitution collapsed.

General Charles de Gaulle, a wartime hero, was put in charge and immediately had a new Constitution written. The new Constitution (of the Fifth French Republic) reduced the powers of the legislature and increased those of the President.[9] Despite lip service to the principle that power would be divided between the executive and legislature, the Constitution gave the President independent power to appoint the Prime Minister, negotiate treaties, and make war. He can dissolve Parliament except in the first year after an election or during a state of emergency. But, as in other parliamentary systems, the legislature controls the purse strings and the power to tax the people. The President's powers were further augmented in 1962 when an amendment to the Constitution provided for the direct election of the President.

In the present system, the President "designates" the Prime Minister. This has been interpreted to mean that the President may also ask for the Prime Minister's dismissal. From 1986 to 1988, socialist President Francois Mitterand had to "cohabit" with a right-wing Jacques Chirac as Prime Minister. After achieving a socialist victory at the polls, the President first appointed the left-leader Michel Rocard as Prime Minister and then later asked for, and received, his resignation so that he could appoint a new Prime Minister. Rocard immediately complied. In 1992, the President did the same with Edith Cresson and she, too, resigned. From 1993–95 the President again had to share power with a Gaullist Prime Minister—Edouard Balladur. The election of 1995 gave the presidency to Gaullist Jacques Chirac but he had to share power with a left coalition of socialists, communists, greens, and other left-wingers who gained a majority in the legislative election. Once again, "cohabitation" between a conservative President Chirac and a Socialist Prime Minister Lionel Jospin was the French solution to a divided government.

Despite the fact that the party system, too, has evolved into a near two-party system, the French Constitution of 1958 can be said to be successful in that cabinet turnovers and instability in government have declined greatly in this mixed parliamentary and presidential system. However, the President is obviously the most important political actor. The National Assembly may throw out a Prime Minister and cabinet, but it has extremely little power over the President during his seven-year term in office. The President (now Jacques Chirac) also dominates the cabinet and administration. This assertion is also borne out by the 1995 constitutional amendment which enables the President to call referendums on a wide range of political issues and thus have an "exclusive relation-ship" with the people.[10]

The Russian constitutional system accords the President even more power than that of France. The bizarre history of modern executive-legislative relations in Russia began with the August 1991 attempted *coup* against President Gorbachev by a small group of hard-line communists.[11] Many Soviet deputies (including Boris Yeltsin) re-mained inside the Duma and, aided by a few tanks and a number of Moscovites, chal-lenged the *coup* leaders, who eventually gave up their efforts to oust the reformist government. Why they did so and why the USSR ended with such extreme abruptness will be debated for years.[12]

After that period, Gorbachev left office and Boris Yeltsin became President. Shortly thereafter Yeltsin faced a showdown with some members of the Congress of People's Deputies who would not accept Presidential decree No. 1400, which called for elec-tions and a referendum on a new Constitution. In defiance, the anti-Yeltsin forces oc-cupied the "white house," the home of the Duma. Yeltsin used the military to pound Parliament into submission in October 1993. Despite widespread complaints that the elec-tion was rigged, the Constitution was approved in the referendum by a vote of 58% and a new Constitution replaced Soviet-style institutions with new democratic processes.

> "Towering above [Russia's] fractured political system is the enigmatic figure of Boris Yeltsin ... His style of rule is that of a monarch, but his source of legitimacy is public elections. This kind of elective autocracy leads to the worst of both worlds: the instability of periodic elections and the inflexibility of autocratic rule."
>
> Peter Rutland,
> in *Current History*, 1998.

The new Constitution gives inordinate power to the President. The President ap-points the Prime Minister and government, and the Duma needs a two-thirds majority to overrule a presidential veto or initiate impeachment of the President. In the early years, the President could basically determine economic policy on his own. When the Duma failed to approve his economic plan in the summer of 1994, Yeltsin merely waited until the Duma was not in session and then implemented what the Duma had rejected.[13] The Duma cannot compel the government to *enforce* even the laws that survive a pres-idential veto. To reduce presidential power would require a constitutional amendment, but the constitutional amendment process is very rigid. In August 1998, with an ailing President and an economy in crisis, a power struggle left the country (for a few weeks) with no functioning government and a seriously weakened President. The crisis began on August 23 when Yeltsin precipitately dismissed Serei Kiriyenko as Prime Minister and reappointed his predecessor, Viktor Chernomyrdin. The Duma rejected Yeltsin's nom-inee twice, forcing the President to abandon his first choice and name Yevgeny Primakov as Prime Minister. Some commentators believe that, as of early 1999, Yeltsin's illness has forced him to yield all real power to other officials. Under the Constitution, the Prime Minister would assume formal authority in the event of the President's incapacity.

The members of the Duma have focused their attention on constructing an effective parliamentary organization. Committees have been set up, and chairmanships are allocated by the size of the party or what the Duma calls "fractions." The upper house, Federal Council, is not even as strong as the Duma and acts basically as a consultative body. It is not organized along party lines and members retain strong regional ties. A large number of members of the Federal Council are heads of regional administrations, equivalent to the governors of American states or premiers of Canadian provinces.

THE DECLINE OF LEGISLATURES IN DEMOCRACIES

Legislatures are found in almost every country in the world. A handful of feudal monarchies have never had a legislature, and authoritarian regimes, such as those governed by military juntas, may try to do without them. But aside from these exceptions legislatures are ubiquitous.[14] In the 1970s, Jean Blondel calculated that about 90% of the states of the developed North, 90% of Asian and Latin American states, 70% of African states, and 50 to 60% of the Middle East had some form of legislature, Parliament, or assembly.[15] But what is their significance?

In general, the power of executives has been growing at the expense of legislatures around the world. Even in parliamentary democracies—where the government controls and is responsible for parliamentary business, while the opposition has the right to criticize and attempt to modify government actions—the executive dominates. Economic and technological shifts in society have assisted the executive in becoming the principle governing authority in the modern world.

Few legislatures around the world—with the specific exception of the American Congress—have kept up with executives in terms of organization, resources, or influence. The weakness of legislatures stems partly from the fact that their basic structures originated in the eighteenth and nineteenth centuries when a different type of society existed.

The so-called "golden age" of legislatures came in the nineteenth century, when the British Parliament was considered more important than the executive. Since then it can be said that legislatures have undergone a relative decline. Despite executive growth and legislative decline, no democrats believe that there "ought" to be weak legislatures. Despite the reality, there seems to be almost unanimous agreement that legislatures and assemblies should be the most significant bodies in settling philosophical, social, and economic differences. But while there is a lament for legislative weakness, there is also a pessimistic attitude that anything can be done to rectify the situation.

The number of analytic problems in calculating the relative power of the executive and legislature are daunting. Experts count the number of bills initiated by an executive and then passed by a legislature to determine if the executive is in control. But, alas, if the legislature were fully in control, the executive would have to introduce bills that the parliamentarians would accept. Aside from this logical problem for the theories about legislative decline, there are other difficulties. Most countries never had a period, as Britain did, when the legislature was dominant; so there was nothing to decline from. Moreover, in countries with the British model, the constitutional ability of Parliament to unmake executives and even monarchs continues to exist even today even though these powers are almost never used.

There are other considerations, too, about the importance of legislatures. Legislatures have important functions to carry out besides law-making. In many ways they control the executive; they supervise government expenditures, act as sounding boards for public opinion, and are recognized as the most important institutions in times of crisis.

Much of the discussion about the decline of legislatures and their policy-making roles comes down to a debate about the proper role of elected politicians. Should members follow their own consciences or should they be required to follow the opinions of constituents? More concretely, should MPs be instructed by their constituents about how to vote or should they be allowed to vote according to their own judgment? Political scientists call these two possible roles the independent and mandate roles.

The classic statement about such roles came from Edmund Burke, who, in a speech to his electors in Bristol, England, on November 3, 1774, declared that members should be free to use their own judgments.[16] For him, making legislation is a matter of "reason and judgment" and legislators should deliberate and come to a conclusions on their own. They should not accept instructions from their constituents, who have neither heard the debate nor deliberated on the issues. His argument is based on the assumption that government is complex and technical and that constituents are too busy to absorb the information needed to make informed decisions.

The opposite point of view was first put forward by the French philosopher Jean Jacques Rousseau. He argued that democratic representation ought to entail the policy desires of constituents. For him, the representative's vote should mirror the wishes of the constituents; he should be mandated by his constituents on all policy questions.

Both of these positions are too extreme. Or, put another way, both are partially right. As Hanna Pitkin put it, "The man is not a representative if his actions bear no relationship to anything about his constituents, and he is not a representative if he does not act at all."[17] In other words, if members are required to act only on the instructions of their constituents they might be immobile. But if they act without a consideration of the views of their constituents they would be neither representative nor democratic.

Such dilemmas confront politicians more often in undisciplined party systems such as those of the United States than in countries such as Canada and Britain where members are tightly controlled. This debate also overlooks the fact that all representatives in either system ought to listen to the debate in the representative assembly before they determine how they will vote, and that members have obligations to their colleagues in the legislature as well as to their constituents.

LEGISLATURES AND EXECUTIVES IN AUTHORITARIAN SYSTEMS

The Role of Legislatures

As we have seen, legislatures exist in almost all countries. While lacking many of the other institutions of democracy—such as effective courts—most authoritarian regimes find it useful to have a parliament or assembly. These institutions meet and deliberate but rarely are the final arbitrators of policy or law.

But all legislatures have multiple functions to perform. Nelson Polsby first distinguished between legislatures that are "transformative"—those which possess the capacity to transform proposals into laws—and those that are only "arenas" for debate and the consideration of government initiatives.[18] Michael Mezey classified the legislatures of the world in terms of their impact on public policy. He found that legislatures may possess *important, modest,* or *negligible* policy-making powers.[19] In other words, legislatures are not always decision-making bodies. In fact, in most of the world they are not. The purpose of such assemblies is to allow grievances to be aired and to mobilize and organize individuals and opinions. But even in their functions as sounding boards, legislatures remain weak in many authoritarian states, and are often dismissed or suspended by dictatorial executives in their search for absolute power.

The former Soviet Parliament—the Supreme Soviet—was used mainly as a rubber stamp for the Communist Party. It met only twice a year for a few days, heard reports from the Central Committee of the Communist Party, and then ratified decisions which had been taken elsewhere. But this did not mean that the institution was superfluous. It heard citizen complaints, acted as a sounding board for public opinion, and functioned as a legitimizing institution in this otherwise highly fractured society.[20] The present Chinese National People's Congress is the largest and most unwieldy legislature in the world, with several thousand members. It meets only to hear reports from the Communist Party and has little, if any, policy-making power. Like the former Supreme Soviet, it is controlled by the Communist Party.

Executive Authority in Authoritarian States

As shown in Chapter 12, ejecting unwanted leaders in an orderly manner is of great significance in politics everywhere—but particularly in authoritarian states. Every authoritarian regime is headed by leaders who have difficulty accepting that they are not omnipotent. Thus, they hang on to power, often having to be forced out, sometimes even in a body bag. Table 13.1 illustrates the longevity of many authoritarian rulers.

In authoritarian states, the executive is the dominant institution. It controls and/or manipulates the legislature, courts, and interest groups. Richard Neustadt has argued that the power of Presidents in the United States is the power to persuade others. The President must induce others to believe they are acting in their own interests.[21] This is not the case in authoritarian regimes where the top person can on some occasions command others simply by the use of coercion.

Table 13.1	Continuity at the Apex of Political Leadership in Many Arab Countries, 1999
Leader	**Time in Power**
Hussein of Jordan	47 years (died February 1999)*
Hassan II Morocco	38 years
Qadhafi of Libya	30 years
Hussein of Iraq	21 years
Mubarak of Egypt	18 years

*Followed in office by his son.

Research about authoritarian leaders is fascinating. Personalistic rule was characterized by such communist dictators as Lenin and Stalin in the Soviet Union, Mao in China, and Tito in Yugoslavia. The tradition continues today with Castro in Cuba and Marshal Kim Jong Il in North Korea. Allan Bullock's study of the historical parallels in the lives of Hitler and Stalin indicates many similar traits in the two dictators.[22] Both men were acutely suspicious—to the point of paranoia. They worried about the people around them as evidenced by Hitler's anti-Jewish actions and Stalin's purges. They were both fierce in handling rivals, but Stalin was more violent. Almost no one who fought with Stalin during the October 1917 revolution survived him. On the other hand, despite one nearly successful attempt on his life, Hitler was able to keep most of his subordinates in line without killing them.

Authoritarian leaders often clothe themselves in the respectable garb of democratic presidential government. They use the name of the constitutional system both to disguise highly personalized forms of rule and to overcome political defects in their states. Whether such usage is a distortion as some claim, or merely a clever adaptation, is a moot point.

Over the years, most Latin American and some Asian countries have simply copied the U.S. nomenclature. Military states in Latin America, for example, have usually adopted some form of presidential rule—prominent examples included General Pinochet in Chile and General Alfredo Stroessner in Paraguay. In much of Africa, presidential rule is used to hide social divisions in the country and/or to disguise the existence of authoritarian government. All of the former French African colonies, for example, have copied the French Constitution with its strong Presidential system. African parliamentary-type states often identify their leaders by the title President rather than the title of Prime Minister.

In many developing states there is incongruence between the formal constitutional documents and the economic and political power relations in the country.[23] In particular, many parliamentary systems, especially those based on the British model, have often had to adjust their constitutions over time to accommodate stresses and strains within the country. Nigeria, for example, has tried to resolve or hide its ethnic divisions by casting off the British parliamentary model and instituting instead either a presidential system or a military government.

One justification for adopting a presidential-type system is that a single leader with the title of President can centralize authority in one person. It allows the executive to unify the country under one set of symbols and one political force. Often, of course, its use is merely a disguise for arbitrary government. Military leaders, in particular, prefer the presidential to the parliamentary system because it allows them to claim that their power comes directly from the people and is not simply the result of bargaining among legislative elites. In many developing countries, the legislatures simply adopt laws giving general and wide permissive authority to their presidents.

The role of the President of Mexico is an example of authoritarian presidentialism in a democratic state. Backed by the most powerful party in the country, the Institutional Party of the Revolution (PRI), the President is virtually a dictator for the six-year term of office. All government institutions rely on the power of the Mexican President. In theory, the Congress and courts have constitutional independence but in reality all are dominated by the President. After six years of dictatorship the President plays a role in the selection of his or her successor, who then assumes the mantle of the next authoritarian leader. Almost all members of the executive who served the outgoing President then leave office and are replaced by the followers of the new President.

Since 1988, however, this system has begun to crack. The 1994 election shattered the illusion of one-party dominance and the myth of "hombre providencial," a strong man who can provide leadership and direction to Mexico. Coloured by the assassination of Luis Donaldo Colosio (the most popular choice to be leader of the PRI), violent upheaval in the Chiapas, and massive instability in the economy, Ernesto Zedillo won the election by only 51%. However, the Constitution and an array of political forces allow him to continue a one-person regime.

The Mexican system combines the trappings of democracy with a high degree of authoritarianism. Its legal form is that of both a democratic and a presidential system. It provides strong leadership at the top, but this leadership is often accompanied by corruption and cronyism.

Monarchy is another authoritarian form of government. Few absolute monarchies exist today; most that do are in the Arab Gulf states, and little is known about their authority structures. In them, law and policy have traditionally been the sole preserve of the monarch (see Close Up 13.2). Secrecy prevails about final decision-making and even the process itself.

Pressures for relaxation of monarchical absolutism have bought about recent changes in the Gulf's monarchical political systems. Saudi Arabia is an example. In March 1992, King Fahd of Saudi Arabia introduced a new Constitution that reduced the number of years a minister can stay in office. He began to decentralize power in his kingdom and established a bill of rights for the first time.[24] He set up a consultative council to advise the cabinet and review laws. However, the new Constitution does not provide for elections or

CLOSE UP 13.2   The Ruling Sabah Family of Kuwait

In Kuwait, the Constitution of 1962 stipulates that a member of the Sabah family will always rule as Emir. It also says that there will be a freely elected Parliament with the power to censure the government and choose cabinet ministers.

In 1986, the Emir suspended Parliament and imposed censorship of the press. After the 1991 Gulf War was concluded, the Constitution was restored and King Faud authorized the creation of a Consultative Council empowered to initiate laws, review domestic and foreign policies, and scrutinize budgets. As well, a Supreme Council of Islamic Affairs was created to review policies and ensure their accordance with the teachings of Islam. In reality, however, Kuwait continues to be controlled by the Sabah family.

political parties or any other institutions of democracy. King Fahd made it absolutely clear that he does not intend to make Saudi Arabia into a democracy. As Figure 13.2 shows, the King continues to name the members of the council, which cannot overrule the cabinet without the King's approval. However, the council does provide a forum for discussion of policy and could help to counterbalance the royal family's absolute power.

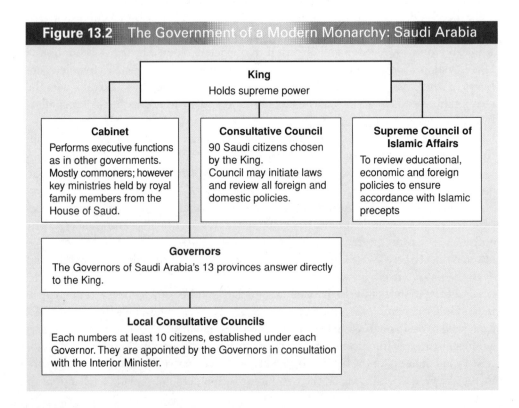

Figure 13.2   The Government of a Modern Monarchy: Saudi Arabia

King
Holds supreme power

Cabinet
Performs executive functions as in other governments. Mostly commoners; however key ministries held by royal family members from the House of Saud.

Consultative Council
90 Saudi citizens chosen by the King. Council may initiate laws and review all foreign and domestic policies.

Supreme Council of Islamic Affairs
To review educational, economic and foreign policies to ensure accordance with Islamic precepts

Governors
The Governors of Saudi Arabia's 13 provinces answer directly to the King.

Local Consultative Councils
Each numbers at least 10 citizens, established under each Governor. They are appointed by the Governors in consultation with the Interior Minister.

The Saudi system of succession to the throne was also changed in 1992. After the tenure of the next Crown Prince (Abdullah is already confirmed as heir to the throne), the King is to be chosen by the equivalent of an electoral college of royal family princes. The King will continue to have the power to appoint and dismiss the Crown Prince, but the Crown Prince will no longer have the automatic right to become King. The new rules therefore create the possibility of altering the line of succession. The move toward re-ducing the King's absolute authority may spur changes in other Arab countries of the Gulf. However, one should not be too optimistic about superficial changes in Saudi Arabia. The Saudi princes permit no free expression of political views, overt opposition, or power-shar-ing in the country.

Absolutist systems of government have continued to decline in the twentieth cen-tury. However they remain prevalent in a few places, based on characteristics of hered-ity, religion, and wealth. Close Up 13.3 describes the unique monarchy of Tonga.

CLOSE UP 13.3   The Monarchy in Tonga: A South Pacific Paradise?

King Taufa'ahau Tupou IV of the Kingdom of Tonga is one of the world's last feu-dal dictators. He is the only surviving monarch in the South Pacific and he is known to the world for unique fund-raising projects such as selling Tongan passports.

The government is controlled by the King. He appoints a Prime Minister and other ministers to a Privy Council which acts as a cabinet. The 31-member Legislature comprises the King, the Privy Council, nine hereditary nobles (chosen by their peers), and nine elected MPs to represent the country's commoners.

In his kingdom the nobility possess political and financial privileges not ac-corded to the commoners. They represent the traditional clan element of Tongan life and reject any suggestions that they should adopt the Western model, as some re-formers suggest. They say it is wrong to apply Western standards in Tonga, be-cause they already have two sorts of representation — nobles represent the traditional kinship groupings and MPs are elected by the people. It is a system, they say, that has worked well for them so why should they change?.

The King's son, Crown Prince Tupouto'a, is in line for the throne.

DISCUSSION QUESTIONS

1. How is the executive controlled in a parliamentary system? In a presidential system?
2. Can governments in communist states control political participation. How? Does it work?
3. Why are presidential systems so prevalent in the Third World?
4. Compare the leadership qualities needed to administer a democratic country with those required in an authoritarian state.
5. Describe how government operates in a monarchical system.

KEY TERMS ▅▅▅▅▅▅▅▅▅▅▅▅▅▅▅▅▅▅▅▅▅▅▅▅▅▅

checks and balances, p. 282
collective ministerial
  responsibility, p. 279
1922 Committee, p. 280
confidence, p. 279
consociational democracies,
  p. 284
the Crown, p. 278
free vote, p. 280

fusion of powers, p. 277
impeach, p. 285
individual ministerial
  responsibility, p. 279
iron triangles, p. 283
issue networks, p. 283
official opposition, p. 280
Parliamentary Labour
  Party, p. 280

party caucus, p. 280
power of the purse, p. 282
private members' bills,
  p. 280
responsible government,
  p. 278
separation of powers,
  p. 277
vote of confidence, p. 282

ENDNOTES

1. Inter-Parliamentary Union, *Parliaments of the World* (Aldershot, Eng.: Gower, 1986).

2. Patrick Weller, *First Among Equals: Prime Ministers in Westminster Systems* (Sydney: George Allen & Unwin, 1985), ch. 4.

3. For comparison of democratic and authoritarian presidents see Juan J. Linz, "The Perils of Presidentialism," *Journal of Democracy*, vol. 9, no. 4 (October 1988), pp. 51–67; and Fred Riggs, "The Survival of Presidentialism in America," *IPSR*, vol. 9, no. 4 (Oct. 1988), pp. 247–49.

4. Arend Lijphart, *Democracy in Plural Societies* (New Haven, Conn.: Yale University Press, 1978); and G. Bingham Powell, Jr., *Contemporary Democracies* (Cambridge, Mass.: Harvard University Press, 1982).

5. Nelson W. Polsby, *Congress and the Presidency*, 4th ed. (Englewood Cliffs, N.J.: Prentice-Hall, 1986).

6. Robert J. Jackson and Doreen Jackson, *Politics in Canada*, 3rd ed. (Scarborough, Ont.: Prentice-Hall Canada, 1994), ch. 7.

7. Richard Rose and Ezra N. Suleiman, eds., *Presidents and Prime Ministers* (Washington, D.C.: American Enterprise Institute, 1980).

8. Robert J. Jackson, "Executive-Legislative Relations in Canada," paper delivered at the 25th anniversary of the Research Branch of the Library of Parliament, October 23–24, 1990.

9. William G. Andrews, *Presidential Government in Gaullist France* (Albany: State University of New York Press, 1982).

10. *The Economist*, August 5, 1995, p. 46.

11. See Zbigniew Brzezinski, "The Premature Partnership," *Foreign Affairs*, vol. 73, no. 2 (March 1994), pp. 67–82.

12. Former United States Ambassador to the USSR, Jack F. Matlock, Jr., has addressed this question in his *Autopsy of an Empire* (New York: Random House, 1995).

13. Michael McFaul, "Russian Politics," *Current History* (October 1994), pp. 313–319.

14. There is a large literature on this topic. See, for example, Michael M. Mezey, *Comparative Legislatures* (Durham, N.C.: Duke University Press, 1979).

15. Jean Blondel, *Comparative Legislatures* (Englewood Cliffs, N.J.: Prentice-Hall, 1973), ch. 1.

16. Edmund Burke, "Address to the Electors of Bristol," *The Works of Edmund Burke*, vol. 1 (New York: Harper, 1855), pp. 219–22.

17. Hanna Pitkin, "The Concept of Representation," in Hanna Pitkin, ed., *Representation* (New York: Atherton, 1969), p. 19.

18. Nelson Polsby, "Legislatures," in Fred I. Greenstein and Nelson W. Polsby, eds., *Handbook of Political Science*, vol. 5, (Reading, Mass.: Addison-Wesley, 1975), pp. 257–319.

19. Mezey, *Comparative Legislatures*.

20. For the period before Gorbachev's reforms see Stephen White, "The U.S.S.R. Supreme Soviet: A Developmental Perspective," *Legislative Studies Quarterly*, vol. 5 (May 1980), pp. 247–74.

21. Richard E. Neustadt, *Presidential Power* (New York: John Wiley, 1979).

22. Alan Bullock, *Hitler and Stalin: Parallel Lives* (London: Alfred A. Knopf, 1991).

23. Allan Kornberg, ed., *Legislatures in Comparative Perspective* (New York: McKay, 1973); G. R. Boynton and Chong Lim Kim, eds., *Legislative Systems in Developing Countries* (Durham, N.C.: Duke University Press, 1975).

24. "Saudis Get Changes in a Royal System," *The New York Times*, March 2, 1992, pp. A1, A8.

FURTHER READING

Bernstein, Carl, and Bob Woodward, *All the President's Men*, (New York, Warner, 1975).

Fenno, Richard, *Home Style: House Members in Their Districts* (Boston: Little, Brown, 1978).

Halpern, Manfred, *The Politics of Social Change in the Middle East* (Princeton: Princeton University Press, 1963).

Hamrin, Carol, and Suisheng Zhao, *Decision-Making in Deng's China* (Armonk: M.E. Sharpe, 1995).

Jackson, R., and C. Rosberg, *Personal Rule in Black Africa* (Berkeley: University of California Press, 1982).

Jones, Charles O. *Separate but Equal Branches: Congress and the Presidency* (Chatham, N.J.: Chatham House Publishers, 1995).

Khadduri, Majid, *Arab Contemporaries: The Role of Personalities in Politics* (Baltimore, Md: Johns Hopkins University Press, 1973).

Lieberthal, Kenneth, and Michael Oksenberg, *Policy Making in China* (Princeton, N.J.: Princeton University Press, 1988).

Linz, Juan, and Arturo Valenzuela, eds., *The Failure of Presidential Democracy: Comparative Perspectives* (Baltimore: Johns Hopkins University Press, 1994).

Manor, James, *From Nehru to Nineties: The Changing Office of the Prime Minister in India* (London: Hurst, 1994).

Neustadt, R., *Presidential Power: Politics of Leadership from FDR to Reagan* (New York: John Wiley, 1990).

Norton, Philip, *Does Parliament Matter?* (Hemel Hempstead, UK: Harvester Wheatsheaf, 1992).

———, *New Directions in British Politics? Essays on the Evolving Constitution* (Aldershot, Eng.: Edward Elgar, 1992).

Pinkney, R., *Right-wing Military Government* (London: Pinter, 1990).

Ranney, Austin, *Pathways to Parliament: Candidate Selection in Britain* (Madison: University of Wisconsin Press, 1965).

Remington, Thomas F., ed., *Parliaments in Transition: New Legislative Politics in Eastern Europe and the Former USSR* (Bolder, Colo.: Westview Press, 1994).

Remmer, K. *Military Rule in Latin America* (Boston: Unwin, 1989).

Salisbury, Harrison E., *The New Emperors: China in the Era of Mao and Deng* (Boston: Little, Brown, 1992).

Shell, Donald, and David Beamish, eds., *The House of Lords at Work* (Oxford: Clarendon Press, 1993).

Teiwes, Frederick, *Politics and Purges in China* (White Plains, N.Y.: M.E. Sharpe, 1979).

Thomas, Norman, and Joseph A. Pika, *The Politics of the Presidency*, 4th ed. (Washington D.C.: QC Press, 1996).

Special issue on "West European Prime Ministers," in *West European Politics*, vol. 14, no. 2 (April 1991).

Wildavsky, Aaron, *The Politics of the Budgetary Process* (New York: New York Times Book, 1987).

Woodward, Bob, *The Agenda: Inside the Clinton Whitehouse* (New York: Simon, 1994).

 ## Weblinks

www.Parliament.uk/
This is the Web Page of the British Parliament.

www.whitehouse.gov/WH/Welcome.html
This is the President of the United States' Web Page.

www.house.gov/CommitteeWWW.html
Information from American congressional committees can be found at this site.

menic.utexas.edu/mes.html
This site describes government structures in the Middle East.

CHAPTER 14

Design of Civilian and Military Public Administration

Executives are ubiquitous in the modern world and so are public servants. Whether the public service consists of civilian, police, or military bureaucrats, their task is to assist in the development and implementation of the country's public policies. In composite these individuals are called the **public administration** of their country, and they constitute what is often referred to as the bureaucracy.

Public administration has been part of the historical development of both Western and non-Western countries. Administrators existed in the great historical states of China, Egypt, and Rome, and in the households of the great feudal monarchies of Britain, France, and Spain. The present Japanese administration can trace its roots to Prussian influence in the nineteenth century.

Today, no modern state is without an extensive public administration. All states use civilians, soldiers, and police officers who are primarily responsible for implementing public policy to uphold the interests of the state. Public employees include all sorts of workers from tax collectors to inspectors of agricultural products, from health-care workers to defence specialists.

PUBLIC ADMINISTRATION TODAY

As the modern state developed it became extensive in the scope of its activities, complex in its organization, and expensive to run.[1] It expanded into new functions and responsibilities, taking on economic tasks earlier associated only with the private sector. The shift in government responsibilities was particularly evident in Western liberal democracies after the two World Wars. In Britain, for example, the government's intervention in controlling citizens' lives during World War II was remarkable: the politicians and civil servants determined what employment people could accept, controlled the industrial sector, and rationed goods and services as well as carrying out the normal functions of directing the war effort.

In communist countries it is practically impossible to distinguish between state and private economics since, in principle, there should be no difference between the two. Consequently, the role of the communist state is extremely large because it carries out functions which, in liberal democratic systems, are part of the private sector. In poorer, developing countries there is much more variety. But there, too, in many areas of the world the expansion of the state has been spectacular. The most widely accepted generalization, however, is that the public sector tends to be much larger in developed than in less economically developed countries regardless of the type of political system.[2]

One way to understand the growth of the public sector is to measure the public expenditure of states. From 1950 to 2000, state activities and responsibilities grew at the expense of the private sphere in all types of democratic systems. Because of this growth in public expenditures and the expansion of government activities, all states have had to employ ever greater numbers of people. This has been the case whether the country is developed or developing, democratic or authoritarian. Facts about the recent efforts to reduce the size of the bureaucracy in several countries are discussed near the end of this chapter. They indicate that there has been an attempt to slow down the growth of bureaucracy during the 1990s but they do not dispute the essential consideration that bureaucracies are extraordinarily large and that, especially at regional and local levels, they continue to grow. Of course, the organization of public servants has taken many forms and styles.

Bureaucratic Organization

The organization of public administration is most significantly affected by the recruitment of its members. Whether they have been appointed for political reasons or selected by objective criteria, the staff who comprise the public administration bring their values, beliefs, and prejudices to their duties. The culture of these public administrators greatly affects how they set out to do their jobs and reflects in the quality of their performance.

As modern public administration developed in the nineteenth century, it adopted a specific form of government organization often known as bureaucracy. The term "bureaucracy" originated as a satirical combination of the French word *bureau* (desk) with the Greek *kratein* (to rule). In 1745 a French physiocrat first used the term "bureaucracy" to describe the eighteenth-century Prussian system of administration.[3] Historically, this system of organization is said to have developed with the French and Prussian armies in the eighteenth and nineteenth centuries. An aphorism often used to depict the strength of the military bureaucracy at that time was: "States often have armies, but the Prussian army has a state." In its more technical meaning today, bureaucracy refers to a specific form of organization. Its form is based on the premise that organizations should be structured to provide as much efficiency as possible, and that this can be accomplished best by setting up a hierarchically structured decision-making process that reduces arbitrary and personal factors to a minimum. Bureaucracy is usually discussed today in terms originated by the German sociologist Max Weber. In his conceptualization, bureaucracy is a complex and hierarchically organized institution. His "ideal-type" of bureaucracy is characterized by:

1. Specialization of official duties;
2. Hierarchical organization of authority;
3. Operations governed by a consistent application of abstract rules to particular cases;
4. Impersonal detachment toward subordinates and clients;
5. Employment based on merit and protection from arbitrary dismissal; and
6. Maximization of technical and organizational efficiency.[4]

In the twentieth century, the popular use of the term bureaucracy conjures up negative images of inefficiency, red tape, and lazy employees. But in a technical sense the term is still used to refer to Weber's notion of a hierarchically organized institution that divides work in such a way as to allow the orders of superiors to be communicated effectively to subordinates. Even in this neutral sense, however, a hierarchically organized public service can be criticized, in particular for not being flexible enough to handle all the administrative requirements of a complex and geographically dispersed society.[5]

In this chapter the term **bureaucracy** is used in this neutral and technical sense of being equal to public administration. However, whether the term used is public service, civil service, or bureaucracy, the idea covers a broad range of types of positions and activities.

Merit versus Patronage

Whereas appointments of public servants in Europe and North America were once made on the basis of family, old-school ties, or the "spoils" gained by the victor after an election, modern public administration insists on fairness in recruitment and promotion. In the eighteenth century, positions in government were treated as property, something that could be purchased or sold. Later, instead of political leaders selling offices in the government or doling them out to friends, the modern system required recruitment to be based on merit, with selection determined by competitive examination.

The desire to both enhance the efficiency of the public service and make it more democratic led to the idea that merit should replace patronage. Ideally, civil servants should be selected on the basis of achievement and merit rather than on ascriptive characteristics such as class, caste, race, gender, or political friendship. The new entrants ought to be the best available or the most qualified individuals. According to the merit principle, applicants should be judged by objective standards such as intelligence, experience, training, and expertise.

Public Servants, Politicians, and Public Policy

Public servants are linked to politicians through their task of making public policies. "Policies" are categorized in at least three different ways—as the *intentions* of politicians, the *actions* of governments, and the *impact* of government on individuals and society. In political science, **policy** is defined as the broad framework within which decisions are taken and action (or inaction) is pursued by governments in relation to political issues.[6]

The development of public policies involves a complex process of interaction between politicians and public servants. But, in very general terms, public policies emerge from relations among historical, geographical, and socioeconomic conditions on mass polit-ical behaviour, elite behaviour, and governmental institutions. For a basic model of the factors involved in policy development see Figure 14.1.

Since both politicians and civil servants are engaged in governing and steering a country, one of the major issues in the study of public administration is whether or not these two roles are similar and compatible. In many respects politicians and public servants do perform the same type of functions, but three important distinctions may be drawn between the political role of the executive and the administrative functions of public servants.

First, there is a difference between the two because of the partisanship of members of the executive and the supposed neutrality of the public service. The second distinction may be made about their tenure. On the whole, political leaders come and go as the re-sult of elections or other forms of changing rulers, while public servants possess tenure or permanence in their positions. And, finally, public servants are to administer the policies of government, not actually make them. The political masters are supposed to make pol-icy and direct the public service in carrying it out. In theory, the task of the public servant is to provide ways to make the plans of politicians feasible and then to implement them.

Such distinctions have not always existed in history, nor do they fit all regimes.[7] In fact, the roles of politicians and public servants are quite blurred both in the real world and in political science literature. For example, the idea that public servants only ad-minister the policies set by politicians has been severely criticized. Few scholars would adhere to the idea that executive, legislative, and judicial functions can be neatly assigned to a particular structure of government or that civil servants' functions can be described as limited to administering the laws. The public service is involved in all forms of gov-ernment activity—it is part of the consultative, deliberative, legislative, and administrative

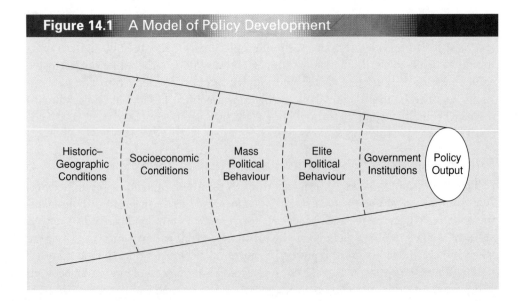

Figure 14.1   A Model of Policy Development

Historic–Geographic Conditions | Socioeconomic Conditions | Mass Political Behaviour | Elite Political Behaviour | Government Institutions | Policy Output

processes. Nevertheless, in liberal democracies there are many formal distinctions between politicians and civil servants. For example, there are important legal and accountability differences between transient politicians and administrators.

Public Service Functions and Controls

Public administrators carry out their functions in departments, ministries, and commissions. In these organizations they perform tasks in such fields as education, welfare, and national defence. They deliberate, organize, regulate, and even legislate in fields as diverse as economic development and health and welfare. Public servants also serve in organizations that cross the line between the public and private sectors. Such independent agencies or commissions often have a large scope of autonomy. In Canada such agencies are called "**Crown Corporations**," (for example, the Canadian Broadcasting Corporation) while in Britain they have been tagged with the wry term "Quangos"— quasi-autonomous nongovernmental organizations. In the United States there are government corporations (such as the Tennessee Valley Authority) that are part government agency and part business corporation.

The functions performed by the top bureaucracy are varied and complex. Besides administering the laws of the state, they also have important policy-making functions. They receive and direct the flow of policy ideas. They consult and negotiate with interest groups. At the top level they assist cabinet Secretaries, ministers, or their equivalents in their executive and legislative functions. They brief top politicians for cabinet meetings and for handling questions in legislatures, in committees, and before the press. It is also a prime function of the public service to assist in the preparation of government budgets.

In order to assess how well bureaucratic functions are performed, it is vital to study the recruitment, organization, and behaviour of these so-called servants of the government. It is also important to reflect on how the bureaucracy carries out its functions. It may be given responsibility to fill out the details of law and/or it may be employed to use strictly financial techniques such as providing tax incentives, giving out loans, or making direct subsidies to companies. The range of its techniques run from moral suasion and exhortation to the use of coercive force.

The political power of civil servants comes from several sources besides their legal authority. Their control of information is vital in policy-making. Even when the executive and politicians insist on making policy themselves, they still have to rely on information provided by the bureaucracy. Another source of bureaucratic power resides in its proximity to interest groups. In their day-to-day practical relations with economic and social interests, bureaucrats become well acquainted with what can, and should, be accomplished. They can mobilize interests to support or deny politicians the policies they want, such as funding their electoral campaigns or providing other forms of political support. Interest group leaders know that individual politicians are usually only transitory while the public service is permanent. They understand that they will have to keep dealing with the same bureaucrats even after the politicians depart. (See Chapters 16 and 17 for a discussion of interest groups.)

The fact that civil servants remain in office longer than most politicians means they can augment their power over time. They acquire information and skills that may not be possessed by transient politicians. As permanent staff they learn how to set the agenda for their political masters. What is more worrisome is that they may dominate politicians with their specialization and control of human and financial resources. The hit British TV comedies *Yes, Minister* and *Yes, Prime Minister* are based on this premise. It is this contention that has led to the charge that bureaucracy subverts democracy because it is based on a belief in maximizing efficiency and hierarchy while democracy is based on principles of equality, majority rule, and responsiveness to the public.

Of particular interest in the bureaucracy are the police and military, who may use their hierarchical discipline and monopoly of legal firepower to dominate the political system. They tend to be even more bureaucratic than civilian authorities because of their rigid adherence to standardization and obedience. For this reason, political scientists often ask if the police and military, indeed any professional public service, can be controlled by democratic politicians. Allegations that Canadian Mounties burned a barn to gain illegal access to the FLQ (Front de Libération du Québec), that the CIA and FBI engaged in wrongdoing in the United States, and that the KGB terrorized democratic forces in the Soviet Union, are all well-known examples.

Certainly there are many obstacles to controlling powerful administrators whether they are civilian, police, or military. This is especially true when the bureaucrats maintain group solidarity against their political masters. Yet the general public and politicians do seem to wish to maintain popular control over their public servants.

How can bureaucrats be persuaded or forced to be accountable and responsive? There are two basic methods of attempting to control public servants or at least make them responsive to public opinion. One approach calls for public servants to be controlled *within* the bureaucracy. The other demands *outside* checks on their behaviour.

Inside Controls

Inside controls are those instruments formulated on the premise that professional standards and methods can provide a check on public servants. Its advocates argue that public servants can be made responsive to public and political interests because of their own feelings of obligation or duty.[8] Inculcating these professional norms can be accomplished many ways: through recruitment, training, and promotion.

In modern bureaucracies the appointment and promotion processes are perhaps the most important devices for controlling public servants. As we have noted, while employees were formerly hired on the basis of partisanship or privilege, today they are expected to be employed on the basis of competitive examinations and to be promoted on the basis of an objective study of their merit. This competitive system is then arranged in a hierarchical manner to promote a career-structured civil service. Of course, this theory does not always work in practice. In Chapter 15 we examine some of the problems in applying this principle.

The professional ethics required in bureaucracy include values such as honesty, industriousness, and the ability to accept political authority, even when that means subordinating personal opinion. In liberal democratic systems public servants are expected to retain a high degree of non-partisanship with regard to political parties and ideologies. When the government changes hands, bureaucrats are expected to be able to work effectively and loyally with the new politicians. In authoritarian systems, on the other hand, commitment to the single party's or a single leader's norms may be required to be a successful civil servant.

In either case there are dangers. Public servants sometimes regard their own impartiality or even commitment to the regime as superior to that of "mere" politicians. In their efforts to defend the "national interest," they may act against the pressure of public influence exerted through the party or political system and become a kind of administrative oligarchy outside of popular control.

Political control over the bureaucracy exists to some degree in all countries. In liberal democracies, the democratic nature of the system is supposed to ensure government control over the bureaucracy. In communist countries party control is demanded by the leaders in power. In most developing countries, even when the state adheres to the liberal democratic model of the government, the leaders often believe they should be able to exercise *personal* control over the bureaucracy. Personal control is certainly the predominant fixture of military and monarchical governments.

Merit versus Representation

Some critics of bureaucratic power allege that the only way to control the public administration is to make it representative of all parts of society. They contend that the composition of the public service should *not* be determined by merit alone because adherence to this principle would not result in a fully representative bureaucracy. Acceptance of this contention has led to demands for affirmative action in many countries.

Advocates of this position argue that bureaucrats should mirror the population as a whole. If a bureaucracy is unrepresentative of some groups, it is argued, it will become insensitive to those denied representation. This idea, among others, has led to the drive in liberal democracies for greater employment of women in higher government positions, as well as demands for equal employment for certain minorities and the handicapped, and for regional representation. In many countries, stress is put on representation based on class and race.[9] But the conundrum is that, unlike politicians, the bureaucracy is not elected but appointed. It is supposed to serve its political masters and at the same time provide services for society in the most efficient and effective manner. Thus, one would theorize that an appointment process based on merit would best serve everyone.

However, there are four arguments for forgoing the merit principle. First, if the recipients of the services are from minority categories then it may be more effective to adopt an **affirmative action** plan that bypasses the merit principle in the recruitment process. In this argument, a **representative bureaucracy** in which the administrators have social and economic characteristics similar to those to whom they administer may be just as important to an efficient administration as one based solely on the merit principle.

A second justification for skirting the merit principle is that greater representativeness in the bureaucracy will assist in altering the economic and social structure of society. In Canada the federal government has affirmative-action plans for women, Native peoples, and the handicapped. In the United States affirmative-action laws are in place at the federal and state levels for various categories of citizens. In India, underprivileged castes are given legal priority in hiring by the government.[10] As B. Guy Peters put it, "hiring minority community members can serve not only to attack any prejudices within society but also to provide a means of economic advancement for members of the minority community."[11] It must be pointed out, however, that hiring based on the principle of representation will not necessarily change a pluralistic society; in fact it is more likely to preserve the status quo.

A third justification for non-adherence to the merit principle is to increase political control of the civil service. For this reason, all states have a mix of merit and political rules for appointments to the public bureaucracy. The top positions, even in liberal democracies, are controlled by politicians. The appointment extremes in liberal democracies can be illustrated by comparing the United States' system, where there are greater political "spoils," to that of Britain. Almost all British senior appointments—and all permanent Secretaries who report directly to cabinet ministers—are made through the regular merit system. Only a handful of political appointments are made in each department. By contrast, in the United States the President controls approximately 2000 political appointments including the top four or five senior positions below the cabinet Secretary. In Britain, therefore, senior public servants deal directly with the minister whereas in the United States they have to go through at least four political appointees to get to the member of cabinet. In Canada, the most senior appointments are **order in council** positions which means that the appointment and tenure of these individuals is at the pleasure of the government—that is, they can be fired without cause. Most senior civil servants come from the public service through merit-hiring procedures but others are brought in as political appointees at the top of the administration.

The fourth argument for bypassing the merit principle is based on an alleged need to overcome the fact that bureaucracies tend to be over-representative of the middle-class. It is argued that if the working-class is to be adequately represented, there will have to be special provisions to induce working-class individuals into the civil service. In Britain, this argument is often expanded by saying that Oxford and Cambridge graduates get a disproportionate share of civil-servant positions and that special recruitment procedures have to be used to attract more students from other, "red brick" universities.[12]

However, most of these techniques to reduce middle-class control of the bureaucracy have failed. In Western liberal democracies middle-class children, on the whole, fare better in school and university than working-class children, and appointment to the public service tends to be judged in terms of educational achievements. Even in the former

Soviet Union the effort to eliminate class barriers failed, as recruits to the bureaucracy tended to come from families that were themselves engaged in middle-class occupations.[13]

By insisting that the members of the public service be "representative" of the population at large and share a high degree of professionalism, it is assumed that they will be made responsive to their political masters and thus to the public. Unfortunately these two principles may conflict, and even when applied successfully neither one seems to be able to eliminate bureaucratic independence. For this reason outside controls are often thought to be necessary to control the bureaucracy.

Outside Controls (Oversight)

In most political systems a hierarchical chain of accountability is instituted from the top elected official, Prime Minister, or President, down through Secretaries or ministers and their top civil servants to the bottom of the bureaucracy. The degree to which the accountability chain, which implies a closely knit superordinate-subordinate relationship, will actually hold public servants responsible in the real world is highly debated. Certainly elected officials such as prime ministers and presidents in liberal democracies are held accountable to a degree through the electoral system and through the attention of the media. The extent to which political leaders can control knowledgeable permanent civil servants is more questionable. At the formal level, accountability links exist in all liberal democracies, but the reality may be quite different. U.S. President Eisenhower once said that it was easier being a General than being President because when he issued orders as General they were carried out, but when he tried to issue similar *commands* as President he was obliged to *persuade* people to carry out his wishes.

In the United States, Congress acts to control senior bureaucrats either at the time of their appointment through scrutiny of their qualifications or later by what is called **oversight**. The latter refers to the ability of Congress to review and judge the work of the administration. The theory is that public servants will act responsibly and in the public interest if they know they are likely to have their actions and decisions checked by Congress at a later date. Congress also holds the power of the purse as a final controlling mechanism over the whole of the bureaucracy. Bureaucrats are well aware that their pet projects may be supported or axed following a congressional review of their budgets.

In British-type parliamentary systems, as we have seen in Chapter 12, ministers who are in charge of the largest departments of government are regularly expected to answer in the legislature for their own and their department's behaviour. In Britain, Canada, Australia, and many other countries, a **question period** is inserted into the parliamentary timetable so that the opposition may review and challenge the government and its functionaries. During this period MPs rise in the House to ask spontaneous, or caucus-planned, questions about government activities.

On the European continent similar devices exist, but they are much less powerful instruments of control over the bureaucracy. In France the **interpellation**, a parliamentary method of demanding ministers to respond to questions and then forcing a general debate and censure motion on the government, proved to be a powerful instrument in the Third and Fourth French Republics. In the Fifth Republic it has been weakened considerably as the current Constitution greatly strengthens the President's executive powers and control over the National Assembly. But even so, this French method is stronger than that used in Germany, where the questions asked, called *Kleine Anfragen* (only requires one member) or *Grosse Anfragen* (requires more than five members, or a "Fraction"), have to be put first in writing and are answered only later at the government's discretion.

Legislatures may require other mechanisms for controlling the executive and administration. While legislators may set the parameters of policy when they enact laws, to a large extent the administration must fill in the details of these policies. In other words, the bureaucracy actually makes laws that are binding on the population, just as politicians do when they pass statutes. This type of legislation passed under the authority of a statute of a legislature is called **subordinate legislation**. Subordinate legislation comes under various names—in Canada and Britain, for example, it is under the rubric of "statutory instruments," whereas in the United States it is called by the generic term "regulations."

In order to maintain control, lawmakers have to find ways to monitor these and other actions of the bureaucracy. If they wish to prevent distortion of what they intend with the law, they must keep careful surveillance of their employees. We have covered this topic in the discussion of committees in the United States House of Representatives and the Senate, but these are unique institutions in the world of legislatures. In Britain and Canada all subordinate legislation must be tabled in the House of Commons where it can be examined by committees or by individual politicians. If the statutory instrument is challenged it can be declared null and void, but the legislatures are normally too weak to take on the executive except in very isolated incidents.

Another well-known device for controlling civil servants is the use of investigations. Legislative committees are often given the power to summon civil servants and witnesses to determine how well the bureaucracy has carried out its tasks. In Canada, the 1991 Al Mashat case, in which a former Iraqi Ambassador was improperly allowed into Canada, was carefully but uniquely investigated by a parliamentary committee. Such committees are very powerful in the United States. Possibly the best known example of committee activity was the McCarthy hearing on communism in the United States in the early 1950s, and the study made by the American Congress of the "arms for hostages" deal made by members of President Ronald Reagan's staff with the Iranian government in the late 1980s. Considerably more powerful in the field of investigations than the United States Congress or British-type legislature is the Swedish *Riksdag*. The *Riksdag* can actually review the minutes of cabinet meetings on an annual basis.[14]

If all else fails, legislatures often use their ability to determine the funding of programs in order to control the bureaucracy. By providing more money for some departments than others, or by eliminating the funds for some programs, they can directly affect the civil servants and force the bureaucracy to be more responsive to political control. In order to control the bureaucracy with such technical devices, politicians need help in the form of the pressure of public opinion. The threat of publicity and exposure acts as a check on bureaucratic power in every country. Civil servants need public approval for their promotions and departmental budgets in the same way that politicians do for elections. Therefore, one way politicians ensure that the bureaucracy will be responsive to public opinion is by setting up institutions to publicize their activities. Two of the best known of these are freedom of information laws and the office of ombudsman.

Freedom of information is a mechanism that requires government private papers and documents to be made public within a specified period and according to legal rules. These rules may concern policies of the government or information on individuals that may have been collected by governmental agencies such as the police or tax collectors. Such laws exist in Canada and the United States, to cite only two of many examples.

The "ombudsman" idea was invented in Sweden in 1809. An **ombudsman** is an official of a Parliament or legislature who is assigned the responsibility of overseeing government officials from "within" the system. He or she may obtain access to secret government documents to determine if citizens' complaints about improper treatment by the administration are valid and set up private investigations to ferret out problems within the administration.

Today, variations of the ombudsmen idea exist in many countries such as Sweden, Britain, Germany, New Zealand, and in individual provinces in Canada and states in the United States. The institution as such does not yet exist at the national level in the United States. Several countries have modified the ombudsman idea for special functions such as overseeing human rights, privacy, or military affairs.[15]

Finally, the political executive may use **counterstaffs** or consultants to help control public servants because counterstaffs provide an alternative source of information to that provided by the permanent bureaucracy. These personally appointed policy staffs from outside the civil service are used to control the flow of information and influence to the politicians. In Canada and Britain the Prime Minister and every cabinet minister has a political staff which he or she personally hires. The President of the United States has an "executive office" and every cabinet Secretary helps to appoint political nominees several layers down into the bureaucracy.[16] In some systems, such as in France, the minister's office may be staffed largely by members of the bureaucracy. But even in such types of arrangements the staff is required to work for the minister directly, and not represent the bureaucracy itself.

Corruption

Another fundamental concern is about corruption in the public service. Since the advent of open competitions and fair examinations in Western democracies, there have been fewer possibilities for petty bribery, but both small- and large-scale corruption continues to exist. Few days go by in any country in which headlines do not point out some ministerial scandal or administrative misdeed.

In some developing countries practices of corruption may not be heavily sanctioned. Bribery may be a normal way of dealing with administrators. Everyone who has travelled to countries such as Nigeria, or read about them, will be familiar with the "dash," a sum of money which must be offered to every minor functionary in order to get things done, from obtaining baggage which had been checked at airports to dealing with allegations of petty crimes. The simple fact is that many countries of the world have not developed an "ethical" model of bureaucratic behaviour, and bribery, and to some degree corruption, are standard methods of getting things accomplished (see Close Up 14.1). Cultural differences, discussed further in Chapter 15, help to explain these practices.

While in liberal democratic countries these matters may be handled by the controls mentioned above, the judicial system is sometimes required. In democratic countries the courts are used to restrain individual government officials from breaking the law or violating the rights of groups or individuals. In some liberal democracies, especially those on continental Europe, special courts, known as administrative courts, are used to judge misdeeds or alleged inappropriate behaviour by administrators. In Canada, Britain, and the United States the regular court system is used to accomplish the same objectives.

Government Restraint, Downsizing, and Renewal

In the past decade there has been a concerted attack on the size and complexity of modern government in most liberal democracies. Bureaucrats are portrayed as being motivated only by their desire to increase their budgets, staffs, and importance. Conservatives, in particular, think that the problems of bureaucracy can be solved by reducing its power. They demand that government administration be made smaller, more decentralized, less expensive, and more flexible in responding to public demands. The

---

CLOSE UP 14.1   Corruption and Violence in Liberia

In the nineteenth century, many freed black American slaves left America and founded Liberia in 1847. They quickly dominated the local Africans. Not until Samuel Doe came to power by a coup in 1980 did a Liberian of local ancestry rule. Considered one of modern Africa's most corrupt and brutal figures, Doe was overthrown by a coup in 1990. The country endured a state of civil war for the next seven years. For most of that time it was in the grip of a clique of evil warlords and teenage gunmen who rampaged the countryside and routinely murdered civilians with machetes. Bribes and procurement kickbacks were central to life, necessary to get a passport, a driver's licence, a birth certificate—even food.

In a relatively peaceful and democratic vote in 1997, the people elected former warlord Charles G. Taylor to be president. Taylor won in spite of his reputation for corruption and brutality during the war. His win was assisted by the fact that he had amassed considerable wealth and control of the former state-radio system.

The election brought some respite from seven years of turmoil and death. However, it is not clear how long the country will have to recover. Corruption is endemic. The fragile state is surrounded by strife, and countries near and far from its borders are competing for influence here and for its wealth of natural resources.

Republican party's Contract for America in the 1994 Congressional election was essentially a set of proposals to weaken Washington bureaucracy.

Such political demands have often been accompanied by grand schemes for reform. The "new public management" school in social science calls for the introduction of business management practices into government.[17] One example would be the claim that "pay for performance" or merit pay should be reinforced in the public sector. This idea is often accompanied by the philosophy that "customer orientation" should be the reigning principle for public servants. Another approach has been to call for the "privatization" of government, either by selling off government enterprises or by "contracting out" services to the private sector. The idea is based on the premise that self-interested decisions in the market place will be made more efficiently than those made by tenured civil servants in the bureaucracy. Probably the clearest example of this philosophy in recent years has been the decision in several countries, including the United States, to privatize some parts of the prison system. Lastly, a case has been made against the centralization of bureaucracies in capital cities. The claim is that better (read "more efficient") decisions would be made if they were made closer to the people that they affect. In other words, decentralization is supposed to enhance decision-making and prevent the waste which is prevalent in large, centralized administrations.

The conundrum inherent to such policies is clear. When the market place is used to enforce efficiency it may be to the advantage of the most conservative forces in society. When governments reduce their size, privatize their functions, and decentralize, do they lose a measure of democratic control? How will democratic responsiveness be enhanced by these new managerial techniques of government? But conservative optimists continue to be led by the ideas put forth by David Osborne and Ted Gaebler in their best-selling popular book *Reinventing Government* in which they argue that "the entrepreneurial spirit" can transform public administration.[18]

THE SPECIAL CASE OF THE POLICE AND THE MILITARY
Police, Prisons, and the Law

Among the state's bureaucrats, the police are the most directly involved both with the citizens and with implementing the laws of the state. The police are responsible for dealing with lawbreakers, and bringing them for prosecution before the courts or other executive agencies. Since the police are always dealing with situations where the law is not respected, they are on the cutting edge between citizens and the law. Unlike the work of most other members of the bureaucracy, police duties are risky and sometimes involve injury and even death.

The organization, training, and effectiveness of police differ greatly from country to country. In liberal democratic countries the state can count on the public's willing acceptance of most of its laws, but in authoritarian countries special or "secret" police may be used for carrying out the leader's demands. The police are agents for the government and are used to suppress political opposition. Crimes against the dictatorial leadership are interpreted as "crimes against the state." Recent examples from authoritarian countries would include the Nazi Gestapo, the Soviet KGB (now the Russian Federal Security Service), and the Iranian Savak.

The standard responsibility of police officers is to enforce the law. But they also have to make their own policies about criminality as not every law can be enforced with the same regularity and consistency. In making choices about what laws to administer and with what resources, they are in effect making policy or law.

Most members of the police, however, spend their time in particular functions, such as patrolling, determining who has committed a crime, arresting suspects, and providing evidence in court. In carrying out these functions they have the invidious but vital mandate to both uphold the law and protect the rights of everyone, including the criminals. In fact, the touchstone of a free society may be the manner in which the police are allowed to do just that. In authoritarian regimes the police allow special rules for special people. When the law does not apply to everyone, it is the beginning of tyranny.

Overlooked in most political science texts is the prison system. This is unfortunate as the corrections system represents the ultimate sanction of the state against a citizen. It represents a failure to socialize all citizens into lawful and peaceful activity. The prison system represents the final proof that even in democratic societies the state retains the ultimate recourse to the use of coercion against its citizens. Hidden from view, the prison system exemplifies what the state is finally all about. Issues about prisons in democracies are obscured by the reluctance of political parties and politicians to regard the prison system as an important instrument of public policy. Left in the shadow of politics it is often overlooked and even despised, but it forms an essential part of the institutions of all countries.

Prisons serve multi-functional and even contradictory purposes. A list of how penitentiary systems function would have to distinguish between their use in democratic and authoritarian countries. Just as the police in authoritarian countries are used to defend political leaders and repression, so are prisons. During the period of communism in the USSR, psychiatric hospitals, prisons, and labour camps were used to punish dissidents. Aleksandr Solzhenitsyn's novels *The Cancer Ward* and *The Gulag Archipelago* show vividly how purges, terror, and prisons were used to defend communism. Even in democracies prisons have the somewhat contradictory purposes of punishing wrongdoers, deterring criminal behaviour, safeguarding society by depriving criminals of their freedom, and providing opportunities to prisoners so they can be successfully reintroduced into society.

Despite the fact that political scientists overlook the role of corrections, prisons are still highly political institutions. Debate about prisons abounds. They cost a lot of money and many citizens argue that the expenditures should be reduced. But how? Some want to privatize them, others seek to reduce prison sentences by encouraging law-makers to use other forms of punishment such as heavy fines and restricting home leaves. Others complain that early-release schemes put violent criminals back in the neighbourhood. Prisoners complain about brutality by prison guards. Corrections guards counter that prison populations are unstable and need constant attention.

Swept under the carpet by politicians and academics, the prison system neverthe-less plays a crucial part in the political system. Law and order is crucial to the func-tioning of both democratic and authoritarian political systems but how it is enforced is always controversial and political.

The Military

Every state also has a military bureaucracy. These officials have even been dubbed "armed bureaucrats."[19] The military bureaucrats differ in degree but not in kind from the police. As Professor S.E. Finer put it, they possess superiority over civilian bureaucracies in the application of force because they have an efficient organization, based on hier-archical authority and military arms.[20] However, his further suggestion that they possess a monopoly of arms is not valid for every country today. The police, or sometimes a paramilitary force, may have arms that are just as lethal as those of the military itself.

In many respects the military acts like any other bureaucracy. It is arranged hierar-chically and employs the same basic pattern as other organizations in an attempt to be efficient and effective. While it may possess lethal arms, it does not necessarily use them. In both democratic and authoritarian countries it is caught up in the contest for resources, personnel, and finances from the government and acts like any other de-partment of state in an effort to obtain these resources. It controls and manipulates in-formation and has direct relations with interest groups concerned with security policies and those who wish to sell military equipment to the government.

In many parts of the world the military takes over and runs the so-called civilian administration permanently or periodically. The liberal democratic assumption that ex-ecutives and their senior administrators control the military is simply invalid in many states. Of course, the military is involved to some extent in the politics of every country.

The degree of civilian control of the military or vice versa varies greatly. In some countries such as the United States the armed forces are directly controlled by elected leaders, but in others the military controls the politicians. In the United States, military power is latent. The President, as Commander-in-Chief of the Armed Forces, and the military are thoroughly involved with decision-making through their roles on the National Security Council and the various Armed Services and Intelligence Committees of Congress. In countries as different as Brazil and South Korea, elected governments have had to obey the military on key political decisions. In still others the military have sim-ply governed the country directly as they do today in Nigeria.

C.E. Welch has drawn up a typology to depict these relationships between military and civilian governments.[21] It can be summarized as follows:

1. **Civilian Control**   In the liberal democratic model, the civilian government main-tains the dominant position. The military acts like any other large bureaucracy. It fights for personnel and resources within the government. It has influence to the extent that it manages to convince the public, government, and politicians that it has the best case.

2. **Civilian Control and Military Participation**   In wartime, for example, military power increases even in liberal democracies. It is not just an equal player with other parts of the bureaucracy—it can insist on having a dominant role in decision-making.

3. **Military Control and Civilian Participation**   When the military takes over the government, it often keeps a degree of civilian participation either for practical or symbolic purposes. To mask the fact that the military is really pulling the strings behind the scenes, civilian leaders may be put at the head of the government.

4. **Direct Military Control**   In such systems the military publicly and unabashedly controls the government. It may employ civilians for tasks in the bureaucracy but clearly the military is the political authority. In such circumstances, either a strong leader becomes a type of military dictator or the military forms a collective leadership often called a "junta." In such cases an officer becomes head of the government, unlike the previous situation where a civilian may remain as the President or Prime Minister.

Civilian Control of the Police and Military

In the liberal democratic model, civilian and police/military organizations and tasks are clearly specified. The civilian agencies are in charge of a set of responsibilities such as economic, social, and foreign policy. The coercive instruments of police and military are responsible for ensuring law and order and protecting the state from foreign aggression. Each may be required to give advice about the others' responsibilities but politicians are supposed to make the final decisions.

In a manner similar to civilian bureaucracy, it is through a career-structured hierarchy, including formalized recruitment, training, and promotions, that police and military are kept in check in liberal democracies. "Inside" and "outside" controls are put in place and a high degree of organizational discipline is required. In other types of states, such as communist, but also in many LDCs, the police and military may be directly involved with the ruling party or apparatus. Eric Nordlinger has called this type of system a "penetration" model.[22] In this model the police and armed forces are inculcated with the ideas and beliefs of the ruling group or class. Recruitment and promotion are dependent on loyalty to the regime and its leaders. A process of indoctrination and even the implantation of "political" members within military and police ranks is used to ensure continued loyalty to the state apparatus.

Other issues including the consequences of military rule and the mechanisms for police or military takeovers of a state (i.e., coups d'état and their consequences) are discussed in the next chapter.

The size of government administration has left citizens with a dual attitude toward public servants, both civilian and military. On one hand, people tend to believe the public service is too powerful, and on the other that it is bogged down in red tape and inefficiency. The larger government grows, the more it seems to be accused of both these failures at the same time.

Economic problems in Western states have strengthened this dual attitude. As government budgets become more constrained, the public reacts by posing even more challenges to the government administration. With scarcity, the public demands both a more efficient organization to provide services and a reduction in the budgets of the bureaucracy. Political analysts, too, are concerned with this dilemma. Samuel Krislov concluded that "Convenience and necessity, not ideology and legitimacy, are their [bureaucrats'] life-blood: they are not loved and respected, but tolerated and depended on."[23]

DISCUSSION QUESTIONS

1. Should public servants be chosen for their professional qualifications? Ethnicity? Gender?
2. Do public servants make policy or are they simply administrators of policies made by politicians?
3. Should public servants be accountable for their actions? In the legislature? In other public forms? Why or why not?
4. Should public officials be elected in democratic states?
5. What controls over the police and military are effective? In democracies? In authoritarian states?

KEY TERMS

affirmative action, p. 305
bureaucracy, p. 301
counterstaffs, p. 309
crown corporations, p. 303
freedom of information,
　p. 309

interpellation, p. 307
ombudsman, p. 309
order in council, p. 306
oversight, p. 307
policy, p. 301
public administration,

p. 299
question period, p. 307
representative bureaucracy,
　p. 305
subordinate legislation,
　p. 308

ENDNOTES

1. The reasons for this growth of the state are the subject of considerable debate. See David Cameron, "The Expansion of the Public Economy: A Comparative Analysis," APSR, vol. 72, no. 4 (December 1978), pp. 1243–61.
2. B. Guy Peters, *The Politics of Bureaucracy*, 3rd ed. (London: Longman, 1989), p. 18. For a general comparison of bureaucracy in developed and developing countries, see Joel D. Aberbach, Robert D. Putnam, and Bert A. Rockman, *Bureaucrats and Politicians in Western Democracies* (Cambridge, Mass.: Harvard University Press, 1981); and Joseph LaPalombara, ed., *Bureaucracy and Political Development* (Princeton, N.J.: Princeton University Press, 1963).
3. Cited in Peter Andrew Simeoni, "Bureaucracy: Its Case, Its Causes, Its Control," *Policy Options*, vol. 12, no. 4 (May 1991), p. 20.

4. Summarized by Peter M. Blau, *Bureaucracy in Modern Society* (New York: Random House, 1956), pp. 28–31. Details are found in Max Weber, *The Theory of Social and Economic Organization*, ed. and trans. by A.M. Henderson and Talcott Parsons (Glencoe, Ill.: Free Press, 1947). For other discussions of this topic of the definition of bureaucracy, see Anthony Downs, *Inside Bureaucracy* (Boston: Little, Brown, 1976); and Peter M. Blau, *The Dynamics of Bureaucracy*, 2nd ed. (Chicago: University of Chicago Press, 1963).

5. For a general critique see Christopher Hood, *The Limits of Administration*, (New York: John Wiley, 1976); and for an application to one country—France—see Michael Crozier, *The Bureaucratic Phenomenon* (Chicago: University of Chicago Press, 1963).

6. For definitions of "policy," see Richard Rose, ed., *Policy-Making in Britain* (London: Macmillan, 1969). See Robert J. Jackson and Doreen Jackson, *Politics in Canada*, 3rd ed. (Scarborough, Ont.: Prentice-Hall Canada, 1994), ch. 13, for elaboration of the theories and models of policy-making.

7. B. Guy Peters, *Public Bureaucracy in Comparative Perspective* (Tuscaloosa: University of Alabama Press, 1988).

8. For an early exponent of this view, see Carl J. Friedrich, "Public Policy and the Nature of Administrative Responsibility," in *Public Policy* (Cambridge, Mass.: Harvard University Press, 1940).

9. For examples of the lack of representativeness in Western democracies, see Mattei Dogan, ed., *The Mandarins of Western Europe* (New York: Wiley, 1975).

10. B.A.V. Sharma, and K.M. Reddy, *Reservation Policy in India* (New Delhi: Light and Life, 1982).

11. Peters, *The Politics of Bureaucracy*, p. 78.

12. For a comparison of elites, see Robert D. Putnam, *The Comparative Study of Political Elites* (Englewood Cliffs, N.J.: Prentice-Hall, 1976).

13. Peters, *The Politics of Bureaucracy*, p. 78.

14. Sigvar Holstad, "Sweden," in Donald C. Rowat, ed., *Administrative Secrecy in Developed Democracies* (New York: Columbia University Press, 1979).

15. Donald C. Rowat, ed., *The Ombudsman: Citizens' Defender* (London: Allen & Unwin, 1965); and Frank Stacey, *The Ombudsman Compared* (Oxford: Clarendon Press, 1978).

16. For details, see Hugh Heclo, *A Government of Strangers* (Washington: The Brookings Institute, 1977).

17. A. Massey, *Managing the Public Sector* (Aldershot: Edward Elgar, 1993), C. Campbell, *Political Leadership in an Age of Constraint* (Pittsburgh: University of Pittsburg Press, 1992), and J. DiIulio, *Deregulating the Public Service: Can Government Be Improved?* (Washington D.C.: The Brookings Institute, 1994).

18. Osborne and Gaebler, *Reinventing Government* (New York: Plume, 1993). Their ideas were foreshadowed by Tom Peters and Robert Waterman in their best-selling book about management in business *In Search of Excellence* (New York: Harper and Row, 1982).

19. As used in Edward Feit, *The Armed Bureaucrats: Military Administrative Regimes and Political Development* (London: Houghton Mifflin, 1973).

20. S.E. Finer, *The Man on Horseback: The Role of the Military in Politics* (Harmondsworth, Eng.: Penguin, 1975).

21. C.E. Welch, Jr., ed., *Civilian Control of the Military* (Albany: State University of New York Press, 1976), *passim*.

22. Eric A. Nordlinger, *Soldiers in Politics: Military Coups and Government* (Englewood Cliffs, N.J.: Prentice-Hall, 1977).

23. Samuel Krislov, *Representative Bureaucracy* (Englewood Cliffs, N.J.: Prentice-Hall, 1974).

FURTHER READING

Bureaucracy

Aberbach, J.D., Robert D. Putnam, and Bert A. Rockman, *Bureaucrats and Politicians in Western Democracies* (Cambridge, Mass.: Harvard University Press, 1981).

Blau, Peter M., *Bureaucracy in Modern Society*, 2nd ed. (New York: Random House, 1971).

Burke, John, *Bureaucratic Responsibility* (Baltimore, Md: Johns Hopkins University Press, 1986).

Camp, Roderic A., *Entrepreneurs and Politics in Twentieth Century Mexico* (New York: Oxford University Press, 1989).

Campbell, C., *Political Leadership in an Age of Constraint* (Pittsburgh: University of Pittsburgh press, 1992).

DiIulio, J. *Deregulating the Public Service: Can Government be Improved?* (Washington D.C.: The Brookings Institute, 1994).

Dogan, Mattei, ed., *The Mandarins of Western Europe: The Political Role of Top Civil Servants* (New York: John Wiley, 1975).

Downs, Anthony, *Inside Bureaucracy* (Boston: Little, Brown, 1976).

Heclo, Hugh, *A Government of Strangers* (Washington, D.C.: The Brookings Institution, 1977).

Heidenheimer, Arnold J., Hugh Heclo, and Carolyn Adams, *Comparative Public Policy*, 2nd ed. (New York: St. Martin's Press, 1983).

LaPalombara, Joseph, ed., *Bureaucracy and Political Development* (Princeton, N.J.: Princeton University Press, 1963).

Massey, Andrew, *Managing the Public Sector* (Aldershot, Eng.: Edward Elgar, 1993).

Osborne, David, and Ted Gaebler, *Reinventing Government* (New York: Plume, 1993).

Peters, B. Guy, *Public Bureaucracy in Comparative Perspective* (Tuscaloosa: University of Alabama Press, 1988).

Rhodes, R.A.W., *Understanding Governance* (Buckingham: Open University Press, 1997).

Self, Peter, *Administrative Theories and Politics*, 2nd ed. (Toronto: University of Toronto Press, 1977).

Sivard, Ruth Leger, *World Military and Social Expenditures* (Washington DC: World Priorities, 1993)

———, *World Military and Social Indicators* (Washington DC: World Priorities, 1993).

Military

Brewer, J. et al, *The Police, Public Order and the State* (Basingstoke: Macmillan, 1988).

Clapham, C. and G. Philip, eds., *The Political Dilemmas of Military Rule* (London: Croom Helm, 1985).

Danapoulos, C., ed., *Military Disengagement from Politics* (London: Routledge, 1988).

Enloe, C.H., *Ethnic Soldiers: State Security in Divided Societies* (Harmondsworth, Eng.: Penguin, 1980).

Huntington, Samuel P., *The Soldier and the State* (Cambridge, Mass.: Harvard University Press, 1957).

Nordlinger, E.A., *Soldiers in Politics: Military Coups and Governments* (Englewood Cliffs, N.J.: Prentice-Hall, 1976).

Perlmutter, Amos, *The Military and Politics in Modern Times* (New Haven, Conn.: Yale University Press, 1977).

Pinkney, R. *Right-wing Military Government* (London: Pinter, 1990).

 **Weblinks**

Canada.gc.ca/depts/major/depind_e.html
The bureaucratic structure of the Canadian government can be found at this site.

www.irlgov.ie/ombudsman/default.htm
This is the Office of the Irish Ombudsman's Web Page.

www.open.gov.uk/index/fiquang.htm
This site identifies many of the Quasi-Autonomous, Non-Government Organisations (QUANGOS) found in Great Britain.

www.ipc.on.ca/
This is the Web Page of the Information and Privacy Commission of Ontario, the office responsible for administering the Ontario Freedom of Information Act.

CHAPTER 15

Design of Civilian and Military Public Administration: Democratic and Authoritarian

Bureaucratic administration is the dominant form of government organization in the contemporary world. It is employed not only in the public sector but also in such private-sector areas as commerce, education, and religion. Whether states are democratic or authoritarian, they all employ some form of bureaucratic power. That power is based on the belief that all social relationships can be organized, calculated, and controlled in order to bring about a rational and efficient use of people and resources. And yet, in contemporary societies bureaucracy is also highly criticized as bringing with it inefficiency, indifference, and red tape.

The organization of public bureaucracies is closely related to the type of political regime and the configuration of societal interests found within each country. It may be highly developed or weakly organized. It may be the dominant structure in the country, or it may be controlled by political parties and their leaders.

The growth of bureaucratic influence in democracies, and especially the uses made of bureaucratic authority, are the focus of this chapter. In authoritarian systems, bureaucracy may be the *raison d'être* of the whole country. Communist countries and military dictatorships epitomize bureaucracy in the complete sense of the word. We examine how these regimes come into being by legitimate or illegitimate means and how they organize their societies and public services. In order to understand fully the nature of bureaucratic power in both the democratic and authoritarian parts of the world, the chapter also examines how bureaucratic processes and instruments have similar characteristics wherever they are found.

THE GROWTH OF BUREAUCRACY

In the last chapter we examined the structure and expansion of government administration. We have seen that bureaucratic growth seems inevitable. But why has public administration—the size of budgets and number of government employees—grown so extensively? Why has this form of organization become predominant in the contemporary world? Can it continue to grow?

Obviously there is no single answer, no consensus, about this significant question. However, B. Guy Peters has summarized the contending arguments to explain this trend toward a larger and more pervasive public bureaucracy.[1] They can be summarized as follows:

1. Citizens have come to expect "entitlements." That is, during good economic times governments extend programs to the public in order to obtain votes. After the buoyant economic period evaporates, politicians are afraid to rescind the programs for fear of retribution from the voters. Thus, a sense of "entitlement" grows in the population, which in turn leads to growth in the public bureaucracy.

2. It is argued that the nature of public sector economics itself leads to an increase in government activities and size. This argument has many forms, but essentially it is based on the contention that an economic law determines that as the economy of a state grows a larger and larger proportion of it will be automatically devoted to the public sector.

3. Government grows because the people demand more and more from their governments. This argument is based on the contention that interest groups have become more powerful and pervasive and that political parties have not been able to prevent these groups from putting pressure on the government to increase payments or services to the public.

4. Lastly, the behaviour of the bureaucracy itself may be a cause of growth in government expenditures. It is argued that civil servants' careers are based on being budget maximizers. That is, they get ahead in their careers by attempting to have bigger budgets and staffs than their competitors. There is evidence both for and against this assertion.[2]

In the final analysis, it may be that no single factor can account for the growth of government. Very likely these four factors, and possibly others, interact to produce the size of government.[3] One might also add that there has been an increase in the number of problems that are difficult to resolve in an interdependent world.

Regardless of the answer to these questions, however, there is no doubt that the basic pattern of growth in the size and costs of public bureaucracies has produced harsh questions for policy-makers and students to contemplate. What are the limits to the size of the state? Can modern governments become so overloaded with responsibilities that they go bankrupt?[4] Will the current neoconservative attack on big government lead to a reduction in the overall size of public bureaucracies? See Close Up 15.1.

RECRUITMENT PATTERNS AND POLITICAL CONTROL IN DEMOCRATIC STATES

The development of a neutral and professional public service emerged alongside, and partly as a consequence of, liberal democracy. A theoretical distinction grew between tran-

CLOSE UP 15.1   Downsizing the Public Service: The Canadian Case

In the 1990s, federal public service jobs were the target of severe cuts in many developed democracies, including Canada. Faced with large deficits and debts, governments turned on the public service and made massive expenditure cuts in order to trim public spending.

In 1986, Canada employed 242 294 federal public servants, not including Crown Corporations or uniformed personnel in the military or the RCMP. By the end of 1995 that number was reduced to 210 517, as projected cuts of 45 000 jobs were put in place. The 1996 budget phased out another 6000 jobs. As well, more government operations were privatized, sending work out of departments to private corporate structures. As part of this arrangement, government job security changed—Canadians in the federal public service have had to choose between being more flexible (even if that means accepting a decline in salaries, benefits, and working conditions) or being laid off.

By these reductions in the size of the public service, cutting other government expenditures, and a growth in the GDP, the government was finally able to reduce the deficit to zero in 1998. Neveretheless, in 1999 the national debt remains at $583 billion, or 71% of the GDP.

sient politicians who come and go on the winds of electoral change and the permanent administrators whose role, in theory, is to carry out the goals and purposes of their political masters.

In the modern state, however, this theoretical dichotomy between "politics" and "administration" is not clear. First, the vastly expanded scope and complexity of contemporary public policy has rendered politicians increasingly dependent upon permanent administrators for information and advice on the formulation, as well as the execution, of government policy. Second, legislators have delegated to the bureaucracy substantial decision-making autonomy in many areas of technical policy-making, such as regulation and administrative procedure. Fears are frequently expressed about an increasingly "political" role of the bureaucracy and especially its recruitment.

The variations in bureaucratic recruitment in democratic and authoritarian countries are not as great as propagandists maintain. There are two points here. First, the social background characteristics of senior bureaucrats are fairly similar throughout the world. Whether they are selected by objective criteria or appointed by government elites, the composition of civil services tends to be similar to the higher social and educational elites of their societies. There are distinctions, of course. British recruiters tend to select generalists who can manage a variety of different functions. Recruitment from the elite universities such as Oxford and Cambridge reinforces this philosophy of administration. The French, German, and to some extent the American administrations tend to hire more people with particular expertise, especially in economics and technology. In authoritarian states, employees are hired and fired because of their commitment to the reigning ideology, party, or leader. Even the police and military are required to work for the goals of the authoritarian leaders. Second, in all states there is a combination of merit appointments and selections made by non-achievement criteria. In other words, there is degree of political control and even manipulation of the selection and composition of the bureaucratic elite even in the most progressive democracies.

The degree of difference is significant, however. In Western liberal democracies, the bureaucracies themselves have obtained the authority to recruit members to their ranks and to train and promote them according to their standards and without reference to party membership, ideology, or commitment to a particular leadership group. This means that non-merit appointments may take place, but when they do, they have the potential to exist in an atmosphere of patronage and corruption. Even if the rules are sometimes broken, objective tests and educational achievement are considered the proper criteria for appointments.

The problem with purely competitive and merit criteria is that the civil service may be insulated from political change. If civil servants are totally secure in their positions, what will make them conform to the direction and control of their masters, the democratically elected politicians?

Among liberal democratic states the degree of political control over the higher bureaucracy is most pronounced in the United States, but it also exists in Germany and France, and to a lesser degree in Canada and Britain.[5] In all of these latter countries recruitment to the upper echelons of the bureaucracy is based on open competition, but politics may still play some role in the selection of the most senior administrators.

In all Western liberal countries recently there appears to be a growth in explicit political appointments to the upper echelon of the bureaucracy. Historically, the United States has been the most developed in this regard. A large number of top administrators change each time the government changes hands. While a core of senior and permanent civil servants remains in place, the major advisors to the new administration come in with each new President. The "spoils system" in which the winners of each election claim the "spoils" of their enemy is well developed in Washington. Incoming American Presidents appoint over 2000 senior bureaucrats to replace those of his or her predecessor, and the President may even control over 20 000 positions in the federal administration as a whole if he or she so chooses. These American political replacements are at the very top of the bureaucracy: Secretaries, deputy under-Secretaries, assistant Secretaries, and bureaucrats whose positions in other countries are usually reserved for career public servants.[6]

In France, Germany, and Japan there are also links between the party that controls government and administrative appointments. In France and Germany, for example, there has been a tendency to place civil servants who have the appropriate sympathies into politically sensitive senior positions. In Germany, political leaders have considerable control over senior appointments in their own departments.[7] In France, the fusion of political and bureaucratic worlds is best exemplified by the system of *cabinets ministeriels* in which each minister has the right to appoint his or her own immediate staff. These posts are extremely powerful in policy elaboration, and the members owe their positions solely to the ministers. The point is, such ministerial personal staffs come essentially from the regular civil service: 80% in the pre-1980 governments and 70% in the post-1981 socialist governments.[8]

In Japan, the bureaucracy is extremely powerful.[9] Even those scholars who deny its sole superiority in policy-making maintain that for years it was part of a "ruling triad," consisting of business, the Liberal Democratic Party (LDP), and the bureaucracy, which dominated policy-making in the country. The Japanese Liberal Democratic Party held power alone from 1955 to 1993. During that time the bureaucracy institutionalized its relations with the LDP. After more than 38 years of working together, the bureaucracy and the party developed smooth working relations. Bureaucrats even went to party headquarters to work out party policy with members of the party apparatus. In other words, the fusion between the two administrations was considerable, and civil servants were well aware that their careers were linked to good relations with the LDP. Because of the reduction of LDP power in the late 1990s, the bureaucracy has had to extend its help to other parties, particularly the socialists, in order to retain a grip on political power in Japan.

In Canada and Britain there is a slower, but nevertheless consistent, trend toward politicizing the higher bureaucracy. In Canada the ministers' political staff—called **exempt** because they are exempt from public service, routine entry requirements—has a high priority for entry into the regular public service after they have served three years with a minister. Moreover, the Prime Minister and his or her cabinet control a few thousand other appointments throughout the bureaucracy. Even in the United Kingdom the strict separation of political and bureaucratic worlds is in transition. Traditionally political leaders have had almost no ability to select the civil servants who were to report to them. But today, senior political appointments are regularly made to the ministers' staff and to the Prime Minister's office. The practice is criticized but it continues to grow. Prime Minister Margaret Thatcher was active in the appointment of new permanent Secretaries during her period in office, and Tony Blair has further "politicized" parts of the bureaucracy.[10]

ADMINISTRATIVE RECRUITMENT AND POLITICAL CONTROL IN AUTHORITARIAN STATES

Authoritarian systems tend to be highly centralized and hierarchically organized. Political leaders want direct and immediate control of the bureaucracy so that they can use it for ideological purposes. Moreover, in authoritarian states, more than in democratic countries, overt political control over the appointment, training, and promotion functions of the bureaucracy is well developed and accepted as normal. Leaders of authoritarian states use basically non-achievement criteria in decisions about who to hire and fire. In effect, in such countries, politicians attempt to subvert administration to politics. In dynasties, military dictatorships, one-party states, communist regimes, and theocracies, there may not be much difference between where administration ends and party or other dictatorial institutions begin.

Some countries have tried and failed to institute actual totalitarian controls, while others continue to attempt this goal. For an understanding of the first category, we shall examine the former Soviet Union, its evolution and demise. We shall then look more closely at the LDCs (less developed countries), especially contemporary China to witness a country that is still attempting to impose total political control while adapting to a market economy.

Communist Bureaucracy

The power of the bureaucracy in communist states tends to be greater than that found in democracies. In addition to the usual functions of the civil service, it also runs all the major business enterprises and planning commissions. Given weak representative institutions, the bureaucracies and military in authoritarian states may be the primary decision-making bodies in the country. In fact, they form the core of authoritarian political systems as other structures, such as parties and legislatures, may be banned altogether.

The transition in communist regimes during the late 1980s is nowhere more evident than in the changing nature of their administrations. The pure model of authoritarian, communist government depicted a hierarchical arrangement of power from the all-powerful leader of the party down to the lowliest citizen. Of course, the real world was much less organized than this model implies. Even in disciplined communist countries political leaders have difficulty controlling the *apparat* or public service, and the *apparat* itself proved incapable of controlling all other relations within society. But let us examine the relations between theory and practice.

After the Russian Revolution of 1917, the Soviet bureaucracy was hailed as the most powerful institution in the country outside of the Communist Party itself. In fact, the two were interwoven to such a degree that it was practically impossible to separate them. One thing is certain: Karl Marx's contention that the state would "wither away" after communist control proved to be singularly incorrect in the Soviet Union. Until the final reforms under Gorbachev in the late 1980s, the Soviet bureaucracy was gigantic. It included millions of ordinary bureaucrats carrying out their multifarious functions, along with the coercive state institutions such as the KGB and the largest military machine in Europe. The Communist Party and the bureaucracy coexisted from local village level through to collective farms, industrial enterprises, and the state and federal bureaucracies.

A dual system of party and *apparatchiks* existed at every level. Historically, the Communist Party controlled this vast machine by use of *nomenklatura, samokritika,* and a coercive system of secret police, regular police, and military which, in its worst characterizations, was called "the terror."

Nomenklatura

Until the democratic reforms of the 1990s, the Central Committee of the Communist Party played the major role of appointing, promoting, and dismissing influential members of the *apparat* or state bureaucracy. Public servants were not appointed by competitive examination. Rather, the party bureaucracy determined the competence and reliability of all would-be functionaries.

The word **nomenklatura** is used by scholars to depict this party control over the selection of senior members of the civil service. This word refers both to the list of all significant party-controlled positions and to the persons deemed suitable to fill them. It is also sometimes used to refer to the composition of the Soviet elite.

Nomenklatura thus refers to a *mechanism* for recruitment into the elite and the sociopolitical *category* of those selected. T.H. Rigby, an Australian political scientist, summarized the importance of *nomenklatura* as "far from being a mere administrative device: it is [was] a basic factor in the distribution and exercise of power and privilege in Soviet Society."[11]

The *nomenklatura* appointments to the bureaucracy were made by the relevant party committee and could not be made without the party's permission. In practical terms this meant that the leader of the party had supreme control. "*Nomenklatura* became a powerful weapon in the hands of those who controlled it, giving them the capacity to make or break careers, to forge alliances and patronage networks, and to discard rivals and challengers to their authority by assigning them to obscure positions, while simultaneously creating all the formal appearances of due process."[12]

Samokritika and Terror

Another tool of administrative control in the former communist Soviet Union was **samokritika**. This concept meant that Soviet citizens were actively encouraged to engage in criticism of individuals, especially officials, and of institutions. While citizens were not free to attack the Communist Party or its leaders, they were asked to point out errors in the behaviour or inefficiencies of farm or factory managers. This information was then used as a controlling device by the party—by firing individuals or by adjusting administrative practices.

During Stalin's tenure, from the late 1920s to his death in 1953, **terror** was also used extensively to keep the authoritarian system in control. The NKVD, or Soviet Secret Police Organization, struck fear into the hearts of all citizens, who feared that they might be arrested, imprisoned, murdered, or sent into exile in Siberia. During the massive efforts to force collectivization on the country, Stalin's orders were responsible for purges and the deaths of up to 20 million people. After the demise of Stalin, the steady erosion in state coercion meant that the terror as such no longer existed, but fear remained one of the major methods for controlling Soviet citizens.

After Stalin's reign, the KGB replaced the NKVD. Its vast organization spread widely and massively throughout the bureaucracy and the Communist Party itself. Until 1991 it remained a political police whose responsibility was the maintenance of the state institutions, and in particular ensuring the political reliability of the military. Since the downfall of communism, the KGB has had a name change—to the Russian Federal Security Service—but many of its functions remain intact. Close Up 15.2 focuses on recent changes in policing in Eastern Europe.

CLOSE UP 15.2   Police in Eastern Europe Today

Following the revolutions in 1989 that brought them democracy, East European countries inherited the regular police and secret police forces that communist structures had put in place more than 40 years earlier. The secret police in particular were widely discredited for having abused their power and for working against their own people.

Significant efforts were needed to reform and democratize internal security forces. To get rid of the corruption and the old communist link in the police, massive reorganization was initiated. Some new departments were created, others were disbanded; purges were undertaken on officials at different levels and new officials were brought in at the top. Police organizations were decentralized and new laws were passed restricting their activities and making them more accountable to their elected assemblies.

However, democratizing the police and the secret police has been difficult. The internal security organizations proved to be very resilient. The secret police force was especially tightly organized and had access to arms. As well, its "degree of fanaticism ... far surpasses that in the party and military."[13]

Many positive changes were made, but other reforms ran into difficulties. It was difficult, for example, to decide how to quickly train new experts to replace those who should be dismissed. It was also difficult for democratic leaders to change the mentality of those who had been faithful servants of the previous communist regimes. Where would they find the money for reforms? In general, the police were left with obsolete equipment and smaller budgets. Yet the police and the secret police are all that the citizens have to protect them against criminals and to safeguard their new democracies. A conundrum indeed!

Perestroika

The political reforms of the 1980s and 1990s in the Soviet Union had a remarkable impact on the older traditions of recruitment, composition and terror.[14] While President Gorbachev never referred to *nomenklatura* specifically, he made vicious attacks on the civil servants appointed through this system.[15] He attacked both the recruitment process and the elite itself. His **perestroika**, or restructuring, was aimed at reforming the very bureaucracy that had been put in place by the older system.

Gorbachev attempted to replace the old system by proposing a greater role for the masses in reform of the system. Instead of replacing the *nomenklatura* system, he proposed supplementing it whenever *elected* officials were to be chosen. The June 1987 local elections introduced a modest reform covering only 5% of the seats. Even this small step began to undermine local officials and the *nomenklatura* system.[16] By 1990, there were further successes in dismantling the system in cities, regions, and states of the Soviet Union. Even within the party itself elections had undermined the *nomenklatura* lists by late 1991 when the Soviet Union disintegrated.

Shifting power from the bureaucracy to the people weakened official control over appointments. As the *nomenklatura* system was replaced by elections and a merit-based selection system, the power of the elite to manipulate future members of its class was reduced. In Russia today, the abandonment of *nomenklatura* as the system of elite recruitment, and a sharp reduction in the privileges that have accrued in the past, may eventually lead to the crystallizing of a political elite comparable with those of Western societies."

ADMINISTRATIVE RECRUITMENT AND POLITICAL CONTROL IN LDCs

The strength of the bureaucracy in the LDCs varies enormously. A very few countries have a competent and honest public administration, but many are extremely weak, characterized by inefficiency and corruption. Some countries, such as India and Pakistan, retain relatively effective administrations from their colonial periods. Others, such as some monarchies, staff the top of the bureaucracy with members of the ruling family and their relatives. Others inherited weak civil services or managed to create them on their own. While the former Soviet Union was evolving somewhat toward a Westernized system of administration before it collapsed, this was not true of much of the rest of the authoritarian world. Especially in some LDCs, where older style colonial administrations were cast off and replaced by purely indigenous structures, there has been a tendency in the opposite direction. Many of these states continue to employ partisan control over the public service for personal purposes.

Public administration in many LDCs is haunted by long-term scarcity, often compounded by poverty and famine. Administrators know that no matter what strategy they employ there will often not be enough resources to feed, clothe, and educate the population let alone to develop the infrastructures and capital required for competition in the modern world. Moreover, in many countries the values and administrative practices of modern administration have not been developed.

In an effort to promote national unity in the face of extreme economic difficulties, many developing countries—especially those with military and one-party systems—have disregarded or never put into place competitive and open examinations for recruitment to the public service. These states prefer a civil service committed to the political leadership rather than one based on achievement criteria.

Central to many of these regimes are ties of kinship or other hierarchical sets of relationships sometimes called "patron-client." These relationships are characterized by a superordinate-subordinate relationship in which relatives or those with higher status provide those with lower status protection, goods, and services in return for loyalty, obedience, and other services such as voting according to instructions during election campaigns.[17] This network of patron-client relationships may be based on economic materialism, but it is also usually linked to kinship lines, sectarian networks, or tribal relations. When modern bureaucratic practices are superimposed on such cultures, distortions occur. Officials from each group or kinship line regard themselves as representatives from that association, and therefore use their office to enhance the well-being of their own people. Subversion of the rules becomes standard as bureaucrats are forced to choose between the principles of rational bureaucracy and the cultural exigencies of their patron-client relationships.

Such distortions occur in economically developed democratic and authoritarian countries, but tribal, kinship, sectarian, and religious bonds remain much stronger in the LDCs. In these countries, the personal rules are simply more important than the impersonal "Weberian" rules of modern bureaucracy. Relatives and patrons are simply expected to find employment and promotion for their friends. Public-office holding is thus a means of legitimately enriching both oneself and one's friends. Westerners are likely to describe these distortions in pejorative terms such as bribery, nepotism, and corruption.

In view of their harsh economic and political realities, post-colonial leaders often attempt to find special ways of building up loyalty to the new regime. One such tactic uses restrictive recruitment rules for entry into the public service. Applicants are selected on the basis of their partisanship or close relations to the leaders of the state. The selection therefore takes place on tribal or ethnic lines rather than competitive examinations. B. Guy Peters quotes Kwame Nkrumah, Ghana's first post-independence leader, as saying:

> It is our intention to tighten up the regulations and to wipe out the disloyal elements of the civil service, even if by so doing we suffer some temporary dislocation of the service. For disloyal civil servants are no better than saboteurs.[18]

There are countries in the non-Western world where these practices are not adopted. While they are especially widespread in Africa,[19] the bureaucracy remains more powerful and less under the tutelage of political parties in South Asia, for example. In India and Pakistan colonial administrations remained in place after independence, and to a large extent continue to thwart some politicians' desires for radical changes in the form of administration.

Many problems of bureaucracy in the LDCs are caused by relatively limited experience with modern administration. With the exception of Latin America, most state institutions in the South were established as copies or hybrids of those of their former colonial masters. This means that many of the regimes were built with little or no relation between their cultures and their state institutions. Only minimal acceptance of the legitimacy of the regime and its system of bureaucratization developed. In other words, the values and political structures were never congruent; rather, a personalistic or patron-client culture remained as a strong competitor to the weaker, modern bureaucratic form. This situation produced high degrees of political instability, military intervention, and revolution in much of Africa and Asia.

Bureaucracy and Ideology: The Case of China

Several developing countries have adopted a Communist party system or socialist model of development in order to escape from the practices of their colonial past. They put the public service in charge of initiating, planning, directing, and implementing developmental programs and projects, sometimes despite the objections of some groups within society. In other words, instead of accepting the incongruence between societal attitudes and state institutions based on Western democratic ideas, they adopted the government or state as their main instrument of change.

The leaders of such countries usually believe they must maintain a strongly partisan civil service to implement their goals and objectives. One of the most effective means of carrying out this task is to infuse the civil service with a strong dose of utopian ideology. Using ideology to control the bureaucracy can be illustrated by the case of China.

For two millennia before the 1949 Communist Revolution, the Chinese bureaucracy had developed one of the most complex and extensive administrations in the world. Before 200 B.C. the Qin dynasty created an empire out of feuding kingdoms. Like the dynasties that followed, it centralized authoritarian rule to build roads, canals, and even the Great Wall. Its centralized empire employed objective, competitive examinations for entry into the administration. It recruited a professional bureaucracy from a distinct and highly trained administrative group, the Mandarin class, which adhered to the Confucian principles of authority and hierarchy. A gentry class under the Mandarins acted as a link between it and the vast and poor peasant class.

After the fall of the last imperial dynasty in 1912, a tumultuous period ensued. The Nationalists under Chiang Kai-shek (now called Jiang Jieshi) almost captured the entire Communist Party, but, led by Mao Tse-tung, the party members escaped in the famous Long March of 1934–35. It was this gruelling, long trek that developed the discipline and the leadership that continues today in the Chinese Communist Party.

After their victory over the nationalists, the communists tried to reform the traditional bureaucracy by adopting a highly centralized Soviet model of government. Mao Tse-tung did not trust the old bureaucracy to carry out the goals of the new communist regime. During his tenure from 1949 to 1976, however, Mao had to shift his policy. In the early stages he attempted to put in place the Russian system of dual party and state bureaucratic organization. But at the same time he sought to weaken central administration and replace it with local structures and control. This contradiction between reliance on centralized bureaucrats and belief in the people's control soon led to major difficulties. When it was obvious the experiment had failed, he instigated the proletarian Cultural Revolution, 1966–68. During this period all authority figures were attacked except military officials. Bureaucrats as well as teachers, intellectuals, artists, and others were publicly humiliated and dismissed from their jobs.

In effect, Mao was trying to replace bureaucratic norms with revolutionary ideology. He failed. In 1976, just before Mao died at the age of 82, Deng Ziaoping took over. He and the army leaders allowed the country to revert to older systems of bureaucratic control and recruitment. Communist ideology continued to be used to guide administrative actions, either directly through party control or indirectly through ideological self-criticism, but it was no longer used to criticize the bureaucracy. Maoism—the ideas of Mao—began to be used selectively, rather than as dogma.

In the 1980s China underwent massive changes, especially in the rural areas. Collectivized agriculture was to some extent replaced with a new "responsibility" system, or what we would call private enterprise. Today, farmers can sell their excess produce on the free market. Small entrepreneurs are allowed to operate in the cities. Private property is still generally not permitted, but industries have been decentralized and can compete with each other in an attempt to make a profit.

In short, China at the beginning of the new millennium is attempting to gain the advantages of bureaucratic organization while retaining some of the ideals of communism. Many scholars doubt that this hybrid system will work over time but Chinese authorities point with pride to the fact that the economy improved tremendously in the 1980s and 1990s. The Chinese continue to consider their country as a member of the developing world, but the life expectancy of Chinese people (67 years) is the highest of the developing world, and its literacy rate (69%) is excellent compared to the poorer parts of the world. The birth of ten million new babies every year, however, makes any prediction about improvement in standard living subject to qualification.[20] The population is rising even as birth rates decline. As the most populous country in the world, China's rise in economic and military power makes this country a central focus of American and Asian foreign policy at the beginning of the new century.

There has been less progress in the political sphere. Attempts at democratization have failed. The massacre of young dissidents at Tiananmen Square in June 1989 ended for some time any hope that the army and communist bureaucracy would be overthrown, or even liberalized in the near future. The leadership of Jiang Zemin, General Secretary of the Communist Party, Chairman of the Military Committee, and President was confirmed with the death of Deng Ziaoping in 1997.

MILITARY BUREAUCRACIES AND COUPS D'ÉTAT

A military government is a special type of highly bureaucratized state. When the armed forces take over a state, they institute hierarchical forms of decision-making and, in alliance with civil service technocrats, attempt to form an administrative state. The various forms and degrees of military control have been discussed in Chapter 14, but the reader should bear in mind that the degree of military involvement varies from supporting a civilian government to direct and total military control. On occasion the army is the backbone behind long-lasting governments such as the monarchy in Morocco.

Military government has been widespread throughout history and around the globe, albeit unevenly distributed geographically. Most of these governments come to office by means of *coups d'état*. The word comes from the French *coup d'état* which means a strike or blow to the state. **Coups d'état** are sudden changes of government leadership through irregular military action. They are launched by the military because they have organizational power, symbolic status, and a near-monopoly on heavy arms (or at least did have until the rise of modern terrorist groups).

Military attempts to take over the organs of government are very common. In fact, in some recent periods more governments changed hands by military takeovers than by elections. In some geographical areas coups become normal, routine ways of changing government. Failed coups, however, outnumber those that are successful.

Some geographical areas are more likely to experience military governments than others. Armed forces interventions tend to occur where governments and democracies are not accorded a high degree of legitimacy.[21] This means that they are found mainly in Africa, Latin America, the Middle East, and to some extent in Asia when civilian governments are considered weak or corrupt. Many of these coups are based on the personal interests of their leaders or their ethnic or tribal groups. Close Up 15.3 summarizes the 1996 Coup in Niger.

In Western Europe, only Greece and Portugal have experienced successful coups since World War II, and in both cases the military went back to the barracks within a short time. Turkey provides a contrast. It has had three coups since World War II. One of these was a famous "coup by memorandum" in which the military merely wrote to the civilian government and asked it to resign. The government complied. Here, as well, civilians were brought back to run the government after only a short period of military control. There have been no military coups in communist countries.

In some countries a kind of "coup culture" exists in which military takeovers are practically institutionalized as a form of governmental change. A vicious cycle of coup after coup occurs. Some countries are particularly prone to military governments. Until

CLOSE UP 15.3 The 1996 Coup in Niger

In January 1996 the military conducted a coup in Niger, ending a brief three-year attempt at democracy. The military placed President Mahamane Ousmne and his Prime Minister under house arrest, outlawed political parties, and suspended the constitution. Colonel Barre Mainassara Ibrahim declared himself head of state, declaring he had done so to save Niger from chaos. He called politicians "greedy, badly prepared, and incapable of adapting to the demands of democratic power," and said it was his "patriotic duty" to stage the coup.

After the coup Colonel Mainassara claimed he did not intend to remain in power long, but as of early 1999 he was still in charge, despite protests and plots against his regime. Niger is one of the world's poorest countries. It is located on the southern edge of the Sahara in western Africa.[22] The GDP per capita is one of the lowest in the world at about $290 (U.S.). Since November 1993 there were also military coups in the neighbouring countries of Gambia and Sierra Leone. As of early 1999 Gambia remains under army control while Sierra Leone is at war.

the 1980s Bolivia, for example, had an average of more than one military takeover a year after becoming a state over 160 years earlier. Syria had more than a dozen coups or attempted coups between World War II and 1973. Coups were endemic to Latin America until well into the 1980s. One Latin American army manual used to describe the presidency of the country as the highest post to which a military officer could aspire.

Explanations and Consequences of Military Governments

The military may intervene directly in the political affairs of a country because of what it perceives as problems in government, or for its own selfish, corporate reasons.[23] In the first case, for example, the military may lose faith in the government's ability to carry out its basic functions such as avoiding economic stagnation, reducing unemployment, reducing inflation, or maintaining order in society. In the second case, it may intervene to maintain the level of the military's budget, prevent its functions from being taken over by another agency, or sometimes to obtain salary raises for army, navy, and air force personnel. Of course, personal ambitions and fears may also play a large part in coups, especially in countries where it has become a standard means of changing rulers, or in those with cyclical patterns of military intervention and then disengagement (coup → civilian government → coup).

When do coups occur? One answer is that they take place when a combination of macro-level factors such as weak economies, high levels of poverty, hunger, unemployment, and underprivilege, and especially fierce competition over land, are present. There is also some evidence that they cluster at certain times and in certain places. There is statistical evidence, for example, that they occur in "broad regional processes." If one country has a coup then its neighbours are more likely to experience one too. This may be explained as "coup contagion" or may be the result of similar socioeconomic processes taking place in the same region at the same time.[24]

Several national characteristics make a successful coup much easier to carry off in some countries than others. "Good" coup countries usually include three characteristics. First, the social and economic conditions of the state confine political participation to only a small fraction of the population. When the bureaucracy issues orders they are either obeyed or evaded; they are never challenged. Second, coup-prone countries must be independent in practice as well as in principle. When foreign troops interfere, they usually attempt to prevent a coup, as they did, for example, in 1964 in Gabon. Thirdly, "good" coup countries should have a well-defined political-economic centre; in other words, a unitary country is more easily controlled. Federal countries are more difficult for the military to take over because constitutional and economic powers tend to be dispersed bureaucratically and geographically. Canada and the United States are therefore difficult coup countries while Portugal and Greece are easier because of the concentration of political and economic control in the capitals, Lisbon and Athens. But it is also true that advanced technology in communications is making it easier to control large tracts of land and dispersed peoples.

The most difficult part of a coup is the dangerous process by which nonparticipating parts of the armed forces are either neutralized or led to join the pro-coup rebels. The troops must be properly positioned to carry this out. In November 1965, a coup failed in Indonesia because the communist troops were in the Borneo jungles and not in Jakarta where they were required.[25] In fast-moving circumstances even seemingly insignificant factors may nullify a coup attempt. In June 1955, an anti-Peron coup in Argentina was prevented because of extensive fog.

In the aftermath of a coup, the leaders must dispose of anti-coup forces and stabilize the lower bureaucracy. Senior civil servants will be afraid to interfere because of the dangers involved in isolated action. The most important event may be the pacification of the masses. The new government will send out a communiqué condemning the old leaders for capricious handling of economic and political affairs, and this will be accompanied with promises of better things to come. Propaganda will be rampant. In 1957, Gamal Abdul Nasser trucked peasants from the Nile Delta to demonstrate in his favour through the streets of Cairo. He then publicized the event on the state broadcasting system.[26]

In the short run after a coup, there is one vital issue: will human rights be abused? The answer is fairly clear, as most military regimes have a poor record on human rights. Massive murder, torture, and imprisonment, to name only a few examples of abuses, resulted from the military control of General Jean Bokassa in the Central African Republic, Idi Amin in Uganda, and, closer to home, by officers in Argentina, Chile, and Uruguay in the 1970s. However, while the deaths that follow a coup are always to be condemned, the most important long-run question is whether or not one coup will simply be followed by another. The likelihood is great that it will be. As a former Prime Minister of Iraq said after his 1968 coup: "I came in on a tank and only a tank will evict me."

The political and policy positions of military governments have been studied from several different angles. On the whole, the military avoids commitment to parties and ideologies. In some cases it rules alone without any political party to hinder its actions. It makes alliances with technocratic elements in the civil service and often eschews politics altogether. Its officers prefer to be "above" politics and their "term of office" is usually quite short. As the military has no process, such as elections, for legitimizing its actions, it cannot maintain support from the people for long periods. Some scholars have estimated the average life span of a military government is only about five years.[27]

When the military associates itself with a political party or movement, it may be either left- or right-wing. In Africa the alliance is often on the left, espousing modernization and development, whereas in Latin America it has been more often associated with the right and conservative forces.[28] Ethnic and regional rivalries also play major roles in coups, especially in Africa. Nigerian coups, for example, always emerge from the rivalries among the Hausa, Fulani, Yoruba, and Ibo ethnic groups. Statistical data, however, affirms that there is little direct new policy direction from military takeovers. Economic growth rates, for example, are usually neither higher nor lower after military interventions.

The world is replete with coups, but there are some relatively poor countries that have never experienced even one. Colombia, Costa Rica, Kenya, Mexico, India, Tanzania, Tunisia, and Venezuela have not had a single successful coup. But, on the whole, governments and bureaucracies in LDCs face extreme challenges in governing without military intervention. It is one of the most persistent problems in the developing world.

BUREAUCRATIC INSTRUMENTS AND THE POLICY PROCESS

The process of public policy-making is not restricted to proposing general objectives such as capitalism or socialism. It also concerns the means by which such ends can be achieved. Political scientists employ the term **governing instruments** to depict the methods used by governments to achieve their goals and policies. The range of instruments varies greatly from one type of state to another and even within countries.

The instruments may be portrayed on a continuum similar to that for democracy and authoritarianism. At one extreme, the state has very little influence on the day-to-day lives of the citizens, while at the other extreme a highly regulated system of authority is present. Within democratic systems the degree of "legitimate" coercion may be the indicator chosen for placing the various types of instruments on a policy dimension. A world sample would not provide such a simple distinction, however. Presumably the amount of coercion used—whether legitimate or not—should be employed for a proper comparison.

The least coercive instrument used by bureaucracies is **exhortation** or symbolic output. This type of bureaucratic behaviour comprises government efforts to induce individuals to comply voluntarily with some objectives. Sometimes known as "suasion," these government actions do not force citizens to comply but merely ask them to do so for the good of the polity.

Such means include symbolic outputs in the form of platitudes or slogans—"We ought to do more for the environment" or "The underprivileged should be compensated." Such statements make governments *appear* to be doing something, but citizens are not harmed by the government's action, and thus it cannot be said to be coercive. However, whether the policies come in the form of government statements, resolutions, or other similar outputs, they are not very effective and often are simply a means of delaying government action. If governments really want to act decisively they spend funds, regulate, legislate, or take over parts of society and the economy.

Another weak, though controversial, coercive method is public expenditure. **Expenditure instruments** comprise such government actions as spending funds on individuals in the form of pensions, child care allowances, unemployment insurance, and so forth. These transfer payments may allow a government to redistribute income to needy citizens. Or, a government may decide to provide the funds directly to companies. These expenditure instruments come in forms such as subsidies, grants, loans, and guarantees.

Another form of expenditure instrument is **tax expenditure**. This type of policy consists of taxes that could be collected by revenue collection agencies, but are not. Tax expenditures provide tax deductions or tax credits to individuals or corporations. They are less visible than other public policies and often receive less criticism than actual expenditures. They may be used to encourage personal or corporate spending on particular social purposes such as pensions, medical care, and child care.

Further up the coercion ladder is the government's use of **regulation** to control behaviour. In the widest sense, regulations comprise all the rules of conduct imposed by government on its individual and corporate citizens. They encompass the civil and criminal laws of a country, the taxation system, and all rules imposed by government agencies. In other words, regulations consist of the rules of the state backed by the legitimate use of state force.[29]

Regulations are used for at least three purposes: to remedy market failures, to serve as instruments of redistribution, and to meet social and cultural goals. In recent years there has been a widespread belief that liberal democracies and communist systems are too heavily regulated. Such beliefs have led to a desire to **deregulate**—that is, reduce the constraints on citizens.

Even in liberal democracies citizens have become more concerned that the bureaucracy over-regulates their lives. Efforts to privatize government functions and deregulate the lives of citizens are tied to a widespread desire to get people out from under the tutelage of bureaucracy.

A fourth level of coercion requires the government to buy or take over enterprises held in the private sector. Of course, such government action is an infringement of the free market. **Public ownership** is particulary abhored by conservatives who view government control of the private sector with distaste.

Arguments about the desirable extent of public enterprise form much of the debate between socialists and conservatives. For socialists, direct intervention in the free market is necessary to create a more egalitarian society, while for conservatives it is a policy that distorts the market and therefore reduces everyone's standard of living.

These four levels of bureaucratic decision-making are basically valid for routine policy-making. In non-routine "crisis" situations such as disasters or riots, the government may have to jump several rungs up this ladder from its symbolic or rhetorical position—over-regulation and pubic ownership—to the most highly coercive forces of police and military. After the crisis has subsided, policy-makers may return to other less coercive forms of policy in order to try to preempt further crises.[30]

When this final policy instrument is used, the political system hovers on the line between democracy and authoritarianism. If the police and military continue to be used, not just for specific crisis events but continually and pervasively, then a democratic state may change into an authoritarian one. If the military assumes power or turns the reins of government over to communists, a single party, a group of religious leaders, or a particular family, an authoritarian regime will have been created.

DISCUSSION QUESTIONS

1. Why do governments always appear to grow in terms of personnel and cost? Is it true?
2. How do communist leaders control their bureaucrats?
3. Are bureaucracies more corrupt in developing countries than in richer states? In communist countries as opposed to democratic ones?
4. What is the role of the military in a *coup d'état*? The public service?
5. Are the military and police under democratic control in your country?

KEY TERMS

coup d'état, p. 330
deregulate, p. 335
exempt staff, p. 323
exhortation, p. 334
expenditure instruments, p. 334

governing instruments, p. 334
nomenklatura, p. 325
perestroika, p. 326
public ownership, p. 335
regulation, p. 335

samokritika, p. 325
tax expenditure, p. 335
terror, p. 325

ENDNOTES

1. B. Guy Peters, *Public Bureaucracy in Comparative Perspective* (Tuscaloosa: University of Alabama Press, 1988), pp. 200 ff. Peters also posits that government grows in the late stages of capitalism, but then dismisses the argument as obviously based on Marxist principles, which he does not accept.
2. For a strong argument in favour of this assertion, see William A. Niskanen, *Bureaucracy and Representative Government* (Chicago: Aldine-Atherton, 1971).
3. See Charles Goodsell, *The Case for Bureaucracy*, 2nd ed. (Chatham, N.J.: Chatham House, 1985).
4. Richard Rose and B. Guy Peters, *Can Government Go Bankrupt?* (New York: Basic Books, 1978).
5. Some cross-national data for liberal democracies is provided in an excellent book by Joel D. Aberbach, Robert D. Putman, and Bert A. Rockman, *Bureaucrats and Politicians in Western Democracies* (Cambridge, Mass.: Harvard University Press, 1981).
6. For a fine overall summary, see Nicholas Henry, *Public Administration and Public Affairs*, 5th ed. (Englewood Cliffs, N.J.: Prentice Hall, 1992).
7. Hans-Ulrich Derlien, "Repercussions of Government Change on the Career Civil Service in Western Germany: The Cases of 1969 and 1982," *Governance*, vol. 1 (1988), pp. 50–78.
8. John Gaffney, "The Political Think-tanks in the UK and the Ministerial Cabinets in France," *Western European Politics*, vol. 14, no. 1 (January 1991), pp. 1–18. And, see Jean-Paul Costa, "Politisation de la fonction publique et alternance en France," *Revue Française d'Administration Publique*, vol. 38 (April–July 1986), pp. 59–65; and Guy Thuillier, *Les Cabinets Ministeriels* (Paris: Presses Universitaires de France, 1982).

9. For a succinct discussion of bureaucrats in Japan see Takashi Inoguchi, "The Nature and Functioning of Japanese Politics," *Government and Opposition*, vol. 26, no. 2 (Spring 1991), pp. 185–98.

10. Peters, *Public Bureaucracy in Comparative Perspective*, p. 254.

11. T.H. Rigby, *Political Elites in the USSR: Central Leaders and Local Cadres From Lenin to Gorbachev* (Aldershot, Eng.: Edward Elgar, 1990), pp. 6-7.

12. Ronald J. Hill and John Lowenhardt, "Nomenklatura and Perestroika," *Government and Opposition*, vol. 26, no. 2 (Spring 1991), p. 232.

13. Quoted by Vladimir Kusin in "The Secret Police: Disliked and Weakened but Not Beaten Yet," in *Report on Eastern Europe*, February 9, 1990, p. 38.

14. The facts for this section are taken from an excellent summary of the recent administration arrangements in the Soviet Union by Hill and Lowenhardt, "Nomenklatura and Perestroika," pp. 228–43.

15. Mikhail Gorbachev, *Perestroika: New Thinking For Our Country and the World* (London: Collins, 1987).

16. Hill and Lowenhardt, "Nomenklatura and Perestroika," p. 236.

17. This type of political system is well-developed in the Philippines. See, for example, Jean Grossholtz, *Politics in the Philippines* (Boston: Little, Brown, 1964); and Carl H. Lande, *Leaders, Factions, Parties* (New Haven, Conn.: Yale University Press, 1965).

18. Peters, *Public Bureaucracy in Comparative Perspective*, p. 103.

19. See Jackton B. Ojwang, "Kenya and the Concept of Civil Service Political Neutrality: A Case of Silent but Determined Politicization," *Indian Journal of Public Administration*, vol. 24 (1978), pp. 430–40.

20. For overviews of modern Chinese politics, see John Fraser, *The Chinese: Portrait of a People* (New York: Summit Books, 1980); B. Michael Frolic, *Mao's People* (Cambridge, Mass.: Harvard University Press, 1980); Lucian W. Pye, *The Dynamics of Chinese Politics* (Cambridge, Mass: Oelgeschlager, 1981); Jonathan D. Spence, *The Gate of Heavenly Peace* (New York: Viking, 1981); and James C.F. Wang, *Contemporary Chinese Politics*, 2nd ed. (Englewood Cliffs, N.J.: Prentice-Hall, 1985).

21. Eric A. Nordlinger has calculated that the military has controlled, directly or indirectly, two-thirds of the states of the Third World in modern times. See his *Soldiers in Politics: Military Coups and Governments* (Englewood Cliffs, N.J.: Prentice-Hall, 1977). On Africa, see Anton Bebler, *Military Rule in Africa* (New York: Praeger, 1972). More generally see Samuel P. Huntington, *The Soldier and the State* (Cambridge, Mass.: Harvard University Press, 1957); and Amos Perlmutter, *The Military and Politics in Modern Times* (New Haven, Conn.: Yale University Press, 1977).

22. Col. Mainassara was quoted by Dalatou Mamane in "Coup Ends Niger's Flirtation with Democracy," *The Globe and Mail*, January 29, 1996.

23. For more information in this area see J.J. Johnson, ed., *The Role of the Military in Underdeveloped Countries* (Princeton, N.J.: Princeton University Press, 1962); and Robert M. Price, "Military Officers and Political Leadership," *Comparative Politics*, vol. 3, no. 3 (April 1971), pp. 361–80.

24. Richard P.Y. Li and William R. Thompson, "The 'Coup Contagion' Hypothesis," *Journal of Conflict Resolution*, vol. 19 (March 1975), pp. 63–88.

25. Edward Luttwak, *Coup d'Etat: A Practical Handbook* (Cambridge, Mass.: Harvard University Press, 1979), p. 66.

26. *Ibid.*, p. 35.
27. Roger Charlton, *Comparative Government* (London: Longman, 1986), p. 164.
28. Henry Bienen, *Military Intervenes: Case Studies in Political Development* (New York: Russell Sage, 1968); and Robert Jackman, "Politicians in Uniform," *APSR*, vol. 70, no. 4 (Dec. 1976), pp. 1098–1109. For an overview of conservative military systems see R. Pinkney, *Right-Wing Military Government* (London: Pinter, 1990).
29. See Robert J. Jackson and Doreen Jackson, *Politics in Canada*, 3rd ed. (Scarborough, Ont.: Prentice-Hall Canada, 1994), ch. 13.
30. Robert J. Jackson, "Crisis Management and Policy-Making," in Richard Rose, ed., *The Dynamics of Public Policy* (London: Sage, 1976).

FURTHER READING

Adie, R., and Paul Thomas, *Canadian Public Administration* (Scarborough: Prentice-Hall, 1987).

Flaherty, David G., *Protecting Privacy in Surveillance Societies: The Federal Republic of Germany, Sweden, France, Canada, and the United States* (Chapel Hill, N.C.: University of North Carolina Press, 1989).

Gruber, Judith, *Controlling Bureaucracies: Dilemmas in Democratic Governance* (Los Angeles: University of California Press, 1987).

Harding, Harry, *Organizing China: The Problem of Bureaucracy* (Stanford, Calif.: Stanford University Press, 1981).

Heclo, Hugh, and Aaron Wildavsky, *The Private Government of Public Money* (Berkeley: University of California Press, 1974).

Hennessy, Peter, *Whitehall* (London: Fontana, 1990).

Henry, Nicholas, *Public Administration and Public Affairs*, 5th ed., (Englewood Cliffs, N.J.: Prentice Hall, 1992).

Kernaghan, Kenneth, and John W. Langford, *The Responsible Public Servant* (Halifax: The Institute for Research on Public Policy, 1990).

Kernaghan, Kenneth, and David Siegal, *Public Administration in Canada: A Text* (Scarborough: Nelson, 1991).

Lefort, Claude, *The Political Forms of Modern Society: Bureaucracy, Democracy, Totalitarianism* (Cambridge, Mass.: MIT Press, 1986).

Morris, Norval and David J. Rothman, eds., *The Oxford History of the Prison* (New York: Oxford University Press, 1996).

O'Donnell, Guillermo, *Modernization and Bureaucratic Authoritarianism: Studies in South American Politics* (Berkeley: Institute of International Studies, University of California, 1973).

Park, Yung H., *Bureaucrats and Ministers in Contemporary Japanese Politics* (Berkeley, Cal.: Institute of East Asian Studies, 1987).

Riggs, Fred, *Administration in Developing Countries* (Boston: Houghton Mifflin, 1964).

Robertson, Davis, and Dennis Judd, *The Development of American Public Policy: The Structure of Policy Restraint* (Glenview, Ill.: Scott, Foresman, 1989).

Stepan, Alfred, *Rethinking Military Politics: Brazil and the Southern Cone* (Princeton, N.J.: Princeton University Press, 1988).

Subramaniam, V., ed., *Public Administration in the Third World: An International Handbook* (Westport, Conn.: Greenwood, 1990).

 **Weblinks**

hav54.socwel.berkeley.edu/resources/govern.htm
This site provides links to many of the United States' social welfare resources.

www.polrisk.com/
This site provides information about the political stability of many of the worlds' nations.

CHAPTER 16

Political Parties and Interest Groups

Groups can provide a mechanism for people to participate in the political system. Often, they are more successful than individuals acting alone to achieve an objective. Some groups in the political arena have a wide range of political goals; others focus narrowly on one specific issue. Some groups are permanent, others more fleeting. This chapter focuses on the nature and activities of two types of groups that are especially active politically; political parties and interest groups.

Political parties are limited in their ability to articulate the interests of citizens. They are by nature very political, very public, and open to criticism. For these reasons, among others, they are often the focus of scandals and disillusionment. However, by their very nature, political parties are flawed, as Lord Macaulay pointed out in this irreverent analogy:

> Every political sect ... has its altars and its deified heroes, its relics and its pilgrimages, its canonized martyrs and confessors, and its legendary miracles.[1]

Political parties in this electronic age still use all the devices of superstition to win converts and maintain their loyalty: conventions are but pilgrimages; heroes and martyrs provide the spiritual glue of the party; relics are the venerated policies and records that provide the proof of vision and ideas of substance. Along with the manipulation, patronage, and distortions, however, parties in democratic systems allow for the orderly election of representatives and leaders to government and are the means by which thousands of citizens can actively participate and express themselves in the political process of their country. They are, in short, a colourful and important part of the democratic process.

POLITICAL PARTIES

Parties are important features of both democratic and authoritarian states. In democracies, parties provide citizens with choices about the personnel and policies of their governments. In authoritarian states they do not. But even when votes are not translated directly into majority government, parties may still provide a link between the mass population and the government. The link lends a vital aura of legitimacy to government actions. The mere existence of parties is often popularly equated with good and democratic government, though that assumption may be far from the case!

Because political parties perform such different functions in the wide spectrum of authoritarian and democratic states, they have many different features and have been defined in a great many ways. Here, we use Giovanni Sartori's very straightforward definition of a **party** as "any political group that presents at elections, and is capable of placing through elections, candidates for public office."[2] The primary goal of political parties is to gain control of the levers of government so that they can realize their policies or programs. In democratic systems, parties compete openly in an electoral process. In authoritarian systems, one party dominates and there is no external competition even though elections may be held; all competition takes place within the one existing party. Or there may be no elections at all. As opposed to other more transitory groups, parties require a permanent organization.

Organized political parties as we know them today are a relatively new phenomenon. They appeared first in the United States and then in France in the eighteenth century in conjunction with the democratic revolutions in 1776 and 1789 respectively. By the end of the nineteenth century, parties were widely established throughout the developed world. In the twentieth century they also became an important feature of emerging communist states, and to a lesser extent were introduced in the developing countries where they were often adopted by leaders of authoritarian regimes who sought to broaden their popular appeal.

Until this new breed of "modern" political party appeared, parties were really just factions or groups. The oligarchic and democratic parties of the ancient Greek city-states, for example, or even the early Liberal-Conservatives and Clear Grits in Canada at the time of Confederation in 1867, were little more than loose coalitions of individuals with few common political interests.

Classifying Parties

Modern political parties evolved quite differently within the broad spectrum of political cultures and political systems of the world's states. It is therefore useful to classify parties in order to compare and understand them. This can be done in a number of ways. Maurice Duverger's classic categorization is *by organization*.[3] He notes that most modern, competitive political parties can be classified as cadre, mass, or devotee, depending on how they are organized. There are two important elements of organization: the relationship between the parliamentary wing of a party and the extra-parliamentary wing; and who controls the process of recruitment and nominations of candidates. Parties within Duverger's classification scheme are best viewed from a historical perspective.

The first modern parties were distinguished from their predecessors by their organization and interests. They originated within representative and legislative bodies, as elected members with common interests began to form loose associations or groups. At the time, elected members were notables who had sufficient leisure to devote to politics and look after a rudimentary group organization, and it was they who financed and led political parties. Suffrage was limited to a small constituency of male landowners, so there was no necessity for those seeking election to have either an elaborate party organization or ambitious ideological justifications. Duverger called this early type of party a **cadre**. Cadre parties are still found today, mostly in the developing world, where cliques and factions dominate, and where there is little party organization.

Over time, as pressures mounted both without and within their elite membership to expand the electoral base of parties and representative governments, the nature of parties changed. Suffrage was extended gradually to include ever larger groups of male and eventually female adults until universal suffrage was reached—before the mid-twentieth century in most developed countries. As the electoral base expanded, the organization and control of parties shifted from inside to outside of the representative institutions, and a new kind of mass party tended to replace elitist cadre parties.

Mass parties originated outside of parliament; they maintained open membership and used an ideological appeal to recruit members. The theoretical rationale behind these parties was that a large membership constructed across broad social categories would help to counter the power of cadre parties, whose leaders were mainly from the economic and social elite of society. In practice, however, their ideological appeal was generally restrictive.

Mass parties are thus the opposite of cadre parties in many respects. From a narrow and well-defined ideological base, they appeal to workers, peasants, and religious groups, and, rather than relying on a parliamentary caucus of party notables for organization, they develop an active and involved bureaucratic hierarchy with "grass roots" branches throughout the country. To recruit members they set up auxiliary organizations that develop recreational, cultural, and sport facilities as well as newspapers. To avoid relying on notables for financial assistance, party membership is formalized, and members pay regular dues.

Duverger's third classification, the devotee party, can be found in both democratic and authoritarian states, although it is more characteristic of the latter. In the **devotee party**, a charismatic leader, along with a ruling elite, directs and controls the party. Rather than having open membership like mass parties, devotee parties are more selective in their recruitment, providing a probationary period to test the prospective member's loyalty and ideological orthodoxy. And, rather than developing branches throughout the electorate and directing them from the centre, they build up a pyramidal structure with a wide base of cells or militia which extends up to the highest leadership. Party rhetoric is revolutionary and forceful. In all, devotee parties are more intensely ideological, more disciplined, and more cohesive than mass parties. The Communist parties of France and Italy after 1945 were typical devotee parties. They were eager to overthrow the governments of their respective countries and replace them with a Soviet-style dictatorship. Hitler's Nazi party is another good historical example of a devotee party.

Another way to categorize parties is by the *type of appeal* that the parties make—that is, whether they are *ideological or non-ideological*. Noncompetitive parties in one-party states may also be meaningfully classified in this way.

In his classification of parties by their ideological basis, Otto Kirchheimer distinguishes the **catch-all party** from those with high degrees of ideology.[4] He notes that the mass party and the cadre party became relatively unsuccessful at the polls because of their limited electoral bases (the working class for the mass party and the establishment class for the cadre party), and tended to expand their appeal to include the maximum number of social groups and therefore be more successful electorally. To do this they followed two strategies. First, they abandoned strong ideological prescriptions in favour of softer lines. Socialist parties in Europe, for example, abandoned the harsher dictates of Marxism and emphasized instead the welfare state. The contemporary Labour Party of Prime Minister Tony Blair has not only abandoned the nationalization of industries but has adopted a so-called "third way" between capitalism and socialism. Similarly, the British Conservative Party abandoned its cries for laissez-faire capitalism and now quietly supports a mixed economy. Second, the parties promised specific rewards to a wide variety of interest groups, from better marketing assistance to farmers and jobs for students to free trade and better conditions for businessmen. Catch-all parties focus above all on maximizing votes; their platforms become like large vats which are filled with as many popular ideas and promises as possible. The Republican and Democratic parties in the United States are classic catch-all parties.

At the opposite extreme from catch-all parties are **ideological parties**. In democratic societies these tend to be narrowly based parties with very specific interests and voter appeal. Parties in totalitarian and authoritarian one-party states are generally highly ideological, although they are immediately distinguishable from ideological parties in democracies by their noncompetitive nature. They differ widely from state to state, particularly in the emphasis they place on indoctrination and mobilization. Totalitarian states use political parties as mobilizing agents to induce intensive participation. The party elite defines the official ideology, and party members attempt to permeate all social activities and institutions to see that the stated ideological goals and policies are understood and followed. Citizens may have a role and opportunities to speak, but only under carefully controlled conditions.

In less extreme authoritarian regimes, on the other hand, mobilization is not a primary feature of the one existing political party. In this case obedience to the dictator, tyrant, military junta, or group of bureaucrats is paramount—not participation. Franco's regime in Spain from 1936 to 1975, for example, avoided popular involvement. Sometimes, particularly in developing countries with authoritarian regimes, a national liberation party plays an important role in gaining independence for the country, but once the mission is accomplished the party is no longer needed as a mobilizing agency, and it atrophies.

Movements and Factions

At this point we must distinguish two phenomena which are close to parties—movements and factions. A **movement** consists of collective behaviour that is ideologically inspired, idealistic, and action oriented. It aims at profound social change, and sometimes even produces revolutionary change. But it does not aspire to govern the country. Some movements have no clear leadership or goals, while others are actively led and directed by ideological guidelines. Sometimes, if it is very successful, a movement will become a party; for example, in India the nationalist movement led by Gandhi became the Congress party after it successfully pressured the British for independence. More recently, in Germany, the environmental movement was transformed into the Green party. In recent years movements have become widespread in Western societies and are having considerable impact on public policy.[5] Some movements such as nationalist movements, civil rights movements, or those concerned with the environment or women's rights are concerned with wide social and political concerns; others such as alcohol prohibition movements are more narrowly focused (see Close Up 16.1). The most radical movements promote fundamental changes in a society and are willing to resort to violent social conflict to achieve their ends.

Movements have proliferated in Western democracies in recent years. Ronald Inglehart offers a compelling theory to explain this phenomenon. He suggests that economic, social, and cultural changes in Western democracies have contributed to a growing politicization of their publics, while at the same time political behaviour is moving outside the constraints of traditional organizations. Elite-directed participation is giving way to ad hoc groups concerned with specific issues and specific policy changes. At the same time, Inglehart suggests, there are growing numbers of **cognitive nonpartisans**; that is, individuals with high political skills without close attachment to any political party.[6] Because of this, he says, the pluralization of politics will continue. There are new social movements and parties on both the left and right wings of the ideological spectrum. Inglehart states that:

> The established political parties came into being in an era dominated by social class conflict and economic issues, and tend to remain polarized on this basis. But in recent years, a new axis of polarization has arisen based on cultural and quality of life issues.[7]

Factions constitute another kind of group which plays an important political role in many countries. A **faction** is an organized group within a political party that has reasonably stable and consistent membership. It may restrain the oligarchic tendencies of party leaders. Some factions are based principally on ideology (within Britain's Conservative and Labour parties); others are based on spoils (within the Liberal Democrats of Italy or the Liberal Democrats of Japan—see Close Up 16.2). Spoils-based factions are encouraged by electoral systems that force candidates from the same party to compete with each other or by one party dominating government over a long period of time.

CLOSE UP 16.1   The Women's Movement

The women's movement is one of the most widespread international movements today. It has been active on and off since the nineteenth century, seeking the right for women to speak out on social issues, to vote, and to have opportunities for paid employment. Because it is composed of many organizations, the international women's movement has no unified political ideology, and there are both liberal and radical versions. The fundamental point of all feminists, however, is that orthodox theories about politics tend to ignore gender and harbour unconscious assumptions about the role of women.

Since the 1960s, one branch of the women's movement has changed its focus from women's rights to women's liberation, denouncing traditions of male supremacy in the family and in political and social structures that assign women an inferior position in society. It has built a solid organization and leadership structure within many countries and also at the international level, increasing membership.

A leftist framework has provided much of the ideological basis for radical feminists. For its advocates, capitalism and its social and political superstructures are identified as the forces behind the oppression of women. It is reasoned that since men control the means of production, they have used their position to institutionalize norms and values that keep women in an inferior condition. The overall goal of the women's movement, shared by both moderates and extremists, is to redress the balance and provide equality for women.

Sometimes women's organizations such as NAC, the National Action Committee on the Status of Women in Canada, are set up to lobby for policy changes. At that point, that branch of the women's movement takes the form of an interest group. To date feminists have sought to influence the policies of existing political parties rather than forming their own. But the approach differs across countries. The Women's Party in Russia is typical of many narrow-interest parties in transitional democratic countries; it runs women candidates and is primarily concerned with improving conditions for women in Russia.[8]

Functions of Political Parties

Political parties perform many useful tasks for society. These vary according to the political system in which the parties operate, but some basic functions are widely shared.[9] Parties normally add an important element of stability to a political system by legitimizing the individuals and institutions that control political power. They also help to organize the government and electorate. For example, they mobilize the electorate by recruiting candidates, conducting campaigns, encouraging partisan attachments, and generally educating the public and stimulating voter participation. As well, they provide varying degrees of policy direction to governments and train and supply potential leaders. In Canada, and in other countries following the British parliamentary form of gov-

CLOSE UP 16.2 Party Factions in Japan

In Japan, from 1955 to 1993 and again after 1996, political factions have been very important in determining who forms the government.

In 1991, for example, major political factions within the governing Liberal Democratic Party withdrew support from Prime Minister Toshiki Kaifu, forcing him to resign immediately before the election. Even though Kaifu was popular with the Japanese public, several LDP factions considered him a transitional Prime Minister who had to give way to a more senior factional leader once the party had shaken off the taint of scandal.

After Japan rid itself of coalition governments in the 1996 elections, the new Prime Minister, Ryutaro Hashimoto, immediately began doling out victory spoils along traditional factional lines. Cabinet members were appointed by the old LDP formula: four posts went to each of the party's four major factions—the Obuchi, Miyazawa, Mitsuzuka and Nakasone, and one to the smaller Komoto faction—and four to senior Liberal Democrats from the upper house.

ernment, the winning party serves to fuse the executive and legislative branches of government, and constitutes the foundation of cabinet government.

Included in the broad task of organizing the electorate and government are several specific party functions that deserve elaboration:

- **Recruitment, nomination, election, and training of political officeholders** Parties recruit, select, and present suitable candidates to represent them in elections. Party positions provide experience for future political leaders. The winning party forms the government and largely decides who will occupy the policy-making posts—the most powerful tool a party controls. Once in power, the party also controls numerous patronage appointments throughout the government structure, enabling it to reward its supporters and extend its influence.

- **Interest aggregation and articulation** Political parties coordinate and refine the demands that are made on the political system, allowing the system to respond more adequately to those demands. Catch-all parties in particular appeal to the various classes, regions, interests, and ethnic groups that make up the country. They help to modify conflict, build coalitions and compromises between contending groups in society, and facilitate decisions.

- **Political socialization** In stable democracies, political parties tend to reinforce the established system indirectly by helping socialize a segment of the population into the prevailing political culture. They assist in inculcating fundamental values and norms. Parties help to create and maintain support for the political system by following accepted rules, thereby contributing to societal acceptance and legitimation of that system. A revolutionary party would, of course, do the opposite.

- **Communication**   Political parties often act as a two-way conduit of communication. They transmit information upward from the grass roots and downward from the government to the public.

- **Policy-making**   Parties that form governments have the initiative in formulating public policy. They present policy platforms to the electorate before elections, but these are rarely restrictive in making policy decisions once the party is elected. The performance of political parties in policy formation varies a great deal from time to time and place to place.[10]

Political parties in one-party authoritarian regimes perform somewhat different functions than those in democracies. Single parties in such regimes provide a mobilizing ideology that they infuse into mass organizations. Political socialization is deliberate and pervasive. All competing elite groups, including the army, are subordinate to it. The party provides support for the government but restricts opportunities for citizen participation.

It is common in authoritarian countries for a party to act as an agent of support for the government while the regime is being established, and then to be purposely weakened by leaders who allow its functions to atrophy until it becomes little more than an extension of the personality of a strong president. Other organizations, including the army, church, bureaucracy, professional groups, and so on, are encouraged to compete with the party as vehicles to assist the regime to maintain its rule and prevent the party from becoming too strong vis-à-vis the president and executive. In parts of Africa, for example, where societies went through rapid and radical change because of their colonial experience and the rise of powerful extremist movements, many parties declined and the army, church, bureaucracy, or other groups usurped their functions.

Often, too, in the fledgling democracies of the democratic world, political parties fail to provide representation for groups such as peasants, oppressed minorities, and women. Too often they represent the narrow interests of the economic or political elite, or a single ethnic group. And frequently a party forms around a charismatic leader who has no clear political program. Once in power such a party may not perform the above functions satisfactorily.

PARTY SYSTEMS

The competition between parties for representation in legislatures affects their relationship with each other and also with government institutions. The network of relationships among parties in a state is known as the **party system**.

There are many **noncompetitive systems** in which a single party is the only legal party and controls every level of government. Regimes such as the People's Republic of China and Cuba are examples. Technically, these states, and also those with no parties, do not have "party systems," because the term implies a competitive situation in which two or more genuinely independent political parties compete in elections for political power. States without political parties, or those that have only one political party, do not engage in party competition, however we include them in Table 16.1 in order to cover the entire spectrum of possible situations.

Competitive party systems are classified by the number of parties that compete for, and have access to, legislative power. In a dominant one-party system, a single party regularly wins almost every election. If three or more parties regularly poll more than 15% a multi-party system is said to exist. No-party systems, and non-competitive systems in which one party dominates, are classified by other variables such as how repressive their governments are.

Between these two types of systems is the **mixed and low-competitive system** category, which includes a few systems that fall between the first two because they include elements of both. Mexico is a good example. One party, the Institutional Revolutionary Party (PRI) dominates to such a degree that the system is almost noncompetitive. When it won the 1994 presidential election it continued 65 years of unbroken rule.

Classification systems such as these are intended to assist gross comparisons between states. Not all countries fit neatly into any one category. Nor do countries necessarily remain in any particular category; they sometimes shift from competitive to

Table 16.1   Party Systems

Type of System	Example
No-Party Systems	Often developing states under military rule (Myanmar)
Noncompetitive Systems (one party)	(1) Communist Authoritarian (China) (2) Conservative Authoritarian (Franco's Spain)
Mixed and Low-Competitive Systems	(1) Low Competition (Mexico)
Competitive Systems (two or more parties)	(1) Dominant One-Party (Japan, 1955–93) (2) Two-Party (United States) (3) Multi-Party Dominant (three or more parties, one usually receives approximately 40% of the vote) (Canada) (4) Multi-Party Loose (three or more parties; none regularly receives 40% of the vote) (Italy)

Source: Adapted from Joseph LaPalombara and Myron Weiner, eds., *Political Parties and Political Development* (Princeton, N.J.: Princeton University Press, 1966) and Joseph LaPalombara, *Politics Within Nations* (Englewood Cliffs, N.J.: Prentice-Hall, 1974), Ch. 13.

noncompetitive systems and vice versa. A prime example is the adoption of competitive systems in new states formed after many years under a classic noncompetitive system.

Parties in Competitive Systems

Parties in competitive political systems place great value on liberal democratic government. In such systems political freedoms are upheld, opposition parties are tolerated, and the verdict of voters is respected. Built into democratic systems is the principle of **loyal opposition**. According to this principle, parties opposing the governing party are considered loyal to the state and its political system. Opposition parties are recognized by law. They have a right to participate freely in politics and to criticize and seek to overthrow the party in power through elections. Theoretically, individuals and groups are free to organize new parties, but in reality they are often difficult to sustain.

Dominant One-Party Systems

A dominant one-party system exists when a single party regularly wins almost every election, even though opposition parties are allowed to function freely. This situation is rather rare. In modern times, Japan provides one of the best examples. Japan was ruled continuously from 1955 to 1993 by the Liberal Democratic Party (LDP). This centre-right party demonstrated a great ability to work with opposition parties sufficiently to undercut their electoral appeal, as well as an ability to act as a catch-all party in responding to new interest groups and demands.[11] Then, in a dramatic realignment which began in 1993, the LDP lost its hegemonic position. Since that crucial election in 1993 Japan has been governed rather unsteadily by a coalition government headed since 1996 by the head of the LDP. Possibly a better current example of a one-party system would be Singapore where Goh Chok Tong's People's Action Party continues to dominate.

Sweden and India are interesting cases as well. The Swedish Social Democratic Party (SDP) holds the record as the longest governing democratically elected party in the Western world. It had been in power nearly 52 years (minus six years: 1976–1982) when it was defeated in 1991, although it almost always governed in coalition with another party. It returned to power in 1994. In India the Congress Party dominated electoral politics from independence in 1947 until 1977. One-party dominance in this case was tied to the charisma of Jawaharlal Nehru, Indira Gandhi and the Gandhi dynasty, and was severely weakened after Mrs. Gandhi and, later, her son Rajiv were assassinated. In 1998 Sonia Gandhi, widow of Rajiv, took up the family tradition as leader of the Congress Party. Her party did not win outright but made significant gains against the ruling BJP (Hindu National Party) and managed to bring it down in 1999.

Two-Party Systems

According to Maurice Duverger, political choice usually takes place in the form of a choice between two alternatives. "A duality of parties does not always exist, but there is almost always a duality of tendencies."[12] Yet, although it is characteristic of much of the English-speaking world, the two-party system is not common worldwide. It appears only in some two dozen countries. In the **two-party system**, two major parties dominate; others have only minor political strength. Four countries—Australia, Great Britain, New Zealand, and the U.S.—are relatively clear-cut cases. The United States has a classic two-party system, although there have been third party or independent candidates such as John Anderson and Ross Perot in recent years. Great Britain, Australia, and New Zealand all have two dominant parties that vie for power as well as a weaker third or even fourth party. In these three countries, many new parties have been formed over time, but few have survived.[13]

The main advantage for the two-party system is that it offers the electorate a choice of policies and leaders and at the same time promotes governmental stability by making it possible for one party to win a majority or near-majority in the legislature.

At various times, Canada has been classified as a two-party system, a two-and-a-half party system, and a multi-party dominant system. Only two parties (the Liberals and Conservatives) have ever formed the federal government, but a third party (the New Democratic Party) has been relatively strong. In recent years two parties representing new ideologies have arisen. The Reform Party campaigns for an American-style conservatism and the Bloc Québécois offers nationalism and independence for Quebec. Since the 1993 general election, the system has conformed best to the multi-party dominant category, discussed below.

Multi-Party Systems

Multi-party systems are characteristic of much of the developed world and also of the newly emerging democracies of Eastern Europe and in the countries formed from the former Soviet Union. In the **multi-party system,** popular support is divided among several parties, so that the largest party must generally form a coalition with one or more other parties to form a government. Advocates of this type of system argue that it allows expression of the many interests of a complex society, including a range of ideological differences, conflicting political values, and philosophies which are based on socioeconomic factors such as language, ethnicity, or religion. This system, of which present-day Austria, Italy, Israel, Spain, the former Third and Fourth French Republics, and Weimar Germany are major examples, is often criticized as being unstable. However, many examples of multi-party systems with stable governments can be found—notably in Switzerland and the Netherlands. Multi-party systems are capable of forming highly stable governments when there are long-standing coalitions between different parties sharing basic values, and when party leaders are willing to negotiate and compromise following elections.

There are two main varieties of multi-party systems. In a **multi-party dominant system**, there are three or more parties but one particular party receives at least 40% of the vote. Sometimes one party dominates, but then the opposition parties tend to form coalitions, and this gives rise to fluctuations in power between the competing parties. Canada is often classified here because the Liberal Party has been the dominant government party throughout the twentieth century, and since 1993 it has had little credible opposition as a national force.

Multi-party loose systems are those in which three or more parties compete but none regularly receives 40% of the vote. They contain parties with a wide range of ideologies or philosophies, which come and go and shift alliances and coalitions with relative frequency. Some parties in multi-party systems have a tendency to be irresponsible. Because they know they can never be brought into the government, they criticize it relentlessly and make outlandish promises which they know they will never have to fulfill. These systems have frequent elections because of the instability of government coalitions. For example, until recently Italy has had a history of extreme government instability. Italian government coalitions have fallen apart 56 times since Italy was set up as a republic in 1946. The Christian Democratic Party that led the government coalitions for most of this time was generally unable to create a firm parliamentary majority because of a lack of continued cooperation with the left-of-centre parties. While elections are not necessarily held every time a new cabinet must be constructed, the frequency and haphazard occurrence of elections for many years made this party system unique among contemporary European states. (Recent electoral reform to ameliorate this problem in Italy are discussed in Chapter 19.)

If political stability is defined in terms of length of government tenure, then countries with multi-party loose systems are in the least-stable category of party systems. On the other hand, even these states generally provide orderly constitutional change of government without violence. However, when governmental instability does result, as in the case of Weimar Germany, the state may be ripe for strong government—even a dictator.

In recent years, political scientists interested in pursuing the effects of multi-party systems have refined the concept of **political fractionalization**. This term refers to the degree to which votes and offices are evenly divided among parties in a state. By measuring the number of parties that receive shares of the popular vote and seats in the legislature and also the relative equality of those shares, Douglas W. Rae came up with a combined score for countries to indicate the degree of party fractionalization.[14]

He found that the least fractionalized party systems were the English-speaking democracies, including Great Britain, Canada, Australia, New Zealand, and the United States. In these countries the parties tended to be moderate, non-ideological, catch-all parties that made broad appeals across social classes and interests. The major parties tended to be remarkably alike in their views and programs. The most fractionalized among the democracies included Belgium, Finland, Denmark, Switzerland, Italy, Netherlands, Israel, and Portugal. Parties in these countries generally ruled by **coalition government**, in which two or more parties formed an alliance to manage the government and share top ministerial posts. Fractionalization obviously does not always result in unstable government, for there have been stable coalitions in a great many of these countries. The term "fractionalization" should not be confused with party factions, which, as we have seen, refers to the existence of powerful groups *within* political parties.

Parties in Noncompetitive Systems

Communist and fascist regimes prior to World War II adopted one-party systems that abided no competition. In each case, the established party determined the conditions of political recruitment, enforced an all-encompassing ideology, and determined the economic and military strategies of the state. In authoritarian states such as the Soviet Union under Stalin and Yugoslavia under Tito, the leaders themselves usurped the function of decision-making, and the party was but an appendage of their will. In China today, the party functions as a permanent institution for which the government is only the administrative agency. The party is the supreme policy-making authority. The state is, ironically, an instrument of the ruling class. Keeping authority within the party framework enables an ideologically united elite to control and supervise the state and ensure the unity of the policy system.

This type of communist one-party state flourishes today in countries such as China, Cuba, North Korea, and Vietnam. Not all one-party states are communist or socialist however. Fascist Italy and Nazi Germany were one-party right-wing dictatorships after World War I, as were the authoritarian governments of Portugal and Spain that expired in the 1970s.

After World War II, as colonialism died, newly independent states proliferated throughout the developing world. Many new states were products of revolutionary upheaval. A high percentage of these states adopted versions of one-party systems. The pre-revolutionary Bolshevik Party and the post-revolutionary CPSU of the former Soviet Union provided a popular prototype and model. In general, being less ideologically orthodox than the Communist Party, these new elitist parties stressed the need for a single party to enforce political integration and socialization in order to counter disunity and separatism. Repression was common, and all party competition was forbidden. Many one-party regimes, both civilian and military existed in Africa before 1990. In Zambia, for example, Kenneth Kaunda ruled for 27 years as head of a one-party state, and in Mali, Moussa Traoru, an army-backed autocrat held power for 23 years. In most of these cases, the leader's political power was buttressed by his absolute control of the economy and state-owed industries.

With the end of the Cold War in the 1990s, democratic values were given new impetus in Africa. Many democrats were eager to dismantle the one-party systems and replace them with multi-party democracies, partly in the hope that democracy would promote economic reforms and bring political stability and prosperity to the continent.

During the early 1990s, most of the former African one-party states drafted new constitutions and allowed multiple parties to exist in law. The results have been mixed. A few leaders, like the presidents of Kenya and Ghana, abandoned economic reforms in order to boost their popularity and win their first multi-party elections in 1992. They won, but drove their countries ever deeper into debt. Others like Zimbabwe's President Robert Mugabe or Senegal's Abdou Diouf retain solid one-party systems behind a multi-party mask. In Central Africa a war ensues among many states. In the so-called Democratic

Republic of the Congo, the self-appointed president, Laurent Kabila, backed by the military, dissolved all of the new democratic institutions in 1997, and is at war in the north, south, and east with both domestic insurgents and foreign troops. In many cases, major political upheavals and flagging committment disrupted political reforms and made economic prosperity elusive. (See Close Up 16.3 for a summary of progress in the African Commonwealth countries.) In assessing their progress to democracy through democratic parties and elections, many of the African leaders contend that, although reform is necessary, each country must follow a reform strategy tailored to its own political and social conditions.

Parties in Mixed and Low-Competitive Systems

Occasionally a government in a noncompetitive system does allow other parties, but only within well-defined limits. The party must be regime-sponsored and operate within strict guidelines that restrict their competitiveness. Some democratic countries have only low competitive systems. An example is Mexico. Since it was founded in 1929, the Institutional Revolutionary Party (PRI) has defeated the three minor parties in every congressional and presidential election. Only since the 1970s have other parties won any appreciable number of seats in the lower house of Congress. In recent years, however, there have been indications that Mexico might be moving toward a more competitive system. In the last decade, the Democratic Revolutionary Party (PRD) and the National Action Party (PAN) have made unprecedented gains in the national legislature

---

CLOSE UP 16.3 Parties and Democracy in Commonwealth Africa

In March 1997, 18 African members of the Commonwealth met to discuss how to improve democracy in Africa. (Nigeria, still a military dictatorship at the time, was not invited.) All 18 countries had undergone momentous change. Ten years earlier, eight of them had been one-party states; three had been military dictatorships; two (South Africa and Namibia) under white rule; one (Swaziland) was a monarchy; five others had held elections, but were not democratic.

Then, between 1990 and 1995 all of these countries except Swaziland had held elections. The outcomes were not all complete victories for democracy, however. South Africa and Namibia ended white rule democratically, but only two of the remaining elections actually changed governments—in Malawi and Zambia. In the others, old dictators and party bosses manipulated things to keep their hold on power. Sierra Leone and Lesotho did end military rule, but since then Sierra Leone has reverted to military control and civil war.

Clearly, establishing multi-party systems is only the beginning of the path to democracy, and most of these Commonwealth countries still have a long way to go.

and state governments. In the July 1997 elections, the PRI lost its majority in the Chamber of Deputies when it took only 39% of the vote, with PAN second at 27% and PRD third at 26%. PAN also took seven of the 31 state governors' elections.

In 1994 presidential elections, Ernesto Zedillo was the PRI stand-in candidate after the assassination of candidate Luis Colosio. Zedillo won an easy victory and assumed the Presidency. The next presidential election will be in the year 2000.

INTEREST GROUPS

Interest groups resemble parties in many respects. In fact, parties and interest groups (often called pressure groups) sometimes overlap. Some narrowly based parties act largely as interest groups, and some interest groups transform themselves into political parties. Sometimes interest groups take part in elections by issuing pamphlets, raising money, and endorsing candidates. However, their goal in doing so is different than that of political parties; they have specific policy issues they want the government to pursue. They want to *influence* government decisions, not run candidates to try to capture government. Interest groups can be distinguished from political parties and other groups by their orientation to the political system.[15] Broadly speaking, parties aggregate interests, while interest groups articulate them. That is, political parties bring together the various interests and expectations of their members and voting constituencies into a policy platform to present to the electorate at election time. If elected to power, parties have the opportunity to put those policies into effect. Interest groups, on the other hand, generally defend specialized interests and causes, and seek a more limited and indirect influence on policies from outside government. Interest groups therefore represent a much narrower range of interests than political parties do.

We can define an **interest group** as an "organized association which engages in activity relative to governmental decisions."[16] This definition includes groups that are relatively transient and issue-oriented as well as those with permanent organizations and general, as well as specific, interests. They do not try to enter government and enact policies themselves, but rather attempt to influence government to act in a specific way. The narrow political activity of an interest group is called **lobbying**, by which we mean seeking to secure favourable policy decisions or the appointment of specific personnel. Sometimes interest groups do their own lobbying—that is, they engage in a range of activities that may include contacting government officials, presenting briefs or petitions, participating in public hearings, soliciting wider public support for their cause, financing court cases, arranging demonstrations and strikes, and so on. Sometimes, however, they hire professional **lobbyists** to conduct these activities for them. And, on occasion, governments themselves set up and even give financial assistance to groups that they want to hear from—for example, NAC (the National Action Committee on the Status of Women). NAC has traditionally received a large percentage of its funds from the federal government. Governments also set up advisory commissions and councils in order to receive input from interest groups.

Lobbying has acquired a bad reputation in many quarters. There is nothing wrong with lobbying—at least not in principle. People who make decisions about public policy should receive as much input from the various interested parties as possible. However, lobbying becomes a bad thing when special interests use money to cross the line between persuading politicians or bureaucrats, for example, bribing them with "entertainment," cash, gifts, donations to a politician's campaign fund, and so on.

Paul Pross identifies four prime characteristics of interest groups:[17]

1. they have a formal structure of organization that gives them continuity;
2. they are able to aggregate and articulate interests;
3. they attempt to act within the political system to influence policy outputs; and
4. they try to influence power rather than exercise the responsibility of government themselves.

The relationship between governments and business leaders and other groups in the economy are of primary importance in developing and maintaining a healthy and prosperous economic environment. That relationship is not one-sided but tends to be mutually beneficial. Interest groups collect information and use it to make coherent demands on political actors. At the same time, they place their technical skills and expert personnel at the disposal of political decision-makers.

Types of Interest Groups

It is evident by now that there are a great many types of interest groups. They can be classed descriptively so that they fall into categories such as: labour unions (Canadian Labour Congress); business organizations (The Chamber of Commerce); public interest groups (Greenpeace); social groups based on gender (National Action Committee on the Status of Women, NAC); professional associations and occupational organizations, and groups based on religion, ethnicity, or age.

In the United States this list could include a category called **political action committees (PACs)**. This particular type of group has mushroomed in significance in American politics since the passage of reform legislation concerning party and campaign finance in the 1970s. PACs are formed by interest groups pooling their members' financial contributions to organize lobbying activities. PACs select particular political candidates whom they want either to elect or defeat, and spend their money to that end. In other words, they spend the money directly, rather than through a political party. By the late 1980s PACs had become the largest single source of campaign fundraising for many seeking legislative office.[18] Some PACs are associated with corporations, others with labour or particular industries (the beer industry is represented by a lobby group called Six PAC), while still others have an ideological orientation.

To compare interest groups across different cultures, it is often best to classify them according their origins and their societal or institutional bases. One relatively simple and widely accepted taxonomy was suggested by Gabriel Almond, who identified four types of interest groups: associational, institutional, non-associational, and anomic.[19]

Associational Interest Groups

Associational interest groups are organized to achieve the specific political objectives of their members, although, they may have other primary purposes. Associational groups tend to be either promotional or protective. **Promotional interest groups** have open membership and specific, limited aims. They are characteristic of interest groups in the developed world where they do not have to be preoccupied with questions of survival and are more concerned with quality of life issues. Promotional groups would include right-to-life or pro-choice groups or those with causes such as preservation of the environment or nuclear disarmament. Typically these groups emerge, change, and even disappear as a reflection of changing political issues and current fads that reflect shifts of public opinion. **Protective interest groups**, on the other hand, have closed membership and are organized to protect common social or economic interests. Trade unions, business groups, or medical associations are examples.

Associational groups tend to be relatively small and less well organized in developing countries, and they also tend to be limited in that they seek solely to protect the interests of their members. Associational groups are rare in communist regimes, where free and open discussion of issues is prevented, and promotional groups are virtually nonexistent because of legal and physical harassment by the state. Protective associations are not tolerated willingly either. In communist states such as China and Cuba, the Communist Party is the exclusive legal representative of the interests of all sectors of society. In the former Soviet Union, promotional groups such as religious groups that predated the communist state were sometimes allowed to continue simply because they proved impossible to eradicate.

Institutional Interest Groups

Institutional interest groups are organizations established for purposes other than political activity. These relatively well-structured and enduring groups become active in order to defend their own interests in the policy decisions of the state. Universities, for example, are established for educational purposes, but may hire lobbyists to defend or attempt to increase their share of the government budget.

Institutional interest groups are the main outlet for diverse interests in communist states. In these states, because the Communist Party has the exclusive right to represent the interests of society, all divisions and diversities tend to be expressed through group action *within* government organizations and institutions. Political discussion and debate are restricted to these areas. As a result, group conflicts in these countries are normally expressed as conflicts between institutions or groups existing within the Communist Party and the civilian and military bureaucracies.

Non–Associational Interest Groups

Non-associational interest groups have no formal organization. They consist of people who share a common interest, and are treated by the state as representing an interest even though they have no formal authorization to do so. Sometimes a loosely structured organization emerges temporarily, but is relatively informal and disappears when the issue is no longer pressing. A good example in Canada would be the temporary and loose bonding together of individuals in the mid/late 1990s to seek compensation for having received tainted blood from the Red Cross.

Non-associational groups are relatively uncommon in developed societies where citizens are used to taking organized collective action. Sometimes they emerge when opinion polls provide information about what people of different backgrounds think. Responses might represent the views of, say, urban or rural constituents, male or female, or different age groups. Non-associational interest groups are more common in developing societies where non-organized groups such as village elders or teachers are approached by the government as though they are leaders of interests. They exist, for example, in the newly independent states of the Southern Hemisphere where modern political institutions have been imposed on traditional economic, social, and political patterns of life. Ethnic, tribal, and kinship associations in Africa also provide the basis of group memberships that have potential for politicization, and their interests are therefore considered by governments. In more developed states, these types of groups have gradually lost their significance, although there are still broad social groups with religious, linguistic, ethnic, and other bases that are not organized into associational pressure groups or even political parties.

Anomic Interest Groups

Interest groups in the **anomic** classification have no formal organizational structures or permanent leaders. They come together only temporarily and act in an ad hoc, uncoordinated fashion, generally as the result of social excitement or turmoil. In May 1968 in France, for example, spontaneous student riots centred in Paris were directed against the government's restrictive, highly centralized education policies.

Contributions of Interest Groups

Because they attempt to exercise influence in the political process, interest groups tend to be credited with sinister instincts and intentions. However, their positive contributions can be considerable, depending in part on the level of socioeconomic development in the state and the relative freedom allowed for them to act.

Their contributions can be summarized as follows:[20]

1. They provide a major source of mediation between government and the individual, articulating aggregated opinions and protecting the individual from undue control by the state.
2. They provide a mechanism for political representation that supplements elections by marshalling support for issues and providing ideas for public policy.
3. They allow the political process to be responsive to social and economic differences in society.

4. They give the government information, both facts and opinions, that can be useful in formulating policies and testing policy proposals. This provides a valuable link between citizens and governments, helping governments keep abreast of shifts of opinion in society.

5. They supplement government agencies. When bureaucrats delegate administrative responsibilities to certain groups, those groups provide the government with an unpaid service.

Problems Created by Interest Groups

Clearly there is a danger that groups with money, social status, better leadership, and political clout will influence the policy process at the expense of weaker groups—that groups will go beyond simply making their voices heard, to distort the democratic process. Interest groups are not equal in the amount of funds they can spend. As one author put it, the "flaw in the pluralist heaven is that the heavenly chorus sings with an upper class accent."[21] And certainly government decision-makers hear more from vested interests who have considerably louder voices than individual taxpayers who cannot afford highly paid lobbyists and lawyers (see Close Up 16.4).

To help level the playing field, governments establish various degrees of control over interest-group activity. Some require lobbyists to register and disclose their lobbying activity. In Canada the Lobbyists Registration Act emphasizes registration and disclosure, but places no significant attention on enforcement. In some other democratic states, where such regulations are very weak, government officials routinely accept money from powerful business interests and then become little more than puppets for special interests. In Mexico, the relationship between the country's major political party and large group interests is extremely close. The Institutional Revolutionary Party (PRI) controls the powerful trade unions, and makes appointments in the public sector down to the level of the traffic police. It also controls the justice system and the majority of media outlets.

CLOSE UP 16.4   Are Interest Groups Responsible for Public Cynicism about Government?

Canadians complain constantly about their government. They say it is too weak, too inert, too venal, too profligate. Yet, these same citizens give money and time to interest groups in order to ensure that the government will not make any changes that will diminish their personal subsidies, social-security cheques, or tax-breaks. These same citizens clamour for more to be done, but they also want lower taxes and cannot accept the elimination of any existing programs. Ordinary citizens organize in associations of pensioners, miners, farmers, and thousands more groups to get their way with the government. And then as individual taxpayers they complain.

Are citizens merely getting the government they deserve, since they are weakening the government through their own collective actions?

Another problem arises from the close relationship between interest group representatives, government personnel, and government regulatory agencies. Many individuals typically work for regulatory agencies for only one or two years and then seek employment in the private sector. The problem is that they know their time in public service will be short, so they are tempted to exploit the situation for their own interests and have little incentive to work in the public interest. Members of Parliament, Senators, and legislative assistants in particular often cap their careers by becoming lobbyists and selling their information and access contacts to special interests.

Interest Groups Revisited

Interest groups clearly are important in the practice of democratic politics. They also play an important role in the *theory* of liberal democracy, which holds that the struggle between individual and group self-interest produces the public good. According to **pluralist theory**, there are many centres of power in society, and public policy reflects the conflict, cooperation, and compromise of independent interest groups. In this theory, interest groups are relatively active while the state is relatively passive in generating public policy. The relative ascendancy of pluralist theory in political science amended classical democratic theory in several ways. Public interest became synonymous with competitive self-interest, and the election process came to be viewed more as a means than an end—as the "competitive struggle for the people's vote."[22] In addition, the theoretical importance of the individual in the political process was reduced as groups became accepted as the decisive actors in formulating public policy.

Corporatist theory presents a contrasting view of the interaction between interest groups, government, and public policy. **Corporatist theory** holds that the state is relatively more autonomous and powerful than interest groups, which are more controlled and passive. According to corporatist theorists, governments grant official recognition to a limited number of interest groups, and these groups are given a virtual monopoly in representing specific sectors of the economy before public authorities.[23] In turn, leaders of these highly recognized and important associations are expected to comply with the policy initiatives of the government.

Corporatist theory is particularly popular with Marxist-oriented scholars who find a remedy for the ills of capitalism in the expanded role of the state. In practice, this theory is useful for understanding the different forms and degrees of interest group activity in both authoritarian and democratic countries where corporatist approaches to policy-making often coexist with independent interest group activity.

DISCUSSION QUESTIONS

1. What is the precise difference between a political party and an interest group?
2. How would you classify Canadian parties? Is this classification relatively stable?
3. Is there such a phenomenon as a two-and-a-half party system?

4. Who should be allowed to join and finance political parties? Join and finance interest groups?

5. Can an interest group ever become a party? If so, give examples.

KEY TERMS

anomic interest group, p. 357

associational interest groups, p. 356

cadre party, p. 342

catch-all party, p. 343

coalition government, p. 351

cognitive nonpartisans, p. 344

competitive party systems, p. 348

corporatist theory, p. 359

devotee party, p. 342

faction, p. 344

ideological parties, p. 343

institutional interest groups, p. 356

interest group, p. 354

lobbying, p. 354

lobbyists, p. 354

loyal opposition, p. 349

mass parties, p. 342

mixed and low-competitive system, p. 348

movement, p. 344

multi-party system, p. 349

non-associational interest groups, p. 356

noncompetitive systems, p. 347

party, p. 341

party system, p. 347

pluralist theory, p. 359

political action committees (PACs), p. 355

political fractionalization, p. 351

promotional interest groups, p. 356

protective interest groups, p. 356

two-party system, p. 349

multi-party dominant system, p. 349

multi-party loose system, p. 351

ENDNOTES

1. Quoted by Neil A. McDonald in *The Study of Political Parties* (New York: Random House, 1955), p. 20.

2. G. Sartori, *Parties and Party Systems* (Cambridge, Mass.: Cambridge University Press, 1976), p. 64.

3. Maurice Duverger, *Political Parties: Their Organization and Activity in the Modern State* (New York: John Wiley, 1963).

4. Otto Kirchheimer, "The Transformation of the Western European Party Systems," in Joseph LaPalombara and M. Wiener, eds., *Political Parties and Political Development* (Princeton, N.J.: Princeton University Press, 1966), pp. 177–200.

5. See Neil J. Smelser, *Theory of Collective Behavior* (New York: Free Press, 1962).

6. Ronald Inglehart, *Culture Shift in Advanced Industrial Society* (Princeton, J.J.: Princeton University Press, 1990), pp. 363–68.

7. Inglehart, *ibid.*, p. 363.

8. See Barbara Deckard Sinclair, *The Women's Movement* (New York: Harper and Row, 1983). Also see the special issue on "Women in Politics" edited by Renata Siemienska, *IPSR*, vol. 6, no. 3 (1985).

9. See Anthony King, "Political Parties in Western Democracies," *Polity*, vol. 11, no. 2 (Winter 1969), pp. 111–41.

10. Anthony King, "Political Parties: Some Skeptical Reflections," in R. Macridis, ed., *Comparative Politics*, 4th ed. (Homewood, Ill.: Dorsey Press, 1972), p. 248.

11. See T.J. Pempel, ed., *Uncommon Democracies: The One-Party Dominant Regimes* (Ithaca, N.Y.: Cornell University Press, 1990).

12. Duverger, *Political Parties*, p. 215.

13. Hugh Berrington "New Parties in Britain: Why Some Live and Most Die" *International Political Science Review*, vol. 6, no. 4, pp. 441–61.

14. Douglas W. Rae, *The Political Consequences of Electoral Laws* (New Haven, Conn.: Yale University Press, 1967), pp. 53–58.

15. Mildred A. Schwartz, "The Group Basis of Politics," in John A. Redekop, ed., *Approaches to Canadian Politics*, 2nd ed. (Scarborough, Ont.: Prentice-Hall Canada, 1983), p. 316.

16. Robert H. Salisbury, "Interest Groups," in Fred I. Greenstein and Nelson W. Polsby, eds., *Handbook of Political Science*, vol. 4 (Reading, Mass.: Addison-Wesley, 1975), p. 175.

17. A. Paul Pross, "Pressure Groups: Adaptive Instruments of Political Communication," in A. Paul Pross, ed., *Pressure Group Behaviour in Canadian Politics* (Toronto: McGraw-Hill Ryerson, 1975).

18. Larry J. Sabato, *PAC Power: Inside the World of Political Action Committees* (New York: W.W. Norton, 1985).

19. Gabriel Almond and G. Bingham Powell, *Comparative Politics* (Boston: Little, Brown, 1966).

20. Adapted from a list by Amitai Etzioni, "Making Interest Groups Work for the Public," *Public Opinion*, vol. 5, no. 4 (August/September 1982), pp. 53–55.

21. E.E. Schattschneider, *The Semisovereign People* (New York: Holt, Rinehart Winston, 1975) p. 35.

22. This definition of elections was offered by Joseph Schumpeter, *Capitalism, Socialism and Democracy* (New York: Harper & Row, 1950), p. 269.

23. Philippe Schmitter and Gerhard Lembruch, eds., *Trends Toward Corporatist Intermediation* (Beverly Hills, Cal.: Sage, 1979).

FURTHER READING

Parties and Movements

Bakvis, Herman, ed., *Canadian Political Parties: Leaders, Candidates and Organization*, Royal Commission on Electoral Reform and Party Financing, vol. 13 (Toronto: Dundurn Press, 1991).

Beck, Paul Allen and Frank Sorauf, *Party Politics in America*, 7th ed. (New York: Harper Collins, 1992).

Carty, K.R., ed., *Canadian Political Party Systems* (Toronto: Broadview, 1992).

Dalton, Russell J., and Manfred Kuchler, *Challenging the Political Order: New Social and Political Movements in Western Democracies* (New York: Oxford University Press, 1990).

Day, Alan, *Political Parties of the World*, 4th ed. (New York: Stockton Press, 1995).

Duverger, Maurice, *Political Parties: Their Organization and Activity in the Modern State* (London: Methuen, 1954).

Eldersveld, Samuel D., *Political Parties in American Society* (New York: Basic Books, 1982).

Epstein, Leon D., *Political Parties in Western Democracies* (New York: Praeger, 1972).

La Palombara, J., and M. Weiner, eds., *Political Parties and Political Development* (Princeton, N.J.: Princeton University Press, 1966).

Laver, Michael, and Norman Schofield, *Multi-Party Government: The Politics of Coalition in Europe* (Oxford: Oxford University Press, 1990).

Lipset, S., and S. Rjokkan, *Party Systems and Voter Alignments* (New York: Free Press, 1967).

Mair, P., *The West European Party System* (Oxford: Oxford University Press, 1990)

Maisel, Sandy L., *The Parties Respond: Changes in the American Party System* (Boulder, Colo.: Westview Press, 1990).

Omvedt, Gail, *Reinventing Revolution: New Social Movements and the Socialist Tradition in India* (London: East Gate, 1993).

Pempel, T.J., ed., *Uncommon Democracies: The One-Party Dominant Regimes*, (Ithaca, N.Y.: Cornell University Press, 1990).

Randall, V. ed., *Political Parties in the Third World* (London: Sage, 1988).

Rose, Richard, *Do Parties Make a Difference?* (Chatham, N.J.: Chatham House Publishers, 1980).

Sartori, Giovanni, *Parties and Party Systems: A Framework for Analysis*, vol. 1 (Cambridge, Mass.: Cambridge University Press, 1976).

Tarrow, Sidney, *Power in Movement: Social Movements, Collective Action and Politics* (New York: Cambridge University Press, 1994).

Thorburn, H.G., ed., *Party Politics in Canada*, 7th ed. (Scarborough: Prentice–Hall Canada, 1996).

Ware, Alan, *Political Parties and Party Systems* (Oxford: Oxford University Press, 1995).

White, S., J. Gardner, G. Schopflin and T. Saitch, *Communist and Post-communist Systems: An Introduction*, 3rd ed. (London: Macmillan 1990).

Interest Groups

Berry, Jeffrey, *Interest Group Society* (Glenview, Ill.: Scott, Foresman, 1988).

Hrebenar, Ronald J. and Ruth K. Scott, *Interest Group Politics in America* (Englewood Cliffs, N.J.: Prentice-Hall, 1990).

Olson, Mancur, *The Logic of Collective Action*, 2nd ed. (Cambridge, Mass.: Harvard University Press, 1971).

 **Weblinks**

www.luna.nl/~benne/politics/parties.html
This site provides links to political parties around the world.

www.democrats.org/
This is the official Web Page of the United States' Democratic Party.

www.rnc.org/
This is the official Web Page of the United States' Republican Party.

www.sphere.ad.jp/ldp/english/e-index.html
This is the official Web Page of the Japanese Liberal Democratic Party.

CHAPTER 17

Political Parties and Interest Groups: Democratic and Authoritarian

The last chapter examined the distinguishing characteristics of parties and interest groups and the roles they play in political systems. We now survey how parties and interest groups function within both democratic and authoritarian states, and consider some of the important political issues associated with their operation.

The chapter pays particular attention to communist parties, tracing the events leading to the dramatic collapse of the Communist Party in the Soviet Union and Eastern Europe. It considers how and why the Communist Party lost its grip on power so unexpectedly as well as issues concerning the fledgling new democratic parties and the party system in contemporary Russia.

POLITICAL PARTIES IN DEMOCRACIES

Most citizens in liberal democratic states tend to identify with, or have some sense of belonging to, a political party. They normally acquire these political identifications relatively early in life from their families and peer groups. As individuals mature and are subject to a wide range of influences, their identification with particular parties may weaken, but early identification still tends to influence voting behaviour and may constitute a stable factor in determining the outcome of free elections. The more intensely people identify with a party, the more likely they are to vote and to participate generally in politics.

Parties in democratic states vary considerably in terms of procedures and organization. However they all operate within the same general parameters and face the same kinds of issues.

Party Membership

Party membership means entails formal attachment to a political party and sharing in the work and benefits associated with it. In most democracies, only about 1% to 3% of adults actually belong to a party, and generally the numbers are declining[1] (see Close Up 17.1). One of the main advantages of a large membership for a party is that it enables the party's viewpoints to be heard more effectively in communities at the grass-roots level. It is a top-down process.

Membership, like other organizational rules, is controlled and enforced by the parties themselves. Sometimes small annual dues or an oath of loyalty is required. In the United States, party membership requirements are unique among democratic states in that the party itself does not control who can become a member. In most American states, party membership requirements are defined by law. A citizen must make a sworn statement of commitment before receiving a ballot to vote in a particular party's direct primary election. Only in a few open-primary states are citizens able to vote without making a public declaration—in which case they may be able to vote in both parties. Critics claim that such wide-open membership rules weaken political parties and prevent them from presenting clear, consistent programs.

In most democratic countries, party supporters can be distinguished as militants or identifiers. **Party militants** devote considerable time and energy to the party and dominate the important business of party associations. **Party identifiers** are members of the electorate who feel attachment to a particular party but participate less within it. Militants exhibit more extreme political philosophies and policy preferences than do party identifiers. A common dilemma for political leaders in democracies is that they depend on political activists but, at the same time, they must maintain the support of more moderate party identifiers in order to win elections.

Party Activities

Candidate selection is a vital process in democracies. Whoever controls the selection process gains leverage in making party policy, distributing patronage, and directing the

---

CLOSE UP 17.1   British Conservatives: A Party in Decline?

Are members of the British Conservative Party becoming an endangered species? A recent study says that following current trends there will be fewer than 100 000 rank-and-file Conservatives by the year 2000—down from about three million after World War II. Similarly, activism and commitment to the cause has plummeted. Only about 28% of members regard their emotional attachment to the party as "very strong."

Some reasons for declining interest are common to other parties in developed democracies—including growth of leisure activities and increased female participation in the work force. Others may be more specific to the Conservative Party such as a desire to move more to the "middle ground" in politics, and the feeling that ordinary party members are ignored and do not matter.[2]

What are the implications of declining party membership for democracy?

party generally. Selection processes vary considerably from one democratic state to another. In some cases they are highly centralized, in others not. Sometimes, for example, a national party agency maintains exclusive power over the selection of party candidates; sometimes regional and local party organizations guard this privilege for themselves. In the former case, a small party elite dominates the selection process, while in the latter all party members may have a vote in selecting their candidates.

The selection process in the United States is quite open and decentralized in this respect; candidate selection for the House of Representatives and Senate is controlled by state, county, and district party organizations. Both the Democratic and Republican parties, however, choose their presidential candidates at national conventions. The convention delegates are selected in a variety of ways. Some states have primaries that bind the delegates to the candidate winning the primary election.[3] Others have preferential primaries that allow the delegates a degree of autonomy in voting at the convention. In still other states, delegates are selected in primaries but they are "unpledged" or free to vote as they wish. Lastly, in some states a number of delegates are chosen in primaries but many others are nominated by state or district party committees. This delegate selection process is discussed in detail in Chapter 19. In Canada, the Canada Elections Act gives all party leaders a veto over the choice of their party's candidates, but only in exceptional cases does the national party headquarters or the party leader interfere with local nominations.

The variety of organizational rules is immense. In Israel, where the entire country is treated as a single parliamentary constituency, candidate selection is made by the party and is comparatively centralized and closed. In Britain, as in Canada, local constituency associations select candidates for Parliament, but the national party organization can veto their decision.

Most democratic parties are active in financing and conducting campaigns to ensure their candidates are elected. In addition to travel costs, candidates have to pay for polls, consultants, advertisements, speechwriters, office space, car rental, and staff.[4] In democratic countries, candidates increasingly hire outside professionals who are specialists in television coverage and image building to play significant roles in political campaigns. In many cases these outsiders have usurped the place of long-time party professionals and reduced their influence.

Party Ideology

Parties in democratic states appeal for votes by presenting platforms based on an ideology or pattern of beliefs. These range from highly ideological tracts (elaborate versions of the ideologies discussed in Chapters 6 and 7) to a hodgepodge of ideas and proposals. Highly ideological parties are concerned primarily with winning converts for their ideologies as well as increasing their number of votes to win office. Less ideological parties such as catch-all parties, on the other hand, are concerned more with attracting a wide range of voters by proposing solutions to specific or timely problems.

Since the 1980s, party systems in many developed democracies have shown patterns of change associated with general and widespread shifts in ideology.[5] The traditional socialist left in several Western European countries has declined somewhat. Even in Britain, when the Labour Party won in 1997, it did so by turning its back on socialist principles. At the same time, there has been a general rise of parties advocating a free-market economy and the privatization of state-owned assets.

Politics has also moved to the right in Canada and the United States in recent years (see Close Up 17.2). In the United States, the Democratic and Republican parties have been so little attached historically to specific ideas that the parties regularly divide into progressive and conservative camps rather than along party lines in Congress. Normally, only in terms of their organizations do these two broad coalitions of interest hang together in a very cohesive fashion. Both claim to represent the vast, mostly moderate body of middle-class voters, but in recent years both parties have been moving to the right of centre.

Running on a right-wing manifesto known as the "Contract for America," the Republicans captured a majority of seats in both the Senate and House of Representatives in the 1994 mid-term congressional elections. This was the first time in 40 years the Republicans held both houses of Congress. The contract committed Republicans to a hard right position on the political spectrum—proposing cuts in what they termed "waste" from the federal budget, and what others called "assistance for the needy." The "Contract" was an electoral gimmick with a number of political objectives. It gave Republican candidates a common theme. It shifted the political discourse significantly to the right. It provided an agenda, a set of priorities, and a timetable for the new Republican majority.

Along with the general shift away from socialism in developed democracies, communist parties with their strict ideologies are also in decline. Their political influence waned almost everywhere throughout the 1980s and 1990s. Following the collapse of communism in Eastern Europe and the Soviet Union, there was bitter in-fighting and disarray in European Communist parties. In France, Spain, Portugal, Italy, and Greece, where Communist parties have played major political roles at various times since World War II, they are far weaker today than a decade ago. They have lost ground to more moderate socialists and social democrats as relative prosperity and the decline of ideology has eroded their base among industrial workers.

As communism has declined there has also been a rise in new parties based on high ideological content such as the environment and women's equality. Such ideas have to a large extent replaced the old issues of class and labour unions. Green socialism is a name sometimes given to ecological or environmental parties and movements that want more radical change in society than the simple platform of ecological awareness would indicate. The basic issues of the importance of ecology and the environment have become widely accepted as part of the political agenda in liberal democracies. In some countries, there are single-interest ecology parties, often a Green Party; in other countries ecological issues have been taken over by established parties. The basic issue has become not *whether*, but *how* to deal with the issues, and this inevitably involves ideological disputes between major political parties.

CLOSE UP 17.2 The Ideological Shift to the Right in Canada

The mid-1990s witnessed a profound ideological change in the Canadian electorate and also in the political parties that represent it. Right-wing populism appeals to those who feel disadvantaged, and Canadians, by 1995, had suffered a decline in real incomes for eight of the previous 13 years. Many Canadians blame big, tax-hungry, debt-ridden governments for a growing gap between rich and poor. In their anger they joined forces with an unlikely ally—the corporate elite—to demand cuts in social services and lower taxes. Political parties scrambled to the right to win public support. The Reform Party was the first party to tap into the ideological shift federally, but the Liberal government also moved to the right very quickly following its 1993 and 1997 victories. The party that once introduced old-age pensions, health care, and other social services took up a new mantra of deficit and debt reduction.

On the far right of the political spectrum, anti-immigration issues are the drawing card of ultra-right-wing parties. Some, such as the National Front in France, led by Jean-Marie Le Pen, are particularly striking in their resurgence and importance.[6] The main emphasis of these extreme right-wing parties throughout Europe tends to be anti-foreigner, often anti-Semitic, populist, and nationalist. The new parties generally protest what they term the "corruption of long-standing power," or "the system," and are fuelled by social problems and pressing issues such as high levels of immigration. They respond to a fear of rising crime rates, inflation, immigration, the erosion of family values, and in some cases of losing national identity to the European Union. Unfortunately, they also attract individuals and groups who advocate intolerance and violence.

Party Organization

Political parties in democracies tend to field candidates in national and also often regional or local district levels. Some, such as the British Labour Party, have a well-defined organizational structure and are fairly centralized, with the central party organization maintaining much influence and control. Others, such as the Democratic and Republican parties in the United States or the Swiss national parties, are highly decentralized with very loose, informal organizational structures. Many conservative parties in Europe, apart from the British Conservative Party, are mere loose federations of local associations and a few well-known individuals. In the United States, even at the national level, Democrats and Republicans are weaker organizationally than most parties in other established democracies. Critics claim that the diffuse structure makes it difficult to develop coherent governmental programs, or for the public to hold a party accountable for its performance in congress.

In Canada, parties are closer to the British than the American model. National associations remain skeletal until election time when the offices are swelled by volunteers and extra staff. Although parties at the provincial level share the same name as those at the national level, they do not necessarily share the same organization or party workers, and often operate, in effect, as different parties. The Liberal Party in Quebec and the national Liberal Party, for example, are two distinct organizations. Figure 17.1 outlines party organization in Canada.

In Canada, each of the major parties represented in Parliament consists of two wings: the parliamentary wing, comprising the party leader and caucus, and a very large extra-parliamentary wing also dominated by the leader. The party structure is pyramidal, with a wide, fluid base of party militants at the foundation and an executive body and a small permanent office at the apex. Between elections, virtually all of the structure below the apex dissolves, and communication with the party must be through the national organization or the parliamentary wing. This is quite different from the situation in Britain and other Western parliamentary democracies, where the extra-parliamentary party remains permanently in place.

Discipline and Cohesion

Within many democratic states debates regularly arise about party discipline. **Party discipline** refers to the ability of the leader to enforce obedience on his or her followers in the legislature and in the party organization. All leaders of democratic political parties possess some means of disciplining their members, but there is considerable difference in the degree to which this is accomplished. In Britain and other Westminster-style parliaments, leaders of major parties routinely instruct their members of Parliament how to vote. This is done via the party "whips" whose function it is to ensure that MPs obey the instructions of the leader and the party. Noncompliance risks a range of punishments from expulsion to ostracism, loss of possibility to advance to ministerial ranks, or loss of "perks." The leader also controls the national party organization and can, through it, veto the renomination of rebellious MPs. Perhaps the greatest inducement for government MPs to vote with their party is to maintain a majority vote in Parliament, so that the Prime Minister will not have to call a new election.

Highly disciplined parties, as in Britain and other Westminster-style parliaments, are very **cohesive**. That is, the elected party members act together on major policy issues. Leaders can count on support of all their members over 95% of the time. Parties in Canada are even more cohesive than those in Britain. At the other extreme, some parliamentary parties in France divide quite regularly. Most parties in the developed democracies fall between these two extremes. Some countries are enigmas in this respect as votes in their legislatures are by secret ballot, and no one can be certain whether parties are voting cohesively or not!

Over the years, parties in the United States have demonstrated remarkably little cohesion, although partisanship pervades much congressional decision-making. E.E.

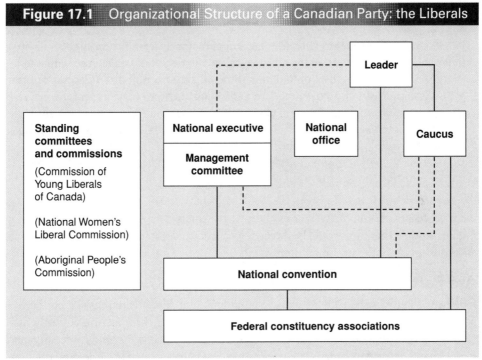

Figure 17.1   Organizational Structure of a Canadian Party: the Liberals

Source: Robert J. Jackson and Doreen Jackson, *Politics in Canada,* 4th ed. (Scarborough, Ont: Prentice-Hall Canada, 1998), p. 402.

Schattschneider argued that parties in the United States should be more tightly disciplined—more like British-type parties—so they could be forced to act more responsibly. Since U.S. parties are not cohesive, the party itself cannot be held responsible for any policies passed or not passed in Congress.[7] As powerful as he or she is in many respects, the President of the United States does not have enough patronage to hand out in order to discipline his or her party. The President can do little more than coax and try to persuade members of the party to vote in a certain way. Members of Congress achieve their power through seniority and congressional influence, not presidential nomination, so they do not depend on the President for advancement or power.

The British, Canadian, Australian, and New Zealand parliamentary systems provide a startling contrast. In these countries the form of government relies on cohesive political parties. The party in power is awarded an electoral mandate to enact a legislative program and its members must support the cabinet and Prime Minister so that the program can be enacted. An MP is not primarily a constituency delegate. In other words, these are not direct democracies. Rather, MPs are elected to serve as members of a particular political party. Within that party the MP is to deliberate and participate in formulating policies, and then to accept and support the majority decision (see Close Up 17.3). If MPs

CLOSE UP 17.3   Party Discipline in Canada

In 1990, a popular Conservative MP in Canada resigned from his party to sit as an Independent. He later joined the Liberals because he strongly disagreed with a tax that the Conservative government was imposing. The argument in favour of his action was that MPs should not be "trained sheep" but free to represent the views of their constituents. Members are, after all, elected by their constituents and should be responsible to them. But others argue that the issue is not that simple: the Canadian form of government relies on cohesive political parties.

Is it an MP's duty to vote for his or her party regardless of personal beliefs?

did not accept decisions arrived at by their party, which groups would they represent? It is quite possible that they would be directed by a particular interest group with a very narrow conception of the national interest.

Are Parties in Decline in Democracies?

Early this century Robert Michels noted a fundamental dilemma of political parties.[8] A political party, he argued, can never retain the program and the constituency for which it was originally founded. In order to win power, parties develop central leadership, and in doing so their party programs inevitably become compromised. This is because the leadership, in trying to build the party, and in working with other parties and interests, develops values and perspectives that are different from the original aims of the party. The validity of Michels' argument has been proven time and again, and some radical parties have even tried to rotate their leadership so that no "leadership class" would develop to compromise the goals of the party. Radical parties that are very quickly successful, as the Nazis were in Germany from 1930 to 1933, are not subject to the dilution of their programs to the same extent as radical parties that attempt to gain power over long periods of time. In the latter case, new radical parties tend to replace the older ones as they become more moderate.

Since the 1950s, political scientists have noted that political parties may not merely be changing, but as institutions they may have entered an era of decline. **Party decline** refers to "the phenomenon in which political parties in general are less determinative of the attitudes and behaviour of political actors on both the mass and elite levels, less highly regarded, and less likely to inspire the electoral act than they once were."[9] In the future, it is argued, parties may play a less significant role in politics than they have throughout the twentieth century. As we have noted, for example, party membership is declining in democracies, and party identification is weakening in most Western industrialized nations.

Political scientists generally agree that a party decline could be unfortunate for democratic political systems. They foresee such negative consequences as governmental incapacity and consequent governmental instability, alienation of citizens from the government and from each other, reduction of accountability of governments to the public, growing conflict within parties, demagoguery, and extremism.[10]

Why are parties declining? A great many contributing factors have been suggested. Often party leaders have amassed power at the expense of party activists. Changing social conditions are also a factor. Conflicts of religion and class have lessened. Fewer people are willing to donate their free time to political parties, and party loyalties have weakened so that voters are more pragmatic and instrumental. Movements and single-issue interest groups, for example, are becoming as adept as catch-all parties in attracting active members. As well, professional bureaucracies are now hired on the basis of objective criteria rather than party patronage, and this has cost parties some adherents. And, finally, the mass media has had a profound impact on parties and elections. To a great extent, television appearances by political leaders have undermined the role of canvassers and caused local party organizations to decline. Television focuses on the party leader, or on a few individuals, and the party tends to be relegated to second place, if it is mentioned at all. When television enters politics, media skills become increasingly important to politicians while party labels become less significant.

Some evidence, on the other hand, indicates that the lament about the demise of parties may be exaggerated. A 1989 study that considered parties in the United States, Great Britain, Sweden, Norway, West Germany, and France cast considerable doubt on the assertion that party decline is universal. It concluded that there is considerable difference in this respect between the countries studied; parties are in decline in some places but not others, and decline does not take the same form in the various places where it does appear. The author claims that the decline of the party should be considered "a nation-specific phenomenon rather than one that applies across most Western industrialized nations and for similar reasons."[11]

It is possible that parties of the "centre" and catch-all parties that have dominated in many Western democracies in recent decades, command fewer passionate supporters. In the late 1990s more ideological parties are back in vogue, and appear to be generating more passion and a greater role for parties once again. Although the role of political parties has changed somewhat in recent decades, they remain the means by which many millions of citizens in a great many of the world's states actively participate and express themselves in the political process. Independent candidates have a difficult time getting elected without a party label and party support. Despite the pessimism about their decline, parties remain a colourful and effective part of the democratic process.

POLITICAL PARTIES IN AUTHORITARIAN STATES

Parties in authoritarian states present a dilemma for political leaders. They are needed to provide support, but participation and mobilization must be strictly controlled to prevent the party from becoming a vehicle which might be used to challenge the leader. Parties are often tightly controlled structures that regiment society and discourage free participation in politics.

When authoritarian regimes are ranged along a no-party, one-party, and multi-party continuum, it is clear that dynastic monarchies and direct military governments generally allow no parties; a great many authoritarian regimes have one party; and very few have multi-party systems. It is also quite common for an authoritarian state to alternate between party governance and military dictatorship as has been the pattern in Turkey, for example. States with single parties that are strongly ideological and nationalist may be transformed into near totalitarian regimes or experience civil war, as has happened for some time in Ethiopia, Mozambique, and Angola.

On occasion, authoritarian states shift in the direction of democracy and allow a competitive two-party or multi-party system to develop. The evolution towards a democratic regime may be a very long process, as it was in Portugal, Greece, and Spain after their periods with authoritarian governments. States sometimes appear to be shifting to competitive parties, but they may not endure when democratic culture and civic traditions are shallow. Such countries can quickly revert to an authoritarian style, as happened in Haiti in 1991 and Algeria in 1992.

The last decade of the twentieth century witnessed dramatic, extraordinary changes in the political systems and political parties of many totalitarian and authoritarian countries around the world. The greatest changes occurred in the Communist countries of Eastern Europe and in the former Soviet Union. To understand the enormity of the change, we first examine the traditional communist party system and then trace its remarkable collapse.

Communist Single-Party Systems

The prototype of single-party systems was that of the Soviet Union from 1918 until about 1986, when it began to "restructure" and crumble. It was a model not only for all communist systems but, in many respects, for other authoritarian regimes as well. As we have noted, political parties within the single-party systems of communist states resemble their counterparts in democracies only superficially. Far from recognizing a loyal opposition, legally only one party is permitted to exist, and all interests must be channelled through it. No opposition is tolerated. Communist theorists maintain that parties represent classes, and since, in a model society, there should be only one class, the "working class," only one party is needed; this is the only "true democracy." To allow another party would be to allow opposition to the interests of the proletariat, and that would be treason.

In 1980, communist governments modelled wholly or partly on the original Soviet system ruled in more than 15 countries. Two decades later the Soviet Union no longer exists, and the few remaining communist states are increasingly isolated—several are trying to reform their systems from within. China is now the only large communist state; with some 50 million members, the Chinese Communist Party (CCP)is the world's largest political organization. Governments in China, Cuba, North Korea, Laos, and Vietnam still share the basic, rigid communist philosophy and one-party systems. To assist their economies, the two largest, China and Vietnam, are pursuing market reforms by introducing some capitalist practices into state-run economies. However North Korea, the third largest, is resisting any change that might trigger the downfall of its Soviet-modelled dictatorship. All three are clinging to rigid communist doctrine and claim that Soviet leaders betrayed the communist cause.

The Soviet Communist Party, 1917–1985

It is important to understand what the Soviet party system was like, and the extensive control of politics that it maintained before restructuring began. The Constitution of the Soviet Union, before the country's collapse in 1991, stated that the Communist Party was:

> ... the ruling and directing force in Soviet society and the core of its political system and of all state and social organizations.

The Communist Party, born of the vision of Karl Marx, was molded by Lenin into a powerful instrument to take over and control an impoverished society in turmoil. It became, as one commentator phrased it, "... church, state, government, watchdog, exclusive club and secret society, a pervasive presence in every aspect of daily life for the millions of people of the Soviet Union."[12] It was the dominant historical force shaping the Soviet Union in the twentieth century.

The Communist Party of the Soviet Union (CPSU) was an elite organization representing, at its height, about 9% of the total population of the USSR, or roughly 19 million persons. Membership was highly restricted; only the most influential members of all occupational and class groups, who were first recommended by three party members of at least three years' standing, and who then passed a series of tests, were allowed to join. Through carefully controlled recruitment, the party maintained members within occupational categories requiring high technical qualifications, or important administrative responsibilities. In this way, it mobilized the population and became the principal means for managing and coordinating society.

The organization of the CPSU, which was highly centralized and disciplined, followed Lenin's formula of **democratic centralism**.[13] The democratic aspect was that party members had the right to participate in discussions and decisions and to elect delegates to conferences, and these delegates in turn had the right to name leaders of higher-level party bodies. Centralism assured unquestioning subordination to the policies adopted in the name of the party. To object was to be expelled. The Communist Party maintained a licensing power over all other social organizations, and regularly broke up those that were deemed to threaten its monopoly over ideological interpretation and policy direction, suppressing, imprisoning, or exiling such group leaders. The highest party organs shared power with the highest governmental bodies, dominating the power structure in the republics, the regions, the cities, and down to the lowest level.

At the apex of the CPSU hierarchy was the **general secretary**, the most powerful figure in the party and therefore of the entire government structure. Below this figure a **Central Committee** of about 240 members divided into several smaller committees including the very powerful Politburo. The **Politburo** was a powerful cabinet, with about

11 members and seven alternates (nonvoting members). As the supreme policy- and decision-making body of the CPSU, it usually met once a week to discuss foreign and domestic matters. The Central Committee's role was to oversee the daily functioning of the party throughout the Soviet Union. It met just a few times a year and elected the general secretary and members of the Politburo. The Central Committee was chosen in turn by the Communist Party Congress, which brought together about 5000 delegates at least once every five years.

Below the Party Congress another level of district, provincial, and republic committees and bureaus existed; at the grass roots a wide range of primary party organizations, or cells, was set up in factories, farms, military units, and other work places. An inner core of full-time party functionaries or **apparatchiks**, (about 200 000) whose exact number, duties, and salaries were secret, ran the party.

The Communist Party, through the Politburo, was the effective ruling institution of the country, even though a parallel government structure existed.

> [The party controlled] ... all the other apparats of the totalitarian state: the armed forces, the courts of 'justice,' the education system, the economic administration, the secret police, in a word the whole state and through it, as Orwell has described it, human society.[14]

CPSU members were required to spend a great deal of time performing political volunteer services and updating their knowledge of Communist Party theory and doctrine. In return for loyalty and performance they enjoyed privileges and benefits such as superior housing, access to scarce goods and medical services, and access to career advancement and social prestige.

The Decline of the Communist Party and the Rise of Democracy in the USSR

Between 1985 and 1989, Soviet leader Mikhail Gorbachev set the forces of democratic change in motion in the USSR. In the face of a deep economic crisis, he undertook to reform communism through controlled liberalization. "Reform communism," with its rallying cry for *perestroika* (restructuring) and *glasnost* (openness), did not aim at full cultural freedom, constitutional government, or a market economy with private property. It absolutely did *not* envisage giving up the hegemony of the Communist Party.

The former Soviet Union also faced the dilemma of how to achieve economic reforms and still retain the tattered remnants of the communist regime. Over a period of six years following the introduction of reform communism in 1985, the Communist Party in the Soviet Union steadily lost authority but still remained entrenched in virtually every branch of the central government.

In 1988 and 1989 President Gorbachev organized partially contested elections in order to create a power base for reform communism separate from the Communist Party. This meant that the party had to give up its constitutional monopoly on power. Following the elections it became the opposition in many major Russian cities, including Moscow.

By June 1989, in the first session of Congress, dissident groups had moved to outright repudiation of the system. Their goal was "to wrest power from the [Communist] Party and to move toward genuine constitutional government, a market system, and private property."[15]

In 1990, Gorbachev created a new office of Soviet President, separate from leadership of the Communist Party. He was duly elected, and as President he was later voted sweeping decree powers. (See Figure 17.2 which outlines the Soviet power structure in 1990.) Meanwhile, with the complete collapse of Eastern European communism in 1990, opposition to the party-controlled system was also mounting in the Soviet Union. Reform communism had brought unprecedented cultural freedom and some semi-free

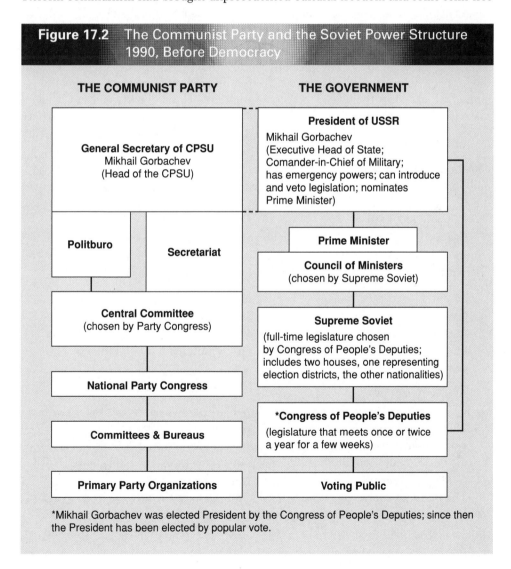

Figure 17.2 The Communist Party and the Soviet Power Structure 1990, Before Democracy

THE COMMUNIST PARTY   **THE GOVERNMENT**

General Secretary of CPSU
Mikhail Gorbachev
(Head of the CPSU)

President of USSR
Mikhail Gorbachev
(Executive Head of State;
Comander-in-Chief of Military;
has emergency powers; can introduce
and veto legislation; nominates
Prime Minister)

Politburo   **Secretariat**

Prime Minister

Council of Ministers
(chosen by Supreme Soviet)

Central Committee
(chosen by Party Congress)

Supreme Soviet
(full-time legislature chosen
by Congress of People's Deputies;
includes two houses, one representing
election districts, the other nationalities)

National Party Congress

*Congress of People's Deputies
(legislature that meets once or twice
a year for a few weeks)

Committees & Bureaus

Primary Party Organizations   **Voting Public**

*Mikhail Gorbachev was elected President by the Congress of People's Deputies; since then the President has been elected by popular vote.

elections, but had permitted only relatively minor economic change. Party leaders resisted reforms that might threaten the *nomenklatura* system (see Chapter 15) and cause the party to lose control over the economy as it had in Poland and Hungary. In spite of this resistance, however, *glasnost* and *perestroika* allowed long pent-up grievances and complaints from the Soviet people to be released. As one observer put it: "The system was desacralized and delegitimized, and by 1990 only criticism of Lenin remained taboo."[16]

In May 1990, Boris Yeltsin, who espoused republican sovereignty and a market economy, was elected chairman of the presidium of the Russian Republic's Parliament in the first major free election in Soviet history, and became leader of Russia's first non-communist government. Within weeks the Russian Parliament declared Russian sovereignty, and Yeltsin resigned dramatically from the Communist Party.

Gorbachev continued to support the Communist Party as he prepared groundwork to reform it, maintaining that the party was essential to keep the Soviet Union together. In July 1991, the party leadership approved a new charter that would transform the former "vanguard of the proletariat" into a broad-based "party of democratic reforms."[17] It called for the CPSU to become an ordinary kind of party with no "leading role." It also called for private property rights and the "separation of economic activity from state management" (no more command economy).[18] As part of the union treaty being worked out with nine of the Soviet republics, Gorbachev also proposed free parliamentary elections and direct presidential elections. Gorbachev also noted that 4.2 million party members had quit over the previous 18 months, reducing membership to the 1973 level of about 15 million, and that resignations continued to pour in at the alarming rate of 2000 a day.[19]

By this time, Boris Yeltsin had won considerable concessions for Russia but was determined to diminish communist authority as quickly as possible. Yeltsin's aim was to end direct party control over the Soviet Union's largest republic. His program

> [essentially jettisoned] many of the dogmas that the Communist party used to justify its iron control over all facets of the nation's life and thought, ranging from its identification as a party of the "working class" through militant atheism, the ideological monopoly of Marxism-Leninism and the imminence of a Communist society.[20]

A government takeover, or coup d'état, staged by hard-line communists against the Soviet leadership on August 19 to 21, 1991, failed, and gave democrats the upper hand politically. On August 22, Yeltsin ordered Communist Party cells in the Soviet armed forces on Russian territory to disband. In response, Communist leaders indicated that they intended "to fight to maintain the privileges, power and wealth" they still enjoyed.[21] They totally rejected Yeltsin's proposal to, in effect, strip the party of its foundations.

The party was, however, tearing itself apart. Despite the attempted coup against him, Gorbachev at first stood by the party saying it had to be purged of reactionaries but could still contribute to reform. On August 23, 1991, Yeltsin suspended *Pravda* and five other Communist Party newspapers. The next day Gorbachev abruptly announced his resignation as leader of the CPSU and recommended that its 300-member inner circle, the Central Committee, be disbanded. By resigning, he effectively decapitated the party and left it to find its own place in the new order. Then, he issued two decrees which amounted to the death blow of the party. First, he ordered an end to all actions by political parties and movements in the military, the security forces, the KGB, and the apparatus of government. Activities of parties or political movements could be carried on only outside of these organs and on their own time. Secondly, he ordered parliamentary deputies to take custody of all the Communist Party's vast holdings.[22]

A few days later the Soviet Parliament held three hours of anguished debate on the fate of the party. Parliament then voted to suspend all activities of the Communist Party pending an investigation of its role in the coup, but it left open the possibility that the party could still return in the future in some social democratic form.[23]

Thus, after more than 74 years, Communist Party rule ended in the Soviet Union, and on Christmas Day 1991, the Soviet Union itself formally ceased to exist. The Communist Party was not declared illegal, because reformers feared the party network and wanted to keep it in the open. It will take years to destroy the grip the party bureaucracy had on the Soviet economy and the apparatus of government. The invisible *nomenklatura* network that buttressed the party may never fade away entirely.

Kremlinologists are still working to explain why the tightly organized, disciplined, and self-perpetuating Communist parties collapsed so unexpectedly. One expert explains it in terms of the collapse of a "totalitarian triangle"—a model that sees the leader at the apex, the bureaucracy and doctrine of Marxism-Leninism as the supporting sides, and the military as the base.[24] Inside this outer triangle is another inner one, made up of the KGB and police systems, which reinforce the outer triangle's ability "to keep society penned in."[25] Roderick MacFarquhar argues that, in the Soviet Union, *glasnost* weakened the doctrinal side of the triangle, while *perestroika* weakened the bureaucratic side. Soviet citizens in effect forced their way out of the weakened triangle. Gorbachev facilitated the breakdown by his decisions to allow party doctrine to be questioned, to encourage an attack on bureaucracies, and to withhold the use of force to the extent that citizens no longer assumed it was inevitable. The Soviet Union and Eastern Europe were broken by blows from the apex, not from internal social pressures.

Fledgling Parties and The Party System of Democratic Russia

In the turbulent years immediately following the breakdown of the Communist Party's hold on the former Soviet Union, Russia struggled toward the democratic ideal of free elections. With no history of democratic parties and elections to guide them, the way has been difficult. New rules had to be devised and put in place for both parties and elections.

The rules for the 1995 Duma election were sufficiently liberal that well over 250 new parties sprang up to run for office. Many were "sofa parties" (so small that their members could all fit on one sofa) unable to collect the 200 000 signatures necessary by the new electoral laws to register. In the end, however, 45 parties were officially registered. Many, such as the Women's Party strictly represents specific group interests. Others were merely vehicles for their leaders—for example, the five top reform politicians all formed their own parties. The number of parties actually making it to the Duma was restricted because of a voting threshold: a party has to secure at least 5% of the national vote before any of its members can win one of the 225 seats elected under proportional representation.

The 1995 campaign was Russia's second post-Soviet election, and the Communists were hopeful because reformed Communists had been highly successful in second post-communist elections throughout Eastern Europe. (The Communists had come in third in Russia's 1993 elections.) This time, the Communists were able to extend their appeal beyond their core groups of support—pensioners, farm workers, and trade unionists of the old agro-industrial complex. They were relatively coherent and united. Fortunately for them, the rules benefited the two parties with the best nationwide organization, themselves and the Liberal Democrats. On election day, disillusioned with economic and social conditions in their fledgling democracy, and crushed by the failure of familiar institutions, Russians voted against the government and moderate reformers in favour of Communists and nationalists. (See chapter 19.) Gennady Zyuganov's Russian Communist Party with its nationalistic rhetoric about "Mother Russia" was the favourite choice of Russia's impoverished pensioners and also of the agrarian vote. The reform ballot was split between five different parties.

The Communists and ultra–nationalists—led by Vladimir Zhirinovsky—now control more than half the seats in the Duma. It is not yet clear what this Communist victory will mean for Russia—whether key reforms will be slowed or reversed. Neither is it clear how, or even whether, the party system will continue to develop along free and democratic lines. The next parliamentary elections will be held in 1999, following a year of political and economic crisis.

Few Russians take elections to the Duma seriously (see Close Up 17.4). Because of the great powers of the President, that election is considered to be by far the most important in determining the course of the country. In June 1996, Russians went to the polls for presidential elections, electing Boris Yeltsin for another term (in spite of his poor health). By the summer of 1998, Yeltsin was very seriously weakened politically, and the country was close to financial collapse.

Communist Parties Outside Europe

Repercussions from the turmoil in the Soviet Union and Eastern Europe were extensive. When communism collapsed, East Bloc aid to developing areas suddenly diminished. Almost overnight many LDCs lost their biggest export market, their main military arms supplier, and their biggest international supporter. In Africa, what one official in the Economic Community of West African States described as an irreversible "hurricane of change" swept the continent. For nearly three decades all but a handful of African nations

CLOSE UP 17.4 Russian Parties in the Run-up to the 1995 Parliamentary Elections

In Russia, as in other developing democracies, hundreds of special interests set up their own political parties. In the 1995 elections to the Duma, there were parties for beer lovers and army officers, to name just two. Their promises ran from the mundane to the exotic ... from lower taxes to raising the temperature to subtropical levels. One party even promised to re-conquer Alaska. There was a flood of new candidates with criminal records who wanted to be elected so they could enjoy immunity from prosecution. Only three parties each won over 10% of the vote, however: the Communist Party (communist); the Liberal Democratic Party (nationalist and xenophobic) and Our Home is Russia (moderate reformist).

had been run, to some degree, as single-party states under a powerful authoritarian leader. Their governments normally changed hands by military coup, or more rarely, when the ruler died in office of natural causes. Suddenly in the first two years of the 1990s, several former one-party states and military dictatorships in Africa were forced to allow some form of political opposition.

In October 1990, Côte d'Ivoire (Ivory Coast) was the first of Africa's old-style single-party governing systems to hold an election following the wave of democratic reform that began sweeping sub-Saharan Africa. Amid charges of cheating and ballot-rigging, 85-year-old President Houphouet-Boigny won his 75-year term against aggressive campaigning by opposition parties. The 1995 elections were equally flawed. By 1992, in southern Africa alone, the Communist states of Angola and Mozambique, as well as one-party Zambia and military states Lesotho and Madagascar had either adopted, or were planning to adopt, multi-party systems. Of the regimes that fell, some were Communist and some were on the right of the political spectrum. Many of the African states that were caught up in a wave of democratic change were acting after years of autocracy. In Benin, Togo, and Zaire, long-ruling leaders were shaken and overthrown by the democratic movement as a new generation of educated Africans rejected the authoritarian politics of the past and sought desperately needed economic reforms that they believed could only come with some measure of political pluralism. Kenya was one of the few African countries south of the Sahara that by late 1995 had still refused to allow a multi-party system. Kenya had become a one-party state in 1982, and the President consistently rejected a multi-party system, calling opposition groups "tribalistic."[26]

Not all Communist systems declined after the breakdown of the Soviet Union. While communism in Eastern Europe waned and the CPSU itself appeared to be on the verge of extinction, the Chinese Communist Party (CPP) was announcing an increase in Party membership to over 50 million people. In July 1991, the CCP celebrated its seventieth birthday. Why did it survive where the others failed? One expert has suggested two major reasons.[27]

Firstly, unlike the communist regimes in Eastern Europe, communism was not imposed on China by Soviet arms, but was indigenous to the country. Therefore, during the 1989 protest in Tiananmen Square, national liberation was not an issue as it was a few months later in Poland, East Germany, Hungary, and the former Czechoslovakia. And because China's hard-line leaders, including the chief reformer Deng Ziaoping, feared the emergence of an independent workers' movement like Solidarity in Poland, they firmly and brutally put down the peaceful student demonstration with military suppression.

Secondly, the Soviet Union needed drastic economic reform that could not be achieved without political reform. In China, however, Deng had spurred China's economy during the 1980s by "unleashing the peasantry from the burdens of soviet-style collectivization." By 1989 "he could reasonably hope that a Communist-led China could be transformed into a powerful modern state" without making fundamental concessions to political reformers.[28]

While Mao's Cultural Revolution had sought to purify the party of "counterrevolutionaries" in 1966, the onslaught weakened the CCP, and it never fully recovered its authority and legitimacy.[29] As one author put it, "the distinction between disgraced leaders and the organization they served was hard to perceive."[30] When Deng became Mao's successor in late 1978, he made the criteria for party leadership economic efficiency and managerial skills, and insisted that the mandate of power was based on competence, thus undermining the strict ideological role of Marxist-Leninist-Maoist thought. Deng did not want the party to be dominated by the leader as it had been under Mao. His volte-face from Maoism and acceptance of a reform program constituted an admission that communist economics did not work.[31]

In his analysis of why the communist regimes collapsed in the Soviet Union and Eastern Europe but not in China, MacFarquhar considers that the weakening of the CCP leadership first by Mao and then by Deng have made the top and sides of the totalitarian triangle in China more fragile, leaving the military as the strong side. As in the Soviet Union and Eastern Europe, he says, the state leadership has contributed to a weakening of the party.

> Totalitarian systems can withstand pressure from social forces; they tend to
> fall apart when their leaders, out of a desire for radical change ignited by
> some external challenge, take actions that help to destroy the system.[32]

For Deng the external challenge was the positive example of the flourishing East Asian economies of Japan, Korea, and others combined with the negative example of the Soviet economic model. For Gorbachev, the comparable image was the superior performance of the Western capitalist system.

In the smaller communist countries of Cuba, Korea, and Laos, communist parties also dominate. In Cuba, for example, the Communist Party (PCC) is still the only authorized political party in the country. Changes to party politics over the past decade have been minor. In 1991 the PCC endorsed the first direct elections to the National Assembly, dropped a rule that excluded all but atheists from party membership, abolished the partly secretariat, and restructured the Politburo. In 1998 elections to the National Assembly, all 601 candidates approved by the PCC received the 50% favourable vote required for election.

Today, as China has become more liberalized, the Chinese Communist Party (CCP) has lost some of its authority in terms of the economy, but political power remains highly centralized in the hands of a very few party individuals. Party membership has grown to an historic high of 58 million compared to 4.5 million in 1949.

The organization of the CPP parallels that of the CPSU in the former Soviet Union. The party and the government are closely intertwined, as evident in Figure 17.3. Jiang Zemin heads both the Communist Party (as General Secretary) and the government (as President). The National People's Congress (NPC), China's Parliament, is the highest organ of state power. It meets annually to enact laws and has the power to amend the Constitution. Deputies in Congress are elected by lower-level legislative bodies and by units of the armed forces. The NPC is guided by a State Council led by the Prime Minister, Li Peng. However the real political power is in the hands of the Politburo of about 18 Party members—and particularly a small core of members of the group who form the Politburo Standing Committee, known as the "magnificent seven." The Standing Committee is headed by the General Secretary, Jiang Zemin, and the Prime Minister, Li Peng, also a member. The group is charge of the military is a party body called the

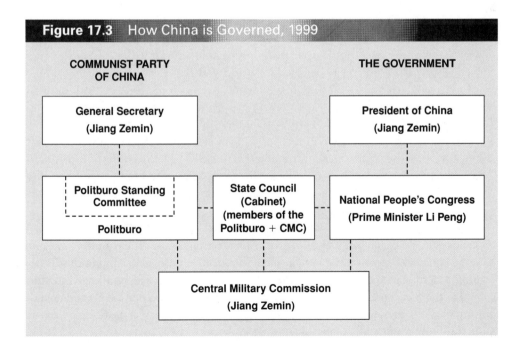

Figure 17.3   How China is Governed, 1999

COMMUNIST PARTY OF CHINA

THE GOVERNMENT

General Secretary
(Jiang Zemin)

President of China
(Jiang Zemin)

Politburo Standing Committee

Politburo

State Council
(Cabinet)
(members of the
Politburo + CMC)

National People's Congress
(Prime Minister Li Peng)

Central Military Commission
(Jiang Zemin)

Central Military Commission (CMC). A parallel CMC under the NPC has the same membership. Both military groups are headed by Jiang Zemin.

China was established as a one-party Communist state, but for many years the regime permitted eight small minority parties to exist. However in December 1998, one party's escalating free speech and criticism drew a backlash from the CPP. Li Peng, leader of the NPC declared that any group opposing the Communist Party "will not be allowed to exist." [33] The leaders of the tiny China Democracy Party were arrested and charged with conspiring to overthrow the state. What the group was working toward was a multi-party system to press for human rights. China's leaders may be ready to allow limited criticsm but certainly not from another political organization.

Single-Party Authoritarian Regimes

Fascist Italy (1922–1944) and Nazi Germany (1930–1945) provide classic historical examples of authoritarian regimes on the right wing of the political spectrum which relied on single-party systems. We noted in Chapter 8 the marked resemblance of these regimes to communist regimes with respect to ideology, centralization, and concentration of power in the hands of the leader and a small, chosen elite. These single-party systems were also organized in a manner similar to their classic communist counterpart.

The organization of these fascist systems was pyramidal and hierarchical with the *Duce* and the *Fuhrer* at the top. Annual party congresses were mere formalities to extol the virtues and policies of the leader. As with the CPSU the party structure ran parallel to governmental structures, and party officials infiltrated the government at all levels, monitoring and controlling its activities. Recruitment to the parties was strictly controlled, and intimidation and force were used readily to exact compliance. Unlike the CPSU, however, these two authoritarian parties did not implode from within. They were destroyed when their armies were defeated in World War II.

Today, single-party systems are less common than before 1990, but still exist in both military and civilian authoritarian regimes such as Syria, Senegal, Zimbabwe, and Tunisia. In these states the single-party systems have different characteristics from those we have just noted. The single political party never attains the dominant position that it does in systems that approximate the totalitarian model. The party is only one important organization among several—including tribes, the army, the bureaucracy, and the church—that are established as agents of support for the government. See Close Up 17.5 for Uganda's unique "no-party" system.

Authoritarian parties are constantly manipulated by individuals in power to counterbalance the power and influence of other organizations within the country.[34] At one period a party may appear to be very influential, but when the leadership finds it is becoming a significant political force, the army or bureaucracy will be allowed to gain ground at the party's expense. In such political systems there tends not to be a strong, mobilizing ideology as there is in totalitarian systems where the party uses ideology to permeate and subordinate all competing elite groups.

CLOSE UP 17.5   "No-Party Democracy" in Uganda

President Yoweri Museveni of Uganda fought his way to power in 1986 in a long guerilla war. He argues (as rulers of authoritarian states often do) that multi-party democracy would divide Uganda society vertically by tribe, region, and religion. According to him, parties work in Western democracies because they are divided primarily horizontally by class, and such horizontal divisions are not as divisive as vertical cleavages. For this reason, Museveni says. he banned political parties.

Museveni held and won presidential elections in 1996 and has generally restored order, but the ban on parties has been extended until at least the year 2000. Meanwhile he has set up what he calls a "no-party democracy" in which candidates stand as individuals, not as party representatives. His critics are less flattering, calling his system a "one-party state with its face washed." In 1999 elections, parties will be allowed, but candidates can stand only as individuals and cannot hold rallies. Museveni will, however, have the machinery of government and his ruling organization behind him.

Given that democracy and economic reform in Uganda seem to be slowly progressing, is Museveni's approach justified?

INTEREST GROUPS IN DEMOCRATIC REGIMES

Interest groups, like political parties, are distinguishing features of democratic regimes. Their operation and significance depend a great deal on the political rules within which they must operate.[35] Interest groups are a vital part of politics in Canada, Britain, and other liberal democracies. However, nowhere in the democratic world are interest groups more significant and widespread than in the United States. In fact they are considered a distinguishing feature of the U.S. government for several reasons. Interest groups accord perfectly with elements of the political culture such as individualism and popular sovereignty. As well, the Constitution makes it relatively easy for pressure groups to influence decisions on behalf of objectives that are often narrow and highly particularistic.[36] For example, the First Amendment protects free speech, press, and assembly as well as the right to "petition Government for a redress of grievances." The fragmented political structure of the United States also contributes to interest-group activity.

Interest groups participate in politics and decision-making in similar ways, adopting similar strategies and tactics. They utilize methods and targets that seem most likely to influence the decision-making process. Within a country these vary from group to group and even from issue to issue for the same group. In different states, interest groups need to adapt their methods and targets to what is allowed or expected in the political culture. The form that pressure-group activity takes, therefore, varies a great deal both within and between states. Across the broad panorama of interest groups the following strategies are common:

- **Direct Political Action**   Methods include petitions, letter writing, demonstrations, and attempts to affect the selection of political authorities and to influence public opinion through the media.
- **Providing Material Resources**   These range from small gifts to multi-million dollar corporate kickbacks, bribes, and favours to targeted decision-makers in return for desired action. Rules about methods and amounts of money or goods that can change hands vary greatly from one country to another.
- **Providing Information**   Interest groups often have specialized data that governments need to formulate public policies.
- **Compliance or Noncompliance**   Political actors benefit from successful policy implementation, and therefore cooperation with interest groups is normally desirable. This allows interest groups considerable influence. On occasion, interest groups may even attempt to force government action by threatening disruption by such means as organizing strikes or boycotts, encouraging intimidation, or engaging in disruptive or violent activity.
- **Litigation**   Some interest groups work within the court system to affect policy. This strategy often involves backing "test cases" to set judicial precedents on an issue.

Several factors help to determine what kind of strategies, tactics, and methods interest groups will pursue. Resources are important, including financial, social, and political resources such as social status, specialized knowledge or skills, capacity for social disruption, and degree of outside support. Such resources vary markedly, and interest-group behaviour depends, to a great degree, upon which are available.

The environment, including the political culture and institutional arrangements of the state, sets the boundaries of acceptable political action. In democratic societies, interests have a wide range of legitimate possibilities to influence policy-making. In authoritarian regimes, as we shall see, the range is extremely limited.

Targets of Interest Group Activity

In seeking access to the political system to further the objectives of their particular cause, interest groups in democracies focus on one or more of four target areas: political parties, the legislature, the executive, and the bureaucracy.[37] There are several access points provided within the political system and to establish mutual consultation.

Interest Groups and Political Parties—Interest groups often attempt to influence party policy resolutions because party decisions may later become government policy decisions. Some interests, particularly labour associations, openly collaborate with specific political parties, and even affiliate with them, providing both financial and political support for the party. This is the case in Canada, for example, where the Canadian Labour Congress is officially affiliated with the New Democratic Party. In multi-party systems, particularly those with proportional representation electoral systems (see Chapter 19), parties tend to become closely associated with one or a few interests on which they rely heavily at election time. Other groups, however, prefer not to identify themselves with one particular political party because governments alternate between or among parties. Parties too are often wary of affiliation with specific group interests, if they think they might alienate voters. They often prefer discreet collaboration and support.

Interest Groups and Legislatures—Interest groups attempt to have input when legislatures make major decisions about allocating resources. Members may approach elected representatives directly or through legislative committees. They often provide background information for committees, or testify before them. They may even prepare draft legislation for law-makers. The impact of interest groups on the legislative process varies depending on the particular rules or organization of the legislative proceedings. In multi-party legislatures, interests that obtain access to party leaders in legislative committees often exercise considerable influence. In countries such as the United States which have uncohesive parties, the relations between legislatures and interest groups is particularly strong.

Interest Groups and Executives—When legislation is initiated by a government that heads a strong, disciplined party, successful interest groups must concentrate on the government or executive. This is the case in Britain, Canada, Australia, and New Zealand, although it is generally difficult for all but the most powerful interest groups to gain access to the executive branch of governments directly. Except for large, national organizations, which tend to have formalized relations and are periodically invited to present briefs to the executive, interest groups normally rely on less formal, direct contacts with government advisors, members, or leaders.

Interest Groups and the Bureaucracy—The relatively permanent bureaucracy is often the most successful arena for pressure group activity. There tends to be a close relationship between civil servants and interest groups. Civil servants initiate and draft, or research and evaluate, policy proposals for the government executive. They advise the government on the public acceptability of these policies and even help educate and inform the public. Bureaucrats, therefore, often seek interest group expertise. Interest groups, for their part, generally cultivate close relations with bureaucrats who can make their case to executives, provide grants and subsidies, and write regulations.

INTEREST GROUPS IN AUTHORITARIAN REGIMES

Interest groups do not thrive in nondemocratic societies. They are, however, tolerated to varying degrees, depending on the country's particular political system and level of economic and political development. Student demonstrations at Tiananmen Square in China in 1989, which would have been routine in Western democracies, were brutally and repressively put down, and the surviving demonstrators severely penalized. Sometimes, on the other hand, interest groups are successful in authoritarian regimes against heavy odds. The Solidarity trade movement in Poland, for example, weathered massive efforts to disband it and eventually transformed itself into a quasi-political party in 1989.

In authoritarian countries, interest groups are often preoccupied with trying to prevent the government from affecting their groups adversely. In countries at the near-totalitarian end of the authoritarian spectrum, any interest groups that are allowed to exist must affiliate with the single party of the state. In the oil-rich, authoritarian states of the Arab world, substantial government income comes from oil rather than taxing wage earners or property owners. Governments pursue policies without consulting domestic interest groups, and are not held accountable to their citizens. In these circumstances interest groups would fail to coalesce around economic issues even if they were allowed to exist.

Many authoritarian states establish political control over interests by using corporatist principles:

> The state organizes certain interests and associations, allows them representation, and gives them policy-making power on matters that concern them. Interests are functionally organized into corporations, in terms of particular economic activities and operations that bring individuals and groups together: agriculture, industry, trade, banking, transportation, etc.[38]

Corporatism provides certain benefits to authoritarian governments. It provides the various interests with well-controlled integration and participation in policy-making. It also permits the state to broaden its supports by incorporating and allowing the participation of new interests in the corporatist network.

Interest Groups in Communist States

According to communist doctrine, interest groups are not necessary because in a communist state antagonistic contradictions should not exist. In the former Soviet Union even differences of opinion about such questions as how best to distribute produce or repair a road were controlled by the party. All economic interests were subordinated to the state and the party. Such interest groups as existed were entirely subordinate to the central authority, and their only recourse for representation of their interests was within and under the CPSU. They had no autonomy or control of their own resources.[39] Even groups such as the police and army, which had a degree of autonomy, had to operate within or under the CPSU. The police force, for example, was a separate organization with its own intelligence network and had agents throughout society. The army maintained its own communication network, trained its recruits, and controlled vast instruments of coercion. In spite of this measure of autonomy, however, neither group was allowed to act only on behalf of the interests of its respective group because many members of the secret police and army were also high-ranking members of the CPSU. It was impossible to tell whether they exercised influence because they represented the interests of their group or those of the party. By penetrating groups this way, the party dominated and tightly controlled the personnel of all subsystems in society. In China, Cuba, Laos, North Korea, and Vietnam the Communist Party–style of organization of interests continues.

In the new states that replaced the former Soviet Union, it is not yet clear how quickly, or to what extent, group interests will conform to the general patterns that we have just described. Socioeconomic, cultural, ethnic, and other groups in these new states are taking independent positions for the first time. In some of these states there is no history of civil society. In Eastern Europe under communism, interest groups were held in such contempt and disrespect that even today, in a democratic regime, there is a psychological bias against many forms of interest group activity. Special interests do form groups, but rather than taking the form of interest groups they tend to form political parties. It is not uncommon in transitional democracies to find literally dozens of small parties. Over time it can be expected that many of these parties will change their focus and turn to more traditional interest group activity.

DISCUSSION QUESTIONS

1. What are some possible consequences of weak party identification and declining party membership? Is the lament about party decline exaggerated?
2. Are communist states and/or communist parties capable of democratic reform?
3. Why did the Communist Party of the USSR lose control of the country even though it controlled all the significant institutions in the country?
4. What is the role of the party in a communist system? In a military regime?
5. What are the prospects for "democracy" and "capitalism" in the states of the former Soviet Union?

KEY TERMS

apparatchiks, p. 374
Central Committee, p. 373
cohesive parties, p. 268
democratic centralism, p. 373

general secretary, p. 373
party decline, p. 370
party discipline, p. 268

party identifiers, p. 264
party militants, p. 264
Politburo, p. 373

ENDNOTES

1. Leon D. Epstein, *Political Parties in Western Democracies* (New Brunswick, N.J.: Transaction Press, 1980), pp. 98–129, 233–60, and 369–77. Richard S. Katz, Peter Mair, et al., "The Membership of Political Parties in European Democracies," *European Journal of Political Research*, vol. 22 (1992), p. 334.
2. See Paul Whitelay, Patrick Seyd and Jeremy Richardson, *True Blues: The Politics of Conservative Party Membership* (Oxford: Clarendon Press, 1994).
3. Primaries are discussed in Chapter 19. For general reference, see Kenneth Prewitt and Sidney Verba, *An Introduction to American Government* (New York: Harper & Row, 1974), chs. 8 and 9.
4. *Ibid.*

5. See, for example, Peter Mair, "The Problem of Party System Change," *Journal of Theoretical Politics*, vol. 1, no. 3 (1989), pp. 251–76.

6. *The Economist*, November 16–22, 1991, p. 15. See the special issue on new political parties edited by Robert Harmel in *IPSR*, vol. 6, no. 4 (1985).

7. E.E. Schattschneider, *Party Government* (New York: Holt, Rinehart and Winston, 1942). On Britain, see Robert J. Jackson, *Rebels and Whips* (London: Macmillan, 1968).

8. Robert Michels, *Political Parties* (New York: Free Press, 1962, first published in 1915).

9. Howard L. Reiter, "Party Decline in the West," *Journal of Theoretical Politics*, vol. 1, no. 3 (July 1989), p. 325.

10. R.J. Dalton, *Citizen Politics in Western Democracies* (Chatham, N.J.: Chatham House, 1988).

11. Reiter, "Party Decline in the West," p. 325.

12. Felicity Barringer, "The Birth and Death of the Party," *The New York Times*, August 25, 1991, p. 17.

13. See Frederick C. Barghoorn and Thomas F. Remington, *Politics in the U.S.S.R.*, 3rd ed. (Boston: Little, Brown, 1986), ch. 3; and Richard Pipes, *The Russian Revolution* (Cambridge, Mass.: Harvard University Press, 1990).

14. Ghita Ionescu, "The Last Convulsion of Totalitarianism," *Government and Opposition*, vol. 25, no. 4 (Autumn 1990), pp. 519–20.

15. Martin Malia, "A New Russian Revolution?" *The New York Review of Books*, vol. xxxviii, no. 13 (July 18, 1991), p. 30.

16. *Ibid.*, p. 29.

17. *The New York Times*, July 27, 1991, p. A5.

18. *The Economist*, July 6–12, 1991, p. 51.

19. *The New York Times*, August 8, 1991, p. A1.

20. *Ibid.*

21. *Ibid.*

22. *The New York Times*, August 25, 1991, p. 14.

23. The resolution passed in the Soviet Parliament stated: "On the basis of evidence in hand on the participation of leading organs of the CPSU in the preparation and implementation of the state coup from the 19th to the 21st of August 1991, the activities of the CPSU on the entire territory of the U.S.S.R. are suspended." *The New York Times*, August 30, 1991, pp. A1 and A10.

24. Roderick MacFarquhar, "The Anatomy of Collapse," *The New York Review of Books*, vol. xxxviii, no. 15 (Sept. 26, 1991), p. 5.

25. *Ibid.*

26. "Defying Kenya's one-party state," *The New York Times*, February 14, 1991.

27. MacFarquhar, "The Anatomy of Collapse," p. 5.

28. *Ibid.* Also see Alan O. Ebenstein, William Ebenstein and Edwin Fogelman, *Today's Isms*, 10th ed. (Englewood Cliffs, N.J.: Prentice Hall, 1994), pp. 174–95.

29. See James R. Townsend and Brantly Womack, *Politics in China*, 3rd ed. (Boston: Little, Brown, 1986), ch. 4.

30. MacFarquhar, "The Anatomy of Collapse," p. 6.

31. Tensions between leftist orthodoxy and modernizing progressivism are discussed in Stuart Schram, "Economics in Command?: Ideology and Policy Since the Third Plenum, 1978–84," *China Quarterly*, no. 99 (Sept. 1984), pp. 417–61.

32. MacFarquhar, "The Anatomy of Collapse," p. 6.

33. *Los Angles Times*, December 2, 1998.

34. See Samuel P. Huntington and Clement Moore, eds., *Authoritarian Politics in Modern Societies* (New York: Basic Books, 1970).

35. See Gabriel Almond and G. Bingham Powell, *Comparative Politics*, 2nd ed. (Boston: Little, Brown, 1979), p. 169 ff.; also see Jack L. Walker, "The Origin and Maintenance of Interest Groups in America," APSR, vol. 77 (1983), pp. 390–406.

36. Robert Dahl, *Dilemmas of Pluralistic Democracy: Autonomy vs Control* (New Haven: Yale University Press, 1982), p. 190.

37. For information specific to the United States, see Kay Lehman Schlozman and John T. Tierney, *Organized Interests and American Democracy* (New York: Harper & Row, 1986).

38. Roy C. Macridis, *Modern Political Regimes* (Boston: Little, Brown, 1986), p. 252.

39. See Gordon Skilling and Franklyn Griffith, eds., *Interest Groups in Soviet Politics* (Princeton, N.J.: Princeton University Press, 1971), ch. XI; and, by the same authors, "Interest Groups and Communist Politics Revisited," *World Politics*, vol. XXXVI, no. 1 (October 1983), pp. 1–27; and Frederick C. Barghoorn and Thomas F. Remington, *Politics in the U.S.S.R.*, 3rd ed. (Boston: Little, Brown, 1986), pp. 250–304.

FURTHER READING

Democratic Parties

Beck, Paul Allen, and Frank Sorauf, *Party Politics in America*, 7th ed. (New York: Harper Collins, 1992).

Bolz, Dan, and Ronald Brownstein, *Storming the Gates: Protest Politics and the Republican Revival* (Boston: Little, Brown, 1995).

Braunthal, Gerard, *Parties and Politics in Modern Germany* (Boulder, CO: Westview Press, 1996).

Christian, William, and Colin Campbell, *Political Parties and Ideologies in Canada*, 4th ed. (Toronto: McGraw-Hill Ryerson, 1995).

Daalder, H., ed., *Party Systems in Denmark, Austria, Switzerland, The Netherlands and Belgium* (New York: St. Martin's Press, 1987).

Dalton, R.J., and Manfred Kuechler, eds., *Challenging the Political Order: New Social and Political Movements in Western Democracies* (New York: Oxford University Press, 1990).

Eldersveld, Samuel, *Political Parties in American Society* (New York: Basic Books, 1982).

Epstein, L., *Political Parties in the American Mold* (Madison, Wis.: University of Wisconsin Press, 1986).

Featherstone, Kevin, *Socialist Parties and European Integration* (New York: St. Martin's Press, 1988).

Laver, Michael, and Norman Schofield, *Multi-party Government: The Politics of Coalition in Europe* (Oxford: Oxford University Press, 1991).

McDonald, Ronald, and Mark Ruhl, *Party Politics and Elections in Latin America* (Boulder, Colo.: Westview Press, 1989).

McKay, David, *American Polities and Society*, 4th ed. (Oxford: Blackwell, 1997).

Norris, Pippa, and Joni Lovenduski, *Political Recruitment* (New York: Cambridge University Press, 1994).

Padgett, Stephen, ed., *Parties and Party Systems in the New Germany* (Brodefield, Vt.: Dartmouth Publishing, 1993).

Philips, Kevin, *Boiling Point: Republicans, Democrats and the Decline of American Middle Class Prosperity* (New York: Harper Collins, 1993).

Poguntke, Thomas, *Alternative Politics: The German Green Party* (Edinburgh: University of Edinburgh Press, 1993).

Punnett, Malcolm, *Selecting the Party Leader: Britain in Comparative Perspective* (New York: Harvester Wheatsheaf, 1992).

Wattenberg, Martin P., *The Decline of American Political Parties, 1952–88*, 3rd ed. (Cambridge, Mass.: Harvard University Press, 1990).

Whiteley, Paul, and Patrick Seyd, *True Bliss: The Politics of Conservative Party Membership* (Oxford: Clarendon Press, 1994).

Authoritarian Parties

Brzezinski, Zbigniew, *The Grand Failure* (New York: Charles Scribner's, 1989).

Dawisha, Karen, *Eastern Europe, Gorbachev, and Reform* (New York: Cambridge University Press, 1988).

Echikson, William, *Lighting the Night: Revolution in Eastern Europe* (New York: William Morrow, 1990).

Gati, Charles, *The Bloc that Failed: Soviet and East European Relations in Transition* (Bloomington: Indiana University Press, 1990).

Grasso, June, Jay Corrin, and Michael Kort, *Modernization and Revolution in China*, rev. ed. (Armonk, N.Y.: M.E. Shape, 1997).

Hough, Jerry F. *Democratization and Revolution in the USSR, 1985–1991* (Washington, D.C.: Brookings Institution, 1997).

Kiernan, Brendan, *The End of Soviet Politics: Elections, Legislatures and the Demise of the Communist Party* (Boulder, Colo.: Westview Press, 1993).

Li, Cheng, *Rediscovering China: Dynamics and Dilemmas of Reform* (Lanhan, M.D.: Rowland & Littlefield, 1997).

Ost, David, *Solidarity and the Politics of Anti-Politics: Opposition and Reform in Poland Since 1968* (Philadephia: Temple University Press, 1990).

Pipes, Richard, *The Russian Revolution* (New York: Alfred A. Knopf, 1990).

Roskin, Michael G., *The Rebirth of East Europe* (Englewood Cliffs, N.J.: Prentice-Hall, 1991).

Rupnik, Jacques, *The Other Europe* (London: Weidenfled and Nicholson, 1988).

Smith, Hedrick, *The New Russians* (New York: Random House, 1990).

White, Stephen, Graeme Gill, and Darrell Slider, *The Politics of Transition: Shaping a Post–Soviet Future* (Cambridge: Cambridge University Press, 1993).

White, Stephen, Alex Pravda, and Zvi Gitelman, eds., *Developments in Russian and Post–Soviet Politics* (London: Macmillan, 1994).

Women's and other Movements

Dalton, Russell, and Manfred Kuechler, eds., *Challenging the Political Order: New Social and Political Movements in Western Democracies* (New York: Oxford University Press, 1990).

Eyerman, Ron, and Andrew Jamison, *Social Movements: A Cognitive Approach,* (University Park, Penn.: Pennsylvania State University Press, 1991).

Fainsod Katzenstein, Mary, and Carol McClurg Mueller, eds., *The Women's Movements of the United States and Western Europe* (Philadelphia: Temple University Press, 1986).

Lovenduski, Joni, *Women and European Politics: Contemporary Feminism and Public Policy*, (Amherst, Mass.: The University of Massachusetts Press, 1986).

Pilat, J.F., *Ecology Politics: The Rise of the Green Movement* (Beverly Hills: Sage, 1980).

Randall, Vicky, and Joni Lovenduski, *Contemporary Feminist Politics* (Oxford: Oxford University Press, 1993).

Interest Groups

Almanac of Federal PACs, 1994–1995 (Arlington, Vt: Anward Publications, 1994).

Brooks, Stephen, and Andrew Strich, *Business and Government in Canada* (Toronto: Prentice-Hall, 1991).

Cigler, A.J., and B.A. Loomis, eds., *Interest Group Politics* (Washington, D.C.: CQ Press, 1991).

Coleman, William D., *Business and Politics: A Study of Collective Action* (Montreal: McGill-Queen's University Press, 1988).

Grant, Wyn, *Pressure Groups, Policy and Democracy in Britain* (Hemel Hempstead: Philip Allan, 1989).

Hrebenar, Ronald J, *Interest Group Politics in the Midwestern States* (Ames: Iowa State University Press, 1993).

Lehmbruch, Gerhard, and Philippe C. Schmitter, eds., *Patterns of Corporatist Policy-Making* (Beverly Hills, Cal.: Sage, 1982).

Smith, Martin J., *Pressure, Power and Policy: State Autonomy and Policy Networks in Britain and the United States* (New York: Harvester Wheatsheaf, 1993).

Van Schendelen, R., and Robert J. Jackson, eds., *The Politicization of Business in Western Europe* (London: Croom Helm, 1986).

Wolpe, Bruce C., and Bertram J. Levine, *Lobbying Congress: How the System Works*, 2nd ed. (Washington D.C.: Congressional Quarterly Press, 1990).

 **Weblinks**

www.dru.nl/maatschappij/politiek/groenen/intlhome.htm
This site provides links to Green Parties around the world.

www.conservative-party.org.uk
This is the official Web Page of the British Conservative Party.

CHAPTER 18

Elections and Voting Behaviour

Elections are one of the world's most ancient political institutions. As long ago as 500 B.C. an assembly of citizens in Athens elected consuls, tribunes, and other officials. Today, elections are indispensable to democratic government, and are valued even by some of the most repressive regimes in the world. In this chapter we examine the very important role elections play in a state, and then consider some of the other ways citizens participate directly in policy-making.

An **electoral system** is the composite of rules and regulations governing the voting process by which representatives are elected to the legislature and by which presidents achieve office in presidential systems. Political parties develop their tactics and strategies within the rules of the electoral system. Electoral systems vary significantly, and not only affect the immediate results of any particular election but also may have a long-term impact on the nature of the party system. We examine the main types of electoral systems and the relationship between the various electoral and party systems. Finally, there are many factors that shape individual electoral behaviour, and we consider the most significant of them.

ELECTIONS: A MATTER OF CHOICE

Since the cachet of democracy carries wide national and international prestige, it is relatively common for authoritarian governments to hold elections in order to try to claim that they have popular, democratic support. In 1990, for example, the military government of Myanmar, formerly called Burma, gave in to pressures from leaders of pro-democracy movements and agreed to call "free and fair" elections. But, fearful of losing, the government then proceeded to arrest thousands of opposition leaders, impose strict martial law, and forcibly move nearly a million people from pro-opposition constituencies to the countryside. In spite of these precautions, when the vote was held, the Government's National Unity Party was humiliated. It received only 10 seats while the main opposition party won 396 of 489. The military refused to turn over power, and those who objected hid in the jungles or were jailed.[1] In 1999 the military continues to rule without allowing elections.

Without some form of elections there is no democracy. Citizens have no choice, no say in who will govern them. But it is equally true, as the Myanmar example illustrates, that elections themselves are far from a guarantee of democracy. To qualify as democratic, elections must be free, which means they must satisfy certain criteria. These include ample opportunity for citizens to form political parties and put forward candidates. There must also be open and fair competition between those seeking election so that the electorate can be presented with meaningful choices. Candidates must be allowed to campaign freely and within the same set of rules. All adults who satisfy certain broad criteria such as citizenship and age qualifications must have the right to vote, following the principle of universal suffrage. On voting day all who are registered must be allowed free access to vote according to their wishes, without fear of coercion or reprisal of any kind. For that reason, the vote should be by secret ballot. And finally, each ballot should be accorded equal value, and be counted and reported honestly and accurately. When these conditions apply, and elections are held within regular time intervals, citizens are able to remove and replace unpopular governments. This makes governments responsive to their people, and is the basis of democracy.

When authoritarian states hold elections, they frequently manipulate the outcome by corrupting the criteria that make for a free electoral process. Irregular registration procedures may deprive individuals or groups of the right to vote; sometimes literacy or other restrictive criteria for registration disenfranchise otherwise qualified voters, or registers may be mislaid or tampered with. Ingenious methods are often devised to find out how people will or have voted,[2] and voters are bribed or threatened with physical harm if they do or do not vote in specified ways. The voting process itself offers wide possibilities for fraud such as rigged or missing ballots, ballot box stuffing, insufficient or closed polling booths in selected areas, and corrupt tallying and accounting of ballots.[3]

The distortions are legion and not always limited to authoritarian regimes; sometimes corruption appears close to home in established democratic regimes. Around the world, buying votes is a relatively common phenomenon. It sometimes takes bizarre forms. In Turkey's 1991 election campaign, for example, the ruling Motherland Party organized charity circumcision ceremonies, attracting votes from the poor who found it difficult otherwise to pay for the costly religious rite.[4]

The Functions of Elections

Elections do much more than simply determine who will form the next government; they play several important functions in a state. The primary role of elections, of course, is to provide a routine mechanism for recruiting and selecting the individuals who will occupy seats in representative institutions. In liberal democracies they also provide for the orderly succession of governments. Regularly held elections provide citizens with periodic opportunities to review the government's record, assess its mandate, and replace it with an alternative. Sometimes, as in the United States, the political executive (the President) is elected, reconfirmed, or replaced by the people directly through the electoral process. In Canada, and other parliamentary democracies, citizens elect members to a legislature. The political executive, then, is formed from the majority party within that legislature and is subsequently responsible to it for the exercise of executive power until the next election.

In noncompetitive electoral systems, elections are only one means of achieving or retaining power. Revolutions or coups and coercion by military or other social groups represent other possibilities. For this reason the outcomes of elections in states which do not have a strong historical base of liberal democracy are not necessarily final.

Elected governments claim a mandate from the voters to rule on their behalf. The electoral process legitimates the government, and to a large extent the policies that it has been elected to carry out. Authoritarian leaders also find it desirable to have an electoral mandate. Even though autocrats never intend to give voters any meaningful choice, they provide them with opportunities to participate and express their support for the system. Elections also send a signal of good conduct to the outside world and endow states, even in noncompetitive systems, with valuable international legitimation.[5]

In all societies, elections also act as agents of political socialization and political integration, providing a unifying focus for the country. During the election period the whole society joins in the common project of deciding who will form the next government. Issues, individuals, and parties are given extensive media exposure in a process that informs, educates, and involves individuals in a common national purpose. Competitive elections in particular encourage political parties to aggregate interests in order to build their political support as widely as possible. Even where there may be only a single slate of candidates for the voters to ratify, as in communist states, election campaigns provide an important opportunity for political leaders to communicate to the citizens what is expected of them; to provide, as one author expressed it, "an immediate and solemn occasion for the transmission of orders, explanations and cues from the government to the population."[6]

Competitive elections also allow periodic opportunities for smaller parties and independent candidates to air their views. They provide a kind of safety valve, giving voters an opportunity to express dissatisfaction with the major parties and register their protest by voting for fringe parties or candidates. In noncompetitive systems, elections may serve more to "anesthetize" citizens—to get them to "go along with" what the government wants by offering them limited participation in the political process.

Direct Democracy: Referendums, Initiative, and Recall

The eighteenth-century philosopher Jean Jacques Rousseau, among others, believed that true political freedom could exist only in societies that were small enough for all citizens to meet and govern themselves.[7] This form of government is called **direct democracy** in which all citizens in a community have the opportunity to participate personally in collective deliberation and decision-making about how they will be governed. Obviously in today's large states it is not possible for everyone to be directly involved in a face-to-face policy-making process, but Rousseau argued that the next best option was for elected representatives to express the will of the community in an assembly. In modern times this idea has expanded to mean that elected representatives should cast their ballots on issues precisely the way they are *mandated* to by their constituents, otherwise they would be acting as an oligarchy rather than according to the democratic will. If representatives do not like the views of their constituents, so the argument goes, they should swallow their objections and follow the public's will or resign from office.

However, there is a second school of thought on this issue, also with deep historical roots. It was stated in its purest form by Edmund Burke, an eighteenth-century conservative English philosopher. Burke held that the kind of representative system Rousseau and others advocated was impossible. He argued that the complex problems of modern societies need full-time representatives to study and make decisions about them. Representatives must, therefore, be able to initiate legislation and not just accept their constituents' ideas. Elected representatives did not constitute an oligarchy, he maintained, because the constituents still had the basic power to decide who their representatives would be. If members of Parliament did not vote according to their own opinions, Burke said, the determination of an issue would precede the discussion—the representatives would study complex problems, but the constituents would already have told them the "right" answers. Following Burke's logic, therefore, representatives should study the options and then exercise their independent judgment on public questions. If they do not do so wisely, constituents can, and should, vote them out of office at the next election.

It is clear that Rousseau and Burke had different conceptions of what constitutes true representation.[8] For Rousseau, representation meant that the elected individual act only as directed. For Burke, an elected member of Parliament could not be a true representative unless he or she acted after the results of wise deliberation among his or her peers in an assembly. This "representation" dilemma is still debated today. Complete independence for the representative is not considered democratic because elected members would not be responding directly to their citizens. On the other hand, it is not possible for a representative to determine what his or her constituents want on every topic and vote accordingly (although some political scientists envision semi-direct democracy through new technology—see Close Up 18.1). In fact, constituents often do not understand or care about issues that do not affect their personal lives.

The best way out of the dilemma would appear to be to elect representatives wisely and then allow them to exercise their best judgment about what is needed as circumstances arise. Representatives are not puppets, but neither are they completely independent. If constituents have strong views, the representatives will listen if they want to be re-elected.

Many democratic states do offer occasions on which citizens can participate more directly in policy-making than simply by electing a representative. These methods of direct democracy include referendum, initiative, and recall.

The most common form of direct participation is the referendum. A **referendum** is a means by which a policy question can be submitted directly to the electorate rather than

CLOSE UP 18.1   Semi–Direct Democracy in Action— Two Proposals

Authors Alvin and Heidi Toffler argue that voters should be allowed to make *more* policy decisions than at present. They promote a form of "semi-direct democracy" in which cheaper, accessible technologies such as the Internet could be used to give ordinary people more of a voice in politics. They believe that governments should be downsized and decentralized to accommodate this semi-direct democracy.

Political scientists Theodore Becker and Christa Daryl Slaton of Auburn University in Alabama are among those promoting experiments with semi-direct democracy through "televoting" and "electronic town meetings." They propose to have issues debated on television, radio, and newspapers and then send information about the debates to a random sample of voters. These individuals would be contacted later by telephone and "facilitated toward a teleconsensus."

If public views can be tested so frequently and easily by new technologies, why do we need elected representatives at all?[9]

being decided exclusively by the elected representatives. Sometimes a referendum consists of a single direct question or statement requiring a "yes" or "no" vote from the public; sometimes it is presented in the form of alternative policy proposals from which the voter may choose. Some subjects are more amenable than others to a referendum vote. The most suitable are significant constitutional issues (should your country abolish the Senate?) and specific local decisions (should we open a new park this year?) When these responses directly determine the legislation which the government must enact, the results are said to be binding.

Referendums, however, are not always binding on the government. Some are **consultative**, in that they are intended to guide politicians' deliberations, not necessarily determine their final decision. These are sometimes called plebiscites. Others are used as **instruments of ratification**: governments administer these referendums to give the final seal of approval to a decision they have already taken concerning a very important issue such as a constitutional amendment.

Consultative referendums are primarily symbolic devices to give the illusion of popular participation. They are really glorified opinion polls; the government has already decided on its course of action and in all likelihood knows whether the voters approve. The results of this type of referendum are often almost unanimous. In Egypt, for example, nine referendums were held between 1956 and 1976, and all yielded a "yes" vote of 99.8% or more.[10] Binding referendums offer a more meaningful choice to citizens since the government is forced to enact legislation according to the majority decision, whether or not it agrees with the referendum results.

Both types of referendums can be educational, and allow for wide participation, bypassing the political representatives who may or may not accurately represent their opinions.[11] In spite of this, however, referendums are rarities at the national level in liberal democracies. By the mid 1970s only about 500 were known to have been held in the history of the world, and over half of them had been held in Switzerland.[12] The United States has never held any referendums at the national level. Canadians have had only three referendums at the federal level. The first was in 1898, when the federal government was contemplating prohibition of alcohol. The second was during the Conscription crisis of 1942. The third referendum was held in 1992 on a broad constitutional reform package known as the "Charlottetown Accord."[13]

National referendums are relatively rare for several reasons. Critics argue that they detract from the sovereignty of Parliament; legislators are elected to make decisions on behalf of their constituents, and any appeal directly to the voters downgrades the importance of the legislators and the sovereign law-making body. As well, referendums usually force clear-cut "yes-no" decisions, which do not allow for any subtlety. The referendum pits opposing groups against each other, and if the government then acts on the results of the referendum, it endorses total victory for one side and total defeat for the other, exacerbating bitter cleavages in society. Representative democracy, in which politicians are placed between the public and the executive, offers more possibilities of compromise between the extremes of an issue. There is also the possibility that relatively uninformed citizens may not want, or may not be able, to make a wise choice on a complex issue and therefore prefer to delegate most of the business of running the country to specialists. Referendum turnouts are usually lower than in general elections so that a minority of the electorate would likely make the decision. As well, there is always the danger that an unscrupulous politician could use a referendum, as Hitler did in the 1930s, to enlist populist sentiments in support of extremist or nondemocratic measures. Perhaps most serious of all, is the objection that referendums may be used as weapons by majorities to threaten or overrule the interests of minorities (see Close Up 18.2).

For these reasons, most countries use referendums cautiously, and primarily at lower levels of government. At the national level they are used most commonly to ratify constitutional amendments, or decide questions of national importance such as sovereignty, secession, or autonomy. The third most common use of referendums is in allowing citizens to decide "moral" issues such as prohibition, abortion, or nuclear energy. On such controversial subjects, politicians are often pleased to let citizens decide for themselves

CLOSE UP 18.2 **Are More Referendums an Antidote to More Lobbyists?**

Some people advocate holding more referendums in order to prevent rich interest groups from getting their way on public policy at the expense of other citizens.

Before deciding whether or not you agree that referendums should be more widely used, ask yourself a question. Keeping in mind that public opinion can fluctuate dramatically, do you trust your fellow voters enough to give them power to make political decisions by referendum?

rather than being held accountable for them at election time. In the United States, since the 1970s the frequency of referendums at the state level has roughly doubled. In Canada as well, referendums are more likely to be held at the provincial level.

Two other instruments used to provide more direct democracy are "initiative" and "recall." **Initiative** is a procedure that allows a group of citizens to petition for a particular law to be drafted and submitted to the electorate for their decision. It is, in effect, a citizens' request for a referendum. Although not used in Canada, about half of the U.S. states allow proposed laws to be voted on directly by initiative procedures. **Recall**, on the other hand, is a procedure that enables citizens to discipline a representative who does not appear to have performed adequately. Constituents may require that their representative be either reconfirmed in office by a new election or dismissed for not properly representing the wishes of the constituency. Recall has not been widely used, not even in the United States where it first appeared.[14]

These procedures are not used very often in parliamentary democracies because of the conflict between direct democracy and the practice of responsible parliamentary government. In the Westminster model they would "either deny to the cabinet the legislation that the cabinet thinks necessary, or ... impose on the cabinet responsibility for the administration of laws the cabinet dislikes."[15] The logical response would be for a cabinet to resign or call an election—a response that could prove unnecessarily expensive and disruptive. Direct democracy procedures are incompatible with parliamentary democracies in another way as well. In these systems the cabinet must retain the confidence of the legislature. If representatives are forced to vote according to their constituents' desires, and these desires conflict with cabinet decisions, the fundamental confidence rule would have to be abolished (see Chapter 13).

Public opinion is notoriously fickle. See Close Up 18.3 for a look at the down-side of electronic democracy.

CLOSE UP 18.3　The Down-side of Electronic Democracy

Imagine a time and place in the future when voters all have Internet access and direct democracy is in vogue. To make a law all one needs to do is send a proposal onto the information highway. Once a week all adult citizens have an opportunity to vote on that week's proposals.

One week, a race riot takes place and the public is bombarded by grisly pictures and detail. Later that week, overcome by emotion, the people vote to ban all "ethnic" immigrants from entering the country and to restrict the liberty of movement of all ethnic minorities.

What does this tell us about direct democracy?

Can voters be trusted to make sensible decisions? Or, are they malleable and short-sighted? How would fluctuations in public opinion impact on a new, electronic society?

TYPES OF ELECTORAL SYSTEMS

There is an enormous variety of electoral systems; states develop unique electoral arrangements based on culture, political history, and party organizations. The type of electoral system determines both *who* votes and *how* the votes are counted. The results of an election under one set of rules would provide a radically different government composition under other rules. It is important, then, to understand how different systems distort the ideal of representation.[16]

There are three main types of electoral systems: single-member plurality, single-member majoritarian, and proportional representation. There are many variations within these three types, but the essential characteristics are the same within each group. Table 18.1 outlines the main differences between these systems.

Single–Member Plurality

The single-member plurality system, sometimes called "first past the post," is the simplest of designs. A country is divided into separate constituencies, and each constituency chooses one legislative representative. In an election, the winner of a **plurality**, that is, the largest number of votes in each constituency, becomes the representative. The candidate does not need an absolute majority of votes—just more than any other candidate receives. One adaptation of this system is a **two-member plurality system** in which the top two candidates represent the constituency.

The single-member plurality electoral system is in place in three of the Anglo-American democracies—the United Kingdom, the United States, and Canada. It is indeed simple, but not without flaws. It damages smaller parties because voters tend not want to "waste" their ballots by casting them for candidates who have no chance of winning. The plurality system tends, therefore, to produce contests between two leading candidates. In fact, it is fairest as a method when only two parties are competing for office. It can produce bizarre, undemocratic results when there are more than two parties. Often in such cases, the winning candidates receive less than half of the votes cast, so that they do not, in fact, represent the majority of their constituents. There is also the problem that a party may win nearly all of its votes in a few constituencies and therefore elect only a few representatives, even though they would have won a greater number of seats had their support been more evenly dispersed throughout many constituencies. Instead, their supporters' votes were "wasted" by being uselessly concentrated in a few areas. Conversely, a party might have considerable support but, because it is too thinly dispersed across many constituencies, not be able to elect any representatives at all. One extreme example of this problem occurred in 1993 when the Conservatives took 16% of the votes in the Canadian general election but won only 2 seats—0.7% of the total. In the 1997 election they won 19% of the votes but only 6.6% of the seats.

Table 18.1	Types of Electoral Systems and Representation	
Electoral System	**Constituency Representation**	**Party Representation**
Single-Member Plurality	— Maintains traditional link between MP and constituents	— Distortion of votes/ seats ratio
		— Minor parties disadvantaged unless support is regionally concentrated
	— MPs often elected on a minority of total votes	— Discourages multiplication of parties; tendency toward two-party system
Single-Member Majoritarian		
(a) Alternative Vote (AV)	— Both maintain traditional link between MP and constituents	— Distortion of votes/ seats ratio
		— "Wasted vote" thesis does not apply; small parties survive even if unsuccessful
(b) Second Ballot	— Representatives usually elected by a majority	— Tendency toward multi-party system
Proportional Representation (PR)		
(a) Party List	— Individual representatives usually owe election more to party than to voters	— Approximate congruence between vote shares and seat allocations
		— Minor parties usually gain "fair" representation; easy entry for new parties
(b) Single Transferable Vote (STV)	— Representatives forced to compete for "first preference" votes	— Tendency toward multi-party system
Mixed Plurality/PR	— Maintains traditional link between MP and constituents	— Approximate congruence between vote shares and seat allocations
		— Minor parties usually gain "fair" representation

Single–Member Majoritarian

The **single-member majoritarian electoral system** is designed to eliminate the problem of the winning candidate not obtaining an absolute majority of the votes cast in his or her constituency. There are essentially two "majoritarian" formulas: the alternative vote (AV) and the second ballot.

In the **alternative vote system**, voters have the opportunity to rank the candidates. They number the candidates 1, 2, 3, and so on in order of preference. Initially, the first preferences are tallied. If one candidate has an absolute majority of votes, that candidate is declared elected. If no candidate has an absolute majority, the candidate with the least votes is excluded, and his or her ballots are transferred to the remaining candidates according to the second preferences marked. This process continues until one candidate obtains an absolute majority. This complicated, but relatively fair, system of assigning votes is used in elections for the Australian House of Representatives.

The **second ballot system** also assures that each winning candidate obtains an absolute majority of the votes cast. In this case candidates who win an absolute majority on the first ballot are elected. For those who do not, a second ballot is called. On the second ballot, candidates who failed to get a specified proportion of the votes the first time are excluded; usually only the two leading candidates are left, and the winner of the second ballot, therefore, has the support of the majority of voters. This system is used for presidential elections in France.

Multi–Member Proportional Representation

The third main type of electoral system, **proportional representation**, or "**PR**" as it is generally referred to, is designed to ensure that parties, or groups of voters, are represented more fairly and equitably than is often the case under the single-member plurality or majoritarian formulas. PR systems strive to ensure that all parties receive representation in Parliament in relative proportion to their respective shares of the popular vote. However, by better reflecting public opinion, this electoral system encourages the proliferation of parties. A great many states, including Israel, Sweden, and the Republic of Ireland, use PR systems. There are two main types: the party-list and the single transferable vote (STV).

Party list systems assign parties seats in the legislature in direct proportion to the percentage of popular vote received. They do this either by treating the whole country as a single large constituency or by creating several large multi-member constituencies. The electorate is asked to vote for a party or a slate of candidates rather than for one or more individuals. Using one of many technical procedures, seats are then allocated to each party in proportion to its share of the popular vote. Candidates are selected from the top of each list according to the proportion of the votes their party has won. The closer candidates are to the top of the list, the better their chance of being elected. Sometimes the electoral rules permit voters to express preferences for particular candidates and move them up on the party list. Essentially, however, in all party-list systems the election is primarily to ensure that the legislature reflects the relative popularity of the parties; individual candidates are a secondary concern.

The **single transferable vote** or "**STV**" variety of proportional representation, on the other hand, places somewhat greater emphasis on individual candidates than it does on parties. Members are elected from multi-member constituencies, but electors rank order and vote for individual candidates rather than a party list. To be elected, a candidate must receive a certain number of votes known as the "quota." A candidate who receives more first preference votes than the quota is automatically elected, and, by various methods, his or her "extra" votes are transferred to the remaining candidates according to their second preferences. If no candidate receives a quota on the first count, the least popular candidate is excluded and his or her votes are transferred. This process continues until all seats are allocated. This electoral system is used in the lower house in the Republic of Ireland, and for Senate elections in Australia.

Although these three types of electoral systems represent the major possibilities, a number of **mixed systems** combine features of the plurality and PR formulas. The classic example is the German system, which uses both the plurality and PR party-list systems. We examine the advantages and disadvantages of that system in detail in the next chapter.

Critics of proportional representation have sometimes called it the "Trojan horse of democracy" (see Figure 18.1) because it has the potential to destroy democracy from within by creating a fragmented, multi-party system.[17] F.A. Hermens, for example, argued many years ago that PR gives rise to a multi-party system, because it allows small parties to win at least a few legislative seats.[18] Multi-party systems, in turn, may also give rise to extremist or narrow-interest parties, because such parties can easily win seats. Since no party wins a majority of seats in such systems all cabinets must be based on fragile coalitions of parties. This in turn promotes cabinet instability and increases the possibility of governmental problems.

Advocates of PR, on the other hand, note that single-member plurality systems make it almost impossible for small, new parties to win in even a few constituencies. Voters feel they would be wasting their vote if they voted for a small party even though they would prefer to do so. Critics of PR maintain, however, that this argument proves the value of single-member plurality systems which provide built-in encouragement for the two-party system, and in turn provide moderate politics and stable cabinets.

Defenders of PR have shown that the assumptions behind Figure 18.1 are oversimplified.[19] In fact, PR has produced many long-term, stable governments throughout Western

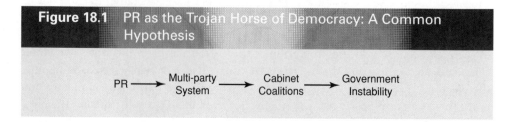

Figure 18.1   PR as the Trojan Horse of Democracy: A Common Hypothesis

PR ⟶ Multi-party System ⟶ Cabinet Coalitions ⟶ Government Instability

Europe. Electoral systems are only one factor affecting party systems: culture, history, and social cleavages also help to determine the number of parties that will prosper and be elected. Societies that are deeply divided along several ethnic, cultural, or religious lines, for example, will be predisposed to multipartism regardless of the type of electoral system. An accurate synthesis of the literature may be that PR retards the development of a two-party system, and it has a slight multiplying effect on the number of parties.[20]

Just as the Trojan horse theory about PR systems must be qualified, so must its counterpart about single-member plurality systems (see Figure 18.2). Not all such electoral systems have produced two-party systems. In Canada, for example, what for years had been a "two-party system" has fragmented into a multi-party dominant system despite the fact that there has been no change in the electoral system (see Chapter 16).

Figure 18.2 The Effects of Single-Member Plurality Systems

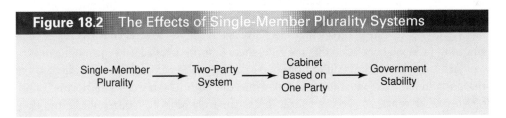

VOTERS AND VOTING BEHAVIOUR

Analysts of electoral behaviour attempt to learn how and why people vote as they do and what their opinions are about specific political events, personalities, and issues. They focus on the voting behaviour of individuals and groups, and the electoral patterns of party support. The topic is amenable to quantification so studies of voting behaviour can apply survey techniques. In order to answer the "how" and "why" questions about opinion and behaviour, public opinion polls are administered to selected samples of the electorate. The "why" questions are more difficult, and more costly to answer. They usually involve taking random samples of people over several time periods to establish why they voted, whether their political attitudes changed over time, and, if they changed, why. Although such behavioural research produces quantifiable results, the quality of the study hinges on the rigours of the research design: a) the sample must be meticulously drawn and extrapolated cautiously to the population as a whole; b) the responses obtained must be honest, freely given, and based on clear and accurate memory; and c) the analysis must be based on objective, scientific methodologies.

Voter Turnout in Democratic Elections

Voting in elections is one of the most basic forms of political participation. It has been a matter of concern in many democratic states, therefore, that the percentage of citizens exercising that right has been low in recent decades. Voting in many cases has become an elite activity, with those in the higher income and educational brackets voting more frequently than their opposites. In most developed democracies, between about 47% and 95% of the electorate vote. Several factors have been associated with low voting turnouts. Sometimes individuals and groups are alienated and feel powerless to influence the political system. Citizens are often cynical about politics and politicians in general, disillusioned by widely publicized scandals and misdemeanours by politicians. The growth of governments has also brought unpopular tax burdens and created the impression that governments are aloof and uncaring. And, in modern, complex societies citizens have many interests and activities with which they are preoccupied, preferring to leave politics to others as long as the government does not seem to be damaging them personally.

What are the reasons for such discrepancies in turnout across countries? In a classic study, Robert W. Jackman found that voter turnout has little to do with political culture factors. Americans generally score higher than citizens of other countries on the perception of voting as a civic duty, they still have a lower turnout rate than most other Western democracies. About 53% vote in presidential elections, and only 35% to 40% vote in congressional elections. Jackman concluded that the differences in turnout reflect five main influences.[21]

First, registration laws differ from one country to the next. These rules affect voter turnout and render cross-country comparisons difficult. In some cases authorities register voters automatically; in others it is left to the individual to register, and often they do not bother. In the United States, for example, where 49 states (North Dakota is the exception) require voters to register before they vote, only about 60% do. This leads to a lower calculation of voter turnout than when traditional measures are used. A U.S. humourist once described elections in his country in these terms: an elected official gets 51% of the vote cast by 40% of the 60% of the prospective voters who are registered! When the vote is calculated as a percentage of registered voters we find that the United States moves up considerably in the comparison.

The second influence Jackman found was that the greater the likelihood that the party in power might be defeated, the higher the turnout. Third, the closer the proportion of the offices won by each party to its share of the popular vote, the higher the turnout. Fourth, elections that are likely to produce a clear winning party produce higher turnouts. And, fifth, turnouts are higher in countries where there is only one legislative house with real power, and lower in countries where power is shared between two houses.

To these five influences on turnout might be added the structural condition of compulsory voting. This operates in several countries including Australia, Belgium, Italy, Greece, and Spain. When compulsory voting was introduced in Australia, turnout jumped from 64% to 95%. Advocates of compulsory voting argue that it strengthens democracy, and that nonparticipants are like a time bomb waiting to disrupt the system.[22] Detractors argue that such compulsion takes away the citizen's right to abstain, and that excessive participation can cause excesses in politics. Seymour M. Lipset, for example, found that the high turnout in the German elections of 1932 and 1933 helped bring Adolf Hitler to power. Gabriel Almond and Sidney Verba argued the middle ground on this issue, taking the stand that the ideal citizen is one who participates up to a point but then sits back and trusts the elected government.[23]

Does nonvoting make a difference? The act of voting itself is important; apathy and indifference destroy democracy from within. Groups that do not vote weaken their collective voice in government. Many candidates win or lose an election by a mere handful of votes, so higher participation could make a difference. Without introducing compulsory voting there are steps that could be taken to encourage voluntary participation. Simpler registration procedures, less negative campaigns, and better voter education about complex issues are some of the possible ways to entice citizens to be participants rather than spectators.

Theories of Voting Behaviour

Modern quantitative studies of voting behaviour have produced various models to explain electoral behaviour:[24]

- **"Supermarket" voting**   This early model suggested that rational voters examine the options and make their selection on voting day just as they choose among products in a supermarket. However, it was soon discovered that many, if not most, individuals make their choice based on brand loyalty—a strong preference for a political party. Their minds are already made up concerning what they will "buy," or who they will vote for.

- **Social group voting**   Another early model suggested that people vote according to their affiliation with social and economic groups, including their social class, education, ethnicity, income, religion, rural or urban residence, etc. While many studies were able to make significant statistical correlations, a high degree of variability over time weakened the analytic power of this model.

- **Attitudinal voting**   Yet another model suggested that attitudes are the most important influence in determining how individuals vote in elections. There are three important components to such attitudes: the effect of the issues; the effect of the candidates and party leaders; and the strength of the individual's party identification—the sense of belonging to a political party. In this model it is postulated that strong party partisans are unlikely to change their vote, while weaker partisans are more likely to determine their votes on the basis of issues, leaders, or other short-term factors.

At the cross-national level, none of the three models has been able to provide definitive explanations about why individuals, groups, or regions vote certain ways. In fact, it is doubtful that such social science precision is possible for all 192 world states. However, single-country studies in this field have been very instructive in identifying patterns of electoral behaviour that are unique to particular states.[25] These explanations have even proved useful to strategists in calculating party appeals at election times.

Influences on Voting Behaviour

Following the attitudinal voting model, influences on voting behaviour can be grouped loosely into two main types—long-term and short-term factors as indicated in Table 18.2.

Long-term factors contribute to an individual's party identification. They include such socioeconomic indicators as class, religion, gender, ethnicity, and so on. In some countries

Table 18.2   Influences on Voting Behaviour

Long-term	Social cleavages and socioeconomic factors	(class, religion, ethnicity gender, region, urban/rural, etc.)
	Electoral rules	
	Political socialization	
	Political parties	(ideology, cohesion)
Short-term	Electoral campaign	(issues, political events, leaders, candidates, media)
	Political parties	(leadership, images projected)

a breadth of factors or cleavages has contributed to a correspondingly wide range of political parties; in other countries fewer of these long-term factors may appear to contribute significantly to electoral behaviour. Short-term factors arise from the specific election in question. It is important to understand the effects of both kinds of factors in order to understand voters' final decisions. It is possible to visualize these factors as a funnel, with the long-term and then the short-term factors flowing into the funnel, and the vote emerging at the tip, as shown in Figure 18.3.

The long-term factors begin early in each individual's life, as attitudes to politics and political parties are acquired through socialization and social group factors. To varying degrees some of these factors have a bearing on party identification and voting intentions. Long before an election campaign starts, an individual may already have acquired a degree of party identification. During the campaign, short-term factors begin to influence the voter. Some personalities, issues, and policies become particularly influential, while others become irrelevant, thereby narrowing the range of influence on the individual's vote on election day.

Figure 18.3   Funnel of Influence in Voting Behaviour

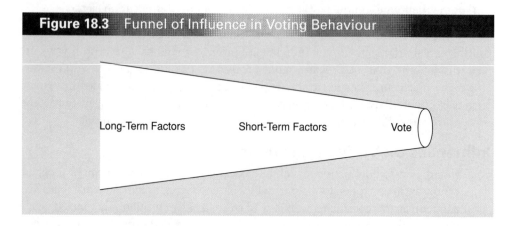

Long-Term Factors   Short-Term Factors   Vote

The influence of long-term factors on voting behaviour is diminishing in some states. Some authors maintain that the most important electoral trend of the postwar years has been the decline in the power of long-term social factors to determine a voter's choice.[26] Changing patterns of campaigning and media, especially television, are often used to explain the reduction in the importance of long-term factors in favour of those that are short-term.

DISCUSSION QUESTIONS

1. Do elections have any real value or are they merely window dressing for political elites?
2. What would happen if your country changed its electoral laws and adopted some form of proportional representation?
3. Do you believe "the Trojan horse" hypothesis is valid? Why or why not?
4. In what respect can elections be more or less democratic? Consider how votes are counted, who runs for office, who is allowed to vote, and how governments are formed.
5. Do you foresee an increased use of direct democracy in your country? Referendums? Recall?
6. Do electoral results determine or influence public policy?

KEY TERMS

alternative vote system, p. 401
consultative, p. 395
direct democracy, p. 392
electoral system, p. 392
instruments of ratification, p. 396
initiative, p. 398

mixed systems, p. 402
plurality, p. 399
party list systems, p. 401
proportional representation, p. 401
recall, p. 398
referendum, p. 395

second ballot system, p. 401
single-member majoritarian electoral system, p. 401
single transferable vote, p. 402
two-member plurality system, p. 399

ENDNOTES

1. "Myanmar Is Different from other Lands," *The New York Times*, August 26, 1990.
2. In the Philippines, for example, it was not uncommon at one time for voters to be paid a bribe after they produced a carbon copy of their ballot.
3. For a survey of such problems see T.E. Smith, *Elections in Developing Countries* (New York: St. Martin's Press, 1960).
4. *The Economist*, October 5–11, 1991, p. 57.
5. Guy Hermet, "State Controlled Elections: A Framework," in G. Hermet et al., eds., *Elections Without Choice* (London: Macmillan, 1978), p. 15.
6. *Ibid.*, pp. 13–14.

7. See A.H. Birch, *Representation* (London: Pall Mall, 1971), p. 35.

8. See Edmund Burke, "Address to the Electors of Bristol," in *The Works of Edmund Burke*, vol. 1 (New York: Harper, 1955), pp. 219–22; and Jean Jacques Rousseau, *Considerations on the Government of Poland* (many editions).

9. See *The Economist*, June 17, 1995, p. 23; and Alvin and Heidi Toffler, *Creating Civilization, The Politics of the Third Wave* (Atlanta: Turner, 1995).

10. David Butler and Austin Ranney, eds., *Referendums: A Study in Practice and Theory* (Washington, D.C.: American Enterprise Institute, 1978), p. 232.

11. Arguments in favour of referendums are made by Robert Moss in *The Collapse of Democracy* (New Rochelle, N.Y.: Arlington House, 1976), pp. 236–47.

12. See Butler and Ranney, eds. *Referendums*.

13. Robert J. Jackson, and Doreen Jackson, *Politics in Canada*, 4th ed. (Scarborough: Prentice Hall, 1998), pp. 420–424.

14. Thomas E. Cronin, *Direct Democracy: The Politics of Initiative, Referendum and Recall* (Cambridge, Mass.: Harvard University Press, 1989).

15. J.A. Corry, *Democratic Government and Politics* (Toronto: University of Toronto Press, 1951), p. 294.

16. See, for example, Vernon Bogdanor and David Butler, eds., *Democracy and Elections: Electoral Systems and Their Political Consequences* (New York: Cambridge University Press, 1983); and Bernard Grofman and Arend Lijphart, eds., *Electoral Laws and Their Political Consequences* (New York: Agathon Press, 1986).

17. See F.A. Hermens, "The Dynamics of Proportional Representation," in D. Apter and H. Eckstein, eds., *Comparative Politics* (New York: Free Press, 1964).

18. *Ibid.*, p. 255.

19. For an analysis of different electoral systems and their impact on political integration within Western, Communist, and developing countries, see A.J. Milnor, *Elections and Political Stability* (Boston: Little, Brown, 1969).

20. Maurice Duverger, *Political Parties* (New York: John Wiley, 1973) p. 215; Arend Lijphart and Bernard Grofman, eds., *Choosing an Electoral System: Issues and Alternatives* (New York: Praeger, 1984).

21. Robert W. Jackman, "Political Institutions and Voter Turnout in the Industrial Democracies," *APSR*, vol. 81, no. 2 (June 1987), pp. 405–53. See also M. Margaret Conway, *Political Participation in the United States* (Washington, D.C.: Congressional Quarterly Press, 1991), p. 111.

22. See E.E. Schattschneider, *The Semisovereign People* (New York: Holt, Rinehart and Winston, 1960).

23. See Seymour M. Lipset, *Political Man* (Garden City, N.Y.: Doubleday, 1960); and Gabriel Almond and Sidney Verba, *The Civic Culture* (Boston: Little, Brown, 1965).

24. The classic study in the United States was Angus Campbell, et al., *The American Voter* (New York: Wiley, 1960); later, in Britain it was David Butler and Donald Stokes, *Political Change in Britain*, 2nd ed. (New York: St. Martin's Press, 1974). More recently, see Michael M. Grant and Norman R. Luttbeg, *American Electoral Behavior* (Itasca, Ill: F.E. Peacock, 1991).

25. A comprehensive series of publications covering the elections held in many democratic regimes in recent years have been edited by Howard Penniman, *At the Polls* (Washington, D.C.: American Enterprise Institute, various years).

26. Martin Harrop and William L. Miller, *Elections and Voters: A Comparative Introduction* (London: Macmillan, 1987), pp. 211–12.

FURTHER READING

Arteron, Christopher, *Teledemocracy: Can Technology Protect Democracy?* (Newbury Park, Calif.: Sage, 1987).

Asher, Herbert, *Presidential Elections and American Politics* (New York: Wadsworth, 1992).

Butler, David, and Austin Ranney, eds., *Referendums Around the World* (Washington, D.C.: The AEI Press, 1994).

——, eds., *Electioneering: A Comparative Study of Continuity and Change* (Oxford: Oxford University Press, 1992).

Cronin, Thomas E., *Direct Democracy: The Politics of Initiative, Referendum and Recall* (Cambridge, Mass.: Harvard University Press, 1989).

Dalton, R.J., Scott C. Flanagan, and Paul Allen Beck, eds., *Electoral Change in Advanced Industrial Societies: Realignment or Dealignment* (Princeton, N.J.: Princeton University Press, 1984).

Franklin, Mark, Tom Mackie, and Henry Valen, *Electoral Change* (New York: Cambridge University Press, 1992).

Ginsberg, Benjamin, *Do Elections Matter?* (New York: M.E. Sharpe, 1991).

Ginsberg, Benjamin, and Martin Shefter, *Politics by Other Means: The Declining Importance of Elections in America* (New York: Basic Books, 1990).

Harrop, Martin, and William L. Miller, *Elections and Voters: A Comparative Introduction* (London: Macmillan, 1987).

Hermet, G., R. Rose, and A. Rouquie eds., *Elections Without Choice* (London: Macmillan, 1978).

Huntington, Samuel P., and Joan M. Nelson, *No Easy Choice: Political Participation in Developing Countries* (Cambridge, Mass.: Harvard University Press, 1976).

Johnston, J. Paul, and H. Pasis, *Representation and Electoral Systems* (Scarborough: Prentice–Hall, 1990).

Lijphart, A., and B. Grofman, eds., *Choosing an Electoral System* (New York: Praeger, 1984).

Lijphart, Arend, *Electoral Systems and Party Systems* (New York: Oxford University Press, 1994).

Polsby, Nelson W., and Aaron Wildavsky, *Presidential Elections: Strategies and Structures of American Politics*, 7th ed. (Chatham N.J.: Chatham House, 1996).

Pomper, Gerald M. ed., *The Election of 1992* (Chatham, N.J.: Chatham House, 1993).

Reeve, Andrew, and Alan Ware, *Electoral Systems: A Comparative and Theoretical Introduction* (New York: Routledge, 1991).

Rose, Richard, and Ian McAllister, *The Loyalties of Voters: A Lifetime Learning Model* (London: Sage, 1990).

Swerdlow, Joel, *Media Technology and the Vote* (Boulder, Colo.: Westview Press, 1989).

Wayne, Stephen J., *The Road to the White House*, 6th ed. (New York: St. Martin's Press, 1997).

Weiner, M., and E. Ozbudun, eds., *Competitive Elections in Developing Countries* (Durham, N.C.: Duke University Press, 1987).

 **Weblinks**

www.keele.ac.uk/depts/po/election.htm
This site provides information about electoral systems and the results of recent elections around the world.

www.umich.edu/~nes/
This is the Web Page for the American National Election Studies, which chronicles American voting behaviour and political attitudes and how they have changed during the last few decades.

www.synapse.net/~radio/refer.htm
This site details the events of the 1995 Quebec Referendum.

CHAPTER 19

Elections and Voting Behaviour: Democratic and Authoritarian

Elections, as we have seen, must satisfy certain criteria to qualify as democratic. Above all, there must be free and open competition allowing for the alternation of individuals and parties in government. Governments in established liberal democracies must be made responsive to shifts in public opinion in order to survive. Regular elections should provide opportunities for citizens to alter party composition of governments and in theory provide shifts in public policy. This is not true in authoritarian systems nor in some LDCs where no choice, or only limited choices, are available in elections. In these circumstances, elections do not provide citizens with an effective voice either about who will form the government or what type of policies the government will enact.

This chapter examines some electoral procedures vital to democratic elections. The procedures themselves vary considerably even within competitive democratic systems, but, in principle, democratic states provide the opportunity for citizen input that noncompetitive systems do not offer. Provisions for regular elections, for example, are vital to democracy, and we consider how different states arrange this. Nomination and selection procedures for candidates are also vital components of free elections. Another important procedure is apportionment—how local areas are assigned the number of representatives they will elect to their legislature.[1] Apportionment is one way that countries attempt to achieve the ideal of all votes counting equally, and we consider how and whether this is accomplished.

The last chapter considered the main theoretical advantages and disadvantages of various types of electoral systems. Here we observe the effects in practice of three types of electoral systems—single-member plurality in Canada, proportional representation in Israel, and a blend of the two systems in Germany. We also examine the unique electoral college system for electing the President of the United States.

Later in this chapter we consider the expression of political freedoms—how political activities are conducted during election campaigns, and on election day. The role of the media in this process is also analyzed and assessed. In the noncompetitive systems of communist states and some of the LDCs, institutions such as the military, the police, and even the judiciary restrict political freedoms and limit the right and ability of individual citizens to express their views openly in elections. The second half of the chapter examines elections in these kinds of states. Since 1985, a dramatic transformation in the political systems of the former Soviet Union and Eastern Europe has radically changed their electoral systems. We trace the remarkable metamorphosis from classic communist-style elections to democratic elections, and consider the hurdles that must still be surmounted in fledgling democratic elections in Russia. Finally, we examine some major problems and issues concerning elections in the developing world.

ELECTORAL PROCEDURES IN DEMOCRACIES
Provisions for Regular Elections

Regular elections ensure that public officeholders can be held accountable to their electorate. Sometimes, electoral dates are predetermined by the constitution and are held regardless of convenience or partisan advantage. In other cases, within maximum time limits, rules allow election dates to be set by the leader or leaders of the governing party. In parliamentary systems there is no restriction on how often an individual may be re-elected as Prime Minister: as the leader of the winning political party, a Prime Minister may stay in office until he or she no longer enjoys the support of the governing party.[2]

In the United States, national elections take place on the exact dates specified in the Constitution—on the first Tuesday after the first Monday in November. They have never been postponed. The timing of state and local contests as well as primary elections (see below) are also determined by law. All members of the House of Representatives and one-third of the Senators are elected every two years. Members of the lower House are elected in single-member constituencies; the Senators represent multi-member districts—two are elected from each state. Presidential elections are held every four years, and winners are restricted to two four-year terms in office.

In Westminster-model countries, electoral dates are more flexible. In Canada, for example, the Prime Minister must ask the Governor General to dissolve Parliament and call an election at least once every five years. Technically the opposition parties have no part to play in the choice of the date. Everything else being equal, the Prime Minister of a majority government makes the decision to call an election some time in the fourth or fifth year, at the most favourable opportunity for his or her party.

Nomination and Candidate Selection

The first step in free elections is the process by which names are recorded on the electoral ballot. Unless candidates are running as independents, they must first be selected by the party they wish to represent and then nominated. **Candidate selection** is the party process of deciding who will be put forward as a candidate. **Nomination** is the legal procedure by which election authorities certify the individuals who are selected, and authorize their names to appear on the ballot. The selection process reduces the alternatives from which the voters will choose to a manageable number, and this makes meaningful choice possible. Within liberal democracies there are three broad categories of candidate selection and nominating procedures: approved self-designation, party-list designation, and the unique direct primary election of the United States.[3]

Approved Self-Designation

The British devised a simple nominating procedure that has been widely followed in other democratic countries. Eligibility rules determine the basic criteria of who may enter their names as candidates. In Britain, a candidate cannot, for example, be a judge, civil servant, member of the clergy or nobility, and must be eligible to vote. Apart from these restrictions, any British citizen may fill in official nomination papers stating their name, address, occupation, and the name of the constituency in which they want to run for office. Two voters from that constituency sign as proposer and seconder, and eight others sign as assentors. This form is filed along with a deposit that is forfeited if the candidate does not win at least 5% of the votes cast. The candidate's name is then authorized to appear on the ballot accompanied by the party designation (if there is one).[4]

This is the same procedure used, with minor variations, in Canada, and in other Commonwealth countries.[5] In Canada, a prospective candidate must file nomination papers with the signatures of 100 other electors and deposit $1000 with a Returning Officer. This low deposit discourages nuisance candidates but does not deter interested citizens from running for office. A prospective candidate does not need the backing of a political party, and need not even reside in the constituency he or she would like to represent. It is extremely difficult in practice, however, for a candidate without party endorsement to be elected in Canada.

Local party organizations in both Britain and Canada control the nominating process for their constituencies, and their exact procedures vary. Generally, they take the initiative in candidate recruitment, holding locally controlled delegate conventions. Only rarely does national party headquarters or the party leader interfere with local nominations.[6] However in Canada a statement signed by the party leader or a designated representative confirming the party endorsement is filed with a candidate's nomination papers, thus leaving open the possibility for the party leader to reject a candidate.

Party-List Designations

In countries that use a party-list system of proportional representation (PR), the authorized agent for each party compiles a rank-ordered list of candidates for each constituency. The initiative for selecting candidates generally rests with party officials and agencies—a procedure that puts enormous power in the hands of the leader. The list is then presented to the election authorities, who verify the eligibility of the suggested candidates and place them on the ballot. This system is in place in Israel, Germany, and the Netherlands for example.

The Direct Primary

Unique to the United States, the **direct primary** is an electoral procedure in which candidates are selected by the voters rather than indirectly by party officials. About two-thirds of the 50 states require direct primaries for nominations for all offices.[7] The rules and significance of these primaries vary considerably from state to state.

The general procedure is as follows: to get his or her name on the ballot, a qualified person files a petition with their name, address, nomination desired, and signatures of a legally designated number of voters who are members of the party whose nomination is sought. Ballots are printed for each party, registering all those who have petitioned to have their names included. In the primary election, voters mark their candidate preferences for each office. The person who receives the largest number of votes for each office on each party's ballot becomes the official candidate for that party, and his or her name goes on the ballot for the ensuing election.

Some primaries are open, and some are closed. In **open primaries** voters do not need to be pre-registered, and can vote in whichever party's primary they choose. In **closed primaries** the vote is restricted to persons pre-registered as members of a particular party. There are other variations. **Crossover primaries** allow citizens to vote in the party primary of their choice after they publicly declare which party they have chosen. **Blanket primaries** allow voters to vote in the primaries of more than one party as long as they restrict their vote for any particular office to only one party.[8]

Presidential Primaries

The best-known and best-publicized primaries are those involving presidential candidates in the United States. Every four years both the Democrats and the Republicans hold national conventions to nominate a presidential and vice presidential candidate. In 1996, for example, Republican delegates in the national convention in San Diego chose Robert Dole as their party's standard bearer. Bill Clinton went through the motions in a parallel procedure before the Democratic convention in Chicago.

Delegates to the presidential conventions are chosen within states. The process is governed by 50 different state laws and varies according to local party rules. Many states, however, choose their delegates by **presidential primaries**. Some states bind all their delegates to the candidate who wins the state primary election, while other states apportion delegates according to the candidates' shares of the vote. The presidential primary system does not provide *all* convention delegates, however. About one-third of the states rely on state caucuses (meetings) to select their national convention delegates. In total, primaries account for about three-quarters of the delegates and caucuses account for the other quarter.

For at least a year before the convention itself, a pre-convention campaign takes place. Candidates for the presidential nomination try to win over party leaders and activists within each state. The larger states—California, New York, and Texas, for example—are seen as being particularly important for a presidential hopeful to win. After the primaries, the next step is for each party to hold its **national convention**, a meeting of party delegates representing each state. Delegates to the national convention vote to determine who the presidential candidate for that party will be. The voting procedure itself is colourful, with a state-by-state roll call and delegate declarations. Because many delegates are committed to vote a certain way, the results of the national convention are generally known before it is even called, but occasionally the vote is too close to call ahead of time.

The national convention is a media event conducted to achieve maximum publicity for the party. The candidates each deliver stylized speeches and receive long ovations. As well as making the final candidate selection, the convention is the supreme governing body of the party, and sets party rules and policy platforms. It is customary to make the vote unanimous as soon as it is clear who the winner is. The campaign trail is long and arduous. The caucuses and primaries leading to the August Republican and Democratic conventions for the 1996 Presidential election began on February 6, 1995, in Louisiana and terminated in California on March 26.

Presidential primaries are often criticized as being somewhat elitist in nature because they attract relatively wealthy, better educated, and older voters.[9] They are also scheduled over a relatively long period of time which tends to exhaust candidates and bore voters. Candidates are subjected to gruelling media examination of their personalities and media skills, but relatively little is conveyed about their positions on vital policy issues. The qualities required to win primaries—ability to raise funds, and skills at the "media game"—are important, but represent only a small part of the skills needed by a President in carrying out the duties of the office.[10]

Apportionment

The principle of "one person, one vote" is one of the foundations of democracy. However, in practice, few electoral systems can stand up to a rigid interpretation of this principle. Israel and the Netherlands come closest, as each operates as one large electoral unit. Other democracies are divided into geographical districts or constituencies, and each constituency elects one or more representatives to the national legislature. Since it is impossible for constituencies to have exactly the same number of voters, a vote in a very heavily populated constituency can be worth considerably less than a vote in a sparsely populated one.

In practice, electoral boundaries are regularly reviewed and adjusted to prevent gross distortions in population size between constituencies. Governments in all established democracies make efforts to adhere to the principle of "rep by pop" and have set up fair-boundary commissions. In Canada, for example, under federal election law, independent, three-member commissions in each province adjust constituency boundaries once every ten years. However, the process is easily manipulated and court surveillance is often required to keep the system fair. The most serious problem is that the political party in power is generally able to influence how boundaries are adjusted and often does so to its own advantage. The process of drawing electoral district boundaries in order to gain an advantage for a political party or interest group is known as **gerrymandering**. This is normally achieved by concentrating large blocs of opposition voters in a few constituencies so they will earn only a few representatives, and distributing large blocs of one's own supporting votes in strategic areas to make best use of them. A certain amount of gerrymandering persists in all democracies—usually to protect incumbents. The only real check on this is public disapproval and, of course, the knowledge that when another party is in power it might act the same.

Electoral Systems in Practice

In the last chapter we considered some of the typical distortions produced by electoral systems. Now we will examine electoral results in four specific countries, each with a different electoral system: Canada, with its single-member plurality system; Israel with proportional representation; and Germany which employs both systems. The United States' presidential electoral system is discussed last.

Single-Member Plurality: Canada

Canada is one of several states, including the United Kingdom and New Zealand, to use a single-member plurality electoral system for elections to its lower house. The United States uses this system for both houses. In those following the Westminster model, the country is divided into a number of constituencies, each of which elects one member to the lower house of the legislature. Each voter casts one ballot, and the winner is determined by a **simple plurality**, that is, by whichever candidate receives the most votes. Members of the U.S. House of Representatives are elected in single-member districts under the plurality rule and each senator is elected separately by plurality in a single state.

Despite the fact that it favours a two-party system, there are some distortions with this electoral system (see Table 19.1). Relatively small swings of votes in single-member plurality systems often result in large numbers of seats changing hands. Perhaps the most outstanding example in Canada occurred in the 1935 general election when the Liberals swept back to power. Their share of the popular vote increased by less than 1%, but their number of seats nearly doubled, from 91 to 173.

Such amplification of small voting shifts into large-scale changes in seat allocation tends to encourage alternation in government between the two dominant parties. On the other hand, it severely penalizes parties that have their votes spread out across the country and cannot obtain the largest number of votes in any particular constituency.

The 1997 election illustrates how this system distorts the translation of percentage votes to percentage seats. The Liberals won the election with 38.3% of the vote. However they were awarded 51.5%, or 155 of the 301 seats, in Parliament. The Reform Party won the next largest percentage of the popular vote, 19.4% and acquired 19.9%, or 60 of the seats. The Progressive Conservatives won the third highest percentage of the popular vote, but because their votes were widely spread out across the country, they won only 20 seats, which translated to only 6.6% of the seats. The Bloc Québécois (BQ) on the other hand, won 10.7% of the vote but acquired 14.6% of the seats. This

Table 19.1	Canadian General Election Results, 1993 (Percentage Shares of Votes and Seats by Party)	
Party	**Votes**	**Seats**
	%	%
Liberals	38.3	51.5
Reform	19.4	19.9
Bloc Québécois	10.7	14.6
New Democratic Party	11.1	7
Progressive Conservatives	18.9	6.6
Other	1.7	0.3

distortion was caused by the fact that the BQ seats are all concentrated in Quebec, and this enables them to win a high number of seats there. As usual in this type of system, the largest party (the Liberals) won a "bonus" of seats, and the smaller parties were penalized in the translation of votes to seats.

Proportional Representation: Israel

The major Western European democracies, with the exception of Britain, use one form or another of promotional representation (PR). It has also been the system preferred by Israel and many newly democratizing Eastern European states.

Israel offers a classic example of PR. It has a party-list, multi-member system of proportional representation. The entire state is handled as one large constituency, which elects all 120 members to the unicameral Knesset. Parties are allowed to submit lists and take part in an election if they possess membership in the outgoing Knesset or obtain the signatures of at least 750 eligible voters. The voter chooses which list to vote for according to which party offers the ideological position he or she prefers. The vote is for a party's entire list; there is no way to designate preference or dislike for any particular individuals on the list, and since the most experienced and influential candidates are at the top of the list, they will be the first chosen to occupy whatever seats the party is awarded.

PR has encouraged the proliferation of parties, and unstable coalition governments have been the rule in Israel. The PR system permits any party that wins at least 2% to have seats in parliament. Following the 1988 elections, representation in the Knesset was shared by 16 parties including four right-wing parties, five left-wing Zionist parties, three left-wing non-Zionist parties, and four religious parties. The right-wing parties, of which Likud was largest, won 47 seats; the Zionist left, of which Labor was the largest, won 48 seats; the non-Zionist left won six seats; the religious parties won 18 seats.[11]

The seats were so evenly divided that the leaders of the Likud and Labor parties alternated as Prime Minister. An election held in 1992, however, broke this stalemate with a clear victory for Labor.

The 1996 election was held under new electoral rules. For the first time, Israelis cast separate votes for a Prime Minister and the Knesset. The Likud's Binyamin Netanyahu was elected Prime Minister and he cobbled together a majority in the Knesset from the Likud, religious parties, the New Immigrant's Party, and the Third Way—a one-issue party opposed to any withdrawal from the Golan Heights. The fragmented party system makes it difficult for either major party—Likud or Labor—to knit together a long-lasting coalition. Close Up 19.1 explores another PR system in transition—that of Italy.

A Mixed Electoral System: Germany

Germany has devised a unique, mixed electoral system. After World War II, West Germany's political leaders were anxious to prevent the kind of political splintering that had served the country so badly and culminated in Hitler's rise to power. After considering the benefits and drawbacks of both plurality and proportional representation electoral systems it was decided to combine the two.

CLOSE UP 19.1   A System in Transition: Italy

Italy has endured notoriously unstable governments since 1946. Backed by the Vatican, Italy's centrist Christian Democrats controlled the government for more than four decades after the 1948 elections. However, their strength was usually based on unstable coalitions. Using a list system of PR, Italians elected about 12 parties, which would then argue over who would be Prime Minister, who would join the ruling coalition, and what the government program would be. In the early 1990s, the situation became so difficult that the electoral laws were changed in an attempt to create a bipolar electoral system with the hope that it would produce more stable governments. The new electoral law created a hybrid system: about one-quarter of the seats in both houses are now elected under the old PR system; the rest are elected under the Anglo-American single-member plurality method.

However, the first election using the new hybrid system still produced a legislature divided among many parties. The electoral change has not been successful. In 1998 the 56th coalition government since the end of World War II was hastily put together when the centre-left coalition was forced to resign. Massimo d'Alema became the first ex-Communist to lead the government of a major West European country. D'Alema headed an eight-party alliance ranging from Communists to centrists.

Many Italians would like to change their electoral law yet again, either to make a single-member plurality system or perhaps, like the French, to have a two-round voting system, which tends to weaken minor parties.

To elect members to the *Bundestag* (the lower House), each *Land* (state) is divided into local constituencies. Half the seats in the *Bundestag* are allocated to these constituencies, the other half to lists of candidates from the political parties. Each citizen casts two votes, one for a local constituency member and one for a political party. Eventually, the number of seats each party receives is determined by a formula which ensures that the *Bundestag* is constituted in proportion to the votes cast in the PR election. If a party proves to be under-represented in the election of constituency members, it is compensated through extra seats from its list.[12] A minimum level of support is required so that only those parties receiving at least 5% of the national vote or at least three members elected in constituencies can obtain representation in the *Bundestag*. As a result of this complex electoral system, significant political groups are represented fairly, but small ones are restricted, so that the number of parties is kept manageable.

The main drawback of this system is its relatively complicated method of translating votes to seats. However, as a method of allocating seats that are proportional to the parties' shares of the votes, it is quite accurate, and is often considered a model system for that reason. It combines overall equity with the possibility of strong local representation and results in quite stable cabinet government.

The 1998 German elections ended the career of Helmut Kohl, who had been Chancellor for 16 years and leader of the Christian Democrats for 25. The new government is a Red-Green coalition headed by Chancellor Gerhard Schroder, leader of the Social Democrats and backed by the Green Party whose leader Joschka Fischer was made foreign minister. The government coalition was made possible by the Green leaders dropping their demands of tripling the price of gasoline and taking Germany out of NATO. The government remains shaky, however, as it tackles the 11% unemployment rate—an intolerable notion for Germans, who are used to low inflation and low unemployment.

Electing the President of the United States

The President of the United States is chosen by an **electoral college** which has a highly complex history. In 1787 when the American Constitution was written, the drafters agreed to have the President elected indirectly—the people would choose electors, and these respected citizens would in turn elect the President. As the democratic philosophy of "one man, one vote" caught on over time, the public came to expect presidential electors to vote for the candidates most popular in their respective states.

Today the process works like this: Americans vote for their choice of President. However the formal decision is in the hands of "electors." Every state is accorded a certain number of electors. This number is achieved by adding the number of Representatives and the number of Senators each state has in Congress. For example, California has 52 Representatives in the House and 2 Senators: thus it gets 54 electors. The candidate who wins the majority of these electors (270 of the 538 electoral votes) becomes the President (see Map 19.1). The mechanics are fairly complicated, however.

In every state, a slate of electors is nominated by each presidential candidate. The candidate who wins a majority (plurality) of the state's popular vote receives that state's entire electoral vote. While electors are not legally bound to vote for the candidate to whom they are pledged, they seldom exercise any personal discretion. Rather, they cast their ballots for the President according to the popular vote in their state. On very rare occasions an elector has not followed the dictates of the popular vote, but such acts of independence have not affected the outcome of a single presidential election in this century.

Those electors chosen in the election send their ballots to the President of the Senate, who officially announces which candidate has received the majority of votes and he or she is duly elected President. However this formal announcement comes as no surprise because once the election for the electors has taken place the press announces who the President will be. It is simply assumed that the electors will vote properly—that is, according to the wishes expressed by the populace. In the 1992 presidential election, Democrat Bill Clinton won 370 electoral votes, Republican George Bush won 168, and Ross Perot, who ran as a Reform Party candidate, won no votes.

If no candidate for President wins a majority of electoral votes—this would require at least a 3-way standoff—the House of Representatives chooses which candidate will become President. In this case, each state gets one vote, and a majority of 26 states in the House is required for victory. The Vice President, too, is elected by the electoral college. If no one receives a majority of electoral votes for the vice presidency, the winner is chosen by the Senate. No President or Vice President has been selected by these complicated methods since 1876.

Electoral Campaigns: Meaningful Choices and the Media

Free electoral competition requires the existence of basic political freedoms, including the right to form political parties, and to play an active role in electing political leaders. It also requires basic civil rights such as the ability to express one's views openly and without fear of retribution. The press and other mass media must also be free from state coercion or direction, and an impartial police force and independent judiciary must be in place to safeguard the rights of individuals and groups.

CLOSE UP 19.2   Electing the U.S. President 1996

After the candidates are chosen at the Democratic and Republican conventions, the real campaign for the presidency began. In 1996 Bill Clinton for the Democratic Party and Robert Dole for the Republicans found themselves competing with third party candidate Ross Perot who ran for the Reform Party. Here were some key dates leading to Bill Clinton's successful attempt to be re-elected as President of the United States:

Labor Day:	The traditional beginning of the actual U.S. presidential campaign
Oct. 6:	The first televised debate between the presidential candidates
Oct. 9:	The vice presidential debate
Oct. 16:	The final presidential "Town Hall" debate
Nov. 5:	Election Day

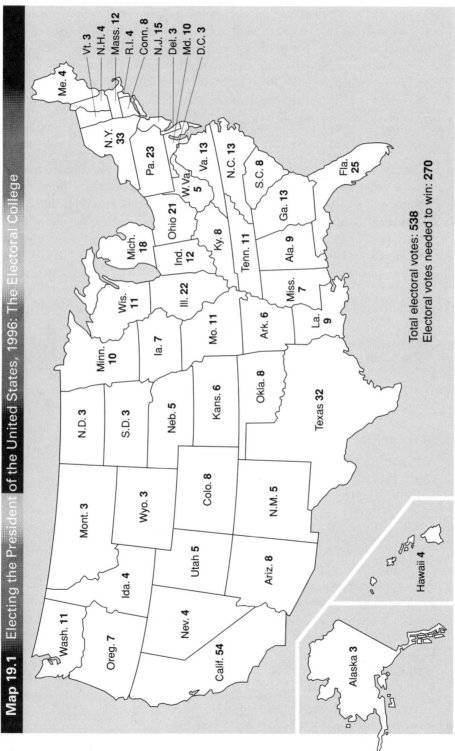

Map 19.1   Electing the President of the United States, 1996: The Electoral College

Vt. 3
N.H. 4
Mass. 12
R.I. 4
Conn. 8
N.J. 15
Del. 3
Md. 10
D.C. 3

Me. 4

N.Y. 33

Pa. 23

W.Va. 5

Va. 13

N.C. 13

S.C. 8

Fla. 25

Ohio 21

Mich. 18

Ind. 12

Ky. 8

Tenn. 11

Ga. 13

Ala. 9

Miss. 7

Wis. 11

Ill. 22

Mo. 11

Ark. 6

La. 9

Minn. 10

Ia. 7

Kans. 6

Okla. 8

Texas 32

N.D. 3

S.D. 3

Neb. 5

Colo. 8

N.M. 5

Mont. 3

Wyo. 3

Wash. 11

Oreg. 7

Ida. 4

Utah 5

Ariz. 8

Nev. 4

Calif. 54

Hawaii 4

Alaska 3

Total electoral votes: **538**
Electoral votes needed to win: **270**

Source: Based on information from United States Bureau of the Census, *Statistical Abstracts of the United States*, 115th ed. (Washington, D.C., 1995).

The ability to conduct electoral campaigns without interference, within established rules, is a recognized political freedom in all democracies. In established democracies, freedom *of* the press is observed, but freedom *from* the press is problematical. New technologies and multiple media ownership enable wealthy individuals or groups to exert significant, undue influence.

It is important to identify the biases of newspapers, radio, and television, and to be aware of their goals and who they are trying to influence. This is particularly true at election time. The media can bias the outcome of campaigns even when they try to be neutral. This happens when they focus public attention on certain candidates or events and ignore others, and when they editorialize about candidates and issues. A common criticism of television coverage of elections is that it treats contenders as part of a "horse race," and judges leadership candidates, in particular, by their appearance and flamboyance rather than by intellectual and leadership qualities. Media in general play for audience appeal by focusing on personalities, and who is winning or losing the "race" rather than on the important issues and how and why the contest is taking a particular form. The substance of campaigns is often ignored, while minor events or peccadillos are sensationalized.

Techniques for winning elections have become very sophisticated and are focused to a large extent around media exposure. The United States is a leader in this respect, but the role of the media in elections has increased in all developed democracies and exercises a very significant impact on campaign organization and the "packaging" and promotion of candidates.[13] New technologies are widely used in election campaigns: computers, campaign agencies, opinion polls, consultants, direct mail, and so on have become, to varying degrees, important factors in manipulating public opinion in modern election campaigns. Media handlers are hired to script candidates, and direct them to create an "event of the day" with an appropriate "10-second clip" that will look and sound good on the evening news. Spontaneity is rare during modern electoral campaigns. Polling is used extensively to determine how voters feel about policy issues, and to target the strengths and weaknesses of candidates and opponents. Paid advertising is geared not only to build up one's own party and candidates but, increasingly, as negative advertisements to attack opponents.

Some commentators believe that modern media campaigns focus public attention on personalities at the expense of parties and issues. And they also fear that the trend for major parties always showing the opposition in the most derogatory light possible is creating an overwhelmingly negative public opinion of politics and politicians. There is no doubt that public opinion is manipulated by the lenses of television cameras and newspaper headlines. Studies show that exactly how much influence they have depends on the characteristics of the person or group being influenced, the nature of the issue, and also the nature of the media in question.[14] The press tends to exercise a continuous long-term influence on opinions.[15] However, higher percentages of citizens rely on television for their news, and television has a greater emotional impact than the print media. Exposure to television news also cuts across educational, social, gender, age, and ethnic groups to a much greater degree than newspapers do.[16]

There is some indication from studies in the United States and elsewhere that the media, and news coverage in particular, influence electoral subgroups differently. Strong party identifiers and activists tend to follow media election coverage most closely, while weaker identifiers, even when they do follow such coverage, tend to base their votes on the issues that are important to them rather than on candidates or parties that the media say will win.[17]

ELECTION PROCESSES IN AUTHORITARIAN SYSTEMS

In authoritarian states, elections may or may not be held, but, regardless of their occurrence, their practical impact is relatively insignificant. In communist states, for example, elections are often held with the trappings of liberal democracy, but they provide no choice of party candidates. A slate of party-chosen nominees is presented and the voters merely confirm the choices—with near-unanimous approval. If there is a choice among candidates it only occurs at the local rather than the state level. The fusion of party and state is thus maintained even when elections take place.

The political role and importance of elections is very different from their counterparts in democratic countries, determining neither who is elected nor what government policies will be adopted, except perhaps at the local level. Since the disintegration of the Soviet Union, the remaining communist countries are, however, facing pressure for change. In Cuba in October 1991, for example, President Fidel Castro announced he would allow non-communists to run in legislative elections and he would resign if the Communist Party (PCC) lost. In 1993, the National Assembly was directly elected for the first time. The only anti-regime option was to vote against the nominees. All were elected. The second direct election to the National Assembly was in early 1998. Once again, all candidates approved by the PCC were elected in a "yes or no" decision. Shortly thereafter the new assembly reappointed Castro to another five-year term as Chairman of the Council of State. Cubans have never been able to vote directly for any senior leaders under President Castro, and such an event is not likely. Cuba is constitutionally a one-party communist state, and Castro has made it clear that it will stay that way, even though he will open Cuba's economy to foreign capital and press the United States to lift its four-decade-old trade embargo against his country.

Elections in the Former Soviet Union

The relative openness of the selection and nomination processes that is characteristic of democracies is absent in authoritarian systems. The former Soviet Union, before Gorbachev became leader of the CPSU in 1985, provides a classic illustration. The Soviets operated a single-candidate system closely controlled by the CPSU. The party apportioned the right to nominate candidates among various trade unions, military units, universities, and other institutions. In practice, however, party members made it clear who the best choice would be, and everyone at each nominating meeting voted for that individual. The local election commission was then informed of the choice, and the commission ratified these submissions and put them on the ballot. One Soviet writer called this past procedure "a hallmark of socialism, a sign that there is not, and cannot be any, discord among our laboring masses, the kind of inner discord that exists within bourgeois society."[18]

Despite the promise of former CPSU Rule 19 that "all leading party bodies are elected," ordinary party members were able to vote directly only at the lowest levels of the party's institutional hierarchy. Above these levels all party elections were indirect— their purpose was to elect individuals who would elect the next rung of officials. The more important the institution, the fewer party members involved in their election. Ordinary party members played no direct part in the election of the party's leaders or in decisions about who would be members of the party's central institutions. These electoral processes were conducted in secrecy and were carefully controlled by the party leadership—a few individuals in the party Secretariat and the party leader. This system provided a very powerful tool for party leaders, enabling them to hold office more or less at will.[19]

Under authoritarian communism, Soviet citizens had two options when they voted. They could only vote for or against the official candidate, and the voting procedure made it obvious to everyone whether the voter had supported the party's choice or not. Voting was compulsory, and turnout regularly exceeded 99%. Candidates almost never failed to be elected.

Shortly after Mikhail Gorbachev came to power in 1985 he initiated electoral reforms which, by 1991, had snowballed and erased most vestiges of the old electoral system throughout the crumbling Soviet state.[20] The new proposals, guaranteed "the right to free and thorough discussion of the political, personal, and professional qualities of candidates and the right to campaign for or against them."[21] The first test of the new law came with the partially competitive elections of March 1989. The Soviet people went to the polls to elect a new 2250-member national parliamentary body, the Congress of People's Deputies.[22] Two-thirds of the Congress's deputies were to be elected by secret ballot in constituency elections.[23]

Gorbachev declared the election results a victory for *perestroika* and a defeat for conservatism. It was, in fact, a carefully guarded experiment with democracy. Since the Communist Party had directly controlled one third of the seats through nominations from national organizations, and exercised its influence over workers' groups and territorial associations, Gorbachev had known that he would be President and his advisors would be elected to serve on the presidium. However, as one expert later noted, "the election marked an irreversible step in the evolution of *perestroika* as politics entered the streets and popular consciousness."[24]

In March 1990, the Congress of People's Deputies ratified a constitutional amendment formally ending the Communist Party's monopoly on political power. That same month, in elections held in the Soviet republics, independent pro-democracy groups achieved major gains in Russia, Ukraine, and Byelorussia (now Belarus), and won outright control of local governments in Moscow, Leningrad, and other cities. Lithuania elected the first non-Communist Premier of a Soviet republic, then voted to secede from the Soviet Union. The 1990 republic and local elections "marked a decisive step towards the pluralisation of Soviet politics and the revival of independent soviets."[25]

ELECTORAL BEGINNINGS IN DEMOCRATIC RUSSIA

Following the rapid disintegration of the Soviet Union, which culminated in December 1991, Russians moved further toward free and democratic elections for the Duma and also for presidential elections. In December 1995, they voted for a new state Duma, the 450-member lower house of parliament. (The upper house does not stand for election.) The infant parties which had been born over the previous few years and months advanced into adolescence in the turbulent months preceding the vote (see Chapter 18). New rules provided for a mixed electoral system: half of Duma members were elected on the basis of party slates, in which 43 parties competed. Only parties winning at least 5% of the nationwide vote could claim any seats. The other half of the deputies were elected as individuals in single-seat constituencies to represent geographic voting districts. Each voter therefore cast two votes: one for a single candidate and one for a party.

The election faced severe logistical problems. About 105 million voters were eligible to vote at one of 94 000 polling stations across 11 time zones. The ballots were long and complicated (see Close Up 19.3). In the end, only four of the 43 parties passed the required 5% threshold allowing them to hold seats in the Duma. The Communists, led by Gennady Zyuganov, emerged as by far the most popular party on the ballot. They won about one-third of the seats—their representation in the Duma went from 10% to 35%. The ultra-nationalist Liberal Democrats, led by Vladimir Zhirinovsky, were second. Our Home Is Russia, the party of Prime Minister Viktor Chernomyrdin, came third. The pro-Western reform-oriented Yabloko Party led by Grigory Yavlinski was fourth (see Table 19.2). The win translated into about one-third of the seats for the Communist Party.

The election campaign showed that the Communist Party, with more than 500 000 members and large numbers of volunteers, is still the biggest and best organized party in

---

CLOSE UP 19.3   Elections Russian Style

The December 1995 Russian election to the Duma was a mix of old traditions and new beginnings. In the Soviet electoral tradition, buffets with cheap food and drinks were set up at polling stations to help attract voters. The oldest voters were given flowers and chocolates. First-time voters got adventure novels.

The ballots were two huge sheets of paper. One listed a confusing array of 43 parties. The other listed the candidates in the local constituency. Many voters were bewildered and had to seek advice from the volunteer election staff or fellow voters. This was hardly surprising since for most voters it was the first time they were allowed to make a genuine choice in an election.

Table 19.2	Results of the Election to the Russian Duma December 17, 1995				
Party	Party-List Votes %	Party-List Seats	Single-Candidate Seats	Total Seats Won in 1995	Total Seats Won in 1993
Communist Party	22.30%	99	58	157	45
Liberal Democratic Party	11.8%	50	1	51	63
Our Home is Russia	10.3	45	10	55	—
Yabloko	6.89	31	14	45	25
Women of Russia	4.61	0	3	3	23
Working Russia	4.53	0	1	1	0
Congress of Russian Communities	4.31	0	5	5	—
Party of Svyatoslav Fyodorov	3.98	0	1	1	—
Democratic Choice of Russia	3.86	0	9	9	76
Agrarian Party	3.78	0	20	20	55
Power to the People	1.61	0	9	9	—
Other parties	unavailable	0	17	17	—
Independents	—	0	77	77	—

Source: Reuters, published in *The New York Times*, December 30, 1995.

Russia. For example, in the last few days of the campaign, Zyuganov withdrew 63 of his candidates from ballots in contests where its left-wing allies had better prospects than the official Communist candidate. This avoided vote splitting and ensured that the leading left-wing candidates would have a much better chance to win. The gamble paid off very well.

Hard liners on both the left and right share a little less than half of the seats in the newly constituted Duma (about 41%), the reformers just over a quarter, and the rest belong to what has been called the centrist "swamp." The Communists dominate the hard-liners' camp because the ultra-nationalist right-wing vote fell by half. The reformers' camp is split evenly between moderate reformists and Mr. Yavlinsky's liberal group. To have a chance to reverse or make significant changes in the direction Russia has been taking on economic reform under President Boris Yeltsin, the Communists and nationalists have to find enough partners to control two-thirds of the votes in the Duma (see Chapter 13). If this occurrs, they could amend the constitution and/or overturn the vetoes that are routinely imposed by the President when he dislikes a parliamentary law.

Several factors contributed to the Communist Party resurgence in the election and afterwards. Economic reforms leading up to the election were harsh and unpopular, and showed few beneficial returns. Many resented falling living standards, and many also were nostalgic for the former glory days of the Soviet Union. The Communist vote dropped dramatically in the presidential elections of June 1996, but the party has made a resurgence since the chaotic economic downturn of 1998.

Boris Yeltsin won a second term as President in the June/July elections in 1996. Communist candidate Gennady Zyuganov was his closest rival, but Yeltsin led in both polls (see Table 19.3). The next presidential election is scheduled for the year 2000.

Table 19.3 Russian Presidential Elections 1996		
Candidate	**% Vote First Ballot**	**% Vote Second Ballot**
Boris Yeltsin	35.3	53.8
Gennady Zyuganov (KPRF)	32.0	40.2
Aleksandr Lebed (KRO)	14.5	–
Grigory Yavlinsky (Yabloko)	7.3	–
Vladimir Zhirinovsky (LDPR)	5.7	–
Others	3.8	–

KPRF – Communist Party of the Russian Federation (communist)
KRO – Congress of Russian Communities (authoritarian)
Yabloko – Apple (liberal reformist)
LDPR – Liberal Democratic Party of Russia (nationalist xenophobic)

Source: DMRI—http://www.agora.stm.it/elections/election/russia.htm.

ELECTIONS IN AUTHORITARIAN LDCs

Elections in some LDCs in Africa, and to a lesser extent in Asia and South America, are held only sporadically. They rarely are competitive or exhibit the open procedures, political freedoms, and civil rights of established democracies.[26] Elections are only one means of attaining political power, so governments tend to be provisional and uncertain in duration. And the elections vary from offering no choice to a limited choice of candidates or parties. In general, the narrowly based governments in some of these countries are more concerned with preserving their own claims to power than they are with broadening the electoral base and allowing freedom of choice to their citizens. Although rhetoric tends to be high in favour of popular sovereignty, as expressed through universal suffrage, mass voting, regular elections, free competition, and honest counting of the ballots, its actual practice leaves much to be desired. Precise, comparable data is scarce for many states so that it is often difficult to measure voter turnout, to know whether opposition parties have been suppressed, or whether illiterate peasants and city workers were coerced by "goon squads" to vote for approved candidates.[27]

This situation has improved slowly, especially in Latin America and, to a growing degree, in Africa and Asia. In the early 1990s, a wave of multi-party democracy swept across a number of developing countries. One-party elections in LDCs are increasingly offering at least a choice between candidates, so that there is some intra-party competition.[28] Single-candidate elections that offer voters no choice at all are becoming less common, except in some presidential systems. And across Africa and South America, dictators have increasingly given way to elected governments.

Latin America is the region where the trend to fully competitive elections was strongest in the last two decades. When Chile's General Pinochet resigned in March 1990, it was the first time in history that elected civilian governments ruled in every country in Latin America, except two: Cuba and Suriname. However, the fact that the generals are gone does not necessarily mean that democracy is fully established in their place; the April 1992 quasi-coup in Peru was a foreboding sign of the fragility of democracy south of the Rio Grande.[29] Elected governments continue to be precarious in several South American states. A few examples of recent LDC elections illustrate the limitations and precariousness of democratic elections in some of these countries in the late 1990s.

Tunisia: In 1987, President Zine El Abidine Ben Ali came to power in Tunisia, promising a "new era" of democracy as he replaced the octogenarian independence leader Habib Bourguiba. Nearly 12 years later his ruling party, the Democratic Constitutional Rally (RCD), still holds almost all of the seats in Tunisia's Parliament. The Islamic opposition is banned, and many of its leaders are in exile, hiding, or prison. The secular opposition is restricted and feeble. They claim that the RCD used its domination of Parliament and government, and its control of the press and television, to rig the 1994 elections and keep their hold on power.

Despite relative improvements in the economy, for many Tunisians under Ben Ali's rule, repression continues. The six legal opposition parties are virtually powerless compared to the RCD, and the country has one of the most powerful security forces in the developing world—80 000 police for a population of only 9 million Tunisians. Nevertheless, there seems to be widespread agreement that Tunisia is not yet ready for full democracy.

Algeria: In neighbouring Algeria, meanwhile, slow and democratic change was taking place in the electoral system. In the spring of 1991, President Chadli Bendjedid attempted to organize an unrigged general election. The National Liberation Front (FLN), which had ruled Algeria since independence in 1962, resented the idea of fighting an election that might not give it an automatic victory. Riots resulted in cancellation of the election when it appeared that the Islamic Salvation Front (FIS) might win. FIS leaders, Islamic fundamentalists, were imprisoned.[30]

However the President did not give up, and a few months later electoral reforms were introduced in the National Assembly. Against great resistance from the FLN, attempts were made to curb some unfair practices that benefited the ruling party. For example, a FLN proposal to increase the number of parliamentary seats and have the extra seats go to rural areas where the FLN had most support was blocked. Proxy voting, a practice that allowed a man to cast his wife's vote, was also eliminated.

Elections were called again. The FIS won the first round of the country's first multi-party national elections. It was expected to form a majority government after the second round of voting scheduled for mid-January 1992. However President Chadli Bendjedid suddenly resigned and the balloting was cancelled. A five-member Council of State was appointed to replace the President without having to endure a "messy election."

Algerian policy after the cancellation of the January election was to "squash the fundamentalists out of existence."[31] By July 1992, FIS leaders were being tried, and several thousand members were incarcerated. The leaderless party retaliated with violence against the basically military regime by assassinating the country's acting President at a public function. The country was torn by a vicious war. In November 1995, with one leading party banned, two others refusing to take part, and terrorist threats to voters, 62% of voters backed incumbent president Liamine Zeroual in another election. This gave Zeroual a mandate to end the fighting and introduce some semblance of democracy. However he was not successful in ending the conflict. In April 1999, a farcical presidential election took place in which all candidates except the military-backed A. Bouteflika withdrew. Not surprisingly Bouteflika won easily. The country is doomed to more years of fighting and repression.

States in Africa: In many sub-Saharan African states, bullets rather than ballots have been the normal method of changing political leaders in the past. In the mid-1990s, for example, Nigeria's army annulled an election when it disliked the results. In Angola rebels returned to their guns when they lost at the polls. However, many military dictatorships and one-party states in Africa have held, or committed themselves to hold, multi-party elections. In Zambia, for example, on October 31, 1991, the country held a general election and President Kenneth Kaunda lost after years of corruption and dictatorship.[32] It was the first time in an English-speaking African country that a President and ruling party were changed by a general election. The multi-party elections were held without violence in the presence of international and Zambian monitoring teams of more than 3000 observers.[33] Other electoral success stories have been in places such as South Africa, Benin (the first country in French-speaking Africa to adopt multi-party democracy), Ghana, and Malawi.[34] In several countries, however, there was widespread electoral fraud—for example in Kenya, Cameroon, Tanzania, and Côte d'Ivoire. The most common fraud was to stuff or steal ballot boxes and then, once in power, to enrich and empower relatives and chosen ethnic groups.

As these examples indicate, government in many LDCs still tend to be by personal rule rather than by institutionalized and regularized forms of government based on democratically accepted rules. Such traditions take a long time to change and many LDCs will suffer reverses on the road to democracy. However, the basic attributes of democratic elections are so widely revered throughout the world today that pressures on the governments of nondemocratic states to provide meaningful choice and open elections are very powerful.

DISCUSSION QUESTIONS

1. Will there ever be competitive democratic elections in every country of the world?
2. Should Canada adopt the PR system of Israel or the mixed system of Germany? Neither?
3. Of what significance are elections in communist countries? In the poorest of the less developed countries?
4. Does the media have too much influence in electoral campaigns?
5. Is the primary system in U.S. presidential elections too cumbersome?

KEY TERMS

blanket primaries, p. 414

candidate selection, p. 412

closed primaries, p. 414

crossover primaries, p. 414

direct primary, p. 414

gerrymandering, p. 416

national convention, p. 415

nomination, p. 412

open primaries, p. 414

presidential primaries, p. 414

simple plurality, p. 416

ENDNOTES

1. One of the best studies of apportionment is by Bernard Grofman, Arend Lijphart, Robert B. McKay, and Howard A. Scarrow, eds., *Representation and Redistricting Issues* (Lexington, Mass: D.C. Heath, 1982).
2. See R. Rose, "Elections and Electoral Systems: Choices and Alternatives," in V. Bogdanor and D. Butler, eds., *Democracy and Elections* (Cambridge: Cambridge University Press, 1983).
3. See Michael Gallagher and Michael Marsh, eds., *Candidate Selection in Comparative Perspective* (Beverly Hills: Sage, 1988).
4. See Austin Ranney, *Pathways to Parliament* (Madison, Wis.: University of Wisconsin Press, 1965).
5. On Canada, see Robert J. Jackson and Doreen Jackson, *Politics in Canada*, 4th ed., (Scarborough, Ont.: Prentice-Hall Canada, 1998), ch. 11.
6. *Ibid.*, ch. 10.
7. See, for example, Larry M. Bartels, *Presidential Primaries and the Dynamics of Public Choice* (Princeton, N.J.: Princeton University Press, 1988).

8. Wayne Parent, C. Jillson, and R. Weber, "Voting Outcomes in the 1984 Democratic Party Primaries and Caucuses," *APSR*, vol. 81, no. 1 (March 1987), pp. 67–84.

9. See Austin Ranney, "Turnout and Representation in Presidential Primary Elections," *APSR*, vol. 66, no. 1 (March 1972), pp. 21–37.

10. See, for example, Barbara Norrander, and Gregg W. Smith, "Type of Contest, Candidate Strategy, and Turnout in Presidential Primaries," *American Politics Quarterly*, vol. 13, no. 1 (January 1985), pp. 28–50.

11. See Tables 12.3b and 12.4b in Thomas T. Mackie and Richard Rose, *The International Almanac of Electoral History*, 3rd ed. (New York: Facts on File, 1988).

12. See the description by Max Kaase, "Personalized Proportional Representation: The 'Model' of the West German Electoral System," in Arend Lijphart and Bernard Grofman, eds., *Choosing an Electoral System: Issues and Alternatives* (New York: Praeger, 1984), pp. 155–64.

13. Doris A. Braber, *Mass Media and American Politics*, 3rd ed. (Washington, D.C.: Congressional Quarterly Press, 1989), offers a comprehensive introduction to the topic in the United States.

14. See Joseph Wagner, "Media Do Make a Difference: The Differential Impact of Mass Media in the 1976 Presidential Race," *AJPS*, vol. 77, no. 3 (August 1983), pp. 407–30.

15. See, for example, Leo Bogart, "The Public's Use and Perception of Newspapers," *Public Opinion Quarterly*, vol. 48, no. 4 (Winter 1984), pp. 709–19.

16. For an excellent examination of the impact of television on politics in the United States see Austin Ranney, *Channels of Power* (New York: American Enterprise Institute, 1983).

17. Michael J. Robinson, "The Media in 1980: Was the Message the Message?" in Austin Ranney, ed., *The American Election of 1980* (New York: American Enterprise Institute 1981), p. 178.

18. P. Tumanov, quoted in John A. Armstrong, *Ideology, Politics and Government in the Soviet Union*, rev. ed. (New York: Praeger, 1967), p. 111.

19. Until Gorbachev resigned, all but one of the leaders, Nikita Khruschev, died in office. See, for example, Frederick C. Barghoorn and Thomas F. Remington, *Politics in the USSR*, 3rd ed. (Toronto: Little, Brown, 1986), ch. 6.

20. See, for example, *Ibid.*; and Z. Brzezinski, *The Grand Failure* (New York: Charles Scribner's, 1989).

21. Quoted in Richard Sakwa, *Gorbachev and his Reforms 1985–1990* (Englewood Cliffs, N.J.: Prentice-Hall, 1991), p. 134.

22. The new Congress was to meet once a year to establish broad economic and social policy, elect a smaller legislative body which would elect a President, and select a presidium, or steering committee.

23. Sakwa, *Gorbachev and his Reforms*, p. 134.

24. Sakwa, *Gorbachev and his Reforms*, p. 139.

25. Sakwa, *Gorbachev and His Reforms*, p. 141.

26. M. Weiner and E. Ozbudun, eds., *Competitive Elections in Developing Countries* (Durham, N.C.: Duke University Press, 1987); Guy Hermet, Richard Rose, and Alain Rouquie *Elections Without Choice* (London: Macmillan, 1978).

27. Raymond D. Gastil, ed., *Freedom in the World: Political Rights and Civil Liberties* (Westport, Conn.: Greenwood Press, 1982), pp. 25–29.

28. See Hermet, Rose, and Rouquie, eds., *Elections Without Choice*, p. 7.

29. See Tina Rosenberg, "Beyond Elections," *Foreign Policy*, no. 84 (Fall 1991), pp. 72–91.

30. *The Economist*, September 28–October 4, 1991, p. 51.
31. *The Economist*, July 4–10, 1992, p. 37.
32. *The New York Times*, Nov. 3, 1991, p. A3.
33. *Ibid*.
34. See "Africa's Role Model," *The Economist*, August 12, 1995, pp. 11, 12.

FURTHER READING

Bibby, John F., *Politics, Parties and Elections in America*, 3rd ed. (Chicago, Ill. Nelson-Hall, 1987)

Booth, John, and Mitchell Seligson, *Elections and Democracy in Central America* (Chapel Hill, N.C.: University of North Carolina Press, 1989).

Boyer, P., *The People's Mandate: Referendums and an More Democratic Canada* (Toronto: Dundurn Press, 1992).

Campbell, Angus, Philip Converse, Warren Miller, and Donald Stokes, *The American Voter* (New York: John Wiley, 1960).

Canada, Royal Commission on Electoral Reform and Party Financing, *Reforming Electoral Democracy* (Ottawa: Supply and Services, 1992).

Canada, Royal Commission on Electoral Reform and Party Financing, *Research Studies* (23 separate collections of research papers prepared by the Royal Commission), (Toronto: Dundurn Press, 1991).

Dominguez, Jorge I., and James A. McCann, *Democratizing Mexico: Public Opinion and Elections* (Baltimore, Md.: Johns Hopkins University Press, 1995).

Fishkin, James S., *The Voice of the People: Public Opinion and Democracy* (New Haven: Yale University Press, 1995).

Flanagan, Scott C., Shinsaku Kohei, Ichiro Miyake, Bradley M. Richardson, and Joji Watanuki, *The Japanese Voter* (New Haven, CT: Yale University Press, 1991).

Flanigan, William, and Nancy Zingale, *Political Behavior of the American Electorate* (Boston: Allyn and Bacon, 1983).

Franklin, Mark N., Thomas T. Mackie, Henry Valin et al, *Electoral Change: Responses to Evolving Social and Attitudinal Structures in Western Countries* (New York: Cambridge University Press, 1992).

Frizzell, Alan, Jon Pammett, and Anthony Westell, *The Canadian General Election of 1997* (Toronto: Dundurn Press, 1997).

Gallagher, Michael, and Michael Marsh, eds., *Candidate Selection in Comparative Perspective: The Secret Garden of Politics* (Beverly Hills: Sage, 1988).

Ginsbert, Benjamin, and Martin Shefter, *Politics by Other Means: The Declining Importance of Elections in America* (New York: Basic Books, Inc., 1990).

Gold, Goward J., *Hollow Mandates: American Public Opinion and the Conservative Shift* (Boulder, Colo.: Westview, 1992).

Himmelweit, Hilde T., et. al., *How Voters Decide*, European Monographs in Social Psychology (London: Academic Press, 1981).

Kiernan, Brendan, *The End of Soviet Politics: Elections, Legislatures and the Demise of the Communist Party* (Boulder, Colo.: Westview, 1993).

King, Anthony, ed., *Britain at the Polls, 1992* (Chatham, N.J.: Chatham House, 1993).

Lijphart, Arend, *Electoral Systems and Party Systems: A Study of 27 Democracies* (New York: Oxford University Press, 1994).

Nie, Norman H., Sidney Verba, and John R. Petrocik, *The Changing American Voter* (Cambridge, Mass.: Harvard University Press, 1976).

Niemi, Richard G., and Herbert F. Wisberg, *Controversies in Voting Behavior*, 2nd ed. (Washington, D.C.: Congressional Quarterly Press, 1984).

Pomper, Gerald M. ed., *The Election of 1992* (Chatham, N.J.: Chatham House, 1993).

Salmore, Stephen A., and Barbara G. Salmore, *Candidates, Parties, and Campaigns* (Washington, D.C.: Congressional Quarterly, 1985).

Scammon, Richard M., and Alice V. McGillivray, *America Votes, 1992* (Washington D.C.: Congressional Quarterly Press, 1993).

White, Stephen, Richard Rose, and Ian McAllister, *How Russia Votes* (Chatham, NJ: Chatham House, 1997).

 Weblinks

www.fec.gov/
This is the Web Page for the United States Federal Electoral Commission.

dodgson.ucsd.edu/lij
The Lijphart Election Archives site provides election results from around the world.

www.neravt.com/left/third.htm
This site provides links to nationalist movements around the world.

CHAPTER 20

Domestic and International Political Change: Development, Political Violence, and Revolution

The field of political science and world politics is characterized to a great degree by the same vital issues that direct the attention of governments and international organizations. Many of these issues concern political change—how states adapt, evolve, fracture, and disappear, and how new countries are created. Topics tend to be about the stability and instability of states and the security of citizens within them. History indicates clearly that nothing about politics is static. Everything about it is dynamic. States emerge, stabilize, and decay. Empires rise and fall. Civilizations come and go.

The desire to understand the growth and change of states has been traced through 2500 years of political thought.[1] During that extensive period, some philosophers have believed that nothing ever really changes, while others have proffered that states develop by evolution or by distinct stages. These two issues of change and decay remain persistent themes of Western thought and political science.

In the fifth century B.C., the Greek philosopher Heraclitus observed that "You can never step in the same river twice"; in other words, all things are in constant flux. On the other side of the coin, Aristotle (384–322 B.C.), for example, examined the reasons for stability along with the characteristics of "good" government in the Greek city-states. He described development in terms of the laws of birth, growth, maturity, and decay. For him states developed in a manner fairly similar to individuals.

In this chapter we examine some of the themes around the two issues of change and decay. In the first section concepts such as development, modernization, and dependency are discussed. In the second section the less seemly side of politics is studied, including discontent, violence, terrorism, coups, and revolution. Of course, this chapter does not exhaustively describe or assess all of the various theories underpinning research on these issues. Rather, it raises questions about these important topics without developing a single theory of political change.

POLITICAL DEVELOPMENT

One of the most important, and most contentious, issues in comparative analysis concerns how states do or do not develop economically and politically. As one looks around the globe it is evident that a minority of states and their citizens are vastly wealthier than the rest. Numerous states endure poverty, unemployment, inadequate housing, poor health, limited education, and impure water. The gap between the richer so-called "developed" states and their "less developed" counterparts is so significant that they are often described as belonging to different worlds.

There are also major differences among states in terms of their politics. Developed countries tend to have fairly stable institutions and governments possessed with legitimacy and the ability to govern. Less developed states are often chronically unstable with contested governments and institutions. In many of these states one ethnic group holds power over others. Many of their governments are repressive and human rights are frequently abused. Political violence, torture, assassinations, and war are prevalent and, except in Latin America, free speech and a free press are often absent.

Every categorization of states is somewhat contentious. But the usual justification for placing some states in the developing category is that almost all of them are relatively quite poor (see Chapters 4 and 5). By comparison with the richer Western countries, the less developed countries (LDCs) are characterized by low incomes, low literacy, high infant mortality rates, and low life expectancy. In some countries, citizens live mainly in rural, agricultural communities, while in others great masses of them scratch out a living in huge cities. Many of these countries have highly vulnerable economies. They are dramatically affected by the changing nature of the international economy, especially if they export only one major commodity.

Of course, there are enclaves of wealth within the LDCs. Exceptionally, some states, such as Saudi Arabia, are placed in this category because of their traditional political processes even though their per capita income is among the highest in the world. On the other hand, some poorer countries in Europe are included in the developed category because of their intermediate position and possibilities for generating wealth.

One of the most significant issues discussed in development studies is **poverty**, defined as a level of income, food, health, education, housing, and quality of life below the minimum standards of life and decency. As Figure 20.1 shows, the richest 20% of the world's population receives 82.7% of the total world income while the poorest 20% receives only 1.4%. Most of the richer people live in northern countries. Global economic growth rarely filters down. Of course, poverty exists in all parts of the world. There are areas of extreme unemployment, homelessness, and even hunger in developed world. But the preponderance of the problem is found in the LDCs or in the South.

Approximately one in every five people on earth lives in poverty. The poorest peoples are found in South Asia (50%), Southeast Asia (25%), and sub-Saharan Africa (16%).[2] With little or no purchasing power, these people are destitute. Approximately one billion humans are malnourished, one and a half billion lack clean drinking water

Figure 20.1   Global Distribution of Income

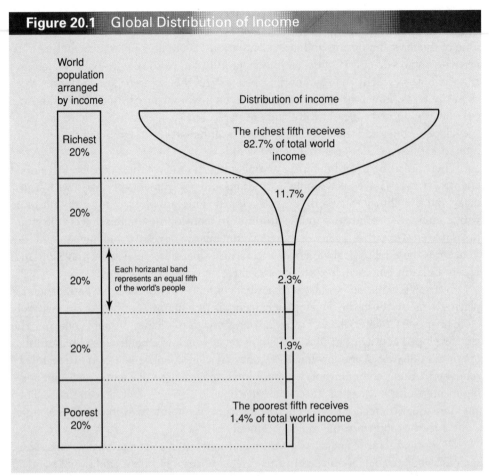

Source: Adapted from *Human Development Report, 1992* by the United Nations Development Programme. Copyright © 1992 by the United Nations Development Programme. Used by permission of Oxford University Press, Inc.

and proper health services, and more than 15 million children a year die before the age of five. The ability of these people to escape from their conditions is minimal. Illiteracy is extremely high (more than half the people of the poorest of the LDCs are illiterate) and they have little chance for employment.

Aggregate income data does not, however, correlate perfectly with poverty or other indications of a deprived life style. The extent of human poverty has little to do with the average level of income. The 1998 **Human Development Index (HDI)** shows, for example, that some 7–17 % of the population in industrial countries is poor. The United Nations constructs this annual index, which includes life expectancy, adult literacy, average years of schooling, and purchasing power. The 1998 HDI rankings are shown in Table 20.1.

Table 20.1 Human Development Index 1998

High Human Development

1 Canada
2 France
3 Norway
4 USA
5 Iceland

6 Finland
7 Netherlands
8 Japan
9 New Zealand
10 Sweden

11 Spain
12 Belgium
13 Austria
14 United Kingdom
15 Australia

16 Switzerland
17 Ireland
18 Denmark
19 Germany
20 Greece

21 Italy
22 Israel
23 Cyprus
24 Barbados
25 Hong Kong, China

26 Luxembourg
27 Malta
28 Singapore
29 Antigua and Barbuda
30 Korea, Rep. of

31 Chile
32 Bahamas
33 Portugal
34 Costa Rica
35 Brunei Darussalam

36 Argentina
37 Slovenia

38 Uruguay
39 Czech Rep.
40 Trinidad and Tobago

41 Dominica
42 Slovakia
43 Uruguay
44 Fiji
45 Panama

46 Venezuela
47 Hungary
48 United Arab Emirates
49 Mexico
50 Saint Kitts and Nevis

51 Grenada
52 Poland
53 Columbia
54 Kuwait
55 Saint Vincent

56 Seychelles
57 Qatar
58 Saint Lucia
59 Thailand
60 Malaysia

61 Mauritius
62 Brazil
63 Belize
64 Libyan Arab Jamahiriya

Medium Human Development

65 Suriname
66 Lebanon
67 Bulgaria
68 Belarus
69 Turkey

70 Saudi Arabia
71 Oman
72 Russian Federation

73 Ecuador
74 Romania
75 Korea, Dem. People's Rep. of
76 Croatia
77 Estonia
78 Iran, Islamic Rep. of
79 Lithuania

80 Macedonia, FYR
81 Syrian Arab Rep.
82 Algeria
83 Tunisia
84 Jamaica

85 Cuba
86 Peru
87 Jordan
88 Dominican Rep.
89 South Africa

90 Sri Lanka
91 Paraguay
92 Latvia
93 Kazakhstan
94 Samoa (Western)

95 Maldives
96 Indonesia
97 Botswana
98 Philippines
99 Armenia

100 Guyana
101 Mongolia
102 Ukraine
103 Turkmenistan
104 Uzbekistan

105 Albania
106 China
107 Namibia
108 Georgia
109 Kyrgyzstan

110 Azerbaijan
111 Guatemala

Table 20.1   Human Development Index 1998 continued

112 Egypt	132 Cameroon	153 Madagascar
113 Moldova, Rep. of	133 Ghana	154 Central African Rep.
114 El Salvador	134 Lesotho	155 Bhutan
115 Swaziland	135 Equatorial Guinea	156 Angola
116 Bolivia	136 Lao People's	157 Sudan
117 Cape Verde	Dem. Rep.	158 Senegal
118 Tajikistan	137 Kenya	159 Haiti
119 Honduras	138 Pakistan	160 Uganda
120 Gabon	139 India	161 Malawi
121 São Tomé and	140 Cambodia	162 Djibouti
Principe	141 Comoros	163 Chad
122 Viet Nam	142 Nigeria	164 Guinea-Bissau
123 Solomon Islands	143 Dem. Rep. of the	165 Gambia
124 Vanuatu	Congo	166 Mozambique
125 Morocco	144 Togo	167 Guinea
126 Nicaragua	145 Benin	168 Eritrea
127 Iraq	146 Zambia	169 Ethiopia
128 Congo	147 Bangladesh	170 Burundi
129 Papua New Guinea	148 Côte d'Ivoire	171 Mali
130 Zimbabwe	149 Mauritania	172 Burkina Faso
	150 Tanzania, U. Rep. of	173 Niger
Low Human Development	151 Yemen	174 Sierra Leone
131 Myanmar	152 Nepal	

Source: United Nations Development Program, *Human Development Report 1998* (New York: Oxford University Press, 1998), pp. 128–130. Copyright © 1998 United Nations Development Program. Used by permission of Oxford University Press, Inc.

Despite some technical difficulties, this index of countries shows clearly that wealth is very unevenly distributed around the world. Of the 20 highest-ranked countries, all but Japan are in Europe, North America, or Australasia. All of the 20 lowest-ranked countries, except Haiti, are in Africa.

Why does there remain basically a rich world and a poor world? In an epoch characterized by a global economy, global communication, global ecology, and global weapons systems, why does such a vast economic imbalance persist? Why, when knowledge, technology, and capital are easily transferable is there not a major shift in world wealth? Table 20.2 offers some clues to help answer this question. During the last decade many U.S. shoe companies have had their shoes produced in poorer countries in the Third World, such as Indonesia, where labour costs are very low compared to the United States or Western Europe. The picture for other manufacturing industries in other Western countries is similar.

Table 20.2	Basketball Shoes and Third World Workers (in U.S. dollars)
U.S. rubber shoe industry average wage	$6.94 per hour
Indonesian rubber shoe industry average wage	$0.14 per hour
Cost of manufacturing 1 pair of Nike basketball shoes in Indonesia	$0.12
Selling price of 1 pair of Nike basketball shoes in the United States	$80.00
Michael Jordan's multi-year endorsement fee for Nike shoes	$2,000,000.00

Source: Data assembled from information in Jeffrey Balinger "The New Free Trade Hell," *Harper's Magazine*, August 1992, pp. 46–57.

Political development is the rubric under which many questions relating to these inequalities throughout the world are placed.[3] It is used both as an umbrella concept for the close-linked phenomena concerning political change everywhere and for the more specific analysis of the growth, or lack of growth and change, in LDCs. It is no wonder, therefore, that there is no accepted definition of "development" and that even the term is criticized by some scholars.[4] There may be considerable agreement that a more developed state should enable its political leaders to accomplish their goals more fully, but there is considerable disagreement about the objectives that should be sought in political development.

Moreover, whether the term used is "development," "developing," or "underdevelopment," the concept is said by some academics to have ideological overtones. There is some validity to this argument. In a nutshell, the question is often put in the following form: Does the economic and political modernization of poorer states necessitate Westernization as well? Do countries that wish to improve the state of their economies and politics necessarily have to follow the same models as those found in Western liberal democracies? Do even communist states such as China—which at times in its history has been more technologically advanced than European countries—have to switch to Western systems in order to develop now?

Many individuals simply assume that economic and political development everywhere should follow the same trajectory that Western states did. But many countries have value systems, cultures, histories, and economies vastly different from those in the Western democratic states. In order to avoid social disruption, they must choose a model for development that is not incompatible with their society. One of the persistent questions, then, is whether political leaders in LDCs can create institutions capable of sustaining economic growth and maintaining political stability.

In the view of some scholars, the focus of study should simply be the "Third World" rather than "development." The problem with using this approach exclusively is that it does not focus on the primary issues of world politics but rather on several specific geographical regions. The approach takes us to the right places—Africa, Asia, Latin

America, the Middle East, and most of the islands of the Pacific Ocean—but it does not tell us what questions to ask when we arrive there. Why do similar circumstances prevail in much of the South? Is it possible for poorer states to move to higher levels of economic and political development? What is the best policy route to escape from these conditions and circumstances?

In many LDCs the characteristic that needs to be eliminated is poverty. However, some of these states, essentially those with rich oil deposits, have escaped from the conditions associated with low economic development and poverty.[5] Even in those states in which poverty is dramatic, the causes differ greatly. The origins of poverty may lie in low productivity, inadequate national resources, famines, wars, or even economic inequality within the country.

MODERNIZATION AND DEPENDENCY THEORIES

Two basic schools of political science clash in explaining *why* some states remain in a less developed condition than others. The two groups may be crudely characterized as following either the traditional theory of political modernization or the more "radical" perspective of dependency theory.[6]

On the whole, the **political modernization** school of comparative and world politics depicts a state's political development in terms of its internal changes over time; in other words, its advocates ask by what processes and institutional changes a traditional state evolves into a developed or modern state.[7] The central question is whether one can account systematically for patterns of political development through its various stages.[8]

Many descriptions of the conditions of developed states have been outlined. They tend to include such social conditions as greater urbanization and higher literacy as well as economic conditions such as greater industrialization and productive capacity. More developed political systems are also associated with organizational sophistication (specialization, differentiation of roles and functions in organizations and government), technological improvement (an increase in means of producing goods and services), and attitudinal differences ("modern" attitudes are characterized by increased knowledge, rationality, secular values, and individualism).[9] These characterizations are used in the specialist literature both to define the *state* of development and the *process* through which states must evolve to become developed.

The political modernization school of thought is based essentially on the idea that LDCs will have to follow the same path that Western states did earlier if they wish to modernize. They will have to accept modern ideas about political processes, education, and the economy. These changes will come about, such theorists argue, if values and structures in these societies can become more like those in the developed countries.

Western or classical economists back up this notion of modernization by arguing that the way for these countries to develop is by competing with developed states in worldwide free trade. If domestic producers in these countries were exposed to international competition, they would be forced to become more efficient and effective: that is, they would have to modernize.

According to this reasoning, the problem with many LDCs is that their leaders have misled them into socialism, state-directed economies, or cronyism and corruption. This argument is backed up by international organizations such as the World Bank and the International Monetary Fund, which lend money only to those countries that conform to certain norms about freedom and capitalism. In the more advanced forms of this argument, advocates proffer the need for governments to foster the development of companies that may be able to compete internationally and then to adopt a laissez-faire doctrine. Japan and South Korea are usually viewed as countries which have successfully adopted this approach of protecting inefficient industries in the expectation that they *will* become competitive. Richer countries, despite giving lip service to this liberal economic theory, actually protect many inefficient industries for security and military reasons.

Many of these arguments, including those of Karl Marx, tend to present a unilinear model of development which is essentially based on Western experiences—in particular, British and American. The idea that the history of states will follow a single, inevitable sequence of stages toward modern development is challenged by most scholars today. In contemporary studies more attention is paid to the key problems in the developmental process and the choices that leaders make to confront these challenges.[10]

The **dependency school**, which is basically Marxist inspired, attempts to describe the situation of LDCs as being caused by their incorporation into the global, capitalist economy during the period of colonization. They reject the idea that LDCs must follow the Western route to development. For them, underdevelopment is seen as a product of unequal relationships between the richer capitalist states and the poorer undeveloped ones. They believe that following the advice to open up markets in the LDCs will only exacerbate the differences between the rich and poor countries. In some of the more radical of these approaches, the world economy is seen as actually creating "underdevelopment" and poverty in the Third World.[11] The capitalist states are said to maintain their economic domination by manipulating factors such as wages, resources, capital, markets, prices, and technologies. The developing states remain as suppliers of raw materials and providers of cheap labour for the benefit of the capitalist states. According to many scholars it is this existence on the periphery that plagues these states.[12]

Assessing the Theories

The tension between these two schools begins with their basic assumptions. The first focuses on modernization while the second focuses on LDCs' dependency on the wealthier states of the world. Both are slippery concepts. What is modern? What is dependency?

The problems with the latter school are just as significant as those with its rival. Strong advocates of dependency theory tend to leave the internal dynamics of each state out of their analysis—internal factors such as class, ethnicity, religion, and particularly culture are simply omitted in the analysis. As Myron Weiner put it:

The rapid modernization of East Asia and portions of Southeast Asia, the emergence of fundamentalism as a major political force in the Middle East, and the failure of class-based movements to replace ethnic movements were among the major political changes not anticipated by most scholars.[13]

Students of the "dependency approach" mistakenly assume that the state of dependency remains unaltered throughout history. They homogenize the experience of all LDCs into one preconceived pattern due to colonization. Some even limit their research to the colonial past and explain how that period created today's world.[14] Others, more nuanced, explain how present-day dependency may be explained by the activities of a particular type of entrepreneurial class—the *comprador* class. Although they are part of the local elite, the *comprador* replace the colonists at the time of national independence and become the managers of the old colonist firms and farms. They then act as intermediaries between the local economy and the international economy which is dominated by the rich countries. The ethos of colonialism and its impact on the local economy thus perpetuates itself even after independence.

Lastly, dependency theorists do not explain why less developed states differ so greatly in their choices about public policy. Some states have been successful in achieving their developmental goals while others have failed. These scholars tend to concentrate on Africa and Latin America to the exclusion of Asia. Ideologically, they seemed to be saying that the poorer states ought to break with the global capitalist system in order to achieve a higher degree of independence.

The simple fact is that both types of theories about development have proven incapable of explaining economic and political development around the world. Clearly, a theory combining the two arguments is required. The emergence of democracy in the states of the former Soviet Union and Eastern Europe as well as earlier in Latin America were certainly not forecast by scholars of either tradition. There is also great interest in the dramatic economic development in certain Asian countries, namely Singapore, South Korea, and Taiwan—the so-called "newly industrializing countries," or "NICs." They have modernized "economically" without adopting Western culture and values. Notwithstanding their difficulties at the end of the 1990s, the NICs have demonstrated that "dependency" can be overcome.

The stability of monarchies in the Gulf, the rise of Islamic fundamentalism throughout the Middle East, and the persistence of prosperous authoritarian regimes in Asia are further examples of the need to reformulate development and dependency theory. As Weiner put it, theories of economic and political development "must take into account both the constraints and opportunities for choice."[15]

To a minor degree these two literatures on development have been synthesized in recent years.[16] Both the impact of the Western world on poorer countries and the internal dynamics of these countries have been recognized as significant. On the other hand, the quest for a universal theory of development which could be replicated from one country to another is in disrepute as scholars search for more middle-range theories regarding specific states or historical periods. It has become clearer that states find themselves confronting industrialization processes at different times and with different effects than earlier universal theories had presupposed.[17]

There seems now to be a rough consensus that attention should be paid to both international *and* domestic factors in explaining political development. The modernization school has accepted the argument that development is affected by international trade patterns, finance, and investment. However, the belief that economic explanations alone could prove conclusive for analyzing developmental processes has also been amended. The dependency school has changed some of its focus from economic growth issues to *economic distribution within LDCs* and the need to study domestic politics. As Samuel P. Huntington maintains, there is a need to explore systematically the relations between culture and development as well as those between the economy and development.[18] In other words, a richer form of explanation is required, which not only respects the findings of area specialists about history, culture, and economics, but also continues the search for meaningful generalizations about political development and the world economy. No one denies that the unequal distribution of wealth and poverty in the world is affected by the attitudes of people and their local elites as well as the domestic and international economy.

POLITICAL VIOLENCE: DOMESTIC AND INTERNATIONAL

Over time, political systems may decay, break apart, or even die. State leaders must constantly make choices about how to maintain order in view of their citizens' demands and expectations. Sometimes such demands cannot be met and order breaks down, giving rise to bombings, kidnappings, riots, and general turmoil. Such political violence cannot be kept within state boundaries today as all crises are internationalized by global communications.

Discontent, strife, and political violence are prevalent in all states, democratic and authoritarian, regardless of their level of development. However, the degree and longevity of such violence differs from state to state. Some countries seem to be in perpetual strife and turmoil while others are more tranquil. But there are no states without some political violence in their history.

The concept of political violence itself is contentious. While, for practical reasons, we employ the word **violence** in this chapter as meaning actual physical force employed for achieving political goals, it can also be useful as a concept referring to *threats* of violence as well as other forms of harassment and manipulation that do not involve physical injury. The word is used in many different ways. As Lewis Carroll put it in *Alice in Wonderland*:

> "When I use a word," Humpty Dumpty said in a rather scornful tone, "it
> means just what I choose it to mean—neither more nor less." "The question
> is," said Alice, "Whether you can make words mean so many different things."
> "The question is" said Humpty Dumpty, "which is to be master—that's all."

Scholars use many techniques in an attempt to understand political violence. Historians describe the trends in political violence over the years, and philosophers try to explain the conceptual underpinnings of the use of violence. The most quantitative/science school of thought in political science, on the other hand, attempts to explain levels of violence by testing hypotheses about the statistical relationships between the attributes of violence and the economic, social, and political conditions that accompany it.[19]

There are many types of political violence. One way to characterize them is by developing a taxonomy to indicate their primary characteristics. Table 20.3 constructs the basic factors (actors and targets) involved in domestic and international political violence, while omitting other items such as the tools used or the degree of organization and participation. As the table indicates, the state may be the recipient or the perpetrator of political violence. **War**, for example, is a type of violence that pits the government of one state against the government of another, while political assassinations concern individual or group violence against other individuals or groups who represent the government or state. (See Close Up 20.1. War is also examined in Chapter 21.) The state may also use violence against its own citizens. When it does so for law enforcement reasons, as when it arrests, detains, imprisons, or even executes criminals, the violence may be considered legitimate. Such violence may be used against those who break the law either in civil or criminal matters. We discussed this type of legitimate violence in Chapters 13 and 14 on public administration.

When violence is used *illegitimately* by the state against its own citizens it is called **internal security**. The state does not simply maintain order but also employs thugs to uphold its authority or repressive laws against those who challenge, or appear to challenge, its right to authority. Examples would include the many "disappearances" of people in Chile, Argentina, El Salvador, and other Latin American countries throughout the 1970s and '80s or the thousands of deaths in Cambodia under the notorious Pol Pot regime. More usual is violence that concerns attacks on the political leaders or the state itself. Unless there are political goals attached to such action, it is normally called **criminal activity**. But when it becomes politicized as in terrorism, coups d'état, or revolutions (all to be discussed below) it is genuine political violence. Other well-known

Table 20.3   Types of Political Violence

Actors \ Targets	Individuals or Groups	State
Individuals or Groups	Political Crime Terrorism Assassinations	Riots Coups d'état
State	Internal Security and Law Enforcement	War

forms of violence are riots and separatist violence. **Riots** are sporadic, disorganized forms of violence. They may involve acts against leaders of government, state institutions, or property. The riots in the 1960s against the Vietnam War by American university students, the continual riots by blacks during apartheid in South Africa, and the urban riots in Los Angeles in 1992 are well-known examples. **Coups d'état**, or sudden forced changes in government leadership through irregular military action, were discussed in Chapters 14 and 15.

When groups wish to form a separate state out of an already existing one, or when regional alienation and desire for increased autonomy are present, it often spills over into political violence. Examples can be found in many countries, including democracies. In Canada during the 1970s, the *Front de Libération du Québec* was involved in bombings, kidnappings, and murder in its quest for an independent Quebec. The Irish Republican Army in Northern Ireland, the Palestinian Liberation Organization in Israel, and the Tamils in Sri Lanka are more recent examples of groups that have used violence for political purposes.

Quantitative Studies of Political Violence

How can political scientists explain the various means of political violence against politicians and the state? The answer is clear. Unless they discuss the details of particular cases, they must revert to some form of quantitative study. The purpose of quantitative analysis is to construct a causal model of strife and thereby determine which variables are the most significant in understanding the causes of political violence. Analysts can then employ these factors along with other more descriptive information to determine whether the state's policies will increase or decrease the level of civil strife.

The likelihood, magnitude, and type of domestic political violence has been most thoroughly examined by American researchers. One of the best known and most explicit research designs is by Ted Gurr.[20] After examining a series of variables in 114 countries, he developed a model that explained two-thirds of the variance of the level of strife among states. In ordinary language that means that most civil strife across countries was explained by or known to be caused by the factors specified in the model.

The basic hypothesis of Gurr's research was that **relative deprivation,** defined as the difference between the expectations of individuals and their ability to satisfy these desires, is a basic precondition for all forms of strife. But, according to Gurr, this discontent is mediated by a number of intervening social conditions. In other words, relative deprivation alone does not cause violence to occur. He defined turmoil, conspiracy, and internal war as the strife-dependent variables. **Turmoil** comprised relatively spontaneous events such as demonstrations, strikes, riots, clashes, and localized rebellions. **Conspiracy** comprised intensively organized, small-scale strife, including assassinations, terrorism, small-scale guerilla wars, coups, and mutinies. **Internal war** included large-scale, organized strife accompanied by extensive violence such as civil wars and large-scale revolts.[21]

Gurr operationalized these concepts into measures of civil strife, providing statistics for such details as the number of participants, number of casualties, property damage, and duration of events.[22] Some of the causal factors and hypotheses examined were:

1. *Persistent Relative Economic Deprivation*—The difference between individuals' expectations (goods and conditions of life) and capabilities (the amount of these goods and conditions that they believe they can obtain).[23]

2. *Participation in Past Strife*—Societies in which strife occurs develop beliefs that justify the use of strife in the future.

3. *Potential Coercion*—The more coercion there is, the less strife there will be. Coercion is operationalized as military participation rates and regime repressiveness.[24]

4. *Institutionalization*— Certain organizational features encourage strife, including external assistance.

5. *Social and Structural Facilitation*—Several factors in this category were examined:

   a) The extent and quality of organization for collective action affecting political strife.

   b) External support for initiators of strife—including symbolic support as well as more concrete support in the form of funds and weapons.

6. *Legitimacy of the Regime*—The lower the support for the regime, the higher the level of strife will be.

When these variables and their interactions were examined for all 114 states, the results provided a causal model of the determinants of civil strife. Gurr showed that three

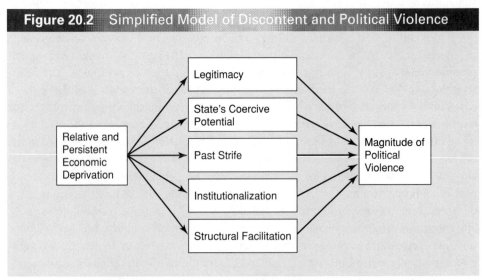

Figure 20.2 Simplified Model of Discontent and Political Violence

Source: Based on T. Robert Gurr's work in John V. Gillespie and Betty A. Nesvold, eds., *Macro-Quantitative Analysis* (Beverly Hills, Cal.: Sage, 1971), pp. 217–49.

variables proved very powerful in explaining strife. Structural facilitation accounted for just under half of the explained variance, while persisting deprivation accounted for a quarter, and legitimacy one-eighth. In other words, while relative deprivation was of continuing importance as a factor producing collective strife, it was not as significant as the other mediating variables that constituted the *mind-set* of participants. Contrary to the initial model, and what one might expect, coercive potential, institutionalization, and past strife turned out to have very little direct and independent effect on the overall level of strife. See Figure 20.2 for a simplified model of Gurr's work.

TERRORISM AND OTHER STRIFE-PRONE ACTIVITY

Political violence can be expressed in many forms. In recent years group-inspired violence, and terrorism in particular, has been a well-used technique of those who wished to influence societies either domestically or internationally. **Terrorism** is the systematic use or threat of violence against individuals or states to obtain political concessions. The word "terrorism" comes from the name given to Robespierre's Committee on Public Safety, which used mass executions to terrorize citizens during the French Revolution.

Today, we are more familiar with hostage-taking and bombing as terrorist weapons than we are with the use of the guillotine, but the results are similar. Terror is used by individuals, groups, and states in order to get governments to alter their policies in the direction the terrorists demand. Examples are legion: Pan American Flight 103 was blown out of the sky over Lockerbie, Scotland, by a concealed bomb; Western hostages were held for many years in Lebanon; a government building was blown up in Oklahoma City in 1995; United States' embassies in Tanzania and Kenya were blown up in 1998; and so on. See Close Up 20.1 for a frightening look at new-wave terrorism.

Research in this field is extremely voluminous, diverse, and often contradictory. For example, well over 6000 books exist on terrorism alone. Unlike the statistical examination of general strife, the study of violence-prone groups is usually based on comparative case studies. The major categories or checklists used by experts to study these cases include organization, leadership, demography, ideology, operations, communications, weapons, funding, and external support.[25] The assumption of much of the research is that the higher the level of structural-facilitation variables, the more likelihood of strife. But studies of group alienation and violence clearly indicate that social-science explanations of terrorism must bear in mind how historical experiences and normative convictions impact on the relative economic deprivation of groups.

One major analytic problem is that many discontented groups do not become violent, even though they possess some, or all, of these required characteristics. How can one determine which groups are inclined to be strife-prone or violent? The answer is conclusive that those groups that seek an ideologically defined transformation of society are more likely to become violent than those that do not.

CLOSE UP 20.1   Modern War: Kosovo, Serbia and NATO

Domestic wars and international wars are often interrelated:

1974   Kosovo becomes an autonomous province within the federal country of Yugoslavia.

1987   Slobodan Milosevic becomes leader of Serbia.

1989   Milosevic revokes Kosovo's autonomy. Ethnic Albanians riot.

1990   Serbia closes Kosovo's parliament. Kosovo Albanians start parallel government.

1991   Slovenia, Croatia and Macedonia secede from the Yugoslav federation. Kosovo Albanians approve independence.

1992-93   Bosnia-Herzegovina declares independence.

1995   NATO begins air campaign against Bosnian Serbs. After 43 months Bosnian war ends with the Dayton Peace Accord.

1996   Pro-independence Kosovo Liberation Army (KLA) emerges.

1998   KLA seizes control of much of Kosovo before being routed by Serbian military. Massacres and fighting start in Kosovo.

1999   Peace talks fail. NATO begins Operation Allied Force against Yugoslavia, bombing throughout the territory. Albanian refugees flee from Kosovo.[26]

Four basic types of discontented groups can be analyzed:

1. *Criminals*—they do not project a vision of a radical transformation of society.
2. *Nihilists*—they want the destruction of society but have no positive goals.
3. *Nationalists with narrow, particularistic goals*—those trying to secede from a state or decentralize a country or oust an occupying power. For example, Quebec or Tamil Tiger separatists.
4. *Nationalists with broad goals*—groups which wish to seize the entire state, as in a revolution.[27]

The third type of these groups appeals to individuals who wish to attack the dominant political structures of a country but do not aim to destroy the state completely. Typically, these groups represent ethno-cultural, nationalist, or racial interests. They question the legitimacy of the state; demanding greater autonomy and self-determination for their groups. These beliefs and demands serve as powerful inducements for political mobilization as the desire for a "homeland" is a powerful rationale for militant action.

If groups become highly alienated then violence is possible.[28] However, this does not mean that alienated groups should be viewed as consisting of criminals and psychotics. In fact, their behaviour is "seldom, if ever, radically senseless or absurd."[29] Instead of dismissing manifestations of violence as being based on deviant personalities or criminal behaviour such groups should be understood in terms of their social psychology.[30] Group membership provides a protective cloak of anonymity; as members of a group, individuals feel free to use violence because the group lends their actions legitimacy. As well, violence-prone individuals believe they are less likely to be punished if they act in a group.[31]

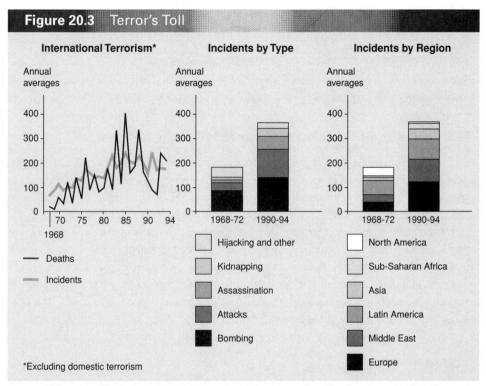

Figure 20.3 Terror's Toll

International Terrorism*

Annual averages

— Deaths

— Incidents

*Excluding domestic terrorism

Incidents by Type

Annual averages

1968-72 1990-94

☐ Hijacking and other

☐ Kidnapping

☐ Assassination

☐ Attacks

■ Bombing

Incidents by Region

Annual averages

1968-72 1990-94

☐ North America

☐ Sub-Saharan Africa

☐ Asia

☐ Latin America

☐ Middle East

■ Europe

Source: University of St. Andrews RAND, "Terrorism: What is terrorism?" as it appeared in *The Economist*, March 2, 1996, p. 24. ©1996 The Economist Newspaper Group Inc. Reprinted with permission. Further reproduction prohibited. **www.economist.com**.

Several conclusions can be reached from the vast literature on the causes of political protest, violence, and terrorism. Since political systems are all based on hierarchies of power, they contain individuals and groups who feel subordinated by the status quo. But, as we have seen in the literature on the magnitude of civil strife, objective conditions of economic deprivation are not a sufficient explanation of strife. As Sederberg expresses it, discontent is a state of mind.[32] Or, as Gurr put it, "what we expect more than what we experience affects our feelings of discontent."[33] In other words, individuals may endure considerable deprivation if they expect little, but may be less willing to endure economic deprivation if they feel their goals are within reach. [34]

Thus, discontent and strife (based on economic deprivation) tend to take place only when an individual or group is affected by ideology and identification. Remember that **ideology** is a relatively organized set of ideas and values that purport to explain and evaluate conditions and propose guidelines for action. **Identification** is defined as how individuals empathize with the political conditions affecting others.[35]

An economically deprived group feels systematically prevented from obtaining what it considers its due. Such discontent—based on ideology and identification—is often found in ethno-cultural groups. Everything being equal, as discontent grows, the level of strife rises. Of course not every discontented group becomes violent. Schwartz has categorized the result of discontent in four forms. A discontented group may:

1. Withdraw—that is, sever all contacts with outside society.
2. Engage in ritualistic conformity—that is, conform while being alienated.
3. Engage in reformism—that is, remain active, but not engage in radical or violent behaviour.
4. Rebel—that is, make attacks, which may be violent, on the system.[36]

The important question is, why do some groups move to category four and use political violence? The answer seems to be related to ideology and to the availability of facilitation structures. The group must have both an ideology that can guide the actions of its members and the necessary resources for analysis, organization, and action.

From this literature on terrorism, we can conclude that the greater the ideological opposition to persisting deprivation, the greater will be the belief in the illegitimacy of the state and its institutions. And, the more this ideology is buttressed by facilitating structures such as a coherent organization, committed leadership, adequate resources such as weapons and funding, geographical proximity and external support, the greater the possibility will be that a strife-prone group will develop.

Such discontented groups may engage in any or all of the following tactics:

- express frustration;
- publicize grievances to national or international audiences;
- publicize the results of resistance to government;
- demystify the power of the state;
- make the territory ungovernable;
- provoke repression which will affect the larger public.

CLOSE UP 20.2   The New Face of Terrorism

"Once upon a time even terrorism was subject to certain rules. True, they were not always observed, but few people boasted of openly defying them. Terrorism was mainly directed against individuals representing tyrannical regimes (or those believed to be tyrannical). If innocent bystanders were killed or wounded, this was not done intentionally."[37]

Today, the author of the above quotation, Walter Laqueur, argues that these rules for terrorism have changed dramatically. The growth of fanaticism and the development of weapons of mass destruction means that a revolution has taken place in terrorism. Innocent bystanders actually become targets.

Do you agree that the threat of terrorism has changed? If so, what can and should be done about it?

Often, oppressed groups feel that only these types of actions, especially shocking ones, can gain them the respect and attention they deserve. There is no doubt that this goal has been achieved by many violence-prone groups over the years. Finally, such groups may engage in turmoil, conspiracy, or civil war to achieve their aims. Depending on the government's response, a retribution-revenge cycle or blood cycle can begin in which the actions of each side are fuelled by demands for vengeance.

Genocide

One of the most abhorrent uses of political violence is genocide. **Genocide** is the deliberate extermination of a race, nation, or other specified group. Etched in our memories is the horror of more than six million Jews being murdered by the Nazis in Germany and Central Europe between 1938 and 1945. But this is not the only example of genocide in the twentieth century. The systematic and deliberate extermination of a people has been continuous. There are many examples. Repatriated nationals and ethnic minorities were systematically put to death in the USSR during and shortly after World War II. According to estimates in the 1970s, the Pol Pot regime in Cambodia killed millions of urbanites. Saddam Hussein dropped nerve gas and mustard gas on Kurd villages in 1988. More recently, in the mid-1990s, "ethnic cleansing" took place in Bosnia where ethnics of another group were expelled or killed by Serbs. Evidence continues to be sought by Serbs to show that Muslims also committed atrocities. Also in the mid-1990s, in Rwanda, members of the Hutu tribe massacred more than a half million members of the Tutsi tribe and antigovernment Hutus (see Table 20.4).

REVOLUTION

Possibly no word in the English language evokes both hope and fear more than revolution. The issue conjures up images of the birth of new nations, the destruction of old empires, and wholesale slaughter of human beings in the name of political ideology. Revolutions are momentous events, involving fundamental economic, social, and political change.

In political science the term **revolution** is used to depict massive or fundamental changes in society based on the use of violence. Sometimes, however, it is used to encompass lesser political events such as nonviolent political change, assassinations of leaders, or coups d'état. Coups may be part of a revolution, but they may be non-revolutionary as well. As discussed in Chapters 14 and 15, a coup is a swift action by an opposition group, usually led by the military, to take over state institutions by force or the threat of force. A coup becomes revolutionary if, after the military has taken over the government, the leader sets out to destroy the existing political and social system in order to create a different one.

The revolutions of France (1789), Russia (1917), and China (1949) are often used to guide thinking about revolutions. In these full-scale revolutions, three characteristics were present. First, violence was used to bring about changes in government leadership.

Table 20.4	Some Major Genocides since 1945	
State	**Genocide Victims**	**Dates**
USSR	Repatriated Nationals and ethnic minorities	1943–47
China	Landlords	1950–51
Sudan	Southern nationalists	1955–72
Sudan	Southern nationalists	1983–98
Indonesia	Communists and ethnic Chinese	1965–66
China	Cultural revolution victims	1966–75
Uganda	Opponents of Idi Amin	1971–79
Pakistan	Bengali nationalists	1971
Cambodia	Educated urbanites	1975–79
Afghanistan	Regime opponents	1978–89
Iraq	Kurds	1984–91
Bosnia	Bosnian Muslims and Croats (pending proof re Serbs)	1991–95
Burundi/Rwanda	Tutsi, Hutu	1993–98

Second, the revolution's immediate target was to make illegal changes in governmental organization, personnel, and policy output. Lastly, the purpose of these revolutions was to make permanent changes in the values and behaviour found in the social system.[38]

This three-part definition (use of violence, capturing of the state apparatus, and changing societal values) wisely restricts the study of revolution. It avoids the wider use of the word "revolution" in reference to changing fads in social norms or even in types of hairstyle. It also avoids the difficulty of combining discordant ideas—as in characterizing the 1960s shift from the sacred to the secular in Quebec society as the "Quiet Revolution."

Thus, on the whole, political scientists restrict the use of the word "revolution" to those situations where there is a fundamental transformation of state organization and class structure in a country.[39] Even with such restrictions there are many difficulties in applying the term to the multifarious events in the real world. Was the nonviolent, but massive, upheaval in the Soviet Union in the late 1980s a revolution?

In order to make sense of the many kinds of revolutions, Chalmers Johnson constructed a useful typology. By studying the ideology, targets, leadership, and degree of spontaneity in revolutions, Johnson found six ideal-types. They were the **Jacquerie**, or mass peasant uprising; the **Millenarian Rebellion**, characterized by the Jacquerie plus charismatic leadership; the **Anarchistic Rebellion**, an attempt to restore a former society; the **Jacobin Communist Revolution**, a spontaneous social and political revolution; the **Conspiratorial Coup d'état**; and the **Militarized Insurrection**, a premeditated nationalist or social revolution.[40]

However, some momentous events do not involve much violence. Some revolutionary transformations seem to emerge directly from the people. The fundamental democratic changes which emerged in the Soviet Union and Eastern Europe in the late 1980s met the conditions for major transformations in these Communist societies and yet there was very little direct violence in most of them. The collapse of communism was brought about by massive economic difficulties, demonstrations against Communist leaders, a failure of Communist ideology, and especially Mikhail Gorbachev's inability or lack of will to govern. In comparison with the degree of change taking place in Communist systems, the amount of violence was comparatively small, the notable exception so far, of course, being war in the former Yugoslavia, Chechnya, and in areas around the Caspian Sea. There have been other such "democratic" revolutions—that is, occasions where a government elected by the people set about to destroy the existing social system and to create new forms of government. Examples from both the right and the left of the political spectrum would include the popular contests that gave rise to Hitler's creation of the German Third Reich in 1933 and Salvadore Allende's Marxist government in Chile in 1970.

Causes of Revolution

The most popular method of studying revolutions is to determine what their causes or conditions are. Both theorists and practitioners (who wish to make or prevent revolutions) would like to know the answers to these perplexing questions. But conclusions on the subject are contested and are often affected by ideological biases.

Certainly, a series of factors tends to coincide with revolutions. These factors include serious economic difficulties, external wars, and a growing acceptance of the use of violence in the pursuit of social transformation. For the most part, the explanations tend to be either ideologically conservative or ideologically progressive. Conservatives tend to believe that revolutions occur when change takes place too rapidly. Progressives base their conclusions on the assumption that revolutions take place when there is not enough change. A few scholars use a combination of conservative and progressive explanations in their theories.

Readers may wish to examine some of the rich theories about the cause of revolution such as those of Hannah Arendt, Chalmers Johnson, Barrington Moore, and Theda Skocpol.[41] But, for introductory purposes, we shall outline only the tenets of the classical works of Karl Marx, Crane Brinton, Alexis de Toqueville, and one modern writer who attempted to combine their ideas, James C. Davies.

Marx's theory of revolutionary change has had a great impact on the history of the world. As an economic determinist, he taught that revolutionary change could be traced to economic causes. The reader will recall from Chapter 8 that, according to Marx's theory of history, the economic forces of a society predetermine the stages of political development. Capitalism is the penultimate stage of economic development in which the increasing degradation of the proletariat causes revolution to erupt. For Marx, capitalists cannot change their exploitive behaviour. The workers will eventually rebel against the status quo, there will be a transformation of the economic system (from one mode of production to another), and a socialist utopia will be constructed. In this final, or Communist, stage the state will wither away and a property-less society will be established.

Marxist thought was incorrect in positing that revolution would take place first in the most advanced capitalist society, Britain. It also did not anticipate the role peasants would play in successful revolutions throughout the world. Such flaws in the analysis prevented the successful prediction of revolutions. But, the ideology did provide a catalyst for some revolutions, as in Russia, China, and Cuba.

Despite the limitations of Marx's theoretical analysis, it was taken up by more pragmatic leaders. Lenin argued that a revolution of the proletariat would occur only if it were led by a disciplined revolutionary "party" dedicated to the violent overthrow of the Russian state. He succeeded in combining workers, peasants, and his militant party to provoke the events that led to the 1917 Russian Revolution. Marxism was also adapted by Mao Tse-tung who, knowing that there was no significant worker proletariat in China, concentrated his activity on the peasants and nationalism to create the 1949 Chinese Revolution.

By contrast with Marx's contention, Crane Brinton found that the revolutions in England, the United States, France, and Russia all took place at a time when the countries showed improvements in their economies. He also found that other factors—such as class antagonism, government financial crises, a transfer of allegiance by the intellectuals, and a loss of self-confidence by the ruling class—were involved in each case.[42] Brinton found that all four revolutions he studied followed the same historical trajectory. Economic problems were compounded when intellectuals refused to support the status quo. Then the governments failed to maintain their legitimacy and were unable to crush their enemies. At this time revolutionaries took over and installed a leadership dominated by moderates. Eventually, the moderates were replaced by extremists who undertook a reign of terror. The last stage was characterized by return to normalcy, and even sometimes by reactionary rule.

The classic position that revolutions may be caused by improving economic standards rather than deterioration was argued by Alexis de Toqueville. He argued that the French Revolution occurred when economic conditions were improving in France, and that there was most discontent in those parts of France where there had been the greatest economic improvements.[43]

How can these two divergent viewpoints be combined? One of the most persuasive accounts of the causes of revolutions is based on both conservative and progressive economic types of explanation. In eight revolutions, James C. Davies found that there had been a prolonged period of economic development followed by a short period of sharp economic reversal just before the revolution broke out. He argued that improving economic conditions increased expectations and that, when they were not satisfied,

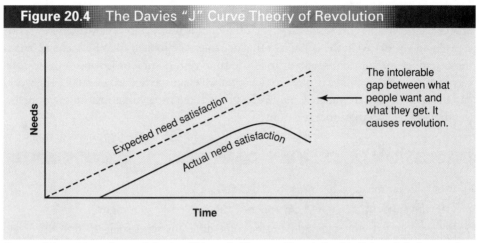

Figure 20.4   The Davies "J" Curve Theory of Revolution

Needs

Expected need satisfaction

Actual need satisfaction

The intolerable gap between what people want and what they get. It causes revolution.

Time

Source: Adapted from James C. Davies, "*Toward a Theory of Revolution,*" in Robert J. Jackson and Michael B. Stein, eds., *Issues in Comparative Politics* (New York: St. Martin's Press, 1971), p. 372.

revolt followed. The psychological mood created the conditions for the revolution. This theory of "rising expectations" is illustrated in Figure 20.4. It indicates that the chief cause of revolutions can be described as a "J" curve. The disparity between the values the people expect and the actual distribution they receive resembles an inverted "J."

As well as these economic and psychological theories of revolution, there have been many attempts to analyze the relations among groups that cause revolutions. Theda Skocpol may be the best known of such contemporary "structural" theorists. She argues that the French, Russian, and Chinese revolutions were all caused by well organized opposition groups who called on peasants to rise against a regime already discredited by war. For her, revolution is best understood as continuing into the period when the new leadership imposes its policies on the new dissidents.[44]

Other explanations of revolution, based on a larger number of examples, concentrate on the long-term commonalities between them—such as economic and societal destabilizing forces—and shorter-term precipitating and immediate events—such as government financial problems or simply incompetence. According to Chalmers Johnson, revolution is a function of positive and negative factors that result in a disequilibreated society; one which can be provoked into a revolution when the elite no longer can uphold its power simply by the use of force—in other words, when it is no longer considered legitimate by the people.[45]

A comprehensive examination of all the issues of comparative and world politics would include more than the study of development, violence, and revolution mentioned above. It would also encompass such topics as class relations, gender differences, and economic inequalities and trans-state concerns. It would assess the degree of integration and political protest in countries as well as the harmony or instability of the international system. The three issues we have chosen to focus on are as old as civilization itself, the others are newer and, in some quarters, are popular today. However, these new concerns should be placed in the context of the fundamental problems that have characterized the discipline of political science since the time of the ancient Greeks—those concerning order and disorder. In the next chapter we examine how the states of the world and the major issues they face domestically are affected by the relations among states— in other words, international relations.

DISCUSSION QUESTIONS

1. What does it mean to be "poor"?
2. Contrast modernization and dependency theories of development.
3. Define political violence and describe some different types such as "terrorism" and "coups d'état."
4. Is violence necessary in every "revolution"?
5. Is a repressive role for the police and military found only in authoritarian countries?

KEY TERMS

Anarchistic Rebellion, p. 453
conspiracy , p. 445
Conspiratorial Coup d'état, p. 453
coups d'état, p. 445
criminal activity, p. 444
dependency school, p. 441
genocide, p. 449
Human Development Index (HDI), p. 436
identification, p. 449

ideology, p. 449
internal security, p. 444
internal war, p. 445
Jacobin Communist Revolution, p. 453
Jacquerie, p. 452
Militarized Insurrection, p. 453
Millenarian Rebellion, p. 452
political development, p. 439

political modernization, p. 440
poverty, p. 435
relative deprivation, p. 445
revolution, p. 451
riots, p. 444
terrorism, p. 447
turmoil, p. 445
violence, p. 443
war, p. 441

ENDNOTES

1. James A. Bill and Robert L. Hardgrave, *Comparative Politics: The Quest for Theory* (Columbus, Ohio: Merrill, 1973), p. 43.

2. World Bank, *World Development Report 1992* (New York: Oxford University Press, 1992); and United Nations Development Program, *Human Development Report 1992* (New York: Oxford University Press, 1992). For overviews, see Paul Harrison, *Inside the Third World: The Anatomy of Poverty*, 2nd ed. (New York: Penguin, 1987); Thomas D. Lairson and David Skidmore, *International Political Economy: The Struggle For Power and Wealth* (New York: Harcourt Brace Jovanovich, 1993).

3. Howard J. Wiarda, "Rethinking Political Development: A Look Backward over Thirty Years, and a Look Ahead," *Studies in Comparative International Development*, vol. 24, no. 4 (Winter 1989–90), pp. 65–82. Wiarda's main point here is that recent events have validated the thesis that there is a relation between economic growth and democracy.

4. For lists of definitions see Fred W. Riggs, "The Rise and Fall of Political Development," in Samuel Long, ed., *The Handbook of Political Behavior*, vol. 4 (New York: Plenum Press, 1981), pp. 289–348; and Samuel P. Huntington, "The Change to Change: Modernization, Development and Politics," *Comparative Politics*, vol. 3, no. 3 (April 1971), pp. 283–322.

5. Christopher Clapham, *Third World Politics* (London: Croom Helm, 1985), p. 2.

6. See Andrew C. Janos, *Politics and Paradigms: Changing Theories of Change in Social Science* (Stanford, Calif.: Stanford University Press, 1986); and Vicky Randall and Robin Theobald, *Political Change and Underdevelopment: A Critical Introduction to Third World Politics* (London: Macmillan, 1989).

7. The best-known exponents of this view are G.A. Almond and G. B. Powell, *Comparative Politics: A Developmental Approach* (Boston: Little, Brown, 1966); and S.P. Huntington, *Political Order in Changing Societies* (New Haven, Conn.: Yale University Press, 1968).

8. The original book on this topic was Gabriel A. Almond and James Coleman, *The Politics of the Developing Areas* (Princeton, N.J.: Princeton University Press, 1960).

9. James A. Bill and Robert L. Hardgrave, Jr., *Comparative Politics* (Columbus, Ohio: Charles E. Merrill, 1973), ch. 2. On the processes of development, see Robert J. Jackson and Michael Stein, eds., *Issues in Comparative Politics* (New York: St. Martin's Press, 1971), ch. 2.

10. Barrington Moore, *The Social Origins of Dictatorship and Democracy* (Cambridge, Mass: Harvard University Press, 1966); and from a different perspective Gabriel A. Almond et al. eds., *Crisis, Choice and Change* (Boston: Little, Brown, 1973).

11. This group would include Immanuel Wallerstein, *The Modern World-System*, 2 vols. (New York: Academic Press, 1980).

12. For example, see F.H. Cardoso and E. Faletto, *Dependency and Development in Latin America* (Berkeley, Calif.: University of California Press, 1979); and *ibid.*, vol. II.

13. Myron Weiner and Samuel P. Huntington, eds., *Understanding Political Development* (Boston: Little, Brown, 1987), p. xiv.

14. For a discussion of the various theories, see Vicky Randall and Robin Theobald, *Political Change and Underdevelopment: A Critical Introduction to Third World Politics* (London: Macmillan, 1985).

15. Weiner and Huntington, p. xxviii.

16. These new approaches include such authors as Joel S. Migdal, *Strong Societies and Weak States* (Princeton, N.J.: Princeton University Press, 1988); and the neo-institutionalists such as Theda Skocpol, *States and Social Revolutions* (Cambridge: Cambridge University Press, 1979); and Peter B. Evans, Dietrich Rueschemeyer, and Theda Skocpol, eds., *Bringing the State Back In* (Cambridge: Cambridge University Press, 1985).

17. See for example, Leonard Binder et al., *Crises and Sequences in Political Development* (Princeton, N.J.: Princeton University Press, 1971).

18. Samuel P. Huntington, "The Goals of Development," in Myron Weiner and Samuel Huntington, eds., *Understanding Political Development* (Boston: Little, Brown, 1987).

19. This is known as a reductionist form of analysis.

20. Ted Robert Gurr, *Why Men Rebel* (Princeton, N.J.: Princeton University Press, 1970), pp. 217–49.

21. Rudolph J. Rummel, "Dimensions of Conflict Behaviour Within and Between Nations," *Yearbook of the Society for General Systems Research*, vol. 8 (1963), pp. 25–26.

22. John V. Gillespie and Betty A. Nesvold, eds., *Macro-Quantitative Analysis* (Beverly Hills: Sage, 1971), p. 195.

23. The Gurr model assumes that aggression is always a consequence of frustration, but although his thesis provides a psychological underpinning to the aggregate data analysis, it has been questioned in the psychological literature. Frustration can lead to non-aggression, aggression can occur without frustration, and in some cultures aggression is not a typical response to frustration. For a more detailed critique of this literature, see Alex P. Schmid and Albert J. Jongman, *Political Terrorism* (Amsterdam: North-Holland, 1988).

24. Also see the literature in Margaret P. Karns, ed., *Persistent Patterns and Emergent Structures in a Waning Century* (New York: Praeger, 1986).

25. Bonnie Cordes, Brian M. Jenkins, and Konrad Kellen, *A Conceptual Framework for Analyzing Terrorist Groups* (Santa Monica, Calif.: Randa, 1985).

26. At the time of writing, the war continues.

27. For an excellent review of these points, see Peter C. Sederberg, *Terrorist Myths* (Englewood Cliffs, N.J.: Prentice-Hall, 1989).

28. The ability of society to adapt to the enduring challenge of diversity is an important variable that cannot be examined in this book. The degree of alienation and its relation to politics is discussed in David C. Schwartz, *Political Alienation and Political Behaviour* (Chicago: Aldine, 1973).

29. Michael Stohl, ed., *The Politics of Terrorism*, 3rd ed., (New York: Marcel Dekker, 1988), pp. 8–11, 77.

30. See, for example, Richard E. Rubenstein, *Alchemists of Revolution* (New York: Basic Books, 1989).

31. Jonathan L. Freedman, J. Merrill Carlsmith, and David O. Sears, *Social Psychology* (Englewood Cliffs, N.J.: Prentice-Hall, 1970).

32. *Ibid.*, p. 85.

33. Gurr, *Why Men Rebel.*

34. James C. Davies, "Toward a Theory of Revolution," in Robert J. Jackson and Michael Stein, eds., *Issues in Comparative Politics* (New York: St. Martin's Press, 1971), pp. 370–84.

35. Sederberg, *Terrorist Myths*, p. 85.

36. Schwartz, *Political Alienation and Political Behaviour.*

37. Walter Laqueur, "The New Face of Terrorism," *The Washington Quarterly*, Autumn 1998, p. 169.

38. For an excellent study of the relation between revolutions and violence see Stephen M. Wat, "Revolution and War," *World Politics*, vol. 44, no. 3 (April 1992), pp. 321–68.

39. Theda Skocpol, *States and Social Revolutions: A Comparative Analysis of France, Russia, and China* (New York: Cambridge University Press, 1979).

40. Chalmers Johnson, *Revolutionary Change* (Boston: Little, Brown, 1966), p. 138; and for a summary of this position and other studies of the types and stages of revolutions see Robert J. Jackson and Michael Stein, eds., *Issues in Comparative Politics* (New York: St. Martin's Press, 1971), ch. V.

41. Hanna Arendt, *The Origins of Totalitarianism* (New York: Meridian, 1958); Chalmers Johnson, *Revolutionary Change* (Boston: Little, Brown, 1966); Barrington Moore, Jr., *The Social Origins of Dictatorship and Democracy* (Boston: Beacon Press, 1966); and Theda Skocpol, *States and Social Revolutions.*

42. Crane Brinton, *The Anatomy of Revolution*, rev. ed. (New York: Random House, 1965).

43. Alexis de Tocqueville, *The Old Regime and the French Revolution* (New York: Doubleday, 1955).

44. Skocpol, *States and Social Revolutions*.

45. Johnson, *Revolutionary Change*.

FURTHER READING

Development

Adams, Nassou A., Worlds Apart: *The North-South Divide and the International System* (London: Zed Books, 1993).

Barber, Benjamin R., *Jihad vs McWorld* (New York: Random House, 1995).

Chilton, Stephen, *Defining Political Development* (Boulder, Col.: Lynne Rienner Publishers, 1988).

Evans, Peter B., Dietrich Rueschemeyer, and Theda Skocpol, eds., *Bringing the State Back In* (Cambridge, Mass.: Cambridge University Press, 1985).

Helleiner, Gerald K., ed., *The Other Side of International Development Policy: The Non-Aid Economic Relations with Developing Countries of Canada, Denmark, the Netherlands, Norway and Sweden* (Toronto: University of Toronto Press, 1990).

Higgott, Richard A., *Political Development Theory: The Contemporary Debate* (London: Croom Helm, 1983).

Huntington, Samuel P., *Political Order and Changing Societies* (New Haven, Conn.: Yale University Press, 1968).

Knopff, Rainer, *Human Rights and Social Technology: The New War on Discrimination* (Ottawa: Carleton University Press, 1989).

Randall, Vicky, and Robin Theobald, *Political Change and Underdevelopment: A Critical Introduction to Third World Politics*, 2nd ed. (London: Macmillan, 1989).

Wallerstein, Immanuel, *The Capitalist World Economy* (Cambridge, Mass.: Cambridge University Press, 1979).

Weiner, Myron, and Samuel P. Huntington, eds., *Understanding Political Development* (Boston: Little, Brown, 1987).

Violence

Anderson, Malcolm, ed., *Policing the World* (Oxford: Clarendon Press, 1989).

Brewer, John D., et al., *The Police, Public Order and the State* (London: Macmillan, 1988).

Combs, Cindy, *Terrorism in the Twenty-First Century* (Upper Saddle River, NJ: Prentice Hall, 1997).

Cooper, Andrew F., *Canadian Foreign Policy* (Scarborough: Prentice Hall, 1997).

Decalo, Samuel, *Coups and Army Rule in Africa*, 2nd ed. (New Haven, Conn.: Yale University Press, 1990).

Fernandez-Armesto, Felipe, *Millenium* (New York: Charles Scribner's Sons, 1994).

Grossman, Dave, *On Killing: The Psychological Cost of Learning to Kill in War and Society* (New York: Little, Brown, 1995).

Gurr, Ted Robert, *Minorities at Risk: A Global View of Ethnopolitical Conflicts* (Washington: U.S. Institute of Peace, 1993).

Heine, Jorge, ed., *A Revolution Aborted: The Lessons of Granada* (Pittsburgh: University of Pittsburgh Press, 1990).

Kagen, Donald, *On the Origins of War and the Preservation of Peace* (New York: Doubleday, 1995).

Lodge, Juliet, ed., *The Threat of Terrorism* (Brighton: Wheatsheaf Books, 1988).

Monurson, Wolfgard J., and Gerhard Hirshfield, eds., *Social Protest, Violence and Terror in Nineteenth- and Twentieth-Century Europe* (London: Macmillan, 1982).

Reich, Walter, ed., *Origins of Terrorism: Psychologies, Ideologies, Theologies, States of Mind* (Cambridge: Woodrow Wilson International Centre for Scholars and Cambridge University Press, 1990).

Reiner, Robert, *The Politics of the Police* (New York: St. Martin's Press, 1985).

Ruane, Joseph, and Jennifer Todd, *The Dynamics of Conflict in Northern Ireland* (New York: Cambridge University Press, 1996).

Skocpol, Theda, *States and Social Revolutions* (Cambridge, Mass.: Cambridge University Press, 1979).

Strange, Susan, *Retreat of the State: The Difference of Power in the World Economy* (Ithaca, NY: Cornell University Press, 1996).

Tucker, H.H., ed., *Combating the Terrorists: Democratic Responses to Political Violence* (New York: Facts on File, 1988).

Vickers, Jeanne, *Women and War* (London: Zed Books, 1993).

Wilkinson, Paul, *Terrorism and the Liberal State* (New York: New York University Press, 1986).

 **Weblinks**

www/cfcsc.dnd.ca/links/index.html
Information about world peace and security can be found at this site.

www.usis.usemb.se/terror/index.html
This site provides information and links to other sites dealing with patterns of world terrorism.

caster.ssw.upenn.edu/~restes/praxis.html
This site provides information about development studies.

www.sipri.se
This is the site of the Stockholm International Peace Research Institute.

www.worldbank.org/
This is the World Bank's Web Page.

jagor.srce.hr/~mprofaca/tribunal.html
This site provides information about international war crime tribunals.

CHAPTER 21

International Relations: Politics Among States

The domestic politics of states is not independent of the relations *among* countries, and international relations is interwoven with the realities of governments throughout the world. As the world grows more interdependent, international politics wields a growing influence on the decision-making of political leaders. No country, however powerful, is totally self-sufficient or independent. The actions of one state have repercussions on others, and there is a kind of globalization process taking place in economics and communications.

The study of **international relations** refers to the broad network of relations among states and includes the activities of their citizens and non-state institutions as well. The global system, therefore, is the result of the behaviour of states and also nongovernmental actors. The **foreign policy** of countries, on the other hand, is more narrow. It depicts any state or government behaviour that has external ramifications. It includes the diplomatic and military relations among states, as well as their cultural, economic, technological, and, increasingly, their ecological interests.

There are basic similarities and dissimilarities between domestic and international affairs. Both consist of the struggle for advantage among organized groups with different interests and values. In neither situation can all the interests and values at stake be satisfied and therefore disputes and conflicts continually erupt. In domestic politics the result of such conflict may extend to violence or revolution. In international politics the result may be warfare among states.

As we shall explain in more detail later in this chapter, the main distinction between the two types of politics is that the international system has no world government to mitigate disputes and determine "who gets what, when, and how." The world's states exist in a kind of *anarchy*, without a higher form of government to guide them. They compete in a world of insecurity and danger. Of course, states sometimes cooperate for their own interests, and in that sense they develop customs and practices that shape their behaviour. The external behaviour of states is thus characterized by legal and political anarchy as well as customs of proper behaviour.

Politics among states takes many forms ranging from diplomacy to war. Routine relations are carried out by negotiations between diplomats and other officials who assert the claims of their states in bilateral (between two of them) and multilateral (among several of them) frameworks.[1] Diplomacy is an old profession. In ancient Greece, passports called "diplomas" existed. These diplomas, made from double metal plates folded and sewn together, were carried by Greek messengers as a sign that they should be given special treatment and travel privileges. Modern diplomacy, as an independent profession with permanent embassies abroad, originated in Italy in the fourteenth century.

Today, "diplomacy" may result in agreement or conflict among states. Treaties and protocols may be negotiated and signed. If agreement cannot be reached among states, other approaches to the disputes may be sought, ranging from public complaints to propaganda, subversion, and even outright war.

Unlike domestic politics, which takes place within a set of more or less developed laws and which is ultimately related to the authority of government and the sovereignty of the territory, international politics possesses no international government that can impose its laws on people everywhere. States may join together in various international organizations for mutual benefit, but few subject themselves to a higher set of decision-makers or laws than those provided by their own domestic authorities.

INTERNATIONAL POLITICS AND LAW

Despite these negative assertions about the politics and conflict among states, a type of law known as **international law** does exist at the global level. This law may be defined as the binding rules of conduct among states, expressed in treaties, the writings of scholars, the rulings of judicial bodies, and in particular by the consistent and established behaviour of states.[2] There is widespread attachment to the principle of *pacta sunt servanda*, which means that treaties ought to be kept. In their ordinary day-to-day activities, states accept and follow international rules and principles. They establish embassies and diplomatic missions in other countries. They sign trade agreements among themselves such as the General Agreement on Tariffs and Trade (GATT), and they form military alliances such as the North Atlantic Treaty Organization (NATO) and the former Warsaw Pact.

This international law is approximately the type of law that existed in "primitive," or what we might call pre-government societies. It developed along three routes: by custom and usage from the negotiations and practices among states; by treaties between two or more states; and by the decisions and actions of higher multilateral organizations such as the United Nations.

Customary law—that is, implicit rules of behaviour and conduct based on usage or practice—exists, but no supra-national government enforces it. In other words, although there are international customs and practices, no political authority or international organization can settle disputes and impose solutions on states based on these rules.

Through centuries of interaction, states have also adopted explicit forms of negotiating and bargaining, which are now part of international law. A **treaty**, essentially a contract between two or more state signatories, binds those countries that sign it to observe the agreement if the proper legal ratification process has been carried out. In international law such treaties impose obligations on the signatory states to comply with the principles and details of the agreement.[3]

Some international institutions also create international law. The United Nations is the best example. It attempts to prevent disputes and preserve law and order. Composed of almost all the states in the world, it attempts to act like a government but does so without the ordinary power of enforcement. The United Nations does not have an army, navy, or airforce. Since no international government can impose the principles of international law, adherence to them is usually contingent on the voluntary compliance of the individual states themselves. But not always. In 1991, the United Nations sanctioned the collective efforts of member states to attack Iraq because of its hostile takeover of Kuwait, but it did *not* fight as an organization. In 1992 it imposed an economic embargo on Libya because Libya refused to hand over two alleged airplane terrorists.

This does not mean that there are no courts higher than domestic ones. At the end of World War II, the victorious countries set up the Nuremberg Court to try Nazi war criminals, and in 1993 the United Nations set up **War Crimes Tribunal** for atrocities such as those in Rwanda, the former Yugoslavia and Kosovo. As well as these extraordinary courts, the European Court successfully imposes community law on citizens inside the states of the European Union (EU). Its decisions must be obeyed even if a member state does not approve.

Less successfully, at the Hague, the **International Court of Justice (ICJ)**, which is part of the United Nations system, hears and adjudicates disputes based on international law. On the whole, this court of 15 judges, appointed by the UN, has studied only minor cases of boundaries and fishing disputes between states. Most states do not accept its compulsory jurisdiction. As the Court has no military or police to ensure that its decisions are carried out, the voluntary compliance of states is required. As an example, the leftist Sandinista government of Nicaragua brought a suit to the Hague in 1984 after the CIA disrupted shipping by mining Nicaraguan harbours. Although the United States was convicted and fined, the American government would not agree that the court had jurisdiction over its actions. There was nothing the court could do to make the U.S. comply. The fine is still unpaid.

However, the rules set by such international bodies as the ICJ do have significant influence because states tend to adhere to the norms set by them. Most court cases, especially in environment and human rights issues, are resolved satisfactorily. In the final analysis, however, if states believe that their interests are badly affected by the results of international law, they tend to disregard its strictures.

This means that states, on occasion, will use nonlegal actions to defend their interests. As J.L. Brierly put it, states normally observe international law when it is convenient to do so, and breaches generally occur "either when some great political issue has arisen between states, or in that part of the system which professes to regulate the conduct of war."[4]

CLOSE UP 21.1 Terrorism, Retaliation, and the International Court of Justice

In 1998, following bombings at American embassies in Kenya and Tanzania, the United States retaliated by sending missiles to devastate a factory in the capital of Sudan and a terrorist training camp in Afghanistan. The primary targets, however, were Usama bin Ladin, whom they believe financed and masterminded the embassy bombings, and a chemical weapons factory he allegedly was financing in Khartoum. Although others were killed, bin Ladin escaped harm. In the aftermath it was not entirely ever clear that the factory the U.S. destroyed was doing more than preparing legal drugs for the country.

Bin Ladin is a wealthy Saudi fundamentalist leader who was stripped of his Saudi citizenship for reportedly having made large sums of money available to militant Islamic causes in a number of countries. Since 1996, bin Ladin is thought to be living in Afghanistan from where he has been urging guerrilla military activity against the United States for maintaining troops in Saudi Arabia.

He is still at large, presumably somewhere in Afghanistan.

Was the United States justified in the 1998 bombings? Could it be brought to the ICJ? Should it be?

THE INTERNATIONAL SYSTEM

The international system is composed of states and other actors such as multinational corporations spread throughout the globe. In 1999, 192 states are sovereign and carry out relations among themselves either directly or through multinational institutions such as the United Nations.

Until World War II (1939–1945), the international system was multipolar—several states competed for power on the international stage. Britain, France, Germany, Italy, Spain, Portugal, Turkey, Austria, and Japan, among others, all had their periods of glory. Alliances were formed and broken, empires created and destroyed. By the mid-nineteenth century, a kind of "balance of power" existed in Europe.[5] In other words, the distribution of power among states provided a rough balance in their competition. Today, the term **balance of power** is used to mean the same thing—a relatively equal distribution of power among states sufficient to maintain security and peace among rivals.

Until World War II, most of the world's wealth and military strength was held in Europe. It was mainly Europeans who "discovered" and conquered most of the globe in the period from the seventeenth to the twentieth century, disseminating their ideas and technology. The First and Second World Wars were fought mainly on European soil. The termination of World War II restructured this Euro-centric international system. After 1945 two new **superpowers**, the United States and the former Soviet Union, dominated the international system. Their strength in international affairs was so profound that scholars refer to this as a period of "bipolar" politics; that is, the two poles were in competition with each other and each attracted its own allies.

A **bipolar** balance of power is therefore one where two superpowers dominate other states in a rivalry over military, economic, political, and ideological goals; each protagonist perceives any gain for its opponent as a loss for itself. The United States at one pole was surrounded by allies in the North Atlantic Treaty Organization (NATO), and the Soviet Union at the other was supported by its alliance with Eastern European countries in the Warsaw Treaty Organization (WTO), commonly known as the Warsaw Pact.

During World War II the United States and the Soviet Union were allies against Hitler's Germany. At the end of the war the United States was the preeminent economic and military power in the West. In Europe, Germany was defeated and divided. Britain, France, and Italy were exhausted. Only the Soviet Union had augmented its military and economic muscle because of the war. In Asia, Japan was occupied by the Americans, and the rest of Asia, particularly China, was in a period of internal change and confusion.

In order to prevent what they regarded as "encirclement" by the West, the Soviet leaders used the Red Army to bring most of Eastern Europe under their control. Winston Churchill called this division of Europe between the forces of democracy in the West and Soviet communism in the East the "**iron curtain**." And in 1947 U.S. President Harry Truman announced a policy of "containment" to prevent the USSR from further aggression in Europe. In the West, NATO was forged to bind democratic states together in an alliance in which they pledged support to each other in the event of external aggression.

From this period, the iron curtain divided the two sides, and for four decades a fairly stable peace existed in Europe. This situation was called the **Cold War** because although the two sides constantly prepared for war no actual "hot" hostilities ever developed. The rivalry was carried out by surrogate armies throughout the developing world—in Angola, Afghanistan, Cuba, Nicaragua, and Zaire, to mention only a few. Direct U.S. force was used in Korea and Vietnam. And, on occasion, such as during 1948 when the Soviet Union blocked access to Berlin, military clashes were narrowly avoided (see Table 21.1 for highlights from the Cold War).

Despite this division of the world into two fairly stable blocs, other disputes, conflicts, and violence erupted throughout the globe without reference to the contest between democracy and communism. In the Middle East, Jews (backed by the United States) and Arabs (backed by the Soviet Union) clashed over territory and the sovereignty of ancient lands. In parts of Asia, peasant communists competed with feudal systems of government. And in many developing countries in Africa, Asia, and Latin America, violent clashes continued over the location of territorial boundaries, forms of government, economic advantage, and even food supplies.

Over time the iron curtain was slowly lifted between East and West Europe, and the Cold War finally ended with the destruction of the Berlin Wall in 1990. Long be-

Table 21.1   Highlights of the Cold War: From Beginning to End

March 1946:	Former British Prime Minister Winston Churchill warns of Soviet expansion and declares that an "iron curtain" has descended over Europe.
July 1947:	George F. Kennan's "X" article in the journal *Foreign Affairs* sets forth "containment" of communism as the major goal of American foreign policy.
June 1948:	The Soviet Union imposes a blockade on West Berlin. The Allies, led by the United States, mount a Berlin Airlift, sending food and other supplies to West Berlin.
June 1950:	North Korea invades South Korea, setting off a three-year war. The U.S. and other pro-Western nations fight for South Korea; Chinese troops aid the North.
November 1956:	Soviet troops crush a popular uprising in Hungary.
October 1957:	U.S. B-52 bombers begin flying on full-time alert; planes carrying nuclear weapons are airborne 24 hours a day.
October 1957:	The Soviet Union announces its successfull launch of the first human-made earth satellite, Sputnik.
April 1961:	CIA-trained Cuban exiles invade Cuba at the Bay of Pigs in a fruitless attempt to overthrow the government of Fidel Castro.
August 1961:	East Germany erects the Berlin Wall.
November 1961:	The Kennedy administration announces that the number of U.S. military advisors in South Vietnam will be increased from 685 to 16 000 by late 1963.
October 1962:	President Kennedy orders an air and naval blockade to force Cuba to remove Soviet missiles from its territory.
August 1964:	Congress passes a resolution authorizing President Johnson to pursue a military buildup in Vietnam.
August 1968:	Soviet troops and tanks roll into Czechoslovakia and crush re-formists' efforts to remodel the communist system.
May 1972:	President Nixon and Leonid I. Brezhnev, the Soviet leader, sign the first treaties setting limits on strategic nuclear arms.
March 1983:	President Reagan says the Soviet Union is "an evil empire."
March 1985:	Mikhail S. Gorbachev becomes Soviet leader and emphasizes the need to reshape the economy and reduce rigidity in the Soviet system, in a process known as *perestroika*.

November 1989:	East Germany lifts restrictions on emigration and travel to the West; after 28 years the Berlin Wall comes down.
August 1991:	The day before President Gorbachev plans to sign a union treaty intended to keep several republics together, hard liners move to overthrow him. The coup fails.
September 1991:	President Bush announces his decision to take B-52 bombers off alert status.
December 1991:	The leaders of Russia, Ukraine, and Byelorussia declare that the Soviet Union has ceased to exist and proclaim a new Commonwealth of Independent States open to all states of the former union.
January 1992:	U.S. President Bush and Russian President Yeltsin declare the Cold War over.

fore that, however, in the 1950s, China and the USSR had become competitors rather than allies. Inside the Soviet empire, as well, cracks had appeared. Force was used to restrain the former Czechoslovakia from drifting away from communism to "socialism with a human face." And one by one the countries of Eastern Europe found ways to escape from Soviet control—Yugoslavia under Tito claimed its independence early; Poland, Czechoslovakia, Hungary, Bulgaria, and Romania had to wait until the late 1980s to split from Soviet domination. By 1990 the disintegration of the Soviet Union itself was in progress.

The 1991 dismantlement of the Warsaw Pact and the increasing economic difficulties of the former Soviet Union have led many commentators to conclude that the world has returned to a multipolar system, or even more often that the United States now stands alone as the single superpower and that we have entered an era of **unipolar** politics. In principle, the change could mean a move toward world government. However, this has not yet occurred, and is unlikely to occur. Certainly the United States has increased its hegemony (or domination) over most of the world in recent years, but only in the military sphere does it remain without peer.

A few years ago many used to argue that the United States was declining as an economic power on the world stage.[6] Thus, for them, the international system was best described as multipolar overall, but with the United States as by far the most powerful country in the military sphere. Such comments are exaggerated as the United States has no significant peers in any major field including economics and technology. U.S. President George Bush may have been premature in 1991 when he declared a **new world order** —a new system of international relations built on the principle of collective security. But the United States remains the preeminent international power. When it wants to act it can. It was, for example, able to use force without Russian objection in the Gulf War, Lebanon, the Dominican Republic, Panama, and Haiti.

International Institutions

Efforts to reduce disputes and conflict within this international system through international law are augmented by the existence of several important international organizations. The most important of these is the United Nations and its specialized multilateral organizations such as the World Health Organization, the International Labour Organization, the International Postal Union, and the International Monetary Fund.

We cannot survey all these institutions here, but it is important to understand the basic structures and functions of the United Nations. The **United Nations** came into existence to provide a forum at which international grievances could be heard and, ideally, peaceful cooperation enhanced. It was not intended to be a government with the ability to use military means to enforce compliance. Neither was it intended to replace the state-based global system nor to become a world government. It neither taxes citizens nor, despite some naive expectations, has it been able to establish a regular army.

During World War II the countries that were fighting Germany and Japan signed a *Declaration of United Nations* in which they pledged not to make separate peace treaties with the enemies. This preliminary step eventually culminated in a *Charter of the United Nations* which 51 states signed between April and June 1945. The UN membership gradually expanded to 185 countries as of 1996.[7] (See Appendix A.) Some countries such as Switzerland never joined the institution, and before its disintegration the USSR had three votes because the Ukraine and Byelorussia (now Belarus), which were republics within the Soviet federation, were given separate seats. Over the years the government of Taiwan was expelled and Indonesia resigned and then later rejoined. In 1991, Russia replaced the former Soviet Union as a member of the UN, and took its seat on the Security Council.

The UN is situated in New York City on international territory. It has its own rules, flag, police force, and multiple decision-making bodies. All members of the UN have seats in the **General Assembly**. As the UN is essentially a deliberating body, its decisions have no legal, binding force on states. The significance of its decisions comes from moral suasion, and its impact on international public opinion. The General Assembly elects new members to the UN on recommendation from the Security Council and approves the overall budget of the association. It also passes resolutions and declarations and sometimes signs conventions or treaties with countries. A two-thirds vote in the Assembly is required for all major decisions.

The **Security Council** is composed of 15 members: five permanent members—France, Great Britain, the People's Republic of China, Russia, and the United States; and ten temporary members elected for two-year terms by the General Assembly. The Security Council was set up to reflect political and military realities. It was given the primary responsibility for action in questions of peace and security. It may consider any action viewed by members as a threat to peace or an act of aggression, and then make recommendations for the resolution of the conflict.

Decisions of the Security Council must be taken by a majority (defined as nine members), but the five permanent members each have a veto over these decisions and

Table 21.2   The United Nations and Related Organizations

Principle Organs

General Assembly

Security Council

Economic and Social Council (ECOSOC)

Trusteeship Council (now defunct)

International Court of Justice (ICJ)

The Secretariat

Subsidiary Organs

General Assembly

    UNICEF: UN Children's Fund

    UNHCR: UN High Commissioner for Refugees

    UNRWA: UN Relief and Works Agency for Palestine Refugees in the Near East

    UNITAR: UN Institute for Training and Research

    UNRISD: UN Research Institute for Social Development

    UNCTAD: UN Conference on Trade and Development

    UNDP: UN Development Program

    UNFPA: UN Population Fund

    UNU: UN University

    UNEP: UN Environment Program

    WFC: World Food Council

Security Council

    All Peacekeeping Forces (16 operational in 1999)

Specialized Agencies

FAO: Food and Agriculture Organization

IBRD/World Bank: International Bank for Reconstruction and Development

ICAO: International Civil Aviation Organization

IDA: International Development Association

IFC: International Finance Corporation

IFAD: International Fund for Agricultural Development

ILO: International Labor Organization

IMO: International Maritime Organization

IMF: International Monetary Fund

ITU: International Telecommunication Union

UNESCO: UN Educational, Scientific and Cultural Organization

UNIDO: UN Industrial Development Organization

UPU: Universal Postal Union

WHO: World Health Organization

WIPO: World Intellectual Property Organization

WMO: World Meteorological Organization

Related Organizations

GATT: General Agreement on Tariffs and Trade

IAEA: International Atomic Energy Agency

WTO: World Trade Organization

IMF: International Monetary Fund

*Organization for Economic Cooperation and Development
Source: Adapted from World Bank data published in *The Globe and Mail*, Oct 4, 1994.

this has often prevented any action. In the past, the United States and the former Soviet Union often blocked implementation of UN resolutions by use of this instrument. Today, many resolutions are simply not put forward because their advocates know that a veto would be used if they were.

Nevertheless, the United Nations is intended as a **collective security organization**, meaning it is an arrangement for states to take collective action against any aggressor member state. A collective security organization is not the same as a **military alliance**. NATO is a military pact, rather than a collective security organization, because it does not include all the countries that could possibly be partners to a conflict. The UN, on the other hand, provides a collective security arrangement because it includes almost all countries in its charter.

The United Nations has a permanent body of over 20 000 international civil servants called the Secretariat, headed by a Secretary-General. Surrounding the UN are several specialized institutions, among which are easily recognized organizations such as the Economic and Social Council, the International Children's Emergency Fund, the World Health Organization, the High Commissioner for Refugees, a Commission on Human Rights, and even a university.

Historically, one of the more interesting departments of the UN was the **Trusteeship Council**. This Council supervised trust territories—those non-self-governing territories of the former League of Nations—and prepared them for independence. Through this process all but one of the earlier territories are now independent, sovereign countries; for example, Tanganyika became Tanzania and New Guinea became Papua New Guinea. The last remaining trust territory, the Palau Islands—a former Japanese possession later administered by the U.S.—became a member of the UN in 1994.

Over the past two decades the UN has been severely criticized, particularly by Western democratic countries, because its large membership with equal voting rights among very unequal states restricts what the organization can accomplish. According to these governments, the UN General Assembly is used too often as a platform for denouncing other states rather than as a forum for rational debate and action on issues.

The United Nations' record in preventing wars has been pitiful (Close Up 21.2 examines the UN's failure in Bosnia). Only on a very few occasions has it been successful in reducing aggression after it had already started. For example, the United Nations played a vital role with its response to war in Korea. For years Korea had been divided between a democratic South and a communist North. By chance, when the North attacked the South in 1950, the USSR delegate at the United Nations was boycotting the organization. Therefore, a U.S. resolution was able to pass the Security Council because the USSR was not there to veto it. A handful of members of the UN, then, decided to act on this Council decision even though the USSR later came back to the meetings in an attempt to prevent it. The Korean War ended in 1953 with an uneasy truce, and advocates argue that this proves the UN was successful in preventing the takeover of South Korea.[8]

In 1991, the Security Council employed an embargo and then authorized member states to use force against Iraq because of its invasion of Kuwait. This policy was possible only because the Soviet Union accepted, and China did not prevent, Operation Desert Storm against Saddam Hussein. Subsequent policies enforced another embargo on Iraq. In 1994 the UN allowed the United States to invade Haiti in order to reinstate Jean-Bertrand Aristide as the democratically elected President of the country (see Close Up 21.3).

Despite these instances of success in the field of war and peace, the UN has not developed into a *world government* and is unlikely to do so. However, no institution has arisen to take its place, and we can be reasonably confident that none will do so for many decades.

CLOSE UP 21.2 Peacekeeping in Bosnia

The humanitarian work of the United Nations in the former Yugoslavia was laudable, but its inaction in preventing war, hostility, displacement of peoples, ethnic cleansing, civilian bombing, and wanton destruction was deplorable. The history of this disaster is beyond the scope of this book, but clearly mistakes were made by almost everyone in the situation (see Close Up 10.1).

The division of the former Yugoslavia into Slovenia, Croatia, Serbia, and Bosnia-Herzegovina and the redivision of these states by aggression was a disaster. The United Nations responded to war between the opponents with relief supplies, economic embargoes, and an arms embargo on Bosnia-Herzegovina. All were unsuccessful except the relief supplies, and even they proved inadequate.

Before the United Nations gave up its responsibilities in Bosnia, almost a quarter of a million people had been killed, the economy was in ruins, and multiple cases of reported ethnic cleansing, mass murder, and rape were disclosed and often confirmed. In 1995, 60 000 NATO troops replaced the United Nations' peacekeepers in an attempt to maintain the peace and restore economic and social stability to the region.

CLOSE UP 21.3 The United Nations and Haiti

The recent history of the troubled republic of Haiti illustrates the role that the United States and the United Nations can and do play in the Caribbean region.

Haiti became independent from France in 1804. Since then, political instability and military interventions have been the norm. Various dictators held the country until the United States' marines occupied it from 1915 to 1934. After alternating civil and military rule, Francois (Papa Doc) Duvalier assumed office in 1957 and became President-for-Life in 1964. His son, Jean-Claude (Baby Doc), succeeded him in 1971 and ruled like his father with repression and corruption until he fled in 1986.

The flight of Baby Doc set off another series of coups and failed elections until 1990, when Father Jean-Bertrand Aristide became the first democratically elected President. Once again the military intervened. In a coup in September 1991, the military forced Aristide from office and into foreign exile. The U.S. refused to recognize the new government. Led by the United States, the United Nations sent military and police peacekeepers to Haiti in September 1994. They reinstated "democracy" by obtaining the resignations of the military officers, returning Aristide to office, and engineering a new round of elections in 1995. The election went well, but instability persisted with three government breakdowns by 1999—and even a period of five months in 1997 without a functioning government. Haiti is paralyzed by a political power struggle that many fear augurs a return to dictatorship. The United Nations continues to have a civilian peace mission in Haiti: there are 282 UN peacekeepers, mostly from Argentina.

The peace-keeping work of the United Nations, such as in Cyprus, Cambodia, the Middle East, and the former Yugoslavia, is at the request or voluntary agreement of the parties to the dispute. Article 43 of the UN Charter calls on all members of the UN to make forces available to the Security Council under "special agreements" for the "maintenance of peace and security." During the period from 1948 to 1999, there have been 49 UN peace-keeping missions, employing well over 750 000 military and other personnel coming from 111 countries. Currently, there are 16 missions in the field.

Regional Organizations

The international system is also composed of many regional organizations. Europe has its **European Union (EU)**, which is a 15-member association formed to promote economic, trade, and political integration. It has a Parliament with elected members from each of the member states and a bureaucracy in Brussels known as the European Commission. Its policies include the Common Agricultural Policy that subsidizes farmers. It enforces its decisions by a European Court, the most powerful interstate court in existence. In December 1992 the EU completed its internal market by abolishing all non-tariff barriers and providing freedom for the movement of all goods, services and capital within Community territory. At that time it became the world's largest trading bloc (see below).

Table 21.3 United Nations Peacekeeping Operations 1999

Africa

Angola – MONUA
   United Nations Observer Mission in Angola
Central African Republic – MINURCA
   United Nations Mission in the Central African Republic
Sierra Leone – UNOMSIL
   United Nations Mission of Observers in Sierra Leone
Western Sahara – MINURSO
   United Nations Mission for the Referendum in Western Sahara

Americas

Haiti – MIPONUH
   United Nations Civilian Police Mission in Haiti

Asia

India/Pakistan – UNMOGIP
   United Nations Military Observer Group in India and Pakistan
Tajikistan – UNMOT
   United Nations Mission of Observers in Tajikistan

Europe

Bosnia & Herzegovina – UNMIBH
   United Nations Mission in Bosnia and Herzegovina
Croatia – UNMOP
   United Nations Mission of Observers in Prevlaka
Cyprus – UNFICYP
   United Nations Peacekeeping Force in Cyprus
Former Yugoslav Republic of Macedonia – UNPREDEP
   United Nations Preventive Deployment Force
Georgia – UNOMIG
   United Nations Observer Mission in Georgia

Middle East

Golan Heights – UNDOF
   United Nations Disengagement Observer Force
Iraq/Kuwait – UNIKOM
   United Nations Iraq-Kuwait Observations Mission
Lebanon – UNIFIL
   United Nations Interim Force in Lebanon
Middle East – UNTSO
   United Nations Truce Supervision Organization

Most other geographical areas also have important international regional organizations but with less centralized authority than the EU. Among the many other institutions, Africa has its **Organization of African Unity (OAU)** and Asia has an **Association of Southeast Asia Nations (ASEAN)**. All the states of North and South America, except Cuba, are joined in the **Organization of American States (OAS)** (see Map 21.1).

Non-regional international actors are also significant. For example, the **British Commonwealth**, which consists of former members of the British Empire, has 51 members

Map 21.1   The Western Hemisphere: A Potential Free Trade Area

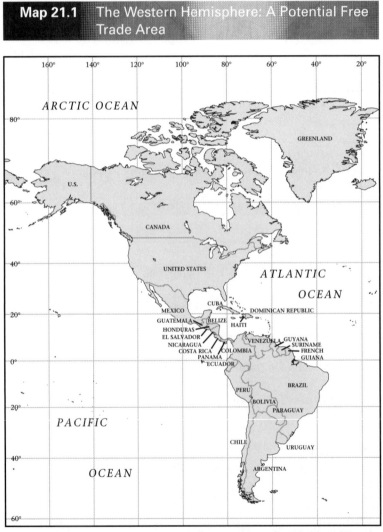

The island states of the Caribbean, not all of which are marked above, consist of Antigua and Barbuda, Bahamas, Barbados, Cuba, Dominica, Dominican Republic, Grenada, Haiti, Jamaica, St. Kitts and Nevis, St. Lucia, St. Vincent and the Grenadines, and Trinidad and Tobago.

spread throughout the world. The **League of Arab States** joins together Arab nations in support of Arab causes and issues.

International Economic Environment

At the end of World War II the leading economic countries met at Bretton Woods in the United States to reorganize the war-torn economies of the trading world. They decided to fix (peg) the exchange rate of the American dollar to the gold standard and other currencies to the dollar. The currencies could be "unpegged" only within stipulated regulations. Eventually, however, the rules unravelled due to pressures on the American dollar, and the entire exchange system became unregulated. Since then, currencies have *floated* freely and states have had little authority to regulate the world economy.

In 1947 the **General Agreement on Tariffs and Trade (GATT)** was established. The GATT is both a treaty and an institution. Its aim is to promote free trade by working to remove barriers to trade such as tariffs, quotas, and legal restrictions. While a few countries such as Russia and some Middle Eastern states are not members, it comprises most of the industrialized countries and covers most world trade. As a treaty, GATT sets out a code of rules for the conduct of trade. As an institution in Geneva it provides a forum for the discussion of trade problems.

The GATT works toward establishing a world trading order based on reciprocity, nondiscrimination, and multilateralism. World trade grew steadily after the GATT was founded and then slowed in the 1970s, with the Organization of Petroleum Export Countries (OPEC) showing the most rapid growth during the decade. In 1981, for the first time since World War II, there was no real growth in world trade. Since then, the world economy has indicated slow market growth, financial instability, and increased international competitiveness.

In its efforts to reduce protectionism, the GATT has held several rounds of negotiations to amend the trading rules. The last of these discussions among 109 states began in 1986 in Uruguay, and thus was named the **Uruguay Round**. This Round lasted seven years and was completed only in 1994. It made major breakthroughs in solving difficulties facing the international trading community. The participants agreed to transform the GATT secretariat into a somewhat more powerful **World Trade Organization (WTO)** and to reduce tariffs on a long list of goods. Technical agreements were also concluded on issues in the service sector, including banking, insurance, telecommunications, broadcasting, and so forth, and on intellectual copyright for subjects such as patents and licences.

Since 1975, the countries of the seven largest economic powers (sometimes called the **G-7**) have been meeting annually at **economic summits** in order to manage the world economy. Although there is no permanent secretariat, the summit has legitimized itself by providing large media events at which the most important economic and even political events of the day are discussed. Since the 1991 summit, Russian leaders have been invited as guests to explain their country's economic needs to the seven leaders from the United States, Britain, France, Germany, Japan, Italy, and Canada. Close Up 21.4

CLOSE UP 21.4 Global Economic Governance?

As the global economy grows, so too does the importance of international economic organizations such as the International Monetary Fund and the World Bank. Both organizations were set up at the end of the World War II.

The purposes of the International Monetary Fund (IMF) are to foster stability in money markets, encourage cooperation among states on monetary matters, aid in the establishment of a payment system, and promote international trade. Currently 179 states are members of this organization, which lends funds to member states and provides technical assistance concerning their economies. The importance of each state in the IMF is measured by its voting strength based on the financial contributions it makes to the Fund. The United States holds about 18% of the votes.

The purposes of the World Bank include lending money to countries or states that commercial banks or other lenders will not support, and generally trying to reduce poverty among its members. A total of 177 countries belong to the World Bank. It makes its decisions in a manner similar to that of the IMF. It tends to support problem projects and has large holdings with India, Brazil, and Indonesia.

provides background information on two other international economic associations: the International Monetary Fund and the World Bank.

States also attempt to gain some economic leverage in the global economy by forming regional trading blocs such as the **European Union**, the **Asian-Pacific Economic Cooperation (APEC)**, and the **North American Free Trade Association (NAFTA)**. The latter includes Canada, Mexico, and the United States, but in time is to be extended to include the entire Western Hemisphere. All three trading blocs continue to be important.

European integration continues to build on earlier successes. In 1952, a European Coal and Steel Community was constructed to bring France and West Germany together in one economic sector. In 1957 the Treaty of Rome was signed bringing six European states together in a **customs union**, a level of economic integration that allows the free movement of goods internally within the union and a common external. Efforts of European countries, especially Britain, to maintain independence from the Treaty of Rome vanished when Britain joined the European Community in 1973.

In 1985, 12 European states signed the **Single European Act (SEA)**, which effectively integrated Western Europe into one economic market by 1992. Three years later, three more countries joined and the European Community grew to 15 members. In the meantime, in 1992, the **Maastricht Treaty** was signed (see Figure 21.1). The treaty provided a framework for further integration by creating a **European Union** of three pillars: The European Community of supranational institutions formed the first pillar and the two other pillars consisted of new forms of intergovernmental cooperation in foreign and home affairs policies. Economically, the EU created a common currency in 1999 and has agreed to endeavour to create a common foreign and security policy. The march to political integration, however,

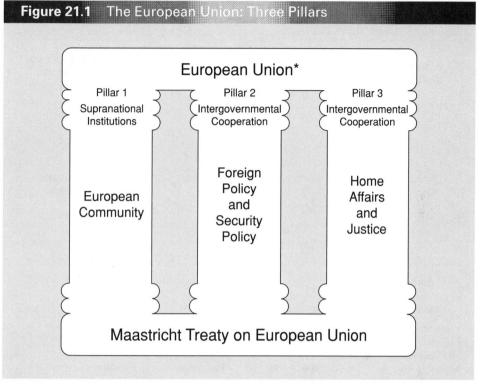

Figure 21.1   The European Union: Three Pillars

European Union*

| Pillar 1 | Pillar 2 | Pillar 3 |
| Supranational Institutions | Intergovernmental Cooperation | Intergovernmental Cooperation |

European Community

Foreign Policy and Security Policy

Home Affairs and Justice

Maastricht Treaty on European Union

*Consisting of the European Council (15 heads of government and President of the Commission, Council (15 ministers), Commissioners (20 commissioners), the European Parliament (626 Euro-MPs), a Court, and various committees.

has not been as quick as many "good Europeanists" would like. Opposition to any further development continues and was strengthened by Britain's decision to opt out of parts of Maastricht and the near rejection of the treaty by Denmark, Britain, and France.

The Maastricht Treaty embraced a timetable for economic and monetary union (EMU) with two institutions—a common bank and a common currency. The **European Central Bank (ECB)** replaced the 11 domestic central banks in 1999 at the same time as the Community adopted of a single currency, the euro. The currencies of the participating members were immediately "fixed" at a specific rate in relationship to the euro. In 2002 the euro will actually replace the deutschemarks, francs, lira, and other national currencies. Of the 15 members of the Union, only Britain, Denmark, Greece, and Sweden have opted out of the common currency and continue to oppose the further economic deepening of European integration.

Before completing this section on international actors, it is wise to remember, as discussed in Chapter 4, that some **multinational corporations (MNCs)** are actually more powerful than many countries. General Motors, for example, is a more important economic actor on the world stage than more than three-quarters of the world's states. These MNCs

Figure 21.2   Primary Institutions of the European Union

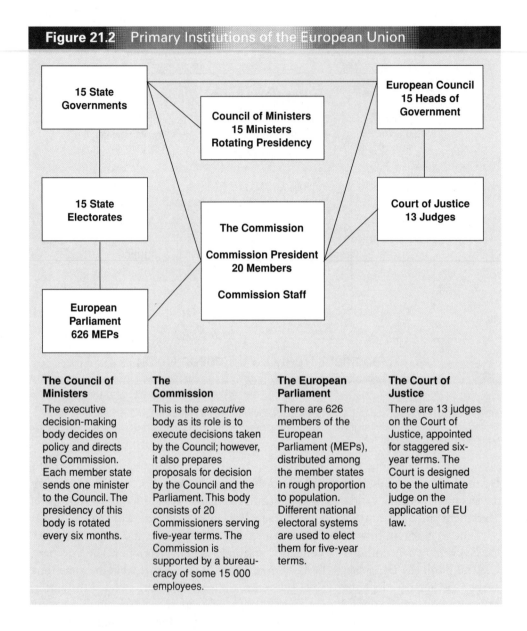

The Council of Ministers

The executive decision-making body decides on policy and directs the Commission. Each member state sends one minister to the Council. The presidency of this body is rotated every six months.

The Commission

This is the *executive* body as its role is to execute decisions taken by the Council; however, it also prepares proposals for decision by the Council and the Parliament. This body consists of 20 Commissioners serving five-year terms. The Commission is supported by a bureaucracy of some 15 000 employees.

The European Parliament

There are 626 members of the European Parliament (MEPs), distributed among the member states in rough proportion to population. Different national electoral systems are used to elect them for five-year terms.

The Court of Justice

There are 13 judges on the Court of Justice, appointed for staggered six-year terms. The Court is designed to be the ultimate judge on the application of EU law.

are economic actors in the international area because they carry out activities beyond the jurisdiction of single states.[9]

They are organized to operate across borders in a number of states. There are approximately 40 000 multinational corporations, the vast majority of which are run from the United States, Japan, and countries of the European Union.

There are also many important international groups such as Amnesty International, Sierra Club, Friends of the Earth, and Greenpeace that are not directly tied to the business community but often have an effect on it. These institutions are **non-governmental organizations (NGOs)**. As their name signifies, they are separate from government and can operate both nationally and globally. They may normally be identified as humanitarian, human rights, and environmental groupings of citizens who desire to have an effect on world politics. The number of NGOs accredited by the United Nations has risen to 1500. In 1998, one of these organizations—the Campaign to Ban Land Mines led by Nobel Peace Prize winner Jodi Williams—persuaded governments to outlaw antipersonnel mines. The treaty came into effect in 1999 without the support of China, Russia, or the USA.

International Strategic Environment

Since no ultimate international authority is in place to enforce the will of the majority of the billions of people in the world, international politics is largely about the power and persuasive capacities of the states that comprise the global system. Conflict between and among states emerges when their national interests are challenged and they respond by employing power in bargaining situations or, occasionally, by threatening military confrontation.

The degree of influence and power a state possesses within the international strategic environment may be measured by its population, territory, economic, military, strategic, and leadership capabilities. One well-known study based on these power criteria named the following ten countries as the most powerful in the world: Australia, Brazil, Canada, China, Germany, Japan, United Kingdom, United States, the former USSR, and West Germany.[10] The remainder of the world was then characterized as forming less significant concentric circles around this core of powerful states.

Until the fragmentation of the Soviet Union in late 1991, the competition between the East and West, or, as it was often phrased, between democracy and communism, was best understood in the context of the historical development of the international system discussed above. The division of Europe by an "iron curtain" gave rise to two powerful military alliances—NATO and the Warsaw Pact. Since the disintegration of the USSR, however, in purely military terms, the basic global pattern can be characterized as one of sharply decreased East-West hostility in the developed world and continuing competition and conflict in many developing countries.

The **North Atlantic Treaty Organization (NATO)** is a defence alliance of Western states set up in 1949 against the perceived threat of communist aggression in Europe and the Atlantic area. As stated in the treaty, "an armed attack against one or more of the parties to the treaty in Europe or North America shall be considered an attack against them all."[11] Fifteen of the 16 members—Belgium, Britain, Canada, Denmark, France, Germany, Greece, Iceland, Italy, Luxembourg, the Netherlands, Norway, Portugal, Spain, Turkey, and the United States—are committed to all parts of NATO. Only France does not belong to the integrated military command structure.

For many years, NATO was confronted with a bloc of communist states linked together under the umbrella of the **Warsaw Pact**. This alliance of Eastern European countries consisted of the USSR and its satellites East Germany, Poland, Czechoslovakia,

Hungary, Bulgaria, and Romania. In 1991, the Warsaw Pact was disbanded when Moscow's authority in Europe, and even within the USSR, evaporated. NATO, too, has had to re-evaluate its role. At its 1991 meeting in Rome, NATO agreed on a new strategic concept to replace its Cold War strategy. The Alliance members concluded that a full-scale, surprise attack on the Eastern fronts had effectively been removed and that the new threats were more multifaceted and multidirectional. Risks, they calculated, were more likely to emerge from economic, social, and political difficulties, including ethnic rivalry and territorial disputes. This strategy led to a reduction in overall size of Allies' forces, a reduced forward presence in central Europe, and a reduced reliance on nuclear weapons. In order to increase cooperation with Russia, it has formed a *Partnership for Peace* with the former members of the Warsaw Pact. In 1995 it deployed 60 000 troops in a peacekeeping mission in Bosnia, and continues to have troops in the area.

NATO's membership has also shifted eastward. In April 1999, Hungary, Poland, and the Czech Republic joined the Alliance, making it an organization of 19 members.[12] This is not the end of the story. Other permanent members of NATO are likely to be admitted within the next decade, and a Euro-Atlantic Partnership Council has emerged—with 44 countries of diverse background and security traditions—as a founder for co-operation on security issues.

NATO is now 50 years old. Although it continues to be based on a treaty which under Article 5 commits each member to come to the defence of the other in the case of an attack from without, this is no longer its primary objective. The organization's purpose began to change with its first-ever violent use of air and naval forces to back up UN peacekeepers in Bosnia-Herzegovina, its first ever ground-force operations in the Dayton Implementation Force (IFOR) and now called the Stabilization Force (SFOR), and its first ever joint operation within Partnership for Peace and other non-NATO countries. In 1999, NATO carried out massive air strikes against Yugoslavia when it did not pull back its forces from attacking Albanians in Kosovo. It was the largest operation NATO had ever carried out. All 19 member states defended these goals: a pull back of Serbian troops from Kosovo; autonomy for the Kosovo Albanian region; and an armed force to monitor the agreement. Such "out-of-area" peacekeeping, peace-making, and peace-enforcement activities are not explicitly mentioned in NATO's legal charter.

The superpower rivalry between the United States and former Soviet Union has terminated, but the two areas still possess the most powerful military machines on earth. The U.S. the European states of Britain, France, Russia, and the Ukraine continue to have numerous conventional and nuclear weapons.

Nuclear weapons profoundly changed the nature of the strategic environment. The *balance of power* concept no longer has the meaning or importance it once had. It has been a half century since President Truman ordered the dropping of nuclear bombs on Hiroshima and Nagasaki to end the war with Japan—the only times the bomb has been employed in hostilities.

The destructive capability of nuclear bombs is well known. Just one 10-megaton nuclear device yields the destructive power of 10 million tons of TNT. It would destroy buildings within a range of 12 miles from the target and produce some 100 000 square miles of radioactive fallout. One nuclear submarine like the Poseidon or Trident carries enough nuclear warheads to destroy every major city in the former USSR. Today, more than 1000 times as much explosive power is stockpiled than was used in all the wars after the invention of gunpowder.

Modern military arsenals may be described by other basic characteristics. One of the most frequently mentioned attributes is the ability of weapons to travel long or short distances. In military language, a **strategic weapon** can travel over large distances to strike at an enemy; intercontinental ballistic missiles or long-range bombers that can travel from the United States to Russia or vice versa are examples. An **intermediate-range weapon**, such as a cruise missile, travels between 500 and 5500 kilometres. A **short-range weapon** is sometimes called a tactical weapon because it travels only short distances, usually less than 500 kilometres. Examples of short-range weapons are artillery shells, mines, or short-range nuclear missiles which can be used as battlefield weapons.[13]

The strategic doctrine underpinning the theoretical use of nuclear weapons during the Cold War was known as the theory of **deterrence**. The paradox of deterrence theory was that for each side to feel secure it had to be made to feel insecure. There had to be a balance of nuclear power. Neither side could be allowed to produce a perfect defence system that would give it an advantage. Deterrence rested on each side being able to deter the other because it, too, possessed nuclear capabilities. Over time, a rough nuclear parity between the United States and the former USSR was established.

Deterrence worked because each side had the capability of obliterating the other side even *after* sustaining a nuclear strike. In military language, deterrence works when each side has a **second-strike capability**; that is, it must have sufficient retaliatory power to withstand a strike from the aggressor and still be able to retaliate at a level unacceptable to the aggressor. Since under these conditions neither side could win a nuclear war, so goes the argument, mutual deterrence is achieved. This theory is called a "game of chicken" by the peace movement, which fears a miscalculation could result in human annihilation. Critics sometimes call this strategic doctrine **Mutual Assured Destruction (MAD)**.

In 1983 the United States announced its **Strategic Defence Initiative (SDI)** or "Star Wars"—which was to replace deterrence theory as a policy. Under this policy the United States was to build a high-technology shield to defend American territory against incoming nuclear missiles. The policy was shown to be an expensive albatross which would never, in the conceivable future, be capable of preventing all missiles from landing on U.S. territory. It is often argued by conservative thinkers that the Soviet Union's economic problems and consequent disintegration emerged from trying to compete with the United States in developing a nuclear arsenal to confront the Star Wars project.

Disarmament and Arms Control

The question of how to maintain security is daunting in the post–Cold-War world. Despite the end of East-West hostilities many states remain armed to the teeth with nuclear and conventional armaments, as well as biological weapons (enhanced bacterial agents like anthrax germs) and chemical weapons (mustard or nerve gas). The **arms race**, in which the two superpowers and their allies sought security by competing to produce more weapons, has been discontinued, but deadly weapons continue to be stockpiled around the world.

The options for reducing the growth of weapons of mass destruction are either general disarmament or arms control. **Pacificists**, who hold the view that all violence and war is morally wrong, uphold the first position. Proponents of **general disarmament** take the view that armaments themselves are the fundamental cause of hostility in international politics. They would prefer that the West take a first step in the peace process by destroying all its weapons to prevent world destruction. However, others fear that such weapons will exist as long as there is hostility between states. Moreover, they argue that even if nuclear weapons were ever totally destroyed they could be remade, and thus states would prepare to produce them again quickly in order to ensure security. Nuclear weapons cannot be "disinvented."

Since no state will accept the vulnerability of total disarmament, the most pragmatic option is for governments to adopt policies of limited disarmament or arms control. Arms control offers a prospect of reducing threats and increasing stability in international affairs without the dangers of outright disarmament.

The use of **arms control** agreements to provide the basis for a more peaceful world are not new. Their use has spanned centuries. As early as 1139, Pope Innocent II called an international conference to control a new, awesome weapon—the crossbow! Other treaties followed.

The **Geneva Protocol** of 1924, signed and ratified by over 110 states, prohibits the use of poisonous gases and liquids in warfare. Since production and stockpiling of such weapons was not prohibited, however, many states continue to possess such weapons. In fact, Iraq used mustard gas on its own Kurdish civilians in 1990.

The 1972 **Biological and Toxin Weapons Convention (BWC)**, ratified by 140 states, commits the signatories to prohibit the development, production, stockpiling, or acquisition of biological agents or toxins. The lack of verification methods in the BWC was rectified in the 1993 **Chemical Weapons Convention (CWC)**, now ratified by 107 states, which prohibits the development, production, acquisition, stockpiling, retention, and use of chemical weapons. It mandates the destruction of all such weapons within 10 years and has unprecedented on-site verification provisions.

Several important arms control treaties about nuclear weapons have been made in the last four decades. In 1968 the nuclear powers signed a **nonproliferation treaty** pledging not to disseminate nuclear devices to non-nuclear countries. As of 1996, 178 states—including all five nuclear weapon states, virtually all of the other industrialized countries, and many developing states—have signed the agreement. Even the nuclear states in the former USSR, the Ukraine, and Tajikistan, have signed. Israel, Pakistan, and India have not acceded to the agreement, however, and Iraq and North Korea have failed to fulfill their obligations under it.

At least seven states are capable of detonating a nuclear bomb: the two superpowers, Britain, France, China, India, and Pakistan. Several other countries have nuclear capability but do not admit it—such as Israel, Brazil, and South Africa. Another half dozen states could develop this capacity—including North Korea, Iran, Iraq, Libya, and Taiwan. In May 1998, India and then Pakistan set off several nuclear devices to the consternation and criticism of the world community.

It is impossible to ascertain whether all of these countries could develop an adequate delivery system for their warheads or whether they would be aggressive enough to use the weapons, but it is clear that the nonproliferation agreement should be strengthened to decrease the possibility of enlarging the nuclear club. One point is clear—the end of the Cold War has not meant the end of nuclear weapons, nor is there any imminent prospect for general nuclear disarmament.

At the strategic level there has been considerable progress. In 1972 the United States and the USSR signed two agreements based on the **Strategic Arms Limitation Talks (SALT I)**. SALT I did not reduce the number of weapons, but slowed the rate of increase. This treaty was followed by the SALT II talks but as of January 1999, the agreement has not been ratified by the Russian Duma. After ten years of intensive discussions, the two superpowers finally managed to sign another strategic agreement on July 31, 1991. This **Strategic Arms Reduction Treaty (START)** reduced, for the first time in history, the number of strategic nuclear weapons that Americans and Russians could aim at each other's territory. The two sides agreed to reduce strategic offensive arms by approximately 30% in three phases over seven years. The rules are complicated but each side was to possess no more than 1600 strategic nuclear delivery vehicles (such as booster rockets or jets) and 6000 "accountable" strategic warheads (actual nuclear bombs).

By early 1999 the U.S. Senate, but not the Russian Duma, had ratified START II. This agreement will reduce U.S. and Russian strategic nuclear forces even further— leaving 3500 long-range nuclear weapons for the U.S. and about 3000 such weapons for Russia. Both sides agreed to the elimination of all MIRVs (multiple independently-targetable re-entry vehicles), MX, and Minuteman missiles for the US, and SS18, SS19, and SS24 missiles for Russia. START II makes two major advances—the number of nuclear weapons will be dramatically reduced and each side can monitor the other's dismantling process. The major fault is that the agreement calls only for the destruction of bombers—missiles and bombers—not the nuclear warheads.

At the level of intermediate-range nuclear forces (INF), the most recent treaty is even more comprehensive and welcome. In December 1987 the U.S. and USSR agreed to eliminate all land-based INF in their arsenals. The treaty included an asymmetrical compromise by the former Soviet Union and a verification regime that included on-site inspection of the destruction process. In May 1991 the destruction of all these missiles in Europe was completed. In practical terms the destruction of 859 U.S. Pershing II and ground-launched Cruise missiles as well as 1752 Soviet SS-20's, SS-5's, and SS-4's means that there are no nuclear-tipped missiles with a range of between 500 and 5500 kilometres left in Europe.

Short-range nuclear forces include all weapons with a range of less than 500 kilometres. In 1989, President George Bush announced that on completion of the Conventional Force Europe agreement (see below), talks would begin on the reduction of short-range nuclear weapons in Europe. NATO agreed with the proposal in June 1990. Finally, the United States, acting on its own, decided to remove these weapons. The basic argument was that such short-range devices in Europe could strike only German territory or the newly founded democracies of Eastern Europe. With Soviet troops removed from Germany and Eastern Europe there would be no purpose to these U.S. weapons. In September 1991 the United States resolved to get rid of all ground-launched nuclear weapons, including artillery shells, and to reduce air-launched missiles in Europe. NATO agreed to limit air-launched nuclear missiles to 1100 by 1994.

At the conventional level, too, there was considerable progress. In November 1990 a **Conventional Force Europe** agreement (**CFE**) was signed between NATO and the Warsaw Pact that sharply reduced conventional force levels in Europe. The treaty limits each defence alignment to equal inventories in five areas—20 000 tanks, 29 000 artillery pieces, 30 000 armored vehicles, 7200 combat aircraft, and 2000 attack helicopters. For all practical purposes this agreement made a NATO or former Warsaw Pact land offensive in Europe impossible. According to the treaty, the 22 participating states had to adhere to the ceiling in Europe from the Atlantic to the Urals and destroy surplus forces. Destruction and verification was conducted under the auspices of the **Organization for Security and Cooperation in Europe** (**OSCE**), which includes all European states plus the United States and Canada.

The continued lessening of tensions between the East and West and the end of Soviet aggressive intentions and capabilities has further affected the arms balance even without the formal ratification of such treaties. The end of the Warsaw Pact in April 1991 weakened Moscow as it removed 500 000 Eastern European troops from its command. Furthermore, as part of the agreement with Germany, the USSR removed all its troops from Eastern Germany by 1994. NATO in response overhauled its military structure, reduced its troops in Europe, set up a rapid reaction corps to handle small confrontations in Europe, and began to invite the participation of Russia and other former Communist countries in its activities.[14]

Arms control measures to reduce weaponry, without going as far as total disarmament, constitute the only pragmatic solution in the contemporary world. Unless and until states learn to live with the values and philosophies that separate them, a sound defence policy accompanied by arms control agreements is the best that can be expected on all sides. This does not mean there cannot be more safeguards. The world would still profit from further reductions in nuclear warheads, a strengthened nuclear nonproliferation treaty, a comprehensive nuclear test-ban treaty, prevention of the arms race in outer space, and a comprehensive treaty for the Arctic region.

North-South Politics

A large majority of the states of the United Nations originated only after 1945 and were former colonies of European empires. In combination with older but equally poor states, they make up the developing world. Since most of them are found in the Southern Hemisphere, their shared problems are often referred to as Southern issues, to distinguish them from the issues of the Northern area of democratic capitalist and former Communist states.

Many of these countries are extremely small and poor. In 1995, the GDP per capita was $233 in the least developed countries, $867 in all the developing countries and $12,764 in the industrialized world.[15] The South is not all poor, however. Some of the states, such as those rich in oil, are quite unlike their poorer cousins even in the same region.[16] Others such as South Korea, Singapore, and Taiwan, or what are known as the **Newly Industrializing Countries (NICs)**, have created the infrastructures of modern industrialized states and compete with the richer countries of the world.[17]

What distinguishes these states, then, is not their low level of economic performance and resultant poverty but their dependence on the richer countries of the industrialized North and their overall approach to world politics. In most of these states a desire for economic improvement is accompanied by a search for identity at home and abroad. In fact, their foreign policies often combine an expression of this need for recognition with a desire to unite their populations.

For this reason, rather than being part of the East-West alliance pattern, most of these states have historically pursued a policy of **nonalignment**; that is, even during the Cold War they did not join either superpower bloc. This one policy united them in the goal of asserting independence even though otherwise their domestic and foreign policies differed and continue to vary greatly.

As a stated policy, nonalignment with the superpowers was first articulated at a 1955 conference at Bandung, Indonesia. The so-called nonaligned movement essentially included more than 100 states ranging from African and Asian countries to Yugoslavia which wished to escape from the clutches of the former Soviet Union, and others such as Cuba that continued to depend on the former Soviet Union for its security.

Regardless of these claims, however, many of these nonaligned states actually relied on one of the greater powers or their allies for economic and military support. Of course, some areas of the world were more closely tied to East-West conflicts than others. For example, on the whole, Latin America and the Middle East experienced more external intervention than Africa.[18] In return for superpower largesse, the satellite LDCs often bought their military equipment and arms from their patron states.

Today, violent conflicts cannot be viewed in these Cold-War terms. Many of the most protracted conflicts relate to local territorial, ethnic, and religious warfare. The most prominent characteristic of LDCs is the similar problems they face. The disastrous effects of high population growth, poverty, and famine, for example, are distinguishing characteristics of most of them.

The LDCs have been particularly prone to the problem of *debt*. In the 1970s many Third World countries borrowed heavily and then in the 1980s found they could not pay their debts. Many states had overestimated their ability to repay the loans and others mismanaged the capital they were lent. More loans were given to offset these debts and a spiral of unpayable debt developed. The situation reached a crisis when Brazil, the world's largest debtor state, began to threaten that it would not pay back the loans at all. In 1982 Mexico, the second largest debtor, announced it could not repay its loans or even the interest on them. This turned many bankers into much more conservative lenders and LDCs found themselves dependent on the IMF and World Bank. The IMF and World Bank, which are controlled by member countries according to their financial commitments, are very conservative institutions, insisting that countries obtaining loans "reinvigorate" their economies, basically by swallowing the bitter pill of economic austerity and forcing the development of capitalism. In order to meet the demands of the IMF and World Bank, it has been necessary for many LDCs to cut public services in fields such as health care and education. In other words, they have been forced to accept the ideas about modernization and development discussed in Chapter 20.

The developing world contains more than three-quarters of the world's population, with China having more than one billion people. Population growth is occurring much more rapidly in the developing areas than in the industrialized Northern countries. Between 1995 and 2015 the industrialized countries are forecast to grow by only 0.2% while the developing countries will grow by 1.5%.[19] The rapid increase in population forecast for the next few decades is so great that it threatens to undermine the governments of many of these countries.

The past century has seen fantastic progress in terms of the longevity and quality of human life. In the economically developed parts of the world, the fall in the death rate and increased life expectancy have been accompanied by low fertility rates. However, these trends have not yet developed in most LDCs, where the population is expected to double during the next century.[20] Finding employment and food for these people may prove impossible. In the large cities overpopulation will lead to even greater problems in housing, transportation, sewage, and garbage collection.

Most states of the world are not yet prepared to take on the issues causing overpopulation. They continue to encourage fertility and large families. Only in a very few places does the state actively intervene to try to reduce fertility rates. Even in China, a "one-child per family" policy is being modified. The government has historically used policies such as birth control programs as well as penalties, and even enforced sterilization and abortion in an attempt to force compliance. Other states have used less intrusive programs. Cuba has restricted movement from rural to urban areas in an attempt to control rapid population growth in certain regions of the country.

While several LDCs have large resources, they are usually very weak in economic terms. Misery is accompanied by hunger and even starvation in many of them. If the data for the world is taken as a whole, there is a satisfactory amount of food for everyone, everywhere. But since food supplies are maldistributed, many people are hungry and many die of starvation. In theory, if a better transportation and distribution system existed, there would be no starvation anywhere today. However, the rapid rise in population predicted for the LDCs during the next century will mean that food production will not keep up with population growth. There simply will not be enough food for everyone even if the distribution and transportation systems are improved and distribution is made more equal.[21] To ensure long-term self-sufficiency and stability, less developed countries must develop their own, independent sources of food and water.

Population and food are only two of the vital issues in LDCs. Pollution of the environment is another obvious problem. In handling these issues, domestic and international politics are interwoven. Many such problems cannot be solved by single states, and only comprehensive changes in the way people govern themselves at the international level will allow satisfactory and permanent solutions. The contests between states, especially those between East and West and between North and South, however, prevent the development of a world government. Nowhere is this more evident than in questions of human rights, environmental protection, health, war, and peace.

HUMAN RIGHTS

Human rights are based on the premise that all people, regardless of their nationality, culture, religion, language, ethnicity, colour, ability, or gender ought to have certain freedoms and privileges. Despite this abstract general agreement, internecine quarrels and violent disputes continue about what these rights entail and under what conditions they should be upheld. There is no universal agreement on what the terms mean. Some interpret human rights very broadly to include topics such as racial or sexual discrimination, while others take a narrower view that human rights should be concerned only with legal rights and remedies.

The philosophy of liberty espoused by Isiah Berlin is often used to sort out the fundamental concepts about human rights.[22] He argued that rights are either *negative* or *positive*. Negative rights imply freedom *from* the restraints of others, including the government. They include such rights as free expression, assembly, press, religion, travel, and the right to a fair trial. Positive rights are those that provide freedom *to* obtain something such as the right to have education, employment, welfare, and hospital care. In other words, the latter include moral and economic obligations rather than merely legal ones.

Many countries list human rights in their constitutions. The United States' Constitution is basically about *negative* rights as the Bill of Rights lists only what the government cannot do. For example, the Constitution states that Congress cannot make a "law respecting an establishment of religion, or prohibiting the free exercise thereof; or abridging the freedom of speech, or of the press ...." On the other hand, the Canadian Constitution provides *positive* rights. It says there must be equality before and under the law and "without discrimination based on race, national or ethnic origin, colour, religion, sex, age or mental or physical disability." But Americans, unlike Canadians, have a constitutional guarantee of the right "to keep and bear arms."

Possibly more germane to this chapter on international affairs are the two declarations of rights found in the 1948 United Nations Universal Declaration on Human Rights, and the International Covenant on Economic, Social and Cultural Rights adopted by the United Nations General Assembly in 1966. These commitments contain both positive and negative ideas about human rights. The Declaration upholds the right to life, liberty, and security as well as the right to a *free* education. The Covenant is more committed to social justice—as in its claim that there should be *fair wages and equal remuneration for work of equal value* and a right to "an adequate standard of living for himself and his family, including adequate food, clothing, and housing, and to the continuous improvement of conditions ..."

Despite these declarations about general human rights, there seems to be more concern in the international community for political topics such as imprisonment, torture, or murder of dissidents because of their political beliefs. One nongovernmental agency vigorously pursuing these topics—Amnesty International—has over a million members.

Genocide—acts such as killing, causing harm, or imposing intolerable conditions on members of specified national, ethnic, racial, or religious groups—has been severely condemned by both governments and nongovernmental agencies. The killing of an estimated six million Jews in Nazi Germany is a pertinent example. More recent events in Cambodia (Kampuchea) illustrate the fact that evil continues to plague the human race. Between 1975 and 1979 the Khmer Rouge Communist government, led by the notorious Pot Pol, killed millions of Cambodians.[23] Other recent examples include the 1990–91 case of Iraq dropping poison gas on its own Kurdish citizens, groups carrying out "ethnic cleansing" from 1992 onward throughout the former Yugoslavia and perhaps the 1998–99 Serbian violence against people of Albanian ethnicity in Kosovo.

In view of these recent atrocities, the United Nations established International Tribunals to try individuals accused of war crimes. In fact, a treaty to establish a "permanent" **International Criminal Court (ICC)** was signed in 1998. The court has jurisdiction to try cases involving genocide, crimes against humanity, and war crimes. The United States, China, Israel and several other countries opposed the establishment of the court on the basis that its citizens could be tried before a "politicized" court.

An important principle of international politics, discussed earlier, is the noninterference of one state in the internal affairs of another. But this principle has often been broken. But should governments take a strict position against other countries for human rights violations? For example, the United States government has often threatened to revoke China's "most favoured nation" trade status because of human rights violations, but it has never carried through with the threat. Even the tragedy at Tiananmen Square in 1989 did not change Chinese–American relations. Should it have?

ENVIRONMENTAL AND HEALTH ISSUES

Concern about the state of the world's environment continues to grow domestically and internationally. The growth of Greenpeace as a movement, the limited success of Green parties in Europe, and legislation to halt the destruction of the environment in most developed democracies are concrete indications of the importance of this policy field. In 1995 the Green Party even shares governmental power in Germany—the first such environmentalist victory in a major industrial country.

The essential problem for the environment comes from the fact that it is a **collective good**. That public goods need to be fostered and preserved is often explained by what is called the "tragedy of the commons." In villages and towns where there are "common lands" these areas are invariably overgrazed by individuals who choose to keep their own lands underutilized while they use the common land extensively. In other words, short-term individual interests tend to prevail over common concerns and issues. On a larger scale, collective goods are not considered as important as the selfish interests of corporations, states or individuals. Thus, people treat the "global commons" in a way that spreads negative consequences for everyone.[24] Parklands are destroyed, the air polluted, and oceans overfished.

The advance of scientific knowledge and technology has brought immeasurable good and bad consequences for humankind. It has been responsible for improvements in health, nourishment, and physical labour, but its side effects are often dangerous. Environmentalists have pointed out many ways that humans are destroying the planet. They have shown that state borders do not count for very much with regard to environmental issues. Policy must, therefore, be developed at a level above the state—in other words, internationally.

Here are some examples of environmental issues that call for global action :

- *Ozone*   The release of harmful synthetic gases is destroying the ozone layer, which protects the earth from ultraviolet rays. In the mid-1980s scientists discovered that this thin layer of ozone encircling the stratosphere was being destroyed by the emission of chlorofluorocarbon (CFC) gases and bromine from halogens into the atmosphere. As the ozone layer is depleted, it allows more ultraviolet light to reach earth, causing increased incidents of in skin cancer, endangering marine life, and possibly affecting the climate. In response, the developed democracies signed and later amended a **Montreal Protocol on Substances that Deplete the Ozone Layer**, which freezes and eventually begins to decrease the use of CFCs and halogen production. Many countries and even subnational authorities have taken action to control the production and use of CFCs and other ozone-depleting substances. The funding of substitute substances, especially for developing countries, is crucial as the economic impacts of the phase-out are significant.

- *Global Warming*   Most experts agree that global warming is taking place at an alarming speed. Some of this so-called greenhouse affect is caused by the release of pollutants—CFCs, methane, nitrous oxide, and ozone—into the atmosphere and by the destruction of the rain forests. The destruction of rain forests reduces the earth's natural ability to extract carbon dioxide from the air. In other words, industrialization (which requires fossil-fuel burning—i.e. the emission of CO_2, which is an inevitable by-product of burning coal, oil, and natural gas) is causing the earth's climatic conditions to change. The rich industrialized countries contain only 25% of the world's population, yet they consume 75% of its energy, 85% of its forest products, and are responsible for 75% of global warming.[25] Country participants at the 1992 Earth Summit in Rio de Janeiro drafted conventions on climate change, biological diversity, and forests. Although governments were satisfied with the enunciated goals, environmentalists criticized the protocols because they contained no targets or timetables.

At the 1997 Kyoto Conference, the rich countries signed a dramatic but vague agreement to cut emissions of greenhouse gases at least five percent below their 1990 levels by 2012. The developing countries would not agree with the accord because they correctly argue that today's problem is essentially due to the excesses of the rich world. The United States alone puts out about a quarter of the world's carbon dioxide emissions. Moreover, the leaders of poorer countries maintained that cutting emissions would reduce economic growth, and they already have a long way to go to catch up with the developed world. China and India even refused to debate the issue.

The future of the accord hinges on a new idea in international relations, and there continues to be considerable discussion about it. The United States wants an international market to trade the right to emit greenhouse gases. This market would allow countries that are above their quota to "buy" emission reduction from other countries. The future and impact of the Kyoto accord will be determined by the decisions on this policy.

- **Renewable Resources**   The earth's vegetation, too, is deteriorating. Forests are being destroyed and plant and animal species are becoming extinct. This waste of renewable resources is the subject of much controversy and is covered by a large variety of international treaties and protocols. Possibly the most important concept in this field is **sustainable development**. In 1987, the authors of *Our Common Future*, published by the UN Commission on Environment and Development, called for a commitment to the idea of sustainable development. It asked states and individuals to understand that the environment must be protected *at the same time* that economic growth takes place. The sustainable development concept calls for both values to be considered in tandem and not in opposition.[26] According to this idea, economic growth should be undertaken only if it does not threaten the environment or deplete resources at a non-renewable rate. But, should Northern countries which have already "developed" by stripping lands of forests and natural resources now "dictate" to Southern countries how they should act? On the whole, developing (usually Southern) states reject the rights of richer countries or environmentalists.

- **Nuclear Issues**   The breakdown of nuclear plants may create deadly radioactivity as happened in the Chernobyl disaster in the former USSR. In addition, states continue to prepare for the non-peaceful use of nuclear energy and nuclear testing continues. In

1995–96 France again tested underground nuclear explosions in the South Pacific. Greenpeace ships tried to sail in the waters but were prevented by French military personnel. Rioting in Papeete, the capital of Tahiti, did not halt the tests, but world pressure finally caused French President Jacques Chirac to cancel the tests as of January 1996 after six explosions. In May 1998 both India and Pakistan conducted above-ground nuclear tests to the anger of most of the world's states.

- *Biology*   Biological research may lead to major international issues. One example is gene splicing (recombinant DNA), which could lead to the inadvertent development of new violent microbes.

These are only some of the international issues concerning the environment—issues only governments and international institutions can solve. But the issues are complex and rife with conflicting values. Should one increase the cost of industrial production in order to eliminate toxic wastes? Should we preserve the Amazon rain forest if it means a reduction of employment for poverty-stricken Brazilians? What role should the United Nations play in protecting the environment?

International Health

Questions about global health are often omitted in books on world politics. By global health we mean such topics as poverty, food production, housing, and disease. However, one disease, acquired immune deficiency syndrome (AIDS), has become so widespread and dangerous that it belongs alongside environmental and population issues as being of world concern. In 1997, 2.3 million people died of AIDS, which is now the fifth largest cause of death worldwide. At the beginning of 1998 more than 30 million people—about 0.5% of the world's population were infected with human immune-deficiency virus (HIV), which is widely accepted as the cause of AIDS. The numbers are much worse in some parts of the world—particularly in Africa. For example, a quarter of the population of Zimbabwe and Botswana is infected.[27]

The AIDs epidemic continues to grow throughout the world. In all cases, HIV damages cells involved in the immune system, which then makes the body vulnerable to infections. AIDS is transmitted from person to person by an exchange of bodily fluids through sexual contact, blood transfusions, shared IV needles, and open sores. The highest rates of AIDS are found among people who do not practise safer sex (i.e., use condoms) and drug abusers.

SECURITY AND PEACE

Despite the fact that nuclear weapons have made outright war between the larger military states impossible, international competition still goes on in other forms. Governments use **tools of statecraft**—instruments to ensure their interests prevail in the world. These include diplomacy as well as more coercive means up to and including war. If a state cannot achieve its aims by negotiation and diplomacy, it may try to convince, influence, induce, manipulate and even coerce states and receptive individuals to its point of view.

All states employ **propaganda**, defined as deliberate distortions of the truth, in their attempts to influence people that their viewpoint is superior to their opponents'. During the height of the Cold War the former Soviet Union used its propaganda agencies to try to convert the world to communism, and the United States employed propaganda about democracy to attempt the opposite.[28]

When such peaceful and overt methods fail, governments may engage in more hostile actions. Again both the United States and the former Soviet Union engaged in what is called **subversion**, defined as foreign support for the rebellious activity of disaffected groups in society. They used secret or covert actions designed to overthrow governments or influence foreign and even domestic policies. U.S. actions in Central America have been well documented, as have similar Soviet efforts in Europe and elsewhere.

War, or outright clashes between two states, is the most violent form of international competition.[29] Whether carried out with nuclear weapons, conventional military arms, or sticks and stones, it has been a horrific part of world history. The world often looks peaceful from the vantage point of North American suburbs, but it is not. Local wars persist in most parts of the world, and currently NATO is at war with Yugoslavia.

Almost all states prepare for war. The estimated world military expenditure reached $1 trillion in 1990 but has been declining in recent years—about a one-third reduction between 1988 and 1997.[30] While nuclear missiles may be especially frightening to the mass public, it is well to remember that about 80% of military expenditure is for conventional weapons and equipment.[31] The international trade in conventional weapons continues to grow, especially in Third World countries. The United States and Soviet Union together supply more than 70% of all arms exported to LDCs. France, Britain, and Italy also share a huge proportion of the total sales.

The death and destruction caused in war is almost beyond description. Modern weapons of mass destruction are horrific. The consequences of the two atomic bombs the United States dropped on Japan in 1945 were terrible: a total of 70 000 died in Hiroshima and 35 000 in Nagasaki. These figures represent only two bombs. Global conflicts killed an estimated 10 million in World War I and 51 million in World War II.[32] And wars continue today throughout the world. It has been estimated by Ploughshares Monitor that there were 250 wars and over 109 million war-related deaths in the twentieth century.[33]

Why have wars occurred continually throughout history and why do they remain with us today? Wars erupt for many reasons and scholars are divided on their causes. Some scholars believe that wars do not develop between democratic states. Indeed, of the 416 wars between sovereign countries between 1816 and 1980 only 12 were "arguably" between democracies.[34] Wars may start by the calculated policy actions of leaders and/or by stupid accidents. Idealists believe that wars are caused by ideologies, nationalism, and poor leadership. Realists believe that states act in the pursuit of security and power, not in the idealistic aims of ethical and legal principles.[35] Why can war neither be avoided nor prevented entirely? The causes of war and conditions of peace are too large a topic to be considered here—it should be pursued in advanced courses in political science. But we can be certain that wars are not aberrations and that—however grim they may be—they have brought beneficial as well as disastrous results.

Wars of independence, or liberation, as they are now called, have helped to draw the map of states as we now find them. The Americans became independent by fighting the British; the Algerians fought the French; the West fought Nazi Germany to free Europe. Violent conflict is endemic to world history.

The destiny of the world may well be an inevitable march toward the interdependence of peoples, nations, and states. Some globalization theorists even argue that individual states and governments have lost control over their own policies and are being dictated to by the global marketplace. But, in the twenty-first century the most important politics will continue to be within states, and political science will provide a most fruitful form of investigation. The past decade has been one of immense change and excitement. As Vaclav Havel, President of the Czech Republic and author, expressed it:

> We playwrights, who have to cram a whole human life or an entire historical era into a two-hour play, can scarcely understand this rapidity [of change] ourselves. And if it gives us trouble, think of the trouble it must give political scientists, who have less experience with the realm of the improbable.[36]

Adrian Raeside © Koko Press Inc.

ADRIAN RAESIDE, Victoria Times-Colonist, Victoria, B.C., Canada

DISCUSSION QUESTIONS ▬▬▬▬▬▬

1. Distinguish between domestic and international law.
2. Is there a "global society"?
3. Do democratic countries go to war with each other? Why or why not?
4. Is world government the answer to problems of the environment? Health? Military security?
5. Is world disarmament possible? Preferable?

KEY TERMS ▬▬▬▬▬▬

Asian-Pacific Economic Cooperation (APEC), p. 476

arms control, p. 482

arms race, p. 482

Association of Southeast Asia Nations (ASEAN), p. 474

balance of power, p. 464

Biological and Toxin Weapons Convention (BWC), p. 482

bipolar, p. 465

British Commonwealth, p. 474

Chemical Weapons Convention (CWC), p. 482

Cold War, p. 465

collective good, p. 489

collective security organization, p. 470

Conventional Force Europe (CFE), p. 484

customary law, p. 462

customs union, p. 476

deterrence, p. 481

economic summits, p. 475

European Central Bank (ECB), p. 477

European Union (EU), p. 472

foreign policy, p. 461

G-7, p. 475

General Agreement on Tariffs and Trade (GATT), p. 475

general disarmament, p. 482

General Assembly, p. 468

Geneva Protocol, p. 482

genocide, p. 488

intermediate-range weapon, p. 481

International Court of Justice (ICJ), p. 463

International Criminal Court (ICC), p. 488

international law, p. 462

international relations, p. 461

"iron curtain", p. 465

League of Arab States, p. 475

Maastricht Treaty, p. 476

military alliance, p. 470

Montreal Protocol on Substances that Deplete the Ozone Layer, p. 489

multinational corporations (MNCs), p. 477

Mutual Assured Destruction (MAD), p. 481

Newly Industrializing Countries (NICs), p. 485

new world order, p. 467

nonalignment, p. 485

non-governmental organizations (NGOs), p. 479

nonproliferation treaty, p. 482

North American Free Trade Association (NAFTA), p. 476

North Atlantic Treaty Organization (NATO), p. 479

Organization for Security and Cooperation in Europe (OSCE), p. 484

Organization of African Unity (OAU), p. 474

Organization of American States (OAS), p. 474

Pacifists, p. 482

propaganda, p. 492

second-strike capability, p. 481

Security Council, p. 468

short-range nuclear forces, p. 483

short-range weapon, p. 481

ENDNOTES

1. For an overview of this fascinating subject see Sir Harold Nicholson, *Diplomacy*, 4th ed. (New York: Oxford, 1988). On the early history of diplomacy, see Frank Adcock, *Diplomacy in Ancient Greece* (New York: St. Martin's Press, 1975).

2. For a contemporary defense of international law see Daniel Patrick Moynihan, *On the Law of Nations* (Cambridge, Mass: Harvard University Press, 1990).

3. See N.J. Rengger, *Treaties and Alliances of the World*, 5th ed., (London: Longman, 1990).

4. J.L. Brierly, *The Law of Nations*, 6th ed. (New York: Oxford, 1963), p. 72. See also Ingrid Detter De Lupis, *The Law of War* (Cambridge, Mass.: Cambridge University Press, 1987).

5. For the classic argument see Hans Morgenthau, *Politics Among Nations*, 5th ed. (New York: Alfred A. Knopf, 1978).

6. The best known exponent of the "declinist" school is Paul Kennedy whose book *The Rise and Fall of the Great Powers* argues that the military power of a state rises and falls because of its relative economic position. (New York: Random House, 1988). For different perspectives on this topic see, for example, Joseph S. Nye, Jr., *Bound to Lead* (New York: Basic Books, 1990); and Robert D. Hormats, "The Roots of American Power," *Foreign Affairs*, vol. 70, no. 3 (Summer 1991) pp. 130–49.

7. A few small territories around the globe have some aspects of sovereignty but have still not joined the United Nations. Kiribati, Nauru, Switzerland, Taiwan, Tonga, Tuvalu, and the Vatican are states which, for one reason or another, are not members of the UN. See J. Denis Derbyshire and Ian Derbyshire, *World Political Systems* (London: Chambers, 1991), Ch. 8.

8. See K.J. Holsti, *International Politics*, 4th ed. (Englewood Cliffs, N.J.: Prentice-Hall, 1983), ch. 15.

9. For more information on non-state actors see Richard Mansbach, Yale Ferguson, et al, *The Web of World Politics: Non-State Actors in the Global System* (Englewood Cliffs, N.J.: Prentice-Hall, 1976).

10. George Thomas Kurian, *The New Book of World Rankings*, 3rd ed., (New York: Facts on File, 1991), p. 47.

11. See K.J. Holsti, *International Politics*, p. 109.

12. Belgium, Britain, Canada, Denmark, France, Iceland, Italy, Luxembourg, the Netherlands, Norway, Portugal, and the U.S. joined in 1949. Greece and Turkey followed in 1952, Germany in 1955, Spain in 1982, and Poland, the Czech Republic, and Hungary in 1999.

13. See Robert J. Jackson, ed., *Europe in Transition: The Management of Security in the Post Cold War Period* (New York: Praeger, 1992). Also see Inis L. Claude, *Swords into Plowshares*, 4th

ed. (New York: Random House, 1981); William Epstein, *The Last Chance: Nuclear Proliferation and Arms Control* (New York: Free Press, 1976); and Harvard Nuclear Study Group, *Living With Nuclear Weapons* (New York: Bantam Books, 1983).

14. See Robert J. Jackson, "The Changing Condition of European Security," in Robert J. Jackson, ed., *Europe in Transition* (New York: Praeger, 1992).

15. *Human Development Report, 1998* (Oxford: Oxford University Press, 1998), p. 206.

16. See Myron Weiner, "Political Change: Asia, Africa and The Middle East," in Myron Weiner and Samuel Huntington, eds., *Understanding Political Development* (Boston: Little, Brown, 1987), pp. 33–64.

17. *Ibid.*

18. Paul Cammack, et al., *Third World Politics* (Baltimore, Md: Johns Hopkins University Press, 1988), p. 244.

19. *Human Development Report, 1998*, p. 200.

20. See Davidson Gwatkin and Sarah Brandel, "Life Expectancy and Population Growth in the Third World," *Scientific American*, 246 (May 1982), pp. 3–11.

21. Vic George, *Wealth, Poverty and Starvation* (New York: St. Martin's Press, 1988).

22. Isiah Berlin, *Four Essays on Liberty* (New York: Oxford University Press, 1960).

23. United States State Department, *Country Reports on Human Rights Practises for 1989* (Washington, D.C.: U.S. Government Printing Office, 1990), p.792.

24. See Will Steger and Jon Bowermaster, *Saving the Earth: A Citizen's Guide to Environmental Action* (New York: Alfred A. Knopf, 1990); and Gareth Porter and Janet Welsh Brow, *Global Environmental Politics* (Boulder, Colo.: Westview Press, 1991).

25. Cited in "Women, Population and the Environment," *Great Decisions: 1991* (New York: Foreign Policy Association), p. 65.

26. World Commission on Environment and Development, *Our Common Future* (New York: Oxford University Press, 1987).

27. Jonathan Mann, Daniel Tarantola, and Thomas Netter, *AIDS in the World: A Global Report* (Cambridge Mass.: Harvard University Press,1992).

28. See Terence H. Qualter, *Propaganda and Psychological Warfare* (New York: Random House, 1962).

29. For significant contributions to the theory and practice of war, see Michael Howard, *The Causes of War* (Cambridge, Mass.: Harvard University Press, 1984); Robert O. Keohane and Joseph S. Nye, *Power and Independence* (Boston: Little, Brown, 1977); and Kenneth N. Waltz, *Theory of International Politics* (Reading, Mass.: Basic Books, 1979).

30. See *SIPRI Yearbook 1998* (Oxford: Oxford University Press, 1998.

31. Michael Bizoska, "Arms Transfer Data Sources," *Journal of Conflict Resolution*, vol. 26 (March 1982), pp. 39–75.

32. David Wood, *Conflict in the Twentieth Century* (London: International Institute for Strategic Studies, 1968) pp. 24–26

33. *World Military and Social Expenditures, 1989*, p. 22; and Francis A. Beer, *Peace Against War* (San Francisco: Freeman, 1981).

34. See *The Economist*, April 1, 1995, p. 17–18.

35. Kenneth N. Waltz, *Theory of International Politics* (New York: McGraw–Hill, 1979); and Hans J. Morgenthau, *Politics Among Nations*, 5th ed., (New York: Alfred A. Knopf, 1973).

36. Vaclav Havel, quoted by James N. Rosenau, in "The Relocation of Authority in a Shrinking World," *Comparative Politics*, vol. 24, no. 3 (April 1992), p. 253.

FURTHER READING

Security

Allison, Graham T., et al., *Avoiding Nuclear Anarchy* (Cambridge, Mass.: MIT Press, 1996).

Bond, Brian, *The Pursuit of Victory: From Napoleon to Saddam Hussein* (Oxford: Oxford University Press, 1995).

Chan, Steve, *East Asian Dynamism: Growth, Order and Security in the Pacific Region* (Boulder, Colo.: Westview Press, 1990).

Dutkiewicz, Piotr, and Robert J. Jackson, eds., *NATO Looks East* (New York: Praeger, 1998).

Enloe, Cynthia, *Bannanas, Beaches, and Bases: Making Feminist Sense of International Politics* (Berkeley: University of California Press, 1990).

————, *The Morning After and Sexual Politics at the End of the Cold War* (Berkeley: University of California Press, 1990).

Halliday, Fred, *Rethinking International Relations* (Vancouver: University of British Columbia Press, 1994).

Hamilton, Keith, and Richard Langhorne, *The Practice of Diplomacy* (London: Routledge, 1995).

Hogan, Michael J., ed., *The End of the Cold War: Its Meanings and Implications* (New York: Cambridge University Press, 1992).

Jackson, Robert J., ed., *Continuity of Discord: Crises and Responses in the Atlantic Community* (New York: Praeger, 1985).

Kennedy, Paul, *The Rise and Fall of Great Powers* (New York: Random House, 1978).

Langille, Howard Peter, *Changing the Guard: Canada's Defence in a World of Transition* (Toronto: University of Toronto Press, 1990).

Light, Margo, and A.J.R. Groom, ed., *International Relations: A Handbook of Current Theory*, 2nd ed. (London: Frances Pinter, 1994).

McNamara, Robert S. *In Retrospect: The Tragedy and Lessons of Vietnam* (New York: Random House, 1995).

Miall, Hugh, *The Peacemakers* (London: Macmillan, 1992).

Nye, Joseph S., Jr., *Bound to Lead: The Changing Nature of American Power* (New York: Basic Books, 1990).

Parsons, Anthony, *From Cold War to Hot Peace* (London: Penguin, 1995).

Ruggie, John Gerard, *Winning the Peace: America and World Order in the New Era* (New York: Columbia University Press, 1996).

Sherry, Michael S., *In the Shadow of War: The United States Since the 1930s* (New Haven, CT: Yale University Press, 1995).

The New Europe

Brezinski, Zbigniew, *The Grand Failure: Communism's Terminal Crisis* (New York: Charles Scribner's, 1989).

Cambone, Stephen A., ed., *NATO's Role in European Stability* (Washington, D.C.: CSIS, 1995).

Crouch, C., and D. Marquand, eds., *The Politics of 1992: Beyond the Single European Market* (Oxford: Basil Blackwell, 1990).

Hoffman, Stanley, and Robert Keohane, eds., *The New European Community* (Boulder, Colo.: Westview Press, 1991).

Jackson, Robert J., ed., *Europe in Transition: The Management of Security in the Post Cold War Period* (New York: Praeger, 1992).

Tismaneanu, Vladimir, *Reinventing Politics: Eastern Europe from Stalin to Havel* (New York: Free Press, 1992).

Economics

Johnson, John J., *A Hemisphere Apart: The Foundations of United States Policy Toward Latin America* (Baltimore, Md.: Johns Hopkins University Press, 1990).

Krugman, P., *Pop Internationalism* (Cambridge, MA: MIT Press, 1996).

Pratt, Cranford, ed., *Middle Power Internationalism: The North-South Dimension* (Montreal: McGill-Queen's University Press, 1990).

 **Weblinks**

www.un.org/
This is the United Nations' Web Page.

ralph.gmu.edu/cfpa/peace/toc.html
This site discusses the United Nations Security Council.

www.eurounion.org
This is the European Union's Web Page.

nuke.handheld.com
This site is a good source on nuclear technology, including nuclear weapons

www.saclant. nato.int/nato.html
Home Pages for the North Atlantic Treaty Organization

www.amnesty.org
This is the site of Amnesty International

www.hrw.org
This is the home page of Human Rights Watch

States of the World

I Seven states of the 192 in the world today are not members of the United Nations: Kiribati, Nauru, Switzerland, Taiwan, Tonga, Tuvalu, and Vatican City.

II The table below lists the 185 states that are members of the United Nations and their dates of admission to the organization.

Member States of the United Nations Organization

1946	Afghanistan	1984	Brunei Darussalam
1955	Albania	1955	Bulgaria
1962	Algeria	1960	Burkina Faso
1993	Andorra	1962	Burundi
1976	Angola	1955	Cambodia
1981	Antigua and Barbuda	1960	Cameroon
1945	Argentina	1945	Canada
1992	Armenia	1975	Cape Verde
1945	Australia	1960	Central African Republic
1955	Austria	1960	Chad
1992	Azerbaijan	1945	Chile
1973	Bahamas	1945	China
1971	Bahrain	1945	Colombia
1974	Bangladesh	1975	Comoros
1966	Barbados	1960	Congo*
1945	Belarus	1945	Costa Rica
1945	Belgium	1960	Côte d'Ivoire
1981	Belize	1992	Croatia
1960	Benin	1945	Cuba
1971	Bhutan	1960	Cyprus
1945	Bolivia	1993	Czech Republic
1992	Bosnia & Herzegovina	1945	Denmark
1966	Botswana	1977	Djibouti
1945	Brazil	1978	Dominica

1945	Dominican Republic	1992	Kazakhstan
1945	Ecuador	1963	Kenya
1945	Egypt	1991	Korea, Democratic People's Republic of
1945	El Salvador		
1968	Equatorial Guinea	1991	Korea, Republic of
1993	Eritrea	1963	Kuwait
1991	Estonia	1992	Kyrgyzstan
1945	Ethiopia	1955	Lao People's Democratic Republic
1970	Fiji		
1955	Finland	1991	Latvia
1945	France	1945	Lebanon
1960	Gabon	1966	Lesotho
1965	Gambia	1945	Liberia
1992	Georgia	1955	Libya
1973	Germany	1990	Liechtenstein
1957	Ghana	1991	Lithuania
1945	Greece	1945	Luxembourg
1974	Grenada	1993	Macedonia, Former Yugoslav Republic of
1945	Guatemala		
1958	Guinea	1960	Madagascar
1974	Guinea-Bissau	1964	Malawi
1966	Guyana	1957	Malaysia
1945	Haiti	1965	Maldives
1945	Honduras	1960	Mali
1955	Hungary	1964	Malta
1946	Iceland	1991	Marshall Islands
1945	India	1961	Mauritania
1950	Indonesia	1968	Mauritius
1945	Iran	1945	Mexico
1945	Iraq	1991	Micronesia, Federated States of
1955	Ireland	1992	Moldova
1949	Israel	1993	Monaco
1955	Italy	1961	Mongolia
1962	Jamaica	1956	Morocco
1956	Japan	1975	Mozambique
1955	Jordan	1948	Myanmar
		1990	Namibia

1955	Nepal	1992	Slovenia
1945	Netherlands	1978	Solomon Islands
1945	New Zealand	1960	Somalia
1945	Nicaragua	1945	South Africa
1960	Niger	1955	Spain
1960	Nigeria	1955	Sri Lanka
1945	Norway	1956	Sudan
1971	Oman	1975	Suriname
1947	Pakistan	1968	Swaziland
1994	Palau	1946	Sweden
1945	Panama	1945	Syria
1975	Papua New Guinea	1992	Tajikistan
1945	Paraguay	1961	Tanzania, United Republic of
1945	Peru	1946	Thailand
1945	Philippines	1960	Togo
1945	Poland	1962	Trinidad and Tobago
1955	Portugal	1956	Tunisia
1971	Qatar	1945	Turkey
1955	Romania	1992	Turkmenistan
1945	Russian Federation	1962	Uganda
1962	Rwanda	1945	Ukraine
1983	Saint Kitts and Nevis	1971	United Arab Emirates
1979	Saint Lucia	1945	United Kingdom
1980	Saint Vincent and the Grenadines	1945	United States of America
		1945	Uruguay
1976	Samoa	1992	Uzbekistan
1992	San Marino	1981	Vanuatu
1975	Sao Tome and Principe	1945	Venezuela
1945	Saudi Arabia	1977	Vietnam
1960	Senegal	1947	Yemen
1976	Seychelles	1945	Yugoslavia**
1961	Sierra Leone	1960	Zaire
1965	Singapore	1964	Zambia
1993	Slovak Republic	1980	Zimbabwe

*   While still at war, Congo has split into Congo-Brazaville and Congo-Zaire

** not permitted to participate in General Assembly deliberations

INDEX

An italic *f* after a page reference indicates a figure; an italic *m* indicates a map; an italic *t* indicates a table; an italic *n* indicates a note; and an italic *w* indicates a Web site.